AF394750

The Yorkshire County Cricket Club Limited

Registered Number 28929R

YEARBOOK
2024

126th EDITION

Editor:
GRAHAM HARDCASTLE

Production Editor:
JAMES M. GREENFIELD

Records and Statistics
Yorkshire First Eleven:
JOHN T. POTTER

Yorkshire Second Eleven:
HOWARD CLAYTON and JOHN VIRR

Official Photographers:
SIMON WILKINSON, ALEX WHITEHEAD
ALLAN MCKENZIE and JOHN CLIFTON *SWpix.com*
and JOHN HEALD

Published by
THE YORKSHIRE COUNTY CRICKET CLUB LTD
HEADINGLEY CRICKET GROUND
LEEDS LS6 3BU
Tel: 0344 504 3099
Website: www.yorkshireccc.com
e-mail: cricket@yorkshireccc.com

TELEPHONE AND FAX NUMBERS

HEADINGLEY CRICKET GROUND

Tel: 0344 504 3099

NORTH MARINE ROAD, SCARBOROUGH   **Tel: 01723 365625**

SHIPTON ROAD, YORK   **Tel: 01904 623602**

© The Yorkshire County Cricket Club Ltd 2024

Produced by:

Great Northern Books
PO Box 1380, Bradford, BD5 5FB
www.greatnorthernbooks.co.uk

ISBN: 978-1-914227-67-7

CONTENTS

Colour Plates — Facing Pages 32 and 256

Officers for 2024

PATRONESS

THE DUCHESS OF KENT

PATRONS

DAVID LASCELLES, EARL OF HAREWOOD   LORD HAWKE
The EARL OF MEXBOROUGH

HONORARY LIFE MEMBERS

Mr J G BINKS
Mr H D BIRD, OBE,
Hon. D (Univ) LLD
Sir GEOFFREY BOYCOTT
Mr D BYAS
Mr G A COPE
Mr D GOUGH MBE
Mr R A HUTTON
Mr D S LEHMANN
Mr R K PLATT
Mr S R TENDULKAR
Mr M P VAUGHAN, OBE

PRESIDENT

DR JANE POWELL

VICE-PRESIDENTS

Mrs J BAIRSTOW
Mr B BOUTTELL
Mr I M CHAPPELL
Mr G A COPE
Mr C J GRAVES CBE
Mr D S HALL, CBE, TD
MR S N HARTLEY
Mr R A HILLIAM
Mr S J MANN
Mr K H MOSS MBE
Mr J W T MUSTOE
Mr D M RYDER
Mr R A SMITH, TD, DL
Mr W B STOTT
Mr K TAYLOR
Mr A L VANN
Mr D WARNER
Mr J D WELCH

THE BOARD

MR COLIN GRAVES CBE (Chair) *
MR PHILLIP HODSON (Deputy Chair) *
MRS LESLIE FERRAR CVO
MR SANJEEV GANDHI *
MR DARREN GOUGH MBE (Managing Director of Cricket)
BARONESS TANNI GREY-THOMPSON DBE DL
MR SANJAY PATEL *
MR STEPHEN VAUGHAN (Chief Executive Officer)

* Pending approval of appointment as directors at the club's next
  Annual General Meeting

MEMBERS' COMMITTEE

Chairman: Mr G GREENFIELD

ELECTED MEMBERS

Ms C EVERS   Ms P BEESLEY
          Mr H RAY

APPOINTED MEMBERS

Mr G GREENFIELD   Mr A KILBURN
          Mr C WOODTHORPE

**Changes announced after February 12 will be recorded in the
2025 edition of the Yorkshire County Cricket Club Yearbook**

Officials of the Yorkshire County Cricket Club

T R Barker	1863	David Jones CBE	2004-6
M J Ellison	1864-97	Robert Appleyard	2006-8
Lord Hawke	1898-1938	Brian Close CBE	2008-10
Rt Hon Sir F S Jackson		Raymond Illingworth CBE	
	1939-1947		2010-2012
T L Taylor	1948-1960	Geoffrey Boycott OBE	
Sir W A Worsley Bart			2012-2013
	1961-1973	Harold 'Dickie' Bird OBE	
Sir K Parkinson	1974-1981		2014-2015
N W D Yardley	1981-1983	John H Hampshire	
The Viscount Mountgarret			2016-2017
	1984-1989	Richard A Hutton	2017-2018
Sir Leonard Hutton	1989-1990	Geoff A Cope	2018-2023
Sir Lawrence Byford		Dr. Jane Powell	2023-
QPM, LLD, DL	1991-1999		
R A Smith			
TD, LLB, DL	1999-2004		

Chair

A H Connell, DL	1971-1979	C J Graves, CBE	2005-2015
M G Crawford	1980-1984	S J Denison	2015-2018
H R Kirk	1984-1985	R A Smith TD, LLB, DL	
B Walsh, QC	1986-1991		2018-2020
Sir Lawrence Byford		C N R Hutton	2020-2021
CBE, QPM, LLD, DL		Lord K Patel OBE	2021-2023
	1991-1998	Baroness T Grey-Thompson	
K H Moss MBE	1998-2002	DBE DL	
GA Cope	2002	(Co and Interim)	2023 and 2024
R A Smith TD, LLB, DL		H Chathli	2023-2024
	2002-5	C J Graves CBE	2024-

Secretary

Geo Padley	1863	J H Nash	1931-1971
J B Wostinholm	1864-1902	J Lister	1972-1991
F C (Sir Fredk.) Toone		D M Ryder	1991-2002
	1903-1930		

Officials of the Yorkshire County Cricket Club

Company Secretary

B Bouttell	2002-5	A Dawson	2023
C Hartwell	2011-14	H Jagpal	2023-
P Hudson	2014-2022		

Captain

R Iddison	1863-1872	D B Close	1963-1970
J Rowbotham	1873	G Boycott	1971-1978
L Greenwood	1874	J H Hampshire	1979-1980
J Rowbotham	1875	C M Old	1981-1982
E Lockwood	1876-1877	R Illingworth	1982-1983
T Emmett	1878-1882	D L Bairstow	1984-1986
Hon M B (Lord) Hawke		P Carrick	1987-1989
	1883-1910	M D Moxon	1990-1995
E J R H Radcliffe	1911	D Byas	1996-2001
Sir A W White	1912-1918	D S Lehmann	2002
D C F Burton	1919-1921	A McGrath	2003
Geoff Wilson	1922-1924	C White	2004-6
A W Lupton	1925-1927	D Gough	2007-8
W A Worsley	1928-1929	A McGrath	2009
A T Barber	1930	A W Gale	2010-16
F E Greenwood	1931-1932	G S Ballance	2017-18
A B Sellers	1933-1947	S A Patterson	2018-22
N W D Yardley	1948-1955	D J Willey	2020-22
W H H Sutcliffe	1956-1957		(T20 only)
J R Burnet	1958-1959	J A Tattersall	2022
J V Wilson	1960-1962	S Masood	2023-

Treasurer

M J Ellison	1863-1893	M G Crawford	1963-1979
M Ellison, jun.	1894-1898	J D Welch	1980-1984
Chas Stokes	1899-1912	P W Townend	1984-2002
R T Heselton	1913-1931		
A Wyndham Heselton			
	1932-1962		

Officials of the Yorkshire County Cricket Club

<table>
<tr><td colspan="2">Chief Executive</td></tr>
<tr><td>C D Hassell</td><td>1991-2002</td><td>Colin J Graves</td><td>2012-13</td></tr>
<tr><td>Colin J Graves</td><td>2002-5</td><td>Mark Arthur</td><td>2013-21</td></tr>
<tr><td>Stewart Regan</td><td>2006-10</td><td>Stephen Vaughan</td><td>2022-</td></tr>
</table>

COUNTY FIXTURES — 2024

All four-day matches. 11am start. *(10.30am in September)*

Date			Opponents	Venue
FRI	**5-8**	**APRIL**	**LEICESTERSHIRE**	**HEADINGLEY**
Fri	12-15	April	Gloucestershire	Bristol
Fri	19-22	April	Middlesex	Lord's
FRI	**26-29**	**APRIL**	**DERBYSHIRE**	**HEADINGLEY**
FRI	**3-6**	**MAY**	**GLAMORGAN**	**HEADINGLEY**
Fri	17-20	May	Sussex	Hove
Fri	24-27	May	Northamptonshire	Wantage Road
SUN	**23-26**	**JUNE**	**GLOUCESTERSHIRE**	**SCARBOROUGH**
Sun	30-3	June/July	Derbyshire	Chesterfield
THU	**22-25**	**AUGUST**	**SUSSEX**	**SCARBROUGH**
THU	**29-1**	**AUGUST /SEPTEMBER**	**MIDDLESEX**	**HEADINGLEY**
Mon	9-12	September	Leicestershire	Grace Road
Thu	17-20	September	Glamorgan	Sophia Gardens
THU	**26-29**	**SEPTEMBER**	**NORTHAMPTONSHIRE**	**HEADINGLEY**

VITALITY BLAST (Twenty20)

All group matches start at 6.30pm floodlit except where stated

THU	**30**	**MAY**	**WORCESTERSHIRE RAPIDS**	**HEADINGLEY**
Fri	31	May	Leicestershire Foxes	Grace Road
Sun	2	June	Northamptonshire Steelbacks *(3.30pm)*	Wantage Road
SUN	**9**	**JUNE**	**DERBYSHIRE FALCONS** *(3pm)*	**HEADINGLEY**
Fri	14	June	Birmingham Bears	Edgbaston
SUN	**16**	**JUNE**	**LEICESTERSHIRE FOXES** *(3pm)*	**HEADINGLEY**
THU	**20**	**JUNE**	**LANCASHIRE LIGHTNING** *(7pm)*	**HEADINGLEY**
Fri	21	June	Durham	Riverside
FRI	**5**	**JULY**	**BIRMINGHAM BEARS**	**HEADINGLEY**
Sun	7	July	Derbyshire Falcons *(2.30pm)*	Chesterfield
THU	**11**	**JULY**	**DURHAM**	**HEADINGLEY**
Fri	12	July	Lancashire Lightning *(7pm)*	Old Trafford
Sun	14	July	Worcestershire Rapids *(2.30pm)*	New Road
FRI	**19**	**JULY**	**NOTTINGHAMSHIRE OUTLAWS**	**(7pm) TRENT BRIDGE**
Tue	3-6	September	Quarter-Finals	
Sat	*14*	*September*	*Finals Day*	*Edgbaston*

METRO BANK ONE-DAY CUP (50-overs)

All matches start at 11am

Thu	25	July	Surrey . . . . .The Oval
Sun	28	July	Nottinghamshire Outlaws . . . . .Welbeck Colliery
WED	**31**	**JULY**	**SUSSEX SHARKS** . . . .**YORK**
FRI	**2**	**AUGUST**	**GLOUCESTERSHIRE** . . . .**YORK**
TUE	**6**	**AUGUST**	**ESSEX EAGLES** . . . .**SCARBOROUGH**
THU	**8**	**AUGUST**	**LEICESTERSHIRE FOXES** . . . .**SCARBOROUGH**
Sun	11	August	Warwickshire . . . . .TBC
Wed	14	August	Glamorgan . . . . .Sophia Gardens
Fri	16	August	Quarter-Finals
Sun	18	August	Semi-Finals
Sun	*22*	*September*	*Final . . . . .Trent Bridge*

OTHER MATCHES

TUE	**26-28**	**MARCH**	**LEEDS/BRADFORD MCCU** . . . . .**HEADINGLEY**
			(Three-Day Friendly)
Sun	21	July	Shropshire . . . . .Wellington CC
			(50-over Friendly)

INTERNATIONAL MATCHES PLAYED AT HEADINGLEY

SUN	**19**	**MAY**	**WOMEN'S IT20** . . . . .**ENGLAND v. PAKISTAN**
WED	**22**	**MAY**	**MEN'S IT20** . . . .**ENGLAND v. PAKISTAN**
SAT	**21**	**SEPTEMBER**	**MEN'S ODI** . . . .**ENGLAND v. AUSTRALIA**

SECOND ELEVEN CHAMPIONSHIP

All four-day matches. 11am start. *(10.30am in September)*

Mon	8-11	April	Lancashire . . . . .TBC
MON	**15-18**	**APRIL**	**SOMERSET** . . . .**HEADINGLEY**
MON	**22-25**	**APRIL**	**LEICESTERSHIRE** . . . .**BRADFORD PA**
Mon	29-1	April/May	Nottinghamshire . . . . .Notts Sports Ground
Mon	17-19	June	Durham (3-day game) . . . . .TBC
Tue	20-23	August	Derbyshire . . . . .Chesterfield
TUE	**27-30**	**AUGUST**	**SURREY** . . . .**YORK**
MON	**2-5**	**SEPTEMBER**	**DURHAM** . . . .**SCARBOROUGH**
Mon	9-12	September	Lancashire . . . . .Southport
Mon	16-19	September	Middlesex . . . . .Merchant Taylors' School

SECOND ELEVEN T20 TROPHY

(DH = double-headers, two fixtures per day)

Wed	29	May	Lancashire . . . . .TBC
THU	**6**	**JUNE**	**DURHAM** . . . .**HEADINGLEY**
FRI	**7**	**JUNE**	**DURHAM** . . . .**WEETWOOD**
Mon	10	June	Leicestershire . . . . .Grace Road
THU	**13**	**JUNE**	**LEICESTERSHIRE** . . . .**WEETWOOD**
Fri	28	June	Derbyshire . . . . .Duffield
TUE	**2**	**JULY**	**LANCASHIRE** . . . .**BARNSLEY**
THU	**4**	**JULY**	**NOTTINGHAMSHIRE** *(DH)* . . . .**WEETWOOD**
Tue	9	July	Derbyshire . . . . .TBC
Tue	*16*	*July*	*Finals Day* . . . .*Wormsley*

<h1 style="text-align:center">SECOND ELEVEN OTHER MATCHES</h1>

(DH = double-headers, two fixtures per day)

Fri	10	May	Leeds/Bradford MCCU *(T20 DH)*	TBC
MON	**13-15**	**MAY**	**SOUTH ASIAN CRICKET ACADEMY**	**BRADFORD PA**
TUE	**21**	**MAY**	**SOUTH ASIAN CRICKET ACADEMY** *(T20 DH)*	**WEETWOOD**
TUE	**25**	**JUNE**	**SOUTH ASIAN CRICKET ACADEMY** *(One-Day)*	**WEETWOOD**
THU	**11**	**JULY**	**ZIMBABWE A** *(One-Day)*	TBC

<h1 style="text-align:center">REGIONAL WOMEN'S FIXTURES, NORTHERN DIAMONDS
RACHAEL HEYHOE FLINT TROPHY (50-OVERS)</h1>

All matches start at 10.30am

Sat	20	April	Lancashire Thunder	Riverside
WED	**24**	**APRIL**	**WESTERN STORM**	**HEADINGLEY**
Sat	27	April	Southern Vipers	Ageas Bowl
WED	**1**	**MAY**	**THE BLAZE**	**SCARBOROUGH**
Sat	4	May	Central Sparks	Edgbaston
Wed	8	May	South East Stars	Beckenham
SUN	**30**	**JUNE**	**CENTRAL SPARKS**	**SCARBOROUGH**
Sun	7	July	Western Storm	Cheltenham College
WED	**10**	**JULY**	**SUNRISERS**	**YORK**
Sun	14	July	The Blaze	Lindum
Mon	26	August	Sunrisers	Chelmsford
Sun	1	September	Lancashire Thunder	Southport
WED	**4**	**SEPTEMBER**	**SOUTHERN VIPERS**	**HEADINGLEY**
Sat	7	September	South East Stars	Riverside
Sat	14	September	Semi-Final	
Sat	*21*	*September*	*Final*	*Grace Road*

<h1 style="text-align:center">CHARLOTTE EDWARDS CUP (TWENTY 20)</h1>

Sun	19	May	Lancashire Thunder	Old Trafford
Thu	23	May	The Blaze	Trent Bridge
MON	**27**	**MAY**	**CENTRAL SPARKS**	**HEADINGLEY**
Fri	31	May	South East Stars	Riverside
Sun	2	June	Sunrisers	Wantage Road
Sat	8	June	Central Sparks	Edgbaston
SUN	**9**	**JUNE**	**THE BLAZE**	**HEADINGLEY**
Fri	14	June	Southern Vipers	Ageas Bowl
SUN	**16**	**JUNE**	**WESTERN STORM**	**HEADINGLEY**
Wed	19	June	Lancashire Thunder	Riverside
Sat	*22*	*June*	*Finals Day*	*Derby*

<h1 style="text-align:center">THE HUNDRED, NORTHERN SUPERCHARGERS</h1>

All fixture dates are double-headers for the men's and women's teams

FRI	**26**	**JULY**	**TRENT ROCKETS**	**HEADINGLEY**
TUE	**30**	**JULY**	**SOUTHERN BRAVE**	**HEADINGLEY**
Fri	2	August	Oval Invincibles	The Oval
SUN	**4**	**AUGUST**	**MANCHESTER ORIGINALS**	**HEADINGLEY**
Tue	6	August	Birmingham Phoenix	Edgbaston
Thu	8	August	Welsh Fire	Sophia Gardens
Sun	11	August	Manchester Originals	Old Trafford
TUE	**13**	**AUGUST**	**LONDON SPIRIT**	**HEADINGLEY**
Sat	17	August	Eliminator	The Oval
Sun	*18*	*August*	*Final*	*Lord's*

YORKSHIRE IN WOMEN'S COUNTY CHAMPIONSHIP
(Group One)

Sun	21	April	North East Warriors *(50 overs)*	TBC
Mon	6	May	Lancashire *(50 overs)*	TBC
Sun	26	May	North East Warriors & Cumbria *(T20 double header)*	TBC
Sun	16	June	Lancashire & Derbyshire *(T20 double header)*	TBC
Sun	30	June	Scotland *(50 overs)*	TBC
Sun	14	July	Derbyshire *(50 overs)*	TBC
Sun	28	July	Nottinghamshire *(T20 double header)*	TBC
Sun	11	August	Scotland & Staffordshire *(T20 double header)*	TBC
Sat	*24-25*	*August*	*Finals Day, T20*	

YORKSHIRE DISABILITY FIXTURES
NATIONAL QUEST LEAGUE
All matches 40-overs per side

Sun	28	April	Middlesex	Higham
Sun	12	May	Hampshire	TBC
Sun	26	May	Surrey	Higham
Sun	9	June	Essex	Harlow
Sun	23	June	Sussex	Ansty
Sun	7	July	Wales	Sudbrook
Sun	21	July	Lancashire	Higham

YORKSHIRE ACADEMY/UNDER-18s
(F denotes Friendly)

Sun	14	April	Barnsley Woolley Miners 50-over F	BWMCC
Sun	14	April	Methley 50-over F	Methley
SUN	**21**	**APRIL**	**YORK 50-over F**	**WEETWOOD**
Sun	21	April	Scarborough 50-over F	Scarborough
Wed	24	April	Worksop College 40-over F	Worksop College
SUN	**28**	**APRIL**	**NOTTINGHAMSHIRE 50-over F**	**WEETWOOD**
Wed	1-2	May	Durham 2-day F	TBC
Mon	6	May	Northamptonshire T20 x2	TBC
Wed	8-9	May	Lancashire 2-day F	TBC
Mon	27	May	Driffield Town T20 x2	Driffield
Wed	29-31	May	ECB T20 North Group Stage	York/Clifton A
Sun	16	June	Lancashire 50-over F	TBC
Fri	21	June	Sedbergh School 1st XI 50-over F	Sedbergh
Tue	25	June	Northamptonshire 50-over F	Peterborough Town
Thu	27	June	Warwickshire 50-over F	TBC
Sun	30	June	Cumbria ECB 50-over Cup	TBC
TUE	**9-11**	**JULY**	**SURREY 3-day F**	**WEETWOOD**
Tue	16-18	July	Lancashire 3-day F	TBC
TUE	**23-25**	**JULY**	**LEICESTERSHIRE U18 CC 3-day**	**WEETWOOD**
Tue	30-1	July/August	Durham U18 CC	Hartlepool
TUE	**6-8**	**AUGUST**	**DERBYSHIRE U18 CC**	**WEETWOOD**
Mon	12-14	August	Lancashire U18 CC	Southport
TUE	**29**	**AUGUST**	**NOTTINGHAMSHIRE U18 CC**	**WEETWOOD**
Sun	1	September	ECB County Cup Final	TBC
Sun	8	September	ECB T20 Finals Day	TBC

Not all Academy/Under-18s fixtures are finalised, and more fixtures are to be added.
Check *https://yorkccc.play-cricket.com/home* for updates.
The ECB T20 North Group stage in late May will be played at York and Clifton Alliance, with six counties involved. The ECB County Cup is an FA Cup style knockout competition with five rounds through to the final.

THE COMPETITIONS EXPLAINED

COUNTY CHAMPIONSHIP

Yorkshire will be aiming for promotion from Division Two in 2024, an eight-team division which will see two teams promoted.

All counties will play each other twice, unlike Division One where there is an uneven split of 14 fixtures because of the 10 teams involved.

Teams gain 16 points for a win and eight for a draw, the draw up from five in 2023. Bonus points are also added, a maximum of five for batting if you reach 450 in 110 overs or three for bowling if you take nine wickets in that same time.

Four rounds in 2024 will see the Kookaburra ball instead of the Dukes used, a move designed in part to prepare prospective England Test players for playing in foreign countries which use that ball more regularly.

VITALITY BLAST

Counties are split into two regional groups of nine, with 14 games. Yorkshire play the majority of their opponents home and away, but not all. The Vikings are aiming to reach Finals Day for a second time in three years.

The top four teams in the two regionalised groups advance to the quarter-finals ahead of Finals Day on Saturday September 14, at Edgbaston. The top two teams — four in total across the North and South — all win the right to host their quarter-final.

Yorkshire will be involved in an extended Blast Off weekend of May 30-June 2 to kick off the competition. Vikings face Northamptonshire at Wantage Road on June 2.

METRO BANK ONE-DAY CUP

The 18 counties have been split into two non-regionalised groups of nine. Each will play eight matches — four at home, four away.

The top three in each table advance to the knockout stages. The top team qualifies direct to the semi-final, while the second and third teams play each other in an effective quarter-final.

The winners advance to the semi-final, with the final played at Trent Bridge on Sunday, September 22.

THE HUNDRED

The Hundred is into its fourth year in 2024. Each game will be 100 balls per side, both for the men and the women, with a number of different playing conditions within that.

The eight teams play eight group fixtures, including their nearest rivals twice. Northern Superchargers play Manchester Originals twice.

Every fixture date will see the men and women play double-headers at the same venue, with the competitions identical in their format.

The top team after the group stage advance directly into the final. The second and third-placed teams play off in an Eliminator for the right to advance to the final.

RACHAEL HEYHOE FLINT TROPHY

The 50-over competition played between the eight women's Regional Centres of Excellence sees the Northern Diamonds seeking to win back the trophy they claimed in 2022.

The trophy, into its fifth season — it started in 2020 — sees all regions play 14 group fixtures, meeting all opponents home and away.

The finals series is exactly the same as the Hundred.

This season the top four teams will qualify for two straight semi-finals, moving to a final at Leicestershire's Grace Road on Saturday, September 21. That is a change from last year, when only the top three teams qualified for knockout cricket.

CHARLOTTE EDWARDS CUP

This regional women's T20 competition has undertaken a significant revamp for 2024.

Instead of all regions playing seven group fixtures they will play 10 this summer. The Diamonds will play everybody once and their closest rivals geographically — Blaze, Central Sparks and Thunder — twice.

The top four teams after the group phase will advance to Finals Day at Derbyshire's County Ground on Saturday, June 22, and face off in two semi-finals before a final, mirroring the men's Blast Finals Day.

This is a change from previous seasons, where only three teams would qualify for the Finals Day. The Diamonds are involved in six double-header days, three of them with Yorkshire's men.

GRAVES PUTS HEART AND SOUL INTO TURNING CLUB AROUND

By Graham Hardcastle

Colin Graves will put his "heart and soul" into transforming Yorkshire's fortunes after agreeing to return and attempt to save the club from its current difficulties, just as he did successfully in 2002.

In January the founder of the Costcutter Supermarkets Group agreed a takeover package with the county, which would see him come back to Headingley as chair.

That deal was given the green light at February's Extraordinary General Meeting, Graves describing the 88 per cent of votes in favour as "phenomenal".

Graves, who left the club in 2015 to be chair of the England and Wales Cricket Board, told how the deal came to fruition and of his confidence in being able to get the club "back on an even keel" quickly.

COLIN GRAVES
Fast track to even keel

Not only do we discuss the financial picture, we talk about his love for cricket and Yorkshire Cricket in particular.

A Dunnington native, where he played for 30-odd years and is now their president, Graves, 76, is backing Yorkshire to secure promotion to Division One of the County Championship in 2024. Women's cricket, the development of Harry Brook and the importance of the Hundred to English Cricket are also topics covered.

"I think we all just want to see Yorkshire Cricket back to where we need it to be," he said. "We've had a turbulent three years, but it's a bit like drawing a line in the sand and saying, 'Let's look forward'.

"I've always been passionate about cricket since I was five. I was brought up with two brothers and my dad — we all played. I've always been a cricket nut. Yorkshire, to me, is special and different. Just walking into this ground, it's different. I put my heart and soul into it in 2002 when I first came here, and I will again. I just couldn't sit and watch the club go bust, basically.

"I think a lot of people outside of cricket don't realise how strong and big Yorkshire Cricket is. The amount played around the county on a Saturday is staggering. It's in our heritage and blood. That's why I'm so passionate about this club and county. We simply cannot let that stop happening. It's an institution. But, as an institution, you still have to pay your way. You have to have a profitable business to do that."

When he left for the ECB, Graves certainly didn't expect to be back at Headingley in a working capacity.

"Not one bit," he continued. "I had no intention of returning to Headingley in any capacity apart from to watch a bit of cricket. Full stop. It never crossed my mind. But things change."

His name has been linked to the club in terms of a takeover deal for the last year to 18 months, with it finally coming to fruition in February of this year, as aforementioned at the start of this piece.

Graves knows the size of the task he and his team face at Headingley: "It's a challenge, but it's not one that worries or over-faces me," he said. "I know I can sort it by working with and getting other people involved to refinance and restructure the club.

"Yes, the figures are bad at the moment because the creditors have built up, and we owe money. From that perspective it's about stopping the haemorrhaging of money going out. In simple terms, we're spending more than we're earning. But I think in a year's time we'll have it on an even keel.

"We have an India Test Match next year, which will be good. We have to make sure next year is profitable and we get back to making profits every year. This year is going to be tough because we haven't got a Test. We had two one-dayers, and that's it. From there, we should be ok.

"It's very similar in some ways to how it was when I first came in. The biggest difference is that we didn't own the ground in 2002. Back then we had an overdraft of £5m and didn't own a blade of grass.

"Now we owe, in total, roughly £20m. But we have an asset in the ground worth roughly £20m. The figures are different, and look bigger, but we have an asset behind us. When I left in 2015 we had bought the ground, we had turned it around and had started with other developments. It was a profitable business paying its way and paying its debts.

"Everything was going great. We had done a load of hard work and got it established. It's just disappointing for the last two or three years that we've had all the issues and the costs incurred with that."

When it comes to cricket administration, Graves has been there, done it and bought the t-shirt.

"I've seen a lot in the last 15 years, chairing the ECB, seeing other counties and getting to know all of the other chairs very well," he said. "I'm pretty experienced and know what it's all about.

"That's the beauty. For example, I know what the North-South Stand is all about. People who don't would come in and it would take them months to get up to speed. All those kind of things will help me get things done quicker."

On the field there were positives in 2023. Yorkshire's men handled significant challenges admirably last year and are eyeing promotion this summer, while the Northern Diamonds are one of the leading lights in the women's game: they won a trophy in 2022 and have a number of young and progressive players.

"Talking to people in and around cricket — I still know a lot around the other counties — it's clear we have a lot of young and exciting players," Graves said of the men. "It's just a matter of keeping them fit.

"We got clobbered a lot by the weather last year. Hopefully, that won't happen again. We definitely have the capabilities of doing well. The main thing is that we need to get out of the second division. Yorkshire should not be in that division. I am definitely confident we can do that."

One of the talented young players at Yorkshire's disposal is England star Brook. "Harry is a phenomenal talent," he said. "It's fantastic what he's done — breaking into all of the England teams and playing the way he has. He's an exceptional player and guy to be able to do that. It's a feather in his cap, but also in Yorkshire's for producing him."

Graves said of the Diamonds: "When I went to ECB one of the first things I did was get the Women's Super League up and running and direct more money into the women's game — pay the players, etc.

"I always thought there was an opportunity to grow the women's game, because we didn't have the amount of girls playing that we needed. It's kicked on from there, and it's been a wonderful achievement what's happened across the board. The Diamonds are one of the leaders in that."

The landscape of women's cricket will change again in 2025, with all counties asked to bid for licenses to host eight tier-one teams in a new and improved domestic structure. Graves is confident Yorkshire will be successful in their bid. He also spoke of the Hundred, driving its creation during his time with the ECB.

"The Hundred, I have always said, would be the jewel in the crown of English Cricket from an asset point of view," he said.

"If you look at it, international cricket isn't owned by the ECB. We have what we're allocated by the ICC, and we live off the back of that. It brings in a lot of money, but it's not under our control.

"Don't get me wrong, we make the best of that, and we want that to continue for as long as it can. If you look at the Championship it doesn't bring in any money. The Blast brings in some money, but it's not an unbelievable amount.

"But the Hundred was something new, and Sky got behind it and invested heavily into it. To me, that's owned by the ECB and should be used to bring extra money into the game and to develop it. It's one of English Cricket's biggest assets."

Graves is clearly a popular figure at Headingley — the weight of member support for his return tells you that. And he will be cheering Yorkshire on alongside those members when time allows this summer.

"I will be around, but I'm not the sort who will be sat watching cricket every day because I have other things to do. I've got a busy life, a busy family — all sorts of things. But I'll get to as much cricket as I can.

HARRY CHATHLI
Handing over the chair

"There will be other people on the board who will be around the grounds. Phillip Hodson, especially, will be very involved with the cricket. He will be our deputy chair. Whether it's me, Phillip, Sanjay Patel or whoever, we'll be here."

Bess the Rock with bat and ball

Dom Bess played winter first-class and List A cricket in Zimbabwe before and after Christmas, returning home for the festive period. Yorkshire's off-spinning all-rounder played for the Southern Rocks team and impressed. At time of writing he had scored three first-class fifties batting at No.3, added to hauls of 5-99 and 4-8.

SHOUT THE GOOD NEWS OF ALL YORKSHIRE'S FANTASTIC THINGS

By Graham Hardcastle

I for one am looking forward to us pushing for promotion. I'm very confident we'll get it as well — Jane Powell, YCCC President

DR JANE POWELL
'A difficult summer...
but we used it well'

Yorkshire President Jane Powell is looking forward to 2024 with supreme confidence, a feeling she shares for not just the men's side but the Northern Diamonds and the county's Disability champions — an area strongly linked to her day job with the England and Wales Cricket Board.

But as she talks for this *Yorkshire Yearbook* feature she also reflects on 2023 — her first year in post — with significant fondness.

"I've had a great time, I really have," she said.

To give her full title, Dr Jane Powell is a former England women's cricket captain. She played in six Test matches, scoring a century against India at Blackpool, and 24 One-Day Internationals between 1984 and 1990. She captained England in a World Cup final at the Melbourne Cricket Ground in 1988, and is a Championship winner with Yorkshire.

Powell, whose twin sister Jill also played Test cricket for England, has played international hockey and badminton at junior representative level and has coached in hockey and cricket as well as working in administration in both sports as well as Lacrosse.

Awards have come along the way for the former batter, perhaps the most significant being in November 2013 when she received an Honorary Doctorate (Doctor of Science) from the University of Worcester for her outstanding contribution to British Sport.

Shortly after being elected as Yorkshire President, she was awarded

MCC Honorary Life Membership.

If you think her career has been a full one so far, you should see her list of presidential duties since taking over from Geoff Cope last March to become Yorkshire's first ever female president.

Functions and dinners attended, matches visited, media interviews, BBC local radio commentary stints undertaken, cricket society chats delivered and awards handed out...it is a list as long as your arm.

"I've done my best to get around, and I've really enjoyed it. That's the top line," she said. "If nothing else, you'll get what you see with me. I won't say something if I'm not going to do it. At times it's been hard work getting to different places. But, ultimately, it's been absolutely worth it. I've really enjoyed meeting a number of different people, all associated with Yorkshire Cricket in many different ways.

"It's just been amazing to see all the work that goes on from so many people who commit vast chunks of their time to promote cricket within our county. I did a South Yorkshire women's presentation evening, and the room was filled. I'm told it's one of the smaller sections, and yet there were 150 people in the room all so passionate about their cricket. It's fascinating to see all the good that's going on."

Powell does not hide away from the fact the county club has endured difficult times over the last few years, but she stressed: "There's loads of good things going on, and we shouldn't be shy to shout about it."

What has she learnt about Yorkshire Cricket during her time in post? "The depth of the impact Yorkshire Cricket has on people for the good," she continued. "I was aware of it, certainly, but the extent of it has pleasantly surprised me. The pathways getting all the free equipment and things like that. What a massive bonus that is for our young players who can play freely without having to worry about being out of pocket.

"The engagement we have with different communities is fantastic. I was lucky enough to be down at Lord's when one of our schools from Batley way finished in the final of the Table Cricket.

"There's stuff that goes on that we just don't know about because there's so much that's going on. I didn't realise all the events the club does for the various faiths: a Diwali dinner, an Iftar for Ramadan, a Christmas gathering.

"I've always known we are a proud county, but I've seen that pride in more ways than I expected. I talk about pride being personal responsibility in delivering excellence, and I think we're making that happen. People are taking responsibility and making sure that the area they're involved in is doing things properly.

"The waiting room which has been done up for the parents who wait for their kids on the pathway is one of those things. It's fantastic, because we don't just want the parents sitting in their cars on cold nights

in the winter. These are the little things which can go amiss, but they're
ones being done properly."

Born in Sheffield — Powell was in the same class at school as Lord
Sebastian Coe — she is based in Silverstone. Formula One country.
Talking of vehicles...upon taking on the role of president the Steel City
native bought a static caravan in Hawkesworth, near Guiseley: "I decided I needed a base up here, so I'm now the proud owner of a brand new
caravan in Moor Valley Country Park. "

Her *to do* list includes trips to watch Yorkshire teams up and down the
country, the first teams of the men and the Diamonds as well as the
Disability D40 national champions. She has also been to men's and
women's second-team fixtures, keeping a keen eye on the next generation of talent.

"We would have finished third in Division Two without the deduction, which is a pretty good effort given the toll it took on the players,"
she said. "We need to get Yorkshire back up to Division One. That's
where we should be.

"We did get scuppered by the weather, but we lacked a bit of a killer
touch at the start of the season. That first game against Leicester, we
bowled poorly and let them back in, and they managed to get over the
line. We did all the hard work, and then let it slip.

"Then there were a few 10th-wicket partnerships which delayed us
here and there. But a lot of the lads are young players, and they'll learn.

"It was actually a big bonus — we were able to give a lot of our
youngsters a real depth of experience. And a number of them came to
the party big time. Look at the partnerships Finlay Bean had with Adam
Lyth. We have an opening partnership there which could really take us
forward. They're starting to be one of those widely renowned opening
partnerships with the weight of runs they scored.

"It was a difficult summer because of the penalties, but we used it
well and will come back stronger this year. I'm hoping that we've turned
a corner now and we can move positively into the new season."

Powell, who was presented with a Diamonds cap by skipper Hollie
Armitage as a welcome gift from the team, said: "I thought they played
some good cricket, but they were unlucky with the weather.

"The one game where things turned in the Rachael Heyhoe Flint
Trophy was the Central Sparks fixture at Headingley when the Sparks
were favoured in a *Duckworth Lewis* chase despite us batting pretty
well. Had that gone our way, I'm sure we'd have made the play-offs.

"But you win or you learn, and that's something Dani Hazell's spoken
a lot about. I think she's quite pleased with the way things are progress-
ing for them. They, like the lads, have a lot of young players coming
through who have got good experience behind them. I just hope they can

make the most of that and get back into contention."

In contention was something Yorkshire's D40 side were in the National Quest League, of course, claiming a stunning title success.

Powell's day job with the England and Wales Cricket Board sees her as Performance Manager for England Disability Cricket, spending a decent portion of her winter travelling to places such as South Africa and India with the respective national teams.

On Yorkshire's triumph, she said: "It was a massive achievement for them, and here's a team who only got promoted last year. They've only gone on and won the County Championship, and what a great credit to everyone they are.

"It was nip and tuck right the way to the end, and there are some great stalwarts there who deserve a lot of recognition. Owen Jervis does some great work behind the scenes, and then you have Gordon Laidlaw who has been around a long time. What a wonderful career he's had. It's just so nice to see them be successful and get the recognition they deserve.

"But it's a tough gig because they'll be expected to do the same. But that's what good teams do. There's no reason why they can't."

More widely on the topic of Disability Cricket, she said: "It's in a very good place. But it's like a lot of things. We need to shout about it, because there are people out there who don't know too much about it. It's almost like a hidden treasure because they get a lot of support from the ECB and can live out all the dreams they have. It's a fantastic environment to be in."

Her international travels either side of Christmas saw her watch the England Learning Disability side win a T20 tri-series in South Africa, seeing off the hosts and Australia. Yorkshire players Alex Jervis and Rob Hewitt were there. She travelled to India with the Physical Disability squad. Yorkshireman Liam Thomas was involved in that series.

Sandwiched in between was due to be the Deaf World Cup in Qatar, for which Yorkshire trio James O'Conner, Cameron Sweeney and Henry Wainman had been selected — the first two for the first time in their careers. However, that competition was called off at the last minute.

Powell, referring to all of Yorkshire's international representatives at all levels, added: "Having played in England teams, you know everyone values the passion that Yorkshire men and women have. You know that if they're selecting a Yorkshire player they'll give it everything to win.

"I grew up at a time of my dad telling me, 'When Yorkshire's strong, England's strong'. It was true then and is now."

President Powell has met the great and good in her first year in post. And another thing is even clearer, there is plenty that is great about Yorkshire Cricket and plenty that is good.

Let's hope that is reflected further in 2024.

SUMMER OF DISCONTENT LEADS TO WINTER THAT SPRINGS HOPE

By Andrew Bosi

This was always going to be a difficult year, with the threat of a points deduction hanging over the side for much of the season. Had we retained Division One status a penalty might have left something to play for — avoiding relegation. In Division Two it left only pride. In many ways the continued uncertainty was the harshest part, and the team did play better once the outcome was known. They went unbeaten throughout September with two wins and two draws in the LV= Insurance County Championship.

The side was further hampered by bad weather — approximately 1,950 overs lost in four-day cricket — and the unexpected international calls on new skipper Shan Masood. The coaching staff hoped to raise morale by using the compensation for Masood to recruit short-term replacement signings, while lamenting the unavailability of long-term international signings. Neil Wagner, for example, was signed for the first 10 four-day games before a torn hamstring rendered him unavailable.

With the exception of Shai Hope, who filled the role behind the timbers when Jonny Tattersall was injured and contributed two scores with the bat, these were largely unsuccessful. The omission of Fin Bean from the starting line up at Durham in mid-May looked more remiss at the end of the season than it did at the time. Based on his average, one more innings would have been sufficient to pass 1,000 runs in his first full season at the top of the order.

Poor weather was not exclusive to Yorkshire, but only one of the 13 games was uninterrupted, and one never began at all — against Gloucestershire at Bristol in April. Thirty-four of the 56 games in the division were drawn, over 60 per cent.

Once the points penalty was known, the agenda shifted to developing a team of the future. Lapses in the field were fewer. Adam Lyth and Bean forged the most successful and settled opening partnership for a decade, and Matthew Revis confirmed his competence with the bat, twice reaching three figures. When he, Bean and George Hill registered centuries against Gloucestershire at Headingley in late June it was the first time in Yorkshire's history that three non-capped players had scored centuries in

Batter or bowler? A good container in some excellent spells...did they impair George Hill's progress with the bat?

the same first-class innings. James Wharton justified the faith shown in him, three times exceeding his previous best and displaying greater fluency in the last two of these innings, including a crucial 89 on the final day of the season when Worcestershire were beaten.

Masood's 60 meant he topped the batting averages (four or more completed innings) and made significant contributions to all three wins. Yorkshire's batting is coming good just as the increased target for maximum batting points (450 in 110 overs) takes effect. Will Luxton, Harry Duke, Yash Vagadia and Noah Kelly are waiting in the wings — the second team, incidentally, finished strongly with three away wins in their Championship competition.

Bowling remained a work in progress. Ben Coad and Matthew Fisher were excellent, sharing 64 wickets, and both played more than in previous seasons. The backup was disappointing. Maybe too much was expected of Jordan Thompson, whose batting possibly declined as a result. Dom Bess endured a lean run, albeit that his batting came to the rescue when Yorkshire needed it most and his bowling contributed with effect in September, yielding 10 wickets in three appearances.

The impression is sometimes given that the grass is always greener on the other side, and some of the bowlers drafted in achieved no more than one would have hoped from our youngsters in the Second Eleven.

Most glaring was the inability to finish sides off: five times the last wicket added more than 50. Derbyshire at Chesterfield recovered from 17-4 to reach 453 in the second innings, and Glamorgan from 100-6 to 273 in the first innings at Cardiff. Hill put in some useful spells with the ball, and seemed most likely to contain the scoring rate when wickets were hard to come by...though some supporters felt bowling so much impaired his progress with the bat.

In the opening match Leicestershire chased down a stiff 389 target, which would have been stiffer but for a rain interruption. Durham suffered their only defeat in this round, which suggested the second division would be competitive. Then Yorkshire endured four blank days at Bristol, and the final day at Hove was washed out when they were in a winning position. A strong Glamorgan had the upper hand at Headingley, where weather interruptions reduced play just enough for Yorkshire to survive on the last day, making their highest fourth innings score to draw in the process. Yorkshire came close to winning against the now runaway leaders at Durham: seeking what would have been the last wicket on the third night was again their undoing.

Derbyshire came back from a seemingly hopeless position at Chesterfield in mid-June, but Yorkshire narrowly prevailed for the first win since April 2022. Then came three rain-ruined games before Derbyshire again — this time at Scarborough in early September — provided the first home win for two years to the day.

A batting paradise at Cardiff was followed by a green top and more rain at Leicester — both draws — before the final game at Headingley saw Yorkshire beat promoted Worcestershire in a contrived chase on the final day. With so much rain this was effectively another three-day match. But a victory gave the Yorkshire's squad significant confidence heading into the winter months.

Gibson with the Giants

Yorkshire coach Ottis Gibson spent a month at the start of 2024 as assistant coach of the Gulf Giants in the UAE's ILT20 event through January and into February. Gibson returned to the Giants as assistant to Andy Flower, having won the inaugural title in 2023. Jordan Thompson also returned to play for the Mumbai Indians Emirates team.

GOLDEN DAYS IN RUN-FILLED SEASON FOR LYTH AND BEAN

By Graham Hardcastle

Adam Lyth hailed the hard work done by his rapidly developing opening partner, Fin Bean, after the pair shone together at the top of Yorkshire's order in 2023. Left-handers Lyth and Bean formed a formidable alliance in the LV= Insurance County Championship, their first full campaign batting together.

The statistics make for impressive reading. Between them they contributed 2,002 runs to Yorkshire's cause — Lyth 1,019 and Bean 983.

As for their opening partnership, they scored 1,278 runs in 20 innings at an average of 63.9. That included stands of 177, 113, 100 and 112 and others of 99, 94 and 98. Their four hundred stands were more for that wicket than any Yorkshire opening partnership had managed in the previous six seasons combined.

Lyth's form was superb, and the 36-year-old has now posted 1,000 Championship runs in a season on four occasions. Bean was particularly impressive, given 2023 was the now 22-year-old's breakthrough year in Yorkshire's first team, having debuted at the back end of 2022.

"We've struck up a nice little partnership at the top of the order," Lyth said. "I think it's the second highest opening partnership in the county season. Hopefully this is something we can build on for years to come.

"I feel for Beany, because he deserved those extra 17 runs (for 1,000). He's played so well. I know he's disappointed, but when he looks back on it he has cemented his place in this team and should be very proud of the way he's played.

"I've had a few partners over the years, but the work Beany's done on a few technical things and what he's figured out, I think it's testament to him that he's cemented his place for a long time.

"We should have had maybe five, six or seven hundred opening partnerships if it wasn't for me getting out. Especially at Scarborough (against Derbyshire in September, 59 and 100), we should have got a load more runs there, and a few other times as well.

"I've been so pleased with and so proud of what Beany's achieved. He should be so proud, too. If he keeps doing that you never know where the celling is for this boy."

Bean started the season on a rookie contract, having posted that record-breaking 441 for the second team against Nottinghamshire last year. But he has since seen that turned into a two-year professional deal.

"I think one of his main strengths is application and concentration," continued Lyth.

"He is a fit young man, so his concentration levels have always been high. He's very good square of the wicket and off his pads. He's a good cutter of the ball.

Starting handle: Fin Bean, left, and Adam Lyth, who forged Yorkshire's most successful and settled opening partnership for a decade.

"We're completely different players, but we complement each other. I'm more of a driver of the ball, he's more of a cutter and clipper through the leg-side. Myself and Leesy did a very good job for a number of years. I think it's quite similar in a way that we've now struck a nice partnership."

Lyth described his own 1,000 runs as a "proud moment", and he owes his performances to a change in mindset: "I've played really, really well most of the season, and have hit the ball well," he said. "I've gone back to my old style of playing. I know I get out a lot driving the ball, but it's my best shot and the shot which gets me the most runs.

"In recent years I've been a bit more tentative in trying not to get out. But my philosophy this year has been, 'I might as well get 50, 60 or 70 and play to my strengths. If I get a good ball, I get a good ball'.

"I've been slightly more attacking than in previous years, and have driven the ball as well as I've ever driven the ball. That's something to look back on for 2024. It's helped that we've played on some pretty nice wickets near enough all year. That gives you a bit more confidence that you can play a more natural, attacking way."

Both players posted three individual centuries, and have been praised to the hilt by teammates, coaches and supporters alike. Captain Shan Masood at one stage said that aiding Bean's development was part of Lyth's legacy at Headingley.

Bean was voted as the Members' Player of the Year during the last-round win over Worcestershire at Headingley, though he couldn't hide his disappointment at missing out on 1,000 runs when he was caught and bowled for 11 in the second innings on the final day of the summer.

"There was obviously frustration," admitted the Harrogate-born star.

Down...and out: Fin Bean dives to catch Worcestershire's Jack Haynes from the bowling of George Hill in Yorkshire's last Championship match of the season at Headingley.

"But speaking to Lythy and Gibbo, they said, 'Try not to look at it from just that final innings, look at from a season's point of view. It's been a successful one'. It's been really enjoyable all year.

"If it's not meant to be, it's not meant to be. I can't look at it too intently. It's more about making your hundreds count. When you get one, go on. It would have been nice to get a 150 or 160 somewhere and not leave it right to the end."

Lyth has praised Bean, so it's time for Bean to return the favour.

He said: "Lythy's ticked it all off. He's opened the batting for the club for many years, he's opened the batting for England. He's done it all. To have him to learn off has been brilliant. I couldn't wish for a better man to have at the other end.

"We have some good fun out there, and it's just great to bat with him. He will come down from the other end sometimes if he sees me trying to crack on. He will say, 'Calm it down'. I try to do the same with him. We've done well."

FIERY WOOD SETS ENGLAND'S *ASHES* HOPES ALIGHT

By Graham Hardcastle

Headingley has seen some classics down the years. *Ashes* Test Matches, other clashes to boot. The 2017 fixture between England and the West Indies springs to mind when Shai Hope — who represented Yorkshire in 2023 as an overseas player — became the first to score two hundreds in the same first-class match at our famous old venue.

This *Ashes* fixture can be added to the list for sure. Things could hardly have worked out better for everyone — for England, for Yorkshire, for a player such as Harry Brook, who got to shine on his home ground, and for teammate Mark Wood, whose searing pace caused Australia all manner of issues.

Richard Robinson, Yorkshire's head of grounds, is another who will remember this occasion for as long as he lives. This was the first Test pitch he had produced, having taken on the role from Andy Fogarty only in the lead-up to the summer.

We shall come back to Robinson and his team later, but let's look at the fixture, one which concluded in an England victory by three wickets inside four days in front of sellout crowd after sellout crowd.

England headed to Leeds in early July on the ropes, the Aussies 2-0 to the good. Ben Stokes and co. had been beaten at Edgbaston and at Lord's. Both matches had been tight affairs, with the hosts having chances to win in each.

Make no mistake: England should have won at Edgbaston. They declared late on Day One of the series at 393-8, a decision which brought about significant discussion. Should they have declared with Joe Root motoring on 118 not out? Why not at least bat out the day and further build the lead? It was England's first sign of Bazball. Would it cost them? Unfortunately, the answer was yes.

Ultimately they set Australia a target of 281 on the final day, reduced them to 209-7 and 227-8...and lost. The first-innings declaration wasn't the only reason for defeat. After all, they should have been able to finish off the last two wickets.

On to Lord's, where Australia were more dominant, driving the contest following a first-innings 416. England collapsed from 188-1, succumbing courtesy of some questionable strokes against the short ball. Their 325 was just not enough, though they managed to stay alive by limiting the visitors to 279 and setting a 371 target on Day Four.

At 193-5 Australia were ahead, but not home and hosed, given Stokes was well set en route to a stunning century and had Yorkshire's Jonny Bairstow for company. Then came the turning point.

It wasn't just the turning point...it was the talking point heading to Leeds.

Bairstow ducked a short ball from Cameron Green, and allowed it to sail through to wicketkeeper Alex Carey.

In a flash he planted his

Player of the Match: Paceman Mark Wood traps Australia's skipper, Pat Cummins, lbw on the way to his first-innings 5.34.

foot behind the crease, and set off to do some mid-pitch gardening and talk to partner Stokes. Carey threw the stumps down, and the Aussies appealed. Out. And captain Pat Cummins decided to follow through with the appeal despite the obvious controversy.

Stokes went on to post 155, but England were bowled out for 327, and lost by 43 runs. The Bairstow dismissal dominated the headlines and media discussion right through to the first morning at Leeds. It wasn't just back page news, it was front.

Thankfully, what followed was just a stunning game of cricket — one which saw no side better Australia's first-innings 263, but England sneak home to keep the series alive at 2-1 heading to Emirates Old Trafford and then the Kia Oval.

The first day set the tone for a nip-and-tuck affair. Stokes won the toss and elected to bowl first, a decision which reaped early rewards as Stuart Broad struck twice to reduce Australia to 85-4. Big guns David Warner, Usman Khawaja and Marnus Labuschagne all departed.

Step forward Mitchell Marsh, the brawny all-rounder whose international career had been stop-start. His talent was undeniable, but here was a man who once said that "most of Australia hates me". He had been brought back into the team in the place of fellow all-rounder Green, and played the knock of his life, a stunning and at times destructive run-a-ball 118 to revitalise the innings and get his side up to a competitive 263. Marsh fell, bowled by the devastatingly pacey Mark Wood, whose 5-34 would set him on the path towards a Player-of-the-Match display.

Marsh's fellow all-rounder, Stokes, then top-scored with a measured 80 for England in a disappointing 237. No other batter reached 40 as another wasted opportunity beckoned. Thankfully, this time England were able to pull it out of the fire.

By this stage we weren't even at the end of Day Two.

Rain played its part — it was always going to, wasn't it? Yorkshire fans would know that was inevitable. There was no play before lunch on Saturday's Day Three.

A tigerish bowling performance limited Australia to 224 all out second time around; Wood adding two more wickets, Moeen Ali matching that haul and new-ball pair Broad and Chris Woakes striking three times apiece. Former Yorkshire overseas batter Travis Head top-scored with a middle order 77 for the visitors, who now had serious work to do to take an unassailable 3-0 lead and thus win the series.

In keeping with recent Ashes battles — Headingley 2019 being the obvious one — this chase was never going to be simple. Yes, Australia didn't have key spin weapon Nathan Lyon to call upon after the offie tore his calf at Lord's. But their attack still included the excellent seamers Cummins, Mitchell Starc — another ex-Tyke — and Scott Boland. This wasn't going to be a walk in the park. So it proved.

As journalist Matt Roller wrote on *Cricinfo*, this was a "white-knuckled run chase". England reached the close on Day Three handily placed at 27-0, but regular wickets fell on Day Four as they slipped from 42-0 to 171-6, four of them going to Starc's left-arm pace, including Stokes and Bairstow.

Starc would get home hero Brook to finish with 5-78, but it was a hollow success for the New South Welshman as Brook had done the bulk of the damage with a typically positive 75 off 93 balls with nine fours. He came in at 93-3, and when he departed they were 230-7, needing just 21 to win, which was achieved with Woakes and Wood at the crease. Woakes hit the winning runs, blazing a boundary through point off Starc to the delight of every English man, woman and child in the ground.

While we will clearly herald Brook as the hero — and we will in just a moment — Durham pacer Wood was absolutely fantastic all match, contributing with bat as well as ball. Added to seven wickets, he hit a quickfire 24 down the order in the first innings and a crucial 16 in the second, sharing a match-clinching unbroken 24 for the eighth wicket with Woakes (32 not out) on Sunday afternoon.

Decade of fun: Harry Brook, whose second-innings top score of 75 was the most important knock of a fledgling career that promises 10 years of excitement ahead.

Brook has clearly played innings of greater substance than this 75. Yorkshire and England fans know that all too well.

After all, he has a Test best of 186 (against New Zealand at Wellington in February of last year) and an overall first-class best of 194 (against Kent at Headingley in April 2022).

But you could make a strong argument for this being the most important knock of a fledgling career, which is going to be such fun to watch over the next decade.

The magnitude of the occasion — on his home ground as well — and the fact he went beyond 1,000 Test runs in only his 17th innings ensured that July 9, 2023, was a day the Burley-in-Wharfedale product will never, ever forget. Brook told *Sky Sports* in a post-match interview: "I know a lot of people in the crowd, and to have done this in front of a home crowd was really nice. The crowd's always special here, whether it's for a T20 Blast game or an England Test Match."

Captain Stokes was glowing in his praise of Headingley as a venue: "We absolutely love coming here, and playing cricket for England. The crowd gets right behind us, and the West Stand are always up with us. It's amazing how this place always has memories that people remember. We just love playing here."

This was the start of a thrilling fightback in a series which ended tied at 2-2, the rivals drawing a rainy fourth Test in Manchester before England won another pulsating affair at the Oval — a fixture which proved to be Broad's swan-song after he surprised everyone by announcing his retirement from cricket.

Behind the scenes, many people at Yorkshire deserve credit for putting on a show. The club's management, office staff, volunteers and stewards. They can all look back on a job very well done.

Which brings us to head of grounds Robinson and his team, who for the week included Keith Boyce, a former Headingley groundsman returning to help out the likes of Andy Fogarty and Jasmine Nicholls.

Make no mistake, the pitch was an absolute belter.

Yorkshire coach Ottis Gibson said: "Richard Robinson coming in, the pitches we've played on this year have been fantastic. I got lots and lots of messages, firstly about the Test pitch — what sort of pitch will it be, what will it do?

"I said, 'The pitch at Headingley will be fantastic'. He has been producing great pitches for us to play on.

Mine! Australia's Mitchell Starc and Pat Cummins, right, almost collide as Cummins catches Harry Brook off Starc's bowling.

"Then, after the Test Match, I was getting text messages from Paul Collingwood, Stuart Broad and all those guys saying, 'What a fantastic pitch that was'. People I know from Australia were also saying, 'Wow, that's a fantastic pitch. Do you guys play on pitches like that all year?' I said, 'Yes, every day'.

"He's left a lot more grass on, which has helped the ball carry through. In that Test I think there were something like 10 catches caught in the slips. Some of these pitches are the best in the country. When you go away from here you play at Scarborough, and the pitches there are also fantastic. We have great practices facilities, and the pitches are great. There are no excuses if you play your cricket here not to excel."

Headingley's one-day international between England and Ireland on September 20 was abandoned without a ball bowled. Persistent morning rain made way for afternoon sunshine, but conditions had not improved enough to enable a start before the 5.32pm cut-off for a 20-over affair.

It was the first of a three-match series which included a host of England's second string players, the senior internationals all preparing for the ODI World Cup in India through October and November.

Joe Root would have played at Headingley, but he was not involved in the solitary England victory at Trent Bridge a few days later. The final match in the series at Bristol was washed out following 31 overs of play.

IMMEDIATE IMPRESSION: Yorkshire captain Shan Masood, who will be hoping to secure four-day promotion this summer — his second campaign in charge. Masood, here celebrating a century during the final -week win over Worcestershire at Headingley in September, was also appointed Pakistan's Test skipper late last year.

OPENING UP IN STYLE: Fin Bean, who enjoyed a superb breakthrough year in Yorkshire's first team in 2023, is handed the Members' Player of the Year award by assistant coach Ali Maiden and the President, Dr Jane Powell. His haul of 983 runs from 13 LV= Insurance County Championship matches at the top of the order included three hundreds, and he was inside the top 10 run-scorers in Division Two.

SHINING BRIGHT: Lauren Winfield-Hill shows us exactly where her allegiances lie.

The Yorkshire legend won three end-of-season trophies at the Diamonds' player of the year awards.

Her 663 runs in 14 innings was the most of any batter across the entire Rachael Heyhoe Flint Trophy in 2023.

She was named the Diamonds' batter of the year, player of the year and Yorkshire members' women's player of the year.

ENGLAND CALLING: Bess Heath, on duty for the Northern Superchargers during last year's Hundred, made her senior England debut in both ODI and T20I cricket in 2023. The dynamic wicketkeeper-batter, 22, has since been handed a full-time development contract with the England and Wales Cricket Board.

NAIL-BITER: Dom Bess slog-sweeps the winning runs as Yorkshire beat Derbyshire by three wickets at Chesterfield in June to seal their first victory in the LV= Insurance County Championship since April 2022. Yorkshire chased down a 212 target after the hosts had fought back from 17-4 in their second innings having conceded a lead of 252.

***

REELING 'EM IN: Matthew Fisher has Brooke Guest caught behind in the first innings of the same Chesterfield game.

The Yorkshire and England seamer took a superb 5-30 as the hosts were bowled out for 111 in the first innings.

FINISH LINE: Jonny Tattersall ends the summer in style with 44 not out to wrap up a Championship triumph against Worcestershire at Headingley.

It was a strange old season for Jonny, who was due to start the season as stand-in captain until the arrival from inter-national duty of Shan Masood.

However, a fin-ger injury meant he didn't play a first-team fixture until late May.

LEGEND LEV: Yorkshire leg-spin ace Katie Levick, who has taken 63 wickets for the Northern Diamonds in 50-over and T20 cricket in the last two seasons — more than any other bowler in regional cricket.

****

FIRST STRIKE: Young seamer Grace Hall celebrates a wicket in her senior regional debut at Headingley against Western Storm in May.

Under the lights Hall returned 2-41 in a high-scoring victory. Quickie Lizzie Scott, left in the cap, joins in the celebrations.

LIGHTNING LIZZIE: England Under-19s fast bowler Lizzie Scott, bowling here in a Rachael Heyhoe Flint Trophy win over South East Stars at Scarborough last May, was awarded her first full-time contract with the Northern Diamonds ahead of 2024.

HONOURED BY THE KING: Leg-spin legend Adil Rashid looks out across the Headingley ground after being awarded the MBE for services to cricket as part of King Charles's first Birthday Honours List. Off the field Adil, a two-time Championship winner with Yorkshire and a double limited-overs World Cup winner with England, has done much work for charity in his home city of Bradford and beyond.

* * *

BLAST OFF: James Wharton celebrates a magnificent century — his first in first-team colours — in Yorkshire's Vitality Blast Headingley win over Worcestershire.

Wharton is wearing a Blast kit including all 632 names of the affiliated league clubs in Yorkshire, the brand child of Yorkshire's creative manager, Adrian Mirfakhrai.

LV= Third Ashes Test Match
England v. Australia

Played at Headingley, Leeds, on July, 6, 7, 8 and 9, 2023
England won by 3 wickets at 3.38 pm on the Fourth Day
Toss won by England

Close of play: First Day, England 68-3 ((Root 19*, Bairstow 1*); Second Day, Australia 116-4 (Head 18*, Marsh 17*): Third Day, England 27-0 (Crawley 9*, Duckett 18*)

AUSTRALIA

First Innings		Second Innings	
D A Warner, c Crawley b Broad	4	(2) c Crawley b Broad	1
U T Khawaja, b Wood	13	(1) c Bairstow b Woakes	43
M Labuschagne, c Root b Woakes	21	c Brook b Ali	33
S P D Smith, c Bairstow b Broad	22	c Duckett b Ali	2
T M Head, c Root b Woakes	39	c Duckett b Broad	77
M R Marsh, c Crawley b Woakes	118	c Bairstow b Woakes	28
§ A T Carey, c Woakes b Wood	8	b Woakes	5
M A Starc, b Wood	2	c Brook b Wood	16
* P J Cummins, lbw b Wood	0	c Bairstow b Wood	1
T R Murphy, b Wood	13	lbw b Broad	11
S M Boland, not out	0	not out	0
Extras b 10, lb 10, nb 3	23	Extras b 5, lb 2	7
Total	263	Total	224

FoW: 1-4 (Warner), 2-42 (Khawaja), 3-61 (Labuschagne), 4-85 (Smith), 5-240 (Marsh),
1st   6-245 (Head), 7-249 (Starc), 8-249 (Cummins), 9-254 (Carey), 10-263 (Murphy)
FoW: 1-11 (Warner), 2-68 (Labuschagne), 3-72 (Smith), 4-90 (Khawaja), 5-131 (Marsh),
2nd   6-139 (Carey), 7-168 (Starc), 8-170 (Cummins), 9-211 (Murphy), 10-224 (head)

	O	M	R	W		O	M	R	W
Broad **	11.4	0	58	2	Broad	14.1	3	45	3
Robinson **	11.2	2	38	0	Woakes	18	0	68	3
Wood	11.4	4	34	5	Wood	17	2	66	2
Woakes	17	1	73	3	Root	1	0	4	0
Ali	9	1	40	0	Ali	17	3	34	2

*** Robinson unable to complete his 12th over,*
  which was completed by Broad

ENGLAND

First Innings		Second Innings	
Z Crawley, c Warner b Marsh	33	c Carey b Marsh	44
B M Duckett, c Carey b Cummins	2	lbw b Starc	23
H C Brook, c Smith b Cummins	3	(5) c Cummins b Starc	75
J E Root, c Warner b Cummins	19	c Carey b Cummins	21
§ J M Bairstow, c Smith b Starc	12	(7) b Starc	5
* B A Stokes, c Smith b Murphy	80	c Carey b Starc	13
M M Ali, c Smith b Cummins	21	(3) b Starc	5
C R Woakes, c Cary b Starc	10	not out	32
M A Wood, c Marsh b Cummins	24	not out	16
S C J Broad, c Smith b Cummins	7		
O E Robinson, not out	5		
Extras b 4, lb 3, w 5, nb 9	21	Extras b 7, lb 7, w 1, nb 5	20
Total	237	Total (7 wkts)	254

FoW: 1-18 (Duckett), 2-22 (Brook), 3-65 (Crawley), 4-68 (Root), 5-87 (Bairstow),
1st   6-131 (Ali), 7-142 (Woakes), 8-167 (Wood), 9-199 (Broad), 10-237 (Stokes)
FoW: 1-42 (Duckett), 2-60 (Ali), 3-93 (Crawley), 4-131 (Root), 5-161 (Stokes),
2nd   6-171 (Bairstow), 7-230 (Brook)

	O	M	R	W		O	M	R	W
Starc	14	3	59	2	Cummins	15	0	77	1
Cummins	18	1	91	6	Starc	16	0	78	5
Boland	10	0	35	0	Boland	11	1	49	0
Marsh	3	1	9	1	Marsh	6	0	23	1
Murphy	7.3	0	36	1	Murphy	2	0	13	0

Player of the Match: M A Wood

Umpires: H D P K Dharmasena and N N Menon   Scorers: J T Potter and J R Virr
Third: J S Wilson   Fourth: M Burns   R S Madugalle

TOP OF THE GROUNDS

Fighting the elements: Head of grounds Richard Robinson tips sawdust onto damp areas of the Headingley outfield.

Richard Robinson, Andy Fogarty, Jasmine Nicholls and Scarborough's John Dodds were all honoured at the ECB's Grounds Manager of the Year awards for 2023.

Robinson, Yorkshire's head of grounds, was recognised for the pitch he produced in this summer's third *Ashes* Test Match, which resulted in a thrilling England victory.

It was the first Test pitch Robinson had produced.

He also finished runner-up in the country's best one-day pitches category, Lee Fortis, of Surrey, taking the top award. Fortis won the top award — the Bernard Flack Memorial Trophy — for the best overall pitches.

Fogarty, who remains a key part of Robinson's excellent groundstaff after stepping down from the lead role earlier last year, was presented with a signed and framed England shirt by the other grounds managers. He was given a standing ovation as recognition of a 40-year career which saw him win the Bernard Flack Memorial Trophy four times, and he was a seven-time one-day award winner.

Dodds also won the award for the best outground pitches in 2023. The awards also celebrated the success of the all-women ground staff team — which Nicholls was part of — who produced the pitch for the England Women's Ashes T20 at Edgbaston in July.

ROOT IN SIGHT OF THE SUMMIT OF ENGLAND'S TEST BATTING

By Graham Hardcastle

This could be the year of Joe Root. The Yorkshire batter could further enhance his legendary status in 2024 by becoming England's leading Test run-scorer — he is 1,004 behind Sir Alastair Cook's total of 12,472, which he amassed between 2006 and 2018.

Root started his year in India for a five-match series, two of which were played before this publication went to print.

Six summer Tests will follow against the West Indies and Sri Lanka through July, August and into September. England then play a further three Tests in Pakistan and New Zealand before the end of the year.

It is not unrealistic to expect that, should Root play them all, 15 more Test Matches will be more than enough for him to score the runs required to usurp the great opener Cook: in 2023, against New Zealand away and Ireland and Australia at home, he scored 787 runs in eight appearances, including a pair of centuries against the Tasman nations.

Last year was a mixture of the good, the bad and the ugly for England, for whom Root, Jonny Bairstow, Harry Brook, Dawid Malan and Adil Rashid played across the various formats.

Their Test cricket was exhilarating, drawing the series in New Zealand 1-1 and at home to Australia 2-2. England were 1-0 up against New Zealand, but 2-0 down in the *Ashes* series...the ebb and flow of that rubber is detailed in our Headingley Test review.

Brook was crowned as the Professional Cricketers' Association men's Player of the Year for 2023 and was honoured by the Cricket Writers' Club, who awarded him the Bob Wills Trophy for being England's Player of the Year — male or female.

Brook's standout innings of the year came against New Zealand at Wellington in February, when he hit a brilliant 186 off 176 balls to help England to recover their first innings of the second Test from 21-3 to 435-8 declared before they went on to lose by one run.

Bairstow came back into England's team at the start of the summer, having recovered from the horror leg injury he suffered playing golf the previous August. And he was handed the wicketkeeping gloves instead of Ben Foakes for the *Ashes*.

His standout innings was 99 not out in the first innings of the fourth Test at rainy Manchester, putting Australia to the sword in typical "Bluey" fashion as the hosts tried to set up the win to level the series at 2-2.

With the inevitable bad weather around later in the game, England needed to push on and give themselves enough time to force a result.

They did push on. The rain still thwarted them, but Bairstow's innings will long be remembered, and the way he came back to perform in such a way from a career-threatening injury deserves praise.

Turning the page: Joe Root batting in the Third Test v. Australia at Headingley. He could update the record books in 2024 by becoming England's highest Test run-scorer.

Unfortunately, England's white-ball crown not only slipped but fell off, and it was a difficult time for all of Yorkshire's players involved in a team which failed to reach the one-day World Cup semi-finals in India in November, winning only three of their nine matches.

It means they go into the mid-summer T20 World Cup in the USA and Caribbean, for which they are defending champions, with significant pressure on their shoulders. Quite how many of Yorkshire's players will be involved remains to be seen. Malan was left out of the end-of-year white-ball tour against the West Indies.

England lost the three-match ODI series against the hosts 2-1, and in the T20 series they slipped to 2-0 behind before Brook hit a stunning 31 not out off seven balls in game three to halve the arrears. England were chasing 223, and needed 21 off the last over. Brook got all of them, and the series finished 3-2.

Matthew Fisher played England Lions cricket, including a tour of India at the start of this year. He is becoming much more of a senior figure and a leader in that set-up, and he will be hoping he can push on to add to the solitary Test cap he won in Barbados at the start of 2022.

Off the field, Adil Rashid was awarded a mid-year MBE in King

Charles's first Birthday Honours List, while he alongside Bairstow and Brook were given the Freedom of the City of Bradford.

Northern Diamonds' wicketkeeper-batter Bess Heath made her senior England ODI and T20I debuts towards the back end of 2023. Heath played against Sri Lanka at Leicester in 50-over cricket last September, contributing an aggressive 21 late in the innings as the hosts completed a victory. She then played against India in the T20 series at the Wankhede Stadium in December, making one in a defeat.

Heath will be hoping to be a part of England's squad which tackles the next ICC tournament, the T20 World Cup in Bangladesh scheduled to be played in September and October.

It is by no means out of the question that Heath's fellow Diamond Hollie Armitage will be part of that tournament, for the regional captain and all-rounder progressed her career to play for England's A side at home and abroad in 2023 before being called into the senior squad for the first time for a T20 series in New Zealand in March this year.

Armitage played against their Australian counterparts on home soil during the summer, and then against India in Mumbai during the first half of the winter. In all, across 50-over and T20 cricket she posted 190 runs in six appearances with two half-centuries.

Outgoing Diamonds director of cricket James Carr said: "For such a young person, Hollie brought strong leadership skills to our region. She's a real battler, but she's got such a calm manner. She's brought out the best in senior and junior players, and that's an art in itself.

"She's developed her T20 game and is quite dominant now. Hopefully, she can go and have an illustrious England career."

ENGLAND'S YORKSHIRE LEADERS
IN ONE-DAY WORLD CUPS

BATTING

Player	Dates	Runs	Matches	Best
J E Root	2015, 2019, 2023	1,034	26	121
J M Bairstow	2019, 2023	747	20	111
D J Malan	2023	404	9	140
M P Vaughan	2003, 2007	348	14	79

BOWLING

Player	Dates	Wkts	Matches	Best
A U Rashid	2019, 2023	26	20	3-42
C M Old	1975, 1979	16	9	4- 8
D Gough	1996, 1999	15	11	4-34
T T Bresnan	2011	9	5	5-48

WOMEN NEAR THE PINNACLE AS MEN FALL TO FLOOR

By Graham Hardcastle

The women's side flew the flag impressively for the Northern Superchargers in last season's Hundred, with Hollie Armitage's team reaching August's Lord's final where they were beaten by Southern Brave. It was the first time that either the men or the women had reached the knockout stages in three seasons of the competition, bettering a plethora of mid-table finishes.

Unfortunately for the men, they finished bottom of the table, winning only two of eight matches. They won against the Trent Rockets and the Southern Brave, both away from home, while their standout individual performance came in a home defeat to Welsh Fire at Headingley.

Harry Brook hit a remarkable 105 not out off only 42 balls, the highest score of the season by any batter in that format, as he lifted the hosts from 92-7 to 158-7. But the Fire won by eight wickets.

The struggles for the men forced a change in coach, with James Foster departing after one summer in charge. In his place comes Lancashire legend Andrew Flintoff, whose return to cricket has gathered pace over recent months.

Ex-England all-rounder Flintoff suffered horrendous facial injuries during a crash while filming the *Top Gear* TV programme, for which he was a host. He recovered away from the public limelight before deciding that he wanted to return to the game which brought him and others watching him so much joy. He has worked with England's senior and Lions teams since the end of last summer.

Only three Yorkshire players featured for the Superchargers men in 2023: Brook with 238 runs — the third-best haul across the competition — Adam Lyth and Adil Rashid. Lyth played only four matches following injury, while Rashid impressed with 11 wickets.

Jonny Bairstow (Welsh Fire), Jafer Chohan and Matthew Fisher (both Southern Brave), Dawid Malan and Joe Root (both Trent Rockets) and Jordan Thompson (London Spirit) all played away from Headingley.

The women's competition saw the Superchargers finish second in the table behind the Brave, winning six of their eight group matches. They

HOLLIE ARMITAGE
"Breath of fresh air" as
Superchargers captain.

then advanced beyond the semi-final eliminator against the Welsh Fire. which was washed out without a ball bowled at the Oval on August 26, because they had finished higher in the league table than their opponents.

In the Lord's final the following day Armitage's side were bowled out for 105 chasing a target of 140.

The Superchargers had a touch more local representation, starting with Northern Diamonds skipper Armitage, coach Dani Hazell and Leah Dobson, Bess Heath and fledgling seamer Grace Hall.

Australian overseas batter Phoebe Litchfield starred with 279 runs.

When you think of Flintoff coming in to lift the men it is interesting that one of the women's standout players in 2023 was another Lancashire legend, Kate Cross.

The England seamer has built her impressive career on the wrong side of the Pennines, both with Lancashire and now Thunder in regional cricket, but she was signed in the pre-tournament draft to play in purple, having not been retained by Manchester Originals. And she claimed 10 wickets.

Cross heaped praise on Armitage as captain, saying: "I found her to be a breath of fresh air, and she really helped me with my game. That was great. I would have her up there as one of the best captains in the tournament. Tactically, she's right up there, and she really impressed me with how calm she was in pressure situations.

"She's got a lot more to give with the bat as well. She will probably hold her hands up and admit that she didn't have her best tournament with the bat. But the games in which she didn't contribute with the bat she did in the field and with her captaincy.

"It's very exciting for her to see where she can get to."

THE DAY TEARS TURNED
TO CHAMPIONSHIP JOY

By Graham Hardcastle

All successes are special, given the hard work required.

Ups, downs, blood, sweat and tears aplenty in every single one across all sports...but now and again come triumphs which stop you in your tracks: Leicester City taking the Premier League title in 2015-16 springs to mind; so, too, does Emma Raducanu winning the US Open women's tennis title in 2021, having entered the main draw as a qualifier.

There will have been plenty of other great underdog tales down the years as well — and you can put Yorkshire's D40 National Quest League title from 2023 in the same bracket.

Granted, this didn't get the same notoriety as the aforementioned remarkable British sporting moments...but there is no question that the exploits of Gordon Laidlaw's side were last summer's grand success story of Yorkshire cricket. And a most unexpected one at that.

That is not to detract from the fantastic work of Yorkshire's Over-50s team, who won their own national title and make up the next feature in this *Yearbook,* but they are a side seen as one of the best in county cricket. They were expected to be there and thereabouts. Not being there would have been a disappointment.

For captain Laidlaw — who has since retired — and his team challenging for the title last season was not part of the initial plan.

Rewind to September 2022, and the D40 team are getting set for a promotion decider against Middlesex seconds from the Pursuit League. Winning it, which they duly did, would secure promotion to the top flight of English cricket. Despite representing a cricket powerhouse of a county, here was a team — a whole disability structure, in fact — which was emerging and developing.

Two teams — one at the S9 softball level and one at D40 — had become three for 2023, an extra D40 side added to meet the increase in number and quality of players. Effectively, the D40 second team would play in the Pursuit League, which the firsts had just come out of.

The hard work of the Jervis's, Owen and Alex, was a big part in this. Father Owen as team manager had been working feverishly behind the scenes, be it on finding players, fixture logistics or lobbying for more

Showpiece champions. Yorkshire's D40 side play the Lord's Taverners at Tring. Back Row, left to right: Dr Jane Powell (Yorkshire County Crickety Club President), Monty Panesar (Lord's Taverners), James O'Conner, William Baxter, Archie Atkins Sloan, Matthew Bateman, David Gower (Lord's Taverners umpire), Cameron Sweeney, Adam Marshall, Kyle Clayton and Callum Robertson (coach). Front row: Robert Hewitt, Jasper Spooner, John Kenwood-Nash, Cameron Cooper, Luke Riley, Owen Morris and Alex Jervis.

exposure. When you think of the type of work which is crucial but goes unnoticed it's likely he's done it.

All-rounder Matt Bateman, Yorkshire's new D40 Quest League captain for 2024, said: "A lot of credit goes to Owen. Alex has had a lot to do with it from the playing side, but the way Owen goes about getting a team on the park and getting us organised, lobbying for better things to happen in the background, he deserves a massive amount of credit.

"He doesn't like taking credit, but things don't happen without him, if that makes sense."

Alex's influence on the field has been significant. He has been playing for Yorkshire for 15 years, and has been an England Learning Disability international since debuting in 2015. He has recruited players, coached them and guided them on the field as well as being a reliable seam-bowling spearhead.

Others must also be mentioned. Coach Callum Robertson is one. We will get onto Laidlaw a bit later, but he was one of three captains last season, including Bateman as a stand-in and fellow all-rounder James O'Conner, who started the season as permanent skipper, having led the side to promotion in 2022.

It was a fair old year for O'Conner, a rollercoaster ride without doubt. He started it as Yorkshire captain, stepped down owing in large parts to other commitments away from the game, and continued to perform on the field, helping to win the title before earning a maiden England call-up for the Deaf World Cup in Qatar in December. Unfortunately, that competition was cancelled at the last minute. The close proximity to Israel and Palestine was a factor, but O'Conner's time in an England shirt will come. Of that there's no doubt.

The support of the Yorkshire Cricket Board, the County Club and the England and Wales Cricket Board has been a significant driver behind the development of disability cricket in England, and not just in the Broad Acres.

The Quest season saw Yorkshire start with a *Roses* defeat against Lancashire and end with a showpiece game against the Lord's Taverners at Tring, the annual reward for the county champions. Former international Monty Panesar played for the Taverners, while ex-England captain David Gower was a guest umpire for the day.

Of the serious stuff Yorkshire won three of their six 40-over matches, with the other two abandoned. They recovered from defeat against the *Red Rose* to win the title by two points from Middlesex, while Lancashire were third. One of Yorkshire's rained off games was away to Surrey during the final round of matches on Sunday, July 30. Had Lancashire won their game at home to Sussex they would have been champions...but they were bowled out for 82, chasing only 94.

Yorkshire victories came away against Sussex, when they travelled down to Ansty with only nine men and won by two runs defending a target of 191, and against defending champions Hampshire and Essex.

"There were a few really key moments," Bateman said. "Losing to Lancashire at the start was an eye-opener. That refocused everybody. We just weren't at it that game, and we needed to improve. Going to Sussex and winning with nine men gave everybody the belief we could win from any situation. Then we turned Hampshire, the reigning champions, over quite convincingly.

"We should have beaten Lancashire in that first game. We were defending 235, and that should be enough in any game. But it definitely refocused us. We knew we had to improve."

As for the title-deciding day Yorkshire were 123-2 after 26 overs when heavy rain hit the south and the game was abandoned instantly. "When we were rained off and we thought that was it, we couldn't win it, the lads in the changing room were mortified," recalled Bateman, who went on to win the Players' Player of the Year award.

"I was devastated, but I was trying to keep a brave face on for some of the lads. There were tears, anger, a few things going around the changing room. We just felt the umpires called it off too soon. As it goes, they made the right decision. It started raining, they pulled the stumps out and said, 'That's it, lads'. I was like, 'What do you mean, that's it?

"'Are we not going to at least wait a little bit?

"It felt like it had been ripped away from us through no fault of our own. I can't see we would have lost that game. We were rattling along.

"But just seeing what it meant to the guys in the changing room was quite humbling.

"Then Kyle Clayton, who the season before played for Lancashire, got some updates and found out they'd thrown it away a bit against Sussex. We'd gone from tears of disappointment to tears of joy.

" It was amazing."

Captain Laidlaw, a former England Physical Disability World Cup winner, said: "We probably set off two years ago thinking it would take

Tragedy to triumph: Alex Jervis, left, holds the championship trophy with all-rounder Matt Bateman, the county's D40 Quest League captain for 2024, after learning they had won the title they thought had gone.

five years to get to where we are now. The key moment was probably the realisation that we could do it. Whether that was at Sussex or even against Lancashire. Even though we got beat in that game, we knew we should have won it. The big thing has been the fact we've put runs on the board. We've 200 in almost every game, and have maxed out on our batting points. We've then bowled really tight to back that up."

For *Ashes*-winning bowler Jervis this was an emotional success. There was a stage pre-Covid that Yorkshire didn't field a hardball team, with Jervis lobbying the Yorkshire Cricket Board for its inclusion. It is very much worth mentioning the hard work of Donna Staniland and Shakil Manir, the YCB's head of operations and disability manager.

"Seeing the team we put out three years ago to the one we've got now, it's unbelievable," Alex said. "It's not as high as I've got to in my career, but as an achievement it's definitely right up there.

Jervis had actually spoken at the start of 2023 about considering giving up cricket, only for a trip to Kenya promoting the game with the Cricket Without Boundaries charity relighting his fire for the game: "I'm glad I didn't give up now," he added.

Before the final game at Surrey the squad were sent good luck messages from Yorkshire captain Shan Masood and Katie Levick. Owen Jervis said: "It was great to have those messages. When we played those to the players they seemed to get it that the big players within the club know we're playing and are behind us. It made a big difference.

"It's clearly been a difficult time at Headingley over the last couple of years. So for us to be able to bring back some silverware is fantastic. It's a fantastic achievement for everyone. I want to mention those behind the scenes as well, and I've already nominated them for an award. We wouldn't be where we are without the people behind the scenes — officials, umpires, scorers, parents — all those who make the game tick."

For all-rounder Bateman, who has taken over the Quest captaincy for 2024, it will be only his second season playing disability cricket. He found out only in the winter of 2022-23 that his Kohler's Disease qualified him to play disability cricket. It is a childhood disease where the bones and legs do not grow straight.

Bateman was a former Hampshire School of Excellence player who has lived in the Worksop area for 23 years. He ended last summer named as Yorkshire's Quest bowler of the season, thanks to nine wickets, and was also named as Players' Player of the Year, having added 241 in eight games with the bat.

Looking ahead to next season, he said of a title-defence: "That will be the plan. We'll certainly not be going in thinking, 'We've won it once, that was nice'. It will be a case of, 'Let's go and try to win it again'. Teams like Lancashire, Middlesex, Hampshire...they'll have a target on us now. Everybody wants to beat the reigning champions."

His predecessor, Laidlaw, stepped away from the game following a legendary career capped in a special way with this triumph. It followed him winning the Physical Disability World Cup with England in Bangladesh in 2015.

Upon retirement in December, Laidlaw said: "I always said I wanted to play cricket to enjoy it, and this summer hasn't been as enjoyable as I'd want. The success we had was unbelievable, and I loved that. But physically not being able to do what I'd want to as well as I'd want to was a bit of a frustration.

"I wanted to help Yorkshire to win the Pursuit League and get back to competing nationally at least. We're ahead of the game with winning it, and that's amazing."

Owen Jervis said of the summer: "We have been measuring our success on trophies and medals, which is only part of the story."

On that basis it is worth noting that Yorkshire Cricket have seen a host of players gain England recognition.

Alex Jervis and Rob Hewitt helped England to win a Learning Disability T20 tri-series against South Africa and Australia in South Africa in November.

O'Conner, wicketkeeper-batter Cameron Sweeney and Henry Wainman — he hasn't played much county cricket for Yorkshire in favour of using his time to play mainstream Premier League club cricket — gained recognition in the Deaf World Cup squad.

Liam Thomas, an England

The man who makes it happen. Name a job and Owen Jervis, above, has probably done it.

Physical Disability cricketer who, like Wainman, hasn't played much county cricket for Yorkshire, went to India at the start of this year.

Another important part of the development of Yorkshire's players and those nationally is the ECB's Disability Premier League, a late-summer competition with many similarities to the Hundred: it aims to pit the country's best players against each other across four manufactured teams — the Black Cats, Tridents, Pirates and Hawks.

Yorkshire had significant representation in that competition, including six players involved in the early-September final between the triumphant Hawks and Pirates at Derbyshire's Incora County Ground, which was televised live by *Sky Sports*. Wainman, Kyle Clayton and Yorkshire's D40 Pursuit captain, Owen Morris, played for the Hawks, and Thomas, Jervis and Laidlaw all represented the Pirates.

It all added up to one remarkable season for disability cricket in Yorkshire. Now they will hoping to build on the significant momentum they have created, and push on to be a sustained powerhouse of the English game. What is it they say? *Strong Yorkshire, strong England.*

INDIAN SUMMER PLAYERS
SHINE FOR YORKSHIRE

By Graham Hardcastle

A period of domination is the target for Yorkshire Over-50s after last year's thrilling title win. That is the aim for the next few summers, says Steve Wales, who has tasted success as county captain and now team manager. The *White Rose* beat Bedfordshire by 146 runs in September's rain-reduced final, bowling their opponents out for just 62 as they replied to a commanding 40-over score of 222-3.

That was a landslide success, as many of Yorkshire's 10 victories were. They lost one and had another cancelled in the group stage.

But the thrilling part was undoubtedly the semi-final victory over Cambridgeshire at Fitzwilliam College in late August, when captain Steve Foster — a superstar at this level — and his team won via fewer wickets lost on a tie as both teams totalled 174.

Cambridgeshire made 174-9 from their 45 overs before Yorkshire replied with 174-5, gaining 11 of the 12 runs needed off the last over, including two off the last ball. What was it Ian Smith said about the 2019 World Cup final? "By the barest of margins." That fits.

There was also an emotional sense of *deja vu* about that fixture: "It was a game where it could have been, 'Oh no, what have we done — we've got to the semi-final and thrown it away'," said Wales, a former Yorkshire and England captain. "Fortunately, we scraped home.

"Then, in the final against Bedfordshire at Wormsley, we were just too dominant. Talking about the tied semi-final...We played against Essex in 2017 at the same stage at Elland, and tied that and won on fewer wickets lost.

"The gentleman who bowled the last over was Dave Burden, and he bowled it at Mel Hussain — Nasser's brother. They wanted five to win off the last over with four wickets in hand. They got four runs, but lost three wickets in doing it.

"Dave, unfortunately, died a couple of years ago following a brain tumour, and it's been a bit like Seve Ballesteros on your shoulder just as the Ryder Cup guys have had in golf. Everyone has a unique Yorkshire number, and we put his on our shirt this year. That win was dedicated to him. I would say that semi-final he starred in was one of the greatest

Over-50s Champions: Back row, left to right: Craig Russell (Hanging Heaton CC), Iqbal Khan (Heckmondwike and Carlinghow), Nick Gaywood (Sheffield Collegiate), Stuart Hudson (Beckwithshaw) and Tom Watkin (Hull Zingari). Middle row: Steve Wales (North Leeds, manager), Lesroy Weekes (Eckington), Muhammad Shahnawaz (Heckmondwike and Carlinghow), Jason Meadows (Elsecar) and Leigh Beaumont (Stockton). Front row: Andy Robertson (Birstall), Babar Butt (Pudsey Congs), Steve Foster (Treeton, captain), Haider Jahangir (Barnsley Woolley, vice-captain), Luke Jarvis (Collingham) and Bandula Ranjith (Hollandswaine).

games I've played in for any side. It was like, 'How the hell did we win that?' I still get goosebumps thinking about it, and it was very similar this year against Cambridgeshire."

Should Yorkshire build on this success in 2024 they will repeat the feat achieved in 2017 and 2018, when they claimed back-to-back Over-50s triumphs under the captaincy of Wales, who played for most of his career for North Leeds in the Aire Wharfe League. He won three national-al titles with Yorkshire, and also captained England sporadically between 2016 and 2018.

"I'm chuffed to bits to have captained my county and my country," he said. "I wasn't good enough to do it at open age, but it just shows what opportunities are about if you look after yourself.

"I initially hung around to play some league cricket with my son. But then, at this stage in your life, when you think you've had your best days, to be able to go again and play in this Yorkshire team, it was up there among my proudest moments. I've played, and now I'm managing, and it's a bit addictive. It's so much fun with these guys, because they're turning up and wanting to win. It's fantastic. It was Peter Graham, former Northern Diamonds bowler Phoebe's late father, who initially told me I should think about putting my name forward to play, and it was the best bit of advice I've ever been given."

Wales says there will be some turnover in Yorkshire's squad — they use 15-16 players — for the coming summer, but nothing too drastic: "Generally our players are 50-55, but we do have a couple of guys who are older. We have Nick Gaywood, who opens the batting and has just turned 60. He used to open with Joe Root at Sheffield Collegiate, and has played for Devon. He is now playing for England 60s. He's a very good, tall, strong, left-handed batter who has just kept going.

"He's huge for us. He got 70-odd in the final and a couple of hundreds through the year. If they're still playing at 55-60 these guys are serious competitors. We've got two or three ex-Pakistani first-class players. Babar Butt, who bats and kept wicket in the final for us, is one of the legends of the Bradford League.

"Our captain is Steve Foster, who captained England 50s when they won the World Cup in South Africa earlier this year. He is ranked as the best Over-50s player in the world.

"We're constantly looking to evolve, and not sit back just because we've won. Because we've done well people hear about it, and want to join us. We'll be blooding some new lads this year, and there will be a few who step aside. That's just normal progression.

"There will be good, healthy competition for places as many are definitely still good enough to go again. It's a bit like junior cricket in that you will get a good group coming through and will do well, but then it goes quiet for a while. Thankfully, we've managed to maintain a group who have been up there for a long time.

"The idea now is to go for a bit of domination," Wales said. "We were the best side last year, but it won't be easy this year. We can't be complacent because there are some good sides out there.

"This is proper competitive environment. It's certainly not for a faint-hearted 50-something-year-old. A lot of counties are bringing in ex-England players. We've played against Kim Barnett in the past, and Mark Alleyne...Nasser Hussain's brother as well."

Talking of Nasser's brother, Mel, brings us to the fact that Essex are one of Yorkshire's main rivals, the counties having probably been the two most consistent teams over the last 10 years. Essex beat Yorkshire in the 2019 final, but Yorkshire gained some revenge in 2023 by beating them in the quarter-finals at Colchester and East Essex CC.

"We got 291-5, and played really well in that game, and we felt that was the big scalp," said Wales, a national sales manager in construction. "Nick Gaywood got a hundred, and Steve Foster 50. Then we bowled them for 201. Then we played Cambridgeshire, and nearly undid all that good work. Thankfully, we just got through and won the final."

Wales describes the competition as "tough", not just because of the quality of cricket, but also because of the logistics. "You're dealing with guys who are still working," he said. "In the group stages we play every Wednesday over a 12-week period with a few gaps in between. Then the knockout stages are played through the holiday season, when you have to try and keep your strongest side together.

"I must pay tribute to Robin Benyon, who has played a massive part in the organisation and administration for the team. He's made things a lot easier.

"The idea of the group stage is to finish top of the group, and Yorkshire have always finished first or second in the time I've been involved. Second means your first knockout tie — the last 16 — is at home. Then the next two could be away, as happened this year.

"Every county is represented. We had Cornwall playing us in a quarter-final at Malton, so it gives you an idea of the travelling involved. If you're in the top two in the country you tend to get home draws through to the final. We lost to Lancashire in the first game of the season, and were pretty poor, but we won every game after that. It was absolutely fantastic."

White's rose changes colour...

Former Yorkshire captain and England all-rounder Craig White has been appointed as Lancashire's bowling coach.

White was already a full-time staff member at Emirates Old Trafford before his December appointment, having worked as an assistant coach for the Thunder women.

He has replaced Graham Onions in the men's role, linking up with new head coach Dale Benkenstein, whom he had previously worked with at Hampshire.

SPINNER MORIARTY HOMES STRAIGHT IN ON FIVE-FOR

By Graham Hardcastle

DAN MORIARTY: Goggles off as he thanks the applauding fans after taking five wickets in his Yorkshire LV= Insurance Championship debut.

Yorkshire signed left-arm spinner Dan Moriarty on a three-year contract ahead of 2024 after an encouraging short-term loan spell through late June and July.

The then Surrey bowler took five wickets on debut in the LV= Insurance County Championship draw against Gloucestershire at Headingley.

The rest of Moriarty's four-game loan spell was decimated by the weather, but Ottis Gibson and Darren Gough were keen to recruit the 24-year-old to add what they believe is the missing piece in their spin bowling jigsaw.

In Dom Bess they have an off-spinner added to a pair of leg-spinners in Jafer Chohan and England white ball legend Adil Rashid.

Off-spinner Jack Shutt was one of two departures from the Yorkshire squad at the end of 2023, with home-grown batter Will Fraine released having joined the county from Nottinghamshire at the end of 2018.

Shutt, who came through the age-groups and Academy system at Yorkshire, and Fraine have both found first-team opportunities limited, showing only flashes of promise when given the chance. Fraine hit a stunning Championship century against a Morne Morkel-led Surrey attack at Scarborough in 2019 as an opener, but he was unable to find a

WILL FRAINE   **JACK SHUTT**   **JAMES CARR**

permanent home anywhere in the order. At his best he was scintillating either at the top of the order in 50-over cricket or as a finisher in T20. But the hierarchy have opted to look beyond the 27-year-old from Huddersfield, who was educated at Malvern College and spent time in Worcestershire's Academy and second team before his initial move to Trent Bridge.

Shutt, 27 this summer and from Barnsley, has been a one-county man. He has played only 32 times across all formats at first-team level, with a superb best of 5-11 in a Vitality Blast win at Durham in 2019.

At the time of writing, Moriarty's arrival was the only significant arrival in Yorkshire's first-team, with Gibson and Gough biding their time on the overseas front until later in the winter. They already have Pakistan Test captain Shan Masood nailed down for another season, with the possibility of supplementing him with another arrival across the trio of competitions.

Off the field the most significant cricket-related winter departure was James Carr as director of cricket for the Northern Diamonds. He left in December, having taken up his role at the start of the regional era in March 2020. His successful tenure was highlighted by the Diamonds winning the Rachael Heyhoe Flint Trophy in 2022.

Carr also helped to pave the way for Bess Heath to progress through to senior cricket with England, with whom she is now centrally contract-ed: "I'd like to say thank you to an outstanding staff team that work tire-lessly behind the scenes and across the pathway," Carr said. "They each offer great skills, knowledge and insight that has contributed hugely to raising the standards and improving performance.

"I've really enjoyed my time working with such outstanding people."

Also departing from the playing staff were all-rounders Yvonne Graves and overseas South African international Chloe Tryon.

Graves played only three competitive fixtures for the Diamonds, having joined from the Lightning side ahead of the 2022 summer, while Tryon hit 279 runs and took 14 wickets in 16 appearances, including bests of 63 and 4-16.

The Diamonds recruited skilful seam bowler Sophia Turner, aged 20, on a pay-to-play contract from rivals Thunder after she took a wicket in each of two end-of-season 50-over games while on loan in September.

Blackburn-born Turner found game time limited at Emirates Old Trafford, though she took 1-4 from four overs in a T20 win against the Diamonds at Headingley in 2021.

WILLIAM (Will) ALAN RICHARD FRAINE
FIRST-CLASS CRICKET FOR YORKSHIRE

Right-hand batter	Right-arm medium-pace bowler	
Born: Huddersfield	June 13, 1996	
Debut for Yorkshire:	v. Essex at Leeds	June 3, 2019
Last played:	v. Surrey at The Oval	September 20, 2022

BATTING AND FIELDING

Matches	Innings	NO	Runs	HS	Avge	100s	50s	Ct
21	38	2	663	106	18.41	1	1	17

Century (1)

2019	106	v. Surrey	at Scarborough

LIST A CRICKET FOR YORKSHIRE

Debut for Yorkshire	v. Durham at Leeds	May 6, 2019
Last played:	v. Hampshire at York	August 17, 2023

BATTING AND FIELDING

Matches	Innings	NO	Runs	HS	Avge	100s	50s	Ct
22	20	2	613	143	34.05	1	2	11

Century (1)

2022	143	v. Northamptonshire	at York

T20 CRICKET FOR YORKSHIRE

Debut for Yorkshire	v. Durham at Chester-le-Street	August 23, 2019
Last played	v. Durham at Chester-le-Street	June 23, 2023

BATTING AND FIELDING

Matches	Innings	NO	Runs	HS	Avge	100s	50s	Ct
29	27	10	362	44*	21.29	0	0	16

JACK WILLIAM SHUTT

FIRST-CLASS CRICKET FOR YORKSHIRE

Right-hand batter   Right-arm off-break bowler
Born: Barnsley   June 24, 1997
Debut for Yorkshire   v. Somerset at Scarborough   August 1, 2020
Last played: v. Essex at Leeds   September 14, 2022

BATTING AND FIELDING

Matches	Innings	NO	Runs	HS	Avge	100s	50s	Ct
5	7	5	12	7*	6.00	0	0	3

BOWLING

Overs	Maidens	Runs	Wkts	Avge	Best	5Wi
38.2	1	200	5	40.00	2-14	0

LIST A CRICKET FOR YORKSHIRE

Debut for Yorkshire   v. Surrey at York   July 22, 2021
Last played: v. Middlesex at Radlett   August 22, 2023

BATTING AND FIELDING

Matches	Innings	NO	Runs	HS	Avge	100s	50s	Ct
14	6	4	9	6*	4.50	0	0	7

BOWLING

Overs	Maidens	Runs	Wkts	Avge	Best	4Wi
78.4	0	437	15	29.13	4-46	2

4 wickets in an innings (2)

2022	4-46	v. Glamorgan	at Cardiff
2023	4-49	v. Middlesex	at Radlett

T20 CRICKET FOR YORKSHIRE

Debut for Yorkshire   v. Lancashire at Leeds   July 25, 2019
Last played   v. Durham at Chester-le-Street   June 17, 2022

BATTING AND FIELDING

Matches	Innings	NO	Runs	HS	Avge	100s	50s	Ct
13	4	3	0	0*	0.00	0	0	3

BOWLING

Overs	Maidens	Runs	Wkts	Avge	Best	4Wi
42	0	327	16	20.43	5-11	2

4 wickets in an innings (2)

2019	5-11	v. Durham	at Chester-le-Street
2022	4-35	v. Durham	at Chester-le-Street

CHAMPIONSHIP HAT-TRICK AT END OF A BUMPY RIDE

By Anthony Bradbury

Having won the County Championship in 1922 and 1923, Yorkshire were keen to obtain a hat-trick of successes when the 1924 season started in early May. Yorkshire were to achieve that triumph after 30 Championship games, but only after a bumpy ride to finish ahead of Middlesex with whom there were two very difficult matches.

Yorkshire had a settled side, sometimes playing exactly the same team, as in some of the 1923 matches — namely Holmes, Sutcliffe, Oldroyd, Leyland, Rhodes, R Kilner, Robinson, Mr G Wilson (captain), Macaulay, Waddington and Dolphin. When Test calls for England — who played South Africa — took Sutcliffe, Kilner and Macaulay away none of the Yorkshire debutants, Mr S Allen, Mr C E Anson, L Ryder, Harry Taylor and I Turner made any impact, and Allen, Anson, Ryder and Turner made their first and last Championship appearances in 1924.

The side started imperiously, winning four of their first five Championship matches, the other being drawn. They then played Middlesex at Lord's without Sutcliffe, Holmes, Kilner and Macaulay, all playing in a Test Trial. For the same reason Middlesex did not have Hendren and J W Hearne. The confident Yorkshire professionals may have been disdainful of a Middlesex side containing eight amateurs, but if so they were soon to suffer. Yorkshire were bowled out for 192, and Middlesex responded with 465-8 declared.

The talented Greville Stevens scored 114, putting on 151 with his captain, F T Mann, in 95 minutes. *Wisden* records that Mann struck four sixes off Wilfred Rhodes, two of them onto the pavilion roof.

Can that be correct?

Rhodes recovered to bowl 52 overs for 102 runs, but the damage was done. Yorkshire capitulated to 121 all out in their second innings and Middlesex, champions in 1920 and 1921, won by an innings and 152 runs. Yorkshire would have travelled home in a bewildered state.

The next disaster came in early June in the much anticipated clash with Lancashire at Headingley. The cricket on the opening day, a Saturday, was slow and tenacious. Lancashire were bowled out for 113, Macaulay taking 6-40, but Herbert Sutcliffe was out for 0 before the end of the day. On the Monday, Yorkshire were tied down by fine bowling and were all out for 130.

Yet that same evening all must have seemed rosy when Lancashire collapsed to 74 all out, Macaulay taking 4-19 and 10 wickets in the match.

With 58 to score for a win on the Tuesday morning, but on a wicket that gave much help to bowlers, Yorkshire were shot out for only 33 runs in 65 minutes with Richard Tyldesley taking 6-18.

Lancashire had won by 24 runs. Yorkshire's 33 remains their lowest-ever score against their great rivals.

It is not the lowest score in a *Roses* match. That "honour" goes to Lancashire with 30 all out at Holbeck in 1868.

Yorkshire then returned to more expected winning ways. Their next home match, at Dewsbury, was against a Somerset side containing nine amateurs.

HERBERT SUTCLIFFE: Topped Yorkshire batting before a triumphant tour of Australia.

(Photo: Mick Pope Archive)

Yorkshire crushed them. Somerset scored 132 and 100, with Yorkshire making 434-8 declared. Sutcliffe struck 213 of those runs, and a few weeks later he scored another double-century, this time 255 not out against Essex at Southend. This was then his highest score, but he did better in 1932 with 313, also against Essex in the famed 555 partnership with Percy Holmes.

Meanwhile, Middlesex were themselves very much in the hunt for Championship success. Both they and Yorkshire were well aware of the key match between the two clubs to take place at Bramall Lane, Sheffield, in early July. The Yorkshire crowds, 30,000 in all over three days with the bulk there on the first day, were also only too conscious of the importance of the fixture. Unhappily, the Middlesex team found

Champion County 1924. Back row, left to right: Edgar Oldroyd, Roy Kilner, Herbert Sutcliffe, George Macaulay, Maurice Leyland, Emmott Robinson and William Ringrose (scorer). Front row: Abe Waddington, Wilfred Rhodes, Geoffrey Wilson (captain), John Stephenson — what blazer is he wearing? — Arthur Dolphin and Percy Holmes.

(Photo: Mick Pope Archive)

themselves facing considerable animosity from the spectators when they were asked to bat when Yorkshire won the toss. In no time the two Middlesex amateurs heading their innings had put on a 50 partnership. Abe Waddington, the Yorkshire left-arm fast-medium bowler, then thought he had Stevens caught at the wicket. Stevens did not move, and the umpire did not give him out.

Waddington reacted petulantly, and some of the crowd were unsparing in abuse. Though Middlesex then lost wickets their middle-order revived their position and they went on to score 358. The normally popular Patsy Hendren was run out for 99, which may have caused more crowd excitement.

After the Sunday rest day crowd trouble flared again on the Monday as Yorkshire sought and failed to overtake Middlesex. Having had a reasonable start they lost three successive players in short order to lbw decisions. Waddington was one of that trio, lbw for 0, and he demonstrated his unhappiness at the decision. The crowd took its cue from Waddington and jeering rang out against the Middlesex team.

The Yorkshire captain, Geoffrey Wilson, came and went, also for 0. Only a modest revival from the last pair took Yorkshire into the final day, and on to 334. Middlesex batted solidly throughout much of that

ABE WADDINGTON: Censured and forced to apologise after fractious game against Middlesex at Bramall Lane.

(Photo: Ron Deaton Archive)

day, leaving Yorkshire no chance of victory and the crowd simmering with discontent.

The umpires made complaint about all these circumstances to MCC, and Yorkshire held a special committee meeting to which Waddington was summoned. Yorkshire asked that MCC conduct an inquiry.

The Middlesex committee also considered the whole matter, suggesting that several Yorkshire players had misbehaved in reactions to decisions.

Middlesex then expressed unwillingness to play Yorkshire in 1925. As for the 1924 season they had no fixtures at all against Derbyshire, Glamorgan, Leicestershire, Northants or Worcestershire perhaps a suggestion that they now would not play Yorkshire did not amount to very much.

An MCC Committee eventually prepare a report indicating that Waddington had shown dissent to the umpires. Lord Hawke censured Waddington, Waddington issued a personal apology, and Yorkshire apologised to Middlesex.

Not a word of this was specifically referred to in the Yorkshire Annual Report dated December 31, 1924. However an announcement was made in that Report that a game with Middlesex in 1925 would be played in Leeds for the Benefit of Roy Kilner and "it is hoped the members and general public will....co-operate to make the match a great success".

The 1925 drawn match was certainly a success for Kilner as his benefit raised £4,017 — a record at the time.

The one regrettable casualty of the unpleasant Middlesex match was that it led at the end of the season to the resignation of the captain, Wilson, a mild-mannered man who may have found the turbulence of his professional team too much to handle. Only a very select few have led Yorkshire to a Championship treble in successive seasons, and

Wilson was one of them. He was still captain when Yorkshire won their last two Championship matches of 1924, defeating Hampshire by 10 wickets and Sussex by an innings and 110 runs.

In those two games alone Kilner took 23 wickets, and the two county opponents were dismissed for totals of 74, 97, 60 and 83.

In a season where the counties could a play a different number of games, and the Championship had to be decided on a percentage basis — points obtained over points possible — Yorkshire had 76.52, with 16 wins in 30 games, and Middlesex 69.00 with 11 wins in 22.

In this era when bowling skills predominated over batting ability George Macaulay took 159 championship wickets at 11.73, and Kilner 113 wickets at 12.12.

Sutcliffe topped the Championship batting averages with 1,342 runs at 46.27, and Edgar Oldroyd – who never played for England – was next with 1,373 runs at 37.10 in his 42 championship innings, more than any other player. Yorkshire's All First Class list was headed by Sutcliffe, Holmes and Oldroyd.

EDGAR OLDROYD: Second in Yorkshire's Championship batting averages behind Sutcliffe, but never a Test call. This study has been taken from cigarette cards issued by Godfrey Phillips Ltd. in 1924.

(Photo: Ron Deaton Archive)

As the year of 1924 ended Lord Hawke had published his *Recollections and Reminiscences.* The opening portrait shows the noble Lord in shooting jacket and trousers with spats, and with a shotgun under an arm, No sign of a cricket bat or ball. There are, even so, many references to two of his greatest players, Hirst and Rhodes, but none to

PRESIDENT IN SPATS: Lord Hawke joins his team at Scarborough, where the only piece of kit missing appears to be a gun under his arm. Note the upper deck of the pavilion when tiered seating was in place where the lounge and bar are today. Left to right: Roy Kilner, Arthur Dolphin, Lord Hawke, Wilfred Rhodes, George Macaulay, Emmott Robinson, Edgar Oldroyd, Geoffrey Wilson (captain), Herbert Sutcliffe, Percy Holmes, Abe Waddington and John Stephenson. This would have been Wilson's final game for Yorkshire on home soil, but he played one more first-class match for Yorkshire against Rest of England at The Oval.

(Photo: Ron Deaton Archive)

some of the cricketing successes of 1924 — Macaulay, Kilner or Oldroyd. Waddington is also nowhere mentioned.

Interestingly Lord Hawke did make a comparison between opening batsmen J T Brown and John Tunnicliffe before the Great War and Holmes and Sutcliffe after that war.

Hawke wrote: "It is true that the latter have achieved more hundred-run partnerships in five years than the former in 19 years. But the quality of the opposing bowling was certainly higher in the case of the seniors. I have not seen so much of the play of the splendid pair who now go in first as I did of the elder couple (who did once have a partnership of 554). What I have seen I admire highly, though I think the old-time pair could make runs faster, and had the more commanding dominance."

Hawke was writing just before Sutcliffe toured Australia and played in the 1924-25 Tests against Australia, scoring 734 runs at an average of

HEROES IN YOUR POCKET

W RHODES

P HOLMES

A DOLPHIN

Lighting up the day: Packets of cigarettes have carried Government health warnings for many years...but 100 years ago the dangers were little understood, and the smoker's cough may have seemed a small price to pay for precious moments of relaxation for men lucky enough to have emerged from the First World War with little more than trench feet. Cigarette-card sets were much prized, and they document popular culture from the beginning of the 20th Century, often depicting the period's actresses, costumes and sports teams. We here present three more for 1922 from the album of Yorkshire cricket archivist *Ron Deaton*.

81.55. Might Hawke have then revised his opinion? In his book royalty and peers known to him were named in some number. Naturally, and fairly, there is mention of Admiral Hawke — the first of those to receive the title of Lord Hawke and who through his victory over the French at Quiberon Bay in 1759 secured the family wealth and title which the cricketing Hawke was still enjoying in 1924.

Our Lord Hawke, as President of Yorkshire, was to reign supreme over Yorkshire county cricket for another 14 years. In that time there were plenty more Yorkshire Championship crowns to come and to be still heralded as this *Yearbook* may progress through more articles of *100 Years Ago*. Sadly, *50 Years Ago* may generally portray a less dominant history of Yorkshire County Cricket Club.

YORKSHIRE'S FIRST CLASS HIGHLIGHTS OF 1924

Wins by an innings (7)

Somerset (132) and (100) lost to Yorkshire (434-8 dec) by an innings and 202 runs at Dewsbury

Yorkshire (300-7 dec) defeated Derbyshire (111) and (78) by an innings and 189 runs at Huddersfield

Yorkshire (275) defeated Glamorgan (48) and (50) by an innings and 177 runs at Cardiff

Essex (132) and (208) lost to Yorkshire (471-5 dec) by an innings and 131 runs at Southend-on-Sea

Sussex (60) and (83) lost to Yorkshire (253-9 dec) by an innings and 110 runs at Hove

Glamorgan (116) and (106) lost to Yorkshire (248-3 dec) by an innings and 26 runs at Bradford

Cambridge University (111) and (117) lost to Yorkshire (234-8 dec) by an innings and 6 runs at Cambridge

Win by 200 or more runs (1)

Yorkshire (200) and (343-3 dec) defeated (Sussex (192) and (125) by 226 runs at Sheffield

Wins by 10 wickets (3)

Hampshire (74) and (97) lost to Yorkshire (136) and (38-0) at Portsmouth

Northamptonshire (163) and (187) lost to Yorkshire (328) and (23-0) at Dewsbury

Warwickshire (170) and (107) lost to Yorkshire (275) and (4-0) at Sheffield

Totals of 400 and over (2)

471-5 dec v. Essex at Southend-on-Sea

434-8 dec v. Somerset at Dewsbury

Opponents dismissed for under 100 (13)

42   v. Gloucestershire 2nd innings at Gloucester *

48   v. Glamorgan 1st innings at Cardiff *

50   v. Glamorgan 2nd innings at Cardiff *

60   v. Sussex 1st innings at Hove ***

68   v. Gloucestershire 1st innings at Gloucester *

71   v. Leicestershire at Bradford

74   v. Lancashire at Leeds

74   v. Derbyshire at Chesterfield

74   v. Hampshire 1st innings at Portsmouth ***

83   v. Sussex 2nd innings at Hove ***

84   v. Northamptonshire at Northampton **

92   v. Nottinghamshire at Bradford **

97   v. Hampshire 2nd innings at Portsmouth ***

*, **, and ***

consecutive matches

Century Partnerships (16)

For the 1st wicket (4)

195	P Holmes and H Sutcliffe	v. Sussex at Sheffield
122	P Holmes and M Leyland	v. Kent at Maidstone
110	P Holmes and H Sutcliffe	v. Warwickshire at Birmingham
107	P Holmes and H Sutcliffe	v. Glamorgan at Bradford

For the 2nd wicket (5)

314	H Sutcliffe and E Oldroyd	v. Essex at Southend-on-Sea
165	H Sutcliffe and E Oldroyd	v. Somerset at Dewsbury
156	P Holmes and E Oldroyd	v. Derbyshire at Huddersfield
130	P Holmes and E Oldroyd	v. Middlesex at Sheffield
107	P Holmes and E Oldroyd	v. Sussex at Hove

For the 3rd wicket (2)

205	E Oldroyd and M Leyland	v. Hampshire at Harrogate
107	H Sutcliffe and M Leyland	v. Warwickshire at Sheffield

For the 4th wicket (2)

129	H Sutcliffe and W Rhodes	v. Somerset at Dewsbury
117	E Oldroyd and W Rhodes	v. South Africans at Sheffield

For the 5th wicket (1)

102	E Oldroyd and R Kilner	v. Surrey at Leeds

For the 6th wicket (1)

142	M Leyland and E Robinson	v. Kent at Hull

For the 9th wicket (1)

110	M Leyland and A Waddington	v. Sussex at Sheffield

Centuries (15)

H Sutcliffe (5)

255 *	v. Essex at Southend-on-Sea
213	v. Somerset at Dewsbury
160	v. Sussex at Sheffield
108 *	v. Cambridge University at Cambridge
108	v. MCC at Scarborough

P Holmes (4)

118 *	v. Glamorgan at Bradford
112	v. Nottinghamshire at Nottingham
107	v. Derbyshire at Huddersfield
105 *	v. Kent at Maidstone

E Oldroyd (3)

138	v. Essex at Southend-on-Sea
122 *	v. Hampshire at Harrogate
103	v. Surrey at Leeds

M Leyland (2)

133 *	v. Lancashire at Manchester
100 *	v. Hampshire at Harrogate

W Rhodes (1)

100	v. Somerset at Weston-Super-Mare

5 wickets in an innings (33)

G G Macaulay (13)

    7 -21   v. Gloucestershire 2nd innings at Gloucester
    7 -31   v. Leicestershire at Bradford
    7 -66   v. Warwickshire at Sheffield
    6 -26   v. Northamptonshire at Northampton
    6 -30   v. MCC at Scarborough
    6 -40   v. Lancashire at Leeds
    6 -66   v. South Africa at Bradford
    6 -72   v. Nottinghamshire at Nottingham
    5 -15   v. Glamorgan at Cardiff
    5 -19   v. Gloucestershire 1st innings at Gloucester
    5 -31   v. Hampshire at Portsmouth
    5 -60   v. Sussex at Sheffield
    5 -73   v. Essex at Hull

R Kilner (10)

    7 -37   v. Sussex 2nd innings at Hove
    6 -15   v. Hampshire 2nd innings at Portsmouth
    6 -48   v. Warwickshire at Birmingham
    5 -18   v. Sussex 1st innings at Hove
    5 -25   v. Glamorgan at Cardiff
    5 -33   v. Hampshire 1st innings at Portsmouth
    5 -34   v. Northamptonshire at Northampton
    5 -48   v. Kent at Maidstone
    5 -58   v. Surrey 1st innings at The Oval
    5 -95   v. Surrey 2nd innings at The Oval

W Rhodes (5)

    6 -22   v. Cambridge University at Cambridge
    6 -25   v. Derbyshire at Huddersfield
    6 -40   v. Northamptonshire at Dewsbury
    5 -28   v. Somerset at Weston-super-Mare
    5 -30   v. Nottinghamshire at Bradford

E Robinson (3)

    6 -87   v. Sussex at Sheffield
    5 -59   v. Middlesex at Sheffield
    5 -84   v. Kent at Maidstone

A Waddington (3)

    7 -43   v. Leicestershire at Leicester
    6 -87   v. MCC at Scarborough
    5 -57   v. Leicestershire at Bradford

10 wickets in a match (7)

G G Macaulay (4)

    12 - 40   (5-19 and 7-21)   v. Gloucestershire at Gloucester
    11 -123   (4-57 and 7-66)   v. Warwickshire at Sheffield
    10 - 59   (6-40 and 4-19)   v. Lancashire at Leeds
    10 - 68   (6-26 and 4-42)   v. Northamptonshire at Northampton

10 wickets in a match *(Continued)*

R Kilner (3)

10 -153   (5-58 and 5-95)   v. Surrey at The Oval **
11 - 48   (5-33 and 6-15)   v. Hampshire at Portsmouth **
12 - 55   (5-18 and 7-37)   v. Sussex at Hove **
** Consecutive matches*

3 catches in an innings (6)

R Kilner (1)

4   v. Northamptonshire at Northampton

A Waddington (1)

4   v. Warwickshire at Sheffield

A Dolphin (1)

3   v. Hampshire at Portsmouth

M Leyland (1)

3   v. Hampshire at Portsmouth

G G Macauley (1)

3   v. Gloucestershire at Gloucester

E Oldroyd (1)

3   v. Essex at Southend-on-Sea

3 dismissals in an innings (3)

A Dolphin (3)

4 (1ct + 3st) v. Glamorgan at Bradford
4 (0ct + 4st) v. Surrey 2nd innings at The Oval
3 (2ct + 1st) v. Surrey 1st innings at The Oval

5 stumpings in a match (1)

A Dolphin (1)

1 + 4   v. Surrey at the Oval

5 catches in a match ((2)

A Waddington (1))

6 (2 + 4)   v. Warwickshire at Sheffield

R Kilner (1)

5 (1 + 4)   v. Northamptonshire at Northampton

Debuts (5)

In First Class cricket (5): S Allen, H Taylor, F I Turner, C E Anson and L Ryder

Caps awarded (none)

100 YEARS AGO

YORKSHIRE AVERAGES 1924

ALL FIRST-CLASS MATCHES

Played 35　　　　Won 18　　　　Lost 4　　　　Drawn 13

County Championship: Played 30　　　Won 16　　　Lost 3　　　Drawn 11

BATTING AND FIELDING *(Qualification 10 completed innings)*

Player	M.	I.	N.O.	Runs	H.S.	100s	50s	Avge	ct/st
H Sutcliffe	28	42	6	1720	255*	5	7	47.77	17
P Holmes	33	50	5	1610	118*	4	9	35.77	18
E Oldroyd	35	51	6	1607	138	3	6	35.71	20
M Leyland	33	46	7	1203	133*	2	6	30.84	12
E Robinson	35	41	9	903	95*	0	6	28.21	36
W Rhodes	35	46	7	1030	100	1	6	26.41	20
R Kilner	29	33	3	537	50	0	1	17.90	19
G G Macaulay	32	34	3	382	44	0	0	12.32	28
H Taylor	6	11	0	125	36	0	0	11.36	1
G Wilson	34	36	6	283	37	0	0	9.43	13
A Dolphin	35	34	11	216	33	0	0	9.39	31/31
A Waddington	31	34	8	181	35	0	0	6.96	28

Also batted

Player	M.	I.	N.O.	Runs	H.S.	100s	50s	Avge	ct/st
A Mitchell	2	2	1	26	19	0	0	26.00	0
T J D Birtles	1	2	0	42	33	0	0	21.00	0
C E Anson	1	2	0	27	14	0	0	13.50	1
J Drake	1	2	1	10	9*	0	0	10.00	0
F I Turner	5	7	0	33	12	0	0	4.71	2
S Allen	1	2	0	8	6	0	0	4.00	0
J S Stephenson	6	8	0	18	9	0	0	2.25	1
L Ryder	2	2	1	1	1	0	0	1.00	2

BOWLING

(Qualification 10 wickets)

Player	Overs	Mdns	Runs	Wkts	Avge	Best	5wI	10wM
G G Macaulay	1121.3	320	2282	184	12.40	7 -21	13	4
R Kilner	1046	432	1744	134	13.01	7 -37	10	5
W Rhodes	660.5	219	1420	96	14.79	6 -22	5	0
H Waddington	556.2	125	1410	65	21.69	7 -43	3	0
E Robinson	565.2	182	1283	55	23.32	6 -87	3	0

Also bowled

Player	Overs	Mdns	Runs	Wkts	Avge	Best	5wI	10wM
E Oldroyd	3.1	0	16	2	8.00	2 -16	0	0
H Sutcliffe	4	0	24	2	12.00	2 -24	0	0
L Ryder	48	3	151	4	37.75	2 -75	0	0
S Allen	36	6	116	2	58.00	2-116	0	0
J Drake	17	2	51	0	—	0 -51	0	0
M Leyland	23	9	41	0	—	0 - 3	0	0
J S Stephenson	6	1	23	0	—	0 -23	0	0
G Wilson	3	0	11	0	—	0 -11	0	0

BOYCOTT DIGS IN TO PUT HIS COUNTY BEFORE COUNTRY

By Anthony Bradbury

In 1973 Yorkshire had a shocking Championship season, finishing in 14th position. So in May 1974 hopes were high for a significant improvement...hopes that were rather dashed as the first 10 games came and went without a win. There was a flicker of hope and momentum as the next two games were won by an innings, but the early-season pattern of disappointment was then resumed. More hopes arose as Yorkshire won two of their last three matches, including a splendid innings victory at Bradford Park Avenue against Surrey, but it was too late to make much difference to their final placement which was to be in 11th place. They finished 81 points behind Worcestershire, who had 11 victories.

The pre-season team photograph of 18 players published in *Wisden* 1975 showed a front row of Chris Old, Don Wilson, Philip Sharpe, Geoffrey Boycott (captain), Tony Nicholson, and John Hampshire. Surely a formidable sextet to form the base of a powerful Yorkshire side. The middle row included the promising left-armer Phil Carrick, Richard Hutton, Richard Lumb and Geoff Cope, and the back row included young hopefuls Peter Squires, Jim Love and Graham Stevenson.

The only player in that photograph never to play for a Yorkshire First Eleven was opening batsman Philip Hodson, who played in the Second team and later became President of MCC, a very rare honour for any Yorkshireman.

Yet Old was often unavailable because of England calls for Tests against India and Pakistan, and Hampshire missed seven weeks through injury. Hutton, Sharpe and Wilson had seasons well below expectations of the Yorkshire members and, no doubt, their own hopes. Sadly, they all left the Yorkshire playing staff at the end of the season. Hutton went on to pursue other interests but, very happily, years later became President of the Yorkshire Club. He remains Patron of the Yorkshire Southern Group. Sharpe, who was to play for Derbyshire for two seasons, will always be remembered for some sterling batting for Yorkshire and England and an amazing 526 catches for Yorkshire, most of them taken in the slips and with the greatest of ease and skill. Only John Tunnicliffe (665), Wilfred Rhodes (586) and Brian Close (564) took more catches for Yorkshire, and Vic Wilson held on to 520. The jovial and much liked Don Wilson became an outstanding Head Coach of MCC for 13 years.

The Annual Report for 1974 recognised, with gratitude to this trio, their great services to Yorkshire Cricket.

Some had successful seasons. Boycott may not regard an average for Yorkshire of over 58 as especially successful but, when he stood down from England selection and preference was given to David Lloyd of Lancashire, he became available for most matches.

Bill Bowes, writing in *Wisden*, also gave credit to Boycott "for field placings, especially for run savings, [as being] very good".

Boycott made 1,220 runs for the county with three hundreds. It is difficult to explain how one day he could rapidly score 149 not out of 251-4 declared against Derbyshire and later, less quickly than his batting partners, 142 not out of 343-5 *innings closed* — a strange 100-over experiment to curtail a Championship first innings — against Surrey.

No doubt there are appropriate explanations for speed and slowness, but without any doubt Boycott provided consistent backbone to the side. 1974 was his Benefit Year. The membership and supporters provided him with £20,538 – very tangible recognition of his ability.

Hampshire, despite his injury which cost him six games, scored 879

First generation: Wicketkeeper David Bairstow nets with opening batter Richard Lumb. David's son, Jonny, and Richard's son, Michael, were both to play for Yorkshire and England, and the Lumbs became only the fourth father-and-son pair to score centuries for Yorkshire. Jonny remains central to the England squad, both with the bat and behind the wicket.

(Photo: Mick Pope Archive)

runs at an average of nearly 55 including two very fine consecutive centuries of 157 not out and 158 in victories against Nottinghamshire and Gloucestershire.

Lumb played consistently, and was given his county cap. Barry Leadbeater, batting with customary doggedness, scored 99 not out against Kent at Scarborough.

Under that rule that closed a first innings after 100 overs he had 10 final overs to score 17 for a maiden century...but he could not manage the last and always difficult run.

The holiday crowd must have been so disappointed,

Spin duo: Phil Carrick, left, who inherited the left-armer's role from Don Wilson and was to be Yorkshire captain from 1987 to 1989, and Geoff Cope, the off-breaker whose many roles over the next 50 years were to include the Presidency from 2019 to 2023.
(Photo: Mick Pope Archive)

though they may have accepted that 41 year old Colin Cowdrey had earlier scored a very fine 122.

Cope, having had to change his action, performed well as the off-spinner, taking 64 Championship wickets and becoming the leading Yorkshire wicket-taker. Bowes wrote of him: "By far the most successful bowler who returned to form most encouragingly and is to be congratulated on his determination to succeed after two years in the wilderness." It is wonderful that Cope had many roles with Yorkshire cricket over the next 50 years, and became a most successful and appreciated President of the club.

The left-armer Carrick, still in the early days of his career, also did well. He never obtained an England cap, and so Don Wilson remains, 50 years later, the last (so far) of the England and Yorkshire left-arm spin bowlers. Cope and the now well established David Bairstow, behind the stumps, were the only two players to participate in all 19 Championship matches. Steve Oldham made his debut for Yorkshire in his mid-twenties, the start of a long and distinguished career, mainly for Yorkshire, and in a match against Gloucestershire had figures of 4.5-3-7-3.

There was an unusual statistic in the game against Nottinghamshire at Worksop. In the Nottinghamshire first innings Denis Schofield, in his last match for Yorkshire, and Arthur "Rocker" Robinson each took five wickets — Robinson including a hat-trick — and in the second innings of Nottinghamshire Cope and Wilson each took five wickets. Nicholson

ARTHUR ROBINSON
Hat-trick for 'Rocker'
(Mick Pope Archive)

was not really at his best in the Championship matches, though he took 44 wickets, and Old in eight such matches took 33 wickets at 17.18.

The four victories were against Nottinghamshire, Gloucestershire, Derbyshire and Surrey.

It is rather sad to mention one of the defeats: in Yorkshire's first innings of just 108 at Leicester they lost all 10 wickets to ex-Yorkshire players — three to Ray Illingworth and seven to Jackie Birkenshaw, who had left Yorkshire in 1960.

To rub salt into that wound ex-Yorkshire player Chris Balderstone took four wickets in the second innings as Yorkshire crumbled.

Inevitably, there was some discussion about Yorkshire's unwillingness to engage overseas players. The Committee were firmly against that possibility, and were probably generally supported by the membership.

Yet their opponents collectively included more than 20 distinguished players from overseas countries including Alvin Kallicharran, Rohan Kanhai, Clive Lloyd, Intikab Alam, Vivian Richards, Mike Proctor, Gordon Greenidge, Srinivasaraghavan Venkataraghavan, Lawrence Rowe, Glen Turner...and, of course — Garfield Sobers. How Cope must have celebrated when he once in 1974 bowled Sobers for 0!

In contrast Clive Lloyd scored 258 runs in four innings, being dismissed just three times. The presence of these great players in opposition teams must have been a huge handicap for the Yorkshire side.

There is little newsworthy to write about Yorkshire's one day cricket in 1974, save it may be startling to recall that Yorkshire's early-round win over Hampshire in the Gillette Cup was their first win in that competition since 1969. In the John Player League there were eight wins in 16 matches and a final place of seventh. As always there were some close results — losing to Somerset by four runs, to Worcestershire by

Moving on. Left to right: Richard Hutton, Don Wilson and Philip Sharpe, whose careers with Yorkshire ended in 1974.
(Photos: Mick Pope Archive)

one run and to Hampshire by one run. Yet other counties would have had some similar results.

Boycott had an average of over 40 in these games – next best being Old at 27.62. Five bowlers took their wickets at less than 20 runs each.

Two former players died in 1974. Horace Fisher, back in

Moving up: Sir Kenneth Parkinson, who was to become President of Yorkshire following the death of Sir William Worsley.

1932, became the first bowler to take a hat-trick comprising three lbws when playing at Sheffield against Somerset. The other death was of Arthur Booth, the slow left-arm bowler who, perhaps in consequence of the death of Hedley Verity in the Second World War, played throughout the 1946 season. At the age of 43 he topped the national averages with 111 wickets at 11.61. What a performance.

Following the death of Sir William Worsley in late 1973, the new President of the club was Sir Kenneth Parkinson, the first non first-class cricketer to be President since M J Ellison in 1897. He was a successful businessman, born in Bradford, and long a member of the county club.

His own cricket was played enthusiastically at club level. His Presidential term was to coincide in part with a very unhappy period in Yorkshire cricket, though *Fifty Years Ago – the Season of 1975* may reveal a much better year for the Yorkshire First Eleven.

YORKSHIRE'S FIRST CLASS HIGHLIGHTS OF 1974

Wins by an innings (4)

Oxford University (106 and 67) lost to Yorkshire (342-9 dec) by an innings
and 169 runs at Oxford
Yorkshire (406-8 dec) defeated Gloucestershire (71 and 170) by an innings
and 165 runs at Harrogate
Nottinghamshire (94 and 87) lost to Yorkshire (250-7 dec) by an innings
and 69 runs at Worksop
Surrey (204 and 137) lost to Yorkshire (343-8 dec) by an innings
and 2 runs at Bradford
at Middlesbrough

Total of 400 and over (1)

406-8 dec   v. Gloucestershire at Harrogate

Opponents dismissed for under 100 (4)

67   v. Oxford University at Oxford
71   v, Gloucestershire at Harrogate
87   v. Nottinghamshire 2nd innings
                    at Worksop

94   v. Nottinghamshire 1st innings
                    at Worksop

Century Partnerships (13)

For the 1st wicket (4)

171	G Boycott and R G Lumb	v. Derbyshire at Chesterfield
130	G Boycott and R G Lumb	v. Lancashire at Manchester
104	G Boycott and R G Lumb 1st innings	v. Sussex at Leeds
104	G Boycott and R G Lumb 2nd innings	v. Sussex at Leeds

For the 2nd wicket (2)

158	G Boycott and P J Sharpe	v. Oxford University at Oxford
136	G Boycott and P J Sharpe	v. Derbyshire at Abbeydale Park, Sheffield

For the 3rd wicket (2)

136	G Boycott and J H Hampshire	v. Surrey at Bradford
103 *	B Leadbeater and P J Squires	v. India at Bradford

For the 4th wicket (1)

114	J H Hampshire and B Leadbeater	v. Gloucestershire at Harrogate

For the 6th wicket (3)

143	R A Hutton and D L Bairstow	v. Somerset at Bath
106	D L Bairstow and G A Cope	v. Middlesex at Lord's
101	B Leadbeater and D L Bairstow	v. Gloucestershire at Harrogate

For the 7th wicket (1)

104	R G Lumb and R A Hutton	v. Northamptonshire at Northampton

Centuries (10)

   G Boycott (4))

      149 * v. Derbyshire at Abbeydale Park, Sheffield
      140   v. Cambridge University at Cambridge
      117   v. Sussex at Leeds
      142 * v. Surrey at Bradford

   J H Hampshire (2)

      157 * v. Nottinghamshire at Worksop **
      158   v. Gloucestershire at Harrogate **
              ** *Consecutive innings*

   R G Lumb (2)

      123 * v. Northamptonshire at Northampton
      100   v. Derbyshire at Chesterfield

   R A Hutton (1)

      102 * v. Somerset at Bath

   C M Old (1)

      116   v. India at Bradford

5 wickets in an innings (15)

   G A Cope (5)

      7 -101   v. Middlesex at Middlesbrough **
      5 - 16   v. Nottinghamshire at Worksop
      5 - 19   v. Oxford University 2nd innings at Oxford
      5 - 46   v. Oxford University 1st innings at Oxford
      5 -100   v. Derbyshire at Abbeydale Park, Sheffield **
          ** *Consecutive matches*

   P Carrick (2)

      6 -43   v. Surrey at Bradford
      6 -46   v. Derbyshire at Chesterfield

   C M Old (2)

      5 -30   v. India at Bradford
      5 -50   v. Somerset at Bath

   A L Robinson (2)

      6 -61   v. Surrey at The Oval
      5 -27   v. Nottinghamshire at Worksop

   R A Hutton (1)

      6 -85   v. Essex at Leyton

   A G Nicholson (1)

      5 -74   v. Lancashire at Manchester

   D Scofield (1)

      5 -42   v. Nottinghamshire at Worksop

   D Wilson (1)

      5 -36   v. Nottinghamshire at Worksop

10 wickets in a match (2)

   P Carrick (1)

      10 - 115   (6-46 and 4-69) v. Derbyshire at Chesterfield

   G A Cope (1)

      10 -65   (5-46 and 5-19) v. Oxford University at Oxford

3 catches in an innings (10)

D L Bairstow (7)

5	v. Cambridge University at Cambridge
4	v. Somerset at Bath
4	v. Glamorgan at Scarborough
3	v. Northamptonshire at Northampton
3	v. Derbyshire at Abbeydale Park, Sheffield
3	v. Lancashire 1st innings at Manchester
3	v. Lancashire 2nd innings at Manchester

P Carrick (1)

3	v. Derbyshire at Chesterfield

C M Old (1)

3	v. Lancashire at Leeds

P J Sharpe (1)

3	v. Northamptonshire at Northampton

3 dismissals in an innings (4)

D L Bairstow (4)

3 (2ct + 1st)	v. Northamptonshire at Northampton
3 (1ct + 2st)	v. Oxford University at Oxford
4 (3ct + 1st)	v. Lancashire at Manchester
3 (1ct + 2st)	v. Surrey at Bradford

5 catches in a match (2)

D L Bairstow (2)

7 (2 + 5)	v. Cambridge University at Cambridge
6 (3 + 3)	v. Lancashire at Manchester

Debuts (2

In First Class cricket: S Oldham and R A J Townsley

Cap awarded: (1): R G Lumb

As one steps down another steps up...

As one former Yorkshire player ended his international career another hopefully started one during the later part of 2023. David Wiley retired from England duty after November's World Cup in India, but just a couple of months earlier Tom Kohler-Cadmore was selected for the ODI squad to face Ireland as a late injury replacement. He didn't play, but hopefully that will happen sooner rather than later.

Both left Headingley at the end of the 2022 summer.

LIST A HIGHLIGHTS OF 1974

Win by 9 wickets (1)

Minor Counties North (109) lost to Yorkshire (110-1) at Leeds

— Benson & Hedges Cup

Win by over 100 runs (1)

Yorkshire (148) defeated Middlesex (23) by 125 runs at Leeds

— John Player League.

Totals of 200 and over (3)

233-6   v. Hampshire at Bradford (won) — John Player League
220   v. Somerset at Bath (lost) — John Player League
201   v. Surrey at The Oval (lost) — Benson & Hedges Cup

Opponents dismissed for under 100 (1)

23   Middlesex at Leeds — John Player League

Match aggregates of 400 and over (3)

444   Somerset (224-4) defeated Yorkshire (220) by 4 runs at Bath

— John Player League

426   Surrey (225-7) defeated Yorkshire (201) by 24 runs at The Oval

— Benson & Hedges Cup

425   Yorkshire (233-6) defeated Hampshire (192) by 41 runs at Bradford

— John Player League

Century Partnerships (none)

Centuries (1)

G Boycott (1)

108 *   v. Northamptonshire at Huddersfield — John Player League

4 wickets in an innings (6)

R A Hutton (1)

4-19   v. Derbyshire at Chesterfield — Benson & Hedges Cup

A G Nicholson (1)

4-15   v. Kent at Leeds — John Player League

S Oldham (1)

4-21   v. Nottinghamshire at Scarboroughs — John Player League

A L Robinson (1)

4-25   v. Surrey at The Oval — John Player League

A Sidebottom(1)

4-40   v. Lancashire at Manchester — John Player League

G B Stevenson (1)

4-57   v. Lancashire at Leed — Gillette Cup

3 catches in an innings (4)

D L Bairstow (2)

4   v. Lancashire at Leeds   — Gillette Cup
3   v. Lancashire at Bradford   — Benson & Hedges Cup

C Johnson (1)

4   v. Northamptonshire at Huddersfield   — John Player League

P J Sharpe (1)

3   v. Minor County North at Leeds   — Benson & Hedges Cup

3 dismissals in an innings (None)

List A Debuts (2): A Sidebottom and S Oldham

50 YEARS AGO

YORKSHIRE AVERAGES 1974

ALL FIRST-CLASS MATCHES

Played 23   Won 6   Lost 7   Drawn 9   Abandoned 1

County Championship: Played 20   Won 4   Lost 7   Drawn 8   Abandoned 1

BATTING AND FIELDING *(Qualification 10 completed innings)*

Player	M.	I.	N.O.	Runs	H.S.	100s	50s	Avge	ct/st
G Boycott	18	30	5	1478	149*	4	8	59.12	6
J H Hampshire	14	23	6	901	158	2	3	53.00	10
B Leadbeater	19	31	4	804	99*	0	5	29.77	10
R G Lumb	18	31	2	763	123*	2	2	26.31	14
C M Old	11	15	0	387	116	1	1	25.80	9
P Carrick	12	13	3	196	46	0	0	19.60	11
R A Hutton	17	25	5	376	102*	1	0	18.80	15
D L Bairstow	22	31	2	533	79	0	4	18.37	50/11
P J Squires	13	21	3	329	67	0	2	18.27	6
P J Sharpe	17	29	2	474	83	0	2	17.55	17
G A Cope	22	24	7	275	43	0	0	16.17	1
C Johnson	8	12	1	173	60	0	1	15.72	5

Also played

Player	M.	I.	N.O.	Runs	H.S.	100s	50s	Avge	ct/st
A G Nicholson	16	16	8	153	50	0	1	19.12	3
A L Robinson	16	9	4	43	17*	0	0	8.60	6
D Wilson	8	12	4	64	22	0	0	8.00	1
G B Stevenson	4	4	0	25	18	0	0	6.25	4
R A J Townsley	1	2	0	2	2	0	0	1.00	0
M K Bore	2	2	0	1	1	0	0	0.50	1
S Oldham	2	1	1	5	5*	0	0	—	1
H P Cooper	1	1	1	8	8*	0	0	—	1
D Schofield	1	1	1	6	6*	0	0	—	0

BOWLING *(Qualification 10 wickets)*

Player	Overs	Mdns	Runs	Wkts	Avge	Best	5wI	10wM
C M Old	334	103	736	46	16.00	5 -30	2	0
P Carrick	405.4	167	840	47	17.87	6 -43	2	1
A L Robinson	375.5	103	880	43	20.46	6 -61	2	0
G A Cope	743.5	260	1681	77	21.83	7-101	5	1
A G Nicholson	471	152	1100	44	25.00	5 -74	1	0
R A Hutton	259.2	70	620	24	25.83	6 -85	1	0
D Wilson	157.4	39	469	17	27.58	5 -36	1	0

Also bowled

Player	Overs	Mdns	Runs	Wkts	Avge	Best	5wI	10wM
D Scholfield	16.2	3	52	5	10.40	5 -42	1	0
S Oldham	20.5	5	69	4	17.25	3 - 7	0	0
H P Cooper	21	8	54	2	27.00	1 -23	0	0
G B Stevenson	29	9	88	2	44.00	2 -43	0	0
M K Bore	44.1	17	129	0	—	0 -20	0	0
J H Hampshire	11	7	6	0	—	0 - 6	0	0
C Johnson	4	2	6	0	—	0 --6	0	0

50 YEARS AGO

YORKSHIRE AVERAGES 1974

LIST A

Played 22   Won 12   Lost 9   No Result 1   Abandoned 1

John Player League: 6th = (17)   Benson & Hedges Cup: Quarter-Final

Gillette Cup: Quarter-Final

BATTING AND FIELDING *(Qualification 10 completed innings)*

Player	M.	I.	N.O.	Runs	H.S.	100s	50s	Avge	ct/st
G Boycott	16	16	2	574	108*	1	3	41.00	9
J H Hampshire	15	14	2	361	87*	0	2	30.08	2
C M Old	15	14	1	359	82	0	2	27.61	5
R G Lumb	16	16	3	343	65	0	2	26.38	3
B Leadbeater	15	14	0	288	90	0	2	20.57	5
D L Bairstow	22	18	4	228	50	0	1	16.28	22
P J Sharpe	18	18	1	258	50	0	1	15.17	13
C Johnson	14	12	0	158	54	0	1	13.16	7
P J Squires	15	14	1	171	52	0	1	13.15	4

Also played

Player	M.	I.	N.O.	Runs	H.S.	100s	50s	Avge	ct/st
A Sidebottom	7	5	4	37	12*	0	0	37.00	0
R A Hutton	15	12	3	160	60	0	1	17.77	5
G B Stevenson	13	10	2	100	27	0	0	12.50	6
A L Robinson	22	12	5	54	18*	0	0	7.71	3
G A Cope	5	4	1	21	16*	0	0	7.00	2
A G Nicholson	19	8	5	19	8	0	0	6.33	2
S Oldham	8	4	1	13	6	0	0	4.33	0
H P Cooper	2	1	0	0	0	0	0	0.00	0
M K Bore	4	1	1	7	7*	0	0	—	1
P Carrick	1	1	1	0	0*	0	0	—	0

BOWLING *(Qualification 4 wickets)*

Player	Overs	Mdns	Runs	Wkts	Avge	Best	4wI	RPO
S Oldham	48	3	181	13	13.92	4-21	1	3.77
G B Stevenson	91	7	340	22	15.45	4-57	1	3.73
A G Nicholson	145	24	388	25	15.52	4-15	1	2.67
C M Old	137.5	21	446	24	18.58	3-51	0	3.23
R A Hutton	103.4	14	408	21	19.42	4-19	1	3.93
A L Robinson	183.5	23	592	28	21.14	4-25	1	3.22
A Sidebottom	61.4	2	261	11	23.72	4-40	1	4.23

Also bowled

Player	Overs	Mdns	Runs	Wkts	Avge	Best	4wI	RPO
H P Cooper	20,2	1	54	4	13.50	3-22	0	2.65
B Leadbeater	14.5	0	73	4	18.25	3-47	0	4.92
M K Bore	36.4	6	148	6	24.66	3-29	0	4.03
G A Cope	36	5	154	3	51.33	2-22	0	4.27

EVEN LORD HAWKE BATTLED FOR BRIGHTER CRICKET

Cricket is going through a period of great upheaval. The drive to appeal to a wider audience, the greater focus on ever-shorter formats, and the dramatically increased scoring rates by England in Test cricket are all attempts to liven up the game and compete for attention alongside other forms of entertainment.

Although these are contemporary concerns they also echo the *brighter cricket* debate of the early 1930s. Many consider the inter-war period a *golden age* of cricket, and in 1930 the prospect of seeing Bradman and the Australian tourists certainly generated excitement.

Nevertheless, the decade was marked by widespread concern about the state of the game. In Yorkshire there was particular anxiety at not having won the Championship since 1925, and at a lack of victories — 45 out of the last 67 matches had been drawn — but more generally there was a sense that interest in cricket was declining.

At Yorkshire's AGM in 1930 Lord Hawke observed there was concern "that first-class cricket might be losing its hold on the affections of the general public". Some considered the game was taken too seriously, with teams too focused on avoiding defeat or securing first-innings points, leading to tedious play.

Well-prepared wickets were seen as too easy for cautious batters to score runs on. People with little spare time did not want to watch inconclusive cricket, which contrasted with 90 minutes of concentrated football action. Others disliked the tone of notices on county grounds:

> *Photography forbidden*
> *No Smoking*
> *No autographs*
> *No moving behind the bowler's arm.*

Cost was also an issue: many complained at the 2s minimum to watch the Australians. In 1925 a total of 326,000 paid to see Yorkshire, but in 1929 only 135,000 did.

Some of the declining interest was outside the control of the counties. Whereas in the past people had had fewer distractions, by 1930 increased motor car use and cheap train excursions to the coast enabled them to travel further at the weekend, and tennis, speedway, rambling,

Dashing captains: Alan Barber, left and Frank Greenwod.
(Photos: Ron Deaton and Mick Pope Archives)

golf, dog-racing and the cinema competed with cricket. County clubs continued to grapple with which days were best for spectators. Monday and Thursday starts risked no Saturday play; Wednesday starts were designed to take advantage of half-day holidays, but these weren't the same everywhere. Call-ups for Tests and other representative fixtures also meant county matches lacked some of the greatest personalities.

While many were reluctant to make changes others recognised the game could not stay the same. In 1929 experiments took place with a larger wicket and a new lbw law. Some even suggested Sunday play, although this generated considerable opposition.

In local cricket more 20-over evening leagues were formed, even though some feared they would degenerate into indiscriminate slogging. In the Bradford League rule changes meant all hits over the boundary counted as six. Some leagues merged to try to bring new impetus to the game and restore old rivalries.

In 1930 Lord Hawke appealed to Yorkshire county cricketers to play "brighter cricket" and said no member of the side should fear a "carpeting" following a defeat if the right spirit had been shown. Yorkshire's new young captain, Alan Barber, said brighter cricket did not mean hitting every ball for six, but rather "our first consideration will be to win the game outright, and the first-innings points will be a secondary consideration". Barber said he was determined to end the "safety-first" allegations made against the Yorkshire side in recent years.

Hawke's plea for brighter cricket was heeded immediately at Lord's, when a match destined for a draw was transformed as Yorkshire bowled out MCC for 67 and scored the necessary 87 runs in 43 minutes, having taken the extra half hour. Against Leicestershire one report said the innings victory "provided all the thrills that the most ardent advocates of brighter cricket could desire". Playing Warwickshire, Barber was praised for declaring rather than batting on before enforcing the follow-on in what was described as "brighter and more forceful cricket".

Yorkshire scored 478 in six hours against Hampshire, "batting in a most refreshing fashion". The spirit infected even the *Roses* match, where Leyland made the highest score ever in these matches, and Yorkshire were praised for scoring at over a run a minute.

The 1930 peak was reached in late June, when one headline read *Hawke's Brighter Cricket Slogan in Force at Bradford* as Yorkshire thrashed the Somerset bowling, 169 runs being added in an hour by Holmes, Mitchell and Leyland. The *Yorkshire Post* called it a "reply to the dirt-track". In the next match Barber made a sporting declaration against Middlesex, who needed to score at a feasible 64 runs per hour. It led to a thrilling 29-run victory five minutes into the extra half hour.

A corner had been turned: Yorkshire drew four fewer matches than the previous year.

Although the county did not win the Championship in 1930 Barber's approach was reportedly "greatly appreciated by the supporters". Described by *Wisden* as the best leader Yorkshire had had in several years, Barber was considered a rare county captain who appreciated that the "very essence of true sport must the hazard of it", and Yorkshire a side which "deserves unstinted praise for the way in which they kept on fighting" despite the bad weather.

Over the winter changes were made to the points system for deciding the Championship. They were designed to encourage captains to go for a win and make sporting declarations, and to reduce the incentive to gain a first-innings lead. The idea of a two-division Championship was raised again, although not pursued.

Not everyone was keen on *brighter cricket*. Lord Harris regretted that some English batters had responded to calls from the crowd to "have a go" and lost their wickets.

Barber was unable to continue in full-time cricket, and was replaced by Frank Greenwood as Yorkshire captain for 1931. Lord Hawke reiterated his call for brighter cricket, backed by Arthur Sellers, chairman of the Cricket Committee, who urged Greenwood to take risks to win and assured him of his support.

Yorkshire also opposed the "doping" of wickets which was seen as making them too batter-friendly.

Under Greenwood the county continued the more energetic approach in most of its play, even if the crowd at the Whitsun *Roses* match cheered when it was announced that stumps would be drawn early, and he was asked to explain slow scoring.

Purposeful batting was allied to risk-taking. In July against Surrey the

> # BRIGHTER CRICKET WANTED.
>
> ## No Playing for First Innings Points.
>
> ## LORD HAWKE'S PLEA.
>
> The Yorkshire County cricket practices at Headingley were concluded yesterday, and, following the practice of recent years, the players, members of the County Committee, and Press were entertained at lunch in the Pavilion.
>
> Lord Hawke, who presided, joined in the

Yorkshire Post. April 24, 1930.
(Mick Pope Archive)

captain declared on the last day, and Bowes and Verity bowled the visitors out for 61 under time pressure, to win by an innings. Against Gloucestershire at Bristol he declared 64 runs behind to get his opponents in just before the close, and won the match easily.

Even in the August *Roses* match brighter cricket was seen as Holmes and Sutcliffe completed a record 323 opening partnership, and nearly 400 runs were scored on the first day. *Wisden* described as "refreshing" Greenwood's leadership, which had included sending the opposition in on five occasions and imbuing his side with "a spirit of adventure".

There were limits, however, to how far more traditional opinion would allow *brighter cricket* to go. At the start of June, after two days had been lost to rain in the match between Yorkshire and Gloucestershire, the captains agreed to declare after one ball each and move straight to a one-innings match. To some this was an obvious response to five points for a first-innings win but 15 for outright victory, and the result was "a wonderful day, brim full of clean, sporting cricket".

Even though Yorkshire lost for the first time in 25 matches by 47 runs, Greenwood received numerous messages of praise for his approach.

In August a similar situation in the match between Yorkshire and Northamptonshire prompted a similar response. This time Yorkshire won after two days had been lost, and a large crowd turned up anticipating an exciting one-innings duel. The *Yorkshire Post* enthused that the game must not be hide-bound by rules which had no connection with the real spirit of the game, and Greenwood said it was a way of making a rain-affected match profitable.

Others were far less happy. While younger voices and "the man in the street" were said to be in favour, more traditional opinion feared it might encourage collusion between captains and was outside the spirit of the game. MCC and Lord Hawke sought explanations from the captains, and *Wisden* condemned "freak" declarations involving two "farcical processions" to the wicket.

It concluded that "possibly no great harm was done" but argued that a tighter Championship might have been reduced to "an absurdity".

Yorkshire won the Championship in dramatic style in 1931, kicking off a decade of triumph. But the experience of the early 1930s shows that anxiety about the state of cricket has a long history. Many past concerns remain with us today — that matches can be inconclusive and lack excitement; that people do not have the time to attend the long-format game; that greater urgency is desirable on the field;and that greater balance between bat and ball is needed.

Brian Sellers gets much praise for Yorkshire's success in the 1930s, but the contributions of Barber and Greenwood in injecting new life into the side should not be forgotten. They showed that leadership matters, that not worrying about defeat allows risks to be taken, and that management backing provides the necessary confidence to act differently. Just as with England in 2022, so a change of mindset in the early 1930s helped Yorkshire to turn a corner.

Jeremy Lonsdale has written numerous books on the history of cricket in Yorkshire, all published by ACS Publications and Pitch Publishing.

Yorkshire warm up in the desert

Yorkshire prepared for the 2024 season with a mid-March tour to Abu Dhabi, just short of a fortnight in length. The likes of Essex and Somerset also travelled to the Arabian Desert.

It was a change in destination from the previous two years, the squad having toured Dubai and then Cape Town under Ottis Gibson's leadership.

GREENFIELD A DELIGHT THAT FELL TO THE _RED ROSE_

By Michael Pulford

"We are always glad to come to Greenfield". So said both Wilfred Rhodes and Maurice Leyland in 1938, following what had become an annual end-of-season fixture played by Yorkshire Elevens at Greenfield CC, one of seven clubs in Saddleworth, the outlying West Riding parish bordering the historic counties of Lancashire and Cheshire, but since 1974 administered by Oldham Council within Greater Manchester.

Yorkshire CCC's connections with Saddleworth are strong, and go back 150 years. Four local cricketers have represented the county, from 1874 to 2003, whilst inter-war fixtures were staged there between 1923 and 1938, and benefit matches for Yorkshire players were held in the parish in the 1970s and 80s — for Tony Nicholson, John Hampshire, Chris Old, Barry Leadbeater, David Bairstow and Phil Carrick, at both Greenfield and Delph and Dobcross.

Alas, Yorkshire has had no effective say in cricketing matters in Saddleworth since the 1980s, when it fell under the newly introduced Lancashire Cricket Board, following the consequences of the 1974 Local Government Act — this despite a local plebiscite having voted to go under the proposed West Yorkshire authority rather than Greater Manchester. Consequently, the best young cricketers have represented Lancashire's age-group sides over the last five decades.

Recent changes in the league cricket structure by the Lancashire Cricket Board appear to have placed Saddleworth even more firmly in _Red Rose_ system, for they brought about the end of the long-standing Saddleworth League. Six of the seven local clubs — Austerlands, Friarmere, Greenfield, Saddleworth, Springhead and Uppermill now play in the Greater Manchester League.

Though two links with Yorkshire still exist: Delph and Dobcross are Huddersfield League members, and Friarmere's age-group sides play in the Halifax Junior League.

Saddleworth's first direct link with Yorkshire came about through mill owner J L Byrom, who was strongly associated with Friarmere and played twice for Yorkshire in 1874. Byrom had a two-storey pavilion built at Friarmere's ground, which is still standing, and is said to have developed the venue with the intention of it being a Yorkshire Colts

Upstairs, downstairs...The two-storey pavilion J L Byrom built at Friarmere as a possible base for Yorkshire Colts.

base. He is also reputed to have recommended both Hirst and Rhodes to Yorkshire.

Lees Whitehead, a medium-fast bowler born at Friarmere, made 119 appearances for Yorkshire between 1889 and 1904, while in 1898 John Thewlis was appointed groundsman at Greenfield after he had been found by A W Pullin (Old Ebor) poverty-stricken and carrying baskets of washing from Oldham into Manchester to make ends meet, as record-ed in *Talks With Old Yorkshire Cricketers.*

In 1923 the first of the inter-war matches involving Yorkshire crick-eters and then Yorkshire Elevens was held in Saddleworth, as lovingly recorded in Phil Taylor's excellent book *Over the Hill by Way of Highmoor — The Centenary History of Saddleworth and District Cricket League.* It began as a specially arranged benefit match for an injured Greenfield player, when Maurice Leyland, Edgar Oldroyd, George Hirst, Percy Holmes and Emmott Robinson joined in two teams alongside local players. The following year Rhodes and Arthur Dolphin played in another end-of-season match at Greenfield, though not a ben-efit fixture, and in 1925 Herbert Sutcliffe, George Macaulay and Roy Kilner joined in the proceedings.

Then, in 1926 the fixture became Saddleworth and District against a Yorkshire Eleven, with all of the county side's leading players making appearances over the following years, including Leonard Hutton, Hedley Verity and Bill Bowes. A crowd of almost 4,000 saw the last such game.

Leyland thanked Messrs. John E and Harold A Tanner for their inter-est and hospitality that included a first-class prematch lunch and after-match tea, which doubtless encouraged Yorkshire players to attend. The brothers were mill owners and local club cricketers, Harold being Greenfield captain in 1923. It was he who initiated the tradition.

Two years later he presented a trophy to the league, the Tanner Cup, played for until recently on a knockout basis.

Hirst said after another of the annual fixtures: "Local cricket owed a great deal to these gentlemen".

Harold Tanner became a Yorkshire Committee member in the post-war years, representing Huddersfield District until his death in 1952. A third Saddleworth-born cricketer, J P (John) Whitehead — no relation to Lees — appeared for the county in the immediate post-war years until 1951.

John was a fast-medium bowler, who came to attention playing for Oldham CC, so he was initially selected by Lancashire in a one-day "friendly" in 1945.

Yorkshire were quickly made aware of Whitehead's

Generation game: Scott and father Mike Richardson opening for Werneth CC in the Central Lancashire League — Scott in *Red Rose* colours, Mike in Yorkshire's.
(Photo: Oldham Chronicle)

origins, and a fortnight later he appeared for his native county.

Saddleworth's direct connection with Yorkshire was broken by Harold Tanner's death and Whitehead's departure to Worcestershire, while any chance of it being restored in during the 1960s was ended by an illness of promising batter Mike Richardson, who had represented Yorkshire's age-group sides. His son, Scott, was to play for the county.

Yorkshire abandoned their county-born selection tradition in the 1990s, and in 2000 they signed Scott, who was Oldham-born but Saddleworth-raised. He progressed through Lancashire's age-groups, but found it necessary to move to Leicestershire to further his career.

A contract was not forthcoming, but Scott played professionally in the Huddersfield League with such success that he came to Yorkshire's attention. He made 13 appearances for Yorkshire, including seven in the 2001 Championship-winning season, but was always remarked upon as a Lancashire product rather than the Saddleworth player he also was.

In recent years two Yorkshire campaign groups who lobby for a better appreciation of the Historic County of Yorkshire, the Yorkshire Ridings Society and the Saddleworth White Rose Society, have funded annual coaching days for young cricketers from Saddleworth School with Pro-Coach Yorkshire at Headingley.

The initiative was interrupted by Covid, but it is hoped this can start again in 2024 and help to maintain an unofficial link between the parish and Yorkshire cricket, one which goes back 150 years.

John Whitehead, right, at The Oval in 1953 in Worcestershire colours.

(Photo kindly forwarded by Tim Jones of Worcestershire Cricket Archives)

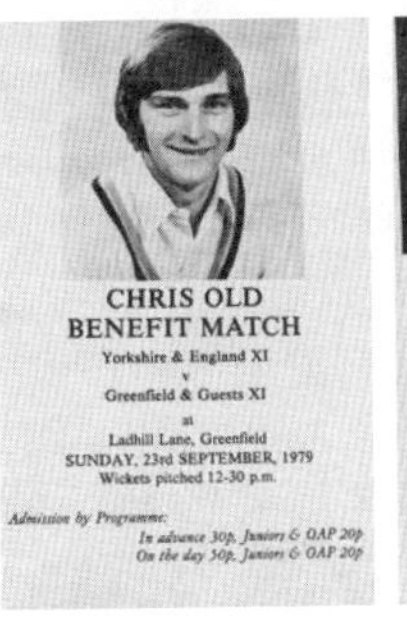

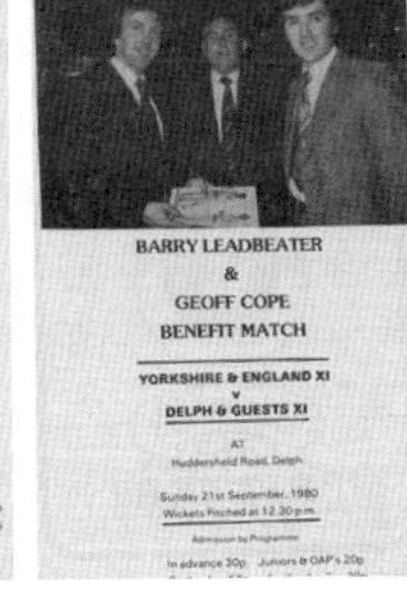

When the stars turned out: Benefit-match covers for Chris Old, Barry Leadbeater, Geoff Cope and David Bairstow.

DOUG PADGETT

By David Warner

Former Yorkshire and England batter Doug Padgett, right, who was employed by the county club throughout his working life, died on January 20, aged 89.

Born in Bradford on July 30, 1934, Padgett was brought up in Idle. He became Yorkshire's youngest player when he made his first-class debut in 1951 at the age of 16 years and 321 days, and he remained the youngest until Paul Jarvis's debut in 1981, aged 16 years and 75 days.

Padgett went on to play in 487 first-class matches for Yorkshire before retiring

at the end of the 1971 season when he was not retained, despite captain Geoffrey Boycott urging the committee to keep him on because of his experience and the strength he could still bring to the batting.

By that time he had scored 20,306 first-class runs for Yorkshire with 29 centuries and a top score 161 not out against Oxford University at The Parks in 1959.

His close association with Yorkshire was still far from over, because he went on to captain the Second XI with distinction, and was appointed club coach, a position he held until his retirement.

Padgett was a "players' player", admired for his exemplary technique and sheer love of the game. He was not a cricketer who yearned for the bright lights on away trips, and he was never happier than upon settling in the bar on a night to discuss cricket and tactics.

Padgett played in two home Test Matches for England against South Africa in 1960 with only moderate success, but many felt that a player of his class was deserving of more chances. He also toured New Zealand with the MCC in 1960-61 on the first tour by aeroplane, but he was not selected for the Test series.

Padgett will best be remembered for the outstanding part he played in Yorkshire's Championship-winning days, which began in the late 1950s and continued well into the 60s — by which time they had clinched the title on seven occasions.

Needle clash: Yorkshire's games against Surrey when both were prime contenders for the Championship could be as tense as the traditional *Roses* rivalry. Padgett tucks one away in 1967 as Ken Barrington watches from first slip with Derek Taylor at the wicket. (Photo: Mick Pope Archive)

And it was he and fellow batter Bryan Stott who got the ball rolling with their magnificent stand of 141 in the second innings against Sussex at Hove in 1959 to bring the first of these Championship successes.

It was Padgett during his time as Yorkshire coach who first spotted the potential of Michael Vaughan. Doug was on the balcony at Abbeydale Park, Sheffield, during the tea interval of a Yorkshire match when he spotted the schoolboy batting on the outfield.

He made enquiries, and as a result Vaughan was signed up to join the Yorkshire Academy and become the first player in recent times to be signed by Yorkshire who had not been born inside the county.

Vaughan was among those who paid tribute when the club announced Doug's death in January, writing on social media platform X: "RIP Doug…I will be forever grateful for the knowledge you passed onto me.

Such a great character who adored Yorkshire Cricket."

Many others responded. Darren Lehmann, the county's overseas professional for seven seasons, said: "RIP. A legend of a man and a gentleman of the game.

"Thanks for everything you did for me, Doug. Our thoughts are with the family at this time."

Kevin Sharp and Ryan Sidebottom were among the other former Yorkshire players who paid tribute.

Sharp wrote: "Thank you, Doug, for believing in me, and providing that guidance and mentoring role that I needed as a young player.

"You were always there to support the lads, and that will never be forgotten by many players.

"Thinking of all the family at this time. RIP." Sidebottom added: "RIP Doug. What a funny, inspiring, passionate coach. Absolutely loved being around him and learning from him growing up at Yorkshire. Wonderful man."

Padgett's loss was also felt on the other side of the Pennines, with former Lancashire and England batter David 'Bumble' Lloyd saying: "An absolute champion...Yorkshire through and through."

Heroes of Hove: Bryan Stott and Doug Padgett in 1959 after the Championship triumph that heralded the golden age of the 1960s.
(Photo: Ron Deaton Archive)

DOUGLAS (DOUG) ERNEST VERNON PADGETT
FIRST-CLASS CRICKET FOR YORKSHIRE 1951 TO 1971

Born Bradford   July 20, 1934   Died: Steeton   January 20, 2024
Right-hand batter.   Right-arm medium-pace bowler
Debut for Yorkshire   v. Somerset at Taunton   June 6, 1951
Last played: v. Somerset at Taunton   July 1, 1962
Last played: v. Hampshire at Dean Park,
                                      Bournemouth   August 25, 1971
          Yorkshire Cap: August 9, 1958

YORKSHIRE BATTING AND FIELDING

Season	M	I	NO	Runs	HS	Avge	100s	50s	Ct
1951	3	4	1	60	25	20.00	0	0	1
1953	2	4	0	38	21	9.50	0	0	0
1955	14	22	1	571	115	27.19	1	2	6
1956	30	44	6	1046	107	27.52	1	6	10
1957	19	31	1	462	48	15.40	0	0	7
1958	24	36	4	685	67	21.40	0	4	12
1959	35	60	8	2158	161*	41.50	4	11	21
1960	31	46	2	1574	146	35.77	5	6	13
1961	37	65	6	1856	114	31.45	4	6	16
1962	34	57	3	1750	125*	32.40	3	11	15
1963	26	39	2	879	142	23.75	2	2	19
1964	33	51	2	1380	112	28.16	2	6	18
1965	32	55	2	1220	91	23.01	0	5	15
1966	31	52	5	1194	79	25.40	0	6	16
1967	30	47	5	1284	139	30.57	2	5	17
1968	32	43	2	1163	136*	28.36	2	8	19
1969	27	45	8	1078	83	29.13	0	7	12
1970	24	38	4	1042	108	30.64	2	6	14
1971	23	35	1	866	133	25.47	1	5	19
	487	774	63	20306	161*	28.55	29	96	250

YORKSHIRE BOWLING

Seasons	Overs	Mdns	Runs	Wkts	Avge	Best
1959	29.1	10	80	1	80.00	1-13
1961	10	2	31	1	31.00	1-14
1962	26.1	15	32	0	—	0- 0
1963	0.5	0	4	1	4.00	1- 4
1964	11	5	27	1	27.00	1- 2
1965	7	5	6	1	6.00	1- 6
1967	8	6	6	1	6.00	1- 6
1968	1	0	11	0	—	0-11
1969	1	0	4	0	—	0- 4
1970	1	0	3	0	—	0- 3
1971	0.3	0	4	0	—	0- 4
	95.4	43	208	6	34.66	1- 2

Centuries (29)

1955	115	v. Warwickshire	at Birmingham
1956	107	v. Scotland	at Hull
1959	161 *	v. Oxford University	at Oxford
	100	v. Lancashire	at Manchester
	122	v. Somerset	at Harrogate
	139 *	v. Nottinghamshire	at Nottingham
1960	130	v. Somerset	at Hull
	146	v. Sussex	at Middlesbrough
	117	v. Surrey	at The Oval
	120	v. Northamptonshire	at Northampton
	113	v. Warwickshire	at Bradford
1961	114	v. Nottinghamshire	at Hull
	112 *	v. Northamptonshire	at Northampton
	106	v. Nottinghamshire	at Nottingham
	101·	v. Somerset	at Taunton

Centuries *(Continued)*

1962	107 *	v. Oxford University	at Oxford
	115	v. Gloucestershire	at Bristol
	125 *	v. Surrey	at Bramall Lane, Sheffield
1963	101	v. Kent	at Hull
	142	v. Derbyshire	at Chesterfield
1964	112	v. Derbyshire	at Chesterfield
	110	v. Nottinghamshire	at Nottingham
1967	111	v. Middlesex	at Bramall Lane, Sheffield
	139	v. Nottinghamshire	at Nottingham
1968	136 *	v. Middlesex	at Leeds
	105	v. Lancashire	at Leeds
1970	106	v. Hampshire	at Bramall Lane, Sheffield
	108	v. Nottinghamshire	at Bramall Lane, Sheffield
1971	133	v. Glamorgan	at Swansea

ENGLAND BATTING AND FIELDING

Season	M	I	NO	Runs	HS	Avge	100s	50s	Ct
1960	2	4	0	51	31	12.75	0	0	0

ENGLAND BOWLING

Seasons	Overs	Mdns	Runs	Wkts	Avge	Best
1960	2	0	8	0	—	0- 8

ALL FIRST-CLASS MATCHES

Matches	Innings	NO	Runs	HS	Avge	100s	50s	Ct
506	806	67	21124	161*	28.58	32	98	261

Overs	Maidens	Runs	Wkts	Avge	Best	5Wi	10Wm
97.4	43	216	6	36.00	1- 2	0	0

LIST A CRICKET FOR YORKSHIRE 1963 TO 1971

Yorkshire debut: Gillette Cup v. Nottinghamshire at Middlesbrough   May 22, 1963

Last played: John Player League v. Northamptonshire at Bradford

September 12, 1971

YORKSHIRE BATTING AND FIELDING

Season	M	I	NO	Runs	HS	Avge	100s	50s	Ct
1963	2	2	0	50	38	25.00	0	0	1
1964	1	1	0	13	13	13.00	0	0	1
1965	4	3	0	56	31	18.66	0	0	0
1966	1	1	0	15	15	15.00	0	0	0
1967	2	1	0	22	22	22.00	0	0	0
1968	1	1	0	34	34	34.00	0	0	0
1969	17	17	1	227	46	14.18	0	0	4
1970	16	15	1	337	68	24.07	0	2	5
1971	13	13	1	315	48	26.25	0	0	2
	57	54	3	1069	68	20.96	0	2	13

YORKSHIRE BOWLING

Seasons	Overs	Mdns	Runs	Wkts	Avge	Best
1970	4	0	25	1	25.00	1-25

ARTHUR *(ROCKER)* ROBINSON

Arthur *(Rocker)* Robinson, left, one of Yorkshire's most popular and big-hearted fast bowlers in the 1970s, died on February 11, aged 77.

Born at Brompton, near Northallerton, on August 17, 1946, Robinson, who made his first-team debut against Oxford University at The Parks in 1971, would claim 196 first-class wickets with his solid left-armers up to the end of 1977, when he was not retained.

Robinson played in one of Yorkshire's less successful periods, but he always gave 100 percent effort and was a totally reliable, proud member of the team.

He took wickets regularly, yet had to wait until the end of the 1976 summer to be awarded his county cap, which he wore with great pride. His career first-class bowling average was a respectable 25.13.

Tall and well-built, Robinson was renowned for his bravery fielding at "Boot Hill", which he did uncomplainingly, despite suffering bruised shins and other regular knocks.

Although a genuine tail-end batter, he still figured in one of Yorkshire's most remarkable century stands when he helped Arnie Sidebottom to put on 144 for the last wicket against Glamorgan at Cardiff in 1977 before Sidebottom was run out for 124, leaving Robinson stranded on 30.

At the time it was Yorkshire's second highest 10th-wicket partnership — and only four runs shy of the 148 by Lord Hawke and David Hunter against Kent at Sheffield in 1898.

Robinson's most successful season came when he captured 43 first-class wickets and 28 in one-day matches in 1974.

Against Surrey at The Oval that summer he returned career-best first-class figures on the Saturday with 6-61 in the Championship and the following day registered his List A best 4-25 in the John Player League.

After playing league cricket for Harlsey and Northallerton, Robinson had two seasons with Leeds at the start of his county career. He returned to Northallerton when his Yorkshire days were over, and became the club's groundsman.

David Warner

ARTHUR LESLIE ROBINSON

FIRST-CLASS CRICKET FOR YORKSHIRE 1971 to 1977

Born: Brompton   August 17, 1946
Died: February 11, 2024
Left-hand batter.   Left-arm medium-pace bowler

Debut for Yorkshire   v. Oxford University at Oxford   May 12, 1971
Last played: v. Derbyshire at Scarborough   September 7, 1977
Yorkshire Cap: October 5, 1976

BATTING AND FIELDING

Season	M	I	NO	Runs	HS	Avge	100s	50s	Ct
1971	3	0	0	0	—	—	0	0	1
1972	1	0	0	0	—	—	0	0	0
1973	11	13	8	73	28*	14.60	0	0	5
1974	16	9	4	43	17*	8.60	0	0	6
1975	18	14	4	101	24	10.10	0	0	16
1976	16	17	11	60	13	10.00	0	0	8
1977	19	16	4	88	30*	7.33	0	0	10
	84	69	31	365	30*	9.60	0	0	46

BOWLING

Seasons	Matches	Overs	Mdns	Runs	Wkts	Avge	Best	5wI	10wM
1971	3	73	24	153	6	25.50	2-22	0	0
1972	1	21	7	42	0	—	0-19	0	0
1973	11	250	69	700	24	29.16	5-56	1	0
1974	16	375.5	103	880	43	20.46	6-61	2	0
1975	18	393.5	101	1031	36	28.63	5-56	1	0
1976	16	379	89	1006	43	23.39	5-78	1	0
1977	19	480.1	139	1115	44	25.34	5-28	2	0
	84	1972.5	532	4927	196	25.13	6-61	7	0

5 wickets in an innings (7)

1973	5-56	v. Surrey	at Leeds
1974	6-61	v. Surrey	at The Oval
	5-27	v. Nottinghamshire	at Worksop
1975	5-56	v. Hampshire	at Abbeydale Park, Sheffield
1976	5-78	v. Worcestershire	at Scarborough
1977	5-28	v. Leicestershire	at Leeds
	5-32	v. Essex at Middlesbrough	

LIST A CRICKET FOR YORKSHIRE 1971 to 1977

Debut for Yorkshire   John Player League v. Middlesex at Lord's   May 16, 1971
Last played: John Player League v. Essex at Scarborough   August 28, 1977

BATTING AND FIELDING

Season	M	I	NO	Runs	HS	Avge	100s	50s	Ct
1971	2	2	0	14	14	7.00	0	0	0
1972	1	0	0	0	—	—	0	0	0
1973	12	4	4	25	10*	—	0	0	2
1974	22	12	5	54	18*	7.71	0	0	3
1975	22	9	4	10	6	2.00	0	0	5
1976	20	4	2	13	6*	6.50	0	0	4
1977	13	5	4	12	5*	12.00	0	0	1
	92	36	19	128	18*	7.52	0	0	15

BOWLING

Seasons	Overs	Mdns	Runs	Wkts	Avge	Best	4wI
1971	16	0	81	6	13.50	4 -38	1
1972	8	0	40	1	40.00	1 -40	0
1973	90	11	290	17	17.05	3 - 3	0
1974	183.5	23	592	28	21.14	4 -25	1
1975	183.5	34	584	19	30.73	2 - 8	0
1976	174.4	23	639	21	30.42	4 -31	1
1977	102.4	12	362	13	27.84	3 -14	-
	759	103	2588	105	24.64	4 -25	3

4 wickets in an innings (3)

1971	4-38	v. Surrey	at The Oval
1974	4-25	v. Surrey	at The Oval
1976	4-31	v. Essex	at Leyton

JOHN WARING

Former Yorkshire fast bowler, John Waring, left, who died on October 1, 2023 — his 81st birthday — made an enormous contribution to cricket, and once even out-shone Freddie Trueman in a sensational *Roses* victory at Headingley.

Born in Ripon, Waring was playing golf there on the day before his death when he suddenly became ill. He was taken to hospital in Harrogate, where he died the following morning.

Educated at Boroughbridge Secondary Modern School, he made his Yorkshire debut against Northamptonshire at Wantage Road in 1963.

Over four seasons he played in 28 first-class matches for his native county, capturing 53 wickets at 21.16.

It was in Yorkshire's Championship-winning season of 1966 – their first of three consecutive title wins – that he rushed Yorkshire to a two-day *Roses* victory at Headingley with match figures of 10-63. Batting first, Lancashire were shot out for 57, Trueman taking 5-18 and Waring 3-23. Yorkshire replied with 196, but Lancashire were again routed by the same new-ball pair, this time Waring returning figures of 7-40 and Trueman 2-26.

Waring, who turned out in one game for Warwickshire in 1967 after being released by Yorkshire, played his early cricket at Dishforth, where he and his wife, Jean, had lived since 1974.

After a spell at Thirsk, he joined Ripon as a 17-year-old, taking 108 wickets for them in 1960 and assisting them in becoming York and District League champions in 1961 and 1962.

There were then spells at Leeds, Harrogate and Scarborough before spending four seasons in the Bradford League with Bingley, where he helped them do the League and Priestley Cup double in 1969. Waring appeared for Cumberland from 1970-1973.

He was always particularly proud of his playing days with Yorkshire, and was a member of the *White Rose* county's Players' Association.

When he retired from cricket he played golf at Ripon City Golf Club, where he served as captain and president.

Waring is survived by wife, Jean, and son, Jonathan.

David Warner

JOHN SHAW WARING

FIRST-CLASS CRICKET FOR YORKSHIRE 1963 to 1966

Born: Ripon   October 1, 1942
Died: Harrogate   October 1, 2023
Right-hand batter.   Right-arm fast-medium bowler
Debut for Yorkshire   v. Northamptonshire at Northampton   May 4, 1963
Last played: v. MCC at Scarborough   September 10, 1966
Last First Class match
was for Warwickshire v. Scotland at Birmingham   August 2, 1967

YORKSHIRE BATTING AND FIELDING

Season	M	I	NO	Runs	HS	Avge	100s	50s	Ct
1963	5	5	2	20	17*	6.66	0	0	5
1964	2	2	0	4	3	2.00	0	0	0
1965	8	7	5	18	6*	9.00	0	0	5
1966	13	13	8	95	26	19.00	0	0	7
	28	27	15	137	26	11.41	0	0	17

YORKSHIRE BOWLING

Seasons	Matches	Overs	Mdns	Runs	Wkts	Avge	Best	5wI	10wM
1963	5	72.3	20	196	13	15.07	5-49	1	0
1964	2	16	4	36	0	—	0-11	0	0
1965	8	128.3	33	348	15	23.20	3-30	0	0
1966	13	206.2	49	542	25	21.68	7-40	1	1
	28	423.2	106	1122	53	21.16	7-40	2	1

5 wickets in an innings (2)

1963	5-49	v. Worcestershire	at Bradford
1966	7-40	v. Lancashire	at Leeds

10 wickets in a match (1)

1966	10-63 (3-23 and 7-40)	v. Lancashire	at Leeds

ALL FIRST-CLASS MATCHES

Matches	Innings	NO	Runs	HS	Avge	100s	50s	Ct/St
29	29	15	152	26	10.85	0	0	17

Overs	Maidens	Runs	Wkts	Avge	Best	5Wi	10Wm
460.2	110	1251	55	22.74	7-40	2	1

For Yorkshire v. Warwickshire at Birmingham on July 14-16, 1965

Matches	Innings	NO	Runs	HS	Avge	100s	50s	Ct/St
1	1	1	1	1*	—	0	0	0

Overs	Maidens	Runs	Wkts	Avge	Best	4Wi
4	1	11	0	—	0-11	0

MINOR COUNTIES CHAMPIONSHIP CAREER

Yorkshire 2nd XI 1961-1966. Cumberland 1970-1973)

Matches	Innings	NO	Runs	HS	Avge	100s	50s	Ct/St
50	62	22	438	67	10.95	0	1	29

Overs	Maidens	Runs	Wkts	Avge	Best	5Wi	10Wm
1215	317	3386	149	22.72	7-57	8	1

SIR MICHAEL PARKINSON

By Chris Waters, *Yorkshire Post*

On the day Sir Michael Parkinson's death was announced, August 17, 2023, it was fitting not only that Yorkshire's cricketers were in action, but also that they were watched by one of their finest sons and one of Parkinson's dearest friends.

Sir Geoffrey Boycott, who played with Parkinson, right, at Barnsley Cricket Club in the 1950s, and who three times appeared on his famous TV chat show, cut a poignant figure in the pavilion at York as Yorkshire played Hampshire in the One-Day Cup. Parkinson had died the previous day, aged 88.

"I knew it was coming because his son, Michael junior, rang me," said Boycott. "I knew he was deteriorating, and it's very sad news."

Boycott, 82, first met Parkinson as a teenager: "I was 15-years-old. I was taken from Ackworth Cricket Club to Barnsley, where Dickie Bird was the star batsman, getting 50 every Saturday. Michael played in the first team. One year, they dropped me for him, and he went and got a hundred against Harrogate. He was a good player."

As their respective careers went in different directions, Parkinson, Boycott and Bird himself, all would become household names. Parkinson did not play first-class cricket like Bird, later to become a legendary umpire, let alone rise to the heights achieved by Boycott, scorer of 48,426 first-class runs and 151 hundreds.

But his broadcasting career was second to none — Parkinson was also a terrific writer — with everyone who was anyone appearing on his show: "I think he was the best interviewer on television, because he liked people," Boycott said. "He actually listened to what they said. When Michael asked a question he actually listened to the person's answer. He warmed to people, and they warmed to him.

"Many of the modern-day interviewers, they interrupt. They make themselves the star of the interview. Michael was different. He once said to me that the star of the Parkinson show was not him, but the person he was interviewing. He said he wanted people to remember the intervie-wee, not the other way round."

Boycott never lost his admiration for Parkinson the man: "He never lost his Yorkshireness, his sense of humour, his sense of honesty. He grew up like all of us in a mining community, and will be sorely missed."

Prior to the One-Day Cup match against Hampshire at Clifton Park, there was a minute's silence in memory of Parkinson, who died after a short illness. The players, coaches and match officials lined up in front of the pavilion to honour a man with lifelong connections to the sport and to Yorkshire cricket.

Parkinson was previously president of Scarborough CC.

Darren Gough, the Yorkshire managing director of cricket, paid trib-ute on the club's behalf: "He was a Barnsley boy, like myself, and it was an absolute pleasure to know him and his family. We are all devastated here at Yorkshire, and the thoughts of everyone at the club are with Sir Michael's family and friends at this sad time."

Parkinson had attended Dickie Bird's 90th birthday party at Headingley on April 17, one of his final public appearances.

Bird said: "His friendship meant more to me than anything else. If I wanted any advice I would ring Parky up. He helped me in so many, many ways. There will never be a chat show host like Michael Parkinson. He was the best. There will never be anyone better than him in your lifetime, my lifetime or anyone else's lifetime."

PETER FRETWELL

Print businessman Peter Fretwell (opposite page), who knocked Freddie Trueman off Yorkshire's General Committee when fresh elections were called in 1984, died on July 3 last year, aged 96.

Yorkshire CCC Vice-President Tony Vann, writes: "Peter led a full life, but cricket was one of his big loves, along with cycling. On the business front he fell into printing quite by chance.

"He was a merchant seaman when the non-appearance of a crew

member in the ship's print room meant he was press-ganged into assisting the ship's printer.

"Not only did he enjoy the work, but he found it quite lucrative. This small beginning led to a career in which he managed printing companies, was a successful print salesman and worked in newspapers on Fleet Street. He bought a print business in Silsden with a partner in 1961, expanding it until he became the sole owner in Keighley in 1980.

"The next stage of his life was about to begin when in September, 1983, Yorkshire sacked Geoffrey Boycott soon after offering him a testimonial for the 1984 season. Some members formed an action group called The Yorkshire Members 1984 Group. A Special General Meeting was called for January 21,1984, at the Harrogate Conference Centre to debate three resolutions:

1 That Geoffrey Boycott should be able to play in 1984.

2 A no-confidence vote against the cricket committee.

3 A no-confidence vote against the General Committee.

"The club lost all three resolutions and fresh elections had to take place. Fretwell stood in Craven District, where he had lived for many years. In one of many surprises he beat Freddie Trueman and was elected for the remaining two years of the cycle.

"He was placed on the Public Relations and Fund Raising sub-committee under the chairmanship of Sidney Fielden. This proved to be a wise move when the sub-committee decided to produce a news magazine for the whole of the membership. His offer that his printing firm would print the first three issues at no charge to the club but thereafter the club would pay the bill was accepted.

"Sadly, Peter by now was 60, and had difficulty listening at the General Committee meetings, even with a hearing aid. He stood down at the end of his two-year term, and did not stand again.

"He was a popular and generous man, who maintained his interest in Yorkshire to the last month of his life. He was always at his happiest watching the team at Scarborough. He lost his wife, Muriel, three years ago. His two sons, Graeme and Des, followed him into the business."

YORKSHIRE'S FIRST-CLASS HIGHLIGHTS OF 2023

Win by 200 runs or more (1)

Yorkshire (297 and 520-9 dec) defeated Derbyshire (247 and 293) by 277 runs at Scarborough

Totals of 400 and over (6)

550-9 dec	v. Gloucestershire at Leeds
517	v. Leicestershire at Leeds
520 - 9 dec	v. Derbyshire at Scarborough **
500	v. Glamorgan at Cardiff **
412- 9	v. Glamorgan at Leeds
407	v. Worcestershire at Worcester

*** Consecutive innings*

Century Partnerships (13)

For 1st wicket (4)

177	A Lyth and F J Bean	v. Worcestershire at Worcester
113	A Lyth and F J Bean	v. Durham at Scarborough
112	A Lyth and F J Bean	v. Leicestershire at Leicester
100	A Lyth and F J Bean	v. Derbyshire at Scarborough

For 2nd wicket (1)

127	F J Bean and Shan Masood	v. Glamorgan at Cardiff

For 3rd wicket (4)

165	F J Bean and D J Malan	v. Leicestershire at Leeds
164	Shan Masood and J H Wharton	v. Worcestershire at Leeds
138	A Lyth and G C H Hill	v. Glamorgan at Leeds
107	J H Wharton and Shan Masood	v. Derbyshire at Scarborough

For 4th wicket (2)

153	F J Bean and G C H Hill	v. Gloucestershire at Leeds
132	Shan Masood and G C H Hill	v. Glamorgan at Cardiff

For 5th wicket (1)

111	G C H Hill and J A Tattersall	v. Gloucestershire at Leeds

For 8th wicket (1)

125	M L Revis and J A Thompson	v. Derbyshire at Scarborough

Centuries (13)

F J Bean (3)

135	v. Worcestershire at Worcester
118	v. Leicestershire at Leeds
114	v Gloucestershire at Leeds

A Lyth (3)

174	v. Glamorgan at Leeds
115	v. Sussex at Leeds
111	v. Durham at Scarborough

D J Malan (2)

132	v. Leicestershire at Leeds
106	v. Derbyshire at Chesterfield

M L Revis (2)

106	v Derbyshire at Scarborough
104 *	v. Gloucestershire at Leeds

Centuries *(Continued)*

Shan Masood (2)

192   v. Glamorgan at Cardiff
123   v. Worcestershire at Leeds

G C H Hill (1)

101   v. Gloucestershire at Leeds

5 wickets in an innings (5)

B O Coad (2)

5 -33 v. Worcestershire at Worcester
5 -54 v. Sussex at Hove

D M Bess (1)

5 -158 v. Leicestershire at Leeds

M D Fisher(1)

5 -30 v. Derbyshire at Chesterfield

M L Revis (1)

5 -50 v Glamorgan at Cardiff

10 wickets in a match (none)

3 catches in an innings (5)

J A Tattersall (3)

4   v. Sussex at Leeds
3   v. Derbyshire at Chesterfield
3   v. Derbyshire at Scarborough

J M Bairstow (1)

3   v. Glamorgan at Leeds

F J Bean (1)

3   v. Worcestershire at Worcestershire

5 catches in a match (2)

J A Tattersall (2)

6 (2 + 4) v. Sussex at Leeds
5 (3 + 2) v. Derbyshire at Scarborough

3 dismissals in an innings (2)

S D Hope (1)

3 (2 ct + 1 st) v. Leicestershire at Leeds

J A Tattersall (1)

3 (2 ct + 1 st) v. Derbyshire at Scarborough

5 dismissals in a match (2)

J A Tattersall (1)

6 (5 ct + 1 st) v. Leicestershire at Leeds

S D Hope (1)

5 (4 ct + 1 st) v. Gloucestershire at Bristol

Debuts (9)

In First Class cricket (1): B M Cliff

In First Class cricket for Yorkshire (8): S D Hope, M E Milnes, M W Edwards, Saud Shakeel, Shan Masood, D T Moriarty, M Steketee and R D Rickelton

Caps awarded (none)

FIRST CLASS FACTFILE
LV= INSURANCE
COUNTY CHAMPIONSHIP 2023
Compiled by John T Potter

Versus LEICESTERSHIRE at Leeds

1. Yorkshire last played a Championship match in Division Two in September 2013.
2. M E Milnes made his First Class debut for Yorkshire.
3. S D Hope made his First Class debut for Yorkshire.
4. J O Hull made his First Class debut.
5. F J Bean (118) scored his maiden First Class century.
6. P S P Handscomb (112) became the 13th player to score a century for and against Yorkshire.
7. Leicestershire's second-innings score (392-7) was the third highest successful fourth-innings chase at Headingley. The two higher were 404-6 by Hampshire in 2006 and 404-3 by Australia against England in 1948.
8. Leicestershire last won a championship match in Yorkshire at Bradford in 1996.
9. This was only Leicestershire's second Championship win at Headingley, the first being in 1910.
10. The total runs scored in this match (1,610) was the second highest in a First Class match involving Yorkshire, the highest being 1,665 against Warwickshire at Birmingham in 2002.

Versus GLOUCESTERSHIRE at Bristol

1. This match was abandoned without a ball bowled before play should have started on the third morning.
2. It was Yorkshire's second match to be abandoned at Bristol. The first was in 1977.

Versus SUSSEX at Hove

1. Yorkshire last played a normal Championship match at Hove in 2015.
2. M W Edwards and Saud Shakeel made their First Class debuts for Yorkshire.
3. J J Carson's 5-79 was his First Class career best.
4. J A Thompson took his 100th Championship wicket.
5. There was no play on the fourth day because of rain.

COUNTY CHAMPIONSHIP FACTFILE *(Continued)*

Versus GLAMORGAN at Leeds

1. Glamorgan last played a normal Championship match at Headingley in 2012.
2. M G Neser took a hat-trick in Yorkshire's first innings — Malan, Hill and Bess. This was the sixth hat-trick against Yorkshire at Headingley.
3. M G Neser's 7-32 was his First Class career best
4. Yorkshire's fourth-innings score of 412-9 was their second highest, the highest being 433 at Edgbaston in 2006 when the lost by 66 runs.

Versus DURHAM at Chester-le-Street

1. Shan Masood made his First Class debut for Yorkshire.
2. B F W de Leede made his Championship debut for Durham.
3. This was Yorkshire's seventh loss by 1 wicket.

Versus DERBYSHIRE at Chesterfield

1. Yorkshire last played a Championship match at Chesterfield in 2013.
2. M D Fisher's 5-30 was his First Class career best. He also took his 100th First Class wicket.
3. Haider Ali's 146 was his maiden Championship century.
4. J L du Plooy's 170 was his highest Championship score.
5. Derbyshire's second-innings fifth-wicket stand of 277 was the highest for this wicket by any team against Yorkshire.

Versus GLOUCESTERSHIRE at Leeds

1. M T Steketee made his First Class debut for Yorkshire.
2. D T Moriarty made his First Class debut for Yorkshire.
3. G Roelofsen made his First Class debut.
4. Yorkshire's first-innings total of 550-9 dec was their highest against Gloucestershire in Yorkshire, passing their 504-7 dec at Bradford in 1905.
5. M L Revis's 104 * was his maiden First Class century.
6. This was the first time three Yorkshire Colts had scored three centuries in the same innings — F J Bean 114, G C H Hill 101 and M L Revis 104 *.
7. Gloucestershire's first-innings seventh-wicket partnership of 162 by O J and T J Price was their highest against Yorkshire.
8. Gloucestershire's first-innings total of 464 was their highest against Yorkshire in Yorkshire, passing their 411 at Leeds 1992.

COUNTY CHAMPIONSHIP FACTFILE *(Continued)*

Versus WORCESTERSHIRE at Worcester

1. R D Rickelton made his First Class debut for Yorkshire.
2. A Lyth passed the total of 13,000 First Class career runs.
3. F J Bean's 138 was his First Class career best.
4. M T Steketee took his 250th First Class wicket.
5. M J Waite's 59* was his maiden First Class fifty.
5. Rain played a big part in this match, with only 229.4 overs bowled in four days.

Versus SUSSEX at Leeds

1. Rain played a big part in this match, with only 237.1 overs bowled. There was no play on the fourth day, as in the match at Hove.

Versus DURHAM at Scarborough

1. Only 120.5 overs were bowled on the first two days. There was no play at all on the third or fourth days.

Versus DERBYSHIRE at Scarborough

1. Derbyshire's previous visit to Scarborough for a Championship match was in July 1991.
2. W L Madsen passed the total of 13,000 First Class runs.
3. Shan Masood passed the total of 9,500 First Class runs.
4. M L Revis's 106 was his highest First Class score.

Versus GLAMORGAN at Cardiff

1. Yorkshire last played a normal Championship fixture at Cardiff in August 1998, when G M Hamilton had a good match with scores of 79 and 70 and bowling analyses of 5-69 and 5-43.
2. B M Cliff made his First Class debut.
3. Shan Masood's 192 was his maiden century for Yorkshire.

Versus LEICESTERSHIRE at Leicester

1. Yorkshire's last Championship visit to Leicestershire was in July 2012, when A Lyth struck 248 * as Yorkshire totalled 486.
2. Leicestershire's 10th-wicket partnership of 93 by H J Swindells and W S Davis was their best against Yorkshire.
3. The weather again spoilt this match with only 148.1 overs bowled and no play on the third day.

COUNTY CHAMPIONSHIP FACTFILE *(Continued)*

Versus WORCESTERSHIRE at Leeds

1. Kashif Ali's 103 was his maiden First Class century.
2. B M T Allinson's 75 was highest First Class score.
3. J Leach took his 450th First Class wicket.
4. J H Wharton's 89 was his highest First Class score.
5. A Lyth passed the total of 1,000 First Class runs for the season. He last achieved this in 2016. Yorkshire's last batsmen to do this were G S Ballance and T Kohler-Cadmore, both in 2019.
6. Yorkshire's fourth-innings match chase of 363-4 was their highest winning chase at Headingley, their only better chases being 400-4 v. Leicestershire at Scarborough in 2005, 402-6 v. Gloucestershire at Bristol in 2012 and 406-4 v. Leicestershire at Leicester in 2005.

Yorkshire Premier League 2023

Champions: Woodlands (Bradford League), Castleford (YPL North), Sheffield Collegiate (YPL South), Saltburn (North Yorkshire South Durham League).

YPL champions: Woodlands; beat Sheffield Collegiate in the final at New Farnley by six wickets chasing 77 on September 16. Collegiate 76 all out (Muhammad Bilal 4-38), Woodlands 78-4 (Tim Jackson 29*).

Semi-Finals: Sheffield Collegiate beat Castleford, Woodlands beat Saltburn.

Title for young Lehmann

Former Yorkshire overseas player Jake Lehmann, the current captain of South Australia, was back in the North last summer as the professional with Bolton side Little Lever, who won the inaugural North West Cricket League title. Lehmann, who briefly represented Yorkshire in late 2016, scored 1,041 runs at an average of 94.64 across all NWCL competitions.

Yorkshire CCC Squad 2024

Captain: S Masood

* Captain

§ Wicket-Keeper

Figures in brackets ( ) indicate position in Second Innings batting order,
where different from First Innings

YORKSHIRE MEN'S SENIOR SQUAD 2024

Player	Date of Birth	Birthplace	First-Class debut for Yorkshire	Date Capped
§ J M Bairstow	September 26, 1999	Bradford	June 11, 2009	July 11, 2011
F J Bean	April 16, 2002	Harrogate	September 5, 2022	
D M Bess	July 22, 1997	Exeter	May 14, 2019	April 8, 2021
H C Brook	February 22, 1999	Keighley	June 26, 2016	Sept 5, 2021
B M Cliff	October 23, 2002	Halifax	September 10, 2023	
B O Coad	January 10, 1994	Harrogate	June 20, 2016	Sept 18, 2018
§ H G Duke	September 6, 2001	Wakefield	May 13, 2021	
M W Edwards	December 23, 1994	Sydney, Aus	April, 20, 2023	
D Ferreira	July 21,1998	Pretoria, SA		
M D Fisher	November 9, 1997	York	April 19, 2015	Sept 26, 2022
G C H Hill	January 24, 2001	Keighley	August 15, 2020	
D J Leech	January 10, 2001	Middlesbrough	August 8, 2020	
W A Luxton	May 6, 2003	Keighley	July 11, 2022	
A Lyth	September 25, 1987	Whitby	May 16, 2007	Aug 22, 2010
D J Malan	September 3, 1987	Roehampton	August 1, 2020	Aug 1, 2020
S Masood	October 14, 1989	Kuwait	May 11, 2023	May 11, 2023
M E Milnes	July 29, 1994	Nottingham	April 6, 2023	
D T Moriarty	February 12, 1999	Reigate	June 25, 2023	
A U Rashid	February 17, 1998	Bradford	July 19, 2006	Sept 18, 2008
M L Revis	November 15, 2001	Steeton	September 16, 2019	
J E Root	December 30, 1990	Sheffield	May 10, 2010	Sept 4, 2012
§ J A Tattersall	December 15, 1994	Harrogate	June 20, 2018	Sept 26, 2022
J A Thompson	October 9, 1996	Leeds	June 10, 2019	July 11, 2022
J H Wharton	February 1, 2001	Huddersfield	April 14, 2022	
Y Vagadia	May 7, 2004	Newcastle Upon Tyne		

LV= INSURANCE COUNTY CHAMPIONSHIP 2023

DIVISION 1

DE   Drawn but team batting last with scores level: 8 points

	P	W	L	D	DE	Abdn	Bonus Points BAT	Bonus Points BOWL	Ded	Points
1 Surrey (Div 1-1) 14	14	8	2	4	0	0	27	41	0	216
2 Essex (Div 1-4) 14	14	7	3	4	0	0	25	39	0	196
3 Hampshire (Div 1-3) ... 14	14	8	4	2	0	0	18	39	3	192
4 Warwickshire (Div 1-8) . 14	14	6	4	4	0	0	22	41	0	179
5 Lancashire (Div 1-2) ... 14	14	3	1	10	0	0	29	35	1	161
6 Nottinghamshire (Div 2-1) 14	14	4	4	6	0	0	18	39	0	151
7 Somerset (Div 1-7) 14	14	3	4	7	0	0	25	40	0	148
8 Kent (Div 1-5) 14	14	2	7	5	0	0	20	34	0	111
9 Middlesex * (Div 2-2) .. 14	14	3	9	1	1	0	5	39	1	104
10 Northamptonshire * (Div 1-6) 14	14	2	8	4	0	0	10	34	0	96

*** Relegated in 2024**

Deductions:

Hampshire	3 points for preparing below-average pitch in match against Essex on July 25, 2023
Lancashire	1 point for slow over-rate in match against Surrey on June 25, 2023
Middlesex	1 point for slow over-rate in match against Somerset on May 18, 2023

DIVISION 2

	P	W	L	D	DE	Abdn	Bonus Points BAT	Bonus Points BOWL	Ded	Points
1 Durham * * (Div 2-6) .. 14	14	7	1	6	0	0	54	39	2	233
2 Worcestershire * * (Div 2-4) 14	14	5	3	6	0	0	21	36	0	167
3 Sussex (Div 2-7) 14	14	3	1	10	0	0	29	39	16	150
4 Leicestershire (Div 2-8) 14	14	3	4	7	0	0	25	35	1	142
5 Glamorgan (Div 2-3) ... 14	14	1	1	12	0	0	29	34	0	139
6 Derbyshire (Div 2-5) ... 14	14	0	4	10	0	0	25	38	0	113
7 Yorkshire (Div 1-9) 14	14	3	2	8	0	1	31	35	50	109
8 Gloucestershire (Div 1-10) 14	14	0	6	7	0	1	23	35	1	97

*** * Promoted in 2024**

Deductions:

Durham	2 points for slow over-rate in match against Derbyshire on April 27, 2023
Sussex	4 points for slow over-rate in match against Yorkshire on April 20, 2023 12 points for three fixed-penalty disciplinary breaches
Leicestershire	1 point for slow over-rate in match against Yorkshire on September 19, 2023
Yorkshire	2 points for slow over-rate in match against Derbyshire on September 3, 2023 48 points for failings identified by the Cricket Discipline Commission enquiry
Gloucestershire	1 point for slow over-rate in match against Sussex on September 26, 2023

LV= Insurance County Championship — Division Two
Yorkshire v. Leicestershire

Played at Headingley, Leeds, on April 6, 7, 8 and 9, 2023
Leicestershire won by 3 wickets at 6.28pm on the Fourth Day

Toss won by Leicestershire — Yorkshire 7 points, Leicestershire 22 points

Close of play: First Day, Yorkshire 285-3 (Malan 91*, Milnes 5*); Second Day, Leicestershire 201-5 (Handscomb 62*, Rehan Ahmed 10*); Third Day, Yorkshire 220-4 (Hope 83*, Hill 57*)

YORKSHIRE

First Innings		Second Innings	
* A Lyth, lbw b Hull	21	c Hull b Finan	0
F J Bean, c Ackermann b Finan	118	c Handscomb b Wright	11
J H Wharton, c Handscomb b Finan	24	c and b Rehan Ahmed	52
D J Malan, c Mulder b Rehan Ahmed	132	c sub (E Barnes) b Hull	3
M E Milnes, lbw b Finan	75	(10) not out	15
§ S D Hope, c Mulder b Ackermann	13	(5) c Patel b Hull	83
G C H Hill, st Handscomb b Rehan Ahmed	3	(6) c Ackermann b Wright	67
M L Revis, c Budinger b Wright	27	not out	22
D M Bess, b Rehan Ahmed	49	c Handscomb b Finan	2
J A Thompson, c Hill b Wright	26	(7) c Rehan Ahmed b Hull	13
B O Coad, not out	1		
Extras b 8, lb 7, w 1, nb 12	28	Extras lb 6, nb 12	18
Total	517	Total (8 wkts dec)	286

Bonus points — Yorkshire 5, Leicestershire 3

FoW: 1-35. (Lyth), 2-104 (Wharton), 3-269 (Bean), 4-363 (Malan), 5-388 (Hope),
1st 6-393 (Hill), 7-439 (Milnes), 8-445 (Revis), 9-485 (Thompson), 10-517 (Bess)
FoW: 1-0 (Lyth), 2-26 (Bean), 3-29 (Malan), 4-125 (Wharton), 5-220 (Hope),
2nd 6-236 (Thompson), 7-260 (Hill), 8-263 (Bess)

	O	M	R	W		O	M	R	W
Wright	27	2	128	2	Finan	12	0	59	2
Finan **	22.4	3	109	3	Wright	9	2	52	2
Hull	15	1	64	1	Hull	8	0	68	3
Salisbury **	7.2	0	43	0	Rehan Ahmed	14	1	67	1
Rehan Ahmed	15	0	89	3	Ackermann	11	1	34	0
Ackermann	15	1	69	1					

*** Salisbury unable to complete his 8th over,
which was finished by Finan*

LEICESTERSHIRE

First Innings		Second Innings	
R K Patel, c and b Thompson	28	c Hope b Coad	125
S G Budinger, c Revis b Milnes	21	c Thompson b Bess	41
* L J Hill, c Lyth b Coad	7	c Hope b Bess	3
C N Ackermann, c and b Milnes	67	lbw b Bess	72
§ P S P Handscomb, lbw b Coad	112	not out	68
P W A Mulder, c Hope b Milnes	1	c Thompson b Bess	11
Rehan Ahmed, c Hill b Thompson	85	st Hope b Bess	10
C J C Wright, not out	66	(9) not out	40
M G A Finan, lbw b Thompson	0	(8) c Bean b Milnes	5
J O Hull, c Bess b Revis	15		
M E T Salisbury, c Hope b Revis	1		
Extras b 3, lb 1, nb 8	12	Extras b 2, lb 10, w 5	17
Total	415	Total (7 wkts)	392

Bonus points — Leicestershire 3, Yorkshire 2

Score at 110 overs: 392-8

FoW: 1-28 (Budinger), 2-51 (Hill), 3-64 (Patel), 4-185 (Ackermann), 5-187 (Mulder), 6-328
1st (Handscomb), 7-332 (Rehan Ahmed), 8-332 (Finan), 9-397 (Hull), 10-415 (Salisbury)
FoW: 1-80 (Budinger), 2-88 (Hill), 3-201 (Ackermann), 4-269 (Patel), 5-298 (Mulder),
2nd 6-318 (Rehan Ahmed), 7-327 (Finan)

	O	M	R	W		O	M	R	W
Coad	28	7	73	2	Coad	14	5	55	1
Milnes	24	6	72	3	Milnes	12	0	62	1
Revis	19.1	1	81	2	Thompson	11.5	2	58	0
Thompson	23	6	86	3	Bess	32	1	158	5
Hill	9	3	30	0	Revis	5	0	21	0
Bess	11	0	69	0	Hill	11	4	26	0

Umpires: B J Debenham and P R Pollard

Scorers: J T Potter and P J Rogers

Century-old record falls

DAWID MALAN
Top score at a gallop

Yorkshire failed to convert dominance at the opening fixture's midway point as the Foxes recovered to secure a remarkable heist, chasing 387 to win by three wickets on day four.

Centuries from opener Fin Bean (118) and Dawid Malan (132), Bean's first in first-team cricket, gave Yorkshire the ideal start at 517 all out, having been inserted on an unexpectedly batter-friendly pitch.

Bean hit the lion's share of 22 off England teenager Rehan Ahmed's first of four overs on day one before nightwatchman Matt Milnes completed a debut 75 on day two.

A run-rate just over five an over mirrored England's new brand of attacking Test cricket. Instead, it was dominance without breaking any sweat against an impotent Leicestershire...but the same criticism could be levelled at Yorkshire's bowlers.

Yorkshire failed to capitalise on having their visitors 187-5 in reply. Leicestershire's fightback was led by Australian Peter Handscomb, a 2017 Headingley overseas player, who hit a determined 112 and shared 141 for the sixth wicket with Ahmed, who batted with youthful exuberance for 85. Troublesome tail-ender Chris Wright also added 66 unbeaten in a 415 reply for a side winless in 2022.

Even so, Yorkshire held sway as they built their lead through the second half of day three. Debutant West Indian overseas Shai Hope's 83 was supported by James Wharton's maiden fifty, 52, and George Hill's 67. At 286-8 declared seven overs into day four a 389 target was set in 87 overs. Yet the pitch remained excellent for batting, and Leicestershire's chances of a first Championship win at Headingley since 1910 were not impossible.

Despite 5-158 for Dom Bess, the Foxes scurried away with 22 points. Opener Rishi Patel's 125 marked his maiden first-class century, while Colin Ackermann made an important 72. Handscomb, 68 not out, and Wright, 40 not out, shared a crucial eighth-wicket stand of 65 in only eight overs to seal victory with seven balls remaining.

Maiden first-team century: Fin Bean, whose 118 against the Foxes, mirrored England's new brand of attacking cricket.

At Seat Unique County Ground, Bristol, on April 13, 14, 15 and 16, 2023
Match abandoned at 9.45am on the Third Day without a ball bowled

Toss: None

Yorkshire 5 points, Gloucestershire 5 points

Umpires: P R Pollard and B V Taylor

Scorers: J T Potter and A J Bull

First washout for five years

Rain and a wet outfield at the Seat Unique Stadium in Bristol meant not a ball was bowled across the four days.

Persistent wet weather across the South West in the buildup to this fixture forced the cancellation of Day One, with umpires Paul Pollard and Billy Taylor making their decision at 9.45am in bright sunshine.

Heavy rain the following day, the Friday, meant Day Two was called off at 9.30am, and fears were already growing about the rest of the contest. And so it proved.

At their 9am Saturday inspection — in bright sunshine like Thursday — Pollard and Taylor called the whole game off, with particular concerns about the condition of the bowlers' run-ups at the Ashley Down Road end of the ground.

Both sides took five points, Yorkshire's first complete washout since Essex at Headingley in April 2018.

Washout for Yorkshire women

Yorkshire women had all six of their County Championship T20 group-stage matches washed out last April and May, going on to win one and lose one against Cumbria and North East Warriors at a Group 1B Finals Day at Casterton School, Sedbergh, on May 14.

LV= Insurance County Championship — Division Two
Sussex v. Yorkshire

Played at 1st Central County Ground, Hove, on April 20, 21, 22 and 23, 2023
Match drawn at 4.40pm on the Fourth Day

Toss won by Sussex

Yorkshire 9 points, Sussex 11 - 4 = 7 points

Close of play: First Day, Sussex 275-5 (Carter 60*, Hudson-Prentice 32*); Second Day, Yorkshire 216-7 (Thompson 15*, Fisher 0*); Third Day, Yorkshire 138-3 (Lyth 69*, Hope 53*); Fourth Day, no play

SUSSEX

First Innings		Second Innings	
A G H Orr, c Bean b Thompson	20	run out (Coad)	26
T J Haines, lbw b Bess	48	c Hope b Thompson	23
T P Alsop, c Bess b Hill	95	lbw b Coad	0
* C A Pujara, lbw b Thompson	18	lbw b Thompson	13
T G R Clark, b Coad	1	lbw b Bess	4
§ O J Carter, c Bean b Coad	64	lbw b Bess	19
F J Hudson-Prentice, c Lyth b Coad	32	lbw b Fisher	30
N J McAndrew, c Hope b Fisher	23	lbw b Fisher	0
J J Carson, lbw b Coad	26	lbw b Bess	1
O E Robinson, c Lyth b Coad	1	c Lyth b Edwards	1
H T Crocombe, not out	25	not out	8
Extras b 1, lb 7	8	Extras b 8, lb 4	12
Total	361	Total	137

Bonus points — Sussex 3, Yorkshire 3

Sussex deducted 4 points for slow over-rate

FoW: 1-48 (Orr), 2-83 (Haines), 3-123 (Pujara), 4-124 (Clark), 5-218 (Alsop), 6-279
1st (Hudson-Prentice), 7-302 (McAndrew), 8-302 (Carter), 9-304 (Robinson), 10-361 (Carson)

FoW: 1-41 (Orr), 2-42 (Alsop), 3-61 (Haines), 4-66 (Pujara), 5-66 (Clark), 6-105
2nd (Hudson-Prentice), 7-107 (McAndrew), 8-118 (Carson), 9-121 (Robinson), 10-137 (Carter)

	O	M	R	W		O	M	R	W
Coad	21.3	8	54	5	Coad	10	1	30	1
Fisher	20	6	81	1	Fisher	8	1	30	2
Thompson	18	4	72	2	Bess	16.1	4	36	3
Edwards	19	2	63	0	Thompson	5	1	23	2
Bess	17	3	60	1	Edwards	4	1	6	1
Hill	7	1	23	1					
Saud Shakeel	1	1	0	0					

YORKSHIRE

First Innings		Second Innings	
* A Lyth, lbw b McAndrew	24	not out	69
F J Bean, c Carter b Carson	49	b McAndrew	3
Saud Shakeel, b Crocombe	3	c Clark b Hudson - Prentice	6
D J Malan, b Carson	37	c Carter b Hudson - Prentice	2
§ S D Hope, b Carson	38	not out	53
G C H Hill, b Robinson	8		
D M Bess, c Carson b Crocombe	13		
J A Thompson, lbw b Carson	22		
M D Fisher, c Pujara b McAndrew	9		
M W Edwards, not out	19		
B O Coad, b Carson	45		
Extras b 4, lb 11, nb 16	31	Extras lb 5	5
Total	298	Total (3 wkts)	138

Bonus points — Yorkshire 1, Sussex 3

FoW: 1-52 (Lyth), 2-65 (Saud Shakeel), 3-136 (Bean), 4-147 (Malan), 5-158 (Hill),
1st 6-198 (Bess), 7-216 (Hope), 8-223 (Thompson), 9-239 (Fisher), 10-298 (Coad)
2nd 1-14 (Bean), 2-31 (Saud Shakeel), 3-39 (Malan)

	O	M	R	W		O	M	R	W
Robinson	15	3	52	1	Robinson	8	1	29	0
McAndrew	16	1	67	2	McAndrew	9	1	28	1
Hudson-Prentice	9	2	28	0	Hudson-Prentice	7	2	19	2
Crocombe	10	4	49	2	Crocombe	6	0	30	0
Haines	3	0	8	0	Carson	10	0	27	0
Carson	21	2	79	5					

Umpires: N J Pratt and R A White

Scorers: J T Potter and G J Irwin

So near...and yet so far

Sixty-three more runs...

That was all Yorkshire needed to win on the final day, with seven wickets remaining. But rain brought more frustration for Ottis Gibson and company as the day was washed out, umpires Neil Pratt and Rob White making their decision at 4.30pm after multiple inspections.

Yorkshire felt they would have needed only an hour to seal their first win of the campaign, with Adam Lyth unbeaten on 69 and West Indian overseas player Shai Hope on 53 not out in his last appearance of a short stint.

There is no doubt it begs the question: should Yorkshire have tried to wrap up victory on Saturday's third evening when

BEN COAD: All-round star

chat of Sunday rain was prominent? Yorkshire's 201 target was set at tea, with 42 overs remaining in the day. In the modern era of aggressive batting it wasn't out of the question.

The loss of three cheap wickets — Fin Bean, Saud Shakeel and Dawid Malan — was a problem as they slipped to 39-3, meaning Lyth and Hope had to consolidate. In truth, completing the chase on the third evening never looked likely, with Hope surviving a controversial run-out appeal on nine: Sussex wicketkeeper Oli Carter threw the ball back at the stumps after Hope had left the ball, grounded his bat and then lifted it again in one motion. It was given not out, with opinion split as to whether the Bajan was lucky to be still there.

He was, helping Yorkshire to 138-3 at the close.

Yorkshire battled back brilliantly on day three from conceding a first-innings lead of 63 — bowled out for 298 replying to 361. Ben Coad, with 5-54 and 45, was their first innings star. Dom Bess was excellent in the second innings with 3-36 and building pressure as Sussex were bowled out for 137, while Mickey Edwards claimed a debut wicket, having been unlucky not to strike in the first innings.

LV= Insurance County Championship — Division Two
Yorkshire v. Glamorgan

Played at Headingley, Leeds, on May 4, 5, 6 and 7, 2023
Match drawn at 6.50pm on the Fourth Day

Toss won by Yorkshire   Yorkshire 8 points, Glamorgan 8 points

Close of play: First Day, Yorkshire 62-5 (Bairstow 2*, Malan 8*); Second Day, Glamorgan 57-2 (Labuschagne 7*, Northeast 0*); Third Day, Glamorgan 352-4 dec (Labuschagne 170*, Root 51*)

GLAMORGAN

First Innings		Second Innings	
* D Lloyd, c Bairstow b Coad	0	(2) c sub (J A Tattersall) b Edwards	33
A G Salter, lbw b Coad	0	(1) lbw b Thompson	15
M Labuschagne, c Bairstow b Hill	65	not out	170
S A Northeast, c Bean b Edwards	49	c Saud Shakeel b Thompson	66
K S Carlson, c Bairstow b Hill	16	c Bairstow b Fisher	0
W T Root, c sub (J A Tattersall) b Edwards	24	not out	51
§ C B Cooke, c Fisher b Thompson	7		
M G Neser, b Edwards	9		
T van der Gugten, not out	35		
J A R Harris, c Lyth b Fisher	6		
J P McIlroy, c Bean b Hill	10		
Extras b 9, lb 6, w 5, nb 4	24	Extras b 7, lb 7, w 1, nb 2	17
Total	245	Total (4 wkts dec)	352

Bonus points — Yorkshire 3

FoW:
1st   1-0 (Lloyd), 2-1 (Salter), 3-83 (Northeast), 4-135 (Carlson), 5-154 (Labuschagne), 6-161 (Cooke), 7-174 (Neser), 8-199 (Root), 9-228 (Harris), 10-245 (McIlroy)
2nd   1-44 (Salter), 2-57 (Lloyd), 3-205 (Northeast), 4-222 (Carlson)

	O	M	R	W		O	M	R	W
Coad **	9.5	2	18	2	Fisher	17	5	44	1
Fisher **	18.1	3	58	1	Thompson	20	4	68	2
Thompson	14	4	38	1	Edwards	15	2	74	1
Edwards	15	2	54	3	Hill	16	1	53	0
Hill	14.5	3	62	3	Bess	10	0	23	0
					Saud Shakeel	4	0	23	0

*** Coad unable to finish his 10th over,
which was completed by Fisher*

YORKSHIRE

First Innings		Second Innings	
* A Lyth, lbw b van der Gugten	17	lbw b McIlroy	174
F J Bean, b van der Gugten	11	lbw b van der Gugten	21
Saud Shakeel, lbw b Neser	19	(6) c Labuschagne b Harris	35
D J Malan, lbw b Neser	25	(5) lbw b Harris	17
M W Edwards, c Labuschagne b Neser	2	(10) b van der Gugten	13
M D Fisher, c Northeast b Neser	0	(9) lbw b Harris	0
§ J M Bairstow, not out	20	(3) c Labuschagne b van der Gugten	0
G C H Hill, b Neser	0	(4) c Cooke b van der Gugten	60
D M Bess, b Neser	0	(7) lbw b McIlroy	0
J A Thompson, c Cooke b Neser	5	(8) not out	55
B O Coad, run out (Carlson)	0	not out	0
Extras lb 5, nb 2	7	Extras b 25, lb 5, w 1, nb 6	37
Total	106	Total (9 wkts)	412

Bonus points — Glamorgan 3

FoW:
1st   1-21 (Lyth), 2-46 (Bean), 3-51 (Saud Shakeel), 4-59 (Edwards), 5-59 (Fisher), 6-90 (Malan), 7-90 (Hill), 8-90 (Bess), 9-102 (Thompson), 10-106 (Coad)
FoW:
2nd   1-99 (Bean), 2-105 (Bairstow), 3-243 (Hill), 4-281 (Malan), 5-325 (Lyth), 6-325 (Bess), 7-377 (Saud Shakeel), 8-377 (Fisher), 9-408 (Edwards)

	O	M	R	W		O	M	R	W
Neser	11	1	32	7	van der Gugten	24	1	72	4
van der Gugten	13	4	46	2	McIlroy	20	3	57	2
Harris	5	1	15	0	Neser	23	5	91	0
McIlroy	2	0	8	0	Harris	22	4	97	3
					Lloyd	4	1	28	0
					Salter	2	0	21	0
					Labuschagne	1	0	16	0

Umpires: H M S Adnan and I D Blackwell   Scorers: J T Potter and A K Hignell

Heroics mask a failure

Yorkshire's wait for a first Championship victory since the opening game of 2022 continued as they failed to make the most of winning the toss and bowling in helpful conditions.

New groundsman Richard Robinson left more grass on the Headingley surface, and Adam Lyth electing to bowl should have been the perfect outcome.

Instead, Yorkshire's bowlers were not at their best as Glamorgan engineered a 245 total thanks to a dogged 65 from Australian linchpin Marnus Labuschagne, the world's No.1 ranked Test batter.

Ben Coad struck twice inside the first five overs — Glamorgan were 1-2 — before going down in his 10th over with a groin injury which ruled him out of the rest of the game.

In the day's final 22 overs, Glamorgan pressed ahead by reducing the hosts to 59-5, including two nightwatchmen — Mickey Edwards and Matthew Fisher — as they were surprisingly employed to protect fit-again Jonny Bairstow.

On day two things got worse. Australian fringe seamer Michael Neser, who had

ADAM LYTH: 174 hls record for Headingley

claimed Edwards and Fisher, claimed a hat-trick as three big in-duckers trapped Dawid Malan lbw and bowled George Hill and Dom Bess who offered no shots. His career-best 7-32 despatched Yorkshire for 106. Bairstow was 20 not out in his first innings since the previous August.

Labuschagne hit a more expansive 170 against a wilting attack, and Glamorgan's 352-4 declared set a 492 victory chase at tea on day three. It did not start until the beginning of day four due to rain, but when it did stand-in captain Lyth led an impressive batting display with a fluent 174 — his highest first-class score at Headingley.

Bairstow was elevated to No.3 from 99-1 at lunch to push the chase, but fell for a duck. Yorkshire slipped from 240-2 at tea to 412-9, including Lyth's loss, fifty-maker Jordan Thompson batting out the last over against Neser. This was Headingley's highest ever fourth-innings total.

LV= Insurance County Championship — Division Two
Durham v. Yorkshire

Played at Seat Unique Riverside, Chester-le-Street, on May 11, 12, 13 and 14, 2023

Durham won by 1 wicket at 11.50 am on the Fourth Day

Toss won by Yorkshire

Durham 19 points, Yorkshire 4 points

Close of play: First Day, Durham 42-2 (Borthwick 21*, Potts 2*); Second Day, Yorkshire 91-3 (Malan 33*, Bairstow 16*); Third Day, Durham 213-8 (Raine 32*, Potts 13*)

YORKSHIRE

First Innings		Second Innings	
A Lyth, c Clark b Potts	0	c Bedingham b Raine	0
* Shan Masood, b Potts	44	b Potts	10
Saud Shakeel, c de Leede b Potts	8		
D J Malan, c Jones b Carse	36	c Robinson b Raine	44
§ J M Bairstow, b de Leede	27	c Robinson b Raine	36
G C H Hill, c de Leede b Raine	28	c Bedingham b Potts	51
M L Revis, b Raine	21	b de Leede	8
D M Bess, c Carse b Potts	13	lbw b Potts	0
J A Thompson, b Carse	2	lbw b Potts	7
M D Fisher, not out	27	not out	8
M W Edwards, c Robinson b Raine	13	lbw b Raine	5
F J Bean *(concussion replacement)*		(3) c Robinson b Carse	22
Extras b 16, lb 9, w 2, nb 8	35	Extras b 19, lb 6, nb 2	27
Total	254	Total	218

Bonus points — Yorkshire 1, Durham 3

F J Bean was a concussion replacement for Saud Shakeel from Day 2 onwards.

FoW: 1st — 1-2 (Lyth), 2-27 (Saud Shakeel RH), 2-81 (Shan Masood), 3-132 (Malan), 4-132 (Bairstow), 5-181 (Revis), 6-202 (Bess), 7-202 (Hill), 8-202 (Saud Shakeel), 9-218 (Thompson), 10-254 (Edwards)

FoW: 2nd — 1-0 (Lyth), 2-18 (Shan Masood), 3-41 (Bean), 4-136 (Malan), 5-145 (Bairstow), 6-186 (Revis), 7-197 (Bess), 8-198 (Hill), 9-207 (Thompson), 10-218 (Edwards)

	O	M	R	W		O	M	R	W
Raine	19.3	5	59	3	Raine	19	2	36	4
Potts	22	6	49	4	Potts	20	3	61	4
de Leede	12	3	40	1	de Leede	12	4	44	1
Carse	17	3	60	2	Carse	5	1	16	1
Patel	10	2	21	0	Patel	11	2	36	0

DURHAM

First Innings		Second Innings	
A Z Lees, lbw b Hill	15	b Fisher	38
M A Jones, c Bairstow b Thompson	2	lbw b Fisher	56
* S G Borthwick, c Lyth b Fisher	35	c Bess b Thompson	11
M J Potts, lbw b Thompson	7	(10) lbw b Hill	25
D G Bedingham, lbw b Thompson	6	(4) c Bairstow b Hill	19
§ O G Robinson, c Bairstow b Revis	44	(5) c Lyth b Fisher	13
G Clarke, c Lyth b Hill	33	(6) b Thompson	9
B A Carse, lbw b Hill	14	(11) not out	2
B F W de Leede, not out	22	(7) b Fisher	4
B A Raine, b Hill	4	(8) not out	50
A Y Patel, b Fisher	34	(9) lbw b Thompson	0
Extras b 4, lb 5, nb 2	11	Extras b 7, lb 12	19
Total	227	Total (9 wkts)	246

Bonus points — Yorkshire 3

FoW: 1st — 1-12 (Jones), 2-38 (Lees), 3-61 (Potts), 4-65 (Borthwick), 5-71 (Bedingham), 6-132 (Robinson), 7-160 (Clark), 8-167 (Carse), 9-173 (Raine), 10-227 (Patel)

FoW: 2nd — 1-47 (Lees), 2-82 (Borthwick), 3-126 (Bedingham), 4-147 (Robinson), 5-150 (Jones), 6-154 (de Leede), 7-173 (Clark), 8-173 (Patel), 9-244 (Potts)

	O	M	R	W		O	M	R	W
Fisher	17.5	4	55	2	Fisher	22	4	64	4
Thompson	15	3	55	3	Thompson	14	1	55	3
Edwards	8	1	36	0	Hill	20	5	42	2
Hill	15	2	43	4	Edwards	4	0	21	0
Revis	9	2	29	1	Revis	5	0	18	0
					Bess	16	4	27	0

Umpires: P K Baldwin and B J Debenham

Scorers: J T Potter and W R Dobson

Hopes dashed to the depths

Yorkshire should have won.

Durham, set a target of 246, slipped to 173-8 late on day three in challenging conditions, but the Division Two leaders scrambled to a one-wicket victory thanks to a ninth-wicket partnership of 71 between Ben Raine and Matthew Potts.

You might say: "It never Raines but it pours" for Yorkshire, the all-rounder finishing on 50 not out off 114 balls and injured fast bowler Brydon Carse squirting the winning runs to third-man off George Hill.

GEORGE HILL: Standout player

It took Durham 50 minutes on day four to triumph. They started on 216-8, needing 33. With two needed to win Hill trapped Potts lbw for 25 to heighten tensions on a pitch which offered signs of uneven bounce to start with before becoming low and slow. Chop-ons were regular.

Hill was Yorkshire's standout player in a match which saw Shan Masood captain the county for the first time and fellow Pakistani Saud Shakeel drop out on day one with concussion after being struck on the helmet by a Potts bouncer. Hill claimed a first-innings 4-43 as Durham replied to Yorkshire's should-have-been-better 254 with 227.

Masood top-scored with 44 after winning the toss in a Yorkshire innings beset by batters not converting starts.

Day three started with the visitors 91-3 in their second innings and Dawid Malan and Jonny Bairstow together, but a slip from 136-3 to 218 all out against an attack minus Carse with a trunk injury was defining. Potts, for the second time in the match, claimed four wickets, and Raine matched him. Hill made 51, the fixture's first of only three fifties.

Alex Lees blazed 38 out of the first 47 runs in Durham's chase, but his departure to Matthew Fisher slowed the rate. Fisher struck three times more after tea as Durham fell from 126-2 to 173-8. But they recovered to win for the third time in five matches.

Yorkshire dropped to the foot of Division Two.

LV= Insurance County Championship — Division Two
Derbyshire v. Yorkshire

Played at Queen's Park, Chesterfield, on June 11, 12, 13 and 14, 2023

Yorkshire won by 3 wickets at 11.56am on the Fourth Day

Toss won by Yorkshire   Yorkshire 22 points, Derbyshire 3 points

Close of play: First Day, Yorkshire 272-5 (Malan 76*, Revis 0 *); Second Day, Derbyshire 248-4 (du Plooy 96*, Haider Ali 129*); Third Day, Yorkshire 147-6 (Shan Masood 68*

DERBYSHIRE

First Innings		Second Innings	
H R C Came, c Tattersall b Fisher	7	lbw b Coad	2
Haider Ali, lbw b Coad	0	(6) lbw b Hill	146
§ B D Guest, c Tattersall b Fisher	4	(7) c sub (B M Cliff) b Bess	42
W L Madsen, b Coad	4	c Hill b Coad	0
* J L du Plooy, lbw b Thompson	28	c Lyth b Bess	170
M J Lamb, c Hill b Fisher	4	(3) c Hill b Fisher	8
L M Reece, lbw b Coad	0	(2) lbw b Fisher	2
A T Thomson, c and b Thompson	20	not out	39
M R J Watt, c Tattersall b Fisher	15	c Tattersall b Bess	7
B W Aitchison, b Fisher	12	c Revis b Fisher	9
R A S Lakmal, not out	12	retired not out	10
Z J Chappell			
Extras lb 5	5	Extras b 10, lb 2, nb 6	18
Total	111	Total	453

Bonus points — Yorkshire 3

Z J Chappell was a concussion replacement for R A S Lakmal in Yorkshire's Second Innings

FoW: 1-1 (Haider Ali), 2-8 (Guest), 3-15 (Madsen), 4-15 (Came), 5-23 (Lamb),
1st 6-24 (Reece), 7-55 (du Plooy), 8-76 (Thomson), 9-94 (Watt), 10-111 (Aitchison)
FoW: 1-4 (Came), 2-4 (Reece), 3-5 (Madsen), 4-17 (Lamb), 5-294 (Haider Ali), 6-367 (Guest),
2nd 7-404 (du Plooy), 8-416 (Watt), 9-431 (Aitchison), 9-453 (Lakmal retired not out)

	O	M	R	W		O	M	R	W
Coad	10	2	28	3	Coad	23	8	54	2
Fisher	10.4	2	30	5	Fisher	22.5	5	70	3
Hill	5	1	15	0	Bess	38	1	190	3
Thompson	6	0	33	2	Thompson	12	0	44	0
					Revis	8	0	41	0
					Hill	15	1	42	1

YORKSHIRE

First Innings		Second Innings	
A Lyth, c Madsen b Aitchison	48	lbw b Watt	30
F J Bean, c Aitchison b Reece	28	c du Plooy b Thomson	19
* Shan Masood, c and b Watt	67	not out	95
D J Malan, c Lakmal b Watt	106	(8) c Lamb b Watt	0
G C H Hill, c Haider Ali b Watt	7	(4) run out (Aitchison/Guest)	0
§ J A Tattersall, c and b Reece	24	(5) lbw b Thomson	22
M L Revis, c Guest b Aitchison	32	c Madsen b Watt	0
D M Bess, b Thomson	2	(9) not out	41
J A Thompson, c du Plooy b Watt	17		
M D Fisher, c Haider Ali b Watt	0	(6) b Watt	4
B O Coad, not out	0		
Extras b 4, nb 18	22	Extras lb 2, nb 2	4
Total	353	Total (7 wkts)	215

Bonus points — Yorkshire 3, Derbyshire 3

FoW: 1-61 (Bean), 2-112 (Lyth), 3-200 (Shan Masood), 4-212 (Hill), 5-266 (Tattersall),
1st 6-325 (Malan), 7-328 (Bess), 8-351 (Thompson), 9-353 (Revis), 10-353 (Fisher)
FoW: 1-38 (Bean), 2-63 (Lyth), 3-84 (Hill), 4-140 (Tattersall), 5-145 (Fisher),
2nd 6-147 (Revis), 7-147 (Malan)

	O	M	R	W		O	M	R	W
Lakmal	19	2	77	0	Chappell	8	0	30	0
Aitchison	10	1	61	2	Watt	18	5	74	4
Reece	9	1	56	2	Reece	6	0	24	0
Thomson	22	1	72	1	Thomson	15.1	1	63	2
Watt	25.3	8	83	5	Aitchison	3	0	22	0

Umpires: T Lungley and C M Watts   Scorers: J T Potter and J E M Hough

Good things come to those...

MATTHEW FISHER: Eight wickets and career-best

Championship victory came to Yorkshire for the first time since their opening fixture of 2022 against Gloucestershire at Bristol.

Seventeen matches had come and gone — 18 if you count this season's abandonment at Bristol.

Victory was achieved in quite the way. After little over four sessions Yorkshire fans were checking hotel cancellation policies, such was the dominance.

Derbyshire, inserted, were skittled for 111 before lunch on day one thanks to Matthew Fisher's career-best 5-30 from 10.4 overs. In reply Dawid Malan's languid 106 underpinned 353 all out before lunch on day two, also including Shan Masood's 67.

Second time around the hosts slumped to 17-4 in bowler-friendly conditions, Fisher and new-ball partner Ben Coad, who had taken three first-innings wickets, uniting with gusto once more to leave Derbyshire 225 behind and reeling...but the match was about to turn.

Fifth-wicket pair Haider Ali, the Pakistani overseas batter dropped down from opening to No. 6, and captain Leus du Plooy counter-attacked, taking 95 from Dom Bess's first 15 overs. Ali, 146, and du Plooy, 170. batted until late morning on day three to share a stand of 277, the highest ever fifth-wicket partnership against Yorkshire.

Batting conditions eased, and Yorkshire lacked potency. Derbyshire increased their lead, while Bess, with 3-190 from 38 overs, recovered admirably, ousting du Plooy. The hosts were prised out for 453, last man Suranga Lakmal retiring hurt after being struck by a Fisher bouncer. Concussion substitute Zak Chappell's superior batting ability meant he couldn't go in as an identical replacement for the Sri Lankan seamer.

Derbyshire were confident, Yorkshire nervous. Those nerves heightened when Scottish left-arm spinner Mark Watt sparked a loss of four wickets for seven runs from 140-3 late on day three to early day four. Malan fell caught at short-leg off day four's first ball. But unbeaten Masood's busy 95 against his former county was ably supported by Bess's run-a-ball 41 not out to seal victory.

LV= Insurance County Championship — Division Two
Yorkshire v. Gloucestershire

Played at Headingley, Leeds, on June 25, 26, 27 and 28, 2023

Match drawn at 4.50pm on the Fourth Day

Toss won by Yorkshire — Yorkshire 13 points, Gloucestershire 12 points

Close of play: First Day, Yorkshire 393-6 (Revis 25*, Fisher 8*); Second Day, Gloucestershire 232-5 (Hammond 84*. O J Price 1*); Third Day, Gloucestershire 421-8 (O J Price 97*, Taylor 4*)

YORKSHIRE

First Innings		Second Innings	
A Lyth, c O J Price b Taylor	14	c O J Price b Zaman Akhter	55
F J Bean, c Charlesworth b Zaman Akhter	114	c Bracey b Zafar Gohar	38
* Shan Masood, lbw b Taylor	0	b Zafar Gohar	32
D J Malan, c Bracey b Charlesworth	28	c Bracey b Zafar Gohar	20
G C H Hill, c Bracey b O J Price	101	c O J Price b Dent	25
§ J A Tattersall, c O J Price b Taylor	79	c O J Price b Charlesworth	1
M L Revis, not out	104	not out	21
M D Fisher, c Bracey b Taylor	8	not out	0
D J Leech, c Hammond b O J Price	32		
M T Steketee, st Bracey b Zafar Gohar	26		
D T Moriarty, not out	4		
Extras b 9, lb 19, nb 12	40	Extras b 4, nb 4	8
Total (9 wkts dec)	550	Total (6 wkts dec)	200

Bonus points — Yorkshire 5, Gloucestershire 2

Score at 110 overs: 466-7

FoW: 1-33 (Lyth), 2-33 (Shan Masood), 3-90 (Malan), 4-243 (Bean), 5-354 (Hill),
1st 6-368 (Tattersall), 7-396 (Fisher), 8-467 (Leech), 9-534 (Steketee)

FoW: 1-73 (Bean), 2-129 (Lyth), 3-135 (Shan Masood), 4-160 (Malan), 5-161 (Tattersall),
2nd 6-200 (Hill)

	O	M	R	W		O	M	R	W
T J Price	14	1	70	0	Taylor	6	3	10	0
Taylor	27	7	70	4	T J Price	9	0	41	0
Zaman Akhter	28	5	101	1	Zaman Akhter	9	0	44	1
Zafar Gohar	30	2	118	1	Zafar Gohar	18	0	63	3
Charlesworth	11	0	70	1	O J Price	1	0	10	0
O J Price	11	0	51	2	Charlesworth	4	0	28	1
van Buuren	9	0	42	0	Dent	0.3	0	0	1

GLOUCESTERSHIRE

B G Charlesworth, c Lyth b Moriarty	35
C D J Dent, c Lyth b Leech	34
G Roelofsen, lbw b Moriarty	19
M A H Hammond, c Leech b Moriarty	92
* G L van Buuren, c Tattersall b Moriarty	12
§ J R Bracey, c Hill b Lyth	44
O J Price, b Moriarty	113
T J Price, b Hill	59
Zafar Gohar, c Tattersall b Leech	3
M D Taylor, c Hill b Leech	4
Zaman Akhter, not out	26
Extras b 7, lb 13, w 1, nb 2	23
Total	464

Bonus points — Gloucestershire 5, Yorkshire 3

FoW: 1-45 (Dent), 2-80 (Roelofsen), 3-93 (Charlesworth), 4-125 (van Buuren), 5-221 (Bracey),
6-246 (Hammond), 7-408 (T J Price), 8-413 (Zafar Gohar), 9-425 (Taylor), 10-464 (O J Price)

	O	M	R	W
Fisher	17	2	63	0
Leech	16	2	78	3
Steketee	17	1	82	0
Moriarty	34.2	9	139	5
Lyth	11	0	50	1
Hill	8	0	32	1

Umpires: P J Hartley and N A Mallender

Scorers: J T Potter and A J Bull

Centuries record for uncapped

Whether it was a trio of first-innings centuries for Fin Bean, George Hill and Matthew Revis — or whether it was a five-wicket haul for debutant loanee spinner Dan Moriarty — this match provided a glimpse into the future of Yorkshire cricket as the Division Two campaign reached its halfway mark.

Opener Bean with 114 and all-rounders Hill and Revis with 101 and 104 respectively — all similarly well-paced innings — underpinned Yorkshire's first-innings 550-9 declared.

It was the first time in the county's history that three non-

TON UP: Matthew Revis celebrates his century with debutant teammate Dan Moriarty.

capped players had scored centuries in the same first-class innings. Yet it didn't lead to a victory as Gloucestershire responded strongly with the bat to take significant time out of the contest.

Left-arm spinner Moriarty, in his first of four matches on loan from county champions Surrey and who would later sign for three years at Headingley, claimed four of the first six wickets to fall as the visitors fell to 125-4 and 246-6, but it was a case of the *Price is Right* for Gloucestershire as brothers Ollie and Tom combined to thwart Shan Masood and co.

The Prices attacked to share 162 inside 33 overs for the seventh wicket on day three, a record partnership for that wicket for Gloucestershire against Yorkshire. Ollie was 97 not out overnight and reached his maiden century in day four's opening over. Older brother Tom, who achieved the same feat earlier in the summer, added 59 in 464 all out. Ollie, 113, was bowled by Moriarty, who finished with 5-139 inside 35 overs.

Gloucestershire avoided the follow-on late on day three, and it was all but game over. Yorkshire cruised to 200-6 in their second innings on day four, and Adam Lyth top-scored with a half-century. Rain stopped play at 4.30pm, and no more play was possible.

Yorkshire claimed 13 points from their third draw in seven matches.

LV= Insurance County Championship — Division Two
Worcestershire v. Yorkshire

Played at New Road, Worcester, on July 10, 11, 12 and 13, 2023

Match drawn at 5.02pm on the Fourth Day

Toss won by Worcestershire   Yorkshire 12 points, Worcestershire 8 points

Close of play: First Day, Yorkshire 154-0 (Lyth 77*, Bean 69*); Second Day, Worcestershire 46-2 (Azhar Ali 14*, Haynes 12*); Third Day, Worcestershire (following on) 22-0 (Gibbon 13*, Finch 7*)

YORKSHIRE

A Lyth, lbw b Gibbon	79
F J Bean, lbw b Finch	135
J H Wharton, lbw b Waite	18
R D Rickelton, c Roderick b Waite	6
G C H Hill, c Roderick b Baker	53
* § J A Tattersall, lbw b Finch	16
M L Revis, c Waite b Finch	31
M D Fisher, c Roderick b Finch	2
B O Coad, c Haynes b Gibbon	41
M T Steketee, b Finch	3
D T Moriarty, not out	1
Extras b 1, lb 5, nb 16	22
Total	407

Bonus points — Yorkshire 4, Worcestershire 3

FoW: 1-177 (Lyth), 2-222 (Wharton), 3-234 (Rickelton), 4-275 (Bean), 5-315 (Tattersall), 6-327 (Hill), 7-330 (Fisher), 8-399 (Coad), 9-406 (Steketee). 10-407 (Revis)

	O	M	R	W
Leach	22	4	76	0
Gibbon	20	1	101	2
Waite	17	2	49	2
Finch	17.1	0	100	5
Baker	15	0	72	1
Libby	1	0	3	0

WORCESTERSHIRE

First Innings		Second Innings	
§ G H Roderick, c Bean b Fisher	4	(3) not out	34
* J D Libby, c Wharton b Coad	9	(4) not out	61
Azhar Ali, c Hill b Coad	22		
J A Haynes, lbw b Coad	29		
A J Hose, b Fisher	38		
E J Pollock, c Lyth b Steketee	0		
M J Waite, c Bean b Steketee	11		
J Leach, c Bean b Coad	33		
J O Baker, c Rickelton b Coad	12		
A W Finch, c Tattersall b Steketee	24	(2) run out (Steketee/Fisher)	15
B J Gibbon, not out	41	(1) c Hill b Coad	15
Extras lb 5, nb 14	19	Extras b 2, lb 3, nb 12	17
Total	242	Total (2 wkts)	142

Bonus points — Yorkshire 3

FoW: 1st 1-11 (Roderick), 2-15 (Libby), 3-63 (Haynes), 4-71 (Azhar Ali), 5-87 (Pollock), 6-119 (Waite), 7-139 (Hose), 8-170 (Baker), 9-179 (Leach), 10-242 (Finch),

2nd 1-31 (Finch), 2-32 (Gibbon)

	O	M	R	W		O	M	R	W
Coad	21	11	33	5	Coad	10	4	19	1
Fisher	21	6	73	2	Fisher	11	0	41	0
Revis	8	1	22	0	Steketee	7	3	16	0
Steketee	15.3	4	55	3	Revis	6	0	27	0
Hill	5	1	27	0	Moriarty	7	2	11	0
Moriarty	14	5	21	0	Lyth	6	0	18	0
Lyth	5	3	6	0	Wharton	1	0	5	0

Umpires: D J Millns and C M Watts   Scorers: J T Potter and S M Drinkwater

Openers wave Malvern magic

FIN BEAN: His third century of the season and a career-best.

Yorkshire made a superb start to a match which ultimately finished in a draw, with Adam Lyth and Fin Bean sharing an unbroken 154 in only 33.3 overs of play possible on day one.

Worcestershire will have rued their decision to bowl when the left-handed openers went on to make their partnership worth 177 early on day two. Lyth made 79 and Bean a career-best 135.

Bean reached his third Championship century of the summer off 140 balls during the second morning, and slog-swept a six off left-arm spinner Josh Baker in the same over he reached three figures.

That Yorkshire missed out on the maximum of five batting bonus points when bowled out for 407 was a frustration given their early dominance.

Seamer Adam Finch finished with five wickets, and it wasn't his only contribution. Yorkshire's South African overseas debutant Ryan Rickelton made six.

Matthew Fisher and Ben Coad struck once apiece as Worcestershire closed day two — another weather-affected day — on 46-2, and Coad continued an impressive game with four more wickets as Yorkshire strengthened their grip on day three. At 179-9 the hosts were wobbling thanks to the new-ball seamer's brilliant 5-33 from 21 overs after he had smacked 41 on day two.

Coad's tail-end heroics were usurped by Worcester's last-wicket pair of Finch, 24, and Ben Gibbon, 41 not out, as they united for almost 36 overs either side of tea on day three to share 63. Yorkshire were still able to enforce the follow-on, but the damage had been done.

Such was the success of Gibbon and Finch they opened in the second innings and shared 31 inside 12 overs into the early stages of day four. Gareth Roderick, 34 not out, and Jake Libby, 61 not out, shared an unbroken stand of 110 for the third wicket from 32-2.

More rain meant more than 130 overs were lost across four days and left Yorkshire contemplating another stalemate.

LV= Insurance County Championship — Division Two
Yorkshire v. Sussex

Played at Headingley, Leeds, on July 19, 20, 21 and 22, 2023
Match drawn at 12.30 pm on the Fourth Day

Toss won by Sussex

Yorkshire 11 points, Sussex 7 points

Close of play: First Day, Sussex 120-6 (Hudson-Prentice 29*, McAndrew 25*); Second Day, Yorkshire 286-4 (Malan 51*, Tattersall 19*); Third Day, Sussex 236-7 (Hudson-Prentice 43*, Carson 19*)

SUSSEX

	First Innings		Second Innings	
T G R Clark, c Lyth b Coad	1	c Tattersall b Lyth	58
T J Haines, c Tattersall b Fisher	17	c Tattersall b Steketee	11
* T P Alsop, c Rickelton b Fisher	35		
C J Tear,		c Tattersall b Coad	5
J M Coles, b Fisher	0	c Bean b Thompson	4
§ O J Carter, b Coad	2	c Moriarty b Thompson	58
D K Ibrahim, c Tattersall b Fisher	6	c Hill b Coad	0
F J Hudson-Prentice, c sub (M L Revis) b Moriarty	73	not out	43
N J McAndrew, b Steketee	47	c Tattersall b Steketee	23
J J Carson, not out	20	not out	19
A Karvelas, c Fisher b Thompson	0		
H T Crocombe, lbw b Moriarty	0		
Extras lb 9, nb 6	15	Extras b 2, lb 1, w 2, nb 10	15
Total	216	Total (7 wkts)	236

Bonus points —Yorkshire 3

C J Tear was a concussion replacement for T P Alsop from Day Two

FoW: 1st 1-6 (Clark), 2-18 (Haines), 3-18 (Coles), 4-41 (Carter), 5-57 (Ibrahim), 6-76 (Alsop), 7-170 (McAndrew), 8-210 (Hudson - Prentice), 9-211 (Karvelas), 10-216 (Crocombe)

FoW: 2nd 1-31 (Haines), 2-42 (Tear), 3-48 (Coles), 4-126 (Clark), 5-127 (Ibrahim), 6-154 (Carter), 7-189 (McAndrew)

	O	M	R	W		O	M	R	W
Coad	16	8	28	2	Coad	17	6	30	2
Fisher	16	5	69	4	Fisher	13	2	40	0
Steketee	12	4	46	1	Steketee	14	0	51	2
Hill	4	2	7	0	Thompson	10	2	25	2
Thompson	10	1	35	1	Hill	3	1	10	0
Moriarty	11.5	3	22	2	Moriarty	16	4	52	0
					Lyth	8	3	17	1
					Malan	3	0	8	0

YORKSHIRE

A Lyth, c Coles b Carson	115
F J Bean, c Coles b McAndrew	45
R D Rickelton, c Clark b Karvelas	46
D J Malan, c and b McAndrew	92
G C H Hill, c Clark b Carson	0
* § J A Tattersall, c Hudson-Prentice b Karvelas	41
J A Thompson, c Coles b Karvelas	0
M D Fisher, not out	10
B O Coad, c Haines b Karvelas	0
M T Steketee	
D T Moriarty	Did not bat
Extras b 8, lb 5, nb 2	15
Total (8 wkts dec)	364

Bonus points — Yorkshire 3, Sussex 2

FoW: 1-94 (Bean), 2-178 (Rickelton), 3-258 (Lyth), 4-258 (Hill), 5-347 (Tattersall), 6-347 (Thompson), 7-363 (Malan). 8-364 (Coad),

	O	M	R	W
McAndrew	16	3	49	2
Karvelas	16.2	1	76	4
Crocombe	8	0	50	0
Hudson-Prentice	11	3	52	0
Haines	2	0	11	0
Carson	18	1	75	2
Coles	12	2	38	0

Umpires: P K Baldwin and J D Middlebrook

Scorers: J T Potter and G J Irwin

Cheated by the rain again

Century beckons: Adam Lyth on the way to his side's top-score of 115.

Yorkshire, as at Hove in April, had got themselves into a winning position ahead of day four, which was then washed out, forcing the hosts to settle for draw number six.

Sussex led by 88 in their second innings with only three wickets left before rain forced the abandonment at 12.30pm on a soggy Saturday.

The weather had played its part earlier in the match, and such was the certainty of the forecast for day four Yorkshire tried to win it in three.

Matthew Fisher set the tone with four early wickets as Sussex slipped to 76-6 on day one, though all-rounder Fynn Hudson-Prentice counterpunched with 73 — his first of two useful innings — to fashion a 216 total after the promotion-chasing visitors had surprisingly elected to bat on a green-tinged pitch.

Adam Lyth's measured 115 in reply was supported by a much speedier 92 for Dawid Malan. Fin Bean, Ryan Rickelton and Jonny Tattersall contributed scores in the 40s to make it 364-8 declared. But that wasn't the full story.

Yorkshire started day three on 286-4, a lead of 70, and with the promise of last-day rain they opted to try to beat the weather as well as their opponents. The opening 9.2 overs saw 78 runs to set up the declaration, with Malan and stand-in captain Tattersall accelerating — Shan Masood was away with Pakistan.

Tattersall made 41 in a shot-a-ball passage of play, while Malan hit two fours and a six in the day's first four balls from off-spinner Jack Carson to move from 51 to 92 in 20 balls.

But Yorkshire could only chip away at the second-innings wickets. Opener Tom Clark and wicketkeeper Oli Carter made 58 apiece and Hudson-Prentice 43 not out, lifting unbeaten Sussex from 48-3 to 236-7 at the close. It was enough to move them up to second in the table with a ninth draw in 10 games.

LV= Insurance County Championship — Division Two
Yorkshire v. Durham

Played at North Marine Road, Scarborough, on July 25, 26, 27 and 28, 2023
Match drawn at 1.15 pm on the Fourth Day

Toss won by Durham   Yorkshire 7 points, Durham 8-1 = 7

Close of play: First Day, Yorkshire 142-2 ((Lyth 75*, Rickelton 0*); Second Day, Durham 106-1 (Lees 65*, Borthwick 29*); Third and Fourth Day, no play

YORKSHIRE

A Lyth, c Robinson b Raine		111
F J Bean, lbw b Potts		46
G C H Hill, lbw b Potts		7
R D Rickelton, lbw b Raine		13
M L Revis, c Robinson b Potts		15
* § J A Tattersall, b de Leede		18
J A Thompson, c Pretorius b Potts		54
B O Coad, c Raine b de Leede		19
M D Fisher, lbw b Raine		24
M T Steketee, c Pretorius b Raine		2
D T Moriarty, not out		2
Extras b 11, lb 6, nb 12		29
Total		340

Bonus points — Yorkshire 2, Durham 3   *Durham deducted 1 point for slow over rate*

FoW: 1-113 (Bean), 2-141 (Hill), 3-176 (Rickelton), 4-212 (Lyth), 5-234 (Revis), 6-236 (Tattersall), 7-260 (Coad), 8-306 (Fisher), 9-312 (Steketee), 10-340 (Thompson)

	O	M	R	W
Raine	28	4	111	4
Potts	25.5	6	93	4
Pretorius	16	3	45	0
de Leede	16	3	70	2
Parkinson	2	0	4	0

DURHAM

A Z Lees, not out		65
M A Jones, c Tattersall b Thompson		8
* S G Borthwick, not out		29
D G Bedingham		
§ O G Robinson		
G Clark		
M Pretorius		
B F W de Leede		
B A Raine		
M J Potts		
M W Parkinson		
Extras nb 4		4
Total (1 wkt)		106

FoW: 1-42 (Jones)

	O	M	R	W
Coad	11	3	35	0
Fisher	8	4	27	0
Thompson	7	1	20	1
Steketee	5	1	22	0
Hill	2	1	2	0

Umpires: S Shanmugam and S J O'Shaughnessy   Scorers: J T Potter and W R Dobson

Points deduction the dampener

No play was possible on the final two days of a clash with champions-to-be Durham.

Yorkshire's tally of overs lost in the 2023 Championship campaign hurtled up to 1,521 as the last game before the break for the Metro Bank One-Day Cup ended in a forgettable draw.

Yet to say there was little to write home about would be

Peppering the sixes: Jordan Thompson bombards the houses on his way to 54.

a disservice to a handful of players who impressed on days one and two, chiefly home bird Adam Lyth. On the ground where he learnt his trade as a prolific opening batter the left-hander underpinned Yorkshire's 340 all out with 16 fours in a drive-dominated 111.

Jordan Thompson peppered the houses which surround the North Marine Road ground, hitting four sixes in 54 down the order — all of them heaved over the leg-side, the last one taking him to his fifty. Ben Raine and Matthew Potts claimed four wickets apiece before Thompson bagged the only wicket to fall in Durham's 106-1 response when he had Michael Jones caught behind.

Lyth and Alex Lees had formed a formidable opening partnership during Yorkshire's Championship-winning years of 2014 and 2015, regularly posting hundreds together, and in this match they looked likely to do it for opposite sides. Lees was enjoying a stunning summer for the runaway Division Two leaders, and his unbeaten 65 put him on course for a fifth century in six Championship innings. The weather thwarted him.

Umpire Steve O'Shaughnessy would have missed day three had there been any play due to a bout of sickness, so Durham legend Phil Mustard had been called in to replace him.

Shortly after day four had been abandoned at 1pm Yorkshire were deducted 48 points by the ECB because of the widely reported issues of racism. The county dropped to the foot of the Division Two table.

LV= Insurance County Championship — Division Two
Yorkshire v. Derbyshire

Played at North Marine Road, Scarborough, on September 3, 4, 5 and 6, 2023
Yorkshire won by 277 runs at 2.16pm on the Fourth Day

Toss won by Derbyshire   Yorkshire 20-2 = 18 points, Derbyshire 3 points

Close of play: First Day, Derbyshire 47-1 (Wagstaff 32*, Guest 13*); Second day, Yorkshire 179-2 ((Wharton 29*, Shan Masood 41*); Third Day, Derbyshire 65-1 (Came 33*, Guest 16*)

First Innings	YORKSHIRE		Second Innings	
A Lyth, lbw b Dal	32		c Madsen b Thomson	43
F J Bean, lbw b Dal	41		run out (Thomson)	64
* Shan Masood, c Guest b Conners	8		(4) c and b Thomson	86
J H Wharton, c Guest b Dal	58		(3) c Madsen b Conners	38
G C H Hill, c Guest b Scrimshaw	11		c Madsen b Wagstaff	79
§ J A Tattersall, c Guest b Dal	45		lbw b Thomson	15
M L Revis, c Guest b Dal	1		c Scrimshaw b Thomson	106
D M Bess, c Wagstaff b Scrimshaw	20		c Dal b Wagstaff	0
J A Thompson, c Dal b Thomson	32		c Scrimshaw b Thomson	64
M D Fisher, not out	37		not out	11
B O Coad, c Guest b Scrimshaw	0			
Extras lb 8, nb 4	12		Extras b 6, lb 4, nb 4	14
Total	297		Total (9 wkts dec)	520

Bonus points — Yorkshire 1, Derbyshire 3

FoW: 1-59 (Lyth), 2-88 (Shan Masood), 3-98 (Bean), 4-129 (Hill), 5-200 (Wharton),
1st   6-204 (Revis), 7-213 (Tattersall), 8-242 (Bess), 9-286 (Thompson), 10-297 (Coad)
FoW: 1-100 (Lyth), 2-116 (Bean), 3-223 (Wharton), 4-238 (Shan Masood), 5-272 (Tattersall),
2nd   6-366 (Hill), 7-366 (Bess), 8-491 (Thompson), 9-520 (Revis)

	O	M	R	W		O	M	R	W
Chappell	15	5	36	0	Chappell	17	2	85	0
Conners	18	5	61	1	Conners	19	5	68	1
Scrimshaw	13.5	1	79	3	Scrimshaw	10	0	56	0
Dal	20	4	72	5	Dal	4	0	28	0
Thomson	10	3	41	1	Thomson	38.4	1	190	5
					du Plooy	4	0	24	0
					Wagstaff	13	0	59	2

First Innings	DERBYSHIRE		Second Innings	
H R C Came, c Tattersall b Coad	0		lbw b Thompson	58
M D Wagstaff, c Revis b Fisher	52		lbw b Bess	9
§ B D Guest, c Tattersall b Thompson	13		c Lyth b Coad	20
W L Madsen, c Bean b Hill	93		lbw b Bess	93
* J L du Plooy, c Hill b Thompson	30		lbw b Bess	0
M J Lamb, b Fisher	10		c Tattersall b Thompson	3
A K Dal, b Fisher	1		st Tattersall b Bess	38
A T Thomson, b Revis	6		c Tattersall b Revis	4
Z J Chappell, c Shan Masood b Thompson	20		c Bess b Revis	33
S Conners, c Tattersall b Revis	15		c sub (B M Cliff) b Revis	1
G L S Scrimshaw, not out	0		not out	0
Extras lb3, nb 4	7		Extras b 16, lb 2, nb 16	34
Total	247		Total	293

Bonus points — Yorkshire 3

FoW: 1-0 (Came), 2-47 (Guest), 3-103 (Wagstaff), 4-173 (du Plooy), 5-191 (Lamb),
1st   6-193 (Dal), 7-209 (Thomson), 8-209 (Madsen), 9-247 (Conners), 10-247 (Chappell),
FoW: 1-24 (Wagstaff), 2-71 (Guest), 3-198 (Came), 4-198 (Madsen), 5-201 (du Plooy),
2nd   6-201 (Lamb), 7-211 (Thomson), 8-289 (Chappell), 9-293 (Conners), 10-293 (Dal)

	O	M	R	W		O	M	R	W
Coad	17	2	63	1	Coad	11	4	36	1
Fisher	16	3	54	3	Hill	11	1	59	0
Thompson	20.1	9	48	3	Bess	24.2	4	79	4
Hill	13	2	41	1	Thompson	13	5	35	2
Revis	8	0	38	2	Revis	12	1	66	3

Umpires: A C Harris and N Pratt   Scorers: J T Potter and J E M Hough

Revved up...and the Bess

Festival ace: Matthew Revis on his way to 106 as Yorkshire set mission impossible.

Clicking through the Festival gears drove Yorkshire to a comfortable 277-run victory — their second against Derbyshire on outground territory in 2023 after success down at Chesterfield in mid-June.

James Wharton's 58 was the best of a number of solid contributions as inserted Yorkshire made an opening day 297 all out, their progress stymied by Anuj Dal's skilful medium paced 5-72. Both counties would have been satisfied with their early work — but Yorkshire then seized the initiative on a spongier North Marine Road surface than usual.

Matthew Fisher and Jordan Thompson contributed important thirties to give Yorkshire's first innings a late boost, and they led the way on day two with three wickets apiece as Derbyshire conceded a 50 lead with 247. Two top-order batters at ends of their career, Mitch Wagstaff and Wayne Madsen, contributed 52 and 93. It was only Wagstaff's second first-class career appearance but Madsen's 200th for Derbyshire.

On days two and three Yorkshire put the game beyond their visitors with a mammoth 520-9 declared to set an almost impossible 571 target. Matthew Revis played the fixture's standout innings, 106 off 142 balls, backed up by half-centuries from Bean, Masood, Hill and Thompson.

Yorkshire could have declared at least an hour earlier and still had enough on the board, but they opted to grind their opponents and give themselves the opportunity to set attacking fields with plenty of room for manoeuvre.

Derbyshire actually started confidently, with Madsen's second 93 much more aggressive than his first. They were 198-2 late on the fourth morning, only to crumble to 201-6 just after lunch and then 293 all out. Off-spinner Dom Bess, going through a challenging summer, impressed with 4-79 as coach Ottis Gibson celebrated his first home Championship success since taking charge in March 2022.

LV= Insurance County Championship — Division Two
Glamorgan v. Yorkshire

Played at Sophia Gardens, Cardiff, on September 10, 11, 12 and 13, 2023
Match drawn at 4.20pm on the Fourth Day

Toss won by Yorkshire   Yorkshire 13 points, Glamorgan 8 points

Close of play: First Day, Yorkshire 330-3 (Shan Masood 113*, Hill 51*); Second Day, Glamorgan 150-6 (Carlson 53*, Douthwaite 17*); Third Day, Glamorgan *following on* 120-2 (Byrom 52*, Northeast 45*)

YORKSHIRE

A Lyth, b McIlroy	49
F J Bean, c Ingram b Carlson	93
* Shan Masood, c Northeast b Harris	192
J H Wharton, lbw b McIlroy	3
G C H Hill, lbw b Harris	71
§ J A Tattersall, c Cooke b Gorvin	6
M L Revis, b Carlson	28
D M Bess, not out	28
J A Thompson, lbw b Harris	0
B O Coad, c Ingram b Carlson	4
B M Cliff, run out (ul Hassan)	1
Extras b 5. lb 12, nb 8	25
Total	500

Bonus points — Yorkshire 5, Glamorgan 2   Score at 110 overs: 460-6

FoW: 1-98 (Lyth), 2-225 (Bean), 3-240 (Wharton), 4-372 (Hill), 5-393 (Tattersall) 6-446 (Revis), 7-482 (Shan Masood), 8-482 (Thompson), 9-495 (Coad), 10-500 (Cliff)

	O	M	R	W
McIlroy	25	5	65	2
Harris	28	0	131	3
Kellaway	7	0	21	0
ul Hassan	12	0	50	0
Gorvin	16	1	69	1
Carlsen	34	1	147	3

GLAMORGAN

	First Innings		Second Innings	
Z ul Hassan	b Coad	8	c Hill b Coad	0
E J Byrom	c Bean b Revis	40	b Bess	101
C Ingram	b Thompson	5	c Lyth b Bess	16
S A Northeast	b Bess	16	not out	166
* K S Carlson	c Wharton b Revis	64	c Tattersall b Cliff	52
W T Root	c Tattersall b Revis	4	b Wharton	45
§ C B Cook	lbw b Revis	4	not out	3
D A Douthwaite	lbw b Coad	37		
A W Gorvin	b Revis	47		
J A R Harris	b Coad	0		
J P McIlroy	not out	30		

B I Kellaway   *replaced by D A Douthwaite due to concussion*

Extras b 9, lb 5, nb 4		18	Extras b 5, lb 1, nb 12	18
Total		273	Total (5 wkts dec)	401

Bonus points — Glamorgan 1, Yorkshire 3

FoW: 1-10 (ul Hassan), 2-19 (Ingram), 3-55 (Northeast), 4-82 (Byrom), 5-96 (Root),
1st   6-100 (Cooke), 7-173 (Carlson), 8-217 (Douthwaite), 9-217 (Harris), 10-273 (Gorvin)
2nd   1-0 (ul Hassan), 2-30 (Ingram), 3-208 (Byrom), 4-305 (Carlson), 5-396 (Root)

	O	M	R	W		O	M	R	W
Coad	10	3	17	3	Coad	11	2	44	1
Thompson	11	0	42	1	Thompson	11	2	47	0
Cliff	8	1	41	0	Bess	41	8	112	2
Bess	33	9	72	1	Cliff	11	0	48	1
Revis	16.2	3	50	5	Revis	13	2	57	0
Hill	9	1	33	0	Lyth	17	1	52	0
Lyth	2	1	4	0	Tattersall	4	0	19	0
					Hill	7	2	11	0
					Wharton	2	1	1	1
					Bean	1	0	4	0

Umpires: P J Hartley and M Newell   Scorers: J T Potter and A K Hignell

Masood heroics unrewarded

For the second match running Yorkshire posted 500 in an innings. While their 520-9 in the win over Derbyshire came in the second innings, this 500 all out was in the first as captain Shan Masood cruised to a superb 192 — his first Yorkshire century — on a turgid Cardiff surface which ultimately produced a draw.

Masood shared 127 for the second wicket with opener Fin Bean, who fell narrowly short of a fourth summer century with 93 as the visitors eased to 330-3 from 78 overs on day one, having elected to bat.

George Hill completed a useful 71 early on day two as Yorkshire made the early running in search of back-to-back victories.

Things looked good when Matthew Revis continued his superb all-round form with 5-50 from 16.2 overs to bowl Glamorgan out for 273 midway through the third afternoon.

There would have been some frustration for Yorkshire, their hosts starting day three on 150-6, but contributions from Kiran Carlson, 64, Dan Douthwaite, 37 — a day two concussion substitute for Ben Kellaway — 47 for Andy Gorvin and Jamie McIlroy's 30 not out revived the Welshmen.

SHAN MASOOD
Cruised to 192

If Yorkshire are to be promoted in 2024 they must develop a ruthless streak to finish teams off. A 56 partnership between Gorvin and McIlroy, both posting career-bests wasn't the first time the last wicket had frustrated Ottis Gibson and co this summer. Yorkshire still made Glamorgan follow-on as Revis, fresh from a century against Derbyshire, claimed his maiden five-for with an excellent spell of hit-the-pitch bowling.

Glamorgan, reduced to 0-1, started day four on 120-2, still trailing by 107, but former Yorkshire loanee Sam Northeast ground out 166, well supported by opener Eddie Byrom's 101 as they ended the day on 401-5 declared. Fledgling seamer Ben Cliff took a debut wicket on day four.

LV= Insurance County Championship — Division Two
Leicestershire v. Yorkshire

Played at Uptonsteel County Ground, Leicester, on September 19, 20, 21 and 22, 2023
Match drawn at 5pm on the Fourth Day

Toss won by Leicestershire

Yorkshire 8 points, Leicestershire 8-1 = 7 points

Close of play: First Day, Yorkshire 155-9 (Thompson 2*, Cliff 0*); Second Day, no play; Third Day, Yorkshire 113-1 (Lyth 51*, Coad 1*)

YORKSHIRE

First Innings		Second Innings	
A Lyth, c Kimber b Currie	16	lbw b Davis	60
F J Bean, c Cox b Davis	40	b Scriven	43
* Shan Masood, lbw b Wright	34	(4) c Kimber b Scriven	10
J H Wharton, b Davis	1	(5) not out	58
G C H Hill, c Cox b Scriven	1	(6) not out	32
§ J A Tattersall, c Patel b Scriven	6		
M L Revis, c Cox b Currie	20		
B W M Mike, b Davis	25		
J A Thompson, c Cox b Scriven	2		
B O Coad, c Hill b Davis	6	(3) b Wright	3
B M Cliff, not out	0		
Extras b 4	4	Extras b 1, lb 18	19
Total	155	Total (4 wkts)	225

Bonus points — Leicestershire 3

FoW:
1st 1-45 (Lyth), 2-79 (Bean), 3-91 (Wharton), 4-96 (Hill), 5-98 (Shan Masood), 6-112 (Tattersall), 7-147 (Revis), 8-147 (Mike), 9-155 (Coad), 10-155 (Thompson)
2nd 1-112 (Bean), 2-119 (Coad), 3-130 (Shan Masood), 4-140 (Lyth)

	O	M	R	W		O	M	R	W
Wright	12	2	44	1	Wright	16	6	38	1
Scriven	12.2	0	47	3	Scrivens	18.4	2	67	2
Currie	7	1	32	2	Currie	9	0	46	0
Davis	8	1	28	4	Davis	11	2	47	1
					Umar Amin	1	0	8	0

LEICESTERSHIRE

R K Patel, lbw b Coad	0
S T Evans, lbw b Hill	15
* L J Hill, c Tattersall b Hill	42
Umar Amin, lbw b Hill	10
L P J Kimber, c Bean b Cliff	4
H J Swindells, c Tattersall b Revis	73
§ O B Cox, lbw b Hill	13
T A R Scriven, b Thompson	17
C J C Wright, c Lyth b Thomson	0
S W Currie, b Cliff	0
W S Davis, not out	44
Extras b 1, lb 12, nb 2	15
Total	233

Bonus points — Yorkshire 3

Over rate deduction 1 point

FoW: 1-0 (Patel), 2-58 (Hill), 3-65 (Evans), 4-70 (Umar Amin), 5-89 (Kimber), 6-97 (Cox), 7-139 (Scriven), 8-139 (Wright), 9-140 (Currie), 10-233 (Swindells)

	O	M	R	W
Coad	14	2	47	1
Thompson	12	0	61	2
Hill	16	4	69	4
Cliff	7	0	27	2
Revis	4.1	1	16	1

Umpires: N L Bainton and N Pratt

Scorers: J T Potter and P J Rogers

Rain defeats both sides

Games which saw ball dominate bat in 2023 were scarce. There had been flashes of it, but nothing prolonged.

This last-but-one fixture was proving to be a rarity, though rain ultimately ruined a good contest as more than 230 overs were lost.

No play was possible on day two, and limited play on day four, which ended farcically with no prospect of a result, yet Leicestershire wanted to wait around for conditions to let them back on

JAMES WHARTON: Steadied the ship.

to rectify a slow over-rate, which saw them deducted a point.

The Foxes needed to win to keep alive their slim promotion chance, and their hopes were raised when they bowled Yorkshire out for 155 on a green-tinged pitch on day one. Seamer Will Davis claimed a season's best 4-28, while Fin Bean's 40 featured for the visitors.

Yorkshire, led by George Hill's excellent 4-69, bounced back strongly on day three by reducing the hosts to 140-9, only for Harry Swindells and Davis (44) to share 93 for the 10th wicket — a record partnership for that wicket in this fixture's history.

Swindells hit a brisk 73 just a few days after his match-winning century in the One-Day Cup final against Hampshire at Trent Bridge, and he and Davis took the aggressive route before becoming more measured as the field spread and Yorkshire's frustrations grew.

A total of 233 gave Leicestershire a 78 lead instead of a first-innings deficit which once looked likely. Yorkshire ended day three on 113-1, 35 ahead, and were targeting victory via conventional means despite the prospect of a contrived finish coming into view.

If Yorkshire just held sway at the start of day four Lewis Hill's side bounced back, reducing them to 140-4 during the morning — a lead of 62. James Wharton's 58 settled the situation, but a three-and-a-half-hour rain delay from just after lunch proved decisive.

LV= Insurance County Championship — Division Two
Yorkshire v. Worcestershire

Played at Headingley, Leeds, on September 26, 27, 28 and 29, 2023
Yorkshire won by 6 wickets at 5.20pm on the Fourth Day

Toss won by Yorkshire   Yorkshire 20 points, Worcestershire 5 points

Close of play: First Day, Worcestershire 280-5 (D'Oliveira 90*, Allinson 31*); Second Day, Yorkshire 24-0 (Lyth 10*, Bean 12*); Third Day, Worcestershire 18-2 ((Libby 4*, Haynes 6*)

	First Innings	WORCESTERSHIRE	Second Innings	
§ G H Roderick, c Bean b Coad	5		c Shan Masood b Coad	0
J D Libby, lbw b Hill	32		not out	109
Azhar Ali, c Lyth b Coad	4		c Lyth b Milnes	8
J A Haynes, c Bean b Hill	14		not out	113
Kashif Ali, c and b Bess	93			
* B L D'Oliveira, lbw b Milnes	103			
B M J Allinson, b Bess	75			
J O Baker, c Revis b Milnes	2			
J Leach, c Coad b Bess	36			
B J Gibbon, c Tattersall b Revis	3			
D Y Pennington, not out	0			
Extras lb 14, nb 8	22		Extras nb 2	2
Total	389		Total (2 wkts dec)	232

Bonus points — Worcestershire 3, Yorkshire 3

FoW: 1-14 (Roderick), 2-22 (Azhar Ali), 3-50 (Libby), 4-67 (Haynes), 5-222 (Kashif Ali),
1st 6-299 (D'Oliveira), 7-301 (Baker), 8-380 (Allinson), 9-383 (Gibbon), 10-389 (Leach)
2nd 1-0 (Roderick), 2-9 (Azhar Ali)

	O	M	R	W		O	M	R	W
Coad	19	4	52	2	Coad	6	2	12	1
Milnes	19	1	79	2	Milnes	5	1	11	1
Hill	16	5	54	2	Bean	10	0	101	0
Thompson	16	2	73	0	Wharton	9.1	0	108	0
Revis	11	3	62	1					
Bess	21	5	55	3					

	First Innings	YORKSHIRE	Second Innings	
A Lyth, c Roderick b Leach	11		c Haynes b Baker	51
F J Bean, b Gibbon	31		c and b Pennington	11
* Shan Masood, c Baker b Gibbon	19		c Gibbon b Baker	123
J H Wharton, b Pennington	8		b Baker	89
G C H Hill, lbw b Leach	52		not out	38
§ J A Tattersall, b Pennington	21		not out	44
M L Revis, not out	51			
D M Bess, not out	48			
J A Thompson				
B O Coad	Did not bat			
M E Milnes				
Extras b 4, lb 5, nb 12	21		Extras b 4, lb 1, nb 2	7
Total (6 wkts dec)	262		Total (4 wkts)	363

Bonus points — Yorkshire 1, Worcestershire 2

FoW: 1-32 (Lyth), 2-60 (Bean), 3-67 (Shan Masood), 4-92 (Wharton), 5-134 (Tattersall),
1st 6-177 (Hill)
2nd 1-22 (Bean), 2-110 (Lyth), 3-274 (Wharton), 4-279 (Shan Masood)

	O	M	R	W		O	M	R	W
Leach	17	4	81	2	Leach	8	1	26	0
Pennington	12	2	49	2	Pennington	13	2	62	1
Gibbon	11	0	63	2	Allinson	12	0	61	0
Allinson	10	4	22	0	Gibbon	11	0	73	0
Baker	9	0	36	0	Baker	21	0	117	3
Kashif Ali	1	0	2	0	Kashif Ali	2	0	19	0

Umpires: S J O'Shaughnessy and S Shanmugam Scorers: J T Potter and S M Drinkwater

A bite out of the Pears

Oozing class: Skipper Shan Masood's 123 leads Yorkshire's victory charge.

Shan Masood's brilliant 123 gave Yorkshire a happy ending to a challenging season as they chased down a 360 target to beat promoted Worcestershire, avoiding bottom place in Division Two.

Masood oozed class in a 131-ball innings, well supported by a career-best 89 from James Wharton. They shared 164 for the third wicket from 110-2 after both teams had agreed to contrive a finish for the final 70 overs.

Yorkshire won for the third time this season, leapfrogging Gloucestershire to finish second bottom. On the second morning in a weather-affected match the Pears achieved promotion by reaching 300 for a second batting bonus point.

Masood opted to bowl, and Ben Coad and George Hill struck twice apiece as Worcestershire slipped to 67-4, only for skipper Brett D'Oliveira to see them to 389 with his 103, well supported by career-bests for Kashif Ali, 93 and Ben Allison, 75.

Dom Bess impressed with 3-55 before Yorkshire recovered from 177-6 to avoid the follow-on and declare at 262-6. Hill top-scored with a measured 52, while unbeaten Matthew Revis, 51, and Bess, 48, were more aggressive as they shared 85.

Gareth Roderick drilled Coad to mid-off with the first ball of Worcestershire's second innings before Matt Milnes, playing his first match since early April following a back-stress fracture, despatched Azhar Ali to make it 9-2. Bad light for the rest of the third evening effectively ruined Yorkshire's chances of a conventional victory.

Fin Bean and Wharton fed meaningless centuries to Jake Libby and Jack Haynes on the fourth morning as Worcester advanced to 262-2 declared. Adam Lyth set the tone in Yorkshire's chase with 51, passing 1,000 runs for 2023, only for Bean to narrowly miss out on that same milestone. But Masood and Wharton were the heroes.

YORKSHIRE AVERAGES 2023

COUNTY CHAMPIONSHIP

Played 14   Won 3   Lost 2   Drawn 8   Abandoned 1

BATTING AND FIELDING
(Qualification 10 completed innings)

	M	I	N O	Runs	H S	100s	50s	Avge	ct/st
Shan Masood	7	13	1	720	192	2	3	60.00	2
A Lyth	13	22	1	1019	174	3	5	48.52	18
F J Bean	13	21	0	983	135	3	2	46.80	14
M L Revis	10	15	4	487	106	2	1	44.27	4
D J Malan	7	13	0	542	132	2	1	41.69	0
G C H Hill	13	21	2	694	101	1	7	36.52	11
J A Tattersall	9	13	1	338	79	0	1	28.16	24/1
J A Thompson	11	14	1	299	64	0	3	23.00	4
D M Bess	8	13	3	216	49	0	0	21.60	5

Also played

	M	I	N O	Runs	H S	100s	50s	Avge	ct/st
M E Milnes	2	2	1	90	75	0	1	90.00	1
S D Hope	2	4	1	187	83	0	2	62.33	6/1
J H Wharton	6	10	1	349	89	0	4	38.77	2
D J Leech	1	1	0	32	32	0	0	32.00	1
J M Bairstow	2	4	1	83	36	0	0	27.66	7
B W M Mike	1	1	0	25	25	0	0	25.00	0
R D Rickelton	3	3	0	65	46	0	0	21.66	2
M D Fisher	9	14	6	140	37*	0	0	17.50	2
Saud Shakeel	3	5	0	71	35	0	0	14.20	1
B O Coad	11	12	3	119	45	0	0	13.22	1
M W Edwards	3	5	1	52	19*	0	0	13.00	0
M T Steketee	4	3	0	31	26	0	0	10.33	0
B M Cliff	2	2	1	1	1	0	0	1.00	0
D T Moriarty	4	3	3	7	4*	0	0	—	1

BOWLING
(Qualification 10 wickets)

Player	Overs	Mdns	Runs	Wkts	Avge	Best	5wI	10wM
B O Coad	279.2	84	728	36	20.22	5 -33	2	0
M D Fisher	238.3	52	799	28	28.53	5 -30	1	0
J A Thompson	249	47	918	30	30.60	3 -48	0	0
M L Revis	124.4	14	528	15	35.20	5 -50	1	0
G C H Hill	206.5	41	681	19	35.84	4 -43	0	0
D M Bess	259.3	39	934	22	42.45	5-158	1	0

Also bowled

Player	Overs	Mdns	Runs	Wkts	Avge	Best	5wI	10wM
D J Leech	16	2	78	3	26.00	3 -78	0	0
M E Milnes	60	8	224	7	32.00	3 -72	0	0
D T Moriarty	83.1	23	245	7	35.00	5-139	1	0
B M Cliff	26	1	116	3	38.66	2 -27	0	0
M T Steketee	70.3	13	272	6	45.33	3 -55	0	0
M W Edwards	65	8	254	5	50.80	3 -54	0	0
A Lyth	49	8	147	2	73.50	1 -17	0	0
J H Wharton	12.1	1	114	1	114.00	1 - 1	0	0
F J Bean	11	0	105	0	—	0 - 4	0	0
D J Malan	3	0	8	0	—	0 - 8	0	0
Saud Shakeel	5	1	23	0	—	0 - 0	0	0
J A Tattersall	4	0	19	0	—	0 -19	0	0

YORKSHIRE'S VITALITY BLAST HIGHLIGHTS OF 2023

Totals of 150 and over (10)

166	v. Birmingham Bears at Birmingham (lost)
175-9	v Worcestershire at Worcester (lost)
189-7	v. Durham at Leeds (lost)
182-7	v. Nottinghamshire at Nottingham (won)
195-6	v. Lancashire at Leeds (won)
170-3	v. Derbyshire at Leeds (won)
156-7	v. Leicestershire at Leicester (won)
224-4	v. Worcestershire at Leeds (won)
197-2	v. Leicestershire at Leeds (won)
176-8	v. Birmingham Bears at Leeds (lost)

Match aggregates of 350 and over (8)

422	Yorkshire (224-4) defeated Worcestershire (198-6) by 26 runs at Leeds
406	Durham (217-3) defeated Yorkshire (189-7) by 28 runs at Leeds
392	Leicestershire (195-5) lost to Yorkshire (197-2) by 8 wickets at Leeds
375	Yorkshire (195-6) defeated Lancashire (180-8) by 15 runs at Leeds
366	Birmingham Bears (200-6) defeated Yorkshire (166) by 34 runs at Birmingham
356	Yorkshire (182-7) defeated Nottinghamshire (174-4) by 8 runs at Nottingham
356	Birmingham Bears (180-7) defeated Yorkshire 9176-8) by 4 runs at Leeds
352	Yorkshire (175-9) lost to Worcestershire (177-8) by 2 wickets at Worcester

Century Partnerships (2)

For 1st wicket (1)

158   A Lyth and D J Malan v. Leicestershire at Leeds

For 2nd wicket (1)

159   D J Malan and J H Wharton v. Worcestershire at Leeds

Centuries (1)

J H Wharton (1)

111 * v. Worcestershire at Leeds

4 wickets in an innings (2)

J A Thompson (2)

5 -21   v. Leicestershire at Leiceste

4 -34   v. Worcestershire at Leeds

3 catches in an innings (2)

B W M Mike (1)

3   v. Leicestershire at Leicester

J A Thompson (1)

3   v. Worcestershire at Worcester

3 dismissals in an innings (none)

T20 Debuts (2): J A Chohan and W A Luxton

T20 Debuts for Yorkshire (3): B W M Mike. Shan Masood and D Wiese

VITALITY BLAST in 2023

WINNERS: **Somerset** (145) defeated Essex Eagles (131) by 14 runs

NORTH GROUP

		P	W	L	T	NR/A	Adj	PTS	NRR
1	Birmingham Bears * (1)	14	11	3	0	0	0	22	0.819
2	Lancashire Lightning * (2)	14	8	5	0	1	0	17	0.427
3	Worcestershire Rapids * (9)	14	8	5	1	0	0	17	0.349
4	Notts Outlaws * (5)	14	8	6	0	0	0	16	-0.222
5	Derbyshire Falcons (3)	14	6	7	1	0	0	13	0.397
6	Northamptonshire Steelbacks (7) ...	14	6	8	0	0	0	12	0.274
7	Durham (8)	14	4	7	2	1	0	11	0.077
8	**Yorkshire Vikings (4)**	**14**	**6**	**6**	**0**	**2**	**-4**	**10**	**-0.737**
9	Leicestershire Foxes (6)	14	2	12	0	0	0	4	-1.402

Adjustments:
Yorkshire: 4 points deducted for failings identified by the Cricket Discipline Commission enquiry

SOUTH GROUP

		P	W	L	T	NR/A	Adj	PTS	NRR
1	Somerset * (2)	14	12	2	0	0	0	24	1.460
2	Hampshire Royals * (4)	14	9	5	0	0	0	18	0.820
3	Surrey * (1)	14	8	6	0	0	0	16	1.192
4	Essex Eagles * (3)	14	8	6	0	0	0	16	0.088
5	Kent Spitfires (9)	14	7	7	0	0	0	14	0.287
6	Sussex Sharks (7)	14	6	8	0	0	0	12	-0.871
7	Gloucestershire (5)	14	5	9	0	0	0	10	-0.993
8	Glamorgan (6)	14	5	9	0	0	0	10	-1.060
9	Middlesex Panthers (8)	14	3	11	0	0	0	6	-0.932

** Qualified for Quarter-Finals (Four)*

Harold Galley, stalwart for the young

Harold Galley, the former president of Yorkshire Schools Cricket Association, who died in Huddersfield on January 12, 2024 aged 86, was a former secretary of the association and an ex-chairman of the English Schools' Cricket Association.

Galley, a retired teacher, was heavily involved at Yorkshire Academy level as administrator, scorer and umpire. He played cricket for Hall Bower and Kirkburton in the Huddersfield League, and was a referee and linesman on the Football League list, officiating at many top venues.

VIKINGS LEFT SHORT-CHANGED AFTER MILLION-DOLLAR DAYS

By Graham Hardcastle

Rollercoaster ride. That best sums up Yorkshire's campaign in the Vitality Blast.

At times they looked a million dollars...but at others the contrast could not have been greater. Ultimately. it was disappointment for skipper Shan Masood and coach Ottis Gibson as the Vikings missed out on knockout cricket.

At the heart of the campaign the county won six successive games, equalling a club record run in this format. The previous six-match winning streak came in 2012, when the likes of Mitchell Starc and David Miller were the stars.

Unfortunately, this winning streak was sandwiched in between a pair of three defeats in a row, and the final two games were abandoned due to rain, including the *Roses* clash at Emirates Old Trafford on June 30 when not a ball was bowled.

Yorkshire finished eighth out of nine in the North Group with 10

DAWID MALAN: Yorkshire's stand-out run-scorer.

points, owing much to their four-point ECB-imposed deduction. They otherwise would have finished fifth. Birmingham, Lancashire, Worcestershire and Nottinghamshire all qualified for the quarter-finals from the North Group.

Somerset won the competition for the second time, beating Essex in the final at Edgbaston on July 15, when former Viking Tom Kohler-

Cadmore was in the title-winning team — and took the catch which sealed victory, a stunning one-handed dive at short third.

For Yorkshire the highlight was undoubtedly the *Roses* victory over a star-studded Lancashire at Headingley by 15 runs on June 1. Jos Buttler was in the Lightning team — so, too, Phil Salt, Daryl Mitchell and Liam Livingstone. It was *White Rose* success for only the second time in *Roses* cricket since the start of the 2018 Blast.

Dawid Malan was Yorkshire's standout player with 546 runs. He was the sixth leading run-scorer in the competition, contributing five fifties with a best of 95 not out. Jordan Thompson led the way with the ball, taking 20 wickets.

Birmingham v. Yorkshire: Edgbaston, May 20.

Yorkshire were unable to take advantage of a super start with the ball, including 2-25 for the impressive Matthew Revis, as Birmingham battled back from 51-4 to post 200-6 and win the main event at *Blast Off* by 34 runs.

Sam Hain's fabulous 83 not out was the key performance for the Bears, who then reduced their visitors to 34-5 and 166 all out, Opener Dawid Malan top-scored with 43 off 29 balls for the Vikings, while Dom Bess finished on 42 not out and Jafer Chohan added 37 on debut.

Blast Off was the ECB's new innovation, starting the competition with a televised Saturday double-header. Lancashire beat Derbyshire in the afternoon fixture.

Worcestershire v. Yorkshire: New Road, May 26.

Worcestershire seamer Adam Finch hit three sixes off the first five balls from Matthew Fisher in the final over as the Rapids chased down 176 and 19 off the last over to win by two wickets with one ball to spare.

Overseas all-rounder David Wiese had claimed three wickets on an impressive debut after the Vikings had posted 175-9, including 42 from Matthew Revis.

Yorkshire looked set for their first win of the season, only for No. 9 Finch to whack 30 off 10 balls and turn the game on its head. When he came to the crease the Rapids were 145-7 after 17.3, but he hit his sixes over long-on and long-off to break Yorkshire's hearts.

Both sides recovered from early issues with the bat: the Vikings 10-2 and the Rapids 8-2.

Yorkshire v. Durham: Headingley, May 28.

Alex Lees posted an excellent career-best 90 off 53 balls against his home county as Durham racked up an imposing 217-3, and defended it comfortably to win by 28 runs and consign Yorkshire to a third straight North Group defeat.

JONNY TATTERSALL

DAVID WIESE

Jonny Tattersall top-scored with 39 off 33 balls in the hosts' 189-7.

Lees shared partnerships of 85 for the second wicket with Michael Jones and 111 for the third with Ollie Robinson, who also posted a career-best 64 not out in 30 balls.

Chasing 218, Yorkshire were off to a flyer at 30-0 after nine balls, but they slipped to 65-3 inside seven overs to undermine their chances of a first win of any sort in 2023. This was the first part of a T20 Sunday double-header with the Northern Diamonds women.

Nottinghamshire v. Yorkshire: Trent Bridge, May 30.

Yorkshire tasted victory for the first time in any competition in 2023 — in fact since August 21 the previous year — by beating Nottinghamshire by eight runs in an enthralling clash.

Malan's brilliant unbeaten 95 led the way to 182-7 before an on-point bowling and fielding display limited the hosts to 174-4 to ensure victory. Yorkshire's innings maintained a good pace all the way through, with Malan's 56-ball effort including four leg-side sixes at the heart of it.

On-loan Jack Brooks claimed 4-51 against his former county, who expertly held their nerve in defence as David Wiese claimed 2-32 and Jordan Thompson defended 20 off the last over.

Yorkshire v. Lancashire: Headingley, June 1.

Malan celebrated his 300th T20 appearance with a superb 83 off 50 balls as Yorkshire secured a rare *Roses* Blast win to breathe life into their summer.

England white ball captain Jos Buttler made just one off two balls in his first county appearance of 2023 as hot favourites Lancashire were sent back across the M62 with their tails between their legs.

Malan underpinned Yorkshire's commanding 195-6 with his second successive fifty.

A sellout 16,000 crowd — a number of whom missed the start due to traffic issues — saw Yorkshire win by 15 runs, only their second *Roses* triumph since the start of 2018. The Lightning finished on 180-8, with Ben Mike and Wiese each claiming 2-31.

Yorkshire v. Derbyshire: Headingley, June 3.

Wayne Madsen fell six runs short of becoming the first man in T20 history to score six successive fifties as his Derbyshire side went down by seven wickets to a revitalised Yorkshire.

The Vikings finished strong with the ball to limit Falcons to 166-8, including a county-best 3-39 for Mike, before Malan continued his fine form with a sumptuous unbeaten 81 off 57 balls to seal the two points.

Derbyshire should have got more runs following Pakistan opener Haider Ali's 74 and Madsen's 44, which took them to 147-2 in the 17th over, but Mike removed Haider, and later in the 18th over captain Leus du Plooy, paving the way for a routine chase.

Leicestershire v. Yorkshire: Grace Road, June 6.

Yorkshire recovered brilliantly from 78-7 batting first to win yet again, getting up to 156-7 before defending it comfortably to romp home by 30 runs as Leicestershire were bowled out for 126 inside 20 overs.

Wiese hit a superb unbeaten 50 off 32 balls in front of the *Sky Sports* cameras before Jordan Thompson starred with his maiden five-wicket haul, 5-21 from 3.3 overs. Supplementing his efforts with the ball was Jafer Chohan, who returned an excellent 1-16.

Yorkshire's total was revitalised by all-rounders young and old, Ben Mike (30) and Wiese, who shared an unbroken 78 in the last 38 balls of the innings for the eighth wicket — a Vikings T20 record.

Yorkshire v. Worcestershire: Headingley, June 9.

Centurion James Wharton and Malan shared 159 for the second wick-et — Yorkshire's all-time highest T20 partnership — as part of a high-scoring win. Wharton, 22, and in only his fourth career T20 match,

JAMES WHARTON

JORDAN THOMPSON

blazed a fabulous 111 not out off 56 balls, and was more than ably supported by Malan's excellent 79 off 48 in a monumental 224-4 batting first. Despite typically excellent Headingley batting conditions, it proved a target beyond the Rapids, who battled to 198-6.

Wharton, who reached his hundred in 51 balls, had been on course to better Yorkshire's fastest-ever century off 47 scored by Ian Harvey against Derbyshire in 2005. Jordan Thompson later returned 4-34 in defence, and took his tally to nine wickets in two games.

Yorkshire v. Leicestershire: Headingley, June 16.

Malan's fifth Blast fifty of the season — a superb 79 off 45 balls — helped Yorkshire to a record-equalling sixth straight T20 win as they chased down 196 with eight wickets and 11 balls remaining.

Louis Kimber bludgeoned a career-best unbeaten 59 to power the Foxes to 195-5, but Malan united with fellow fifty-maker Adam Lyth, the left-handers sharing a superb Club record opening stand of 158 in 14 overs. Unbeaten Lyth went on to top-score with a season's best 90 off 50 balls as the pair fell one run short of equalling the partnership record set by Malan and James Wharton a week before. Mike earlier struck twice with the ball against his former county.

Derbyshire v. Yorkshire: Chesterfield, June 18.

Yorkshire endured a disastrous day as, chasing 213, they were bowled out for 68 inside 12 overs, halting their six-game winning run with a defeat of record proportions.

Leus du Plooy and Haider Ali crashed half-centuries to boost the Falcons to 212-4 before a flurry of wickets consigned the Vikings to their fourth defeat in 10 in the North Group.

Derbyshire had a mixed first 10 overs of their innings, reaching 70-3, but they took 142 off the next 10, including 31 off the last over with five sixes from Mike, whose 1-74 from four overs was Yorkshire's most expensive-ever T20 spell.

The 144-run margin was the county's heaviest-ever defeat.

Yorkshire v. Northamptonshire, Headingley, June 20.

Yorkshire's batting caught them out for the second game running as they failed to chase 181 and suffered a significant setback in their quarter-final qualification hopes.

The Vikings lost their fifth game in 11 and their second on the bounce, bowled out for 102 inside 16 overs to lose by 78 runs after the visitors had posted 180-6 with Justin Broad's unbeaten 47 and two wickets for Thompson, who was overshadowed by fellow seamer Tom Taylor's superb career-best 5-28.

Ex-Vikings captain David Willey had a productive return to the club he left in late 2022: skippering the Steelbacks, he hit a late 28 and took two new-ball wickets. Only Malan (34) made it beyond 20 in pursuit.

Yorkshire v. Birmingham: Headingley, June 22.

Yorkshire oh so nearly chased 181 against the North Group leaders. Needing 27 off the last over with two wickets left, Wiese hit Henry Brookes for three sixes, and the target was 12 off two balls. But they finished on 176-8 to lose by four runs, and were left needing to win their last two games to have any chance of qualifying.

Birmingham posted 180-7 thanks to a measured 66 from opener Rob Yates, though they could have got more but for some excellent bowling from miserly trio Dom Bess, Wiese and Matthew Fisher.

In reply Yorkshire slipped to 87-5 in the 13th over before some powerful striking from Thompson and Matthew Revis revived things with knocks of 34 and 32. They shared 54, but both fell before Wiese cut loose to take the target to 12 off two balls. Brookes then looked as if he had bowled a wide, which wasn't given, before closing out an away win.

Snaring a Fox: Ben Mike pounces against Leicestershire.

Durham v. Yorkshire: Riverside, June 23.

North East rain prevented Yorkshire from pursuing a crucial victory in the bid for quarter-final qualification as only 8.1 overs were bowled.

The Vikings took one point from their last-but-one North Group fixture, meaning a top-four finish was now dependent on a win in their last match against Lancashire and other results going their way.

When rain hit the ground just before 7pm — a couple of hours earlier than expected — Yorkshire were 49-1, with Shan Masood unbeaten on a campaign best 35 from 27 balls. Umpires Steve O'Shaughnessy and Neil Pratt abandoned the match shortly after 8.40pm.

Lancashire v. Yorkshire: Old Trafford, June 30.

More weather frustration as the Manchester *Roses* clash was abandoned without a ball bowled — an outcome which knocked the Vikings out of the competition. Rain throughout the day got lighter as the 7pm start time approached, but it didn't abate.

Umpires Michael Gough and Graham Lloyd called the match off just after 8.40pm. This was the third *Roses* Blast match at Emirates Old Trafford abandoned without a ball bowled following 2012 and 2019.

Yorkshire, already eliminated from the competition, were deducted four points by the ECB on July 28 as part of the punishments for the club's involvement in English cricket's racism scandal.

Vitality T20 Blast — North Group
Birmingham Bears v. Yorkshire

Played at Edgbaston, Birmingham, on May 20, 2023
Birmingham Bears won by 34 runs

Toss won by Yorkshire   Birmingham Bears 2 points, Yorkshire 0 points

BIRMINGHAM BEARS

P R Stirling, b Revis	10
R M Yates, c Shan Masood b Mike	9
* § A L Davies, b Thompson	9
S R Hain, not out	83
D R Mousley, b Bess	11
C G Benjamin, c Bess b Revis	46
C R Woakes, c Revis b Leech	4
H J H Brookes, not out	10
D R Briggs	
J B Lintott Did not bat	
C N Miles	
Extras b 1, lb 3, w 10, nb 4	18
Total (6 wkts, 20 overs)	200

FoW: 1-15 (Yates), 2-30 (Stirling), 3-32 (Davies), 4-51 (Mousley), 5-148 (Benjamin), 6-158 (Woakes)

	O	M	R	W
Leech	4	0	44	1
Mike	4	0	45	1
Revis	4	0	25	2
Thompson	4	0	41	1
Bess	2	0	19	1
Chan	2	0	22	0

YORKSHIRE

A Lyth, c Davies b Woakes	1
D J Malan, lbw b Lintott	43
§ J M Bairstow, c Davies b Brookes	7
* Shan Masood. b Woakes	5
W A R Fraine, b Brookes	0
M L Revis, c Briggs b Mousley	10
B W M Mike, c Brookes b Miles	12
J A Thompson, c Briggs b Miles	0
D M Bess, not out	42
J A Chohan, b Brookes	37
D J Leech, b Brookes	0
Extras lb 1, w 8	9
Total (19,5 overs)	166

FoW: 1-2 (Lyth), 2-9 (Bairstow), 3-15 (Shan Masood), 4-20 (Fraine), 5-34 (Revis), 6-66 (Mike), 7-66 (Thompson), 8-104 (Malan), 9-166 (Chohan), 10-166 (Leech)

	O	M	R	W
Woakes	4	0	34	2
Brookes	3.5	0	32	4
Miles	4	1	25	2
Mousley	3	0	14	1
Briggs	2	0	15	0
Lintott	3	0	45	1

Player of the Match: S R Hain

Umpires: M Burns and G D Lloyd   Scorers: J T Potter and M D Smith
Third Umpire: P K Baldwin

Vitality T20 Blast — North Group
Worcestershire v. Yorkshire

Played at New Road, Worcester, on May 26, 2023
Worcestershire won by 2 wickets

Toss won by Yorkshire — Worcestershire 2 points, Yorkshire 0 points

YORKSHIRE

A Lyth, c Mir b Pennington	4
D J Malan, c Cox b Pennington	0
* Shan Masood, c Brown b D'Oliveira	31
§ J A Tattersal, c Pennington b D'Oliveira	29
M L Revis, run out (Finch>Cox)	42
J A Thompson, c Finch b Bracewell	36
D Wiese, c Haynes b Brown	15
B W M Mike, c Haynes b Brown	2
D M Bess, not out	12
J A Chohan, b Brown	2
M D Fisher Did not bat	
Extras w 2	2
Total (9 wkts, 20 overs)	175

FoW: 1-1 (Malan), 2-10 (Lyth), 3-57 (Tattersall), 4-68 (Shan Masood), 5-124 (Thompson), 6-142 (Wiese), 7-144 (Mike), 8-173 (Revis), 9-175 (Chohan)

	O	M	R	W
Pennington	2	0	11	2
Finch	4	0	45	0
Brown	3	0	28	3
Bracewell	4	0	28	1
Mir	4	0	24	0
D'Oliveira	3	0	39	2

WORCESTERSHIRE

M G Bracewell, c Tattersall b Fisher	3
* B L D'Oliveira, c Revis b Wiese	2
J A Haynes, c Bess b Chohan	32
A J Hose, c and b Thompson	44
Kashif Ali, c Malan b Thompson	24
§ O B Cox, c Thompson b Revis	26
E J Pollock, b Wiese	1
U Mir, c Thompson b Wiese	9
A W Finch, not out	30
D Y Pennington, not out	0
P R Brown Did not bat	
Extras lb 1, w 5	6
Total (8 wkts, 19.5 overs)	177

FoW: 1-7 (D'Oliveira), 2-8 (Bracewell), 3-86 (Hose), 4-98 (Haynes), 5-130 (Cox), 6-131 (Pollock), 7-135 (Mir), 8-157 (Kashif Ali)

	O	M	R	W
Fisher	3.5	0	45	1
Wiese	4	0	18	3
Revis	4	0	36	1
Thompson	4	0	40	2
Chohan	3	0	26	1
Mike	1	0	11	0

Umpires:R K Illingworth and A G Wharf — Scorers: J T Potter and S M Drinkwater

Vitality T20 Blast — North Group
Durham v. Yorkshire

Played at Headingley, Leeds, on May 28, 2023
Durham won by 28 runs

Toss won by Yorkshire$\qquad\qquad\qquad$Durham 2 points, Yorkshire 0 points

DURHAM

G Clark, c Tattersall b Fisher	0
* A Z Lees, c Chohan b Mike	90
M A Jones, c Lyth b Bess	43
§ O G Robinson, not out	64
A J Turner, not out	7

B F W de Leeds
L Doneathy
L Trevaskis$\qquad$Did not bat
B A Raine
N A Sowter
B D Glover

Extras lb 4, w 5, nb 4 ... 13
Total (3 wkts, 20 overs) ... 217

FoW: 1-1 (Clark), 2-86 (Jones), 3-197 (Lees)

	O	M	R	W
Fisher	3	0	24	1
Wiese	4	0	42	0
Revs	1	0	12	0
Thompson	4	0	51	0
Bess	3	0	31	1
Chohan	3	0	25	0
Mike	2	0	28	1

YORKSHIRE

A Lyth, c Robinson b Glover	24
D J Malan, c Clark b Sowter	26
* Shan Masood, c Turner b de Leede	6
§ J A Tattersall, c Turner b Raine	39
M L Revis, run out (Lees/Robinson)	14
J A Thompson, lbw b Raine	33
D Wiese, c Trevaskis b Raine	28
B W M Mike, not out	5
D M Bess, not out	0

J A Chohan
M D Fisher$\qquad$Did not bat

Extras b 2, lb 4, w 8 ... 14
Total (7 wkts, 20 overs) ... 189

FoW: 1-30 (Lyth), 2-37 (Shan Masood), 3-65 (Malan), 4-94 (Revis), 5-141 (Tattersall), 6-157 (Thompson), 7-188 (Wiese)

	O	M	R	W
de Leede	4	0	47	1
Glover	3	0	35	1
Raine	4	0	27	3
Sowter	4	0	30	1
Turner	3	0	27	0
Trevaskis	2	0	17	0

Umpires: T Lungley and D J Millns$\qquad\qquad$Scorers: J T Potter and W R Dobson

Vitality T20 Blast — North Group
Nottinghamshire v. Yorkshire

Played at Trent Bridge, Nottingham, on May 30, 2023
Yorkshire won by 8 runs

Toss won by Yorkshire

Yorkshire 2 points, Nottinghamshire 0 points

YORKSHIRE

A Lyth, c Carter b Brooks	12
D J Malan, not out	95
W A Luxton, c Munro b Brooks	0
* Shan Masood, c James b Montgomery	34
D Wiese, c Clarke b Patel	11
M L Revis, c Hales b Brooks	9
J A Thompson, c Carter b Shaheen Afridi	1
B W M Mike, c Montgomery b Brooks	15
D M Bess, not out	0
J A Chohan	
§ J A Tattersall	Did not bat
Extras lb3, w 2	5
Total (7 wkts, 20 overs)	182

FoW: 1-41 (Lyth), 2-41 (Luxton), 3-91 (Shan Masood), 4-109 (Wiese), 5-151 (Revis), 6-152 (Thompson), 7-169 (Mike)

	O	M	R	W
Shaheen Afridi	4	0	29	1
Carter	4	0	33	0
Brooks	4	0	51	4
Mullaney	2	0	15	0
Patel	3	0	28	1
Montgomery	2	0	18	1
James	1	0	5	0

NOTTINGHAMSHIRE

J M Clarke, c Tattersall b Wiese	8
A D Hales, c Luxton b Wiese	53
C Munro, c Shan Masood b Thompson	46
M Montgomery, c Malan b Mike	28
§ T J Moores, not out	15
L W James, not out	11
* S J Mullaney	
S R Patel	
M Carter	Did not bat
Shaheen Afridi	
J A Brooks	
Extras lb 4, w 7, nb 2	13
Total (4 wkts, 20 overs)	174

FoW: 1-15 (Clarke), 2-99 (Hales), 3-134 (Munro), 4-157 (Montgomery)

	O	M	R	W
Bess	4	0	31	0
Wiese	4	0	32	2
Mike	2	0	18	1
Thompson	4	0	33	1
Chohan	2	0	22	0
Revis	4	0	34	0

Umpires: T Lungley and S J O'Shaughnessy

Scorers: J T Potter and R Marshall

Played at Headingley, Leeds, on June 1, 2023
Yorkshire won by 15 runs

Toss won by Lancashire   Yorkshire 2 points, Lancashire 0 points

YORKSHIRE

A Lyth, c Hartley b de Grandhomme	32
D J Malan, c Salt b Livingstone	83
W A Luxton, c Wood b de Grandhomme	4
M L Revis, not out	24
* Shan Masood, c Hartley b de Grandhomme	15
J A Thompson, c Buttler b Mitchell	18
D Wiese, c Wood b Mitchell	2
B W M Mike, not out	6
§ J A Tattersall	
D M Bess	Did not bat
J A Chohan	
Extras lb 4, w 3, nb 4	11
Total (6 wkts, 20 overs)	195

FoW: 1-88 (Lyth), 2-106 (Luxton), 3-134 (Malan), 4-165 (Shan Masood), 5-187 (Thompson), 6-189 (Wiese)

	O	M	R	W
Wood	4	0	55	0
Bailey	1	0	10	0
Livingstone	3	0	22	1
Mitchell	4	0	33	2
Parkinson	1	0	14	0
Wells	2	0	20	0
de Grandhomme	4	0	24	3
Hartley	1	0	13	0

LANCASHIRE

P D Salt, c and b Mike	16
§ J C Buttler, c Shan Masood b Bess	1
S J Croft, c Wiese b Thompson	22
L W P Wells, c Luxton b Mike	21
D J Mitchell, c Wiese b Chohan	21
* L S Livingstone, c Tattersall b Wiese	15
C de Grandhomme, c Tattersall b Wiese	12
T W Hartley, run out (Mike/Tattersall/Revis)	39
L Wood, not out	24
T E Bailey, not out	3
M W Parkinson	Did not bat
Extras lb 1, w 5	6
Total ((8 wkts, 20 overs)	180

FoW: 1-4 (Buttler), 2-37 (Croft), 3-61 (Wells), 4-64 (Salt), 5-97 (Mitchell), 6-101 (Livingstone), 7-149 (de Grandhomme), 8-157 (Hartley)

	O	M	R	W
Wiese	4	0	31	2
Bess	2	0	19	1
Mike	3	0	31	2
Thompson	4	0	39	1
Revis	4	0	36	0
Chohan	3	0	23	1

SKY TV Player of the Match: D J Malan

Umpires P J Hartley and S J O'Shaughnessy   Scorers: J T Potter and C Rimmer
Third Umpire: S Redfern

Played at Headingley, Leeds, on June 4, 2023
Yorkshire won by 7 wickets

Toss won by Yorkshire   Yorkshire 2 points, Derbyshire 0 points

DERBYSHIRE

L M Reece, c Chohan b Mike	6
Haider Ali, c Wiese b Mike	74
T A Wood, c Luxton b Chohan	17
W L Madsen, c Malan b Wiese	44
* J L du Plooy, b Mike	1
§ B D Guest, not out	4
M H McKiernan, b Thompson	11
Z J Chappell, c Tattersall b Revis	1
M R J Watt, run out (Thompson/Revis)	0
G L S Scrimshaw	
Zaman Khan	Did not bat
Extras b 5, lb 2, w 1	8
Total (8 wkts, 20 overs)	166

FoW: 1-18 (Reece), 2-59 (Wood), 3-147 (Madsen), 4-149 (Haider Ali), 5-150 (du Plooy), 6-161 (McKiernan), 7-164 (Chappell), 8-166 (Watt)

	O	M	R	W
Wiese	4	0	30	1
Bess	2	0	8	0
Mike	4	0	39	3
Thompson	4	0	36	1
Revis	4	0	32	1
Chohan	2	0	14	1

YORKSHIRE

A Lyth, b Wood	31
D J Malan, not out	81
W A Luxton, c Madsen b Scrimshaw	7
D Wiese, c Wood b Chappell	30
B W M Mike, not out	9
J A Thompson	
* Shan Masood	
M L Revis	Did not bat
§ J A Tattersall	
D M Bess	
J A Chohan	
Extras w 6, nb 6	12
Total (3 wkts, 18.2 overs)	170

FoW: 1-83 (Lyth), 2-110 (Luxton), 3-158 (Wiese)

	O	M	R	W
Watt	2	0	12	0
Zaman Khan	3.2	0	37	0
Chappell	4	0	34	1
Scrimshaw	4	0	33	1
Wood	2	0	17	1
McKiernan	2	0	21	0
Reece	1	0	16	0

Umpires: H M S Adnan and J D Middlebrook   Scorers: J T Potter and J E M Hough

Vitality T20 Blast — North Group
Leicestershire v. Yorkshire

Played at Uptonsteel County Ground, Leicester, on June 6, 2023

Yorkshire won by 30 runs

Toss won by Yorkshire

Yorkshire 2 points, Leicestershire 0 points

YORKSHIRE

A Lyth, b Naveen ul Haq	5
D J Malan, c Rehan Ahmed b Parkinson	2
J H Wharton, b Rehan Ahmed	26
* Shan Masood, c Hill b Hull	23
§ J A Tattersall, c and b Rehan Ahmed	0
M L Revis, c Hill b Hull	10
J A Thompson, c Finan b Rehan Ahmed	2
D Wiese, not out	50
B W M Mike, not out	30
D M Bess	
J A Chohan — Did not bat	
Extras b 4, lb 2, nb 2	8
Total (7 wkts, 20 overs)	156

FoW: 1-10 (Malan), 2-21 (Lyth), 3-57 (Wharton), 4-57 (Tattersall), 5-63 (Shan Masood), 6-68 (Thompson), 7-78 (Revis)

	O	M	R	W
Finan	4	0	40	0
Parkinson	4	0	20	1
Hull	4	0	30	2
Naveen ul Haq	4	0	39	1
Rehan Ahmed	4	0	21	3

LEICESTERSHIRE

N R Welch, c Tattersall b Bess	0
* § L J Hill, c Mike b Thompson	13
R K Patel, lbw b Thompson	36
P W A Mulder, c Mike b Thompson	46
L P J Kimber, b Chohan	1
Rehan Ahmed, c Wharton b Revis	1
A M Lilley, c and b Mike	2
M G A Finan, c and b Thompson	20
Naveen ul Haq, c Wharton b Thompson	0
C F Parkinson, c Wiese b Mike	1
J O Hull, not out	2
Extras w 4	4
Total (19.3 overs)	126

FoW: 1-1 (Welch), 2-34 (Hill), 3-73 (Patel), 4-77 (Kimber), 5-80 (Rehan Ahmed), 6-84 (Lilley), 7-114 (Mulder), 8-114 (Naveen ul Haq), 9-124 (Parkinson), 10-126 (Finan)

	O	M	R	W
Wiese	3	1	22	0
Bess	1	0	7	1
Mike	4	0	37	2
Thompson	3.3	0	21	5
Revis	4	0	23	1
Chohan	4	0	16	1

SKY TV Player of the match: D Wiese

Umpires: D J Millns and R A White

Scorers: J T Potter and P J Rogers

Third Umpire: S Redfern

Vitality T20 Blast — North Group
Yorkshire v. Worcestershire

Played at Headingley, Leeds, on June 9, 2023
Yorkshire won by 26 runs

Toss won by Yorkshire   Yorkshire 2 points, Worcestershire 0 points

YORKSHIRE

A Lyth, c D'Oliveira b Bracewell	2
D J Malan, c Hose b Bracewell	79
J H Wharton, not out	111
* Shan Masood, c D'Oliveira b Santner	4
D Wiese, run out (Cox)	15
J A Thompson, not out	2
§ J A Tattersall	
M L Revis	
B W M Mike	Did not bat
D M Bess	
J A Chohan	
Extras b 1, lb 1, w 9	11
Total (4 wkts)	224

FoW: 1-11 (Lyth), 2-170 (Malan), 3-175 (Shan Masood), 4-222 (Wiese)

	O	M	R	W
Pennington	2	0	21	0
Bracewell	4	0	39	2
Finch	4	0	45	0
Brown	4	0	56	0
Santner	4	0	40	1
D'Oliveira	2	0	21	0

WORCESTERSHIRE

M G Bracewell, retired not out	11
* B L D'Oliveira, c Mike b Revis	47
J A Haynes, c Shan Masood b Wiese	6
A J Hose, c Tattersall b Thompson	11
M J Santner, c Lyth b Thompson	27
Kashif Ali, not out	48
§ O B Cox, c Mike b Thompson	35
E J Pollock, c Revis b Thompson	0
A W Finch, not out	1
D Y Pennington	
P R Brown	Did not bat
Extras b 2, lb 4, w 2, nb 4	12
Total (6 wkts)	198

FoW: 1-14 (Bracewell rno), 1-28 (Haynes), 2-48 (Hose), 3-107 (D'Oliveira), 4-109 (Santner), 5-190 (Cox), 6-190 (Pollock)

	O	M	R	W
Wiese	4	0	40	1
Bess	4	0	36	0
Mike	3	0	26	0
Thompson	4	0	34	4
Revis	3	0	35	1
Chohan	2	0	21	0

Umpires: H M S Adnan and S J O'Shaughnessy   Scorers: J T Potter and S M Drinkwater

<h1 style="text-align:center">Vitality T20 Blast — North Group
Yorkshire v. Leicestershire</h1>

Played at Headingley, Leeds, on June 16, 2023
Yorkshire won by 8 wickets

Toss won by Yorkshire   Yorkshire 2 points, Leicestershire 0 points

LEICESTERSHIRE

N R Welch, c Bess b Thompson	40
§ H J Swindells, c Lyth b Wiese	39
R K Patel, c Shan Masood b Mike	9
* C N Ackermann, c Thompson b Mike	0
L P J Kimber, not out	59
P W A Mulder, c Mike b Revis	31
Rehan Ahmed, not out	5
C F Parkinson	
J O Hull	
M G A Finan	Did not bat
Naveen ul Haq	
Extras b 3, lb 2, w 3, nb 4	12
Total (5 wkts)	195

FoW: 1-65 (Welch), 2-82 (Patel), 3-82 (Ackermann), 4-110 (Swindells), 5-163 (Mulder)

	O	M	R	W
Wiese	4	0	44	1
Bess	4	0	22	0
Mike	3	0	43	2
Revis	2	0	25	1
Thompson	4	0	28	1
Chohan	3	0	28	0

YORKSHIRE

A Lyth, not out	90
D J Malan, c Kimber b Finan	79
J H Wharton, c Swindells b Finan	3
D Wiese, not out	13
* Shan Masood	
J A Thompson	
§ J A Tattersall	
M L Revis	Did not bat
B W M Mike	
D M Bess	
J A Chohan	
Extras lb 1, w 11	12
Total (2 wkts, 18.1 overs)	197

FoW: 1-158 (Malan), 2-165 (Wharton)

	O	M	R	W
Parkinson	4	0	28	0
Hull	3	0	44	0
Ackermann	3	0	36	0
Naveen ul Haq	2	0	15	0
Finan	3.1	0	35	2
Rehan Ahmed	3	0	38	0

Umpires: P J Hartley and J D Middlebrook   Scorers: J T Potter and P N Johnson

Vitality T20 Blast — North Group
Derbyshire v. Yorkshire

Played at Queen's Park, Chesterfield, on June 18, 2023
Derbyshire won by 144 runs

Toss won by Yorkshire — Derbyshire 2 points, Yorkshire 0 points

DERBYSHIRE

L M Reece, c Wiese b Bess	12
H R C Came, c Shan Masood b Mike	27
Haider Ali, c Chohan b Thompson	59
W L Madsen, run out (Thompson)	0
* J L du Plooy, not out	66
§ B D Guest, not out	39
M H McKiernan	
Z J Chappell	
A T Thomson	Did not bat
G L S Scrimshaw	
Zaman Khan	
Extras lb 1, w 6, nb 2	9
Total (4 wkts)	212

FoW: 1-21 (Reece), 2-48 (Came), 3-49 (Madsen), 4-119 (Haider Ali)

	O	M	R	W
Wiese	4	0	29	0
Bess	4	0	33	1
Thompson	4	0	49	1
Mike	4	0	74	1
Revis	4	0	26	0

YORKSHIRE

A Lyth, c du Plooy b Thomson	0
D J Malan, b Thomson	3
J H Wharton, c and b Chappell	1
* Shan Masood, c Reece b Chappell	13
§ J A Tattersall, c Haider Ali b Chappell	1
M L Revis, c Chappell b Scrimshaw	21
D Wiese, c du Plooy b McKiernan	13
B W M Mike, c Haider Ali b McKiernan	1
J A Thompson, c Haider Ali b Scrimshaw	8
D M Bess, b Zaman Khan	1
J A Chohan, not out	4
Extras w 2	2
Total ((11.2 overs)	68

FoW: 1-0 (Lyth), 2-1 (Wharton), 3-6 (Malan), 4-7 (Tattersall), 5-20 (Shan Masood), 6-35 (Wiese), 7-37 (Mike), 8-62 (Thompson), 9-63 (Bess), 10-68 (Revis)

	O	M	R	W
Thomson	3	0	22	2
Chappell	2	0	16	3
McKiernan	2	0	10	2
Zaman Khan	2	0	12	1
Scrimshaw	2.2	0	8	2

Umpires: H M S Adnan and P J Hartley — Scorers: J T Potter and J E M Hough

Vitality T20 Blast — North Group
Yorkshire v. Northamptonshire

Played at Headingley, Leeds, on June 20, 2023
Northamptonshire won 78 runs

Toss won by Northamptonshire   Northamptonshire 2 points, Yorkshire 0 points

NORTHAMPTONSHIRE

R S Vasconcelos, c Malan b Thompson	37
E N Gay, c Shan Masood b Thompson	40
C A Lynn, c Lyth b Chohan	3
J Broad, not out	47
S A Zaib, run out (Shan Masood)	5
* D J Willey, run out (Bess/Tattersall)	28
A J Tye, run out (Thompson)	12
§ L D McManus, not out	1
T A I Taylor	
B W Sanderson Did not bat	
F J Heldreich	
Extras lb 2, w 5	7
Total (6 wkts)	180

FoW: 1-55 (Vasconcelos), 2-70 (Lynn), 3-88 (Gay), 4-94 (Zaib), 5-144 (Willey), 6-168 (Tye)

	O	M	R	W
Bess	4	0	32	0
Wiese	4	0	45	0
Mike	1	0	7	0
Thompson	4	0	42	2
Chohan	4	0	13	1
Revis	3	0	39	0

YORKSHIRE

A Lyth, c Vasconcelos b Sanderson	1
D J Malan, b Taylor	34
J H Wharton, c McManus b Willey	0
* Shan Masood, b Willey	2
M L Revis, b Sanderson	7
§ J A Tattersall, c Vasconcelos b Taylor	13
D Wiese, b Taylor	0
B W M Mike, b Taylor	4
J A Thompson, c Sanderson b Taylor	13
D M Bess, not out	6
J A Chohan, b Tye	11
Extras lb 6, w 3, nb 2	11
Total (15.2 overs)	102

FoW: 1-6 (Lyth), 2-7 (Wharton), 3-15 (Shan Masood), 4-22 (Revis), 5-49 (Tattersall), 6-49 (Wiese). 7-68 (Mike), 8-73 (Malan), 9-88 (Thompson), 10-102 (Chohan)

	O	M	R	W
Willey	4	1	15	2
Sanderson	4	1	22	2
Taylor	4	0	28	5
Tye	2.2	0	26	1
Broad	1	0	5	0

Umpires: R A Kettleborough and G D Lloyd   Scorers: J T Potter and Q L S Jones

Vitality T20 Blast — North Group
Yorkshire v. Birmingham Bears

Played at Headingley, Leeds, on June 22, 2023
Birmingham Bears won by 4 runs

Toss won by Birmingham Bears   Birmingham Bears 2 points, Yorkshire 0 points

BIRMINGHAM BEARS

R M Yates, run out (Wharton/Tattersall)	66
* § A L Davies, c Bess b Revis	15
C G Benjamin, c Wiese b Thompson	45
G J Maxwell, b Revis	21
D R Mousley, run out (Wharton/Tattersall)	6
E G Barnard, c Malan b Bess	10
J G Bethell, c Wharton b Wiese	3
C R Woakes, not out	10
H J H Brookes	
D R Briggs Did not bat	
J B Lintott	
Extras b 1, lb 1, w 2	4
Total (7 wkts)	180

FoW: 1-37 (Davies), 2-97 (Benjamin), 3-123 (Maxwell), 4-136 (Mousley), 5-157 (Barnard), 6-164 (Bethell), 7-180 (Yates)

	O	M	R	W
Fisher	4	0	26	0
Wiese	4	0	26	1
Revis	3	0	36	2
Chohan	3	0	36	0
Thompson	3	0	38	1
Bess	3	0	16	1

YORKSHIRE

A Lyth, c Woakes b Mousley	34
D J Malan, c Mousley b Maxwell	13
J H Wharton, c Yates b Woakes	4
* Shan Masood, b Lintott	21
§ J A Tattersall, lbw b Mousley	2
J A Thompson, c Bethell b Mousley	34
M L Revis, c Bethell b Woakes	32
D Wiese, not out	20
D M Bess, b Mousley	10
J A Chohan, not out	1
M D Fisher Did not bat	
Extras b 2, lb 2, w 1	5
Total (8 wkts)	176

FoW: 1-23 (Malan), 2-32 (Wharton), 3-71 (Lyth), 4-73 (Shan Masood), 5-87 (Tattersall), 6-141 (Revis), 7-143 (Thompson), 8-153 (Bess)

	O	M	R	W
Woakes	4	0	22	2
Brookes	4	0	51	0
Maxwell	4	0	32	1
Lintott	2	0	18	1
Briggs	2	0	21	0
Mousley	4	0	28	4

Umpires: N A Mallender and P R Pollard   Scorers: J T Potter and M D Smith

Vitality T20 Blast — North Group
Durham v. Yorkshire

Played at Seat Unique Riverside, Chester-le-Street, on June 23, 2023
No result

Toss won by Durham   Durham 1 point, Yorkshire 1 point

YORKSHIRE

A Lyth, c Carse b Raine	1
D J Malan, not out	8
* Shan Masood, not out	5
W A R Fraine	
§ J A Tattersall	
J A Thompson	
M L Revis	Did not bat
D Wiese	
D M Bess	
J A Chohan	
M D Fisher	
Extras b 4, lb 1	5
Total (1 wkt, 8.1 overs)	49

FoW:- 1-1 (Lyth)

	O	M	R	W
Drissell	3.1	0	6	0
Raine	2	1	15	1
Turner	2	0	15	0
Sowter	1	0	8	0

DURHAM

G Clark
* A Z Lees
M A Jones
B A Carse
§ O G Robinson
A J Turner
J J Bushell
L Trevaskis
B A Raine
N A Sowter
G S Drissell

Umpires: S J O'Shaughnessy and N J Pratt   Scorers: J T Potter and W R Dobson

Lancashire v. Yorkshire

At Emirates Old Trafford, Manchester, on June 30, 2023
Match abandoned without a ball bowled

Toss — none   Yorkshire 1 point, Lancashire 1 point

Umpires: M A Gough and G D Lloyd   Scorers: J T Potter and C Rimmer
Third Umpire: S J O'Shaughnessy

YORKSHIRE VIKINGS AVERAGES 2023

VITALITY BLAST

Played 13   Won 6   Lost 6   No Result 1   Abandoned 1

BATTING AND FIELDING

(Qualification 4 completed innings)

Player	M.	I.	N.O.	Runs	H.S.	100s	50s	Avge	ct/st
D J Malan	13	13	3	546	95*	0	5	54.60	5
J H Wharton	6	6	1	145	111*	1	0	29.00	3
D Wiese	12	11	3	197	50*	0	1	24.62	6
M L Revis	13	9	1	169	42	0	0	21.12	3
A Lyth	13	13	1	237	41	0	1	19.75	4
Shan Masood	13	11	1	189	35*	0	0	18.90	7
B W M Mike	11	9	4	84	30*	0	0	16.80	7
J A Thompson	13	10	1	147	36	0	0	16.33	5
J A Tattersall	12	6	0	84	39	0	0	14.00	8

Also played

Player	M.	I.	N.O.	Runs	H.S.	100s	50s	Avge	ct/st
D M Bess	13	7	5	71	42*	0	0	35.50	4
J A Chohan	13	5	2	55	37	0	0	18.33	3
J M Bairstow	1	1	0	7	7	0	0	7.00	0
W Luxton	3	3	0	11	7	0	0	3.66	3
W A R Fraine	2	1	0	0	0	0	0	0.00	0
D Leech	1	1	0	0	0	0	0	0.00	0
M D Fisher	4	0	0	0	—	0	0	—	0

BOWLING

(Qualification 4 wickets)

Player	Overs	Mdns	Runs	Wkts	Avge	Best	4wI	RPO
J A Thompson	46.3	0	452	20	22.60	5-21	2	9.72
B W M Mike	31	0	359	13	27.61	3-39	0	11.58
D Wiese	43	1	359	11	32.63	3-18	0	8.34
M L Revis	40	0	359	9	39.88	2-25	0	8.97
D M Bess	33	0	254	6	42.33	1- 7	0	7.69
J A Chohan	31	0	246	5	49.20	1-13	0	7.93

Also bowled

Player	Overs	Mdns	Runs	Wkts	Avge	Best	4wI	RPO
D Leech	4	0	44	1	44.00	1-44	0	11.00
M D Fisher	10.5	0	95	2	47.50	1-24	0	8.76

METRO BANK ONE-DAY CUP HIGHLIGHTS OF 2023

Total of 250 and over (1)

253 v. Middlesex at Radlett (lost)

Match aggregates of 450 and over (2)

484 Surrey (241) lost to Yorkshire (243-9) by 1 wickets at York

507 Yorkshire (253) lost to Middlesex (254-5) by 5 wickets at Radlett

Century Partnerships (none)

4 wickets in an innings (4)

D M Bess (1)

 5-37 v Essex at Chelmsford

B W M Mike (1

 4-40 v. Surrey at York

M L Revis (1)

 4-54 v. Essex at Chelmsford

J W Shutt (1)

 4-49 v. Middlesex at Radlett

3 catches in an innings (1)

H G Duke (1)

 3 v. Kent at Scarborough

3 dismissals in an innings (none)

List A Debuts (2): D J Leech and J H Wharton

List A Debuts for Yorkshire (2): B W M Mike and Shan Masood

Metro Bank One-Day Cup

FINAL TABLES 2023

WINNERS: **Leicestershire** (267-5) defeated Hampshire (265-8) by 2 runs

GROUP A

		P	W	T	L	NR	A	PTS	NRR
1	Leicestershire (A 2)	8	7	0	1	0	0	14	1.302
2	Hampshire * (B 1)	8	7	0	1	0	0	14	1.048
3	Lancashire * (B 2)	8	4	0	2	1	1	10	0.827
4	Kent (B 3)	8	4	0	4	0	0	8	-0.331
5	Nottinghamshire (A 3)	8	3	0	4	0	1	7	-0.274
6	**Yorkshire (B 5)**	**8**	**2**	**0**	**4**	**0**	**2**	**6**	**-1.051**
7	Middlesex (A 4)	8	2	0	5	0	1	5	0.104
8	Surrey (A 7)	8	2	0	5	0	1	5	-1.250
9	Essex (B 6)	8	1	0	6	1	0	3	-0.774

GROUP B

		P	W	T	L	NR	A	PTS	NRR
1	Warwickshire (B 6)	8	7	0	1	0	0	14	1.301
2	Gloucestershire * (A 5)	8	6	0	2	0	0	12	0.804
3	Worcestershire * (B 9)	8	6	0	2	0	0	12	0.533
4	Glamorgan (B 4)	8	4	0	3	0	1	9	-0.065
5	Durham (A 9)	8	3	0	4	0	1	7	-0.841
6	Northamptonshire (B 8)	8	3	0	5	0	0	6	0.391
7	Somerset (A 8)	8	3	0	5	0	0	6	-0.285
8	Derbyshire (B 7)	8	2	0	6	0	0	4	-0.470
9	Sussex (A 1)	8	1	0	7	0	0	2	-1.388

** Qualified for Quarter-Finals (Two)*
Last year's positions in brackets

THE BAD, THE WET — AND ONE OF THE BEST DAYS OF SUMMER

By Graham Hardcastle

Yorkshire's One-Day Cup campaign was a real mixed bag of the good, bad and the wet — including more *Roses* disappointment as the fixture at Scarborough was abandoned without a ball bowled after torrential rain in the build-up. They were eliminated before their final-round clash with Middlesex at Radlett, one of three defeats on the bounce to end the campaign with a whimper.

Nine players were missing to the Hundred, counting the likes of Jonny Bairstow and Joe Root in that number, but Yorkshire should still have been better than they were, especially late in the competition with the bat when they were bowled out for less than 200 in successive defeats at home to Hampshire and away to Leicestershire.

This was still an enjoyable month of cricket, watching young players up and down the county circuit among outground settings. The one-wicket victory over Surrey in the sunshine of York when Harry Duke starred with an unbeaten 93 in pursuit of 242 was one of the best days of the entire summer.

Yorkshire finished sixth in the table with as many points, including two wins, four defeats and a pair of no-results. Leicestershire ended up as champions. They beat Hampshire in the September final at Trent Bridge, a popular triumph among county supporters as this was the Foxes' first piece of List A silverware in 38 years.

For Yorkshire captain Shan Masood top-scored with 217 runs from six matches, while wicketkeeper-opener Duke was close behind with 201 from the same number of appearances. That no Viking scored a century through the tournament was an obvious issue, while only six half-centuries were scored across the squad.

Matthew Revis led the way with the ball. The all-rounder claimed 10 wickets with his improving seamers, including an opening day hat-trick against Kent at Scarborough. Dom Bess claimed a career best 5-37 in victory over Essex by five wickets at Chelmsford.

Cheshire v. Yorkshire: Nantwich, July 30.

Rain at the mid-innings interval limited Yorkshire's National Counties warm-up to 50 overs with no result. Cheshire posted a compet-

Highlight of summer: Harry Duke on the way to his unbeaten 93 at York as Surrey wicketkeeper Josh Blake looks on.

itive 268-9. George Hill captained Yorkshire for the first time in the absence of Shan Masood, who had just landed back in England following international duty with Pakistan in Sri Lanka.

Off-spinner Dom Bess claimed standout figures of 4-41 from eight overs, backed up by Dom Leech's 3-32 from nine. Captain Harry Dearden top-scored with 76 for Cheshire, who were invited to bat.

Yorkshire v. Kent: Scarborough, August 1

Ben Coad's superb three-wicket new-ball spell and a Matthew Revis hat-trick were not enough to prevent Yorkshire from losing a rainy competition opener on Yorkshire Day. The Vikings were set an initial 283 target before mid-innings rain and then a little bit more revised the target three times on *DLS* to 261 in 43 overs, 235 in 35 and then 181 in 24.

Yorkshire were 53-2 after 11 overs when further rain hit. Upon the resumption they raced to 117-4 after 17, with Hill crashing 35 off 18 balls. More rain left the hosts three runs short of a winning target.

Kent, inserted, posted a competitive 282-9 from their 50 overs, recovering from 49-4, thanks to contrasting hundreds from aggressive Joey Evison and measured Ben Compton. Coad claimed 3-16 from 10 overs, bowling straight through.

Revis underpinned the fall of five wickets in the final 15 balls: in the 49th over he had fellow all-rounders James Bazley and Grant Stewart caught at deep square-leg before bowling Hami Qadri.

To celebrate Yorkshire Day the hosts wore a remake of the 1993 *Axa League* shirt, the county's first ever piece of coloured clothing.

Yorkshire v. Lancashire: Scarborough, August 3.

The eagerly anticipated *Roses* clash at North Marine Road was abandoned without a ball bowled. Heavy rain throughout the previous day made way for overcast conditions on the morning of play, but water had got under the covers at the Peasholm Park End of the cut pitch.

The groundstaff attempted to dry the problem area by draping it in towels and going over it with the heavy roller, only for a 1.15pm abandonment to follow four inspections. This was the third attempt to play a *Roses* match at Scarborough in either Championship or List A cricket since 2020, the previous two cancellations being Coronavirus related.

Nottinghamshire v. Yorkshire: Trent Bridge, August 5.

Heavy rain forced the abandonment of Yorkshire's second successive fixture, this one called off at 12.40pm. It was Yorkshire's 10th straight game across all competitions, including the friendly at Cheshire, affected by weather. The last fixture played without being affected was against Birmingham on June 22 in the Vitality Blast.

Essex v. Yorkshire: Chelmsford, August 13.

Dom Bess and Matthew Revis shared nine wickets to inspire a brilliant come-from-behind victory by five wickets against the Eagles.

Both recorded their best List A figures as Essex crashed from 103-0 in the 10th over to 221 all out — Bess taking 5-37 from 7.4 overs and Revis 4-54 from eight. Essex flew out of the blocks having elected to bat, with opener Michael Pepper hitting 63 off 34 balls. But they lost all 10 wickets for 118 runs and their last seven for 46, slipping from 175-3.

Captain Shan Masood and James Wharton then anchored the chase with 54 apiece, Wharton the more aggressive — his 49-ball innings representing a career best. The pair shared 68 for the fifth wicket to advance decisively from 112-4. Earlier off-spinner Bess stood out, taking four of the last five wickets to fall.

Yorkshire v. Surrey: York, August 15.

Tenth-wicket heroes Harry Duke and Dom Leech carried Yorkshire to a nail-biting one-wicket victory after the Vikings, chasing 242 to win their second match in five, they slipped from 141-3 to 210-9 to seriously undermine their chances.

Unbeaten wicketkeeper-opener Duke, who finished with a brilliant and calm 93 off 132 balls, and last man Leech gained the 32 runs

Brilliance with bat and ball: Ben Coad, left, and Dom Leech

required, winning with nine balls remaining. Duke was Yorkshire's standout performer at sun-kissed Clifton Park, where a 3,000-strong crowd cheered wildly as Leech swung away the winning boundary.

Leech started and ended this game brilliantly. Surrey posted 241 all out, having been 0-2 as the quick struck twice in two balls in the second over of the match. Fellow quick Ben Mike also impressed with a career best 4-40 from 7.5 overs, all of his wickets coming inside the innings' last seven overs. One of them was Ben Geddes, who led Surrey's recovery from 0-2 and 79-5 with an excellent middle-order 92.

Yorkshire v. Hampshire: York, August 17.

Yorkshire were unable to chase 312 against qualification-rivals Hampshire as they were bowled out for 134 to go down by 177 runs and undermine their chances of progression.

Former England Under-19s captain Tom Prest revived a Hampshire innings which had crept to 108-4 in the 26th over, including two wickets for Ben Mike, with an excellent 105 off 118 balls.

Shan Masood elected to bowl on the same pitch used for the Surrey win, and Ben Coad was brilliant with 0-21 from 10 overs bowled straight through, but Prest — with help from Joseph Eckland's career-best 72 off 55, changed the complexion of the contest to push Hampshire up to 311-6. Yorkshire crumbled to 36-7 inside 15 overs, and therefore never threatened.

Leicestershire v. Yorkshire: Grace Road, August 20.

Yorkshire's second successive defeat — their third in all — ended their chances of List A silverware. They lost by six wickets after being bowled out for 184, the Foxes reeling in that target inside 43 overs.

Australian overseas wicketkeeper-batter Peter Handscomb anchored the chase with a measured 60 off 97 balls for the champions-to-be.

Yorkshire fell to 91-8, having been inserted, but their total was more than doubled by the last two wickets, while Leicestershire fell to 15-2 chasing. Ben Coad was Yorkshire's standout performer with an innings-high 45 off 52 balls from No.10 added to 2-33 from 10 overs with the new ball. Dom Bess hit 40 off 50 balls.

Middlesex v. Yorkshire: Radlett, August 22.

Quick-fire half-centuries from opener Joe Cracknell and ex-England Test batter Sam Robson ensured Middlesex successfully chased 254 as Yorkshire ended their campaign with a dead-rubber five-wicket defeat.

Cracknell's List A best 87 off 65 balls overshadowed Shan Masood's measured 96 off 129 for Yorkshire, the overseas captain posting his highest score in his first season with the county.

Masood held Yorkshire together on a tricky pitch, the county slipping to 29-3 batting

SHAN MASOOD: 5,000 runs

first. Robson finished with 62 unbeaten. There were sporadic signs of uneven bounce and a two-paced nature about the surface at Middlesex's leafy Hertfordshire outground, where just short of 2,000 watched on a warm and sunny day.

Upon reaching 84 Masood also recorded his 5,000th run in his 112th List A appearance — but he missed out on a century, trapped lbw as one of four wickets to fall in Yorkshire's last over to seamer Ryan Higgins, 4-39. Yorkshire's bowlers erred, and weren't able to take advantage of any help on offer from the pitch.

Metro Bank One-Day Cup — Group A
Yorkshire v. Kent

Played at North Marine Road, Scarborough, on August 1, 2023
Kent won by 2 runs (DLS method)

Toss won by Yorkshire   Kent 2 points, Yorkshire 0 points

KENT

M K O'Riordan, c Fraine b Coad	2
B G Compton, run out (Bess/Mike)	103
* J A Leaning, c Duke b Coad	14
A J Blake, c Duke b Hill	4
§ H Z Finch, c Duke b Coad	0
J D M Evison, c Revis b Leech	136
J J Bazley, c Wharton b Revis	0
G Stewart, c Wharton b Revis	0
Hamidullah Qadri, b Revis	0
M R Quinn, not out	8
M W Parkinson Did not bat	
Extras lb 5, w 6, nb 4	15
Total (9 wkts)	282

FoW: 1-6 (O'Riordan), 2-36 (Leaning), 3-44 (Blake), 4-49 (Finch), 5-268 (Evison), 6-270 (Bazley), 7-270 (Stewart), 8-270 (Qadri), 9-282 (Compton)

	O	M	R	W
Coad	10	3	16	3
Leech	10	0	60	1
Hill	10	1	40	1
Revis	8	0	57	3
Bess	7	0	54	0
Mike	5	0	50	0

YORKSHIRE

F J Bean, c Qadri b Bazley	2
§ H G Duke, c Blake b Parkinson	31
* Shan Masood, run out (Evison)	31
G C H Hill, c Finch b Bazley	35
W A R Fraine, not out	15
J H Wharton, not out	1
B W M Mike	
M L Revis	
D M Bess Did not bat	
B O Coad	
D J Leech	
Extras w 2	2
Total (4 wkts, 17 overs)	117

DLS par score at final rain interruption: 119-4

FoW: 1-3 (Bean), 2-52 (Shan Masood), 3-68 (Duke), 4-111 (Hill)

	O	M	R	W
Bazley	5	0	20	3
Stewart	4	0	29	0
Quinn	3	0	16	0
Evison	3	0	23	0
Parkinson	2	0	29	1

Umpires: N A Mallender and S Shanmugam   Scorers: J T Potter and L A R Hart

Yorkshire v. Lancashire

At North Marine Road, Scarborough, on August 3, 2023
Match abandoned without a ball bowled

Toss — none   Yorkshire 1 point, Lancashire 1 point
Umpires:N Ashraf and S Redfern   Scorers: J T Potter and C Rimmer

Metro Bank One-Day Cup — Group A
Nottinghamshire v. Yorkshire

At Trent Bridge, Nottingham, on August 5, 2023
Match abandoned without a ball bowled

Toss — none   Yorkshire 1 point, Nottinghamshire 1 point
Umpires: R J Bailey and N A Mallender   Scorers: J T Potter and A Cusworth

Essex v. Yorkshire

Played at The Cloud County Ground, Chelmsford, on August 13, 2023
Yorkshire won by 5 wickets

Toss won by Essex   Yorkshire 2 points, Essex 0 points

ESSEX

M S Pepper, c Bean b Bess	63
R J Das, c and b Revis	36
* T Westley, c Duke b Revis	17
B J Webster, c Duke b Bess	39
L M Benkenstein, c Coad b Revis	27
S R Harmer, c Fraine b Revis	3
C W J Allison, lbw b Shutt	13
§ W J Buttleman, b Bess	3
J A Richards, c and b Bess	7
A P Beard, not out	0
A S S Nijjar, b Bess	0
Extras w 13	13
Total (35.4 overs)	221

FoW: 1-103 (Pepper), 2-124 (Westley), 3-125 (Das), 4-175 (Benkenstein), 5-181 (Harmer), 6-202 (Allison), 7-212 (Webster), 8-220 (Richards), 9-221 (Buttleman), 10-221 (Nijjar)

	O	M	R	W
Leech	7	1	45	0
Coad	4	0	44	0
Bess	7.4	0	37	5
Revis	8	0	54	4
Shutt	8	0	40	1
Hill	1	0	1	0

YORKSHIRE

F J Bean, b Webster	39
§ H G Duke, b Nijjar	42
* Shan Masood, c Buttleman b Westley	54
G C H Hill, c Webster b Nijjar	1
W A R Fraine, c and b Harmer	2
J H Wharton, not out	54
M L Revis, not out	21
J W Shutt	
D M Bess Did not bat	
B O Coad	
D J Leech	
Extras lb 4, w 5	9
Total (5 wkts, 45.5 overs)	222

FoW:-1-80 (Bean), 2-103 (Duke), 3-107 (Hill), 4-112 (Fraine), 5-180 (Shan Masood)

	O	M	R	W
Richards	3	0	13	0
Beard	5	1	21	0
Nijjar	10	0	43	2
Harmer	10	0	33	1
Webster	8	0	60	1
Westley	9.5	0	48	1

Umpires: J D Middlebrook and P Mustard   Scorers: J T Potter and A E Choat

Metro Bank One-Day Cup — Group A
Yorkshire v. Surrey

Played at Clifton Park, York, on August 15, 2023
Yorkshire won by 1 wicket

Toss won by Yorkshire   Yorkshire 2 points, Surrey 0 points

SURREY

D P Sibley, c Bess b Revis	30
R S Patel, c Wharton b Leech	0
* R J Burns, c Bean b Leech	0
B T Foakes, lbw b Hill	25
C T Steel, b Hill	12
B B A Geddes, b Mike	92
§ J W Blake, c and b Revis	25
C McKerr, b Mike	32
L A Griffiths, not out	12
D T Moriarty, c Wharton b Mike	3
G S Virdi, c Duke b Mike	0
Extras lb 3, w 3, nb 4	10
Total (47.5 overs)	241

FoW: 1-0 (Patel), 2-0 (Burns), 3-41 (Foakes), 4-59 (Steel), 5-79 (Sibley), 6-124 (Blake), 7-218 (McKerr), 8-231 (Geddes), 9-241 (Moriarty), 10-241 (Virdi)

	O	M	R	W
Coad	10	1	40	0
Leech	8	1	34	2
Hill	6	0	32	2
Revis	10	1	53	2
Mike	7.5	0	40	4
Bess	6	0	39	0

YORKSHIRE

F J Bean, b McKerr	10
§ H G Duke, not out	93
* Shan Masood, b Virdi	11
G C H Hill, c Blake b Griffiths	30
W A R Fraine, st Blake b Patel	32
J H Wharton, c Sibley b Virdi	4
B W M Mike, st Blake b Steel	7
M L Revis, c and b Steel	1
D M Bess, c Geddes b Steel	26
B O Coad, b Moriarty	2
D J Leech, not out	18
Extras w 1, nb 8	9
Total (9 wkts, 48.3 overs)	243

FoW: 1-12 (Bean), 2-29 (Shan Masood), 3-80 (Hill), 4-141 (Fraine), 5-150 (Wharton), 6-159 (Mike), 7-163 (Revis), 8-197 (Bess), 9-210 (Coad)

	O	M	R	W
Virdi	10	0	48	2
McKerr	10	0	59	1
Moriarty	10	0	47	1
Griffiths	4	0	24	1
Steel	10	0	49	3
Patel	4.3	0	16	1

Umpires: N A Mallender and S Shanmugam   Scorers: J T Potter and D Beesley

Metro Bank One-Day Cup — Group A
Yorkshire v. Hampshire

Played at Clifton Park, York, on August 17, 2023
Hampshire won by 177 runs

Toss won by Yorkshire   Hampshire 2 points, Yorkshire 0 points

HAMPSHIRE

F S Middleton, b Leech	5
* N R T Gubbins, c Duke b Hill	30
T J Prest, c Leech b Mike	105
§ B C Brown, c Duke b Mike	19
A H T Donald, c Bean b Mike	7
J R Eckland, c Bean b Revis	72
F S Organ, not out	32
I G Holland, not out	3
D C Kelly	
E V Jack Did not bat	
S W Currie	
Extras b 4, lb 10, w 14, nb 10	38
Total (6 wkts)	311

FoW: 1-24 (Middleton), 2-47 (Gubbins), 3-94 (Brown), 4-108 (Donald), 5-233 (Eckland), 6-307 (Prest)

	O	M	R	W
Coad	10	1	21	0
Leech	7	0	43	1
Hill	8	0	42	1
Revis	10	0	70	1
Mike	10	0	84	3
Bess	5	0	37	0

YORKSHIRE

F J Bean, c Brown b Holland	4
§ H G Duke, c Organ b Kelly	0
* Shan Masood, c Brown b Holland	18
G C H Hill, c Prest b Kelly	0
W A R Fraine, c Currie b Holland	9
J H Wharton, c Brown b Jack	4
B W M Mike, b Jack	0
M L Revis, c Middleton b Organ	23
D M Bess, c Prest b Currie	24
B O Coad, not out	16
D J Leech, c Kelly b Jack	23
Extras b 4, lb 1, w 6, nb 2	13
Total (31.1 overs)	134

FoW: 1-4 (Duke), 2-4 (Bean), 3-6 (Hill), 4-27 (Fraine), 5-36 (Wharton), 6-36 (Mike), 7-36 (Shan Masood), 8-90 (Revis), 9-92 (Bess), 10-134 (Leech)

	O	M	R	W
Holland	8	2	12	3
Kelly	7	0	22	2
Jack	5.1	1	31	3
Curries	5	0	34	1
Organ	6	1	30	1

Umpires: N Ashraf and S J O'Shaughnessy   Scorers: J T Potter and F C Newnham

Metro Bank One-Day Cup — Group A
Leicestershire v. Yorkshire

Played at Uptonsteel County Ground, Leicester, on August 20, 2023
Leicestershire won by 6 wickets

Toss won by Leicestershire — Leicestershire 2 points, Yorkshire 0 points

YORKSHIRE

F J Bean, lbw b Salisbury	28
§ H G Duke, c Handscomb b Wright	4
* Shan Masood, c Kimber b Wright	7
W A Luxton, b Wright	0
J H Wharton, c Walker b Davis	26
M L Revis, c Patel b Davis	18
G C H Hill, c Handscomb b Salisbury	0
B W M Mike, lbw b Salisbury	0
D M Bess, c Handscomb b Mulder	40
B O Coad, st Handscomb b Kimber	45
J W Shutt, not out	6
Extras b 1, lb 3, w 6	10
Total (47.5 overs)	184

FoW: 1-11 (Duke), 2-24 (Shan Masood), 3-24 (Luxton), 4-60 (Bean), 5-78 (Wharton), 6-79 (Hill), 7-83 (Mike), 8-91 (Revis), 9-166 (Bess), 10-184 (Coad)

	O	M	R	W
Mulder	10	2	34	1
Wright	10	2	31	3
Walker	6	0	41	0
Salisbury	10	1	28	3
Davis	9	0	41	2
Kimber	2.5	0	5	1

LEICESTERSHIRE

R K Patel, c Bess b Hill	1
S B Budinger, c Duke b Coad	9
* L J Hill, lbw b Coad	21
§ P S P Handscomb, c Duke b Bess	60
P W A Mulder, not out	51
L P J Kimber, not out	30
S T Evans	
R I Walker	
C J C Wright — Did not bat	
W S Davis	
M E T Salisbury	
Extras lb 9, w 3, nb 2	14
Total (4 wkts, 42.2 overs)	186

FoW: 1-9 (Patel), 2-15 (Budinger), 3-57 (Hill), 4-137 (Handscomb)

	O	M	R	W
Coad	10	0	33	2
Hill	8	1	27	1
Revis	5	1	21	0
Bess	10	0	41	1
Mike	3.2	0	30	0
Shutt	6	0	25	0

Umpires: S J O'Shaughnessy and N J Pratt — Scorers: J T Potter and P J Rogers

Metro Bank One-Day Cup — Group A
Middlesex v. Yorkshire

Played at Radlett Cricket Club, Radlett, on August 22, 2023
Middlesex won by 5 wickets

Toss won by Yorkshire

Middlesex 2 points, Yorkshire 0 points

YORKSHIRE

W A Luxton, c Simpson b Bamber	5
J H Wharton, c de Caires b Cullen	0
* Shan Masood, lbw b Higgins	96
F J Bean, c Stoneman b Cullen	7
M L Revis, run out (Hollman)	51
D M Bess, c Andersson b de Caires	51
§ H G Duke, c Stoneman b Bamber	31
B W M Mike, c Simpson b Higgins	5
D J Leech, not out	1
J W Shutt, b Higgins	0
B M Cliff, c Cracknell b Higgins	0
Extras b 1, lb 1, w 4	6
Total (50 overs)	253

FoW: 1-0 (Wharton), 2-22 (Luxton), 3-29 (Bean), 4-114 (Revis), 5-197 (Bess), 6-239 (Duke), 7-252 (Mike), 8-253 (Shan Masood), 9-253 (Shutt), 10-253 (Cliff)

	O	M	R	W
Bamber	10	2	36	2
Cullen	8	1	32	2
Andersson	8	0	62	0
Higgins	10	0	39	4
Hollman	6	0	43	0
de Caires	8	0	39	1

MIDDLESEX

* M D Stoneman, c Duke b Leech	16
J B Cracknell, lbw b Shutt	87
S D Robson, c Luxton b Shutt	62
R F Higgins, c Wharton b Shutt	4
§ J A Simpson, not out	29
J L B Davies, c Luxton b Shutt	0
M K Andersson, not out	36
L B K Hollman	
J M de Carries	
E R Bamber	
B C Cullen	
Extras lb 10, w 4, nb 6	20
Total (5 wkts, 34.3 overs)	254

Did not bat: L B K Hollman, J M de Carries, E R Bamber, B C Cullen

FoW: 1-52 (Stoneman), 2-171 (Cracknell), 3-177 (Higgins), 4-201 (Robson), 5-201 (Davies),

	O	M	R	W
Cliff	4.3	0	40	0
Leech	4	0	42	1
Mike	4	0	33	0
Revis	6	0	42	0
Shutt	10	0	49	4
Bess	6	0	38	0

Umpires R J Bailey and N L Bainton

Scorers: J T Potter and D K Shelley

YORKSHIRE VIKINGS AVERAGES 2023
METRO BANK ONE-DAY CUP

Played 8   Won 2   Lost 4   Abandoned 2

BATTING AND FIELDING

(Qualification 4 completed innings)

Player	M	I	N O	Runs	H S	100s	50s	Avge	ct/st
H G Duke	6	6	1	201	93*	0	1	40.20	11
Shan Masood	6	6	0	217	96	0	2	36.16	0
D M Bess	6	4	0	141	51	0	1	35.25	3
M L Revis	6	5	1	114	51	0	1	28.50	3
J H Wharton	6	6	2	89	54*	0	1	22.25	5
F J Bean	6	6	0	90	39	0	0	15.00	4
G C H Hill	5	5	0	66	35	0	0	13.20	0
B W M Mike	5	4	0	12	7	0	0	3.00	0

Also played

Player	M	I	N O	Runs	H S	100s	50s	Avge	ct/st
D J Leech	5	3	2	42	23	0	0	42.00	1
B O Coad	5	3	1	63	45	0	0	31.50	1
W A R Fraine	4	4	1	58	32	0	0	19.33	2
J W Shutt	3	2	1	6	6*	0	0	6.00	0
W A Luxton	2	2	0	5	5	0	0	2.50	2
B M Cliff	1	1	0	0	0	0	0	0.00	0

BOWLING

(Qualification 4 wickets)

Player	Overs	Mdns	Runs	Wkts	Avge	Best	4wI	RPO
J W Shutt	24	0	114	5	22.80	4-49	1	4.75
G C H Hill	33	2	142	5	28.40	2-32	0	4.30
M L Revi	47	2	297	10	29.70	4-54	1	6.31
B O Coad	44	5	154	5	30.80	3-16	0	3.50
B W M Mike	30.1	0	237	7	33.85	4-40	1	7.85
D M Bess	41.4	0	246	6	41.00	5-37	1	5.90
D K Leech	36	2	224	5	44.80	2-34	0	6.22

Also bowled

Player	Overs	Mdns	Runs	Wkts	Avge	Best	4wI	RPO
B M Cliff	4.3	0	40	0	—	0-40	0	8.88

First Metro Bank One-Day International
England v. Ireland

At Headingley, Leeds, on September 20, 2023
Match abandoned without a ball bowled
Toss: None

Umpires: Ahsan Raza and M Burns

Scorers: J R Virr and A Hinchliffe

Third: R J Tucker

Fourth: D J Millns

Referee: B C Broad

National Counties Showcase One-Day Match
(Not List A)
Cheshire v. Yorkshire

Played at Nantwich Cricket Club, Nantwich, on July 30, 2023
No result

Toss won by Yorkshire

CHESHIRE

B Kohler-Cadmore, c Bess b Leech	13
S J Perry, c Bean b Hill	50
H J Dobson, c Duke b Leech	1
* H E Dearden, c Bess b Cliff	76
§ W J Evans, c Hill b Bess	2
A M Money, lbw b Bess	6
N D Anderson, b Bess	17
L Young, b Bess	1
C W G Sanders, not out	61
S Green, c Wharton b Leech	18
J J Williams, not out	1
Extras b 5, lb 9, w 8	22
Total (9 wkts)	268

FoW: 1-27 (Kohler-Cadmore), 2-33 (Dobson), 3-123 (Perry), 4-130 (Evans), 5-145 (Money), 6-174 (Anderson), 7-182 (Young), 8-194 (Dearden), 9-258 (Green)

	O	M	R	W
Leech	9	1	32	3
Cliff	7	0	32	1
Revis	7	1	45	0
Mike	6	0	40	0
Hill	6	0	28	1
Shutt	7	0	36	0
Bess	8	0	41	4

YORKSHIRE

§ H G Duke
F J Bean
J H Wharton
W A R Fraine
* G C H Hill
B W M Mike   Did not bat
M L Revis
D M Bess
D J Leech
J W Shutt
B M Cliff

Umpires: S J O'Shaughnessy and J Pitcher

Scorers: J T Potter and I A F Bevers

NORTHERN DIAMONDS

Captain: Hollie Armitage

Director of Cricket: To be confirmed   Coach: Danielle Hazell

Academy Head Coach: Tom Cant

CHARLOTTE EDWARDS CUP 2023

Final: Southern Vipers (118-3) defeated The Blaze (114-8) by 7 wickets

		P	W	L	T	NR/A	BP	PTS	NRR
1	The Blaze *	7	7	0	0	0	4	32	1.765
2	Southern Vipers * *	7	5	2	0	0	2	22	0.940
3	Thunder **	7	4	3	0	0	2	18	0.331
4	Northern Diamonds	7	4	3	0	0	1	17	-0.129
5	South East Stars	7	3	4	0	0	0	12	-0.096
6	Western Storm	7	3	4	0	0	0	12	-0.512
7	Central Sparks	7	2	5	0	0	0	8	-0.558
8	Sunrisers	7	0	7	0	0	0	0	-1.717

*   *Qualified for Final*

* * *Qualified for Semi-Final (One)*

RACHAEL HEYHOE FLINT TROPHY 2023

Final: The Blaze (200-8) lost to Southern Vipers (203-5)) by 5 wickets

		P	W	T	L	NR	A	BP	PTS	NRR
1	Southern Vipers (3)	14	7	1	4	1	1	4	38	0.457
2	The Blaze * (6)	14	7	0	4	1	2	4	38	0.173
3	South East Stars * (2)	14	7	0	6	1	0	6	36	0.583
4	Sunrisers (8)	14	6	0	5	1	2	2	32	-0.006
5	Central Sparks (5)	14	6	1	5	1	1	1	31	-0.233
6	Northern Diamonds (1)	14	6	0	7	1	0	4	30	-0.206
7	Thunder (7)	14	3	2	5	1	3	2	26	-0.111
8	Western Storm (4)	14	2	0	8	3	1	0	16	-1.068

* *Qualified for Semi-Final (One)*

NORTHERN DIAMONDS 2024 SQUAD (* denotes contracted player)

Player	Date of Birth	Birthplace	Role
H J Armitage (Captain) *	June 14, 1997	Huddersfield	RHB, LB
L Dobson *	June 10, 2001	Scarborough	RHB
R E Duckworth	October 30, 2000	Preston	RHB
G E Hall	December 24, 2002	York	RHB, RAMF
B A M Heath	August 20, 2001	Chesterfield	WK, RHB
A Glen	April 2, 2001	Leeds	RHB, RAMF
S L Kalis *	August 30, 1999	Delft, NL	RHB
B A Langston *	September 6, 1992	Harold Wood	RAF, RHB
K A Levick *	July 17, 1991	Sheffield	LB
E K Marlow *	April 12, 2004	Harrogate	OB
L E Scott *	September 1, 2004	Hexham	RAMF
R Slater *	November 20, 2001	Glens Falls, USA	LAMF
P E Turner *	August 1, 2003	Northallerton	RHB, RAMF
S Turner	April 23, 2023	Blackburn	RHB, RAM
L Winfield-Hill *	August 16, 1990	York	RHB, WK
J A Woolston	February 25, 2003	Stockton-on-Tees	RHB, RAMF

Bess Heath holds a development contract with the England and Wales Cricket Board

YOUNG ONES A SILVER LINING AS VIPERS POISON CUP HOPES

By Graham Hardcastle

Diamonds were unable to defend the title they won, oh so gloriously, in September 2022, missing out on the knockout stage with only six wins from 14 matches.

Hollie Armitage's squad finished sixth in the table, six points adrift of third placed South East Stars, who qualified alongside the Blaze and eventual champions Southern Vipers — who completed the regional double, courtesy of another success in the Charlotte Edwards Cup.

Many will look at last summer as a failure, but that far from tells the whole story. Here was a team starting to rebuild, having lost experienced heads such as former England international Jenny Gunn, who retired, and Linsey Smith. A much younger group of players showed at stages that they can compete.

The Diamonds enjoyed a productive first half of the 50-over campaign, winning four of the first seven matches until early July. Things didn't go so well through the second half of the campaign.

A home defeat against the Vipers at South Northumberland on September 5 was particularly costly: it was the first game back after the Hundred, and the Diamonds — chasing 262 — failed to get the nine runs needed off the last over despite having captain Armitage at the crease on 103 alongside Leah Dobson on 20.

Had they won that fixture, it would have set the platform for a run at qualification during the final three rounds of the campaign. It just wasn't meant to be.

Lauren Winfield-Hill was the region's standout player — in fact, the competition's standout batter. Nobody scored more runs than her 663 with one hundred and five fifties. Leg-spinner Katie Levick claimed 24 wickets — the second best haul in the competition.

Both were rewarded by being named in the Metro Bank women's national team of the year, an eleven selected via the Professional Cricketers Association's Most Valuable Player rankings system.

Northern Diamonds v. Western Storm: Headingley, April 22.

The Diamonds began the defence of their title with a thumping 105-run victory over a Storm side including prospective England debutants Lauren Filer and Danielle Gibson, who would both break into interna-

Up and away: Standout Northern Diamonds batter Lauren Winfield-Hill on her way to a top-score 75 against Western Storm at Headingley as wicketkeeper Nat Wraith looks on.

tional cricket in 2023. Half-centuries from Winfield-Hill (75), Bess Heath (71) and South African debutant Chloe Tryon (63) took Diamonds to a commanding 290-8 total off a rain-reduced 37 overs.

Leg-spinner Levick then claimed 4-36, including her 300th career wicket across all formats, as Storm fell well short of the target at 185 all out. Rain fell throughout the morning, but the players finally took to the field at 1pm, and a 109-run partnership for the fourth wicket from 91-3 between Winfield-Hill and Heath — another prospective England debutant — was key to the result of this fixture.

Central Sparks v. Northern Diamonds: New Road, April 29.

A damaging batting collapse led to the Diamonds' first 50-over defeat since the 2022 final against the Vipers at Northampton as they went down by seven wickets.

Inserted, the defending champions built a good platform at 50-0 through Winfield-Hill and Sterre Kalis, but they then lost all 10 wickets for only another 111 runs. Winfield-Hill was the first, bowled by Issy Wong for an innings-high 42, and Armitage with 37 was the only other batter to make it beyond 30. Off-spinner Georgia Davis claimed 4-19 from 7.4 overs before a routine chase was led by captain Eve Jones's determined opening 67 not out.

Sunrisers v. Northern Diamonds: Chelmsford, May 1.

Superb bowling in helpful conditions ensured the Diamonds got back to winning ways with victory by five wickets on Bank Holiday Monday, with Scottish international all-rounder Katherine Fraser making a triumphant debut.

Winfield-Hill led the chase of 158 with a typically free-flowing 51 off 43 balls — her eighth score of 50 or more in her last 10 RHFT innings, dating back to the start of 2022.

But this victory — secured with a bonus point — was set up by the bowlers, who combined to put the hosts under severe pressure after they had surprisingly elected to bat on a grey Essex morning.

Jess Woolston (2-18 from seven overs) and Lizzie Scott (2-27 from 10) were outstanding with the new ball, backed up impressively by fellow seamer Abi Glen with two wickets, but Levick returned the pick of the figures in Sunrisers' 157 all out with 3-23 from eight overs.

Northern Diamonds v. The Blaze: Riverside, May 6.

South African seamer Nadine de Klerk starred with a career-best 7-33 as the Blaze claimed victory by four wickets, a margin much tighter than had once looked likely.

De Klerk was relentless. She removed key duo Winfield-Hill and Armitage before pressing on to bowl the Diamonds out for 62 inside 19 overs. No batter made it into double figures.

But just when you thought a procession to the points was inevitable for the Midlanders they only stumbled across the line, falling from 25-0 to 58-6, with all six wickets falling to spin. De Klerk's compatriot and international teammate, Tryon, starred with her left-arm spinners, returning 4-16 from 7.5 overs, and Levick chipped in with two wickets, but it wasn't to be.

Northern Diamonds v. South East Stars: Scarborough, May 10.

Jess Woolston's brilliant career-best 5-37 outshone a recovering century from England batter Sophia Dunkley as the Diamonds won an entertaining fixture by three wickets *(DLS)*.

New-ball seamer Woolston claimed all five top-order wickets to leave the Stars staring down the barrel at 55-5 inside only 11 overs. It was the match-deciding performance, but the Diamonds were made to work as No.4 Dunkley hit a run-a-ball unbeaten 101 to fashion a total of 223.

A wet outfield delayed the start, forcing a 46-over game, and further rain revised the target to 178 in 36 overs. Openers Sterre Kalis, who top-

STERRE KALIS

KATIE LEVICK

scored with an excellent 66 not out, and Winfield-Hill (45) shared 88 for the first wicket, but Winfield-Hill was one of seven wickets to fall around Kalis, who held firm to secure victory with two balls left.

South East Stars v. Northern Diamonds: Beckenham, July 2.

Grace Hall's senior best return of 4-33 from eight overs preceded a fabulous unbeaten 116 from Winfield-Hill as they set up a convincing seven-wicket Diamonds win as 50-over cricket returned to the schedule after a month-and-a-half break for T20s.

This was Hall's competitive 50-over debut for the Diamonds — and the 20-year-old seamer also affected a run-out as the Stars were bowled out for 205, having elected to bat.

A clash between two sides affected by England call-ups, with the Diamonds missing captain Armitage and Bess Heath due to A-team duty, was decided by a player who was released by the national management.

Winfield-Hill arrived from England's senior T20 squad just in time to toss up as stand-in skipper, and she played a captain's knock, including 15 fours and a six in 100 balls, to seal a success watched by Yorkshire chair Harry Chathli, whose daughter, Kira, played for the Stars.

The Blaze v. Northern Diamonds: Chesterfield, July 7.

The Diamonds went down by nine wickets in their top-of-the-table clash with the league leaders as failure to build on an excellent start with the bat proved costly.

Winfield-Hill top-scored with 56, and she shared 55 inside 12 overs for the first wicket with Kalis, but the Diamonds, having elected to bat, slipped to 147-9 before a late rally boosted them to 185 all out. Last-wicket pair Hall and Woolston shared 38, but that was in vain as Blaze knocked off the runs at a parched Queen's Park to win their fifth game in seven and consign the Diamonds to a third defeat.

England opener Tammy Beaumont top-scored with a destructive, unbeaten 83, and shared an unbroken 156 for the second wicket with Sarah Bryce (53 not out).

Northern Diamonds v. Thunder: York, July 11.

Arch-rivals Thunder claimed their first 50-over win of the summer as Naomi Dattani impressed with bat and ball at Clifton Park.

Dattani claimed four wickets with her left-arm seamers to help to bowl Diamonds out for 167, and played a crucial innings of 46, sharing a 98-run stand with Deandra Dottin — who made 54 not out — as Thunder completed the chase with six wickets and 12.2 overs to spare.

Winfield-Hill top-scored for Diamonds with 33, but their total never appeared enough. It was a story of wickets falling at regular intervals.

Northern Diamonds v. Central Sparks: Headingley, July 15.

The Diamonds were beaten again, their title defence now in jeopardy.

They lost by five wickets *(DLS)* as a rain-ravaged fixture was completed with two balls remaining after showers all day.

Former England all-rounder Katie George starred with 2-46 from seven overs of left-arm seam and then struck 56 off 35 balls as the visitors chased a revised 164 target in 19 overs.

The Diamonds were on a healthy 223-4 from 34 of 37 scheduled overs, with rain returning after a delayed start.

When play resumed the Sparks were set their target, which they reached amidst an entertaining finale, thanks to George's best 50-over score for the Midlanders, whom she joined at the start of 2023. Armitage top-scored with 66 for the Diamonds, and Levick returned 3-31.

Southern Vipers v. Northern Diamonds: Arundel, July 22.

The Diamonds suffered their only No Result of the summer, rain limiting play to 25.4 overs. The rain which swept across the country only hit the picturesque Sussex venue just after midday, allowing the inserted Diamonds to reach 105-4. Unfortunately, it didn't stop.

Captain Armitage hit seven fours in a top score of 48 off 64 balls.

Northern Diamonds v. Southern Vipers: South Northumberland, September 5.

Armitage's superb unbeaten 106 off 107 balls wasn't enough to get the Diamonds over the line as they lost their fourth match in five —by only three runs — either side of the break for the Hundred.

Opposing captain Georgia Adams also impressed in this topsy-turvy fixture, and her performance ultimately came in a winning cause — 82

JESS WOOLSTON   **PHOEBE TURNER**

and then 1-34 with her off-spin. Seamers Hall (4-46) and Scott shared seven wickets, with Vipers failing to make the most of a commanding start at 127-1 in the 29th over, finishing with 261-8.

The Diamonds were well set at 203-3 in the 42nd over of their chase, with Armitage going well, but they failed to get nine off the last from Georgia Elwiss, finishing on 258-5.

Northern Diamonds v. Western Storm, Taunton, September 10.

The Diamonds won by 31 runs, their first victory since July 2, to boost their knockout qualification hopes.

Aiming for a top-three finish, Winfield-Hill score a beautifully crafted 83 off 92 balls to underpin a commanding 281-3 from 43 overs. Morning rain forced a reduction in overs, but Winfield-Hill and Kalis (45) shared 101 inside 18 overs for the first wicket, Leah Dobson adding a hard-hitting unbeaten 68.

Storm recovered manfully from 17-2 to 250-7, but they were always too far behind the rate. Captain Sophie Luff made 87, but Scott and Levick decisively struck twice apiece.

Thunder v. Northern Diamonds: Sale, September 13.

Winfield-Hill's barnstorming 89 helped to give the Diamonds back-to-back victories, gaining revenge on their arch-rivals — the Diamonds had lost to Thunder at York earlier in the competition.

But now they claimed a commanding 48-run win, despite a scare in the first half of the fixture when they slipped from 51-1 to 196 all out.

Winfield-Hill hit 14 fours in an opening 90-ball effort before Levick matched Thunder spinner Liv Bell's four wickets to ensure the hosts were humbled. They too started well at 54-1, though crumbled to 148 all out. Phoebe Turner's seam also accounted for three wickets.

Northern Diamonds v. Sunrisers: Riverside, September 16.

The Diamonds saw their title defence ended amid a thrilling final-day six-wicket defeat *(DLS)*.

The defending champions needed to beat the Sunrisers — also eliminated — to have any chance of knockout cricket, but other results also needed to go their way, which they didn't: this was confirmed as the Diamonds were about to start their defence of a revised target of 126 in 18 overs, which came down to the visitors needing 10 off the last.

Rain delayed the start until 2pm, and further interrupted this fixture.

The Diamonds made 114-6 in 18 overs, including Bess Heath's 37 off 21 balls two days after making her senior England debut.

Sunrisers, who needed a bonus victory amid a host of other things to go their way to finish in the top three places, then hunted down their *Duckworth Lewis Stern* target for the loss of four wickets with three balls to spare.

Jo Gardner top-scored with a brisk 30 not out.

England calls captain marvel Hollie

Diamonds captain Hollie Armitage earned her maiden senior England call-up to be part of a March T20 series in New Zealand. Armitage had impressed for England A, including on tour of India in December, and she enjoyed a productive month of domestic T20 cricket in New Zealand in January. Armitage helped Central Districts to reach the Super Smash final, her 10-match haul of 318 runs the third best in the competition.

NORTHERN DIAMONDS AVERAGES 2023

RACHAEL HEYHOE-FLINT TROPHY

Played 14   Won 6   Lost 7   No Result 1

BATTING AND FIELDING
(Qualification 3 completed innings)

Player	M.	I.	N.O.	Runs	H.S.	100s	50s	Avge	ct/st
L Winfield-Hill	14	14	1	663	116*	1	5	51.00	10/4
B A M Heath	9	9	2	286	71	0	1	40.86	1
H J Armitage	13	13	1	384	106*	1	1	32.00	1
C L Tryon	9	9	3	184	63	0	2	30.67	4
E K Marlow	10	10	4	164	25*	0	0	27.33	3
L Dobson	10	7	1	154	68*	0	1	25.67	2
S L Kalis	14	14	1	299	66*	0	1	23.00	4
L E Scott	14	7	2	32	11*	0	0	6.40	1
P E Turner	11	10	2	45	13	0	0	5.63	3
K A Levick	14	6	1	22	11*	0	0	4.40	0
A A Glen	5	4	0	7	5	0	0	1.75	3

Also batted

Player	M.	I.	N.O.	Runs	H.S.	100s	50s	Avge	ct/st
G E Hall	8	3	1	48	21*	0	0	24.00	1
R E Duckworth	6	4	0	55	27	0	0	13.75	1
J A Woolston	12	5	2	25	13	0	0	8.33	6
K J G Fraser	2	2	1	7	4	0	0	7.00	1
S Turner	2	1	1	4	4*	0	0	—	0
R E Slater	1	0	0	0	—	0	0	—	0

BOWLING
(Qualification 3 wickets)

Player	Overs	Mdns	Runs	Wkts	Avge	Best	4wi	RPO
K A Levick	99	6	435	24	18.12	4 -28	2	4.39
A A Glen	25.3	1	132	6	22.00	2 -34	0	5.17
J A Woolaston	66	3	302	13	23.23	5 -37	1	4.57
P E Turner	21	1	120	5	24.00	3 -18	0	5.71
G E Hall	47.4	0	265	11	24.09	4 -33	2	5.55
L E Scott	84.3	2	381	12	31.75	3 -33	0	4.50
C L Tryon	55.3	3	249	6	41.50	4 -16	1	5.71

Also bowled

Player	Overs	Mdns	Runs	Wkts	Avge	Best	4wi	RPO
S Turner	10	0	53	2	26.50	1 -22	0	5.30
E K Marlow	12	0	79	1	79.99	1 -31	0	6.58
H J Armitage	28.1	0	188	2	94.00	1 -26	0	6.67
K J G Fraser	4	0	14	0	—	0 14	0	3.50

Rachael Heyhoe-Flint Trophy
Northern Diamonds v. Western Storm

Played at Headingley, Leeds, on April 22, 2023
Northern Diamonds won by 105 runs

Toss won by Western Storm   Northern Diamonds 5 points, Western Storm 0 points

NORTHERN DIAMONDS

§ L Winfield-Hill, b Griffiths	75
S L Kalis, b Filer	1
* H J Armitage, b Filer	1
P E Turner, run out (Luff)	3
B A M Heath, c Wraith b Skelton	71
C L L Tryon, b Smale	63
A A Glen, b Griffiths	0
L E Scott, b Skelton	8
E K Marlow, not out	17
K A Levick, not out	6
J A Woolston Did not bat	
Extras b 6, lb 2, w 35, nb 2	45
Total (8 wkts, 36 overs)	290

FoW: 1-8 (Kalis), 2-33 (Armitage), 3-71 (Turner), 4-180 (Heath), 5-200 (Winfield-Hill), 6-200 (Glen), 7-241 (Scott), 8-265 (Tryon)

	O	M	R	W
Gibson	8	0	50	0
Filer	7	1	54	2
Holland	3	0	38	0
Griffiths	7	1	40	2
Skelton	6	0	45	2
Smale	4	0	36	1
Thomson	1	0	19	0

WESTERN STORM

A C Griffiths, b Woolston	0
W V Corney, b Scott	2
* S N Luff, st Winfield-Hill b Levick	33
F C Wilson, c Woolston b Glen	43
D R Gibson, lbw b Levick	17
§ N A J Wraith, st Winfield-Hill b Levick	24
N F Holland, run out (Scott/Tryon)	6
S A E Smale, lbw b Levick	0
L L Filer, b Scott	6
C N Skelton, c Tryon b Glen	12
I S Thomson, not out	16
Extras b 6, lb 3, w 16, nb 1	26
Total (33.3 overs)	185

FoW: 1-5 (Corney), 2-8 (Griffiths), 3-97 (Luff), 4-97 (Wilson), 5-125 (Gibson), 6-138 (Holland), 7-148 (Wraith), 8-149 (Smale), 9-160 (Filer), 10-185 (Skelton)

	O	M	R	W
Scott	7	0	17	2
Woolston	5	0	28	1
Marlow	7	0	41	0
Levick	8	0	36	4
Glen	4.3	0	34	2
Tryon	2	0	20	0

Umpires: R Dovey and P R Pollard   Scorers: G Maddison and S Pollard

Rachael Heyhoe-Flint Trophy
Central Sparks v. Northern Diamonds

Played at New Road, Worcester, on April 29, 2023
Central Sparks won by 7 wickets

Toss won by Central Sparks   Central Sparks 5 points, Northern Diamonds 0 points

NORTHERN DIAMONDS

§ L Winfield-Hill, b Wong	42
S L Kalis, c Freeborn b George	16
* H J Armitage, c Perrin b Baker	37
P E Turner, b Wong	4
B A M Heath, lbw b Davis	13
C L L Tryon, c Wong b George	26
A A Glen, b Davis	0
L E Scott, b Baker	2
E K Marlow, not out	7
K A Levick, c Campbell b Davis	1
J A Woolston, c Freeborn b Davis	0
Extras b 1, lb 2, w 8, nb 2	13
Total (36.3 overs)	161

FoW: 1-50 (Winfield-Hill), 2-77 (Kalis), 3-87 (Turner), 4-121 (Heath), 5-123 (Armitage), 6-124 (Glen), 7-127 (Scott), 8-160 (Tryon), 9-161 (Levick), 10-161 (Woolston)

	O	M	R	W
Arlott	4	0	19	0
Potts	5	0	20	0
Wong	8	0	44	2
George	5	0	25	2
Baker	7	1	31	2
Davis	7.3	1	19	4

CENTRAL SPARKS

* E Jones, not out	67
C Brewer, c Tryon b Woolston	4
§ A J Freeborn, run out (Levick)	37
D S T Perrin, st Winfield-Hill b Armitage	30
A Campbell, not out	9
K L George	
E L Arlott	
I E C M Wong Did not bat	
G K Davis	
G E A Potts	
H L Baker	
Extras lb 5. w 10	15
Total (3 wkts, 38.2 overs)	162

FoW: 1-6 (Brewer), 2-104 (Freeborn), 3-149 (Perrin)

	O	M	R	W
Scott	6	0	25	0
Woolston	5	0	21	1
Marlow	1	0	7	0
Glen	6	0	23	0
Levick	7	0	21	0
Tryon	9	0	34	0
Armitage	4.2	0	26	1

Umpires: N Ashraf and J Naeem   Scorers: S M Drinkwater and H Vernon

Rachael Heyhoe-Flint Trophy
Sunrisers v. Northern Diamonds

Played at The Cloud County Ground, Chelmsford, on May 1, 2023
Northern Diamonds won by 5 wickets

Toss won by Sunrisers   Northern Diamonds 5 points, Sunrisers 0 points

SUNRISERS

G E Scrivens, b Woolston	11
C L Griffith, b Woolston	1
J L Grewcock, c Winfield-Hill b Levick	50
M K Villiers, c Fraser b Scott	0
S M Horley, c Armitage b Glen	8
J L Gardner, b Tryon	32
§ A D Carr, c Winfield-Hill b Scott	12
E Gray, lbw b Levick	1
* K S Castle, lbw b Levick	9
K L Coppack, not out	16
A M Maqsood, c Woolston b Glen	0
Extras b 2, w 15	17
Total (46 overs)	157

FoW: 1-11 (Griffith), 2-16 (Scrivens), 3-17 (Villiers), 4-32 (Horley), 5-97 (Gardner), 6-116 (Carr), 7-128 (Grewcock), 8-129 (Gray), 9-149 (Castle), 10-157 (Maqsood)

	O	M	R	W
Scott	10	0	27	2
Woolston	7	1	18	2
Glen	7	1	36	2
Fraser	4	0	14	0
Levick	8	1	23	3
Tryon	10	0	37	1

NORTHERN DIAMONDS

§ L Winfield-Hill, lbw b Villiers	51
S L Kalis, lbw b Castle	14
* H J Armitage, lbw b Villiers	30
P E Turner, b Villiers	13
B A M Heath, not out	32
C L L Tryon, b Gray	12
K J G Fraser, not out	3
A A Glen	
L E Scott Did not bat	
K A Levick	
J A Woolston	
Extras w 5	5
Total ((5 wkts, 28.3 over)	160

FoW: 1-53 (Kalis), 2-88 (Winfield-Hill), 3-105 (Turner), 4-120 (Armitage), 5-139 (Tryon)

	O	M	R	W
Coppack	3	0	25	0
Gray	6.3	0	37	1
Castle	5	0	26	1
Villiers	10	0	42	3
Maqsood	1	0	12	0
Scrivens	3	0	18	0

Umpires: J Ibbotson and R A White   Scorers: H M Hyde and A J Thurgood

Rachael Heyhoe-Flint Trophy
Northern Diamonds v. The Blaze

Played at Seat Unique Riverside, Chester-le-Street, on May 6, 2023
The Blaze won by 4 wickets

Toss won by The Blaze — The Blaze 5 points, Northern Diamonds 0 points

NORTHERN DIAMONDS

§ L Winfield-Hill, c K E Bryce b de Klerk	7
S L Kalis, lbw b Ballinger	6
* H J Armitage, c S J Bryce b de Klerk	8
P E Turner, lbw b de Klerk	8
B A M Heath, c Beaumont b de Klerk	9
C L L Tryon, c S J Bryce b de Klerk	0
K J G Fraser, b Ballinger	4
A A Glen, b Ballinger	2
L E Scott, c S J Bryce b de Klerk	2
K A Levick, c Glenn b de Klerk	1
J A Woolston, not out	5
Extras lb 1, w 4, pen 5	10
Total (18.1 overs)	62

FoW: 1-20 (Winfield-Hill), 2-30 (Armitage), 3-38 (Kalis), 4-42 (Turner), 5-42 (Tryon), 6-47 (Fraser), 7-53 (Heath), 8-53 (Glenn), 9-54 (Levick), 10-62 (Scott)

	O	M	R	W
de Klerk	9.1	3	33	7
Ballinger	9	2	23	3

THE BLAZE

M Kelly, c Woolston b Tryon	15
T T Beaumont, c Turner b Tryon	9
G E B Boyce, c Woolston b Tryon	9
K E Bryce, lbw b Tryon	5
§ S J Bryce, lbw b Levick	0
S Glenn, not out	7
N de Klerk, b Levick	3
L F Higham, not out	3
S E N Munro	
* K L Gordon — Did not bat	
G Ballinger	
Extras b 4, lb 3, w 5	12
Total (6 wkts, 18.5 overs)	63

FoW: 1-25 (Kelly), 2-41 (Beaumont), 3-42 (Boyce), 4-43 (S J Bryce), 5-53 (K E Bryce), 6-58 (de Klerk)

	O	M	R	W
Scott	2	0	16	0
Woolston	3	0	14	0
Tryon	7.5	2	16	4
Levick	6	2	10	2

Umpires: J Naeem and N J Pratt — Scorers: S Blacklock and J D Davidson

Rachael Heyhoe-Flint Trophy
Northern Diamonds v. South East Stars

Played at North Marine Road, Scarborough, on May 10, 2023
Northern Diamonds won by 3 wickets (DLS method)
Toss won by Northern Diamonds Northern Diamonds 4 points, South East Stars 0 points

SOUTH EAST STARS

Start delayed by rain. Match reduced to 46 overs per side

§ K M Chathli, c Winfield-Hill b Woolston	18
A Cranstone, c Dobson b Woolston	5
* B F Smith, c Glenn b Woolston	13
S I R Dunkley, not out	101
A N Davidson-Richards, c Glen b Woolston	5
P J Scholfield, c and b Woolston	0
P A Franklin, c Kalis b Glen	26
N E Farrant, c Kalis b Scott	13
R L Macdonald-Gay, c Heath b Scott	1
F R Davies, c and b Glen	15
D L Gregory, lbw b Levick	0
Extras lb1, w 24, nb 1	26
Total (44.2 overs)	223

FoW: 1-9 (Cranstone), 2-23 (Smith), 3-46 (Chathli), 4-52 (Davidson-Richards), 5-55 (Scholfield), 6-100 (Franklin), 7-145 (Farrant), 8-154 (Macdonald-Gay), 9-222 (Davies), 10-223 (Gregory)

	O	M	R	W
Woolston	9	0	37	5
Scott	7	0	47	2
Tryon	9	0	43	0
Levick	9.2	0	40	1
Glen	8	0	39	2
Armitage	2	0	16	0

NORTHERN DIAMONDS

Revised target to win: 178 runs off 36 overs

§ L Winfield-Hill, b Macdonald-Gay	45
S L Kalis, not out	66
* H J Armitage, c Scolfield b Macdonald-Gay	7
B A M Heath, c Franklin b Gregory	33
C L L Tryon, run out (Scolfield/Chathli)	0
P E Turner, b Davies	4
L Dobson, c Franklin b Smith	7
A A Glen, st Chathli b Smith	5
L E Scott, not out	3
K A Levick	Did not bat
J A Woolston	
Extras lb 2, w 5, nb 1	8
Total (7 wkts, 35.4 overs)	178

FoW: 1-88 (Winfield-Hill), 2-105 (Armitage), 3-146 (Heath), 4-146 (Tryon), 5-150 (Turner), 6-167 (Dobson), 7-175 (Glen)

	O	M	R	W
Davies	7	0	36	1
Franklin	5	0	17	0
Scholfield	6	0	16	0
Davidson-Richards	2	0	21	0
Smith	6.4	0	34	2
Macdonald-Gay	4	0	25	2
Gregory	5	0	27	1

Umpires: P Mustard and J Naeem Scorers: Q L S Jones and S Ward

Rachael Heyhoe-Flint Trophy
South East Stars v. Northern Diamonds

Played at The Kent County Ground, Beckenham, on July 2, 2023
Northern Diamonds won by 7 wickets

Toss won by South East Stars   Northern Diamonds 5 points, South East Stars 0 points

SOUTH EAST STARS

§ K M Chathli, c Winfield-Hill b Woolston	11
A Stonehouse, c Winfield-Hill b Woolston	9
T Brits, lbw b Levick	17
J E M Spence, c Tryon b Levick	13
C A E Hill, c Tryon b Hall	63
K Moore, c Winfield-Hill b Hall	0
M Blinkhorn-Jones, c and b Marlow	10
B J Miles, c Turner b Hall	28
D E M Carter, b Hall	2
P A Chatterji, not out	15
* D L Gregory, run out (Hall)	4
Extras b 4, lb 3, w 25, nb 1	33
Total (46 overs)	205

FoW: 1-13 (Chathli), 2-24 (Stonehouse), 3-49 (Brits), 4-66 (Spence), 5-67 (Moore), 6-91 (Blinkhorn-Jones), 7-172 (Miles), 8-180 (Carter), 9-185 (Hill), 10-205 (Gregory)

	O	M	R	W
Scott	10	1	34	0
Woolston	10	2	29	2
Levick	10	0	37	2
Hall	8	0	33	4
Marlow	4	0	31	1
Tryon	4	0	34	0

NORTHERN DIAMONDS

§ * L Winfield-Hill, not out		116
S L Kalis, run out (Spence/Chathli)		6
E K Marlow, lbw b Carter		20
P E Turner, c Miles b Carter		2
C L Tryon, not out		57
L Dobson		
R E Duckworth		
L E Scott	Did not bat	
K A Levick		
G E Hall		
J A Woolston		
Extras w 5, nb 3		8
Total ((3 wkts, 33 overs)		209

FoW: 1-33 (Kalis), 2-82 (Marlow), 3-86 (Turner)

	O	M	R	W
Stonehouse	4	0	44	0
Miles	8	2	34	0
Chatterji	5	0	29	0
Carter	5	0	31	2
Gregory	7	0	47	0
Moore	4	0	24	0

Umpires: N J Llong and F B Richards   Scorers: L Martin and S E Robinson

Rachael Heyhoe-Flint Trophy
The Blaze v. Northern Diamonds

Played at Queen's Park, Chesterfield, on July 7, 2023
The Blaze won by 9 wickets

Toss won by Northern Diamonds   The Blaze 5 points, Northern Diamonds 0 points

NORTHERN DIAMONDS

§ L Winfield-Hill, b Higham	56
S L Kalis, c Boyce b Gordon	12
* H J Armitage, c Kelly b Gordon	8
E K Marlow, c S J Bryce b Higham	11
B A M Heath, c Kelly b Munro	25
L Dobson, c K E Bryce b McCarthy	24
P E Turner, b Munro	0
L E Scott, b Munro	0
K A Levick, c S J Bryce b McCarthy	1
G E Hall, not out	21
J A Woolston, c Kelly b Graves	13
Extras lb 5, w 8, nb 1	14
Total (45 5 overs)	185

FoW: 1-55 (Kalis), 2-71 (Armitage), 3-92 (Marlow), 4-105 (Winfield-Hill), 5-131 (Heath), 6-131 (Turner), 7-145 (Scott), 8-146 (Dobson), 9-147 (Levick), 10-185 (Woolston)

	O	M	R	W
K E Bryce	6	0	31	0
Munro	10	2	35	3
McCarthy	9	1	17	2
Gordon	10	1	38	2
Higham	8	1	35	2
Graves	2.5	0	24	1

THE BLAZE

M Kelly, b Levick		16
T T Beaumont, not out		83
§ S J Bryce, not out		53
G E B Boyce		
K E Bryce		
M L Kirk		
T M Graves	Did not bat	
S E N Munro		
L F Higham		
* K L Gordon		
C M McCarthy		
Extras lb 12, w 25		37
Total (1 wkt, 24.5 overs)		189

FoW: 1-33 (Kelly)

	O	M	R	W
Scott	4	0	25	0
Woolston	6	0	43	0
Levick	6	0	40	1
Hall	4	0	32	0
Armitage	4.5	0	37	0

Umpires: J D Middlebrook and F B Richards   Scorers: I Howe and S J Stringfellow

Rachael Heyhoe-Flint Trophy
Northern Diamonds v. Thunder

Played at Clifton Park, York, on July 11, 2023
Thunder won by 6 wickets

Toss won by Thunder

Thunder 5 points, Northern Diamonds 0 points

NORTHERN DIAMONDS

§ L Winfield-Hill, c Threlkeld b Dattani	33
S L Kalis, b Jackson	21
* H J Armitage, b Dattani	6
E K Marlow, run out (Heap/Threlkeld)	9
B A M Heath, run out (Dottin/Threlkeld)	17
C L Tryon, b Morris	14
L Dobson, c Smale b Heap	13
L E Scott, c Dottin b Heap	6
K A Levick, c Morris b Dattani	11
G E Hall, c Threlkeld b Dattani	13
J A Woolston, not out	4
Extras b 1, lb 2, w 17	20
Total (43.5 overs)	167

FoW: 1-58 (Winfield-Hill), 2-58 (Kalis), 3-73 (Armitage), 4-88 (Marlow), 5-110 (Heath), 6-117 (Tryon), 7-135 (Dobson), 8-136 (Scott), 9-160 (Levick), 10-167 (Hall)

	O	M	R	W
Gaur	6	0	20	0
Norris	5	0	20	0
Dattani	6.5	1	16	4
Jackson	3	0	21	1
Morris	10	3	27	1
Lamb	6	0	29	0
Heap	4	1	11	2
Dottin	3	0	20	0

THUNDER

E L Lamb, lbw b Levick	21
S A Smale, b Scott	15
N D Dattani, lbw b Tryon	46
F M K Morris, b Levick	0
D J S Dottin, not out	54
* § E Threlkeld, not out	10
D L Collins	
L N Heap	
T G Norris	Did not bat
M Gaur	
L E Jackson	
Extras b 5, lb 3, w 13, nb 1	22
Total (4 wkts, 38.4 overs)	168

FoW: 1-32 (Smale), 2-58 (Lamb), 3-58 (Morris), 4-156 (Dattani)

	O	M	R	W
Scott	10	0	42	1
Woolston	8	0	32	0
Levick	8	0	43	2
Hall	3	0	14	0
Tryon	9.4	1	29	1

Umpires: A E Clark and A C Harris

Scorers: M Brooks and S Pollard

Rachael Heyhoe-Flint Trophy
Northern Diamonds v. Central Sparks

Played at Headingley, Leeds, on July 15, 2023
Central Sparks won by 5 wickets (DLS method)

Toss won by Central Sparks   Central Sparks 4 points, Northern Diamonds 0 points

NORTHERN DIAMONDS

§ L Winfield Hill, b Davis	28
S L Kalis, c Freeborn b George	36
* H J Armitage, c Burns b Davis	66
E K Marlow, c Ellis b George	22
B A M Heath, not out	49
C L Tryon, not out	1
L Dobson	
L E Scott	
K A Levick	Did not bat
G E Hall	
J A Woolston	
Extras b 1, lb 4, w 14, nb 2	21
Total ((4 wkts, 34 overs)	223

FoW: 1-60 (Winfield-Hill), 2-83 (Kalis), 3-131 (Marlow), 4-197 (Armitage)

	O	M	R	W
Potts	5	0	28	0
Wong	5	1	36	0
George	7	0	46	2
Davis	4	0	40	2
Ellis	5	0	26	0
Burns	8	0	42	0

CENTRAL SPARKS

Target to win 164 runs off 19 overs

* E Jones, c Woolston b Hall	26
E A Burns, c Marlow b Woolston	10
§ A J Freeborn, b Levick	10
K L George, b Levick	56
A Campbell, b Levick	27
I E C M Wong, not out	1
C R Pavely, not out	2
B L Ellis	
D S T Perrin	Did not bat
G K Davis	
G E A Potts	
Extras b 8, lb 8, w 16	32
Total (5 wkts, 18.4 overs)	164

FoW: 1-41 (Burns), 2-60 (Freeborn), 3-89 (Jones), 4-161 (George). 5-162 (Campbell)

	O	M	R	W
Woolston	4	0	24	1
Scott	2	0	21	0
Tryon	4	0	36	0
Levick	3.4	0	31	3
Hall	2	0	17	1
Armitage	3	0	19	0

Umpires: G Bambury and S Widdup   Scorers: J R Virr and S Pollard

Rachael Heyhoe-Flint Trophy
Southern Vipers v. Northern Diamonds

Played at Arundel Castle on July 22, 2023
No result

Toss won by Southern Vipers   Northern Diamonds 2 points, Southern Vipers 2 points

NORTHERN DIAMONDS

§ L Winfield-Hill, b Taylor	8
S L Kalis, c Adams b Brown	3
* H J Armitage, c Southby b Adams	48
E K Marlow, not out	25
R E Duckworth, b Adams	0
C L Tryon, not out	11
L Dobson	
L E Scott	
K A Levick	Did not bat
R E Slater	
J A Woolston	
Extras lb 2, w 8	10
Total (4 wkts, 25.4 overs)	105

FoW: 1-5 (Kalis), 2-24 (Winfield-Hill), 3-82 (Armitage), 4-82 (Duckworth)

	O	M	R	W
Brown	4	1	14	1
Smith	5	1	13	0
Taylor	3	0	10	1
Dean	7	0	29	0
Monaghan	2	0	14	0
Adams	4.4	0	23	2

SOUTHERN VIPERS

E M McCaughan	
M E Bouchier	
* G L Adams	
E L Windsor	
F G Kemp	
C E Dean	Did not bat
M J Brown	
L C N Smith	
A Z Monaghan	
§ R M Southby	
M L L Taylor	

Umpires: A C Harris and B J Peverall   Scorers: C L Green and R V Isaacs

Rachael Heyhoe-Flint Trophy
Northern Diamonds v. Southern Vipers

Played at Roseworth Terrace, Gosforth, on September 5, 2023
Southern Vipers won by 3 runs

Toss won by Southern Vipers   Southern Vipers 4 points, Northern Diamonds 0 points

SOUTHERN VIPERS

E M McCaughan, c and b Hall	47
A E M Norgrove, b Scott	6
* G L Adams, b Turner	82
G A Elwiss, c Winfield-Hill b Hall	22
E L Windsor, c Turner b Hall	39
N M Faltum, c sub (E Whiting) b Scott	7
N H Harman, lbw b Scott	1
A Z Monaghan, c Scott b Hall	8
M L L Taylor, not out	3
§ R M Southby, not out	15
A G Lee Did not bat	
Extras b 3, lb 5, w 22, nb 1	31
Total ((8 wkts, 50 overs)	261

FoW: 1-18 (Norgrove), 2-127 (McCaughan), 3-169 (Adams), 4-207 (Elwiss), 5-226 (Faltum), 6-228 (Harman), 7-242 (Windsor), 8-245 (Monaghan)

	O	M	R	W
Scott	9	1	33	3
Woolston	5	0	29	0
Turner	10	0	64	1
Levick	10	2	43	0
Hall	10	0	46	4
Armitage	6	0	38	0

NORTHERN DIAMONDS

§ L Winfield-Hill, lbw b Lee	29
S L Kalis, lbw b Adams	37
* H J Armitage, not out	106
E K Marlow, c and b Harman	20
R E Duckworth, c Harman b Monaghan	23
L Dobson, b Elwiss	20
P E Turner, not out	2
G E Hall	
L E Scott Did not bat	
K A Levick	
J A Woolston	
Extras b 3, lb 1, w 17	21
Total (5 wkts)	258

FoW: 1-52 (Winfield-Hill), 2-98 (Kalis), 3-159 (Marlow), 4-203 (Duckworth), 5-254 (Dobson)

	O	M	R	W
Taylor	10	0	57	0
Adams	10	0	34	1
Lee	10	1	32	1
Monaghan	8	0	54	1
Elwiss	7	0	46	1
Harman	5	0	31	1

Umpires: A E Clark and J D Middlebrook   Scorers: G Maddison and P Summerside

Rachael Heyhoe-Flint Trophy
Western Storm v. Northern Diamonds

Played at The Cooper Associates County Ground, Taunton, on September 10, 2023
Northern Diamonds won by 31 runs

Toss won by Western Storm   Northern Diamonds 4 points, Southern Vipers 0 points

NORTHERN DIAMONDS

§ L Winfield-Hill, c Wilson b Robbins	83
S L Kalis, run out (Robbins)	45
* H J Armitage, c Griffiths b Robbins	45
L Dobson, not out	68
E K Marlow, not out	23
R E Duckworth	
P E Turner	
G E Hall Did not bat	
L E Scott	
K A Levick	
S Turner	
Extras b 4, lb 4, w 9	17
Total (3 wkts)	281

FoW: 1-101 (Kalis), 2-177 (Armitage), 3-288 (Winfield-Hill)

	O	M	R	W
Robbins	9	1	41	2
Lane	5	0	35	0
Smale	5	0	34	0
Griffiths	9	0	69	0
Skelton	6	1	38	0
Harvey	7	0	37	0
Holland	2	0	19	0

WESTERN STORM

A C Griffiths, lbw b Scott	1
E V Corney, c Winfield-Hill b S Turner	10
* S N Luff, st Winfield-Hill b Levick	87
F C Wilson, c Duckworth b Armitage	57
N F Holland, b Levick	5
§ N A J Wraith, c Kalis b Scott	61
S A E Smale, run out (Scott)	5
C N Skelton, not out	9
N Harvey, not out	1
M J Robbins	
G L Lane Did not bat	
Extras lb 3, w 10, nb 1	14
Total (7 wkts, 43 overs)	250

FoW: 1-8 (Griffiths), 2-44 (Corney), 3-124 (Wilson), 4-135 (Holland), 5-204 (Luff), 6-239 (Wraith), 7-241 (Smale)

	O	M	R	W
S Turner	7	0	31	1
Scott	7	0	30	2
Hall	9	0	51	0
Levick	9	0	61	2
P E Turner	3	0	22	0
Armitage	8	0	52	1

Umpires: R Dovey and S Widdup   Scorers: L M Rhodes and Szczepanski

Rachael Heyhoe-Flint Trophy
Thunder v. Northern Diamonds

Played at Sale Cricket Club on September 13, 2023
Northern Diamonds won by 48 runs

Toss won by Thunder   Northern Diamonds 5 points, Thunder 0 points

NORTHERN DIAMONDS

§ L Winfield-Hill, b Norris	89
S L Kalis, b Graham	8
* H J Armitage, b Jones	9
E K Marlow, lbw b Jones	10
R E Duckworth, b Bell	27
L Dobson, c Heap b Bell	6
P E Turner, c Dattani b Bell	9
L E Scott, not out	11
G E Hall, c and b Bell	2
K A Levick, b Dattani	14
J A Woolston, b Dattani	3
Extras lb 2, w 6	8
Total ((46.4 overs)	196

FoW: 1-23 (Kalis), 2-51 (Armitage), 3-83 (Marlow), 4-129 (Duckworth), 5-151 (Winfield-Hill), 6-151 (Dobson), 7-163 (Turner), 8-169 (Levick), 9-188 (Hall), 10-196 (Woolston)

	O	M	R	W
Norris	6	0	35	1
Graham	6	0	32	1
Jones	10	2	34	2
Dattani	4.4	0	33	2
Morris	10	0	28	0
Bell	10	0	32	4

THUNDER

S A Smale, c Winfield-Hill b Turner	33
L N Heap, b Woolston	14
N D Dattani, c Winfield-Hill b Levick	16
F M K Morris, lbw b Levick	0
* § E Threlkeld, c Marlow b Turner	31
L K Delany, not out	23
D E Mullan, b Turner	0
T G Norris, lbw b Levick	1
P C Graham, lbw b Levick	0
O N Bell, run out (Armitage/Winfield-Hill)	8
H L Jones, run out (Dobson/Winfield-Hill)	2
Extras lb 1, w 19	20
Total (33.4 overs)	148

FoW: 1-27 (Heap), 2-54 (Dattani). 3-54 (Morris), 4-92 (Smale), 5-110 (Threlkeld), 6-110 (Mullan), 7-114 (Norris), 8-114 (Graham), 9-140 (Bell), 10-148 (Jones)

	O	M	R	W
Scott	7	0	38	0
Woolston	4	0	27	1
Levick	10	1	28	4
Hall	7.4	0	36	0
Turner	5	1	18	3

Umpires: J Ibbotson and N Ashraf   Scorers: I A F Bevers and M U Naeem

Rachael Heyhoe-Flint Trophy
Northern Diamonds v. Sunrisers

Played at Seat Unique Riverside, Chester-le-Street, on September 16, 2023
Sunrisers won by 6 wickets (DLS method)

Toss won by Sunrisers   Sunrisers 4 points, Northern Diamonds 0 points

NORTHERN DIAMONDS

§ L Winfield-Hill, b Gray	1
S L Kalis, c Castle b Grewcock	28
* H J Armitage, b Gray	13
R E Duckworth, c Scrivens b Castle	5
B A M Heath, c Miller b Villiers	37
L Dobson, c Villiers b Scrivens	16
P E Turner, not out	0
S Turner, not out	4
G E Hall	
K A Levick	Did not bat
L E Scott	
Extras lb 1, w 9	10
Total (6 wkts, 18 overs)	114

FoW: 1-4 (Winfield-Hill), 2-26 (Armitage), 3-51 (Kalis), 4-73 (Duckworth), 5-106 (Heath), 6-110 (Dobson)

	O	M	R	W
Gray	5	0	24	2
Coppack	4	0	18	0
Castle	3	0	17	1
Grewcock	2	0	15	1
Villiers	2	0	24	1
Scrivens	2	0	15	1

SUNRISERS

Target to win: 126 runs off 18 overs

* G E Scrivens, b S Turner	11
A Dowse, c Kalis b Hall	27
§ A D Carr, b Hall	29
M K Villiers, c Dobson b P E Turner	1
J L Gardner, not out	30
F H Miller, not out	20
J L Grewcock	
A Surenkumar	
E Gray	Dids not bat
K S Castle	
K L Coppack	
Extras b 2, lb 2, w 4	8
Total (4 wkts, 17.3 overs)	126

FoW: 1-20 (Scrivens), 2-59 (Dowse), 3-60 (Villiers), 4-77 (Carr)

	O	M	R	W
Scott	3.3	0	26	0
S Turner	3	0	22	1
P E Turner	3	0	16	1
K A Levick	4	0	22	0
G E Hall	4	0	36	2

Umpires: G Brown and H M S Adnan   Scorers: G Maddinson and G McGurk

SWAGGER TURNS TO STUMBLE IN HAT-TRICK OF DEFEATS

By Graham Hardcastle

The Diamonds missing out on qualification for Finals Day — what would have been their second appearance in three seasons — was a particular disappointment due to the fast start they had made to a competition sandwiched in between the first and second half of the 50-over Rachael Heyhoe Flint Trophy.

Four wins on the spin through late May were achieved with quality and swagger. They were odds on to qualify for New Road on June 10...but it wasn't to be, and they were pipped to the post by cross-Pennine rivals Thunder, who beat them comfortably in a final day winner-takes-all group-stage contest at Blackpool.

That was the last of three campaign-ending defeats in succession, leaving Thunder, Southern Vipers and group-stage winners the Blaze to contest Finals Day. Defending title-holders the Vipers won again, beating the Blaze during a reserve day after torrential rain had interrupted the Saturday final.

Yet there were still positives for Diamonds coach Dani Hazell to reflect upon.

Captain Hollie Armitage shone with 216 runs in seven matches, including a standout 82 in a thrilling victory over South East Stars at The Oval. She was the fourth leading run-scorer in the competition — and that was where leg-spinner Katie Levick finished on the list of leading wicket-takers: she stood out with 12 victims, including a best of 5-19 in the home win over Sunrisers at Headingley.

Fledgling seamer Grace Hall, in her maiden taste of senior regional cricket, wasn't far behind Levick's success. The then 20-year-old — she celebrated her 21st birthday on Christmas Eve — excelled with 10 wickets from her seven appearances.

York-born Hall has a deceptive, slingy action and all the tricks of the trade required to be a top-drawer short-form bowler, and she broke through into 50-over cricket during the second half of the summer.

Northern Diamonds v. Western Storm: Headingley, May 19.

Brutal innings of 98 and 74 from Lauren Winfield-Hill and Hollie Armitage led Diamonds to a record-breaking 218-3 total in a landslide opening night floodlit victory by 32 runs.

LAUREN WINFIELD-HILL   **GRACE HALL**

Never in two years of regional cricket had a team posted more than the 186-1 Thunder scored against Sunrisers at Emirates Old Trafford in 2021, but the Diamonds cruised beyond that inside only 17 overs, having been inserted.

They took advantage of a short boundary towards the West Stand side and a fast outfield, though captain Armitage hoisted five of her six sixes to the longer leg-side boundary in a 36-ball assault. Winfield-Hill batted with more poise, hitting 21 boundaries in 56 balls.

Storm, minus England captain Heather Knight — she was absent despite being named in the match-day squad — were spirited in response as they totalled 186-8, but no one could support opener Danielle Gibson's 52 as debutant seamer Hall, Lizzie Scott, Levick and Abi Glen all struck.

Central Sparks v. Northern Diamonds: Edgbaston, May 23.

Diamonds won by three runs in a low-scoring thriller. The visitors recovered from losing nine wickets for 62 in 135 all out, and then squeezed the home side's batting on a used surface before South African overseas all-rounder Chloe Tryon successfully defended 13 off the last over with four wickets remaining.

Opener Leah Dobson top-scored with 41, and Tryon claimed 3-30 with her left-arm spin. Approximately 1,500 school children who were invited to watch on a Tuesday morning into the early afternoon saw the Diamonds lose their way against spin from 73-1 in the ninth over. They duly made amends with a tigerish bowling and fielding display.

Abbey Freeborn hit four fours off the otherwise fabulous Lizzie Scott as 20 came from the 18th over to lift the hosts to 118-6 with two overs left. Scott had bowled three overs for 11 runs against a Sparks top order including England's Amy Jones as they slipped to 76-5 in the 15th over of the chase. Levick with 1-21 from four conceded only five runs in the 19th over before Tryon did the trick in the last.

South East Stars v. Northern Diamonds: Kia Oval, May 26.

Captain Armitage and fast bowler Scott — with bat in hand — were the heroes as the Diamonds clinched a last-ball thriller by two wickets to extend their winning start.

Scott hit the fixture's last ball for four when three were needed in pursuit of 139, while Armitage hit a brilliant career-best 82 off 59 balls to anchor the chase before falling as the target became six off the last over with three wickets left. A further wicket fell before Scott carved the last ball from Alice Davidson-Richards over point to spark wild scenes of celebration in the Diamonds' dug-out.

Hall had impressed with 3-20, including the key wicket of England star Sophia Dunkley for 12, as the Stars were restricted to 138-7. Scott bowled three brilliant overs of seam, 1-11, before going in to bat with nine balls remaining and adding a crucial six not out off five balls.

Armitage had that Friday feeling after scoring her second fifty, and international Alice Capsey stood out for the Stars with 71 off 48 balls.

Northern Diamonds v. Sunrisers: Headingley, May 28.

Levick claimed a fabulous 5-19 as the Diamonds won by 35 runs to continue their perfect start to their bid for T20 silverware, this match part of a Sunday double-header with Yorkshire's men.

Dobson's 47 and late firepower from Bess Heath — 31 off 14 balls — lifted the hosts to 172-7, which always appeared a tough ask for a Sunrisers side who had lost their first three matches. A superb bowling display led by Levick ensured Sunrisers fell well short at 137 all out. Heath also claimed three stumpings and a catch behind.

The Diamonds struck at regular intervals. Levick was outstanding with her third career T20 five-for, her first for the Diamonds, and took three wickets in an over as Sunrisers were bowled out inside 19 overs.

Dobson hit four successive boundaries off Eva Gray's seam in the sixth over to take the score to 48-1 after Armitage had elected to bat. She was strong on both sides of the wicket in laying a platform for what proved to be a winning total.

BESS HEATH   **LIZZIE SCOTT**

The Blaze v. Northern Diamonds: Riverside, June 2.

Hollie Armitage's side suffered their first defeat, going down by six wickets to a Blaze side who booked their place at Finals Day, courtesy of success in Durham. The Diamonds were limited to a below-par 129-7, a total the visitors reeled in with ease thanks to Sarah Bryce's opening 67 off 43 balls.

Despite this being a sluggish pitch the visitors' batting should have been better as their top order failed to capitalise on a series of starts. Winfield-Hill top-scored with 40, while Dobson and Heath made 19 apiece, Armitage 23, and Tryon 20.

Tryon's fellow South African international, Nadine de Klerk, impressed with 3-31 for Blaze, including the wicket of her compatriot.

Blaze then raced to their target thanks to Bryce's exploits in a contest which would have seen either side qualify for Finals Day with victory. Unfortunately for the Diamonds, it wasn't them.

Northern Diamonds v. Southern Vipers: Headingley, June 4.

The hosts were beaten by a nail-biting 16-run margin, which saw both sides recover from the loss of early wickets. The Vipers posted 144-6, and defended it to prevent the Diamonds, with 128-9, securing a place at Finals Day with a win.

Diamonds held onto third place in the table ahead of the final round of fixtures, and they knew a win over Thunder would seal a place at Finals Day. This was a see-saw affair, befitting the battles both teams

CHLOE TRYON

LEAH DOBSON

have had across the first three years of regional action.

The Vipers were 49-5 before recovering to set a 145 target, but the Diamonds slipped to 5-3, recovered to 99-4...and slipped to 128-9. England legend Anya Shrubsole claimed a stunning 4-18 in four overs for Vipers, including each of the first three wickets with the new ball.

Levick starred with 2-12 from four overs for the Diamonds, while Sterre Kalis top-scored with 32. It wasn't enough.

Thunder v. Northern Diamonds: Blackpool, June 7.

It was heartache for the Diamonds as they missed out on Finals Day, Thunder qualifying instead courtesy of a victory by seven wickets.

Teenaged Scottish off-spinner Liv Bell starred with 3-9 from three overs in only her third senior regional appearance as the Diamonds were put out for 96. The hosts knocked off the target in 15 overs to secure a five-point victory thanks to an unbeaten 42 off 34 balls from Fi Morris.

Diamonds elected to bat, but Thunder piled on the pressure with some excellent bowling and fielding to hold them to the lowest total of the 2023 competition. Only Sterre Kalis (24) and Chloe Tryon (22) reached 20. All-rounder Morris was one of three bowlers who struck twice apiece before her 42 not out contributed decisively to the chase.

Charlotte Edwards Cup
Northern Diamonds v. Western Storm

Played at Headingley, Leeds, on May 18, 2023
Northern Diamonds won by 32 runs

Toss won by Western Storm   Northern Diamonds 4 points, Western Storm 0 points

NORTHERN DIAMONDS

L Winfield-Hill, c Gibson b Skelton	98
L Dobson, b Filer	25
* H J Armitage, c Gibson b Prendergast	74
§ B A M Heath, not out	8
C L L Tryon, not out	7
S L Kalis	
K J G Fraser	
A A Glen	Did not bat
L E Scott	
K A Levick	
G E Hall	
Extras lb 2, w 2, nb 2	6
Total (3 wkts, 20 overs)	218

FoW: 1-58 (Dobson), 2-197 (Winfield-Hill), 3-202 (Armitage)

	O	M	R	W
Gibson	4	0	28	0
Filer	2	0	30	1
Prendergast	4	0	32	1
Smale	3	0	38	0
Skelton	4	0	35	1
Griffiths	2	0	30	0
Holland	1	0	23	0

WESTERN STORM

§ N A J Wright, c Hall b Scott	16
D R Gibson, c Tryon b Hall	52
O P Prendergast, c Heath b Scott	14
F C Wilson, lbw b Levick	16
* S N Luff, c Hall b Levick	9
A C Griffiths, b Glen	31
L L Filer, c Tryon b Hall	21
N F Holland, c and b Glen	11
K A Jones, not out	4
S A E Smale, not out	1
C N Skelton	Did not bat
Extras w 11	11
Total (8 wkts)	186

FoW: 1-19 (Wraith), 2-35 (Prendergast), 3-73 (Wilson), 4-103 (Luff), 5-121 (Gibson), 6-164 (Griffiths), 7-165 (Filer), 8-184 (Holland)

	O	M	R	W
Hall	4	0	41	2
Scott	4	0	27	2
Tryon	3	0	34	0
Levick	3	0	25	2
Glen	4	0	36	2
Fraser	2	0	23	0

Umpires: H M S Adnan and G Bambury   Scorers: A M Cregan and J R Emmerson

Charlotte Edwards Cup
Central Sparks v. Northern Diamonds

Played at Edgbaston, Birmingham, on May 23, 2023
Northern Diamond won by 3 runs

Toss won by Central Sparks   Northern Diamonds 4 points, Central Sparks 0 points

NORTHERN DIAMONDS

L Winfield-Hill, c Burns b Arlott	0
L Dobson, b Davis	41
* H J Armitage, c E Jones b Burns	27
S L Kalis, st A E Jones b Davis	10
§ B A M Heath, run out (George)	4
C L L Tryon, c George b Davis	2
K J G Fraser, c and b Burns	26
A A Glen, b George	3
L E Scott, c E Jones b Potts	3
K A Levick, not out	1
G E Hall, c Perrin b Arlott	1
Extras b 4, lb 3, w 10	17
Total (19.3 overs)	135

FoW: 1-5 (Winfield-Hill), 2-73 (Dobson), 3-85 (Kalis), 4-91 (Heath), 5-92 (Armitage), 6-113 (Tryon), 7-120 (Glen), 8-126 (Scott), 9-134 (Fraser), 10-135 (Hall)

	O	M	R	W
Potts	4	0	28	1
Arlott	3.3	0	14	2
Wong	2	0	21	0
Davis	4	0	13	3
George	2	0	24	1
Burns	4	0	28	2

CENTRAL SPARKS

* E Jones, c Dobson b Levick	30
D S T Perrin, c Scott b Fraser	1
§ A E Jones, b Tryon	16
E A Burns, c Winfield-Hill b Tryon	12
A Campbell, c Armitage b Hall	8
E L Arlott, not out	28
A J Freeborn, c Kalis b Scott	22
K L George, c Fraser b Tryon	5
I E C M Wong, not out	6
G K Davis	
G E A Potts Dids not bat	
Extras lb 1, w 2, nb 1	4
Total (7 wkts)	132

FoW: 1-10 (Perrin), 2-40 (A E Jones), 3-57 (E Jones), 4-64 (Burns), 5-76 (Campbell), 6-114 (Freeborn), 7-126 (George)

	O	M	R	W
Fraser	3	0	17	1
Scott	4	0	31	1
Tryon	4	0	30	3
Levick	4	0	21	1
Hall	3	0	18	1
Glen	2	0	14	0

Umpires: A C Harris and A Y Harris   Scorers: H S Eccleston and M D Smith

Charlotte Edwards Cup
South East Stars v. Northern Diamonds

Played at The Kia Oval on May 26, 2023
Northern Diamonds won by 2 wickets

Toss won by Northern Diamonds   Northern Diamonds 4 points, South East Stars 0 points

SOUTH EAST STARS

* B F Smith, c Hall b Tryon	14
S I R Dunkley, c Tryon b Hall	12
A R Capsey, c Tryon b Glen	71
N E Farrant, c Dobson b Scott	2
P A Franklin, b Levick	11
P J Scholfield, c Dobson b Hall	6
A N Davidson-Richards, c Glen b Hall	8
§ K M Chathli, not out	3
F R Davies, not out	8
C A R Cooper	
D L Gregory Did not bat	
Extras w 3	3
Total (7 wkts)	138

FoW: 1-22 (Dunkley), 2-28 (Smith), 3-33 (Farrant), 4-76 (Franklin), 5-94 (Scholfield), 6-126 (Davidson-Richards), 7-129 (Capsey)

	O	M	R	W
Fraser	2	0	12	0
Scott	3	0	11	1
Tryon	4	0	31	1
Hall	4	0	20	3
Levick	3	0	29	1
Glen	4	0	35	1

NORTHERN DIAMONDS

L Winfield-Hill, c Capsey b Cooper	1
L Dobson, run out (Davies)	1
* H J Armitage, st Chathli b Davies	82
S L Kalis, b Gregory	18
§ B A M Heath, c Capsey b Cooper	19
C L L Tryon, st Chathli b Cooper	2
K J G Fraser, run out (Dunkley/Davies)	1
A A Glen, c Chathli b Davidson-Richards	1
L E Scott, not out	6
K A Levick, not out	2
G E Hall Did not bat	
Extras lb3, w 4	7
Total (8 wkts)	140

FoW: 1-2 (Dobson), 2-6 (Winfield-Hill), 3-55 (Kalis), 4-93 (Heath), 5-113 (Tryon), 6-121 (Fraser), 7-131 (Armitage), 8-133 (Glen)

	O	M	R	W
Cooper	4	0	12	3
Davies	4	0	30	1
Franklin	2	0	14	0
Davidson-Richards	3	0	23	1
Gregory	2	0	16	1
Scholfield	3	0	27	0
Smith	2	0	15	0

Player of the Match: H J Armitage

Umpires: B J Debenham and A Y Harris   Scorers: D Beesley and M Shepherd

Charlotte Edwards Cup
Northern Diamonds v. Sunrisers

Played at Headingley, Leeds, on May 28, 2023
Northern Diamonds won by 35 runs

Toss won by Northern Diamonds   Northern Diamonds 5 points, Sunrisers 0 points

NORTHERN DIAMONDS

L Winfield-Hill,, c Maqsood b Castle	19
L Dobson, c Miller b Scrivens	47
* H J Armitage, c Castle b Scrivens	8
S L Kalis, st Carr b Villiers	29
§ B A M Heath, st Carr b Castle	31
C L L Tryon, not out	12
K J G Fraser, c Scrivens b Gardner	4
A A Glen, run out (Griffith/Scrivens)	7
L E Scott	
K A Levick Did not bat	
G E Hall	
Extras pen 5, lb 4, w 6	15
Total (7 wkts)	172

FoW: 1-23 (Winfield-Hill), 2-48 (Armitage), 3-111 (Dobson), 4-130 (Kalis), 5-152 (Heath), 6-157 (Fraser), 7-172 (Glen)

	O	M	R	W
Villiers	4	0	24	1
Gray	2	0	21	0
Scrivens	4	0	24	2
Castle	4	0	37	2
Maqsood	3	0	32	0
Gardner	3	0	25	1

SUNRISERS

M K Villiers, lbw b Tryon	6
D van Nierkerk, c Heath b Scott	14
A J MacLeod, b Levick	21
C L Griffith, c Tryon b Levick	18
G E Scrivens, st Heath b Tryon	50
J L Gardner, c Winfield-Hill b Hall	13
E Gray, st Heath b Levick	3
F H Miller, st Heath b Levick	2
§ A D Carr, c Glen b Levick	0
* K S Castle, not out	2
A M Maqsood, c Winfield-Hill b Hall	2
Extras w 6	6
Total (18.4 overs)	137

FoW: 1-20 (van Nierkerk), 2-30 (Villers), 3-41 (MacLeod), 4-74 (Griffith), 5-103 (Gardner), 6-125 (Gray), 7-127 (Miller), 8-127 (Carr), 9-131 (Scrivens), 10-137 (Maqsood)

	O	M	R	W
Fraser	3	0	39	0
Scott	4	1	18	1
Tryon	4	0	22	2
Levick	4	0	19	5
Hall	2.4	0	27	2
Glen	1	0	12	0

Umpires: P Mustard and S Widdup   Scorers: J T Potter sand A Hinchliffe

Charlotte Edwards Cup
Northern Diamonds v. The Blaze

Played at Seat Unique Riverside, Chester-le-Street, on June 2, 2023
The Blaze won by 6 wickets

Toss won by Northern Diamonds   The Blaze 5 points, Northern Diamonds 0 points

NORTHERN DIAMONDS

L Winfield-Hill, b Munro	40
L Dobson, b Gordon	19
* H J Armitage, c Kirk b Gordon	23
§ B A M Heath, c Gordon b de Klerk	19
C L L Tryon, b de Klerk	20
S L Kalis, run out (Gordon)	0
K J G Fraser, not out	5
L E Scott, b de Klerk	0
A A Glen	
K A Levick Did not bat	
G E Hall	
Extras w 3	3
Total (7 wkts)	129

FoW: 1-33 (Dobson), 2-80 (Armitage), 3-100 (Winfield-Hill), 4-117 (Heath), 5-117 (Kalis), 6-129 (Tryon), 7-129 (Scott)

	O	M	R	W
Higham	4	0	23	0
Ballinger	3	1	10	0
de Klerk	4	0	31	3
Gordon	4	0	29	2
Bryce	2	0	12	0
Groves	1	0	9	0
Munro	2	0	15	1

THE BLAZE

M Kelly, b Scott	19
§ S J Bryce, not out	67
G E B Boyce, b Tryon	15
K E Bryce, b Glen	2
M L Kirk, b Glen	0
N de Klerk, not out	21
S E N Munro	
L F Higham	
* K L Gordon Did not bat	
J P Groves	
G Ballinger	
Extras b 4, lb 1, w 4	9
Total (4 wkts, 15.4 overs)	133

FoW: 1-28 (Kelly), 2-88 (Boyce), 3-96 (K E Bryce), 4-96 (Kirk)

	O	M	R	W
Tryon	3.4	0	29	1
Scott	3	0	26	1
Fraser	1	0	10	0
Levick	2	0	19	0
Hall	3	0	21	0
Glen	3	0	23	2

Umpires: J Ibbotson and S Widdup   Scorers: S Blacklock and G Maddinson

Charlotte Edwards Cup
Northern Diamonds v. Southern Vipers

Played at Headingley, Leeds, on June 4, 2023
Southern Vipers won by 16 runs

Toss won by Southern Vipers   Southern Vipers 4 points, Northern Diamonds 0 points

SOUTHERN VIPERS

E M McCaughan, c Hall b Tryon	8
M E Bouchier, c Armitage b Hall	24
§ N L Faltum, c Fraser b Scott	4
* G L Adams, not out	42
G A Elwiss, lbw b Levick	2
F G Kemp, b Hall	0
E L Windsor, b Levick	25
N H Harman, not out	32
L C N Smith	
M L L Taylor Did not bat	
A Shrubsole	
Extras lb 1, w 5, nb 1	7
Total (6 wkts)	144

FoW: 1-8 (McCaughan), 2-14 (Faltum), 3-38 (Bouchier), 4-48 (Elwiss), 5-49 (Kemp), 6-92 (Windsor)

	O	M	R	W
Tryon	4	0	33	1
Scott	4	0	20	1
Hall	3	0	33	2
Glen	4	0	37	0
Levick	4	0	12	2
Fraser	1	0	8	0

NORTHERN DIAMONDS

L Winfield-Hill, b Shrubsole	1
L Dobson, c McCaughan b Shrubsole	0
* H J Armitage, c Elwiss b Shrubsole	2
S L Kalis, c Adams b Shrubsole	32
§ B A M Heath, lbw b Taylor	26
C L Tryon, c Smith b Elwiss	30
K J G Fraser, c Kemp b Elwiss	0
A A Glen, not out	13
L E Scott, st Faltum b Adams	5
K A Levick, run out (Faltum)	4
G E Hall, not out	4
Extras lb 2, w 9	11
Total (9 wkts)	128

FoW: 1-1 (Winfield-Hill), 2-2 (Dobson), 3-5 (Armitage), 4-46 (Heath), 5-99 (Tryon), 6-99 (Fraser), 7-105 (Kalis), 8-115 (Scott), 9-123 (Levick)

	O	M	R	W
Smith	4	0	17	0
Shrubsole	4	0	18	4
Adams	4	0	34	1
Taylor	3	0	27	1
Harmon	1	0	10	0
Elwiss	4	0	20	2

Umpires: J Ibbotson and S Widdup   Scorers: J T Potter and S Pollard

Charlotte Edwards Cup
Thunder v. Northern Diamonds

Played at Stanley Park, Blackpool, on June 7, 2023
Thunder won by 7 wickets

Toss won by Northern Diamonds   Thunder 5 points, Northern Diamonds 0 points

NORTHERN DIAMONDS

L Winfield-Hill, c Dattani b Gaur	12
L Dobson, c Bell b Norris	2
* H J Armitage, c Dottin b Norris	0
S L Kalis, c Dattani b F M K Morris	24
§ B A M Heath, b Gaur	1
C L Tryon, b F M K Morris	22
B A Langston, b Bell	2
K J G Fraser, c Dattani b Bell	17
L E Scott, not out	11
K A Levick, c Heap b Bell	0
G E Hall, run out (Heap/Dattani)	0
Extras b 1, w 3, nb 1	5
Total (18.4 overs)	96

FoW: 1-11 (Dobson), 2-11 (Armitage), 3-15 (Winfield-Hill), 4-19 (Heath), 5-46 (Tryon), 6-49 (Langston), 7-74 (Kalis), 8-93 (Fraser), 9-93 (Levick), 10-96 (Hall)

	O	M	R	W
Gaur	4	0	27	2
Norris	4	0	19	2
F M K Morris	3	0	16	2
Bell	3	0	9	3
S Morris	2	0	14	0
Dattani	2.4	0	10	0

THUNDER

N D Dattani, c Levick b Langston	20
L N Heap, c Kalis b Fraser	12
F M K Morris, not out	42
D J S Dottin, st Heath b Levick	9
* § E Threlkeld, not out	4
D L Collins	
S A Smale	
T G Norris	Did not bat
M Gaur	
O N Bell	
S Morris	
Extras b 1, lb 1, w 7, nb 1	10
Total (3 wkts, 15 overs)	97

FoW: 1-30 (Heap), 2-64 (Dattani), 3-90 (Dottin)

	O	M	R	W
Scott	1	0	14	0
Fraser	3	0	14	1
Levick	3	0	19	1
Tryon	4	0	16	0
Langston	3	0	22	1
Hall	1	0	10	0

Umpires: N Ashraf and J Naeem   Scorers: J Egan and C Rimmer

NORTHERN DIAMONDS AVERAGES 2023

CHARLOTTE EDWARDS CUP

Played 7   Won 4   Lost 3

BATTING AND FIELDING
(Qualification 3 completed innings)

Player	M.	I.	N.O.	Runs	H.S.	100s	50s	Avge	ct/st
H J Armitage	7	7	0	216	82	0	2	30.85	2
L Winfield-Hill	7	7	0	171	98	0	1	24.42	3
L Dobson	7	7	0	135	47	0	0	19.28	3
C L Tryon	7	7	2	95	30	0	0	19.00	5
S L Kalis	7	6	0	113	32	0	0	18.83	2
B A M Heath	7	7	1	108	31	0	0	18.00	2/4
K J G Fraser	7	6	1	53	26	0	0	10.60	2
L E Scott	7	5	2	25	11*	0	0	8.33	1
A A Glen	6	4	1	24	13*	0	0	8.00	3

Also batted

Player	M.	I.	N.O.	Runs	H.S.	100s	50s	Avge	ct/st
K A Levick	7	4	2	7	4	0	0	3.50	1
G E Hall	7	3	1	5	4*	0	0	2.50	3
B A Langston	1	1	0	2	2	0	0	2.00	0

BOWLING
(Qualification 3 wickets)

Player	Overs	Mdns	Runs	Wkts	Avge	Best	4wi	RPO
K A Levick	23	0	144	12	12.00	5 -19	1	6.26
G E Hall	20.4	0	170	10	17.00	3 -20	0	8.22
L E Scott	23	1	147	7	21.00	2 -27	0	6.39
C L Tryon	26.4	0	195	8	24.37	3 -30	0	7.31
A A Glen	18	0	157	5	31.40	2 -23	0	8.72

Also bowled

Player	Overs	Mdns	Runs	Wkts	Avge	Best	4wi	RPO
B A Langston	3	0	22	1	22.00	1 -22	0	7.33
K J G Fraser	15	0	123	2	61.50	1 -14	0	8.20

VICTIMS OF OWN SUCCESS AS BEST FLY THE NEST

By John Virr

Defending the four-day Championship title won in 2022 was always going to be a difficult task — but Tom Smith's side were not a million miles away in the end. Also encouragingly, they progressed through to T20 Finals Day, where they were beaten semi-finalists.

The title defence was made much harder when two of the first four Championship games were lost and another decimated by rain. Throughout the 11 four-dayers an incredible 1,159 overs were lost to rain — the equivalent of over 12 full days.

Despite using 29 different players, results improved as the season progressed, with six games won, three lost and two drawn, leaving a finishing place of fifth with almost 13 points per game. The Second XI Championship is decided by average points per game as the counties don't all play the same number of matches. Leicestershire won the competition with an average of 14.75.

There were several areas of note. From 2022 Fin Bean cemented his place in the first team, and further progression was made with appearances from Will Luxton, James Wharton, Dom Leech and Ben Cliff — who made his first-class debut in September at Cardiff.

Younger players Yash Vagadia and Noah Kelly both made impacts. Vagadia made 612 runs at 38.25 with four 50-plus scores, including a highest of 81. Kelly, still in the club's Academy, made 357 runs at 59.50 with three half-centuries, including a best of 79.

Luxton finished as top run-scorer in the Championship, totting up 681 runs at 56.75 with two hundreds and four further half-centuries. He was closely followed by Will Fraine's 639 runs — a player who also finished as joint-highest outfield catcher in the whole competition with 11.

Overall, six hundreds were scored — two from Luxton and one each from Fraine, Ben Mike, George Hill and Matthew Revis.

Leech took 33 wickets at 23.36 to finish as the second highest wicket-taker in the competition, but Jack Shutt wasn't too far behind with 29 at 28.17 and Mike had 25 at 22.68. Shutt had a pair of five-wicket hauls, and there was one for Ben Parker. Mike returned a 6-43 and Hill a 6-45.

Off-spinner Shutt bowled the most overs with 245.4, followed by

NOAH KELLY   **YASH VAGADIA**

Leech with 207.3. We extend thanks and best wishes for the future to Fraine and Shutt, who have both been released by the county. We all hope they make a success of their next moves, wherever they may be.

T20 performances in 2022 were poor, so a semi-final finish last season was clearly progress. Unfortunately, the team lost out in the semi-final at picturesque Wormsley to a Derbyshire side featuring several first-team players, most notably club captain Leus du Plooy.

The second-team competition starts before the first-team Vitality Blast, and many counties take the opportunity to field first-teamers in the early rounds. Yorkshire captain Shan Masood played in one. As it stands any appearance in a group game is enough to qualify a player for Finals Day.

Prior to the semi-final, Luxton and Cliff were awarded their second-team caps.

Again, 29 players were used, and Yorkshire finished top of the North Group with eight wins from 10 matches. All counties are split into three groups, and the Vikings' record was better than that of the other two group winners, Glamorgan in the Central Group and Hampshire in the South. Glamorgan also won eight out of 10 and accrued 16 points, but Yorkshire finished with a superior net run-rate.

Derbyshire went on to win the competition, beating Glamorgan in the final. The Falcons had qualified for Finals Day as the best second-placed finisher across the trio of groups.

Fraine finished as top run-scorer with 350 at an average of 50, and in doing so he became — as far as research shows — the first second-team player ever to score two unbeaten hundreds on the same day, when he made 113 not out and 107 not out against Nottinghamshire at Worksop College.

Wharton made 199 runs, with a strike rate of 174.56, helping him to gain a place in the first-team Blast side at the top of the order. He went on to score that tremendous hundred against Worcestershire Rapids under the Headingley floodlights.

T20 friendlies were played against South Asian Cricket Academy (SACA), and one of these saw Wharton and Luxton produce a remarkable unbeaten opening partnership of 257 – Wharton 139 not out and Luxton 104 not out.

Though the level of opposition was different it is worth looking at global stats for T20 cricket at first-team and international level to get an idea of just how significant the Wharton and Luxton stand was.

WILL LUXTON

At time of writing no pair had ever united to post a partnership higher than 236 in any fixture since the inception of 20-over cricket in the early 2000s.

Cliff was the leading wicket-taker with 15 at 17.13 apiece, and Shutt followed closely behind with 14 at 13.29. Add in the friendlies, and those figures become 20 at 14.65 and 19 at 11.95.

Due to the make-up of the second-team season red ball cricket was played from April to mid-May, followed by T20s until mid-June, returning to red ball until mid-July. Due to the Metro Bank One-Day Cup and the Hundred there is then an almost six-week gap in second-team cricket until it resumes in late August/early September.

When it did resume after the MB50 the three four-day games saw three wins to finish on a positive note.

WATCHING THE STARS COME OUT

Tom Smith hailed the development of a number of Yorkshire's up-and-coming stars as the former England Lions all-rounder turned *White Rose* second-team coach assessed the summer that was 2023.

Smith was pleased with the county's progress just below first-team level, and he highlighted the impressive run of T20 results — Yorkshire won eight of their 10 group fixtures to qualify for Finals Day — as particularly pleasing, given it is an area of the game the county's management, led by Ottis Gibson and Darren Gough, have been targeting.

"Obviously, it was nice to win the Championship in 2022," Smith said. "Of course it was. But I would never want to judge the success of a season in the second team on silverware, because your team can change from week to week.

"I think it was a really good season for a number of different players. The season before last we had a lot of trial players, whereas last year we had a lot more staff or Academy lads playing.

"Someone like young Noah Kelly played six out of the 11 four-day games, and ended up averaging 60 as a 17-year-old (357 runs). He had a really good season as he gets used to professional cricket, and his game has come on leaps and bounds through being in that environment. In all forms of cricket he scored 1,740 runs.

"For a young lad to do that, it's amazing. He's starting to thinking differently about his cricket. In the last game of the season at Durham he was asking, 'What do I need to do differently to play more second-team and then first-team cricket — what are the areas I need to work on?'

"He wants to really move forward quite quickly, and is doing well.

"I look at someone like Will Luxton. He made really good strides with the bat, Yash Vagadia, too (612 runs in the Championship). Harry Duke in white-ball cricket did really well in the first and second team, and Ben Cliff made his first-class debut.

"We have a young leg-spinner on the Academy in Josh Hoyle, who has done well in the T20 stuff in particular. We've also had 16-year-olds playing at times. Will Bennison is one who is doing really well in the pathway and age groups, and he's had a chance.

"The beauty of second-team cricket is that you can create a pathway for those young lads to come in. At the same time we've had a second-team with 11 pros in at times. If we can keep building that, hopefully the club will be very successful over the next 5-10 years."

On T20 cricket, Smith said: "We got through to Finals Day as a first-team in 2022, and as a second-team last season. That's something as a

COACH TOM SMITH

club we're trying to work on.

"We're delivering messages right the way through, to the younger lads on the Academy as well.

"We want them to play white-ball cricket with freedom. That has been shown, at some points to the detriment of our red-ball cricket.

"But the red ball stuff, we played some good cricket throughout the year."

Last season saw the first second-team Championship match played at Headingley since 2018, when Yorkshire beat Nottinghamshire by 205 runs — a match noted for Jonny Bairstow's comeback after following eight months out with a broken leg and dislocated ankle suffered in August 2022.

Bairstow scored 97 and 57.

"We played on the international wicket, and it was a belter of a surface," Smith said. "We had quite a strong team out that week, Jonny, Beany, Hilly, Fish. As a second team goes it wasn't a bad one.

"But, at the same time, we had some young pros and Academy lads in who had never played at Headingley. It was a brilliant experience for them. Jonny was brilliant with the lads. He admitted he was a bit nervous on day one after that much time off. But as soon as he got out there and played he was back to his normal self.

"He was more than happy to chat to the lads about anything they wanted. He gave as much time as he could to those around him. When you see international players doing that, it's really inspiring."

Second Eleven 2023

PLAYERS WHO APPEARED FOR YORKSHIRE SECOND ELEVEN IN 2023
(excluding First Eleven capped players)

Player	Date of Birth	Birthplace	Type
F J Bean *	April 16, 2002	Harrogate	LHB/WK
B M Cliff *	October 23, 2002	Halifax	RHB/RFM
H G Duke *	September 6, 2001	Wakefield	RHB /WK
W A R Fraine *	June 13, 1996	Huddersfield	RHB/RM
G C H Hill *	January 24, 2001	Keighley	RHB/RMF
D J Leech *	January 10, 2001	Midddlesbrough	RHB/RMF
W A Luxton *	May 6, 2003	Keighley	RHB
J W Shutt*	June 24, 1997	Barnsley	RHB/OB
J Akhtar §	November 11, 2005	Pontefract	RHB/OB
J A Anson §	August 9, 1995	Hull	RHB/RFM
W J Bennison	September 10, 2006	Boroughbridge	RHB/LB
J A Chohan §	July 11, 2002	Camden, Middlesex	RHB/LB
A D Cree	October 13, 2004	Pontefract	RHB
M W Edwards §	December 23, 1994	Manly, NSW, Aus	RHB/RFM
J A Gunn	February 3, 2001	Rotherham	RHB/RM
J J Hen-Boisen §	July 17, 2006	Wakefield	RHB/SLA
J J Hoyle §	July 21, 2006	Huddersfield	RHB/LB
N M Kelly	September 21, 2005	Hull	LHB/WK
I F Light	April 12, 2005	Harrogate	RHB/WK
C J McMurran	January 10, 2005	Leeds	RHB/RFM
B W M Mike §	August 24, 1998	Nottingham	RHB/RMF
M E Milnes §	July 29, 1994	Nottingham	RHB/RFM
I Mohammed §	July 12, 2004	Birmingham	RHB/OB
L J Owens §	June 16, 2006	Sheffield	RHB/LFM
B S J Parker §	April 3, 2003	Bath	RHB/RFM
M L Revis	November 15, 2001	Steeton, Keighley	RHB/RM
H H Round	March 1, 2006	Scunthorpe	RHB/RM
A R Shetty §	June 26, 2004	Manchester	RHB/OB
J W Shutt	June 24, 1997	Barnsley	RHB/OB
A J Taylor-Clarke §	September 29, 2002	Middlesbrough	LHB/LFM
Y Vagadia	May 7, 2004	Newcastle upon Tyne	RHB/OB
J H Wharton	February 1, 2001	Huddersfield	RHB/OB

* Second Eleven cap

§ Debutants

SECOND ELEVEN HIGHLIGHTS OF 2023

CHAMPIONSHIP
Century partnerships (11)
For the 1st wicket (2)

111	W A Luxton and Y Vagadia	v. Surrey at Guildford
111	W A R Fraine and N M Kelly	v. Durham at Scarborough

For the 2nd wicket (2)

189 *	W A R Fraine and W A Luxton	v. Derbyshire at Weetwood
117	W A Luxton and A R Shetty	v. Lancashire at Southport

For the 3rd wicket (1)

143	G C H Hill and W A Luxton	v. Northamptonshire at Weetwood

For the 4th wicket (2)

101*	N M Kelly and W A R Fraine	v. Durham at The Riverside
101	W A Luxton and W A R Fraine	v. Surrey at Guildford

For the 6th wicket (2)

103	B W M Mike and I F Light	v. Surrey at Guildford
100	H G Duke and B W M Mike	v. Nottinghasmshire at Headingley

For the 7th wicket (1)

149	N M Kelly and M E Milnes	v. Lancashire at Southport.

(The highest seventh-wicket partnership nationally
in the 2023 Second XI Championship)

For the 8th wicket (1)

126	Y Vagadia and D J Leech	v. Nottinghamshire at Headingley

(The highest eighth-wicket partnership nationally
in the 2023 Second XI Championship)

Centuries (6)

W A Luxton (2)

   115   v. Surrey at Guildford
   102 * v. Derbyshire at Weetwood

G C H Hill (1)

   138   v. Northamptonshire at Weetwood

M L Revis (1)

   112   v. Lancashire at York

B W M Mike (1)

   112   v. Surrey at Guildford

W A R Fraine (1)

   109 * v. Derbyshire at Weetwood

Ten wickets in a match:–. No player achieved this feat in 2023. The best performances were by Mike, with match figures of 7-88 v. Durham at Scarborough and Hill, with 7-65 against Nottinghamshire at Headingley.

Five wickets in an innings (3)

J W Shutt (2)

   5- 41   v. Gloucestershire at Rockhampton
   5- 64   v. Durham at Scarboroug

B S J Parker (1))

   5- 22   v. Gloucestershire at Rockhampton

Five victims in an innings: No player achieved this feat in 2023. The best performance was by H G Duke, who had four victims, all caught, in the *Roses* battle at York..

T20 COMPETITION

Century Partnerships (2)

For the 1st wicket (1)

185 *   W A R Fraine and J H Wharton   v. Nottinghamshire at Worksop College

Ssecond match of two.
This meant that Yorkshire won a 2nd XI T20 game
by 10 wickets for the first time.

For the 3rd wicket (1)

131   W A R Fraine and N M Kelly   v. Nottinghamshire at Worksop College

(First match of two)

Centuries (2)

W A R Fraine (2)

113 *   v. Nottinghamshire at Worksop College
107*   v. Nottinghamshire at Worksop College

5 wickets in an innings: No player achieved this feat in 2023. The closest return was 4-10 by J W Shutt against Derbyshire at Abbeydale Park, Sheffield.

Five victims in an innings: No player achieved this feat in 2023. The best return was four, all caught, by J A Tattersall against Leicestershire at Headingley in the second game of two..

MISCELLANEOUS STATISTICS

1   The highlight of the season was undoubtedly reaching Finals Day in the 2nd XI T20 competition. It was the third time Yorkshire had achieved this but, also for the third time, they failed to progress beyond the semi-final stage, losing to Derbyshire, who were in their first appearance at this stage of the competition and who went on to defeat Glamorgan in the final. Finals Day had been held in the pleasant surroundings of Arundel Castle in Sussex for many years, but was moved in 2023 to Wormsley in Buckinghamshire, the ground built for and owned by the late John Paul Getty.

2   W A R Fraine established a national 2nd XI T20 record when on June 2 at Worksop College he hit a century as an opener in each game of the double-header against Nottinghamshire. This is the first time such a feat has occurred in the competition since its inception in 2011.

3   J W Shutt took his tally to 51 wickets for the 2nd XI, and became the club's leading bowler in this competition.

4   In the Championship W A R Fraine, N M Kelly and W A Luxton all qualified for the national averages. Each had a final batting average of over 50 for the season. D M Leech, J W Shutt and B W M Mike all qualified for the national bowling averages.

5.   W A Luxton scored 681 Championship runs, and was the second highest scorer in the competition behind J Blake, of Surrey, who registered 729 runs.

6.   Y Vagadia, W A Luxton, H G Duke and J H Wharton all passed 1,000 Championship runs. J W Shutt has passed 100 Championship wickets.

7.   Yorkshire's run of four consecutive wins to finish the 2023 season was their best run since they had five consecutive wins in 1977.

7

SECOND ELEVEN CHAMPIONSHIP 2023

Points Awarded: Won (W) 16, Tie (T) 8, Lost (L) 0, Drawn (D) or Abandoned 5
Batting Bonus Points: one point awarded for every 50 runs from 250 to 450
in the first 110 overs of the innings (maximum five points)
Bowling Bonus Points: one point awarded at three, six and nine
wickets taken in the first 110 overs of the innings (maximum three points)

Bonus points are retained irrespective of the result of the match

Order in the table: Position of teams in the table is determined by:
(i) Average points per match and (ii) Games won

FINAL TABLE

		P	W	L	D	Aban	Bat	Bowl	Ded	Points	Per Match
1	Leicestershire	9	5	0	3	1	8	23	8	118	14.75
2	Hampshire	8	4	2	1	1	13	18	0	100	14.29
3	Worcestershire	10	6	2	1	1	6	24	0	136	13.60
4	Sussex	8	4	2	0	2	13	17	0	104	13.00
5	**Yorkshire**	**11**	**6**	**3**	**2**	**0**	**15**	**28**	**7**	**142**	**12.91**
6	Lancashire	12	5	2	3	2	20	25	0	150	12.50
7	Glamorgan	10	5	4	0	1	11	23	0	119	11.90
8	Surrey	9	3	3	3	0	21	23	0	107	11.89
9	Middlesex	9	2	2	2	3	16	16	0	89	9.89
10	Somerset	9	3	4	1	1	11	19	0	88	9.78
11	Durham	8	3	5	0	0	8	20	0	76	9.50
12	Essex	10	2	3	3	2	19	19	1	94	9.40
13	Derbyshire	8	2	3	1	2	8	15	0	70	8.75
14	Warwickshire	10	2	3	3	2	8	19	0	84	8.40
15	Nottinghamshire	10	2	5	3	0	13	23	2	81	8.10
16	Gloucestershire	8	2	4	2	0	2	18	0	62	7.75
17	Northamptonshire	10	2	6	2	0	5	27	0	74	7.40
18	Kent	7	0	5	2	0	10	17	0	37	5.29

(The "Bonus Points" heading spans the Bat, Bowl and Ded columns; the "Average Points" heading spans the Points and Per Match columns.)

Second Eleven Championship
Yorkshire v. Worcestershire

Played at Bradford Park Avenue on April 10, 11, 12 and 13, 2023
Match abandoned as a draw at 10.16 am on the Fourth Day

Toss won by Yorkshire   Yorkshire 7 points, Worcestershire 5 points

Close of play: First Day, Worcestershire 10-0 (T R Cornall 5, RM Edavalath 4; 4.1 overs);
Second Day, Worcestershire 113-6 (H J Cullen 25, R L Evitts 4; 34.3 overs); Third Day, no play.;

WORCESTERSHIRE

T R Cornall, c Duke b Edwards	5
R M Edavalath, c Light b Leech	35
Kashif Ali, b Cliff	1
O H Cox, b Edwards	12
§ O B Cox, c Leech b Cliff	8
H J Cullen, not 0ut	25
O J Walker, c Cliff b Mike	12
R L Evitts, not out	4
J O Baker	
A W Finch	
C W Jones Did not bat	
* P R Brown	
A R Sylvester	
Extras b 1, lb 6, nb 4	11
Total (6 wkts, 34.3 overs)	113

FoW: 1-13 (T R Cornall); 2-20 (Kashif Ali); 3-49 (O H Cox); 4-66 (R M Edalavath); 5-70 (O B Cox), 6-97 (O J Walker)

	O	M	R	W
Cliff	10	4	17	2
Leech	7	1	32	1
Edwards	7	0	21	2
Shutt	2.3	1	9	0

YORKSHIRE

* W A R Fraine
W A Luxton
Y Vagadia
§ H G Duke
I F Light
A D Cree
B W M Mike
M W Edwards
J W Shutt
B M Cliff
J A Chohan
D J Leech

Umpires: |N Ashraf and I Rich   Scorers: J R Virr and P M Mellish

Second Eleven Championship
Leicstershire v. Yorkshire

Played at Kibworth on April 17, 18, 19 and 20, 2023
Leicestershire won by 6 wickets at 12. 15pm on the Fourth Day

Toss won by Leicestershire

Leicestershire 17 points, Yorkshire 3 points

Close of play: First Day, no play; Second Day, Leicestershire (1) 105-7 (T A R Scriven 27, S B Wood 0; 38 overs); Third Day, Leicestershire (2) 117-2 (L P J Kimber 41, H J Swindells 22; 26 overs)

YORKSHIRE

First Innings		Second Innings	
* W A R Fraine, lbw b Walker	16	c Davis b Scriven	71
Y Vagadia, b Barnes	8	c Swindells b Finan	4
J H Wharton, b Walker	0		
W A Luxton, b Walker	1	(3) c Davis b Sullivan	27§
§ H G Duke, lbw b Davis	21	(4) lbw b Finan	43
B W M Mike, not out	72	(5) b Sullivan	1
A D Cree, b Kimber	12	(6) b Sullivan	7
J A Chohan, c Swindells b Kimber	0	lbw b Finan	0
D J Leech, b Barnes	0	b Sullivan	0
J W Shutt, lbw b Barnes	0	not out	1
B M Cliff, lbw b Barnes	1	b Finan	4
I F Light	Did not bat	(7) c Swindells b Finan	4
C J McMurran			
Extras b 12, lb 2, w 1, nb 6	21	Extras b 6, lb 12, nb 12	30
Total (49.2 overs)	152	Total (57.5 overs)	192

FoW: 1-26 (Vagadia); 2-29 (Fraine); 3-31 (Luxton); 4-34 (Wharton); 5-99 (Duke),
1st 6-129 (Cree); 7-129 (Chohan); 8-134 (Leech); 9-144 (Shutt); 10-152 (Cliff)
FoW: 1-6 (Vagadia); 2-83 (Luxton); 3-137 (Fraine); 4-150 (Mike); 5-170 (Cree),
2nd 6 183 (Light); 7 183 (Chohan); 8-184 (Leech); 9-186 (Duke); 10-192 (Cliff)

	O	M	R	W		O	M	R	W
Davis	11	2	23	1	Davis	5	0	12	0
Barnes	10.2	3	30	4	Finan	10.5	1	43	5
Kimber	6	2	24	2	Kimber	9	0	37	0
Walker	8	2	22	3	Barnes	5	0	17	0
Scriven	6	4	15	0	Sullivan	15	5	31	4
Sullivan	8	1	24	0	Walker	6	0	14	0
					Scriven	7	3	20	1

LEICESTERSHIRE

First Innings		Second Innings	
S T Evans, c Duke b Cliff	6	lbw b Cliff	7
S Steel, lbw b Leech	0	b Shutt	46
L P J Kimber, lbw b Shutt	36	c Fraine b Leech	52
§ H J Swindells, lbw b Mike	11	not out	51
N R Welch, lbw b Mike	0	c Fraine b Shutt	14
T A R Scriven, not out	55	not out	13
E Barnes, st Duke b Shutt	1		
R I Walker, b Shutt	5		
S B Wood, c Cliff b Mike	0		
* W S Davis, c Luxton b Leech	27		
H A Sullivan, b Leech	0		
M G A Finan	Did not bat		
Extras b 7, lb 6, nb 6	19	Extras b 1, lb 2	3
Total (54 overs)	160	Total (4 wkts; 45.1 overs)	186

FoW: 1-0 (Steel); 2-6 (Evans); 3-51 Swindells); 4-51 (Welch); 5-79 (Kimber),
1st 6-85 (Barnes); 7-99 (Walker); 8-110 (Wood); 9-158 (Davis); 10-160 (Sullivan)
2nd 1-42 (Evans); 2-61 (Steel); 3-137 (Kimber); 4-164 (Welch)

	O	M	R	W		O	M	R	W
Cliff	6	1	17	1	Cliff	8.1	0	30	1
Leech	11	4	22	3	Leech	12	3	42	1
McMurran	5	1	14	0	Mike	4	0	22	0
Mike	10	0	30	3	Shutt	17	1	63	2
Shutt	16	4	47	3	Chohan	4	0	17	0
Chohan	6	0	17	0					

Umpires: A C Harris and R J Bailey

Scorers: P N Johnson and J R Virr

Leicestershire originally gained 19 points from the game, but were deducted two for a slow over rate.
I F Light replaced J H Wharton as full substitute at the end of Day 2 for Yorkshire.

Second Eleven Championship
Yorkshire v. Nottinghamshire

Played at Headingley, Leeds, on April 25, 26, 27 and 28
Yorkshire won by 205 runs at 4.59 pm on the Fourth Day

Toss won by Yorkshire   Yorkshire 24 points, Nottinghamshire 4 points

Close of play: First Day, Yorkshire (1) 437-7 (Y Vagadia 30, D J Leech 18; 96 overs); Second Day, Nottinghamshire (1) 313-9 (J P H Hayes 1, T H S Pettman 1; 70 overs); Third Day, Yorkshire (2) 266-5 (W A R Fraine 16, Y Vagadia 10; 46.2 overs)

First Innings	YORKSHIRE		Second Innings	
F J Bean, c Schadendorf b Giles	70		c Harrison b Raheem Ahmed	40
J H Wharton, c Schadendorf b Stone	11		b Loten	35
G C H Hill, c Martindale b Pettman	34		run out (Raheem Ahmed)	88
J M Bairstow, c Harrison b Stone	97		lbw b Harrison	57
W A R Fraine, b Harrison	26		not out	16
§ * H G Duke, lbw b Pettman	46		c Schadendorf b Stone	3
B W M Mike, c Hayes b Pettman	60			
Y Vagadia, c Schadendorf b Loten	69		(7) not out	10
D J Leech, lbw b Carter	47			
J W Shutt, not out	2			
B M Cliff, not out	6			
B S J Parker	Did not bat			
M D Fisher				
Extras b 7, lb 33, nb 18	58		Extras lb 9, nb 6	15
Total (9 wkts dec, 120 overs)	526		Total (5 wkts dec, 46.2 overs)	266

FoW: 1-18 (Wharton), 2-109 (Hill), 3-182 (Bean), 4-266 (Bairstow), 5-280 (Fraine),
1st   6-380 (Mike),, 7-383 (Duke), 8-509 (Leech), 9-517 (Vagadia)
2nd: 1-81 (Bean), 2-93 (Wharton), 3-184 (Bairstow), 4-246 (Hill), 5-251 (Duke)

	O	M	R	W		O	M	R	W
Pettman	24	3	86	3	Stone	9.2	3	35	1
Stone	20	6	43	2	Pettman	8	0	48	0
Hayes	17	2	93	0	Raheem Ahmed	4	1	20	1
Raheem Ahmed	7	0	45	0	Hayes	3	0	22	0
Loten	16	0	69	1	Loten	7	0	36	1
Giles	8	1	43	1	Carter	9	1	48	0
Harrison	10	2	57	1	Giles	4	0	24	0
Carter	18	2	50	1	Harrison	2	0	24	1

Second Eleven Championship
Yorkshire v. Nottinghamshire *(continued)*

First Innings	NOTTINGHAMSHIRE	Second Innings
B J R Martindale, b Parker 66		c Shutt b Cliff 38
§ D J Schadendorf, c Bean b Leech 0		b Fisher 0
C G Harrison, c Wharton b Leech 0		c Cliff b Fisher 4
T W Loten, b Parker 30		c Bairstow b Leech 8
S I M King, c Bean b Cliff 0		lbw b Hill 5
F W McCann, c Fraine b Cliff 70		c Cliff b Hill 4
* O P Stone, c Mike b Cliff 65		c and b Hill 4
M Carter, b Mike 32		c Duke b Hill 102
Raheem Ahmed, c Fraine b Mike 16		c Bairttow b Hill 14
J P H Hayes, not out 15		c sub b Hill 54
T H S Pettman, b Hill 5		not out 3
T O Giles Did not bat		
Extras b 6, lb 10, nb 16 32		Extras b 10, lb 4, nb 16 20
Total (76.3 ovs) 331		Total (57.1 ovs) 256

FoW: 1-24 (Schadendorf), 2-24 (Harrison), 3-102 (Martindale),4-103 (Loten), 5-103 (King).
1st 6-259 (Stone), 7-260 (McCannn), 8-307 (Carter), 9-310 (Raheem hmed), 10-331 (Pettman)
FoW: 1-1 (Schedendorf), 2-25 (Harrison), 3-55 (Martindale), 4-63 (Loten), 5-63 (King),
     6-67 (Stone), 7-72 (McCann), 8-108 (Raheem Ahmed), 9-235 (Carter). 10-256 (Hayes)

	O	M	R	W			O	M	R	W
Cliff	18	4	79	3	Fisher		10	2	43	2
Leech	10	1	61	2	Leech		14	1	50	1
Mike	11	2	38	2	Cliff		9	2	36	1
Parker	12	2	69	2	Parker		9	1	41	0
Hill	12.3	4	20	1	Hill		11.1	1	45	6
Shutt	13	0	48	0	Shutt		4	0	27	0

J M Bairstow kept wicket from lunch to tea on Day 2
H G Duke resumed these duties after tea to close of play
M D Fisher replaced B W M Mike on Day 3
Yorkshire`s substitute fielder on Day 4 was H H Round
G C H Hill`s return of 6-45 was his best in the 2nd XI Championship,
beating his previous best of 3-21 v. Nottinghamshire at York CC in 2021
J M Bairstow kept wicket in Nottinghamshire`s second innings

Umpires: H M S Adnan and J C Tredwell   Scorers: J R Virr and Mrs A Cusworth

Second Eleven Championship
Yorkshire v. Lancashire

Played at York on May 1, 2, 3 and 4, 2023
Lancashire won by 10 wkts at 6.02pm on the Third Day

Toss won by Yorkshire

Yorkshire 3 points, Lancashire 23 points

Close of play: First Day, Lancashire (1) 370-4 (M F Hurst 21, T H Aspinwall 13 ; 96 overs); Second Day, Yorkshire (2) 73-2 (M L Revis 26; 18.5 overs).

LANCASHIRE

First Innings		Second Innings	
H Singh, c Duke b Cliff	59	not out	23
C J Dickinson, c Revis b Mike	184	not out	44
§ G I D Lavelle, c Leech b Chohan	69		
* D J Lamb, c Leech b Cliff	4		
M F Hurst, c Duke b Revis	21		
T H Aspinwall, c Wharton b Leech	30		
J M Blatherwick, c Mike b Cliff	11		
J P Morley, c Duke b Revis	0		
A R Shetty, not out	22		
K N Watson, lbw b Leech	0		
C R Barnard, c Duke b Mike	5		
W Vause	Did not bat		
Extras b 12, lb 6, w 2. nb 8	28	Extra nb 6	6
Total (120.4 overs)	433	Total (0 wkts, 14.3 overs)	73

FoW: 1-130 (Singh), 2-254 (Lavelle), 3-324 (Lamb), 4-342 (Dickinson), 5-370 (Hurst),
1st   6-395 (Blatherwick), 7-402 (Morley), 8-402 (Aspinwall), 9-402 (Watson, 10-433 (Barnard)

	O	M	R	W		O	M	R	W
Cliff	20	7	38	3	Mike	6	0	28	0
Leech	17	2	63	2	Taylor-Clarke	4	0	16	0
Revis	24	3	80	2	Shutt	3	0	17	0
Mike	21.4	1	70	2	Chohan	1.3	0	12	0
Taylor-Clarke	10	0	54	0					
Shutt	11	1	55	0					
Chohan	17	2	55	1					

YORKSHIRE

First Innings		Second Innings	
J H Wharton, c Hurst b Blatherwick	0	c Lavelle b Blatherwick	0
W A Luxton, lbw b Lamb	7	b Morley	44
M L Revis, c Lavelle b Aspinwall	19	lbw b Morley	112
§ * J A Tattersall, lbw b Morley	38	c Lavelle b Lamb	1
H G Duke, c Hurst b Aspinwall	8	c Dickinson b Aspinwall	66
Y Vagadia, c Hurst b Aspinwall	74	c Singh b Lamb	38
B W M Mike, c Watson b Morley	4	b Barnard	1
D J Leech, st Hurst b Morley	18	b Morley	13
J A Chohan, c Lavelle b Lamb	0	b Lamb	14
J W Shutt, c Hurst b Lamb	1	c Lavelle b Aspinwall	17
B M Cliff, not out	4	not out	2
A J Taylor-Clarke	Did not bat		
Extras b 1, lb 2, nb 8	11	Extras b 3, w 1, nb 8	12
Total (47.1 overs)	184	Total (98.4 overs)	320

FoW: 1-0 (Wharton),   2-16 (Luxton), 3-44 (Revis), 4-78 (Tattersall), 5-78 (Duke),
1st   6-91 (Mike), 7-145 (Leech), 8-146 (Chohan), 9-152 (Shutt), 10-184 (Vagadia)
FoW: 1-0 (Wharton), 2-73 (Luxton), 3-80 (Tattersall), 4-213 (Duke), 5-247 (Revis)
2nd   6-252 (Mike), 7-273 (Leech), 8-293 (Vagadia), 9-304 (Chohan), 10-320 (Shutt)

	O	M	R	W		O	M	R	W
Blatherwick	11	3	38	1	Blatherwick	19	4	74	1
Lamb	12	1	42	3	Lamb	23	1	57	3
Aspinwall	8.1	3	25	3	Aspinwall	16.4	4	47	2
Watson	2	0	12	0	Vause	3	0	22	0
Morley	14	0	64	3	Morley	29	4	93	3
					Watson	3	0	8	0
					Barnard	6	1	16	1

Lancashire substituted M F Hurst for G I D Lavelle § as wicketkeeper
*Yorkshire substituted H G Duke for J A Tattersall * § as wicketkeeper*

Umpires: J Montgomery-Else and Miss S Redfern

Scorers: J R Virr and G L Morgan

Second Eleven Championship
Yorkshire v. Northamptonshire

Played at Weetwood, Leeds, on June 19, 20, 21 and 22, 2023
Match drawn at 5.01pm on the Fourth Day

Toss won by Northamptonshirere   Northamptonshire 9 points, Yorkshire 8 points

Close of play: First Day, Northamptonshire (1) 147-5 (L A Procter 39, R Upadhyay 6; 47.4 overs),
Second Day, no play; Third Day, Yorkshire (1) 36-1 (N M Kelly 12, G C H Hill 8; 18 overs)

NORTHAMPTONSHIRE

M H Azad, c Duke b Hill	18
S M Whiteman, c Hill b Leech	30
* L A Procter, c Duke b Leech	141
A U Buchake, c Duke b Shutt	2
§ H O M Gouldstone, c Kelly b Leech	1
G K Berg, c Luxton b Gunn	34
R Udaphyay, c Hill b Shutt	123
S C Kerrigan, c Cliff b Shutt	0
C J White, not out	18
G P H Weldon, not out	33
R R L Bailey	
B J Wightman Did not bat	
G E Gowler	
Extras b 5, lb 15, w 2, nb 2	24
Total (8 wkts dec, 121 overs)	424

FoW: 1-39 (Whiteman), 2-77 (Azad), 3-80 (Buchake), 4-81 (Gouldstone), 5-139 (Berg), 6-352 (Procter); 7-353 (Kerrigan); 8-380 (Udaphyay)

	O	M	R	W
Leech	25	7	68	3
Cliff	24	6	112	0
Gunn	18	3	56	1
Hill	22	5	43	1
Shutt	26	9	103	3
Hen-Boisen	6	1	22	0

YORKSHIRE

F J Bean, c Azad b Berg	16
N M Kelly, b Weldon	20
* G C H Hill, c Azad b Wightman	138
W A Luxton, b Weldon	38
§ H G Duke, c Azad b B|erg	31
Y Vagadia, c Gouldstone b Bailey	23
W J Bennison, not out	17
D J Leech, c Procter b Azad	42
J W Shutt, not out	1
B M Cliff	
J Hen-Boisen Did not bat	
J A Gunn	
Extras b 4, lb 9	13
Total (7 wkts, 98 overs)	339

FoW: 1-27 (Bean), 2-73 (Kelly), 3-216 (Hill), 4-242 (Luxton), 5-279 (Vagadia), 6-281 (Duke), 7-335 (Leech)

	O	M	R	W
White	7	1	18	0
Berg	16	5	36	2
Procter	9	0	34	0
Kerrigan	21	6	55	0
Weldon	11	0	38	2
Wightman	13	2	63	1
Bailey	10	0	40	1
Gowler	7	2	26	0
Azad	4	0	15	1

Northamptonshire full substitute: G E Gowler for S M Whiteman at start of Day 3

Umpires: I G Warne and R G Eagleton   Scorers: J R Virr and Q L S Jones

Second Eleven Championship
Yorkshire v. Derbyshire

Played at Weetwood, Leeds, on June 26, 27, 28 and 29, 2023
Yorkshire won by 6 wickets at 6.07pm on the Fourth Day

Toss won by Derbyshire   Yorkshire 18 points, Derbyshire 5 points

Close of play: First Day, Derbyshire (1) 395-6 (A Harrison 42, V V Kelley 0, 96 overs), Second Day, no play; Third Day, Yorkshire (1) 225-1 (W A R Fraine 109, W A Luxton 71, 46 overs)

DERBYSHIRE

First Innings		Second Innings	
M D Wagstaff, c Light b Mike	18	not out	67
T R McGladdery, c Duke b Gunn	64	b Coad	7
E A Brookes, lbw b Cliff	8	not out	53
T A Wood, lbw b Cliff	167		
B Walkden, c Duke b Mike	22		
* M H McKiernan, c Duke b Mike	49		
A Harrison, not out	57		
§ V V Kelley, c Cliff b Mike	38		
H E Broderick, not out	1		
B S J Parker			
H A Sullivan	Did not bat		
J B Fallows			
Extras b 10, lb 7, w 1, nb 8	26	Extras nb 2	2
Total (7 wkts dec, 103 overs)	450	Total (1 wkt dec, 19 overs)	125

FoW: 1st 1-51 (Wagstaff), 2-67 (Brookes), 3-117 (McGladdery), 4-191 (Walkden), 5-271 (M H McKiernan), 6-389 (Wood), 7-449 (Kelley)
2nd 1-7 (T R McGladdery)

	O	M	R	W		O	M	R	W
Cliff	23	5	82	2	Coad	5	2	3	1
Mike	22	4	73	4	Gunn	4	0	14	0
Gunn	16	2	86	1	Wharton	5	0	54	0
Shutt	25	4	86	0	Luxton	5	1	54	0
Chohan	14	0	72	0					
Coad	3	0	34	0					

YORKSHIRE

First Innings		Second Innings	
W A R Fraine, not out	109	(5) c Brookes b Fallows	58
J H Wharton, b Parker	8	(1) c Broderick b Parker	87
W A Luxton, not out	71	not out	102
§ * H G Duke		(2) c Broderick b Brookes	26
Y Vagadia		(4) c Wagstaff b Parker	46
N M Kelly		not out	5I
I F Light			
J W Shutt			
B M Cliff			
J A Gunn	Did not bat		
B W M Mike			
J A Chohan			
B O Coad			
Extras b 4, lb 3, nb 30	37	Extras b 6, lb 11, nb 12	29
Total (1 wkt dec, 46 overs)	225	Total (4 wkts, 73.1 ovs)	353

FoW 1st: 1-36 (Wharton)
2nd 1-82 (Duke), 2-155 (Wharton), 3-243 (Vagadia), 4-347 (Fraine)

	O	M	R	W		O	M	R	W
Fallows	8	1	34	0	Fallows	11.1	1	70	1
Parker	11	0	72	1	Parker	13	1	62	2
Brookes	13	2	49	0	Harrisom	11	0	38	0
Broderick	6	0	26	0	Brookes	13	0	55	1
Sullivan	8	1	37	0	McKiernan	13	1	48	0
					Sullivan	10	0	59	0
					Wagstaff	2	0	4	0

Yorkshire substituted B O Coad for J A Chohan at the start of Day 2

Umpires: S Widdup and D M Jones   Scorers: J R Virrand J A Wallis

Second Eleven Championship
Yorkshire v. Durham

Played at Scarborough on July 11, 12, 13 and 14, 2023
Durham won by 131 runs at 2.15pm on the Fourth Day

Toss won by Yorkshire

Yorkshire 3 points, Durham 19 points

Close of play: First Day, Durham (1) 164-5 (H M Crawshaw 83, G S Drissell 17; 51.2 overs); Second Day, Durham (2) 105-1 (Crawshaw 33; 31 overs); Third Day, Yoskshire (2) 200-2 (W A R Fraine 61, y Vagadia 19; 39 overs)

DURHAM

First Innings		Second Innings	
H M Crawshaw, c Light b Mike	83	st Duke b Shutt	129
* B S McKinney, c Fraine b Cliff	4	c Parker b Shutt	66
R G Whitfield, c Duke b Mike	35	c Duke b Mike	15
L Trevaskis, c Parker b Mike	35	c Fraine b Shutt	101
J J Bushnell, lbw b Mike	0	lbw b Shutt	0
§ H S Mustard, c Duke b Parker	3	(7) c Kelly b Cliff	40
G S Drissell, b Mike	22	(8) c Duke b Leech	5
G Darwood, c Fraine b Mike	4	(9) not out	18
D Hogg, c Fraine b Cliff	21	(10) c Mike b Leech	0
B D Glover, c Mike b Leech	3		
O J Gibson, not out	0	b Shutt	0
P Coughlin	Did not bat	(6) c Light b Leech	10
Extras b 6, lb 2, nb 12	20	Extras b 5, lb 8, nb 6	19
Total (62.3 overs)	204	Total (95.4 overs)	403

FoW: 1-5 (McKinney), 2-64 (Whitfield, 3-105 (Trevaskis), 4-105 (Bushnell), 5-122 (Mustard),
1st 6-168 (Crawshaw), 7-174 (arwood), 8-177 (Drissell), 9-188 (Glover), 10-204 (Hogg)
FoW: 1-105 (McKinney), 2-126 (Whitfield), 3-323 (Crawshaw), 4-328 (Trevaskis), 5-331 (Bushnell),
2nd 6-352 (Coughlin), 7-374 (Drissell), 8-388 (Mustard), 9-393 (Hogg), 10-403 (Gibson)

	O	M	R	W		O	M	R	W
Cliff	16.3	4	57	2	Cliff	22	2	78	1
Leech	16	3	43	1	Leech	16	4	60	3
Parker	10	2	35	1	Mike	16	4	45	1
Mike	13	2	43	6	Shutt	16.4	3	64	5
Shutt	7	0	18	0	Parker	8	1	39	0
					Chohan	12	0	85	0
					Y Vagadia	5	0	19	0

YORKSHIRE

First Innings		Second Innings	
W A R Fraine, c Bushnell b Hogg	17	c Mustard b Drissell	90
N M Kelly, lbw b Hogg	27	c Mustard b Bushnell	74
§ * H G Duke, c Mustard b Hogg	1	b Gibson	20
Y Vagadia, c Bushnell b Darwood	26	c Drissell b Darwood	34
B W M Mike, c Hogg b Glover	4	c Mustard b Darwood	0
I F Light, c Drissell b Glover	0	lbw b Bushnell	0
A D Cree, lbw b Bushnell	12	lbw b Glover	16
D J Leech, not out	18	c Whitfield b Glover	21
J A Chohan,.lbw b Bushnell	0	c Mustard b Glover	7
J W Shutt, c Glover b Bushnell	15	not out	8
B M Cliff, c Trevaskis b Gibson	7	lbw b Darwood	4
B S J Parker	Did not bat		
Extras b 8, lb 2, w 1, nb 18	29	Extras b 18, lb 5, w 1, nb 22	46
Total (39.5 overs)	156	Total (76.1 overs)	320

FoW: 1-31 (Fraine), 2-38 (Duke), 3-86 (Vagadia), 4-93 (Mike), 5-93 (Light),
1st 6-112 (Kelly), 7-112 (Cree), 8-112 (Chohan), 9-130 (Shutt), 10-156 (Cliff)
FoW: 1-111 (Kelly), 2-164 (Duke), 3-241 (Vagadia), 4-243 (Mike), 5-252 (Light),
2nd 6-254 (Fraine), 7-287 (Cree), 8-302 (Leech), 9-303 (Chohan), 10-320 (Cliff)

	O	M	R	W		O	M	R	W
Gibson	7.5	0	52	1	Gibson	16	2	100	1
Hogg	11	5	23	3	Hogg	9	2	31	0
Glover	9	2	28	2	Bushnell	13	5	23	2
Darwood	6	0	26	1	Glover	12	2	68	3
Bushnell	6	1	18	3	Trevaskis	3	0	14	0
					Daewood	13.1	4	32	3
					Drissell	10	2	29	1

Umpires: I P Laurence and B Jones

Scorers: J R Virr and W K Telford

Second Eleven Championship
Gloucestershire v. Yorkshire

Played at Rockhampton on July 17, 18, 19 and 20, 2023
Yorkshire won by 156 runs at 4.39pm on the Third Day

Toss won by Yorkshire   Gloucestershire 3 points, Yorkshire 19 points

Close of play: First Day, Yorkshire (1) 160-9 (H G Duke 60, B M Cliff 1; 72 overs), Second Day, Yorkshire (2) 206-4 (H G Duke 40, A D Cree 1; 43 overs)

First Innings	YORKSHIRE		Second Innings	
W A R Fraine, c Wells b Davies	13	c Boorman b Middleton		40
B W M Mike,b Tagg	13	c Wells b Syed		69
W A Luxton, run out (Baker/Wells)	1	b Syed		31
§ * H G Duke, not out	64	lbw b Syed		49
Y Vagadia, c Taylor b Syed	43	b Syed		8
A D Cree, c Wells b Muchall	1	c Dunne b Syed		16
W J Bennison, c Dunne b Muchall	1	lbw b Middleton		16
D J Leech, run out (Baker/Wells)	1	lbw b Middleton		7
J A Chohan, c Middleton b Davies	2	c Taylor b Middleton		3
J W Shutt, lbw b Middleton	16	not out		16
B M Cliff, b Syed	1	b Foreman		15
B S J Parker	Did not bat			
Extras b 1, w 1, nb 6"	8	Extras b 9, lb 8, nb 8		25
Total (75.3 overs)	164	Total (73.4 overs)		295

FoW: 1-17 (Fraine), 2-18 (Luxton), 3-32 (Mike), 4-101 (Vagadia), 5-106 (Cree),
1st   6-112 (Bennison, 7-115 (Leech), 8-118 (Chohan), 9-155 (Shutt, 10-164 (Cliff)
FoW: 1-90 (Fraine), 2-126 (Mike), 3-169 (Luxton), 4-199 (Vagadia), 5-220 (Duke),
2nd   6-235 (Cree), 7-251 (Bennison), 8-259 (Chohan), 9-260 (Leech), 10-295 (Cliff)

	O	M	R	W		O	M	R	W
Muchall	13	1	31	2	Davies	14	0	65	0
Davies	15	2	40	2	Muchall	5	0	22	0
Tagg	10	3	17	1	Tagg	3	0	17	0
Baker	3	1	7	0	Baker	4	0	21	0
Middleton	14	4	33	1	Middleton	16	3	51	4
Syed	15.3	1	29	2	Syed	24	3	80	5
Taylor	3	0	4	0	Taylor	5	0	21	0
Smith	2	0	2	0	Boorman	0.4	0	1	1

First Innings	GLOUCESTERSHIRE		Second Innings	
E W O Middleton, b Parker	26	lbw b Mike		29
T W Boorman, c Vagadia b Cliff	7	c Fraine b Leech		8
§ B J J Wells, c Duke b Mike	28	(5) b Parker		0
J M R Taylor, c Duke b Parker	15	b Shutt		23
A M Syed, b Parker	13	(6) b Shutt		3
M A J Dunne, not out	38	(7) lbw b Shutt		18
Z A Sharif, c Mike b Parker	0	(3) lbw b Shutt		17
* T M J Smith, lbw b Parker	0	not out		27
P B Muchall, c Parker b Leech	5	b Shutt		10
J A Davies, b Leech	0	c Duke b Chohan		0
I J Tagg, c Vagadia b Leech	7	c Luxton b Chohan		2
R T Baker	Did not bat			
Extras b 10, lb 4, nb 2	16	Extras b 1, lb 10		11
Total (39.3 overs)	155	Total (44 overs)		148

FoW: 1-11 (Boorman), 2-60 (Middleton), 3-68 (Wells), 4-85 (Syed), 5-92 (Taylor),
1st   6-92 (Sharif), 7-92 (Smith), 8-125 (Muchall), 9-131 (Davies), 10-155 (Tagg)
FoW: 1-28 (Boorman), 2-59 (Middleton), 3-83 (Sharif), 4-86 (Taylor), 5-86 (Wells),
2nd   6-104 (Syed), 7-111 (Dunne), 8-139 (Muchall), 9-140 (Davies), 10-148 (Tagg)

	O	M	R	W		O	M	R	W
Cliff	11	0	58	1	Parker	8	2	20	1
Leech	11.3	2	40	3	Mike	6	1	17	1
Parker	9	2	22	5	Cliff	5	1	8	0
Mike	8	2	21	1	Leech	5	0	19	1
					Shutt	14	2	41	5
					Chohan	6	0	32	2

Gloucestershire substituted B J J Wells for Z A Shafi as wicketkeeper

Umpires: J C Tredwell and K Sumra   Scorers : C Jones and J R Virr

Second Eleven Championship
Lancashire v. Yorkshire

Played at Southport and Birkdale CC on September 4, 5, 6 and 7, 2023
Yorkshire won by 316 runs at 4.15pm on the Third Day

Toss won by Yorkshire   Lancashire 3 points, Yorkshire 23 points
Close of play: First Day, Yorkshire (1) 433 (J W Shutt 6*; 95 overs); Second Day, Yorkshire (2) 137-5 (W A R Fraine 18, N M Kelly 0; 29 overs)

First Innings	YORKSHIRE	Second Innings	
* W A Luxton, st Hurst b Singh	70	b Morley	68
Y Vagadia, lbw b Boyden	22	b Morley	40
A R Shetty, c Hurst b Birkman	72	lbw b Morley	2
§ H G Duke, c Dickinson b Birkman	2	b Morley	0
W A R Fraine, lbw b Dunn	38	c Hurst b Morley	21
B W M Mike, c Selby b Singh	26	b Dickinson	3
N M Kelly, c Lavelle b Birkman	79	c Hurst b Singh	45
M E Milnes, c Singh b Dunn	91	c Selby b Singh	34
D J Leech, run out (Walker/Singh)	12	b Singh	15
M W Edwards, c Hurst b Dunn	0	not out	14
J W Shutt, not out	6	not out	2
C J McMurran	Did not bat		
Extras b 7, lb 2, nb 6	15	Extras b 5, lb 1, w 1, nb 2	9
Total (95 overs)	433	Total 9 wkts dec, 54 overs)	253

FoW: 1-38 (Vagadia), 2-155 (Shetty), 3-157 (Duke), 4-193 (Luxton), 5-239 (Mike),
1st   6-239 (Fraine), 7-388 (Kelly), 8-406 (Leech), 9-410 (Edwards), 10-433 (Milnes)
FoW: 1-81 (Vagadia), 2-89 (Shetty), 3-89 (Duke), 4-124 (Luxton), 5-135 (Mike),
2nd   6-144 (Fraine), 7-219 (Milnes), 8-220 (Kelly), 9-247 (Leech)

	O	M	R	W		O	M	R	W
Birkman	16	2	53	3	Chapple	3	0	24	0
Boyden	10	2	40	1	Birkman	3	0	19	0
Chapple	9	4	29	0	Morley	24	4	79	5
Walker	10	0	59	0	Dunn	3	0	24	0
Dunn	12	1	69	3	Singh	12	2	53	3
Hussain	9	0	50	0	Dickinson	9	0	48	1
Singh	21	2	99	2					
Dickinson	8	0	25	0					

First Innings	LANCASHIRE	Second Innings	
H P N Singh, c Kelly b Vagadia	75	(2) lbw b Milnes	7
§ M F Hurst, c Shetty b Leech	0	(1) c Luxton b Leech	14
* G I D Lavelle, c Edwards b Leech	0	c Mike b Milnes	35
C J Dickinson, c Duke b Edwards	13	b Leech	0
G K Reddy, lbw b Edwards	0	lbw b McMurran	20
L B Selby, c Leech b Mike	11	c Leech b Shutt	27
J Chapple, c Edwards b McMurran	18	b Shutt	0
J P Morley, b Shutt	57	c and b Vagadia	21
H D Walker, not out	2	c McMurran b Vagadia	26
H A Hussain, lbw b Shutt	1	lbw b Shutt	5
H M Birkman, lbw b Shutt	0	not out	0
J A Boyden	Did not bat		
Extras b 1, w 1, nb 6	8	Extras b 11, lb 6, nb 8, pen 5	30
Total (64.3 overs)	185	Total (42 overs)	185

FoW: 1-7 (Hurst), 2-7 (Lavelle), 3-31 (Dickinson), 4-31 (Reddy), 5-54 (Selby),
1st   6-81 (J Chapple), 7-182 (Morley), 8-182 (Singh), 9-183 (Hussain), 10-185 Birkman)
FoW: 1-29 (Singh), 2-29 (Hurst), 3-39 (Dickinson), 4-79 (Reddy), 5-124 (Selby),
2nd   6-128 (Lavelle), 7-132 (Chapple), 8-168 (Walker), 9-177 (Morley), 10-185 (Hussain)

	O	M	R	W		O	M	R	W
Leech	7	2	30	2	Milnes	7	2	14	2
Milnes	10	1	28	0	Leech	7	0	37	2
Edwards	12	6	30	2	Edwards	6	2	16	1
Mike	9	2	32	1	Mike	4	1	23	0
McMurran	1	0	6	1	McMurran	5	0	13	1
Shutt	16.3	5	38	3	Shutt	10	1	47	3
Y Vagadia	9	3	20	1	Y Vagadia	3	0	13	2

*In Yorkshire's second innings Lancashire substituted G I D Lavelle * for M F Hurst† as wicketkeepe*
Umpires: B Shafayat and J P Prince   Scorers: J Egan and J Virr

Second Eleven Championship
Surrey v. Yorkshire

Played at Guildford on September 11, 12, 13 and 14, 2023
Yorkshire won by 7 wickets at 2.34pm on the Fourth Day

Toss won by Surrey   Surrey 6 points, Yorkshire 23 points
Close of play: First Day, Surrey (1) 348-8 (O F M Sykes 6, G S Virdi 0; 96 overs); Second Day, Yorkshire (1) 332-5 (B W M Mike 57, I F Light 2; 79 overs); Third Day, Surrey (2) 156-6 (B S Sudharson 56, T M Ealham 7; 52 overs)

First Innings	SURREY		Second Innings	
A S Gill, lbw b Gunn	30	b Milnes	5
* B B A Geddes, lbw b Leech	15	lbw b Leech	16§
§ J W Blake, c Luxton b Milnes	142	c Duke b Milnes	1
B S Sudharsan, lbw b Milnes	6	c Fraine b Leech	60
S P van der Merwe, c Duke b Leech	111	run out (Mike)	23
O F M Sykes, c Duke b Leech	55	c Leech b Shutt	10
D T Moriarty, c Kelly b Shutt	1	c Gunn b Shutt	18
T M Ealham, c Duke b Shutt	5	not ou t	36
M P Dunn, b Mike	1	b Leech	0
G S Virdi, c Shutt b Gunn	29	b Mike	21
S H Stuart-Reckling, not out	0	b Mike	0
A M French	Did not bat		
Extras b 14, lb 3, w 3, nb 12	32	Extras b 16, lb 3, w 5	24
Total (110.1 overs)	427	Total (72 overs)	214

FoW: 1-32 (Geddes), 2-80 (Gill), 3-98 (Sudharsan), 4-327 (van der Merwe), 5-333 (Blake),
1st   6-335 (Moriarty), 7-347 (Ealham), 8-348 (Dunn), 9-427 (Sykes), 10-427 (Virdi
FoW: 1-8 (Gill), 2-22 (Blake), 3-22 (Geddes), 4-72 (van der Merwe), 5-99 (Sykes),
2nd   6-136 (Moriarty), 7-174 (Sudharson), 8-184 (Dunn), 9-214 (Virdi), 10-214 (Stuart-Reckling)

	O	M	R	W		O	M	R	W
Milnes	16	4	44	2	Milnes	11	1	32	2
Leech	15	1	80	3	Leech	16	1	68	3
McMurran	10	0	42	0	Gunn	9	1	19	0
Mike	21	3	65	1	Mike	13	3	33	2
Gunn	8.1	0	29	2	Shutt	18	6	26	2
Shutt	35	3	108	2	McMurran	5	2	17	0
Y Vagadia	5	0	42	0					

First Innings	YORKSHIRE		Second Innings	
W A Luxton, c Geddes b Virdi	115	c Dunn b Sudharsan	58
Y Vagadia, b Moriarty	56	c Moriarty b Sudharsan	81
N M Kelly, b Ealham	18	not out	22
§ H G Duke, c Gill b Ealham	8	lbw b Sudharsan	0
W A R Fraine, b Moriarty	67	not out	4
B W M Mike, c Moriarty b Ealham	112		
I F Light, c Ealham b Moriarty	27		
M E Milnes, st Blake b Moriarty	36		
D J Leech, c Geddes b French	2		
J W Shutt, not out	9		
C J McMurran, lbw b Moriarty	0		
J A Gunn	Did not bat		
Extras b 11, lb 4, w 2, nb 10	27	Extras b 1, lb 2	3
Total (121 overs)	477	Total (3 wkts, 29.5 overs)	168

FoW: 1-64 (Vagadia), 2-120 (Kelly), 3-151 (Duke), 4-252 (Luxton), 5-300 (Fraine),
1st   6-403 (Light), 7-419 (Mike), 8-432 (Leech), 9-477 (Milnes), 10-477 (McMurran)
2nd   1-111 (Luxton), 2-164 (Vagadia), 3-164 (Duke)

	O	M	R	W		O	M	R	W
Dunn	13	2	66	0	Dunn	3	1	22	0
French	15	0	96	1	Moriarty	9	1	36	0
Moiarty	40	6	102	5	Stuart-Reckling	5	1	29	0
Stuart-Reckling	14	2	46	0	Ealham	7	0	55	0
Virdi	14	0	69	1	Sudharsan	5.5	0	23	3
Ealham	23	1	86	3					
Sudharsan	2	1	1	0					

Umpires: P D Nicholls and D R Turl   Scorers: D J Hagger and J R Virr

Second Eleven Championship
Durham v. Yorkshire

Played at the Riverside, Chester-le-Street, on September 18, 19, 20 and 21, 2023
Yorkshire won by 7 wkts at 5.19pm on the Fourth Day

Toss won by Yorkshire
Durham 0 points, Yorkshire 18 points
Close of play: First Day, Durham (1) 145-7 (G A Darwood 17, S J C McAlindon 13; 56 overs), Second Day, no play; Third Day, no play

First Innings	DURHAM		Second Innings	
H M Crawshaw, c Duke b Milnes		5	c Duke b Milnes	0
J J Kelly, b Gunn		27	lbw b McMurran	11
R G Whitfield, c Fisher b Gunn		23	c Kelly b Leech	15
C Gaffney, b Milnes		20	c Duke b Leech	25
L Trevaskis, c Fraine b Shutt		22	c Light b Fisher	20
L Symington, b Milnes		3	b Milnes	7
§ H S Mustard, b Milnes		0	not out	7
G A Darwood, not out		17	c McMurran b Luxton	4
S J C McAlindon, not out		13		
L S Robinson				
B D Glover	Did not bat			
O J Gibson				
Extras 9 b, lb 4, w 2		15	Extras b 1, lb 1	2
Total (7 wkts dec, 56 overs)		145	Total (7 wkts dec, 33 overs)	91

FoW: 1-6 (Crawshaw), 2-51 (Whitfield), 3-75 (Kelly), 4-92 (Gaffney), 5-100 (Symington),
1st 6-100 (Mustard), 7- 119 (Trevaskis)
FoW: 1-0 (Crawshaw), 2-26 (Kelly), 3-26 (Whitfield), 4-55 (Gaffney), 5-69 (Symington),
2nd 6-76 (Trevaskis), 7- 91 (Darwood)

	O	M	R	W		O	M	R	W
Milnes	15	8	26	4	Milnes	10	5	11	2
Leech	12	3	30	0	Fisher	12	3	36	1
Gunn	10	2	28	2	McMurran	4	1	11	1
McMurran	7	1	28	0	Leech	6	1	26	2
Shutt	11	2	20	1	Luxton	1	0	6	1
Y Vagadia	1	1	0	0					

YORKSHIRE
(First Innings forfeited)
Second Innings

* W A Luxton, b Glover		48
Y Vagadia, b Glover		30
N M Kelly, not out		67
§ H G Duke, b Gibson		28
W A R Fraine, not out		53
I F Light		
M D Fisher		
D J Leech		
M E Milnes	Did not bat	
J W Shutt		
C J McMurran		
J A Gunn		
Extras b 1, lb 6, nb 4		11
Total (3 wkts, 45.5 overs)		237

FoW: 1-80 (Vagadia), 2-87 (Luxton); 3-136 (Duke)

	O	M	R	W
Robinson	10	2	44	0
Darwood	7.5	1	45	0
Glover	9	2	44	2
Gibson	9	0	53	1
McAlindon	3	0	12	0
Trevaskis	5	1	15	0
Symington	2	0	17	0

Umpires: S Widdup and J Montgomery-Else   Scorers: G Maddison and J R Virr

SECOND ELEVEN CHAMPIONSHIP
AVERAGES 2023

Played 11   Won 6   Lost 3   Drawn 2

BATTING AND FIELDING
(Qualification 5 innings)

Player	M.	I.	N.O.	Runs	H.S.	Avge	100s	50s	ct/st
N M Kelly	6	9	3	357	79	59.50	0	3	5
W A R Fraine	9	15	4	639	109 *	58.09	1	5	11
W A Luxton	9	14	2	681	115	56.75	2	4	5
Y Vagadia	11	17	1	612	81	38.25	0	4	3
B W M Mike	9	12	1	365	112	33.18	1	3	6
H G Duke	11	17	1	418	66	26.12	0	2	28/2
J W Shutt	11	13	8	94	17	18.80	0	0	2
D J Leech	10	13	1	196	47	16.33	0	0	6
A D Cree	4	6	0	64	16	10.67	0	0	0
B M Cliff	8	9	3	44	15	7.33	0	0	6
J A Chohan	6	8	0	26	15	3.25	0	0	0

Also played

Player	M.	I.	N.O.	Runs	H.S.	Avge	100s	50s	ct/st
I F Light	6	4	0	31	27	7.75	0	0	5
C J McMurran	4	1	0	0	0	0.00	0	0	2
J A Gunn	4	0	0	0	—	—	0	0	1
M E Milnes	3	3	0	161	91	53.67	0	1	0
B S J Parker	3	0	0	0	—	—	0	0	3
F J Bean	2	3	0	126	70	42.00	0	1	2
W J Bennison	2	3	1	34	17 *	17.00	0	0	0
M W Edwards	2	2	1	14	14 *	14.00	0	0	2
M D Fisher	2	0	0	0	—	—	0	0	1
G C H Hill	2	3	0	260	138	86.67	1	1	5
J M Bairstow	1	2	0	154	97	77.00	0	2	2
B O Coad	1	0	0	0	—	—	0	0	0
J J Hen-Boisen	1	0	0	0	—	—	0	0	0
M L Revis	1	2	0	131	112	65.50	1	0	1
A R Shetty	1	2	0	74	72	37.00	0	1	1
J A Tattersall	1	2	0	39	38	19.50	0	0	0
A J Taylor-Clarke	1	0	0	0	—	—	0	0	0

BOWLING
(Qualification 10 wickets)

Player	Overs	Mdns	Runs	Wkts	Avge	Best	5wI	10wM
M E Milnes	69	21	155	12	4-26	12.91	0	0
B W M Mike	172.4	26	567	25	6-43	22.68	1	0
D J Leech	207.3	36	771	33	3-22	23.36	0	0
J W Shutt	245.4	33	817	29	5-41	28.17	2	0
B M Cliff	172.4	36	621	17	3-38	36.25	0	0

Also bowled

Player	Overs	Mdns	Runs	Wkts	Avge	Best	5wI	10wM
J A Chohan	60.3	2	290	3	96.67	2-32	0	0
B O Coad	8	2	37	1	37.00	1- 3	0	0
M W Edwards	25	8	67	4	16.75	2-21	0	0
M D Fisher	22	5	79	3	26.33	2-43	0	0
J A Gunn	65.1	8	232	6	38.67	2-28	0	0
J J Hen-Boisen	6	1	22	0	—	—	0	0
G C H Hill	45.4	10	108	8	13.50	6-45	0	1
W A Luxton	6	1	60	1	60.00	1- 6	0	0
C J McMurran	37	5	131	3	43.67	1- 6	0	0
B S J Parker	56	10	226	9	25.11	5-22	0	1
M L Revis	24	3	80	2	40.00	2-80	0	0
A J Taylor-Clarke	14	0	70	0	—	—	0	0
Y Vagadia	23	4	94	3	31.33	2-13	0	0
J H Wharton	5	0	54	0	—	—	0	0

SECOND ELEVEN T20 IN 2023

Two matches versus the same opponents at the same venue on the same day.

SEMI-FINALS

Yorkshire 160-4	lost to Derbyshire	161-4	by 6 wickets
Glamorgan 202-7	beat Hampshire	133	by 69 runs

FINAL

Derbyshire 192-3	beat Glamorgan	187	by 5 runs

*All matches played at Sir John Paul Getty's ground
at Wormsley, Buckinghamshire, on June 15, 2023*

NORTHERN GROUP FINAL TABLE

		P	W	L	Points	Net Run Rate
1	**Yorkshire**	**10**	**8**	**2**	**16**	**1.624**
2	Derbyshire	10	7	3	14	1.000
3	Lancashire	10	5	5	10	-0.025
4	Nottinghamshire	10	4	6	8	-0.490
5	Leicestershire	10	3	7	6	-0.647
6	Durham	10	3	7	6	-1.447

CENTRAL GROUP FINAL TABLE

		P	W	L	Points	Net Run Rate
1	Glamorgan	10	8	2	16	0.780
2	Warwickshire	10	5	5	10	0.746
3	Gloucestershire	10	5	5	10	-0.023
4	Somerset	10	5	5	10	-0.200
5	Worcestershire	10	4	6	8	-0.502
6	Northamptonshire	10	3	7	6	-0.847

SOUTHERN GROUP FINAL TABLE

		P	W	L	Points	Net Run Rate
1	Hampshire	10	7	3	14	0.397
2	Sussex	10	6	4	12	0.887
3	Essex	10	6	4	12	0.388
4	Kent	10	5	5	10	0.162
5	Surrey	10	4	6	8	0.100
6	Middlesex	10	2	8	4	-1.959

PREVIOUS WINNERS

2011	**Sussex**, who beat Durham by 24 runs
2012	**England Under-19s**, who beat Sussex by eight wickets
2013	**Surrey**, who beat Middlesex by six runs
2014	**Leicesterhire**, who beat Somerset by 11 runs
2015	**Middlesex**, who beat Kent by four wickets
2016	**Middlesex**, who beat Somerset by two wickets
2017	**Sussex**, who beat Hampshire by 24 runs
2018	**Lancashire**, who beat Essex by 25 runs
2019	**Glamorgan**, who beat Hampshire by 1 run
2020	*No competition because of the Coronovirus epidemic*
2021	**Warwickshire**, who beat beat Sussex by 54 runs
2022	**Glamorgan**, who beat Leicestershire by 5 wkts

SECOND ELEVEN T20 AVERAGES 2023

Played 11   Won 8   Lost 3

BATTING AND FIELDING

(Qualification 3 innings)

Player	M	I	N.O	Runs	H.S	Avge	30s	50s	Ct/St
W A R Fraine	9	9	2	350	113 *	50.00	1	0	8
J H Wharton	6	6	1	199	68 *	39.80	1	2	3
N M Kelly	5	4	1	117	42	39.00	2	0	4
H G Duke	7	6	1	150	50 *	30.00	2	1	3/1
W A Luxton	7	7	0	158	42	22.57	3	0	2
B W M Mike	3	3	1	45	25 *	22.50	0	0	4
F J Bean	8	7	0	153	54	21.85	2	1	7
J A Tattersall	4	4	1	59	34	19.67	1	0	7
D M Bess	4	3	1	37	21	18.50	0	0	0
J W Shutt	9	3	2	15	10 *	15.00	0	0	3
G C H Hill	7	6	1	63	23 *	12.60	0	0	6
B M Cliff	10	3	1	23	14	11.50	0	0	1
Y Vagadia	9	8	2	56	25	9.33	0	0	2
D J Leech	6	4	1	17	7	5.67	0	0	1

Also played

Player	M	I	N.O	Runs	H.S	Avge	30s	50s	Ct/St
M L Revis	3	2	1	48	44 *	48.00	1	0	1
Shan Masood	2	1	0	43	43	43.00	1	0	0
A Lyth	1	1	0	41	41	41.00	1	0	0
I Mohammed	1	1	0	21	21	21.00	0	0	1
J A Thompson	2	2	0	17	11	8.50	0	0	1
J A Chohan	2	2	0	10	9	5.00	0	0	0
B O Coad	4	2	1	1	1 *	1.00	0	0	2
J J Hoyle	5	1	1	1	1 *	—	0	0	1
L Owens	2	1	1	6	6 *	—	0	0	1
J A Anson	1	1	1	8	8 *	—	0	0	0
M D Fisher	1	1	0	0	0	—	0	0	0
H H Round	2	0	0	0	—	—	0	0	0
C J McMurran	1	0	0	0	—	—	0	0	0

BOWLING

(Qualification 5 wickets)

Player	Overs	Mdns	Runs	Wkts	Avge	Best
J W Shutt	32	0	186	14	13.28	4-10
B W M Mike	10	0	94	7	13.42	3-12
D M Bess	12	0	72	5	14.40	2-19
B M Cliff	32.3	0	257	15	17.13	3-22
G C H Hill	20	0	132	6	22.00	2-15
D J Leech	21	0	177	7	25.28	2-23
B O Coad	15	0	131	5	26.20	2-29

Also bowled

Player	Overs	Mdns	Runs	Wkts	Avge	Best
M D Fisher	4	0	26	3	8.67	3-26
J A Thompson	6.3	0	45	3	15.00	2-29
J A Chohan	6.2	0	55	3	18.33	3-14
M L Revis	9	0	61	3	20.33	2-21
Y Vagadia	13	0	106	4	26.50	2-17
C J McMurran	3	0	29	1	29.00	2-24
L Owens	3	0	29	1	29.00	1-18
J J Hoyle	16	0	131	3	43.67	1-21
H H Round	4	0	45	1	45.00	1-26

STUDENTS NARROWLY MISS OUT ON DOUBLE FIRST

By Graham Hardcastle

The county's fledglings enjoyed an impressive summer in 2023, narrowly missing out on the double. They finished top of their regional three-day Championship group and were beaten national T20 finalists.

The ECB have for the last couple of seasons labelled their Academy competitions as Under-18s events, and Yorkshire can look back on a job well done.

It is often said that below first-team level at Headingley results are far from the be-all-and-end-all. They help massively. Of course they do, but player performance, development and progression is arguably of primary importance.

A number of teenagers shone brightly, including the likes of Noah Kelly and Louie Owens, who in August were called up to an England Under-19s invitational squad to face Australia and Ireland in both red and white-ball cricket.

For batter Kelly, whose summer exploits have been mentioned in our second-team review, you will find many a good judge suggesting he is one to watch in the next few years. All-rounder Owens is from the same Sheffield Collegiate production line as Joe Root.

Further representation came in the form of a sextet of call-ups for the ECB's Super Fours competition at Loughborough in July. Kelly and Owens were joined by Jawad Akhtar, Josh Hoyle, Isaac Light and Harvey Round. The Super Fours pits the best Under-17s and 18s players across the counties against each other, split between four regions.

"They're exciting experiences for the lads, and very exciting for us that we had good representation," said Academy head coach Tom Craddock.

The first half of the Academy summer was white-ball concentrated, the players generally balancing their on-field commitments with education. Despite a could-do-better showing in 50-over cricket, Yorkshire won three of their five T20 matches to qualify for Finals Day, which actually took place in September at Kibworth in Leicestershire to bring the curtain down on the season.

Yorkshire beat Northamptonshire in the morning semi-final before losing to Surrey in the afternoon final. Even though the T20s drew to a close at the end of the season the second half of 2023 was more red ball concentrated when players had finished their exams.

This competition is regionalised, with the furthest a team can go being to win their group, which Yorkshire did impressively as they went unbeaten across five matches to finish top by a point from Nottinghamshire. There were four draws and a win.

"We competed well in all games, which was really cool," said Craddock. "From a performance angle, it's been very nice to see.

"The other thing we managed to do was play 29 players, and being able to balance performance with the development of a lot of our players has been an incredible win for all of us. It's something we're very, very proud of."

As well as the in-competition cricket, Craddock and James Martin, Yorkshire's head of the boys' performance pathway, boosted the Academy's summer schedule with a host of friendlies, a training camp or two and team-building activities.

Prior to the Championship cricket kicking off a couple of away trips to face Surrey and Hampshire were undertaken. The Hampshire fixture at Basingstoke ended up producing one of the matches of the summer, yielding what can only be described as a head-scratching finish. Those who witnessed it will not forget it, though it ended in an away defeat.

Chasing 202, the hosts were cruising at 200-5 before slipping to 201-9, only just stumbling across the line. "Clearly we'd have wanted to win that game," Craddock said. "But it was amazing nevertheless."

A number of Craddock's charges got their chance in the second team.

Will Bennison was one of those, and you can bet your bottom dollar there will be more to shout about in 2024.

Yorkshire Academy 2024

Jawad Akhtar (Wakefield Thornes), Will Bennison (Sheriff Hutton Bridge), Matthew Firbank (Clifton Alliance), Tom Fraine (York), Josh Hoyle (Almondbury Wesleyan), Noah Kelly (Driffield Town), Louie Owens (Sheffield Collegiate), Harvey Round (Barnsley Woolley Miners), Owen Smith (Barnsley Woolley Miners), Joe Thompson (Clifton Alliance) and Alex Wade (Olicanian).

THE MAGNIFICENT SEVEN

The County Age-Group structure was left celebrating a magnificent seven last summer — that being the number of their Under-15s players called up to the prestigious Bunbury Festival.

Peter Greenfield, Abdullah Hussain, Rizwan Ishfaq, Monty Jackson, Dan Longley, Aaron Ratnalingam, Aarush Shinde all took their place in the North Squad at Loughborough, half that total squad.

Before we have a look at some county results it is worth noting some significant individual performances.

Greenfield scored a pair of centuries for Yorkshire Under-15s, the best of which was an unbeaten 179 in a 50-over friendly win over Derbyshire in August. Will Bennison also matched that for the Under-16s, again in a 50-over friendly victory against Northamptonshire.

PETER GREENIELD
Photo: Kidz In Focus

Pleasingly, there are too many five-wicket hauls to mention. This *Yearbook* would be like the Magna Carta if we did! But we can highlight a couple.

Louie Wilson claimed a fabulous 7-56 in the second innings of a two-day Under-14s friendly win over Lancashire at Scarborough in late August after claiming 4-18 in the first innings.

Isaac Wilkes also returned 6-25 for the Under-12s in a 40-over friendly win against Derbyshire.

The performances of Under-13 Safiullah Abrar were highly

LOUIE WILSON
Photo: Kidz In Focus

impressive. He posted 503 runs in all cricket and added 30 wickets. He has been elevated to join the county's Emerging Players Programme in 2024 as its youngest member.

Yorkshire's male County Age-Group system starts aged 12 and runs through to Under-16s.

The highlight for the Under-12s was an unbeaten Festival at Rugby School, where they saw off Warwickshire, Middlesex, Durham and Lancashire.

The Under-14s were in pole position to qualify for the knockout stages of their County Cup, only denied when games against Cumbria and Lincolnshire were rained off.

The Under-16s were beaten finalists in the County Cup by Middlesex for the second year running, having topped Group One with seven wins from eight.

SAFIULLAH ABRAR
Youngest Emerging Player

Yorkshire Emerging Players 2024

Muhammad Safiullah Abrar (Wakefield Thornes), Ibrahim Ahmed (Cleckheaton), Musa Altaf (Sheffield United), Tom Bradley (Sheffield Collegiate), Ed Burch (Hallam), Noah Chapman (Birstall), Monty Dodsworth (Acomb), Peter Greenfield (Harrogate), Josh Hen-Boisen (Wakefield Thornes), Rizwan Ishfaq (Sheffield Collegiate), Harry Pearson (Anston), Aaron Ratnalingam (New Rover), Jack Redshaw (Scarborough), Aarush Shinde (Elsecar), Jay Singh (Hallam), Ben Squires (Scarborough), Alex Strain (York), Bradley Sylvester (Cleckheaton), Charlie Taylor (Honley) and Louie Wilson (Studley Royal).

GEMS WHO SPARKLE THROUGH SUMMER OF STORMS

By Graham Hardcastle

Rain, rain go away...

The Northern Diamonds Academy lost approximately 40 per cent of their playing time to the weather in 2023, highlighted by a ruined early-summer festival at Millfield School in Taunton and a washed-out two-day friendly against Thunder at Weetwood at the start of August.

Yet despite this, there was plenty to look back on with significant encouragement.

Batter Erin Thomas impressed greatly, and in January was called up to an England Under-19s training camp ahead of potential selection for a Sri Lanka tour in March and April. Regional teammates Trudy Johnson and Maddie Ward got the same call.

For wicketkeeper-batter Ward, a new arrival in the Academy from the Blaze, selection came during the same December week that she won the inaugural women's T10 European Championship title with England's National Counties XI in Malaga.

The Millfield School rainy festival was one of two summer Academy festivals there. At the second one in July the Diamonds lost four games and had another rained off, while Thomas was the leading run-scorer across all teams with 139.

It was not a surprise to hear Diamonds senior regional talent manager Tom Cant say: "Erin was a highlight of the festival for us. We'll look back on the festival as a learning curve — the long travel to Millfield, the weather and preparation, etc — and we'll be better for it next year.

"With several new players in the squad and the festival washout in April, it was the first festival with cricket for half the squad, and it ended up being one of those weeks where we kept coming up just short."

Cricket was played across a variety of formats at Academy level, with players crossing over regularly between that side and the second team. Thirteen of the 14 in the 2023 Academy played second-team cricket.

The Academy were at their strongest in 50-over cricket: "We've got a few things to work on in T20 cricket, which is exciting to look forward to as a coach," Cant said.

After the second trip to Millfield and the rained off two-dayer the

Player of the Year: Emily Whiting with Mark Harrison, regional talent manager, left, and Tom Cant, senior regional talent manager.

Diamonds won a pair of 50-over friendlies against the Southern Vipers at Northallerton and Darlington in early August. Another 50-over victory came against Thunder at Ramsbottom when more of a senior presence was evident across both regions — who were giving game time to their players not on duty in the Hundred.

The Diamonds, with 204 all out, won by two runs. Thomas made 57 and Rebecca Duckworth 82 against her home region before Phoebe Turner starred with 5-31 from 10 overs. The hosts were put out for 202.

Performances of note in the games against the Vipers came from the likes of Harriet Robson with a 77, Ellie Nightingale 49 and Emily Whiting, above, and Lucy Lindley with a pair of four-wicket hauls.

North v. North matches were put on by the England management at Loughborough later in the summer as part of their Under-19s Talent Identification process, and six Diamonds players were selected. Thomas and Johnson were added to Olivia Miller, Elicia Pollard, Robson and Grace Thompson, but Thompson was unavailable to take part.

"Three of those five are in their first year on the Academy, which shows the progress they are making," said Cant, who was one of a few members of the Diamonds backroom staff involved at Loughborough.

As for the rained off two-day friendly against Thunder...should there be more longer format cricket at regional level, be it seniors or below? Cant thinks there should: "Longer format cricket is something that looks to be appearing, and is here to stay in the women's game."

PROFESSIONAL — AND IT SHOWS

Last year was marked a crucial one for the professionalisation of the Girls' County Age-Group Pathway in Yorkshire.

Transitioning from the Yorkshire Cricket Board to the county club enabled full-time staff to be dedicated to the girls' pathway for the first time.

This move has proven to pay dividends in the performances of each of those age groups.

The Under-18s finished top of their 40-over ECB Cup group, winning six of eight matches.

Notable performances during the group stage included 111

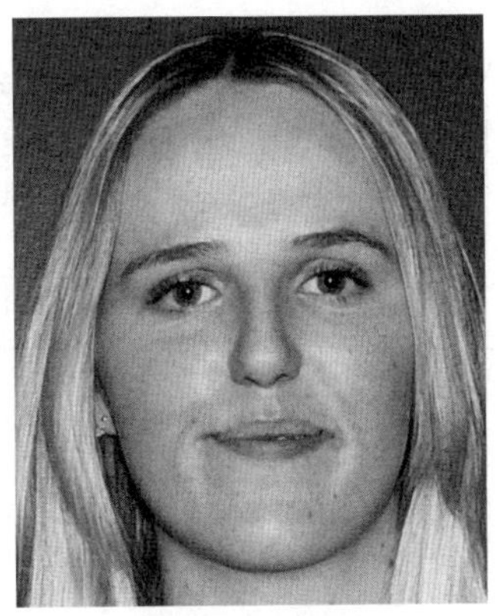

ERIN THOMAS

from Erin Thomas as part of a 193-run partnership with her Northern Diamonds' Academy teammate Frances Lonsdale to beat Lancashire convincingly at Scarborough, while Rhia Sedha and Leah Burkinshaw both claimed five-wicket hauls in the same fixture against Cumbria. Unfortunately, the team were beaten quarter-finalists by eventual champions Staffordshire.

Yorkshire's Under-13s enjoyed a good year, highlighted best by going on an eight-match unbeaten run from late June to early August. Incredibly, that included a pair of T20 ties on the same day against Nottinghamshire at Saxton in early July.

Navya Gutta was a centurion with 102 not out in a 35-over win over Northumberland, as was Amelia Oliver for the Under-15s with an unbeaten 121 in a 40-over win against Lancashire.

The Under-11s, 13s and 15s enjoyed productive summer festivals at Scarborough, Malvern and Rugby.

The Under-11s enjoyed a 20-day programme including a Malvern Festival, where Pippa MacLelland was the standout with a stunning 77 not out in game of 19 overs per side against Durham. Batting at seven, she underpinned a 143-9 total in a game which saw no other teammate make 10. Yorkshire won by 14 runs.

Emily Roberts claimed a superb 6-11 in an Under-18s win over an Australian Wanderers Touring team, while Jeanie Lee (Under-15s), Evie

Hopper (Under-13s) and Jess Thompson (Under-18s) all claimed five-wicket hauls added to the exploits of Sedha and Burkinshaw for the Under-18s.

Northern Diamonds Academy 2024

Mary Butler, Trudy Johnson (both Durham), Lucy Lindley, Frances Lonsdale (both Yorkshire), Olivia Miller (Northumberland), Ellie Nightingale, Amelia Oliver, Elicia Pollard, Lucy Randle-Bissell (all Yorkshire), Harriet Robson, Freya Rook (both Northumberland), Beth Slater, Erin Thomas (both Yorkshire), Grace Thompson (Durham), Maddie Ward (Nottinghamshire) and Emily Whiting (Northumberland).

Northern Diamonds Emerging Players Programme 2024

Alice Acklam, Ines Blackwell (both Yorkshire), Ava Broady (Northumberland), Maiya Charlesworth (Yorkshire), Jess Clarke, Mae Deaville, Grace Denley (all Durham), Clare Fairclough, Izzy Fidler, Georgie Flack (all Yorkshire), Amy Hurst, Ella Jackson (both Durham), Olivia Kibler, Florrie McKenna (both Yorkshire), Kate Million (Durham), Ellis Rawlin, Emily Roberts, Rhia Sedha (all Yorkshire), Naomi Silva (Northumberland), Lily-Mai Taylor, Laura Trotter (both Durham), Sarah Vince (Northumberland), Sarah Wood and Emma Wrightson (both Yorkshire).

Winner Ward

Northern Diamonds Academy wicketkeeper-batter Maddie Ward, an England Under-19s international, helped a National Counties Cricket Association XI — playing under an England XI name — to win the inaugural women's European Championship T10 title in Malaga in the days leading up to Christmas. They beat Netherlands in the final. Ward joined the Academy during the winter following a successful trial.

RECORDS SECTION

All records in this section relate to First-Class Yorkshire matches except where stated

HONOURS

County Champions (34)
1867, 1870, 1893, 1896, 1898, 1900, 1901, 1902, 1905, 1908, 1912, 1919,
1922, 1923, 1924, 1925, 1931, 1932, 1933, 1935, 1937, 1938, 1939,
1946, 1959, 1960, 1962, 1963, 1966, 1967, 1968, 2001, 2014, 2015

Joint Champions (2)
1869, 1949

Promoted to Division 1
2005, 2012

Gillette Cup Winners (2)
1965, 1969

Cheltenham & Gloucester Trophy (1)
2002

Benson & Hedges Cup Winners (1)
1987

John Player Special League Winners (1)
1983

Fenner Trophy Winners (3)
1972, 1974, 1981

Asda Challenge Winners (1)
1987

Ward Knockout Cup (1)
1989

Joshua Tetley Festival Trophy (7)
1991, 1992 (Joint), 1993, 1994, 1996, 1997 and 1998

Tilcon Trophy Winners (2)
1978 and 1988

Pro-Arch Trophy (1)
2007-08

Emirates Airlines T20 (2)
2015 and 2016

Second Eleven Champions (5)
1977, 1984, 1991, 2003, 2002

Joint Champions (1)
1987

Minor Counties Champions (5)
1947, 1957, 1958, 1968, 1971

Under-25 Competition Winners (3)
1976, 1978, 1987

Bain Clarkson Trophy Winners (2)
1988 and 1994

Second Eleven Trophy (1)
2009

YORKSHIRE'S CHAMPIONSHIP CAPTAINS

1867 to 2022

* R Iddison (2)	1867, 1870
Lord Hawke (8)	1893, 1896, 1898, 1900, 1901, 1902, 1905, 1908
Sir Archibald White (1)	1912
D C F Burton (1)	1919
G Wilson (3)	1922, 1923, 1924
A W Lupton (1)	1925
F E Greenwood (2)	1931, 1932
A B Sellers (6)	1933, 1935, 1937, 1938, 1939, 1946
J R Burnet (1)	1959
J V Wilson (2)	1960, 1962
D B Close (4)	1963, 1966, 1967, 1968
D Byas (1)	2001
A W Gale (2)	2014, 2015

Joint Champions

* R Iddison (1)	1869
N W D Yardley (1)	1949

** R Iddison was captain when Yorkshire were Champion county, the County Championship starting in 1890.*

CHAMPION COUNTIES SINCE 1873

The County Championship

The County Championship was officially constituted in 1890, and before that Yorkshire were generally considered Champions by the Press in 1867 and 1870, and equal top in 1869. From 1873 the list was generally accepted in the form as it is today.

		Yorkshire's Position
1873	Gloucestershire / Nottinghamshire	7th
1874	Gloucestershire	4th
1875	Nottinghamshire	4th
1876	Gloucestershire	3rd
1877	Gloucestershire	7th
1878	Middlesex	6th
1879	Nottinghamshire/Lancashire	6th
1880	Nottinghamshire	5th
1881	Lancashire	3rd
1882	Nottinghamshire/Lancashire	3rd
1883	Nottinghamshire	2nd
1884	Nottinghamshire	3rd
1885	Nottinghamshire	2nd
1886	Nottinghamshire	4th
1887	Surrey	3rd
1888	Surrey	2nd
1889	Surrey/Lancashire / Nottinghamshire	7th
1890	Surrey	3rd
1891	Surrey	8th
1892	Surrey	6th
1893	**Yorkshire**	**1st**
1894	Surrey	2nd
1895	Surrey	3rd
1896	**Yorkshire**	**1st**
1897	Lancashire	4th
1898	**Yorkshire**	**1st**
1899	Surrey	3rd
1900	**Yorkshire**	**1st**
1901	**Yorkshire**	**1st**
1902	**Yorkshire**	**1st**
1903	Middlesex	3rd
1904	Lancashire	2nd
1905	**Yorkshire**	**1st**
1906	Kent	2nd
1907	Nottinghamshire	2nd
1908	**Yorkshire**	**1st**
1909	Kent	3rd
1910	Kent	8th
1911	Warwickshire	7th
1912	**Yorkshire**	**1st**
1913	Kent	2nd
1914	Surrey	4th
1919	**Yorkshire**	**1st**
1920	Middlesex	4th
1921	Middlesex	3rd
1922	**Yorkshire**	**1st**
1923	**Yorkshire**	**1st**
1924	**Yorkshire**	**1st**
1925	**Yorkshire**	**1st**
1926	Lancashire	2nd
1927	Lancashire	3rd
1928	Lancashire	4th
1929	Nottinghamshire	2nd
1930	Lancashire	3rd
1931	**Yorkshire**	**1st**
1932	**Yorkshire**	**1st**
1933	**Yorkshire**	**1st**
1934	Lancashire	5th
1935	**Yorkshire**	**1st**
1936	Derbyshire	3rd
1937	**Yorkshire**	**1st**
1938	**Yorkshire**	**1st**
1939	**Yorkshire**	**1st**
1946	**Yorkshire**	**1st**
1947	Middlesex	7th
1948	Glamorgan	4th
1949	**Yorkshire**/Middlesex	**1st**
1950	Lancashire/Surrey	3rd
1951	Warwickshire	2nd
1952	Surrey	2nd
1953	Surrey	12th
1954	Surrey	2nd
1955	Surrey	2nd
1956	Surrey	7th
1957	Surrey	3rd

		Yorkshire's Position			Yorkshire's Position
1958	Surrey	11th	1991	Essex	14th
1959	**Yorkshire**	**1st**	1992	Essex	16th
1960	**Yorkshire**	**1st**	1993	Middlesex	12th
1961	Hampshire	2nd	1994	Warwickshire	13th
1962	**Yorkshire**	**1st**	1995	Warwickshire	8th
1963	**Yorkshire**	**1st**	1996	Leicestershire	6th
1964	Worcestershire	5th	1997	Glamorgan	6th
1965	Worcestershire	4th	1998	Leicestershire	3rd
1966	**Yorkshire**	**1st**	1999	Surrey	6th
1967	**Yorkshire**	**1st**	2000	Surrey	3rd
1968	**Yorkshire**	**1st**	**2001**	**Yorkshire**	**1st**
1969	Glamorgan	13th	2002	Surrey	9th
1970	Kent	4th	2003	Sussex	Div 2, 4th
1971	Surrey	13th	2004	Warwickshire	Div 2, 7th
1972	Warwickshire	10th	2005	Nottinghamshire	Div 2, 3rd
1973	Hampshire	14th	2006	Sussex	Div 1, 6th
1974	Worcestershire	11th	2007	Sussex	Div 1, 6th
1975	Leicestershire	2nd	2008	Durham	Div 1, 7th
1976	Middlesex	8th	2009	Durham	Div 1, 7th
1977	Kent/Middlesex	12th	2010	Nottinghamshire	Div 1, 3rd
1978	Kent	4th	2011	Lancashire	Div 1, 8th
1979	Essex	7th	2012	Warwickshire	Div 2, 2nd
1980	Middlesex	6th	2013	Durham	Div 1, 2nd
1981	Nottinghamshire	10th	**2014**	**Yorkshire**	**Div 1, 1st**
1982	Middlesex	10th	**2015**	**Yorkshire**	**Div 1, 1st**
1983	Essex	17th	2016	Middlesex	Div 1, 3rd
1984	Essex	14th	2017	Essex	Div 1, 4th
1985	Middlesex	11th	2018	Surrey	Div 1, 4th
1986	Essex	10th	2019	Essex	Div 1, 5th
1987	Nottinghamshire	8th	*2020*	*No matches played due to Covid-19*	
1988	Worcestershire	13th	2021	Warwickshire	Div 1, 5th (6)
1989	Worcestershire	16th	2022	Surrey	Div 1, 9th (10)
1990	Middlesex	10th	2023	Surrey	Div 2, 7th (8)

SEASON-BY-SEASON RECORD OF ALL FIRST-CLASS MATCHES PLAYED BY YORKSHIRE 1863-2023

Season	Played	Won	Lost	Drawn	Abd§	Season	Played	Won	Lost	Drawn	Abd§
1863	4	2	1	1	0	1921	30	17	5	8	0
1864	7	2	4	1	0	1922	33	20	2	11	0
1865	9	0	7	2	0	1923	35	26	1	8	0
1866	3	0	2	1	0	1924	35	18	4	13	0
1867	7	7	0	0	0	1925	36	22	0	14	0
1868	7	4	3	0	0	1926	35	14	0	21	1
1869	5	4	1	0	0	1927	34	11	3	20	1
1870	7	6	0	1	0	1928	32	9	0	23	0
1871	7	3	3	1	0	1929	35	11	2	22	0
1872	10	2	7	1	0	1930	34	13	3	18	2
1873	13	7	5	1	0	1931	33	17	1	15	1
1874	14	10	3	1	0	1932	32	21	2	9	2
1875	12	6	4	2	0	1933	36	21	5	10	0
1876	12	5	3	4	0	1934	35	14	7	14	0
1877	14	2	7	5	0	1935	36	24	2	10	0
1878	20	10	7	3	0	1935-6	3	1	0	2	0
1879	17	7	5	5	0	1936	35	14	2	19	0
1880	20	6	8	6	0	1937	34	22	3	9	1
1881	20	11	6	3	0	1938	36	22	2	12	0
1882	24	11	9	4	0	1939	34	23	4	7	1
1883	19	10	2	7	0	1945	2	0	0	2	0
1884	20	10	6	4	0	1946	31	20	1	10	0
1885	21	8	3	10	0	1947	32	10	9	13	0
1886	21	5	8	8	0	1948	31	11	6	14	0
1887	20	6	5	9	0	1949	33	16	3	14	0
1888	20	7	7	6	0	1950	34	16	6	12	1
1889	16	3	11	2	1	1951	35	14	3	18	0
1890	20	10	4	6	0	1952	34	17	3	14	0
1891	17	5	11	1	2	1953	35	7	7	21	0
1892	19	6	6	7	0	1954	35	16	3	16*	0
1893	23	15	5	3	0	1955	33	23	6	4	0
1894	28	18	6	4	1	1956	35	11	7	17	0
1895	31	15	10	6	0	1957	34	16	5	13	1
1896	32	17	6	9	0	1958	33	10	8	15	2
1897	30	14	7	9	0	1959	35	18	8	9	0
1898	30	18	3	9	0	1960	38	19	7	12	0
1899	34	17	4	13	0	1961	39	19	5	15	0
1900	32	19	1	12	0	1962	37	16	5	16	0
1901	35	23	2	10	1	1963	33	14	4	15	0
1902	31	15	3	13	1	1964	33	12	4	17	0
1903	31	16	5	10	0	1965	33	12	4	17	0
1904	32	10	2	20	1	1966	32	16	6	10	1
1905	33	21	4	8	0	1967	31	16	5	10	2
1906	33	19	6	8	0	1968	32	13	4	15	0
1907	31	14	5	12	2	1969	29	4	7	18	0
1908	33	19	0	14	0	1970	26	10	5	11	0
1909	30	12	5	13	0	1971	27	5	8	14	0
1910	31	11	8	12	0	1972	21	4	5	12	1
1911	32	16	9	7	0	1973	22	3	5	14*	0
1912	35	14	3	18	1	1974	22	6	7	9	1
1913	32	16	5	11	0	1975	21	11	1	9	0
1914	31	16	4	11	2	1976	22	7	7	8	0
1919	31	12	5	14	0	1977	23	7	5	11	1
1920	30	17	6	7	0	1978	24	10	3	11	1

SEASON-BY-SEASON RECORD OF ALL FIRST-CLASS MATCHES PLAYED BY YORKSHIRE 1863-2023 *(Contd.)*

Season	Played	Won	Lost	Drawn	Abd§	Season	Played	Won	Lost	Drawn	Abd§
1979	22	6	3	13	1	2001	16	9	3	4	0
1980	24	5	4	15	0	2002	16	2	8	6	0
1981	24	5	9	10	0	2003	17	4	5	8	0
1982	22	5	1	16	1	2004	16	3	4	9	0
1983	23	1	5	17	1	2005	17	6	1	10	0
1984	24	5	4	15	0	2006	16	3	6	7	0
1985	25	3	4	18	1	2007	17	5	4	8	0
1986	25	4	6	15	0	2008	16	2	5	9	0
1986-7	1	0	0	1	0	2009	17	2	2	13	0
1987	24	7	4	13	1	2010	18	6	2	10	0
1988	24	5	6	13	0	2011	17	4	6	7	0
1989	22	3	9	10	0	2012	17	5	0	12	0
1990	24	5	9	10	0	2013	17	8	2	7	0
1991	24	4	6	14	0	2014	17	8	1	8	0
1991-2	1	0	1	0	0	2015	18	12	1	5	0
1992	22	4	6	12	1	2016	18	5	4	9	0
1992-3	1	0	0	1	0	2017	15	5	5	5	0
1993	19	6	4	9	0	2018	13	5	5	3	2
1994	20	7	6	7	0	2019	15	6	4	5	0
1995	20	8	8	4	0	2020	5	3	0	2	0
1995-6	2	2	0	0	0	2021	14	6	3	5	0
1996	19	8	5	6	0	2022	14	1	6	7	0
1997	20	7	4	9	0	2023	13	3	2	8	1
1998	19	9	3	7	0						
1999	17	8	6	3	0		3691	1545	678	1468	41
2000	18	7	4	7	0						

* Includes one tie each season

§ All these matches were abandoned without a ball being bowled, except Yorkshire v Kent at Harrogate, 1904, which was abandoned under Law 9. The two in 1914 and the one in 1939 were abandoned because of war. The four-day matches Yorkshire v. Essex at Leeds in 2018 and Gloucestershire v. Yorkshire at Bristol in 2023 were abandoned without a ball bowled, each side receiving five points in both matches. All these matches are excluded from the total played.

Of the 1,545 matches won 526 have been by an innings margin, 89 by 200 runs or more, and 135 by 10 wickets. Of the 678 lost 114 have been by an innings margin, 17 by 200 runs or more, and 36 by 10 wickets.

ANALYSIS OF RESULTS VERSUS ALL FIRST-CLASS TEAMS 1863-2023

COUNTY CHAMPIONSHIP

Opponents	Played	Won	Lost	Drawn	Tied
Derbyshire	207	105	19	83	0
Durham	38	16	9	13	0
Essex	167	85	29	53	0
Glamorgan	115	53	13	49	0
Gloucestershire	203	103	44	56	0
Hampshire	178	75	22	81	0
Kent	205	86	40	79	0
Lancashire	265	79	53	133	0
Leicestershire	168	84	16	67	1
Middlesex	235	82	59	93	1
Northamptonshire	145	69	26	50	0
Nottinghamshire	259	93	48	118	0
Somerset	181	93	27	61	0
Surrey	250	87	71	92	0
Sussex	203	87	33	83	0
Warwickshire	196	87	33	76	0
Worcestershire	144	72	22	50	0
Cambridgeshire	8	3	4	1	0
Total	3167	1359	568	1238	2

OTHER FIRST-CLASS MATCHES

Opponents	Played	Won	Lost	Drawn	Tied
Derbyshire	3	1	1	1	0
Durham	1	1	0	0	0
Essex	2	2	0	0	0
Hampshire	1	0	0	1	0
Lancashire	13	5	3	5	0
Leicestershire	3	2	1	0	0
Middlesex	1	1	0	0	0
Nottinghamshire	3	2	1	0	0
Surrey	1	0	0	1	0
Sussex	2	0	0	2	0
Warwickshire	2	0	0	2	0
Totals	32	14	6	12	0
Australians	55	6	19	30	0
Indians	14	5	1	8	0
New Zealanders	10	2	0	8	0
Pakistanis	4	1	0	3	0
South Africans	17	1	3	13	0
Sri Lankans	3	0	0	3	0
West Indians	17	3	7	7	0
Zimbabweans	2	0	1	1	0
Bangladesh A	1	1	0	0	0
India A	2	0	0	2	0
Pakistan A	2	1	0	1	0
South Africa A	1	0	0	1	0
Totals	128	20	31	77	0

ANALYSIS OF RESULTS VERSUS ALL FIRST-CLASS
TEAMS 1863-2023 *(continued.)*

Opponents	Played	Won	Lost	Drawn	Tied
Cambridge University/U C C E	88	42	17	29	0
Canadians	1	1	0	0	0
Combined Services	1	0	0	1	0
Durham MCCU	1	1	0	0	0
England XI's	6	1	2	3	0
Hon. M.B. Hawke's XI	1	0	1	0	0
International XI	1	1	0	0	0
Ireland	3	3	0	0	0
Jamaica	3	1	0	2	0
Leeds/Bradford MCCU	6	3	0	3	0
Liverpool and District*	3	2	1	0	0
Loughborough UCCE	2	1	0	1	0
MCC	155	55	40	60	0
Mashonaland	1	1	0	0	0
Matebeleland	1	1	0	0	0
Minor Counties	1	1	0	0	0
Oxford University	44	21	3	20	0
Philadelphians	1	0	0	1	0
Rest of England	16	4	5	7	0
Royal Air Force	1	0	0	1	0
Scotland**	11	7	0	4	0
South of England	2	1	0	1	0
C. I. Thornton's XI	5	2	0	3	0
United South of England	1	1	0	0	0
Western Province	2	0	1	1	0
Windward Islands	1	0	0	1	0
I Zingari	6	2	3	1	0
Totals	364	152	73	139	0
Grand Totals	3691	1545	678	1466	2

*Matches played in 1889, 1891, 1892 and 1893 are excluded. **Match played in 1878 is included

ABANDONED MATCHES (41)

1889 v. MCC at Lord's	1950 v. Cambridge University at Cambridge
1891 (2) v. MCC at Lord's v. MCC at Scarborough	1957 v. West Indians at Bradford
1894 v. Kent at Bradford	1958 (2) v. Nottinghamshire at Hull v. Worcestershire at Bradford
1901 v. Surrey at The Oval	1966 v. Oxford University at Oxford
1902 v. Leicestershire at Leicester (AR)	1967 (2) v. Leicestershire at Leeds v. Lancashire at Manchester
1904 v. Kent at Harrogate (Law 9 — now Law 10)	1972 v. Australians at Bradford
1907 (2) v. Derbyshire at Sheffield v. Nottinghamshire at Huddersfield	1974 v. Hampshire at Bournemouth
1912 v. Surrey at Sheffield	1977 v. Gloucestershire at Bristol
1914 (2) v. England at Harrogate (due to war) v. MCC at Scarborough (due to war)	1978 v. Pakistan at Bradford
1926 v. Nottinghamshire at Leeds	1979 v. Nottinghamshire at Sheffield (AP)
1927 v. Kent at Bradford	1982 v. Nottinghamshire at Harrogate
1930 (2) v. Derbyshire at Chesterfield* v. Northampstonshire at Harrogate*	1983 v. Middlesex at Lord's
1931 v. Sussex at Hull	1985 v. Essex at Sheffield (AP)
1932 (2) v. Derbyshire at Chesterfield v. Kent at Sheffield	1987 v. Sussex at Hastings
1937 v. Cambridge University at Bradford	1992 v. Oxford University at Oxford
1939 v. MCC at Scarborough (due to war)	2018 v. Leeds/Bradford MCCU at Leeds *
	2018 v. Essex at Leeds
	2023 v. Gloucestershire at Bristol

* Consecutive matches

ANALYSIS OF RESULTS ON GROUNDS IN YORKSHIRE USED IN 2023

FIRST-CLASS MATCHES

Ground	Played	Won	Lost	Drawn	Tied
Leeds Headingley 1891-2023	485	181 (37.32%)	86 (17.73%)	218 (44.95%)	0 (0.00%)
Scarborough North Marine Road 1874-2023	264	107 (40.53%)	42 (15.91%)	115 (43.56%)	0 (0.00%)

HIGHEST MATCH AGGREGATES – OVER 1,350 RUNS

Runs	Wkts	
1665	33	Yorkshire (351 and 481) lost to Warwickshire (601:9 dec and 232:4) by 6 wkts at Birmingham, 2002
1606	31	Yorkshire (438 and 363:5 dec) lost to Somerset (326 and 479:6) by 4 wkts at Taunton, 2009
1484	36	Yorkshire (521 and 220) lost to Surrey (515 and 228:6) by 4 wkts at Scarborough, 2022
1479	28	Yorkshire (405 and 333:4 dec) lost to Somerset (377 and 364:4) by 6 wkts at Taunton , 2010
1473	17	Yorkshire (600:4 dec. and 231:3 dec.) drew with Worcestershire (453:5 dec. and 189:5) at Scarborough, 1995.
1442	29	Yorkshire (501:6 dec. and 244:6 dec.) beat Lancashire (403:7 dec. and 294) by 48 runs at Scarborough, 1991.
1439	32	Yorkshire (536:8 dec. and 205:7 dec.) beat Glamorgan (482: 7 dec. and 216) by 43 runs at Cardiff, 1996.
1431	32	Yorkshire (388 and 312:6) drew with Sussex (398 and 333:6 dec) at Scarborough, 2011
1417	33	Yorkshire (422 and 193:7) drew with Glamorgan (466 and 336:6 dec) at Colwyn Bay, 2003
1406	37	Yorkshire (354 and 341:8) drew with Derbyshire (406 and 305:9 dec) at Derby, 2004
1400	32	Yorkshire (299 and 439: 4 dec.) drew with Hampshire (296 and 366:8) at Southampton, 2007
1393	35	Yorkshire (331 and 278) lost to Kent (377 and 407:5 dec) by 175 runs at Maidstone, 1994.
1390	34	Yorkshire (431:8 dec and 265:7) beat Hampshire (429 and 265) by 3 wkts at Southampton, 1995.
1390	33	Durham (573 and 124-3) beat Yorkahire (274 and 419) by 7 wkts at Scarborough, 2013.
1376	33	Yorkshire (531 and 158:3) beat Lancashire (373 and 314) by 7 wkts at Leeds, 2001
1376	20	Yorkshire (677: 7 dec.) drew with Durham (518 and 181:3 dec.) at Leeds, 2006
1374	36	Yorkshire (594: 9 dec. and 266:7 dec.) beat Surrey (344 and 170) by 346 runs at The Oval, 2007
1373	36	Yorkshire (520 and 114:6) drew with Derbyshire (216 and 523) at Derby, 2005
1364	35	Yorkshire (216 and 433) lost to Warwickshire (316 and 399:5 dec.) by 66 runs at Birmingham, 2006
1359	25	Yorkshire (561 and 138:3 dec.) drew with Derbyshire (412:4 dec. and 248:8) at Sheffield, 1996.
1359	30	Yorkshire (358 and 321) lost to Somerset (452 and 228:0) by 10 wkts at Taunton, 2011
1353	18	Yorkshire (377:2 dec. and 300:6) beat Derbyshire (475:7 dec. and 201:3 dec) by 4 wkts at Scarborough, 1990.

LOWEST MATCH AGGREGATES – UNDER 225 RUNS IN A COMPLETED MATCH

Runs	Wkts	
165	30	Yorkshire (46 and 37:0) beat Nottinghamshire (24 and 58 by 10 wkts at Sheffield, 1888.
175	29	Yorkshire (104) beat Essex (30 and 41) by an innings and 33 runs at Leyton, 1901.
182	15	Yorkshire (4:0 dec. and 88.5) beat Northamptonshire (4:0 dec. and 86) by 5 wkts at Bradford, 1931.
193	29	Yorkshire (99) beat Worcestershire (43 and 51) by an innings and 5 runs at Bradford, 1900.
219	30	Yorkshire (113) beat Nottinghamshire (71 and 35) by an innings and 7 runs at Nottingham, 1881.
222	32	Yorkshire (98 and 14:2) beat Gloucestershire (68 and 42) by 8 wkts at Gloucester, 1924.
223	40	Yorkshire (58 and 51) lost to Lancashire (64 and 50)

LOWEST MATCH AGGREGATES – UNDER 325 RUNS IN A MATCH IN WHICH ALL 40 WICKETS FELL

Runs	Wkts	
223	40	Yorkshire (58 and 51) lost to Lancashire (64 and 50) by 5 runs at Manchester, 1893.
288	40	Yorkshire (55 and 68) lost to Lancashire (89 and 76) by 42 runs at Sheffield, 1872.
295	40	Yorkshire (71 and 63) lost to Surrey (56 and 105) by 27 runs at The Oval, 1886.
303	40	Yorkshire (109 and 77) beat Middlesex (63 and 54) by 69 runs at Lord's, 1891.
318	40	Yorkshire (96 and 96) beat Lancashire (39 and 87) by 66 runs at Manchester, 1874.
318	40	Yorkshire (94 and 104) beat Northamptonshire (61 and 59) by 78 runs at Bradford, 1955.
319	40	Yorkshire (84 and 72) lost to Derbyshire (106 and 57) by 7 runs at Derby, 1878.
320	40	Yorkshire (98 and 91) beat Surrey (72 and 59) by 58 runs at Sheffield, 1893.
321	40	Yorkshire (88 and 37) lost to I Zingari (103 and 93) by 71 runs at Scarborough, 1877.
321	40	Yorkshire (80 and 67) lost to Derbyshire (129 and 45) by 27 runs at Sheffield, 1879.

LARGE MARGINS OF VICTORY – BY AN INNINGS AND OVER 250 RUNS

Inns and 397 runs	Yorkshire (548:4 dec.) beat Northamptonshire (58 and 93) at Harrogate, 1921
Inns and 387 runs	Yorkshire (662) beat Derbyshire (118 and 157) at Chesterfield, 1898.
Inns and 343 runs	Yorkshire (673:8 dec) beat Northamptonshire (184 and 146) at Leeds, 2003
Inns and 321 runs	Yorkshire (437) beat Leicestershire (58 and 58) at Leicester, 1908.
Inns and 314 runs	Yorkshire (356:8 dec) beat Northamptonshire (27 and 15) at Northampton, 1908. (Yorkshire's first match v. Northamptonshire).
Inns and 313 runs	Yorkshire (555:1 dec) beat Essex (78 and 164) at Leyton, 1932.
Inns and 307 runs	Yorkshire (681:5 dec.) beat Sussex (164 and 210) at Sheffield, 1897.
Inns and 302 runs	Yorkshire (660) beat Leicestershire (165 and 193) at Leicester, 1896.
Inns and 301 runs	Yorkshire (499) beat Somerset (125 and 73) at Bath, 1899.
Inns and 294 runs	Yorkshire (425:7 dec.) beat Gloucestershire (47 and 84) at Bristol, 1964.
Inns and 284 runs	Yorkshire (467:7 dec) beat Leicestershire (111 and 72) at Bradford, 1932.
Inns and 282 runs	Yorkshire (481:8 dec) beat Derbyshire (106 and 93) at Huddersfield, 1901.
Inns and 280 runs	Yorkshire (562) beat Leicestershire (164 and 118) at Dewsbury, 1903.
Inns and 271 runs	Yorkshire (460) beat Hampshire (128 and 61) at Hull, 1900.
Inns and 271 runs	Yorkshire (495:5 dec) beat Warwickshire (99 and 125) at Huddersfield, 1922.
Inns and 266 runs	Yorkshire (352) beat Cambridgeshire (40 and 46) at Hunslet, 1869.
Inns and 260 runs	Yorkshire (521: 7dec.) beat Worcestershire (129 and 132) at Leeds, 2007.
Inns and 258 runs	Yorkshire (404:2 dec) beat Glamorgan (78 and 68) at Cardiff, 1922. (Yorkshire's first match v. Glamorgan).
Inns and 256 runs	Yorkshire (486) beat Leicestershire (137 and 93) at Sheffield, 1895.
Inns and 251 runs	Yorkshire (550) beat Leicestershire (154 and 145) at Leicester, 1933.

LARGE MARGINS OF VICTORY – BY OVER 300 RUNS

389 runs	Yorkshire (368 and 280:1 dec) beat Somerset (125 and 134) at Bath, 1906.
370 runs	Yorkshire (194 and 274) beat Hampshire (62 and 36) at Leeds, 1904.
351 runs	Yorkshire (280 and 331) beat Northamptonshire (146 and 114) at Northampton, 1947.
346 runs	Yorkshire (594: 9 dec. and 266: 7 dec.) beat Surrey (344 and 179) at The Oval, 2007.
328 runs	Yorkshire (186 and 318:1 dec) beat Somerset (43 and 133) at Bradford, 1930.
328 runs	Yorkshire (280 and 277:7 dec) beat Glamorgan (104 and 105) at Swansea, 2001
320 runs	Yorkshire (331 and 353:9 dec) beat Durham (150 and 214) at Chester-le-Street, 2004
308 runs	Yorkshire (89 and 420) beat Warwickshire (72 and 129) at Birmingham, 1921
308 runs	Yorkshire (89 and 420) beat Warwickshire (72 and 129)
305 runs	Yorkshire (370 and 305:4 dec) beat Hampshire (227 and 143) at Leeds, 2015
305 runs	Yorkshire (282 and 263:4 dec) beat Nottinghamshire (94 and 146) at Scarborough 2016

LARGE MARGINS OF VICTORY – BY 10 WICKETS
(WITH OVER 100 RUNS SCORED IN THE 4th INNINGS)

4th Innings

167:0 wkt	Yorkshire (247 and 167:0) beat Northamptonshire 233 and 180) at Huddersfield, 1948.
147:0 wkt	Yorkshire (381 and 147:0) beat Middlesex (384 and 142) at Lord's, 1896.
142:0 wkt	Yorkshire (304 and 142:0) beat Sussex (254 and 188) at Bradford, 1887.
139:0 wkt	Yorkshire (163:9 dec and 139:0) beat Nottinghamshire (234 and 67) at Leeds, 1932.
138:0 wkt	Yorkshire (293 and 138:0) beat Hampshire (251 and 179) at Southampton, 1897.
132:0 wkt	Yorkshire (328 and 132:0) beat Northamptonshire (281 and 175) at Leeds, 2005
129:0 wkt	Yorkshire (355 and 129:0) beat Durham MCCU (196 and 287) at Durham, 2011
127:0 wkt	Yorkshire (258 and 127:0) beat Cambridge University (127 and 257) at Cambridge, 1930.
119:0 wkt	Yorkshire (109 and 119:0) beat Essex (108 and 119) at Leeds, 1931.
118:0 wkt	Yorkshire (121 and 118:0) beat MCC (125 and 113) at Lord's, 1883.
116:0 wkt	Yorkshire (147 and 116:0) beat Hampshire (141 and 120) at Bournemouth, 1930.
114:0 wkt	Yorkshire (135 and 114:0) beat Hampshire (71 and 176) at Bournemouth, 1948.
114:0 wkt	Yorkshire (135 and 114:0) beat Hampshire (71 and 176)
105:0 wkt	Yorkshire (307 and 105:0) beat Worcestershire (311 and 100) at Worcester, 2015

HEAVY DEFEATS – BY AN INNINGS
AND OVER 250 RUNS

Inns and 272 runs   Yorkshire (78 and 186) lost to Surrey (536)
at The Oval, 1898.

Inns and 261 runs   Yorkshire (247 and 89) lost to Sussex (597: 8 dec.)
at Hove, 2007.

Inns and 255 runs   Yorkshire (125 and 144) lost to All England XI (524)
at Sheffield, 1865.

HEAVY DEFEATS – BY OVER 300 RUNS

433 runs   Kent (482-8 dec and 337-7 dec) defeated Yorkshire (269 and 117)
at Leeds, 2019

376 runs   Essex (227 and 334-7 dec) defeated Yorkshire (111 and 74)
at Chelmsford, 2017

324 runs   Yorkshire (247 and 204) lost to Gloucestershire (291 and 484)
at Cheltenham, 1994.

305 runs   Yorkshire (119 and 51) lost to Cambridge University (312 and 163)
at Cambridge, 1906.

HEAVY DEFEATS – BY 10 WICKETS
(WITH OVER 100 RUNS SCORED IN THE 4th INNINGS)

4th Innings

228:0 wkt   Yorkshire (358 and 321) lost to Somerset (452 and 228:0)
at Taunton, 2011

148:0 wkt   Yorkshire (83 and 216) lost to Lancashire (154 and 148:0)
at Manchester, 1875.

119:0 wkt   Yorkshire (92 and 109) lost to Nottinghamshire (86 and 119:0 wkt)
at Leeds, 1989.

108:0 wkt   Yorkshire (236 and 107) lost to Hampshire (236 and 108:0 wkt)
at Southampton, 2008

100:0 wkt   Yorkshire (95 and 91) lost to Gloucestershire (88 and 100:0)
at Bristol, 1956.

NARROW VICTORIES – BY 1 WICKET

Yorkshire (70 and 91:9) beat Cambridgeshire (86 and 74) at Wisbech, 1867.
Yorkshire (91 and 145:9) beat MCC (73 and 161) at Lord's, 1870.
Yorkshire (265 and 154:9) beat Derbyshire (234 and 184) at Derby, 1897.
Yorkshire (177 and 197:9) beat MCC (188 and 185) at Lord's, 1899.
Yorkshire (391 and 241:9) beat Somerset (349 and 281) at Taunton, 1901.
Yorkshire (239 and 168:9) beat MCC (179 and 226) at Scarborough, 1935.
Yorkshire (152 and 90:9) beat Worcestershire (119 and 121) at Leeds, 1946.
Yorkshire (229 and 175:9) beat Glamorgan (194 and 207) at Bradford, 1960.
Yorkshire (265.9 dec and 191:9) beat Worcestershire (227 and 227) at Worcester, 1961.
Yorkshire (329:6 dec and 167:9) beat Essex (339.9 dec and 154) at Scarborough, 1979.
Yorkshire (Innings forfeited and 251:9 beat Sussex (195 and 55.1 dec) at Leeds, 1986.
Yorkshire (314 and 150:9) beat Essex (200 and 261) at Scarborough, 1998.

NARROW VICTORIES – BY 5 RUNS OR LESS

By 1 run   Yorkshire (228 and 214) beat Middlesex (206 and 235) at Bradford, 1976.
By 1 run   Yorkshire (383 and inns forfeited) beat Loughborough UCCE (93: 3 dec. and 289) at Leeds, 2007.
By 1 run   Yorkshire (206 and 247) beat Northamptonshire (234 and 218) at Leeds, 2021
By 2 runs   Yorkshire (108 and 122) beat Nottinghamshire (56 and 172) at Nottingham, 1870.
By 2 runs   Yorkshire (304:9 dec and 135) beat Middlesex (225:2 dec and 212) at Leeds, 1985.
By 3 runs   Yorkshire (446:9 dec and 172:4 dec) beat Essex (300:3 dec and 315) at Colchester, 1991.
By 3 runs   Yorkshire (202 and 283) beat Somerset (224 and 258) at Taunton, 2017
By 5 runs   Yorkshire (271 and 147:6 dec) beat Surrey (198 and 215) at Sheffield, 1950.
By 5 runs   Yorkshire (151 and 176) beat Hampshire (165 and 157) at Bradford, 1962.
By 5 runs   Yorkshire (376:4 and 106) beat Middlesex (325:8 and 152) at Lord's, 1975
By 5 runs   Yorkshire (323:5 dec and inns forfeited) beat Somerset (inns forfeited and 318) at Taunton, 1986.

NARROW DEFEATS – BY 1 WICKET

Yorkshire (224 and 210) lost to Australian Imperial Forces XI (265 and 170:9) at Sheffield, 1919
Yorkshire (101 and 159) lost to Warwickshire (45 and 216:9) at Scarborough, 1934.
Yorkshire (239 and 184:9 dec.) lost to Warwickshire (125 and 302:9) at Birmingham, 1983.
Yorkshire (289 and 153) lost to Surrey (250:2 dec and 193:9) at Guildford, 1991.
Yorkshire (341 and Inns forfeited) lost to Surrey (39:1 dec and 306:9) at Bradford, 1992.
Yorkshire (234 and 252) lost to Essex (225 and 162:9) at Leeds, 2022

NARROW DEFEATS – BY 5 RUNS OR LESS

By 1 run   Yorkshire (135 and 297) lost to Essex (139 and 294) at Huddersfield, 1897.
By 1 run   Yorkshire (159 and 232) lost to Gloucestershire (164 and 228) at Bristol, 1906.
By 1 run   Yorkshire (126 and 137) lost to Worcestershire (101 and 163) at Worcester, 1968.
By 1 run   Yorkshire (366 and 217) lost to Surrey (409 and 175) at The Oval, 1995.
By 2 runs   Yorkshire (172 and 107) lost to Gloucestershire (157 and 124) at Sheffield, 1913.
By 2 runs   Yorkshire (179:9 dec and 144) lost to MCC (109 and 216) at Lord's, 1957.
By 3 runs   Yorkshire (126 and 181) lost to Sussex (182 and 128) at Sheffield, 1883.
By 3 runs   Yorkshire (160 and 71) lost to Lancashire (81 and 153) at Huddersfield, 1889.
By 3 runs   Yorkshire (134 and 158) lost to Nottinghamshire (200 and 95) at Leeds, 1923.
By 4 runs   Yorkshire (169 and 193) lost to Middlesex (105 and 261) at Bradford, 1920.
By 5 runs   Yorkshire (58 and 51) lost to Lancashire (64 and 50) at Manchester, 1893.
By 5 runs   Yorkshire (119 and 115) lost to Warwickshire (167 and 72) at Bradford, 1969.

HIGH FOURTH INNINGS SCORES – 300 AND OVER

By Yorkshire

To Win:
406:4	beat Leicestershire by 6 wkts at Leicester, 2005
402:6	beat Gloucestershire by 4 wkts at Bristol, 2012
400:4	beat Leicestershire by 6 wkts at Scarborough, 2005
339:6	beat Durham by 4 wkts at Chester-le-Street, 2013
331:8	beat Middlesex by 2 wkts at Lord's, 1910.
327:6	beat Nottinghamshire by 4 wkts at Nottingham, 1990.*
323:5	beat Nottinghamshire by 5 wkts at Nottingham, 1977.
318:3	beat Glamorgan by 7 wkts at Middlesbrough, 1976.
316:8	beat Gloucestershire by 2 wkts at Scarborough, 2012
309:7	beat Somerset by 3 wkts at Taunton, 1984.
305:8	beat Nottinghamshire by 2 wkts at Worksop, 1982.
305:5	beat Hampshire by 5 wkts at West End, Southampton, 2015
305:3	beat Lancashire by 7 wkts at Manchester, 1994.
304:4	beat Derbyshire by 6 wkts at Chesterfield, 1959.
300:4	beat Derbyshire by 6 wkts at Chesterfield, 1981.
300:6	beat Derbyshire by 4 wkts at Scarborough, 1990.*

To Draw:
341:8	(set 358) drew with Derbyshire at Derby, 2004.
333:7	(set 369) drew with Essex at Chelmsford, 2010
316:6	(set 326) drew with Oxford University at Oxford, 1948.
312:6	(set 344) drew with Sussex at Scarborough 2011
316:7	(set 320) drew with Somerset at Scarborough, 1990.
300:5	(set 392) drew with Kent at Canterbury, 2010

To Lose:
433	(set 500) lost to Warwickshire by 66 runs at Birmingham, 2006
380	(set 406) lost to MCC. by 25 runs at Lord's, 1937.
343	(set 490) lost to Durham by 146 runs at Leeds 2011
324	(set 485) lost to Northamptonshire by 160 runs at Luton, 1994.
322	(set 344) lost to Middlesex by 21 runs at Lord's, 1996.
309	(set 400) lost to Middlesex by 90 runs at Lord's 1878.

*Consecutive matches

By Opponents:

To Win:
479:6	Somerset won by 4 wkts at Taunton, 2009
472:3	Middlesex won by 7 wkts at Lord's, 2014
404:5	Hampshire won by 5 wkts at Leeds, 2006
392:4	Gloucestershire won by 6 wkts at Bristol, 1948
364:4	Somerset won by 6 wkts at Taunton, 2010
354:5	Nottinghamshire won by 5 wkts at Scarborough, 1990
337:4	Worcestershire won by 6 wkts at Kidderminster, 2007
334:6	Glamorgan won by 4 wkts at Harrogate, 1955
329:5	Worcestershire won by 5 wkts at Worcester, 1979
321:6	Hampshire won by 4 wickets at Leeds, 2017
306:9	Surrey won by 1 wkt at Bradford, 1992
305:7	Lancashire won by 3 wkts at Manchester, 1980
302:9	Warwickshire won by 1 wkt at Birmingham, 1983

ALL REVVED UP: Matthew Revis celebrates his maiden five-wicket haul, against Glamorgan at Cardiff in September. Earlier in the summer the rapidly developing all-rounder posted his maiden first-class century, against Gloucestershire at Headingley in June.

WINNERS ARE GRINNERS: Harry Duke and Dom Leech, who shared an unbroken last-wicket stand of 33 as Vikings chased down a 242 to beat Surrey by one-wicket in the Metro Bank One-Day Cup clash at York. Opener Duke scored a superb unbeaten 93, while seamer Leech finished 18 not out. Leech said it was his favourite day on a cricket field.

LIKE A BIRD ON THE WING: Adam Lyth takes off to catch Sussex's Tom Haines in their Championship clash at Headingley.

YORKIES ABROAD: The county's four representatives with England's Physical Disability team, who lost a five-match T20 series 3-2 against India in late January and early February. Left to right at the Narendra Modi Stadium in Ahmedabad are assistant coach Jared Warner, head coach Ben Silver, wicketkeeper-batter Liam Thomas and Jane Powell, Yorkshire's President whose day job is the ECB's disability performance manager.

CHANGING OF THE GUARD

WELCOMING A NEW ERA: Yorkshire's members listen to outgoing Chair Harry Chathli speak at February's EGM, which was held to vote in Colin Graves's refinancing package for the county. Approximately 350-400 members attended the meeting in the East Stand Long Room.
BELOW: Graves, third from left, who becomes the new Chair, has Phillip Hodson, prospective Vice Chair, to his immediate left and then Sanjeev Gandhi, a board member. At the end of the front row can be seen Darren Gough, Managing Director of Cricket.

ENGLAND CALLING: Northern Diamonds captain Hollie Armitage, who earned her maiden England call-up for the March T20 series in New Zealand. The Huddersfield-born star has scored 50-over regional centuries in each of the last two seasons. Her Diamonds team-mate Bess Heath was on the tour having made her senior England debut in 2023.

ON A ROLL: John Dodds, left, who won the award for the best outground pitches at the ECB's Grounds Manager of the Year awards, and Headingley's former head groundsman, Andy Fogarty, honoured with a special presentation to mark a much-decorated 40-year career.

PHOTOGRAPHER'S DREAM: John Heald captured this spectacular snap during a weather delay at Leicestershire's Grace Road in September. Will Yorkshire's pot of gold at the end of the rainbow come in the form of promotion in 2024? *Somewhere, over the rainbow...*

ALL UNDER ONE ROOF: A £1.5m 10-lane all-weather cricket dome was opened at Bradford Park Avenue in October. The facility — the first of its kind — is funded by the England and Wales Cricket Board in partnership with Bradford Council, and is set to provide sessions for 10,000 people from the community each year.

BIG BEN CHIMES: Ben Cliff, who made his first-class debut for Yorkshire in September's LV= Insurance County Championship draw against Glamorgan at Cardiff, claimed one second-innings wicket and would add two more scalps to his tally in the draw against Leicestershire at Grace Road the following week. Former Yorkshire loanee batter Sam Northeast is at the crease for Glamorgan.

TEAM WORK MAKES THE DREAM WORK: *SWPix* photographer Allan McKenzie, who captured this image of Yorkshire celebrating their Championship win over Derbyshire at Scarborough, described it as one of his 2024 favourites.

HIGH FOURTH INNINGS SCORES – 300 AND OVER *(Continued)*

By Opponents:

To Draw:

366:8	(set 443)	Hampshire drew at Southampton, 2007.
334:7	(set 339)	MCC. drew at Scarborough, 1911.
322:9	(set 334)	Middlesex drew at Leeds, 1988.
318-7	(set 499)	Northamptonshire at Northampton 2022
317:6	(set 355)	Nottinghamshire drew at Nottingham, 1910.
300:9	(set 314)	Northamptonshire drew at Northampton, 1990.

To Lose:

370	(set 539)	Leicestershire lost by 168 runs at Leicester, 2001
319	(set 364)	Gloucestershire lost by 44 runs at Leeds, 1987.
318	(set 324)	Somerset lost by 5 runs at Taunton, 1986.
315	(set 319)	Essex lost by 3 runs at Colchester, 1991
314	(set 334)	Lancashire lost by 19 runs at Manchester, 1993.
310	(set 417)	Warwickshire lost by 106 runs at Scarborough, 1939.
306	(set 413)	Kent lost by 106 runs at Leeds, 1952.
300	(set 330)	Middlesex lost by 29 runs at Sheffield, 1930.

TIE MATCHES

Yorkshire (351:4 dec and 113) tied with Leicestershire (328 and 136) at Huddersfield, 1954.
Yorkshire (106:9 dec and 207) tied with Middlesex (102 and 211) at Bradford, 1973.

HIGHEST SCORES BY AND AGAINST YORKSHIRE

Yorkshire versus: —

	By Yorkshire:	Against Yorkshire:
Derbyshire:		
In Yorkshire:	677:7 dec at Leeds 2013	491 at Bradford, 1949
Away:	662 at Chesterfield, 1898	523 at Derby, 2005
Durham:		
In Yorkshire:	677:7 dec. at Leeds, 2006	573 at Scarborough, 2013
Away	589-8 dec at Chester-le-Street, 2014	507:8 dec at Chester-le-Street, 2016
Essex:		
In Yorkshire:	516 at Scarborough, 2010	622:8 dec. at Leeds, 2005
Away:	555:1 dec. at Leyton, 1932	521 at Leyton, 1905
Glamorgan:		
In Yorkshire:	580:9 dec at Scarborough, 2001	498 at Leeds, 1999
Away:	536:8 dec. at Cardiff, 1996	482:7 dec. at Cardiff, 1996
Gloucestershire:		
In Yorkshire:	504:7 dec. at Bradford, 1905	411 at Leeds, 1992
Away:	494 at Bristol, 1897	574 at Cheltenham, 1990
Hampshire:		
In Yorkshire:	593:9 dec. at Leeds 2016	498:6 dec at Scarborough, 2010
Away	585:3 dec at Portsmouth 1920	599:3 at Southampton, 2011
Kent:		
In Yorkshire	571 at Leeds 2022	537:9 dec at Leeds, 2012
Away:	559 at Canterbury, 1887	580: 9 dec. at Maidstone, 1998
Lancashire:		
In Yorkshire:	590 at Bradford, 1887	566-9 dec at Leeds, 2022
Away	616:6 dec at Manchester, 2014	537 at Manchester, 2005
Leicestershire:		
In Yorkshire	562 { at Scarborough, 1901 / at Dewsbury, 1903	681:7 dec. at Bradford, 1996
Away:	660 at Leicester, 1896	425 at Leicester, 1906

HIGHEST SCORES BY AND AGAINST YORKSHIRE *(Continued)*

Yorkshire versus: —

	By Yorkshire:	**Against Yorkshire:**
Middlesex:		
In Yorkshire:	575:7 dec. at Bradford, 1899	527 at Huddersfield, 1887
Away	538:6 dec at Lord's, 1925	573:8 dec at Lord's, 2015
Northamptonshire:		
In Yorkshire:	673:8 dec. at Leeds, 2003	517:7 dec. at Scarborough, 1999
Away	546:3 dec at Northampton, 2014	531:4 dec at Northampton, 1996
Nottinghamshire:		
In Yorkshire:	572:8 dec at Scarborough, 2013	545:7 dec at Leeds, 2010
Away	534:9 dec at Nottingham, 2011	490 at Nottingham, 1897
Somerset:		
In Yorkshire:	525:4 dec. at Leeds, 1953	630 at Leeds, 1901
Away:	589:5 dec at Bath, 2001	592 at Taunton, 1892
Surrey:		
In Yorkshire:	582:7 dec. at Sheffield, 1935	516-7 dec at Leeds, 2017
Away:	704 at The Oval, 1899	634:5 dec at The Oval, 2013
Sussex:		
In Yorkshire:	681:5 dec. at Sheffield, 1897	566 at Sheffield, 1937
Away:	522:7 dec. at Hastings, 1911	597:8 dec. at Hove, 2007
Warwickshire:		
In Yorkshire	561:7 dec at Scarborough 2007	482 at Leeds, 2011
Away:	887 at Birmingham, 1896	601:9 dec. at Birmingham, 2002
	(Highest score by a First-Class county)	
Worcestershire:		
In Yorkshire:	600: 4 dec. at Scarborough, 1995	572:7 dec. at Scarborough 2018
Away:	560:6 dec. at Worcester, 1928	456:8 at Worcester, 1904
Australians:		
In Yorkshire:	377 at Sheffield, 1953	470 at Bradford, 1893
Indians:		
In Yorkshire:	385 at Hull, 1911	490:5 dec. at Sheffield, 1946
New Zealanders:		
In Yorkshire:	419 at Bradford, 1965	370:7 dec. at Bradford, 1949
Pakistanis:		
In Yorkshire:	433:9 dec. at Sheffield, 1954	356 at Sheffield, 1954
South Africans:		
In Yorkshire:	579 at Sheffield, 1951	454:8 dec at Sheffield, 1951
Sri Lankans:		
In Yorkshire:	314:8 dec. at Leeds, 1991	422:8 dec. at Leeds, 1991
West Indians:		
In Yorkshire:	312:5 dec. at Scarborough, 1973	426 at Scarborough, 1995
Zimbabweans:		
In Yorkshire:	298:9 dec at Leeds, 1990	235 at Leeds, 2000
Cambridge University:		
In Yorkshire:	359 at Scarborough, 1967	366 at Leeds, 1998
Away:	540 at Cambridge, 1938	425:7 at Cambridge, 1929
Durham MCCU:		
Away:	355 at Durham, 2011	287 at Durham, 2011
Leeds/Bradford MCCU:		
In Yorkshire	543-5 dec at Leeds, 2017	211 at Leeds, 2012
Away	489-8 dec at Weetwood, Leeds, 2019	219 at Weetwood, Leeds, 2019
Loughborough MCCU:		
In Yorkshire:	383:6 dec at Leeds, 2007	289 at Leeds, 2007

HIGHEST SCORES BY AND AGAINST YORKSHIRE *(Continued)*

Yorkshire versus: —

MCC: | **By Yorkshire:** | **Against Yorkshire:**

In Yorkshire: 557:8 dec. at Scarborough, 1933 — 478:8 at Scarborough, 1904

Away: 528:8 dec. at Lord's, 1919 — 488 at Lord's, 1919

Oxford University:

In Yorkshire: 173 at Harrogate, 1972 — 190:6 dec at Harrogate, 1972

Away: 468:6 dec. at Oxford, 1978 — 422:9 dec. at Oxford, 1953

LOWEST SCORES BY AND AGAINST YORKSHIRE

Yorkshire versus:

Derbyshire: | **By Yorkshire:** | **Against Yorkshire:**

In Yorkshire: 50 at Sheffield, 1894 — 20 at Sheffield, 1939

Away: 44 at Chesterfield, 1948 — 26 at Derby, 1880

Durham:

In Yorkshire: 93 at Leeds, 2003 — 125 at Harrogate, 1995

Away: 108 at Durham, 1992 — 74 at Chester-le-Street, 1998

Essex:

In Yorkshire: 31 at Huddersfield, 1935 — 52 at Harrogate, 1900

Away: 50 at Chelmsford, 2018 — 30 at Leyton, 1901

Glamorgan:

In Yorkshire: 83 at Sheffield, 1946 — 52 at Hull, 1926

Away: 92 at Swansea, 1956 — 48 at Cardiff, 1924

Gloucestershire:

In Yorkshire: 61 at Leeds, 1894 — 36 at Sheffield, 1903

Away: 35 at Bristol, 1959 — 42 at Gloucester, 1924

Hampshire:

In Yorkshire: 23 at Middlesbrough, 1965 — 36 at Leeds, 1904

Away: 96 at Bournemouth, 1971 — 36 at Southampton, 1898

Kent:

In Yorkshire: 30 at Sheffield, 1865 — 39 { at Sheffield, 1882 / at Sheffield, 1936 }

Away: 62 at Maidstone, 1889 — 63 at Canterbury, 1901

Lancashire:

In Yorkshire: 33 at Leeds, 1924 — 30 at Holbeck, 1868

Away: 51 { at Manchester, 1888 / at Manchester, 1893 } — 39 at Manchester, 1874

Leicestershire: | By Yorkshire: | Against Yorkshire:

In Yorkshire: 93 at Leeds, 1935 — 34 at Leeds, 1906

Away: 47 at Leicester, 1911 — 57 at Leicester, 1898

Middlesex:

In Yorkshire: 45 at Leeds, 1898 — 45 at Huddersfield, 1879

Away: 43 at Lord's, 1888 — 49 at Lord's in 1890

Northamptonshire:

In Yorkshire: 85 at Sheffield, 1919 — 51 at Bradford, 1920

Away 64 at Northampton, 1959 — 15 at Northampton, 1908
(and 27 in first innings)

Nottinghamshire:

In Yorkshire: 32 at Sheffield, 1876 — 24 at Sheffield, 1888

Away: 43 at Nottingham, 1869 — 13 at Nottingham, 1901
(second smallest total
by a First-Class county)

LOWEST SCORES BY AND AGAINST YORKSHIRE *(continued)*

Yorkshire versus:

Somerset: | **By Yorkshire:** | **Against Yorkshire:**

In Yorkshire: 73 at Leeds, 1895 — 43 at Bradford, 1930
Away: 83 at Wells, 1949 — 35 at Bath, 1898

Surrey:
In Yorkshire: 54 at Sheffield, 1873 — 31 at Holbeck, 1883
Away: 26 at The Oval, 1909 — 44 at The Oval, 1935

Sussex:
In Yorkshire: 61 at Dewsbury, 1891 — 20 at Hull, 1922
Away: 42 at Hove, 1922 — 24 at Hove, 1878

Warwickshire:
In Yorkshire: 49 at Huddersfield, 1951 — 35 at Sheffield, 1979
Away: 54 at Birmingham, 1964 — 35 at Birmingham, 1963

Worcestershire:
In Yorkshire: 62 at Bradford, 1907 — 24 at Huddersfield, 1903
Away: 72 at Worcester, 1977 — 65 at Worcester, 1925

Australians:
In Yorkshire: 48 at Leeds, 1893 — 23 at Leeds, 1902

Indians:
In Yorkshire: 146 at Bradford, 1959 — 66 at Harrogate, 1932

New Zealanders:
In Yorkshire: 189 at Harrogate, 1931 — 134 at Bradford, 1965

Pakistanis:
In Yorkshire: 137 at Bradford, 1962 — 150 at Leeds, 1967

South Africans:
In Yorkshire: 113 at Bradford, 1907 — 76 at Bradford, 1951

Sri Lankans:
In Yorkshire: Have not been dismissed. Lowest is 184:1 dec at Leeds, 1991 — 287:5 dec at Leeds, 1988

West Indians:
In Yorkshire: 50 at Harrogate, 1906 — 58 at Leeds, 1928

Zimbabweans:
In Yorkshire: 124 at Leeds, 2000 — 68 at Leeds, 2000

Cambridge University:
In Yorkshire: 110 at Sheffield, 1903 — 39 at Sheffield, 1903
Away: 51 at Cambridge, 1906 — 30 at Cambridge, 1928

Durham MCCU:
Away 355 at Durham, 2011 — 196 at Durham, 2011

Leeds/Bradford MCCU:
In Yorkshire 135 at Leeds, 2012 — 118 at Leeds, 2013
Away — 118 at Weetwood, Leeds, 2019

Loughborough MCCU:
In Yorkshire 348:5 dec at Leeds, 2010 — 289 at Leeds, 2007

MCC:
In Yorkshire: 46 { at Scarborough, 1876 / at Scarborough, 1877 — 31 at Scarborough, 1877
Away: 44 at Lord's, 1880 — 27 at Lord's, 1902

Oxford University:
In Yorkshire: Have not been dismissed. Lowest is 115:8 at Harrogate, 1972 — 133 at Harrogate, 1972
Away: 141 at Oxford, 1949 — 46 at Oxford, 1956

INDIVIDUAL INNINGS OF 150 AND OVER

**A complete list of all First Class Centuries up to and Including 2020
is to be found in the 2021 edition**

J M BAIRSTOW (7)

205	v. Nottinghamshire	at Nottingham	2011
182	v. Leicestershire	at Scarborough	2012
186	v. Derbyshire	at Leeds	2013
161 *	v. Sussex	at Arundel	2014
219 *	v. Durham	at Chester-le-Street	2015
246	v. Hampshire	at Leeds	2016
198	v. Surrey	at Leeds	2016

G S BALLANCE (5)

174	v. Northamptonshire	at Leeds	2014
165	v. Sussex	at Hove	2015
203 *	v. Hampshire 2nd innings	at West End, Southampton	2017
194	v. Worcestershire	at Worcester	2018
159	v. Kent	at Canterbury	2019

W BARBER (7)

162	v. Middlesex	at Bramall Lane, Sheffield	1932
168	v. MCC	at Lord's	1934
248	v. Kent	at Leeds	1934
191	v. Sussex	at Leeds	1935
255	v. Surrey	at Bramall Lane, Sheffield	1935
158	v. Kent	at Bramall Lane, Sheffield	1936
157	v. Surrey	at Bramall Lane, Sheffield	1938

M G BEVAN (2)

153 *	v. Surrey	at The Oval	1995
160 *	v. Surrey	at Middlesbrough	1996

H D BIRD (1)

181 *	v. Glamorgan	at Bradford	1959

R J BLAKEY (3)

204 *	v. Gloucestershire	at Leeds	1987
196	v. Oxford University	at Oxford	1991
223 *	v. Northamptonshire	at Leeds	2003

G S BLEWETT (1)

190	v. Northamptonshire	at Scarborough	1999

M W BOOTH (1)

210	v. Worcestershire	at Worcester	1911

G BOYCOTT (32)

165*	v. Leicestershire	at Scarborough	1963
151	v. Middlesex	at Leeds	1964
151*	v. Leicestershire	at Leicester	1964
177	v. Gloucestershire	at Bristol	1964
164	v. Sussex	at Hove	1966
220*	v. Northamptonshire	at Sheffield	1967
180*	v. Warwickshire	at Middlesbrough	1968
260*	v. Essex	at Colchester (Garrison Ground)	1970
169	v. Nottinghamshire	at Leeds	1971
233	v. Essex	at Colchester (Garrison Ground)	1971
182*	v. Middlesex	at Lord's	1971
169	v. Lancashire	at Sheffield	1971
151	v. Leicestershire	at Bradford	1971

INDIVIDUAL INNINGS OF 150 AND OVER *(Continued)*

G BOYCOTT *(Continued)*

204*	v. Leicestershire	at Leicester	1972
152*	v. Worcestershire	at Worcester	1975
175*	v. Middlesex	at Scarborough	1975
201*	v. Middlesex	at Lord's	1975
161*	v. Gloucestershire	at Leeds	1976
207*	v. Cambridge University	at Cambridge	1976
156*	v. Glamorgan	at Middlesbrough	1976
154	v Nottinghamshire	at Nottingham	1977
151*	v Derbyshire	at Leeds	1979
167	v Derbyshire	at Chesterfield	1979
175*	v Nottinghamshire	at Worksop	1979
154*	v Derbyshire	at Scarborough	1980
159	v Worcestershire	at Sheffield (Abbeydale Park)	1982
152*	v Warwickshire	at Leeds	1982
214*	v Nottinghamshire	at Worksop	1983
163	v Nottinghamshire	at Bradford	1983
169*	v Derbyshire	at Chesterfield	1983
153*	v Derbyshire	at Harrogate	1984
184	v Worcestershire	at Worcester	1985

T T BRESNAN *(1)*

169*	v. Durham	at Chester-le-Street	2015

H C BROOK *(1)*

194	v. Kent	at Leeds	2022

G L BROPHY *(1)*

177*	v Worcestershire	at Worcester	2011

J T BROWN *(8)*

168*	v Sussex	at Huddersfield	1895
203	v Middlesex	at Lord's	1896
311	v Sussex	at Sheffield	1897
300	v Derbyshire	at Chesterfield	1898
150	v Sussex	at Hove	1898
168	v Cambridge University	at Cambridge	1899
167	v Australians	at Bradford	1899
192	v Derbyshire	at Derby	1899

D BYAS *(5)*

153	v Nottinghamshire	at Worksop	1991
156	v Essex	at Chelmsford	1993
181	v Cambridge University	at Cambridge	1995
193	v Lancashire	at Leeds	1995
213	v Worcestershire	at Scarborough	1995

D B CLOSE *(5)*

164	v Combined Services	at Harrogate	1954
154	v Nottinghamshire	at Nottingham	1959
198	v Surrey	at The Oval	1960
184	v Nottinghamshire	at Scarborough	1960
161	v Northamptonshire	at Northampton	1963

D DENTON *(11)*

153*	v Australians	at Bradford	1905
165	v Hampshire	at Bournemouth	1905
172	v Gloucestershire	at Bradford	1905

INDIVIDUAL INNINGS OF 150 AND OVER *(Continued)*

D DENTON *(Continued)*

184	v Nottinghamshire	at Nottingham	1909
182	v Derbyshire	at Chesterfield	1910
200*	v Warwickshire	at Birmingham	1912
182	v Gloucestershire	at Bristol	1912
221	v Kent	at Tunbridge Wells	1912
191	v Hampshire	at Southampton	1912
168*	v Hampshire	at Southampton	1914
209*	v Worcestershire	at Worcester	1920

A W GALE (4)

150	v. Surrey	at The Oval	2008
151*	v. Nottinghamshire	at Nottingham	2010
272	v. Nottinghamshire	at Scarborough	2013
164	v. Worcestershire	at Scarborough	2015

P A GIBB (1)

157*	v. Nottinghamshire	at Sheffield	1935

S HAIGH (1)

159	v. Nottinghamshire	at Sheffield	1901

L HALL (1)

160	v. Lancashire	at Bradford	1887

J H HAMPSHIRE (5)

150	v. Leicestershire	at Bradford	1964
183*	v. Sussex	at Hove	1971
157*	v. Nottinghamshire	at Worksop	1974
158	v. Gloucestershire	at Harrogate	1974
155*	v. Gloucestershire	at Leeds	1976

I J HARVEY (1)

209*	v. Somerset	at Leeds	2005

LORD HAWKE (1)

166	v. Warwickshire	at Birmingham	1896

G C H HILL (1)

151*	v. Northamptonshire	at Northampton	2022

G H HIRST (15)

186	v. Surrey	at The Oval	1899
155	v. Nottinghamshire	at Scarborough	1900
214	v. Worcestershire	at Worcester	1901
153	v. Leicestershire	at Dewsbury	1903
153	v. Oxford University	at Oxford	1904
152	v. Hampshire	at Portsmouth	1904
157	v. Kent	at Tunbridge Wells	1904
341	v. Leicestershire	at Leicester (Aylestone Road)	1905
232*	v. Surrey	at The Oval	1905
169	v. Oxford University	at Oxford	1906
158	v. Cambridge University	at Cambridge	1910
156	v. Lancashire	at Manchester	1911
218	v. Sussex	at Hastings	1911
166*	v. Sussex	at Hastings	1913
180*	v. MCC	at Lord's	1919

INDIVIDUAL INNINGS OF 150 AND OVER *(Continued)*

P HOLMES (16)

302*	v. Hampshire	at Portsmouth	1920
150	v. Derbyshire	at Chesterfield	1921
277*	v. Northamptonshire	at Harrogate	1921
209	v. Warwickshire	at Birmingham	1922
220*	v. Warwickshire	at Huddersfield	1922
199	v. Somerset	at Hull	1923
315*	v. Middlesex	at Lord's	1925
194	v. Leicestershire	at Hull	1925
159	v. Hampshire	at Southampton	1925
180	v. Gloucestershire	at Gloucester	1927
175*	v. New Zealanders	at Bradford	1927
179*	v. Middlesex	at Leeds	1928
275	v. Warwickshire	at Bradford	1928
285	v. Nottinghamshire	at Nottingham	1929
250	v. Warwickshire	at Birmingham	1931
224*	v. Essex	at Leyton	1932

L HUTTON (31)

196	v. Worcestershire	at Worcester	1934
163	v. Surrey	at Leeds	1936
161	v. MCC	at Lord's	1937
271*	v. Derbyshire	at Sheffield	1937
153	v. Leicestershire	at Hull	1937
180	v. Cambridge University	at Cambridge	1938
158	v. Warwickshire	at Birmingham	1939
280*	v. Hampshire	at Sheffield	1939
151	v. Surrey	at Leeds	1939
177	v. Sussex	at Scarborough	1939
183*	v. Indians	at Bradford	1946
171*	v. Northamptonshire	at Hull	1946
197	v. Glamorgan	at Swansea	1947
197	v. Essex	at Southend-on-Sea	1947
270*	v. Hampshire	at Bournemouth	1947
176*	v. Sussex	at Sheffield	1948
155	v. Sussex	at Hove	1948
167	v. New Zealanders	at Bradford	1949
201	v. Lancashire	at Manchester	1949
165	v. Sussex	at Hove	1949
269*	v. Northamptonshire	at Wellingborough	1949
156	v. Essex	at Colchester (Castle Park)	1950
153	v. Nottinghamshire	at Nottingham	1950
156	v. South Africans	at Sheffield	1951
151	v. Surrey	at The Oval	1951
194*	v. Nottinghamshire	at Nottingham	1951
152	v. Lancashire	at Leeds	1952
189	v. Kent	at Leeds	1952
178	v. Somerset	at Leeds	1953
163	v. Combined Services	at Harrogate	1954
194	v. Nottinghamshire	at Nottingham	1955

R A HUTTON (1)

189	v. Pakistanis	at Bradford	1971

R ILLINGWORTH (2)

150	v. Essex	at Colchester (Castle Park)	1959
162	v. Indians	at Sheffield	1959

INDIVIDUAL INNINGS OF 150 AND OVER *(Continued)*

Hon F S JACKSON (3)

160	v. Gloucestershire	at Sheffield	1898
155	v. Middlesex	at Bradford	1899
158	v. Surrey	at Bradford	1904

P A JAQUES (7)

243	v. Hampshire	at Southampton (Rose Bowl)	2004
173	v. Glamorgan	at Leeds	2004
176	v. Northamptonshire	at Leeds	2005
219	v. Derbyshire	at Leeds	2005
172	v. Durham	at Scarborough	2005
160	v. Gloucestershire	at Bristol	2012
152	v. Durham	at Scarborough	2013

R KILNER (5)

169	v. Gloucestershire	at Bristol	1914
206*	v. Derbyshire	at Sheffield	1920
166	v. Northamptonshire	at Northampton	1921
150	v. Northamptonshire	at Harrogate	1921
150	v. Middlesex	at Lord's	1926

T KOHLER-CADMORE (2)

176	v. Leeds/Bradford MCCU	at Weetwood, Leeds	2019
165*	v. Warwickshire	at Birmingham	2019

F LEE (1)

165	v. Lancashire	at Bradford	1887

A Z LEES (1)

275*	v. Derbyshire	at Chesterfield	2013

D S LEHMANN (13)

177	v. Somerset	at Taunton	1997
163*	v. Leicestershire	at Leicester	1997
182	v. Hampshire	at Portsmouth	1997
200	v. Worcestershire	at Worcester	1998
187*	v. Somerset	at Bath	2001
252	v. Lancashire	at Leeds	2001
193	v. Leicestershire	at Leicester	2001
216	v. Sussex	at Arundel	2002
187	v. Lancashire	at Leeds	2002
150	v. Warwickshire	at Birmingham	2006
193	v. Kent	at Canterbury	2006
172	v. Kent	at Leeds	2006
339	v. Durham	at Leeds	2006

E I LESTER (5)

186	v. Warwickshire	at Scarborough	1949
178	v. Nottinghamshire	at Nottingham	1952
157	v. Cambridge University	at Hull	1953
150	v. Oxford University	at Oxford	1954
163	v. Essex	at Romford	1954

M LEYLAND (17)

191	v. Glamorgan	at Swansea	1926
204*	v. Middlesex	at Sheffield	1927
247	v. Worcestershire	at Worcester	1928
189*	v. Glamorgan	at Huddersfield	1928
211*	v. Lancashire	at Leeds	1930

INDIVIDUAL INNINGS OF 150 AND OVER *(Continued)*

M LEYLAND (Continued)

172	v. Middlesex	at Sheffield	1930
186	v. Derbyshire	at Leeds	1930
189	v. Middlesex	at Sheffield	1932
153	v. Leicestershire	at Leicester (Aylestone Road)	1932
166	v. Leicestershire	at Bradford	1932
153*	v. Hampshire	at Bournemouth	1932
192	v. Northamptonshire	at Leeds	1933
210*	v. Kent	at Dover	1933
263	v. Essex	at Hull	1936
163*	v. Surrey	at Leeds	1936
167	v. Worcestershire	at Stourbridge	1937
180*	v. Middlesex	at Lord's	1939

E LOCKWOOD (1)

208	v. Kent	at Gravesend	1883

J D LOVE (4)

163	v. Nottinghamshire	at Bradford	1976
170*	v. Worcestershire	at Worcester	1979
161	v. Warwickshire	at Birmingham	1981
154	v. Lancashire	at Manchester	1981

F A LOWSON (10)

155	v. Kent	at Maidstone	1951
155	v. Worcestershire	at Bradford	1952
166	v. Scotland	at Glasgow	1953
259*	v. Worcestershire	at Worcester	1953
165	v. Sussex	at Hove	1954
164	v. Essex	at Scarborough	1954
150*	v. Kent	at Dover	1954
183*	v. Oxford University	at Oxford	1956
154	v. Somerset	at Taunton	1956
154	v. Cambridge University	at Cambridge	1957

R G LUMB (2)

159	v. Somerset	at Harrogate	1979
165*	v. Gloucestershire	at Bradford	1984

A LYTH (8)

248 *	v. Leicestershire	at Leicester	2012
230	v. Northamptonshire	at Northampton	2014
251	v. Lancashire	at Manchester	2014
202	v. Surrey	at The Oval	2016
194	v. Leeds/Bradford MCCU	at Leeds	2017
153	v. Nottinghamshire	at Nottingham	2021
183	v. Surrey	at Scarborough	2022
174	v. Glamorgan	at Leeds	2023

D J MALAN (3)

219	v. Derbyshire	at Leeds	2020
199	v. Sussex	at Leeds	2021
152	v.Kent	atLeeds	2022

D R MARTYN (1)

238	v. Gloucestershire	at Leeds	2003

INDIVIDUAL INNINGS OF 150 AND OVER *(Continued)*

A McGRATH (7)

165	v. Lancashire	at Leeds	2002
174	v. Derbyshire	at Derby	2004
165*	v. Leicestershire	at Leicester	2005
173*	v. Worcestershire	at Leeds	2005
158	v. Derbyshire	at Derby	2005
188*	v. Warwickshire	at Birmingham	2007
211	v. Warwickshire	at Birmingham	2009

A A METCALFE (7)

151	v. Northamptonshire	at Luton	1986
151	v. Lancashire	at Manchester	1986
152	v. MCC	at Scarborough	1987
216*	v. Middlesex	at Leeds	1988
162	v. Gloucestershire	at Cheltenham	1990
150*	v. Derbyshire	at Scarborough	1990
194*	v. Nottinghamshire	at Nottingham	1990

A MITCHELL (7)

189	v. Northamptonshire	at Northampton	1926
176	v. Nottinghamshire	at Bradford	1930
177*	v. Gloucestershire	at Bradford	1932
150*	v. Worcestershire	at Worcester	1933
158	v. MCC	at Scarborough	1933
152	v. Hampshire	at Bradford	1934
181	v. Surrey	at Bradford	1934

F MITCHELL (2)

194	v. Leicestershire	at Leicester	1899
162*	v. Warwickshire	at Birmingham	1901

M D MOXON (14)

153	v. Lancashire	at Leeds	1983
153	v. Somerset	at Leeds	1985
168	v. Worcestershire	at Worcester	1985
191	v. Northamptonshire	at Scarborough	1988
162*	v. Surrey	at The Oval	1989
218*	v. Sussex	at Eastbourne	1990
200	v. Essex	at Colchester (Castle Park)	1991
183	v. Gloucestershire	at Cheltenham	1992
171*	v. Kent	at Leeds	1993
161*	v. Lancashire	at Manchester	1994
274*	v. Worcestershire	at Worcester	1994
203*	v. Kent	at Leeds	1995
213	v. Glamorgan	at Cardiff (Sophia Gardens)	1996
155	v. Pakistan 'A'	at Leeds	1997

E OLDROYD (5)

151*	v. Glamorgan	at Cardiff	1922
194	v. Worcestershire	at Worcester	1923
162*	v. Glamorgan	at Swansea	1928
168	v. Glamorgan	at Hull	1929
164*	v. Somerset	at Bath	1930

D E V PADGETT (1)

161*	v. Oxford University	at Oxford	1959

INDIVIDUAL INNINGS OF 150 AND OVER *(Continued)*

R PEEL (2)

158	v. Middlesex	at Lord's	1889
210*	v. Warwickshire	at Birmingham	1896

A U RASHID (3)

157*	v. Lancashire	at Leeds	2009
180	v. Somerset	at Leeds	2013
159*	v. Lancashire	at Manchester	2014

W RHODES (8)

196	v. Worcestershire	at Worcester	1904
201	v. Somerset	at Taunton	1905
199	v. Sussex	at Hove	1909
176	v. Nottinghamshire	at Harrogate	1912
152	v. Leicestershire	at Leicester (Aylestone Road)	1913
167*	v. Nottinghamshire	at Leeds	1920
267*	v. Leicestershire	at Leeds	1921
157	v. Derbyshire	at Leeds	1925

P E ROBINSON (2)

150*	v. Derbyshire	at Scarborough	1990
189	v. Lancashire	at Scarborough	1991

J E ROOT (5)

160	v. Sussex	at Scarborough	2011
222 *	v. Hampshire	at Southampton (West End)	2012
182	v. Durham	at Chester-le-Street	2013
236	v. Derbyshire	at Leeds	2013

2013 innings consecutive

213	v.Surrey	at Leeds	2016

J W ROTHERY (1)

161	v. Kent	at Dover	1908

J A RUDOLPH (5)

220	v. Warwickshire	at Scarborough	2007
155	v. Somerset	at Taunton	2008
198	v. Worcestershire	at Leeds	2009
191	v. Somerset	at Taunton	2009
228*	v. Durham	at Leeds	2010

H RUDSTON (1)

164	v. Leicestershire	at Leicester (Aylestone Road)	1904

J J SAYERS (3)

187	v. Kent	at Tunbridge Wells	2007
173	v. Warwickshire	at Birmingham	2009
152	v. Somerset	at Taunton	2009

A B SELLERS (1)

204	v. Cambridge University	at Cambridge	1936

SHAN MASOOD (1)

192	v. Glamorgan	at Cardiff	2023

K SHARP (2)

173	v. Derbyshire	at Chesterfield	1984
181	v. Gloucestershire	at Harrogate	1986

INDIVIDUAL INNINGS OF 150 AND OVER *(Continued)*

P J SHARPE (4)

203*	v. Cambridge University	at Cambridge	1960
152	v. Kent	at Sheffield	1960
197	v. Pakistanis	at Leeds	1967
172*	v. Glamorgan	at Swansea	1971

G A SMITHSON (1)

169	v. Leicestershire	at Leicester	1947

W B STOTT (2)

181	v. Essex	Sheffield	1957
186	v. Warwickshire	Birmingham	1960

H SUTCLIFFE (39)

174	v. Kent	at Dover	1919
232	v. Surrey	at The Oval	1922
213	v. Somerset	at Dewsbury	1924
160	v. Sussex	at Sheffield	1924
255*	v. Essex	at Southend-on-Sea	1924
235	v. Middlesex	at Leeds	1925
206	v. Warwickshire	at Dewsbury	1925
171	v. MCC	at Scarborough	1925
200	v. Leicestershire	at Leicester (Aylestone Road)	1926
176	v. Surrey	at Leeds	1927
169	v. Nottinghamshire	at Bradford	1927
228	v. Sussex	at Eastbourne	1928
150	v. Northamptonshire	at Northampton	1929
150*	v. Essex	at Dewsbury	1930
173	v. Sussex	at Hove	1930
173*	v. Cambridge University	at Cambridge	1931
230	v. Kent	at Folkestone	1931
183	v. Somerset	at Dewsbury	1931
195	v. Lancashire	at Sheffield	1931
187	v. Leicestershire	at Leicester (Aylestone Road)	1931
153*	v. Warwickshire	at Hull	1932
313	v. Essex	at Leyton	1932
270	v. Sussex	at Leeds	1932
182	v. Derbyshire	at Leeds	1932
194	v. Essex	at Scarborough	1932
205	v. Warwickshire	at Birmingham	1933
177	v. Middlesex	at Bradford	1933
174	v. Leicestershire	at Leicester (Aylestone Road)	1933
152	v. Cambridge University	at Cambridge	1934
166	v. Essex	at Hull	1934
203	v. Surrey	at The Oval	1934
187*	v. Worcestershire	at Bradford	1934
200*	v. Worcestershire	at Sheffield	1935
212	v. Leicestershire	at Leicester (Aylestone Road)	1935
202	v. Middlesex	at Scarborough	1936
189	v. Leicestershire	at Hull	1937
165	v. Lancashire	at Manchester	1939
234*	v. Leicestershire	at Hull	1939
175	v. Middlesex	at Lord's	1939

W H H SUTCLIFFE (3)

171*	v. Worcestershire	at Worcester	1952
181	v. Kent	at Canterbury	1952
161*	v. Glamorgan	at Harrogate	1955

J A TATTERSALL (1)

180*	v.Surrey	at Scarborough	2022

K TAYLOR (8)

168*	v. Nottinghamshire	at Nottingham	1956
159	v. Leicestershire	at Sheffield	1961
203*	v. Warwickshire	at Birmingham	1961
178*	v. Oxford University	at Oxford	1962
163	v. Nottinghamshire	at Leeds	1962
153	v. Lancashire	at Manchester	1964
160	v. Australians	at Sheffield	1964
162	v. Worcestershire	at Kidderminster	1967

T L TAYLOR (1)

156	v. Hampshire	at Harrogate	1901

J TUNNICLIFFE (2)

243	v. Derbyshire	at Chesterfield	1898
158	v. Worcestershire	at Worcester	1900

G ULYETT (1)

199*	v. Derbyshire	at Sheffield	1887

M P VAUGHAN (7)

183	v. Glamorgan	at Cardiff (Sophia Gardens)	1996
183	v. Northamptonshire	at Northampton	1996
161	v. Essex	at Ilford	1997
177	v. Durham	at Chester-le-Street	1998
151	v. Essex	at Chelmsford	1999
153	v. Kent	at Scarborough	1999
155*	v. Derbyshire	at Leeds	2000

E WAINWRIGHT (3)

171	v. Middlesex	at Lord's	1897
153	v. Leicestershire	at Leicester	1899
228	v. Surrey	at The Oval	1899

W WATSON (7)

153*	v. Surrey	at The Oval	1947
172	v. Derbyshire	at Scarborough	1948
162*	v. Somerset	at Leeds	1953
163	v. Sussex	at Sheffield	1955
174	v. Lancashire	at Sheffield	1955
214*	v. Worcestershire	at Worcester	1955
162	v. Northamptonshire	at Harrogate	1957

C WHITE (6)

181	v. Lancashire	at Leeds	1996
172*	v. Worcestershire	at Leeds	1997
186	v. Lancashire	at Manchester	2001
183	v. Glamorgan	at Scarborough	2001
161	v. Leicestershire	at Scarborough	2002
173*	v. Derbyshire	at Derby	2003

INDIVIDUAL INNINGS OF 150 AND OVER *(Continued)*

K S WILLIAMSON (1)

189	v. Sussex	at Scarborough	2014

B B WILSON (2)

150	v. Warwickshire	at Birmingham	1912
208	v. Sussex	at Bradford	1914

J V WILSON (7)

157*	v. Sussex	at Leeds	1949
157	v. Essex	at Sheffield	1950
166*	v. Sussex	at Hull	1951
223*	v. Scotland	at Scarborough	1951
154	v. Oxford University	at Oxford	1952
230	v. Derbyshire	at Sheffield	1952
165	v. Oxford University	at Oxford	1956

M J WOOD (5)

200*	v. Warwickshire	at Leeds	1998
157	v. Northamptonshire	at Leeds	2003
207	v. Somerset	at Taunton	2003
155	v. Hampshire	at Scarborough	2003
202*	v. Bangladesh 'A'	at Leeds	2005

N W D YARDLEY (2)

177	v. Derbyshire	Scarborough	1947
183*	v. Hampshire	Leeds	1951

YOUNUS KHAN (2)

202*	v. Hampshire	Southampton (Rose Bowl)	2007
217*	v. Kent	Scarborough	2007

CENTURIES BY CURRENT PLAYERS

**A complete list of all First-Class Centuries up to and including 2020
is to be found in the 2021 edition**

J M BAIRSTOW (15)

205	v. Nottinghamshire	Nottingham	2011
136	v. Somerset	Taunton	2011
182	v. Leicestershire	Scarborough	2012
118	v. Leicestershire	Leicester	2012
107	v. Kent	Leeds	2012
186	v. Derbyshire	Leeds	2013
123	v. Leeds/Bradford	Leeds	2014
161*	v. Sussex	Arundel	2014
102	v. Hampshire	Leeds	2015
125*	v. Middlesex	Leeds	2015
219*	v. Durham	Chester-le-Street **	2015
108	v. Warwickshire	Birmingham **	2015

*(** consecutive innings)*

139	v. Worcestershire	Scarborough	2015
246	v. Hampshire	Leeds	2016
198	v. Surrey	Leeds	2016

F J BEAN (3)

118	v. Leicestershire	Leeds	2023
135	v. Worcestershire	Worcester	2023
114	v. Gloucestershire	Leeds	2023

CENTURIES BY CURRENT PLAYERS *(Continued)*

H C BROOK (7)

124	v. Essex	Chelmsford	2018
101	v. Somerset	Leeds	2019
113	v. Northamptonshire	Northampton	2021
118	v. Somerset	Scarborough	2021
101	v. Gloucestershire	Bristol	2022
194	v. Kent	Leeds	2022
123	v. Essex	Chelmsford	2022

G C H HILL (3)

151*	v. Northamptonshire	Northampton	2022
131	v. Hampshire	West End, Southampton	2022
101	v. Gloucestershire	Leeds	2023

A LYTH (31)

132	v. Nottinghamshire	Nottingham	2008
142	v. Somerset	Taunton	2010
133	v. Hampshire	Southampton	2010
100	v. Lancashire	Manchester	2010
248 *	v. Leicestershire	Leicester	2012
111	v. Leeds/Bradford MCCU	Leeds	2013
105	v. Somerset	Taunton	2013
130	v. Leeds/Bradford MCCU	Leeds	2014
104	v. Durham	Chester-le-Street	2014
230	v. Northamptonshire	Northampton	2014
143	v. Durham	Leeds	2014
117	v. Middlesex	Scarborough	2014
251	v. Lancashire	Manchester	2014
122	v. Nottinghamshire	Nottingham	2014
113	v. MCC	Abu Dhabi	2015
111	v. Hampshire	Leeds	2016
106	v. Somerset	Taunton	2016
202	v. Surrey	The Oval	2016
114 *	v. Durham	Leeds	2016
194	v. Leeds/Bradford MCCU	Leeds	2017
100	v. Lancashire	Leeds	2017
134 *	v. Hampshire	Leeds	2018
103	v. Lancashire	Leeds	2020
115 *	v. Glamorgan	Leeds	2021
116	v. Kent	Canterbury	2021
153	v. Nottinghamshire	Nottingham	2021
145	v. Warwickshire	Leeds	2022
183	v. Surrey	Scarborough	2022
174	v. Glamorgan	Leeds	2023
115	v. Sussex	Leeds	2023
111	v. Durham	Scarborough	2023

D J MALAN (5)

219	v. Derbyshire	Leeds	2020
199	v. Sussex	Leeds	2021
152	v. Kent	Leeds	2022
132	v. Leicestershire	Leeds	2023
106	v. Derbyshire	Chesterfield	2023

CENTURIES BY CURRENT PLAYERS *(Continued)*

A U RASHID (10)

108	v. Worcestershire	Kidderminster	2007
111	v. Sussex	Hove	2008
117 *	v. Hampshire	Basingstoke	2009
157 *	v. Lancashire	Leeds	2009
180	v. Somerset	Leeds	2013
110 *	v. Warwickshire	Birmingham	2013
103	v. Somerset	Taunton	2013

(2013 consecutive innings)

108	v. Somerset	Taunton	2014
159 *	v. Lancashire	Manchester	2014
127	v. Durham	Scarborough	2015

M L REVIS (2)

104 *	v. Gloucestershire	Leeds	2023
106	v. Derbyshire	Scarborough	2023

J E ROOT (9)

160	v. Sussex	Scarborough	2011
222 *	v. Hampshire	Southampton (West End)	2012
125	v. Northamptonshire	Leeds	2012
182	v. Durham	Chester-le-Street	2013
236	v. Derbyshire	Leeds	2013
213	v. Surrey	Leeds	2016
130 *	v. Nottinghamshire	Nottingham	2019
101	v. Kent	Canterbury	2021
147	v. Lancashire	Leeds	2022

SHAN MASOOD (2)

192	v. Glamorgan	Cardiff	2023
123	v. Worcestershire	Leeds	2023

J A TATTERSALL (2)

135 *	v. Leeds/Bradford MCCU	Weetwood, Leeds	2019
180*	v. Surrey	Scarborough	2022

CENTURIES BY ALL PLAYERS 1863-2023

(Including highest score)

112	H Sutcliffe	313 v. Essex	at Leyton	1932
103	G Boycott	260* v. Essex	at Colchester (Garrison Gd)	1970
85	L Hutton	280* v. Hampshire	at Sheffield	1939
62	M Leyland	263 v. Essex	at Hull	1936
61	D Denton	221 v. Kent	at Tunbridge Wells	1912
60	P Holmes	315 * v. Middlesex	at Lord's	1925
56	G H Hirst	341 v. Leicestershire	at Leicester (Aylestone Rd)	1905
46	W Rhodes	267 * v. Leicestershire	at Leeds	1921
41	M D Moxon	274 * v. Worcestershire	at Worcester	1994
39	A Mitchell	189 v. Northamptonshire	at Northampton	1926
37	E Oldroyd	194 v. Worcestershire	at Worcester	1923
34	J H Hampshire	183 * v. Sussex	at Hove	1971
34	A McGrath	211 v. Warwickshire	at Birmingham	2009
33	D B Close	198 v. Surrey	at The Oval	1960
31	A Lyth	251 v. Lancashire	at Manchester	2014
30	F A Lowson	259 * v. Worcestershire	at Worcester	1953
29	D E V Padgett	161 * v. Oxford University	at Oxford	1959
29	J V Wilson	230 v. Derbyshire	at Sheffield	1952

CENTURIES BY ALL PLAYERS 1863-2023 *(Continued)*

28	D Byas	213	v. Worcestershire	at Scarborough	1995
27	G S Ballance	203 *	v. Hampshire	at West End, Southampton	2017
27	W Barber	255	v. Surrey	at Sheffield	1935
26	D S Lehmann	339	v. Durham	at Leeds	2006
26	W Watson	214 *	v. Worcestershire	at Worcester	1955
25	A A Metcalfe	216 *	v. Middlesex	at Leeds	1988
24	E I Lester	186	v. Warwickshire	at Scarborough	1949
23	J T Brown	311	v. Sussex	at Sheffield	1897
23	P J Sharpe	203 *	v. Cambridge University	at Cambridge	1960
22	R G Lumb	165 *	v. Gloucestershire	at Bradford	1984
22	J T Tunnicliffe	243	v. Derbyshire	at Chesterfield	1898
21	Hon F S Jackson	160	v. Gloucestershire	at Sheffield	1898
20	M P Vaughan	183	v. Glamorgan	at Cardiff (Sophia Gardens)	1996
	and	183	v. Northamptonshire	at Northampton	1996
19	A W Gale	272	v. Nottinghamshire	at Scarborough	2013
19	C White	186	v. Lancashire	at Manchester	2001
18	J A Rudolph	228 *	v. Durham	at Leeds	2010
18	E Wainwright	228	v. Surrey	at The Oval	1899
17	W B Stott	186	v. Warwickshire	at Birmingham	1960
17	N W D Yardley	183 *	v. Hampshire	at Leeds	1951
16	K Taylor	203 *	v. Warwickshire	at Birmingham	1961
16	M J Wood	207	v. Somerset	at Taunton	2003
15	J M Bairstow	246	v. Hampshire	at Leeds	2016
15	R Kilner	206 *	v. Derbyshire	at Sheffield	1920
15	G Ulyett	199 *	v. Derbyshire	at Sheffield	1887
15	B B Wilson	208	v. Sussex	at Bradford	1914
14	R Illingworth	162	v. Indians	at Sheffield	1959
13	J D Love	170 *	v. Worcestershire	at Worcester	1979
12	R J Blakey	223 *	v. Northamptonshire	at Leeds	2003
12	H Halliday	144	v. Derbyshire	at Chesterfield	1950
11	P A Jaques	243	v. Hampshire	at Southampton (Rose Bowl)	2004
11	A Z Lees	275 *	v. Derbyshire	at Chesterfield	2013
11	K Sharp	181	v. Gloucestershire	at Harrogate	1986
10	C W J Athey	134	v. Derbyshire	at Derby	1982
10	Lord Hawke	166	v. Warwickshire	at Birmingham	1896
10	F Mitchell	194	v. Leicestershire	at Leicester	1899
10	A U Rashid	180	v. Somerset	at Leeds	2013
9	D L Bairstow	145	v. Middlesex	at Scarborough	1980
9	M G Bevan	160 *	v. Surrey	at Middlesbrough	1996
9	L Hall	160	v. Lancashire	at Bradford	1887
9	J J Sayers	187	v. Kent	at Tunbridge Wells	2007
8	W Bates	136	v. Sussex	at Hove	1886
8	M J Lumb	144	v. Middlesex	at Southgate	2006
8	J E Root	236	v, Derbyshire	at Leeds	2013
8	T L Taylor	156	v. Hampshire	at Harrogate	1901
7	H C Brook	194	v. Kent	at Leeds	2022
7	J B Bolus	146 *	v. Hampshire	at Portsmouth	1960
7	E Robinson	135 *	v. Leicestershire	at Leicester (Aylestone Rd)	1921
7	P E Robinson	189	v. Lancashire	at Scarborough	1991
6	T Kohler-Cadmore	176	v. Leeds/Bradford MCCU	at Weetwood, Leeds	2019
6	E Lockwood	208	v. Kent	at Gravesend	1883
6	R Peel	210 *	v. Warwickshire	at Birmingham	1896
6	W H H Sutcliffe	181	v. Kent	at Canterbury	1952
5	T T Bresnan	169 *	v. Durham	at Chester-le-Street	2015

CENTURIES BY ALL PLAYERS 1863-2023 *(Continued)*

5	D J Malan	219	v. Derbyshire	at Leeds	2020
5	C M Old	116	v. Indians	at Bradford	1974
4	I Grimshaw	129 *	v. Cambridge University	at Sheffield	1885
4	S Haigh	159	v. Nottinghamshire	at Sheffield	1901
4	S N Hartley	114	v. Gloucestershire	at Bradford	1982
4	R A Hutton	189	v. Pakistanis	at Bradford	1971
4	J A Leaning	123	v. Somerset	at Taunton	2015
4	A B Sellers	204	v. Cambridge University	at Cambridge	1936
3	F J Bean	135	v. Worcestershire	at Worcester	2023
3	G L Brophy	177 *	v. Worcestershire	at Worcester	2011
3	P Carrick	131 *	v. Northamptonshire	at Northampton	1980
3	A J Dalton	128	v. Middlesex	at Leeds	1972
3	A Drake	147 *	v. Derbyshire	at Chesterfield	1911
3	G C H Hill	151 *	v. Northamptonshire	at Northampton	2022
3	F Lee	165	v. Lancashire	at Bradford	1887
3	G G Macaulay	125 *	v. Nottinghamshire	at Nottingham	1921
3	R Moorhouse	113	v. Somerset	at Taunton	1896
3	R M Pyrah	134 *	v. Loughborough MCCU	at Leeds	2010
3	J W Rothery	161	v. Kent	at Dover	1908
3	J Rowbotham	113	v. Surrey	at The Oval	1873
3	T F Smailes	117	v. Glamorgan	at Cardiff	1938
3	Younus Khan	217 *	v. Kent	at Scarborough	2007
2	M W Booth	210	v. Worcestershire	at Worcester	1911
2	D C F Burton	142 *	v. Hampshire	at Dewsbury	1919
2	K R Davidson	128	v. Kent	at Maidstone	1934
2	P A Gibb	157 *	v. Nottinghamshire	at Sheffield	1935
2	P J Hartley	127 *	v. Lancashire	at Manchester	1988
2	I J Harvey	209 *	v. Somerset	at Leeds	2005
2	C Johnson	107	v. Somerset	at Sheffield	1973
2	S A Kellett	125 *	v. Derbyshire	at Chesterfield	1991
2	N Kilner	112	v. Leicestershire	at Leeds	1921
2	B Parker	138 *	v. Oxford University	at Oxford	1997
2	M L Revis	106	v. Derbyshire	at Scarborough	2023
2	A Sellers	105	v. Middlesex	at Lord's	1893
2	Shan Masood	192	v. Glamorgan	at Cardiff (Sophia Gardens)	2023
2	E Smith (Morley)	129	v. Hampshire	at Bradford	1899
2	G A Smithson	169	v. Leicestershire	at Leicester	1947
2	G B Stevenson	115 *	v. Warwickshire	at Birmingham	1982
2	F S Trueman	104	v. Northamptonshire	at Northampton	1963
2	J A Tattersall	180*	v. Surrey	at Scarborough	2022
2	C Turner	130	v. Somerset	at Sheffield	1936
2	D J Wainwright	104 *	v. Sussex	at Hove	2008
2	T A Wardall	106	v. Gloucestershire	at Gloucester (Spa Ground)	1892
1	Azeem Rafiq	100	v. Worcestershire	at Worcester	2009
1	A T Barber	100	v. England XI	at Sheffield	1929
1	H D Bird	181 *	v. Glamorgan	at Bradford	1959
1	T J D Birtles	104	v. Lancashire	at Sheffield	1914
1	G S Blewett	190	v. Northamptonshire	at Scarborough	1999
1	J A Brooks	109 *	v. Lancashire	at Manchester	2017
1	M T G Elliott	127	v. Warwickshire	at Birmingham	2002
1	T Emmett	104	v. Gloucestershire	at Clifton	1873
1	G M Fellows	109	v. Lancashire	at Manchester	2002
1	A J Finch	110	v. Warwickshire	at Birmingham	2014
1	W A R Fraine	106	v. Surrey	at Scarborough	2019

1	J N Gillespie	123 *	v. Surrey	at The Oval	2007
1	D Gough	121	v. Warwickshire	at Leeds	1996
1	A K D Gray	104	v. Somerset	at Taunton	2003
1	A P Grayson	100	v. Worcestershire	at Worcester	1994
1	F E Greenwood	104 *	v. Glamorgan	at Hull	1929
1	G M Hamilton	125	v. Hampshire	at Leeds	2000
1	P S P Handscomb	101 *	v. Lancashire	at Manchester	2017
1	W E Harbord	109	v. Oxford University	at Oxford	1930
1	R Iddison	112	v. Cambridgeshire	at Hunslet	1869
1	W G Keighley	110	v. Surrey	at Leeds	1951
1	R A Kettleborough				
		108	v. Essex	at Leeds	1996
1	B Leadbeater	140 *	v. Hampshire	at Portsmouth	1976
1	J S Lehmann	116	v. Somerset	at Leeds	2016
1	D R Martyn	238	v. Gloucestershire	at Leeds	2003
1	G J Maxwell	140	v. Durham	at Scarborough	2015
1	S E Marsh	125 *	v. Surrey	at The Oval	2017
1	J T Newstead	100 *	v. Nottinghamshire	at Nottingham	1908
1	L E Plunkett	126	v. Hampshire	at Leeds	2016
1	C A Pujara	133 *	v. Hampshire	at Leeds	2015
1	R B Richardson	112	v. Warwickshire	at Birmingham	1993
1	H Rudston	164	v. Leicestershire	at Leicester (Aylestone Rd)	1904
1	A Sidebottom	124	v. Glamorgan	at Cardiff (Sophia Gardens)	1977
1	I G Swallow	114	v. MCC	at Scarborough	1987
1	S R Tendulkar	100	v. Durham	at Durham	1992
1	J Thewlis	108	v. Surrey	at The Oval	1868
1	C T Tyson	100 *	v. Hampshire	at Southampton	1921
1	H Verity	101	v. Jamaica	at Kingston (Sabina Park)	1935/36
1	A Waddington	114	v. Worcestershire	at Leeds	1927
1	W A I Washington				
		100 *	v. Surrey	at Leeds	1902
1	H Wilkinson	113	v. MCC	at Scarborough	1904
1	W H Wilkinson	103	v. Sussex	at Sheffield	1909
1	K S Williamson	189	v. Sussex	at Scarborough	2014
1	E R Wilson	104 *	v. Essex	at Bradford	1913
1	A Wood	123 *	v. Worcestershire	at Sheffield	1935
1	J D Woodford	101	v. Warwickshire	at Middlesbrough	1971

SUMMARY OF CENTURIES
FOR AND AGAINST YORKSHIRE 1863-2023

FOR YORKSHIRE				AGAINST YORKSHIRE		
Total	In Yorkshire	Away		Total	In Yorkshire	Away
113	67	46	Derbyshire	59	27	32
33	17	16	Durham	25	13	12
77	34	43	Essex	49	21	28
71	40	31	Glamorgan	28	16	12
91	44	47	Gloucestershire	56	28	28
103	44	59	Hampshire	61	27	34
86	39	47	Kent	65	33	32
119	60	59	Lancashire	123	61	62
99	54	45	Leicestershire	48	25	23
97	49	48	Middlesex	92	38	54
83	35	48	Northamptonshire	53	25	28
132	60	72	Nottinghamshire	88	33	55
107	54	53	Somerset	63	23	40
122	53	69	Surrey	116	42	74
92	44	48	Sussex	78	34	44
107	37	70	Warwickshire	77	31	46
77	33	44	Worcestershire	48	20	28
1	1	0	Cambridgeshire	0	0	0
1610	765	845	**Totals**	**1129**	497	632
9	9	0	<u>Australians</u>	16	16	0
9	9	0	Indians	7	7	0
8	8	0	New Zealanders	3	3	0
5	5	0	Pakistanis	1	1	0
9	9	0	South Africans	7	7	0
5	5	0	Sri Lankans	1	1	0
5	5	0	West Indians	6	6	0
1	1	0	Zimbabweans	0	0	0
3	3	0	Bangladesh 'A'	1	1	0
0	0	0	India 'A'	3	3	0
1	1	0	Pakistan 'A'	1	1	0
45	1	44	Cambridge University	20	2	18
2	2	0	Combined Services	0	0	0
1	0	1	Durham MCCU	1	0	1
4	3	1	England XIs	3	2	1
0	0	0	International XI	1	1	0
1	0	1	Ireland	0	0	0
3	0	3	Jamaica	3	0	3
10	8	2	Leeds/Bradford MCCU	0	0	0
1	0	1	Liverpool and District	0	0	0
2	2	0	Loughborough MCCU	1	1	0
1	0	1	Mashonaland	0	0	0
2	0	2	Matabeleland	1	0	1
54	38	16	MCC	52	34	18
39	0	39	Oxford University	11	0	11
6	0	6	Rest of England	15	0	15
9	5	4	Scotland	1	0	1
3	3	0	C L Thornton's XI	4	4	0
0	0	0	Western Province	1	0	1
1	1	0	I Zingari	1	1	0
239	118	121	**Totals**	**161**	91	70
1849	883	966	**Grand Totals**	**1290**	588	702

FOUR CENTURIES IN ONE INNINGS

1896 v. Warwickshire at Birmingham	F S Jackson ....117 E Wainwright ....126 Lord Hawke ....166 R Peel *210

(First instance in First-Class cricket)

THREE CENTURIES IN ONE INNINGS

1884 v. Cambridge University ....
at Cambridge
- L Hall 116
- W Bates 133
- I Grimshaw 115

1887 v. Kent ....
at Canterbury
- G Ulyett 124
- L Hall 110
- F Lee 119

1897 v. Sussex ....
at Sheffield
- J T Brown 311
- J Tunnicliffe 147
- E Wainwright *104

1899 v. Middlesex ....
at Bradford
- F S Jackson 155
- D Denton 113
- F Mitchell 121

1904 v. Surrey ....
at The Oval
- D Denton 105
- G H Hirst 104
- J Tunnicliffe *139

1919 v. Gloucestershire ....
at Leeds
- H Sutcliffe 118
- D Denton 122
- R Kilner *115

1925 v. Glamorgan ....
at Huddersfield
- P Holmes 130
- H Sutcliffe 121
- E Robinson *108

1928 v. Middlesex ....
at Lord's
- P Holmes 105
- E Oldroyd 108
- A Mitchell 105

1928 v. Essex ....
at Leyton
- H Sutcliffe 129
- P Holmes 136
- M Leyland *133

1929 v. Glamorgan ....
at Hull
- E Oldroyd 168
- W Barber 114
- F E Greenwood *104

1933 v. MCC ....
at Scarborough
- H Sutcliffe 107
- A Mitchell 158
- M Leyland 133

1936 v. Surrey ....
at Leeds
- H Sutcliffe 129
- L Hutton 163
- M Leyland *163

1937 v. Leicestershire ....
at Hull
- H Sutcliffe 189
- L Hutton 153
- M Leyland *118

1947 v. Leicestershire ....
at Leicester
- L Hutton 137
- N W D Yardley 100
- G.A Smithson 169

THREE CENTURIES IN ONE INNINGS *(Continued)*

			J H Hampshire	*116
1971	v.	Oxford University	R A Hutton	101
		at Oxford	A J Dalton	111
			G Boycott	141
1975	v.	Gloucestershire	R G Lumb	101
		at Bristol	J H Hampshire	*106
			M D Moxon	130
1995	v.	Cambridge University	D Byas	181
		at Cambridge	M G Bevan	*113
			M J Wood	102
2001	v.	Leicestershire	M J Lumb	122
		at Leeds	D S Lehmann	104
			C White	183
2001	v.	Glamorgan	M J Wood	124
		at Scarborough	D Byas	104
			J A Rudolph	122
2007	v.	Surrey	T T Bresnan	116
		at The Oval	J N Gillespie	*123
			A Lyth	130
2014	v.	Leeds/Bradford MCCU	G S Ballance	101
		at Leeds	J M Bairstow	123
			A Lyth	111
2016	v.	Hampshire	J M Bairstow	246
		at Leeds	L E Plunkett	126
			G S Ballance	111
2019	v.	Somerset	T Kohler-Cadmore	102
		at Leeds	H C Brook	101
			F J Bean	114
2023	v.	Gloucestershire	G C H Hill	101
		at Leeds	M L Revis	* 104

CENTURY IN EACH INNINGS

D Denton	107 and 109*	v. Nottinghamshire at Nottingham, 1906
G H Hirst	111 and 117*	v. Somerset at Bath, 1906
D Denton	133 and 121	v. MCC at Scarborough, 1908
W Rhodes	128 and 115	v. MCC at Scarborough, 1911
P Holmes	126 and 111*	v. Lancashire at Manchester, 1920
H Sutcliffe	107 and109*	v. MCC at Scarborough, 1926
H Sutcliffe	111 and 100*	v. Nottinghamshire at Nottingham, 1928
E I Lester	126 and 142	v. Northamptonshire at Northampton, 1947
L Hutton	197 and 104	v. Essex at Southend, 1947
E I Lester	125* and 132	v. Lancashire at Manchester, 1948
L Hutton	165 and 100	v. Sussex at Hove, 1949
L Hutton	103 and 137	v. MCC at Scarborough, 1952
G Boycott	103 and 105	v. Nottinghamshire at Sheffield, 1966
G Boycott	163 and 141*	v. Nottinghamshire at Bradford, 1983
M D Moxon	123 and 112*	v. Indians at Scarborough, 1986
A A Metcalfe	194* and 107	v. Nottinghamshire at Nottingham, 1990
M P Vaughan	100 and 151	v. Essex at Chelmsford, 1999
Younus Khan	106 and 202*	v. Hampshire at Southampton, 2007
G S Ballance	148 and 108*	v. Surrey at The Oval, 2013
G S Ballance	108 and 203*	v. Hampshire at West End, 2017

HIGHEST INDIVIDUAL SCORES
FOR AND AGAINST YORKSHIRE

Highest For Yorkshire:
341 G H Hirst v. Leicestershire at Leicester, 1905
Highest Against Yorkshire:
318* W G Grace for Gloucestershire at Cheltenham, 1876

Yorkshire versus:

Derbyshire
For Yorkshire:	300 — J T Brown at Chesterfield, 1898
Against:	270* — C F Hughes at Leeds, 2013
Most Centuries *For Yorkshire:*	G Boycott 9
Against:	K J Barnett and W Storer 4 each

Durham
For Yorkshire:	339 — D S Lehmann at Leeds, 2006
Against:	221* — K K Jennings at Chester-le-Street, 2016
Most centuries *For Yorkshire*	A McGrath 5
Against	M J Di Venuto and M D Stoneman 4

Essex
For Yorkshire:	313 — H Sutcliffe at Leyton, 1932
Against:	219* — D J Insole at Colchester, 1949
Most Centuries *For Yorkshire:*	H Sutcliffe 9
Against:	F L Fane, K W R Fletcher, G A Gooch and D J Insole 3 each

Glamorgan
For Yorkshire:	213 — M D Moxon at Cardiff, 1996
Against:	202* — H Morris at Cardiff, 1996
Most Centuries *For Yorkshire:*	G Boycott, P Holmes and H Sutcliffe 5 each
Against:	H Morris 5

Gloucestershire
For Yorkshire:	238 — D R Martyn at Leeds, 2003
Against:	318*— W G Grace at Cheltenham, 1876
Most Centuries *For Yorkshire:*	G Boycott 6
Against:	W G Grace 9

Hampshire
For Yorkshire:	302* — P Holmes at Portsmouth, 1920
Against:	300* — M A Carberry at Southampton, 2011
Most Centuries *For Yorkshire:*	G S Ballance 7
Against:	C P Mead 10

Kent
For Yorkshire:	248 — W Barber at Leeds, 1934.
Against:	237 — D I Stevens at Leeds, 2019
Most Centuries *For Yorkshire:*	A McGrath 6
Against:	F E Woolley 5

Lancashire
For Yorkshire:	252 — D S Lehmann at Leeds, 2001 —
Against:	238 — K K Jennings at Leeds, 2022
Most Centuries *For Yorkshire:*	G Boycott and H Sutcliffe 9 each
Against:	M A Atherton and C H Lloyd 6 each.

Leicestershire
For Yorkshire:	341— G H Hirst at Leicester, 1905
Against:	218— J J Whitaker at Bradford, 1996
Most Centuries *For Yorkshire:*	H Sutcliffe 10
Against:	J J Whitaker and C J B Wood 5 each

Middlesex
For Yorkshire:	315*— P Holmes at Lord's, 1925
Against:	243*— A J Webbe at Huddersfield, 1887
Most Centuries *For Yorkshire:*	P Holmes and H Sutcliffe 7 each
Against:	M W Gatting 8

Northamptonshire
For Yorkshire:	277* — P Holmes at Harrogate, 1921
Against:	235 — A J Lamb at Leeds, 1990
Most Centuries *For Yorkshire:*	H Sutcliffe 5
Against:	W Larkins 5

HIGHEST INDIVIDUAL SCORES FOR AND AGAINST
YORKSHIRE *(continued)*

Yorkshire versus

Nottinghamshire
- *For Yorkshire:* 285 — P Holmes at Nottingham, 1929
- *Against:* 251* — D J Hussey at Leeds, 2010

Most Centuries
- *For Yorkshire:* G Boycott 15
- *Against:* R T Robinson 6

Somerset
- *For Yorkshire:* 213 — H Sutcliffe at Dewsbury, 1924
- *Against:* 297 — M J Wood at Taunton, 2005

Most Centuries
- *For Yorkshire:* G Boycott 6
- *Against:* L C H Palairet, IVA. Richards, M E Trescothick 5 each

Surrey
- *For Yorkshire:* 255 — W Barber at Sheffield, 1935
- *Against:* 273 — T W Hayward at The Oval, 1899

Most Centuries
- *For Yorkshire:* H Sutcliffe 9
- *Against:* J B Hobbs 8

Sussex
- *For Yorkshire:* 311 — J T Brown at Sheffield, 1897
- *Against:* 274* — M W Goodwin at Hove, 2011

Most Centuries
- *For Yorkshire:* L Hutton 8
- *Against:* C B Fry 7

Warwickshire
- *For Yorkshire:* 275 — P Holmes at Bradford, 1928
- *Against:* 225 — D P Ostler at Birmingham, 2002

Most Centuries
- *For Yorkshire:* G Boycott and H Sutcliffe 8 each
- *Against:* D L Amiss, H E Dollery, R B Khanhai and W G Quaife 4 each.

Worcestershire
- *For Yorkshire:* 274* — M D Moxon at Worcester, 1994
- *Against:* 259 — D Kenyon at Kidderminster, 1956

Most Centuries
- *For Yorkshire:* M Leyland 6
- *Against:* D Kenyon and G M Turner 5 each

Australians
- *For Yorkshire:* 167 — J T Brown at Bradford, 1899
- *Against:* 193* — B C Booth at Bradford, 1964

Most Centuries
- *For Yorkshire:* G Boycott and D Denton 2 each
- *Against:* N C O'Neill 2

Indians
- *For Yorkshire:* 183* — L Hutton at Bradford, 1946
- *Against:* 244* — V S Hazare at Sheffield, 1946

Most Centuries
- *For Yorkshire:* M D Moxon 2
- *Against:* V S Hazare, VMankad, PR Umrigar D K Gaekwad, G A Parkar and R Lamba 1 each

New Zealanders
- *For Yorkshire:* 175 — P Holmes at Bradford, 1927
- *Against:* 126 — W M Wallace at Bradford, 1949

Most Centuries
- *For Yorkshire:* L Hutton and DB Close 2 each
- *Against:* H G Vivian, WM Wallace and J G Wright 1 each

Pakistanis
- *For Yorkshire:* 197 — P J Sharpe at Leeds, 1967
- *Against:* 139 — A H Kardar at Sheffield, 1954

Most Centuries
- *For Yorkshire:* P J Sharpe 2
- *Against:* A H Kardar 1

South Africans
- *For Yorkshire:* 156 — L Hutton at Sheffield, 1951
- *Against:* 168 — I J Seidle at Sheffield, 1929

Most Centuries
- *For Yorkshire:* L Hutton 2
- *Against:* H B Cameron, J D Lindsay, B Mitchell, D P B Morkel, I J Seidle, L J Tancred, C B van Ryneveld 1 each

HIGHEST INDIVIDUAL SCORES FOR AND AGAINST
YORKSHIRE *(continued)*

Yorkshire versus

Sri Lankans	*For Yorkshire:*	132 — M D Moxon at Leeds, 1988
	Against:	112 — S A R Silva at Leeds, 1988
Most Centuries	*For Yorkshire:*	K Sharp 2
	Against:	S A R Silva 1
West Indians	*For Yorkshire:*	112* — D Denton at Harrogate, 1906
	Against:	164 — S F A Bacchus at Leeds, 1980
Most Centuries	*For Yorkshire:*	M G Bevan, D Denton, L Hutton, R G Lumb and A A Metcalfe 1 each
	Against:	S F A Bacchus, C O Browne, S Chanderpaul P A Goodman, C L Hooper and G St A Sobers 1 each
Zimbabweans	*For Yorkshire:*	113 — M D Moxon at Leeds, 1990
	Against:	89 — G J Whittall at Leeds, 2000
Most Centuries	*For Yorkshire:*	M D Moxon 1
	Against:	None
Cambridge University	*For Yorkshire:*	207* — G Boycott at Cambridge, 1976
	Against:	171* — G L Jessop at Cambridge, 1899
		171 — P B H May at Cambridge, 1952
Most Centuries	*For Yorkshire:*	H Sutcliffe 4
	Against:	G M Kemp 2
Durham MCCU	*For Yorkshire:*	139 — J J Sayers at Durham, 2011
	Against:	127 — T Westley at Durham, 2011
Most Centuries	*For Yorkshire:*	J J Sayers 1
	Against:	T Westley 1
Leeds Bradford MCCU	*For Yorkshire:*	194 — A Lyth at Leeds, 2017
	Against:	69 — A MacQueen at Leeds, 2012
Most Centuries	*For Yorkshire:*	A Lyth, 3
Loughborough MCCU	*For Yorkshire:*	134* — R M Pyrah at Leeds, 2010
	Against:	107 — C P Murtagh at Leeds, 2007
Most Centuries	*For Yorkshire:*	R M Pyrah 2
	Against:	C P Murtagh 1
MCC	*For Yorkshire:*	180* — G H Hirst at Lord's, 1919
	Against:	214 — E H Hendren at Lord's, 1919
Most Centuries	*For Yorkshire:*	L Hutton 8
	Against:	R E S Wyatt 5
Oxford University	*For Yorkshire:*	196 — R J Blakey at Oxford, 1991
	Against:	201— J E Raphael at Oxford, 1904
Most Centuries	*For Yorkshire:*	M Leyland 4
	Against:	A A Baig and Nawab of Pataudi (Jun.) 2 each

J B Hobbs scored 11 centuries against Yorkshire – the highest by any individual (8 for Surrey and 3 for the Rest of England).

Three players have scored 10 centuries against Yorkshire – W G Grace (9 for Gloucestershire and 1 for MCC). E H Hendren (6 for Middlesex, 3 for MCC and 1 for the Rest of England) and C P Mead (all 10 for Hampshire).

CARRYING BAT THROUGH A COMPLETED INNINGS

Batsman	Score	Total	Against	Season
G R Atkinson	30*	73	Nottinghamshire at Bradford	1865
L Hall	31*	94	Sussex at Hove	1878
L Hall	124*	331	Sussex at Hove	1883
L Hall	128*	285	Sussex at Huddersfield	1884
L Hall	32*	81	Kent at Sheffield	1885
L Hall	79*	285	Surrey at Sheffield	1885
L Hall	37*	96	Derbyshire at Derby	1885
L Hall	50*	173	Sussex at Huddersfield	1886
L Hall	74*	172	Kent at Canterbury	1886
G Ulyett	199*	399	Derbyshire at Sheffield	1887
L Hall	119*	334	Gloucestershire at Dewsbury	1887
L Hall	82*	218	Sussex at Hove	1887
L Hall	34*	104	Surrey at The Oval	1888
L Hall	129*	461	Gloucestershire at Clifton	1888
L Hall	85*	259	Middlesex at Lord's	1889
L Hall	41*	106	Nottinghamshire at Sheffield	1891
W Rhodes	98*	184	MCC at Lord's	1903
W Rhodes	85*	152	Essex at Leyton	1910
P Holmes	145*	270	Northamptonshire at Northampton	1920
H Sutcliffe	125*	307	Essex at Southend	1920
P Holmes	175*	377	New Zealanders at Bradford	1927
P Holmes	110*	219	Northamptonshire at Bradford	1929
H Sutcliffe	104*	170	Hampshire at Leeds	1932
H Sutcliffe	114*	202	Rest of England at The Oval	1933
H Sutcliffe	187*	401	Worcestershire at Bradford	1934
H Sutcliffe	135*	262	Glamorgan at Neath	1935
H Sutcliffe	125*	322	Oxford University at Oxford	1939
L Hutton	99*	200	Leicestershire at Sheffield	1948
L Hutton	78*	153	Worcestershire at Sheffield	1949
F A Lowson	76*	218	MCC at Lord's	1951
W B Stott	144*	262	Worcestershire at Worcester	1959
D E V Padgett	115*	230	Gloucestershire at Bristol	1962
G Boycott	114*	297	Leicestershire at Sheffield	1968
G Boycott	53*	119	Warwickshire at Bradford	1969
G Boycott	182*	320	Middlesex at Lord's	1971
G Boycott	138*	232	Warwickshire at Birmingham	1971
G Boycott	175*	360	Nottinghamshire at Worksop	1979
G Boycott	112*	233	Derbyshire at Sheffield	1983
G Boycott	55*	183	Warwickshire at Leeds	1984
G Boycott	55*	131	Surrey at Sheffield	1985
M J Wood	60*	160	Somerset at Scarborough	2004
J J Sayers	122*	326	Middlesex at Scarborough	2006
J J Sayers	149*	414	Durham at Leeds	2007
A Lyth	248*	486	Leicestershire at Leicester	2012

44 instances, of which L Hall (14 times), G Boycott (8) and H Sutcliffe (6) account for 28 between them.

The highest percentage of an innings total is 61.17 by H. Sutcliffe (104* v. Hampshire at Leeds in 1932) but P Holmes was absent ill, so only nine wickets fell.

Other contributions exceeding 55% are:

59.48%	G Boycott	(138*	v. Warwickshire at Birmingham, 1971)
56.87%	G Boycott	(182*	v. Middlesex at Lord's, 1971)
56.43%	H Sutcliffe	(114*	v. Rest of England at The Oval, 1933)
55.92%	W Rhodes	(85*	v. Essex at Leyton, 1910)

2,000 RUNS IN A SEASON

Batsman	Season	M	I	NO	Runs	HS	Avge	100s
G H Hirst	1904	32	44	3	2257	157	55.04	8
D Denton	1905	33	52	2	2258	172	45.16	8
G H Hirst	1906	32	53	6	2164	169	46.04	6
D Denton	1911	32	55	4	2161	137*	42.37	6
D Denton	1912	36	51	4	2088	221	44.23	6
P Holmes	1920	30	45	6	2144	302*	54.97	7
P Holmes	1925	35	49	9	2351	315*	58.77	6
H Sutcliffe	1925	34	48	8	2236	235	55.90	7
H Sutcliffe	1928	27	35	5	2418	228	80.60	11
P Holmes	1928	31	40	4	2093	275	58.13	6
H Sutcliffe	1931	28	33	8	2351	230	94.04	9
H Sutcliffe	1932	29	41	5	2883	313	80.08	12
M Leyland	1933	31	44	4	2196	210*	54.90	7
A Mitchell	1933	34	49	10	2100	158	53.84	6
H Sutcliffe	1935	32	47	3	2183	212	49.61	8
L Hutton	1937	28	45	6	2448	271*	62.76	8
H Sutcliffe	1937	32	52	5	2054	189	43.70	4
L Hutton	1939	29	44	5	2316	280*	59.38	10
L Hutton	1947	19	31	2	2068	270*	71.31	10
L Hutton	1949	26	44	6	2640	269*	69.47	9
F A Lowson	1950	31	54	5	2067	141*	42.18	5
D E V Padgett	1959	35	60	8	2158	161*	41.50	4
W B Stott	1959	32	56	2	2034	144*	37.66	3
P J Sharpe	1962	36	62	8	2201	138	40.75	7
G Boycott	1971	18	25	4	2221	233	105.76	11
A A Metcalfe	1990	23	44	4	2047	194*	51.17	6

1,000 RUNS IN A SEASON

Batsman		Runs scored	Runs scored	Runs scored
C W J Athey	(2)	1113 in 1980	1339 in 1982	—
D L Bairstow	(3)	1083 in 1981	1102 in 1983	1163 in 1985
J M Bairstow	(2)	1015 in 2011	1108 in 2015	—
G S Ballance	(3)	1363 in 2013	1023 in 2017	1014 in 2019
W Barber	(8)	1000 in 1932	1595 in 1933	1930 in 1934
		1958 in 1935	1466 in 1937	1455 in 1938
		1501 in 1939	1170 in 1946	—
M G Bevan	(2)	1598 in 1995	1225 in 1996	—
R J Blakey	(5)	1361 in 1987	1159 in 1989	1065 in 1992
		1236 in 1994	1041 in 2002	—
J B Bolus	(2)	1245 in 1960	1970 in 1961	—
M W Booth	(2)	1189 in 1911	1076 in 1913	—
G Boycott	(19)	1628 in 1963	1639 in 1964	1215 in 1965
		1388 in 1966	1530 in 1967	1004 in 1968
		1558 in 1970	2221 in 1971	1156 in 1972
		1478 in 1974	1915 in 1975	1288 in 1976
		1259 in 1977	1074 in 1978	1160 in 1979
		1913 in 1982	1941 in 1983	1567 in 1984
		1657 in 1985	—	—
J T Brown	(9)	1196 in 1894	1260 in 1895	1755 in 1896
		1634 in 1897	1641 in 1898	1375 in 1899
		1181 in 1900	1627 in 1901	1291 in 1903
D Byas	(5)	1557 in 1991	1073 in 1993	1297 in 1994
		1913 in 1995	1319 in 1997	—

1,000 RUNS IN A SEASON *(Continued)*

Batsman		Runs scored	Runs scored	Runs scored
D B Close	(13)	1192 in 1952	1287 in 1954	1131 in 1955
		1315 in 1957	1335 in 1958	1740 in 1959
		1699 in 1960	1821 in 1961	1438 in 1962
		1145 in 1963	1281 in 1964	1127 in 1965
		1259 in 1966	—	—
K R Davidson	(1)	1241 in 1934	—	—
D Denton	(20)	1028 in 1896	1357 in 1897	1595 in 1899
		1378 in 1900	1400 in 1901	1191 in 1902
		1562 in 1903	1919 in 1904	2258 in 1905
		1905 in 1906	1128 in 1907	1852 in 1908
		1765 in 1909	1106 in 1910	2161 in 1911
		2088 in 1912	1364 in 1913	1799 in 1914
		1213 in 1919	1324 in 1920	—
A Drake	(2)	1487 in 1911	1029 in 1913	—
A W Gale	(2)	1076 in 2013	1045 in 2015	—
A P Grayson	(1)	1046 in 1994	—	—
S Haigh	(1)	1031 in 1904	—	—
L Hall	(1)	1120 in 1887	—	—
H Halliday	(4)	1357 in 1948	1484 in 1950	1351 in 1952
		1461 in 1953	—	—
J H Hampshire	(12)	1236 in 1963	1280 in 1964	1424 in 1965
		1105 in 1966	1244 in 1967	1133 in 1968
		1079 in 1970	1259 in 1971	1124 in 1975
		1303 in 1976	1596 in 1978	1425 in 1981
Lord Hawke	(1)	1005 in 1895	—	—
G H Hirst	(19)	1110 in 1896	1248 in 1897	1546 in 1899
		1752 in 1900	1669 in 1901	1113 in 1902
		1535 in 1903	2257 in 1904	1972 in 1905
		2164 in 1906	1167 in 1907	1513 in 1908
		1151 in 1909	1679 in 1910	1639 in 1911
		1119 in 1912	1431 in 1913	1655 in 1914
		1312 in 1919	—	—
P Holmes	(14)	1876 in 1919	2144 in 1920	1458 in 1921
		1614 in 1922	1884 in 1923	1610 in 1924
		2351 in 1925	1792 in 1926	1774 in 1927
		2093 in 1928	1724 in 1929	1957 in 1930
		1431 in 1931	1191 in 1932	—
L Hutton	(12)	1282 in 1936	2448 in 1937	1171 in 1938
		2316 in 1939	1322 in 1946	2068 in 1947
		1792 in 1948	2640 in 1949	1581 in 1950
		1554 in 1951	1956 in 1952	1532 in 1953
R Illingworth	(5)	1193 in 1957	1490 in 1959	1029 in 1961
		1610 in 1962	1301 in 1964	—
F S Jackson	(4)	1211 in 1896	1300 in 1897	1442 in 1898
		1468 in 1899	—	—
P A Jaques	(2)	1118 in 2004	1359 in 2005	—
S A Kellett	(2)	1266 in 1991	1326 in 1992	—
R Kilner	(10)	1586 in 1913	1329 in 1914	1135 in 1919
		1240 in 1920	1137 in 1921	1132 in 1922
		1265 in 1923	1002 in 1925	1021 in 1926
		1004 in 1927	—	—
T Kohler-Cadmore	(1)	1004 in 2019	—	—

1,000 RUNS IN A SEASON *(Continued)*

Batsman	*Runs scored*	*Runs scored*	*Runs scored*
A Z Lees	(2) 1018 in 2014	1285 in 2016	—
D S Lehmann	(5) 1575 in 1997	1477 in 2000	1416 in 2001
	1136 in 2002	1706 in 2006	—
E I Lester	(6) 1256 in 1948	1774 in 1949	1015 in 1950
	1786 in 1952	1380 in 1953	1330 in 1954
M Leyland	(17) 1088 in 1923	1203 in 1924	1560 in 1925
	1561 in 1926	1478 in 1927	1554 in 1928
	1407 in 1929	1814 in 1930	1127 in 1931
	1821 in 1932	2196 in 1933	1228 in 1934
	1366 in 1935	1621 in 1936	1120 in 1937
	1640 in 1938	1238 in 1939	—
J D Love	(2) 1161 in 1981	1020 in 1983	—
F A Lowson	(8) 1678 in 1949	2067 in 1950	1607 in 1951
	1562 in 1952	1586 in 1953	1719 in 1954
	1082 in 1955	1428 in 1956	—
M J Lumb	(1) 1038 in 2003	—	—
R G Lumb	(5) 1002 in 1973	1437 in 1975	1070 in 1978
	1465 in 1979	1223 in 1980	—
A Lyth	(4) 1509 in 2010	1619 in 2014	1153 in 2016
....	1019 in 2023	—	—
A McGrath	(3) 1425 in 2005	1293 in 2006	1219 in 2010
A A Metcalfe	(6) 1674 in 1986	1162 in 1987	1320 in 1988
	1230 in 1989	2047 in 1990	1210 in 1991
A Mitchell	(10) 1320 in 1928	1633 in 1930	1351 in 1932
	2100 in 1933	1854 in 1934	1530 in 1935
	1095 in 1936	1602 in 1937	1305 in 1938
	1219 in 1939	—	—
F Mitchell	(2) 1678 in 1899	1801 in 1901	—
R Moorhouse	(1) 1096 in 1895	—	—
M D Moxon	(11) 1016 in 1984	1256 in 1985	1298 in 1987
	1430 in 1988	1156 in 1989	1621 in 1990
	1669 in 1991	1314 in 1992	1251 in 1993
	1458 in 1994	1145 in 1995	—
E Oldroyd	(10) 1473 in 1921	1690 in 1922	1349 in 1923
	1607 in 1924	1262 in 1925	1197 in 1926
	1390 in 1927	1304 in 1928	1474 in 1929
	1285 in 1930	—	—
D E V Padgett	(12) 1046 in 1956	2158 in 1959	1574 in 1960
	1856 in 1961	1750 in 1962	1380 in 1964
	1220 in 1965	1194 in 1966	1284 in 1967
	1163 in 1968	1078 in 1969	1042 in 1970
R Peel	(1) 1193 in 1896	—	—
W Rhodes	(17) 1251 in 1904	1353 in 1905	1618 in 1906
	1574 in 1908	1663 in 1909	1355 in 1910
	1961 in 1911	1030 in 1912	1805 in 1913
	1325 in 1914	1138 in 1919	1329 in 1921
	1368 in 1922	1168 in 1923	1030 in 1924
	1256 in 1925	1071 in 1926	—
E Robinson	(2) 1104 in 1921	1097 in 1929	—
P E Robinson	(3) 1173 in 1988	1402 in 1990	1293 in 1991
J A Rudolph	(4) 1078 in 2007	1292 in 2008	1366 in 2009
	1375 in 2010	—	—

1,000 RUNS IN A SEASON *(Continued)*

Batsman	Runs scored	Runs scored	Runs scored
J J Sayers	(1) 1150 in 2009	—	—
A B Sellers	(1) 1109 in 1938	—	—
K Sharp	(1) 1445 in 1984	—	—
P J Sharpe	(10) 1039 in 1960	1240 in 1961	2201 in 1962
	1273 in 1964	1091 in 1965	1352 in 1967
	1256 in 1968	1012 in 1969	1149 in 1970
	1320 in 1973	—	—
W B Stott	(5) 1362 in 1957	1036 in 1958	2034 in 1959
	1790 in 1960	1409 in 1961	—
H Sutcliffe	(21) †1839 in 1919	1393 in 1920	1235 in 1921
	1909 in 1922	1773 in 1923	1720 in 1924
	2236 in 1925	1672 in 1926	1814 in 1927
	2418 in 1928	1485 in 1929	1636 in 1930
	2351 in 1931	2883 in 1932	1986 in 1933
	1511 in 1934	2183 in 1935	1295 in 1936
	2054 in 1937	1660 in 1938	1416 in 1939

† First season in First-Class cricket – The record for a debut season.

Batsman	Runs scored	Runs scored	Runs scored
W H H Sutcliffe	(1) 1193 in 1955	—	—
K Taylor	(6) 1306 in 1959	1107 in 1960	1494 in 1961
	1372 in 1962	1149 in 1964	1044 in 1966
T L Taylor	(2) 1236 in 1901	1373 in 1902	—
S R Tendulkar	(1) 1070 in 1992	—	—
J Tunnicliffe	(12) 1333 in 1895	1368 in 1896	1208 in 1897
	1713 in 1898	1434 in 1899	1496 in 1900
	1295 in 1901	1274 in 1902	1650 in 1904
	1096 in 1905	1232 in 1906	1195 in 1907
C Turner	(1) 1153 in 1934	—	—
G Ulyett	(4) 1083 in 1878	1158 in 1882	1024 in 1885
	1285 in 1887	—	—
M P Vaughan	(4) 1066 in 1994	1235 in 1995	1161 in 1996
	1161 in 1998	—	—
E Wainwright	(3) 1492 in 1897	1479 in 1899	1044 in 1901
W A I Washington	(1) 1022 in 1902	—	—
W Watson	(8) 1331 in 1947	1352 in 1948	1586 in 1952
	1350 in 1953	1347 in 1954	1564 in 1955
	1378 in 1956	1455 in 1957	—
W H Wilkinson	(1) 1282 in 1908	—	—
B B Wilson	(5) 1054 in 1909	1455 in 1911	1453 in 1912
	1533 in 1913	1632 in 1914	—
J V Wilson	(12) 1460 in 1949	1548 in 1950	1985 in 1951
	1349 in 1952	1531 in 1953	1713 in 1954
	1799 in 1955	1602 in 1956	1287 in 1957
	1064 in 1960	1018 in 1961	1226 in 1962
A Wood	(1) 1237 in 1935	—	—
M J Wood	(4) 1080 in 1998	1060 in 2001	1432 in 2003
	1005 in 2005		
N W D Yardley	(4) 1028 in 1939	1299 in 1947	1413 in 1949
	1031 in 1950	—	—

BATSMEN WHO HAVE SCORED OVER 10,000 RUNS

Player	M	I	NO	Runs	HS	Av'ge	100s
H Sutcliffe	602	864	96	38558	313	50.20	112
D Denton	676	1058	61	33282	221	33.38	61
G Boycott	414	674	111	32570	260*	57.85	103
G H Hirst	717	1050	128	32024	341	34.73	56
W Rhodes	883	1195	162	31075	267*	30.08	46
P Holmes	485	699	74	26220	315*	41.95	60
M Leyland	548	720	82	26180	263	41.03	62
L Hutton	341	527	62	24807	280*	53.34	85
D B Close	536	811	102	22650	198	31.94	33
J H Hampshire	456	724	89	21979	183*	34.61	34
J V Wilson	477	724	75	20548	230	31.66	29
D E V Padgett	487	774	63	20306	161*	28.55	29
J Tunnicliffe	472	768	57	19435	243	27.33	22
M D Moxon	277	476	42	18973	274*	43.71	41
A Mitchell	401	550	69	18189	189	37.81	39
P J Sharpe	411	666	71	17685	203*	29.72	23
E Oldroyd	383	509	58	15891	194	35.23	37
J T Brown	345	567	41	15694	311	29.83	23
W Barber	354	495	48	15315	255	34.26	27
R Illingworth	496	668	131	14986	162	27.90	14
D Byas	268	449	42	14398	213	35.37	28
G Ulyett	355	618	31	14157	199*	24.11	15
R J Blakey	339	541	84	14150	223*	30.96	12
A McGrath	242	405	29	14091	211	37.47	34
W Watson	283	430	65	13953	214*	38.22	26
F A Lowson	252	404	31	13897	259*	37.25	30
Lord Hawke	510	739	91	13133	166	20.26	10
R Kilner	365	478	46	13018	206*	30.13	15
D L Bairstow	429	601	113	12985	145	26.60	9
A Lyth	207	347	17	12894	251	39.07	31
K Taylor	303	505	35	12864	203*	27.37	16
N W D Yardley	302	420	56	11632	183*	31.95	17
R G Lumb	239	395	30	11525	165*	31.57	22
E Wainwright	352	545	30	11092	228	21.53	18
S Haigh	513	687	110	10993	159	19.05	4
E I Lester	228	339	27	10616	186	34.02	24
A A Metcalfe	184	317	19	10465	216*	35.11	25
C White	221	350	45	10376	186	34.01	19
Hon F S Jackson	207	328	22	10371	160	33.89	21
J D Love	247	388	58	10263	170*	31.10	13

PLAYERS WHO HAVE SCORED CENTURIES
FOR AND AGAINST YORKSHIRE

Player		For	Venue	Season
C W J Athey (5)	114*	Gloucestershire	Bradford	1984
(10 for Yorkshire)	101	Gloucestershire	Gloucester	1985
	101*	Gloucestershire	Leeds	1987
	112	Sussex	Scarborough	1993
	100	Sussex	Eastbourne	1996
M G Bevan (1)	142	Leicestershire	Leicester	2002
(9 for Yorkshire)				
J B Bolus (2)	114	Nottinghamshire	Bradford	1963
(7 for Yorkshire)	138	Derbyshire	Sheffield	1973
D B Close (1)	102	Somerset	Taunton	1971
(33 for Yorkshire)				
M T G Elliott (1)	125	Glamorgan	Leeds	2004
(1 for Yorkshire)				
P A Gibb (1)	107	Essex	Brentwood	1951
(2 for Yorkshire)				
P S P Handscomb	112	Leicestershire	Leeds	2023
(1 for Yorkshire)				
P A Jaques (1)	222	Northamptonshire	Northampton	2003
(7 for Yorkshire)				
N Kilner (2)	119	Warwickshire	Hull	1932
(2 for Yorkshire)	197	Warwickshire	Birmingham	1933
A Z Lees (1)	106	Durham	Chester-le-Street	2020
(11 for Yorkshire)				
M J Lumb (1)	135	Nottinghamshire	Scarborough	2013
(8 for Yorkshire)				
P J Sharpe (1)	126	Derbyshire	Chesterfield	1976
(23 for Yorkshire)				
K S Williamson (1)	111	Gloucestershire	Bristol	2012
(1 for Yorkshire)				

RECORD PARTNERSHIPS FOR YORKSHIRE

1st wkt	555	P Holmes (224*)	and H Sutcliffe (313)	v. Essex at Leyton	1932
2nd wkt	346	W Barber (162)	and M Leyland (189)	v. Middlesex at Sheffield	1932
3rd wkt	346	J J Sayers (173)	and A McGrath (211)	v. Warwickshire at Birmingham	2009
4th wkt	372	J E Root (213)	and J M Bairstow (198)	v. Surrey at Leeds	2016
5th wkt	340	E Wainwright (228)	and G H Hirst (186)	v. Surrey at The Oval	1899
6th wkt	305	A Lyth (183)	and J A Tattersall (180*)	v. Surrey at Scarborough,	2022
7th wkt	366*	J M Bairstow (219*)	and T T Bresnan (169*)	v, Durham at Chester-le-Street	2015
8th wkt	292	R Peel (210*)	and Lord Hawke (166)	v. Warwickshire at Birmingham	1896
9th wkt	246	T T Bresnan (116)	and J N Gillespie (123*)	v. Surrey at The Oval	2007
10th wkt	149	G Boycott (79)	and G B Stevenson (115*)	v. Warwickshire at Birmingham	1982

RECORD PARTNERSHIPS AGAINST YORKSHIRE

1st wkt	372	R R Montgomerie (127)	and M B Loye (205)	for Northamptonshire at Northampton	1996
2nd wkt	417	K J Barnett (210*)	and TA Tweats (189)	for Derbyshire at Derby	1997
3rd wkt	523	M A Carberry (300*)	and N D McKenzie (237)	for Hampshire at Southampton	2011
4th wkt	447	R Abel (193)	and T Hayward (273)	for Surrey at The Oval	1899
5th wkt	277	J L du Plooy (170)	and Haider Ali (146)	for Derbyshire at Chesterfield	2023
6th wkt	346	S W Billings (138)	and D I Stevens (237)	for Kent at Leeds	2019
7th wkt	315	D M Benkenstein (151)	and O D Gibson (155)	for Durham at Leeds	2006
8th wkt	178	A P Wells (253*)	and B T P Donelan (59)	for Sussex at Middlesbrough	1991
9th wkt	233	I J L Trott (161*)	and J S Patel (120)	for Warwickshire at Birmingham	2009
10th wkt	132	A Hill (172*)	and M Jean-Jacques (73)	for Derbyshire at Sheffield	1986

CENTURY PARTNERSHIPS FOR THE FIRST WICKET IN BOTH INNINGS

128	108	G Ulyett (82 and 91)	and L Hall (87 and 37)	v. Sussex at Hove	1885

(First instance in First-Class cricket)

138	147*	J T Brown (203 and 81*)	and J Tunnicliffe (62 and 63*)	v. Middlesex at Lord's	1896

(Second instance in First-Class cricket)

105	265*	P Holmes (51 and 127*)	and H Sutcliffe (71 and 131*)	v. Surrey at The Oval	1926
184	210*	P Holmes (83 and 101*)	and H Sutcliffe (111 and 100*)	v. Nottinghamshire at Nottingham	1928
110	117	L Hutton (95 and 86)	and W Watson (34 and 57)	v. Lancashire at Manchester	1947
122	230	W B Stott (50 and 114)	and K Taylor (79 and 140)	v. Nottinghamshire at Nottingham	1957
136	138	J B Bolus (108 and 71)	and K Taylor (89 and 75)	v. Cambridge University at Cambridge	1962
105	105	G Boycott (38 and 64)	and K Taylor (85 and 49)	v. Leicestershire at Leicester	1963
116	112*	K Taylor (45 and 68)	and J H Hampshire (68 and 67*)	v. Oxford University at Oxford	1964
104	104	G Boycott (117 and 49*)	and R G Lumb (47 and 57)	v. Sussex at Leeds	1974
134	185*	M D Moxon (57 and 89*)	and A A Metcalfe (216* and 78*)	v. Middlesex at Leeds	1988
118	129*	G S Ballance (72 and 73*)	and J J Sayers (139 and 53*)	v. Durham MCCU at Durham	2011

CENTURY PARTNERSHIPS FOR THE FIRST WICKET IN BOTH INNINGS BUT WITH CHANGE OF PARTNER

109		W H H Sutcliffe (82) and F A Lowson (46)
	143	W H H Sutcliffe (88) and W Watson (52) v. Canadians at Scarborough, 1954
109		G Boycott (70) and R G Lumb (44)
	135	G Boycott (74) and J H Hampshire (58) v. Northamptonshire at Bradford, 1977

CENTURY PARTNERSHIPS

FIRST WICKET (Qualification 200 runs)

555	P Holmes (224*) and H Sutcliffe (313) v. Essex at Leyton, 1932
554	J T Brown (300) and J Tunnicliffe (243) v. Derbyshire at Chesterfield, 1898
378	J T Brown (311) and J Tunnicliffe (147) v. Sussex at Sheffield, 1897
375	A Lyth (230) and A Z Lees (138) v. Northamptonshire at Northampton, 2014
362	M D Moxon (213) and M P Vaughan (183) v. Glamorgan at Cardiff, 1996
351	G Boycott (184) and M D Moxon (168) v. Worcestershire at Worcester, 1985
347	P Holmes (302*) and H Sutcliffe (131) v. Hampshire at Portsmouth, 1920
323	P Holmes (125) and H Sutcliffe (195) v. Lancashire at Sheffield, 1931
315	H Sutcliffe (189) and L Hutton (153) v. Leicestershire at Hull, 1937
315	H Sutcliffe (116) and L Hutton (280*) v. Hampshire at Sheffield, 1939
309	P Holmes (250) and H Sutcliffe (129) v. Warwickshire at Birmingham, 1931
309	C White (186) and M J Wood (115) v. Lancashire at Manchester, 2001
290	P Holmes (179*) and H Sutcliffe (104) v. Middlesex at Leeds, 1928
288	G Boycott (130*) and R G Lumb (159) v. Somerset at Harrogate, 1979
286	L Hutton (156) and F A Lowson (115) v. South Africans at Sheffield, 1951
282	M D Moxon (147) and A A Metcalfe (151) v. Lancashire at Manchester, 1986
281*	W B Stott (138*) and K Taylor (130*) v. Sussex at Hove, 1960
279	P Holmes (133) and H Sutcliffe (145) v. Northamptonshire at Northampton, 1919
274	P.Holmes (199) and H Sutcliffe (139) v. Somerset at Hull, 1923
274	P Holmes (180) and H Sutcliffe (134) v. Gloucestershire at Gloucester, 1927
272	P Holmes (194) and H Sutcliffe (129) v. Leicestershire at Hull, 1925
272	M J Wood (202*) and J J Sayers (115) v. Bangladesh 'A' at Leeds, 2005
270	A Lyth (143) and A Z Lees (108) v. Durham at Leeds, 2014
268	P Holmes (136) and H Sutcliffe (129) v. Essex at Leyton, 1928
267	W Barber (248) and L Hutton (70) v. Kent at Leeds, 1934
265*	P Holmes (127*) and H Sutcliffe (131*) v. Surrey at The Oval, 1926
264	G Boycott (161*) and R G Lumb (132) v. Gloucestershire at Leeds, 1976
253	P Holmes (123) and H Sutcliffe (132) v. Lancashire at Sheffield, 1919
248	G Boycott (163) and A A Metcalfe (122) v. Nottinghamshire at Bradford, 1983
245	L Hutton (152) and F A Lowson (120) v. Lancashire at Leeds, 1952
244	J A Rudolph (149) and J J Sayers (86) v Nottinghamshire at Nottingham, 2009
241	P Holmes (142) and H Sutcliffe (123*) v. Surrey at The Oval, 1929
240	G Boycott (233) and P J Sharpe (92) v. Essex at Colchester, 1971
238*	P Holmes (126*) and H Sutcliffe (105*) v. Cambridge University at Cambridge, 1923
236	G Boycott (131) and K Taylor (153) v. Lancashire at Manchester, 1964
235	P Holmes (130) and H Sutcliffe (132*) v. Glamorgan at Sheffield, 1930
233	G Boycott (141*) and R G Lumb (90) v. Cambridge University at Cambridge, 1973
233	H Halliday (116) and W Watson (108) v. Northamptonshire at Northampton, 1948
231	M P Vaughan (151) and D Byas (90) v. Essex at Chelmsford, 1999
230	H Sutcliffe (129) and L Hutton (163) v. Surrey at Leeds, 1936
230	W B Stott (114) and K Taylor (140*) v. Nottinghamshire at Nottingham, 1957
228	H Halliday (90) and J V Wilson (223*) v. Scotland at Scarborough, 1951
228	G Boycott (141) and R G Lumb (101) v. Gloucestershire at Bristol, 1975
227	P Holmes (110) and H Sutcliffe (119) v. Leicestershire at Leicester, 1928
225	R G Lumb (101) and C W J Athey (125*) v. Gloucestershire at Sheffield, 1980
224	C W J Athey (114) and J D Love (104) v. Warwickshire at Birmingham, 1980
222	W B Stott (141) and K Taylor (90) v. Sussex at Bradford, 1958
221	P Holmes (130) and H Sutcliffe (121) v. Glamorgan at Huddersfield, 1925
221	M D Moxon (141) and A A Metcalfe (73) v. Surrey at The Oval, 1992
221	A Lyth (111) and A Z Lees (121) v. Leeds/Bradford MCCU at Leeds, 2013
219	P Holmes (102) and A Mitchell (130*) v. Somerset at Bradford, 1930
218	M Leyland (110) and H Sutcliffe (235) v. Middlesex at Leeds, 1925
218	R G Lumb (145) and M D Moxon (111) v. Derbyshire at Sheffield, 1981
210*	P Holmes (101*) and H Sutcliffe (100*) v. Nottinghamshire at Nottingham, 1928
210	G Boycott (128) and P J Sharpe (197) v. Pakistanis at Leeds, 1967
209	F A Lowson (115) and D E V Padgett (107) v. Scotland at Hull, 1956

208	A Mitchell (85) and E Oldroyd (111) v. Cambridge University at Cambridge, 1929
207	A Mitchell (90) and W Barber (107) v. Middlesex at Lord's, 1935
206	G Boycott (118) and R G Lumb (87) v. Glamorgan at Sheffield, 1978
204	M D Moxon (66) and A A Metcalfe (162) v. Gloucestershire at Cheltenham, 1990
203	L Hutton (119) and F A Lowson (83) v. Somerset at Huddersfield, 1952
203	M D Moxon (117) and S A Kellett (87) v. Somerset at Middlesbrough, 1992
203	M D Moxon (134) and M P Vaughan (106) v. Matebeleland at Bulawayo, 1996
200*	P Holmes (107*) and H Sutcliffe (80*) v. Oxford University at Oxford, 1930

Note: P Holmes and H Sutcliffe shared 69 century opening partnerships for Yorkshire; G Boycott and R G Lumb 29; L Hutton and F A Lowson 22; M D Moxon and A A Metcalfe 21; J T Brown and J Tunnicliffe 19; H Sutcliffe and L Hutton 15; G Boycott and P J Sharpe 13, and L Hall and G Ulyett 12.

SECOND WICKET (Qualification 200 runs)

346	W Barber (162) and M Leyland (189) v. Middlesex at Sheffield, 1932
343	F A Lowson (183*) and J V Wilson (165) v. Oxford University at Oxford, 1956
333	P Holmes (209) and E Oldroyd (138*) v. Warwickshire at Birmingham, 1922
314	H Sutcliffe (255*) and E Oldroyd (138) v. Essex at Southend-on-Sea, 1924
311	A Z Lees (275*) and P A Jaques (139) v. Derbyshire at Chesterfield, 2013
305	J W.Rothery (134) and D Denton (182) v. Derbyshire at Chesterfield, 1910
302	W Watson (172) and J V Wilson (140) v. Derbyshire at Scarborough, 1948
301	P J Sharpe (172*) and D E V Padgett (133) v. Glamorgan at Swansea, 1971
288	H Sutcliffe (165) and A Mitchell (136) v. Lancashire at Manchester, 1939
280	L Hall (160) and F Lee (165) v. Lancashire at Bradford, 1887
266*	K Taylor (178*) and D E V Padgett (107*) v. Oxford University at Oxford, 1962
264	P A Jaques (152) and K S Williamson (97) v. Durham at Scarborough, 2013
261*	L Hutton (146*) and J V Wilson (110*) v. Scotland at Hull, 1949
260	R G Lumb (144) and K Sharp (132) v. Glamorgan at Cardiff, 1984
258	H Sutcliffe (230) and E Oldroyd (93) v. Kent at Folkestone, 1931
253	B B Wilson (150) and D Denton (200*) v. Warwickshire at Birmingham, 1912
248	H Sutcliffe (200) and M. Leyland (116) v. Leicestershire at Leicester, 1926
244	P. Holmes (138) and E Oldroyd (151*) v. Glamorgan at Cardiff, 1922
243	G Boycott (141) and J D Love (163) v. Nottinghamshire at Bradford, 1976
243	C White (183) and M J Wood (124) v. Glamorgan at Scarborough, 2001
237	H Sutcliffe (118) and D Denton (122) v. Gloucestershire at Leeds, 1919
237	M D Moxon (132) and K Sharp (128) v. Sri Lankans at Leeds, 1988
236	F A Lowson (112) and J V Wilson (157) v. Essex at Leeds, 1950
235	M D Moxon (130) and D Byas (181) v. Cambridge University at Cambridge, 1995
230	L Hutton (180) and A Mitchell (100) v. Cambridge University at Cambridge, 1938
230	M P Vaughan (109) and B Parker (138*) v. Oxford University at Oxford, 1997.
227	M J Wood (102) and M J Lumb (122) v. Leicestershire at Leeds, 2001
225	H Sutcliffe (138) and E Oldroyd (97) v. Derbyshire at Dewsbury, 1928
223	M D Moxon (153) and R J Blakey (90) v. Somerset at Leeds, 1985
222	H Sutcliffe (174) and D Denton (114) v. Kent at Dover, 1919
219	F S Jackson (155) and D Denton (113) v. Middlesex at Bradford, 1899
217	R G Lumb (107) and J D Love (107) v. Oxford University at Oxford, 1978
216	M P Vaughan (105) and D Byas (102) v. Somerset at Bradford, 1994
215	A W Gale (136) and A McGrath (99) v. Lancashire at Manchester, 2008
215	S E Marsh (125*) and A Z Lees (102) v. Surrey at The Oval, 2017
211	J A Rudolph (141) and A McGrath (80) v Nottinghamshire at Leeds, 2010
207	P A Jaques (115) and A McGrath (93) v. Essex at Chelmsford, 2004
206	J Tunnicliffe (102) and F S Jackson (134*) v. Lancashire at Sheffield, 1898
206	H Sutcliffe (187) and M Leyland (90) v. Leicestershire at Leicester, 1931
205	H Sutcliffe (174) and A Mitchell (95) v. Leicestershire at Leicester, 1933
205	G Boycott (148) and P J Sharpe (108) v. Kent at Sheffield, 1970
203	A T Barber (100) and E Oldroyd (143) v. An England XI at Sheffield, 1929
203	J J Sayers (187) and A McGrath (100) v. Kent at Tunbridge Wells, 2007
202*	W Rhodes (115*) and G H Hirst (117*) v. Somerset at Bath, 1906
202	G Boycott (113) and C W J Athey (114) v. Northamptonshire at Northampton, 1978

CENTURY PARTNERSHIPS *(Continued)*

THIRD WICKET (Qualification 200 runs)

346	J J Sayers (173) and A McGrath (211) v. Warwickshire at Birmingham, 2009
323*	H Sutcliffe (147*) and M Leyland (189*) v. Glamorgan at Huddersfield, 1928
317	A McGrath (165) and D S Lehmann (187) v. Lancashire at Leeds, 2002
310	A McGrath (134) and P A Jaques (219) v. Derbyshire at Leeds, 2005
301	H Sutcliffe (175) and M Leyland (180*) v. Middlesex at Lord's, 1939
293*	A A Metcalfe (150*) and P E Robinson (150*) v. Derbyshire at Scarborough, 1990
269	D Byas (101) and R J Blakey (196) v. Oxford University at Oxford, 1991
258*	J T Brown (134*) and F Mitchell (116*) v. Warwickshire at Bradford, 1901
253*	G S Ballance (101*) and J E Root (130*) v. Nottinghamshire at Nottingham, 2019
252	D E V Padgett (139*) and D B Close (154) v. Nottinghamshire at Nottingham, 1959
249	D E V Padgett (95) and D B Close (184) v. Nottinghamshire at Scarborough, 1960
248	C Johnson (102) and J H Hampshire (155*) v. Gloucestershire at Leeds, 1976
247	P Holmes (175*) and M Leyland (118) v. New Zealanders at Bradford, 1927
244	D E V Padgett (161*) and D B Close (144) v. Oxford University at Oxford, 1959
240	L Hutton (151) and M Leyland (95) v. Surrey at Leeds, 1939
237	J A Rudolph (198) and A McGrath (120) v. Worcestershire at Leeds, 2009
236	H Sutcliffe (107) and R Kilner (137) v. Nottinghamshire at Nottingham, 1920
236	M J Wood (94) and D S Lehmann (200) v. Worcestershire at Worcester, 1998
234*	D Byas (126*) and A McGrath (105*) v. Oxford University at Oxford, 1997.
233	L Hutton (101) and M Leyland (167) v. Worcestershire at Stourbridge, 1937
230	D Byas (103) and M J Wood (103) v. Derbyshire at Leeds, 1998
229	L Hall (86) and R Peel (158) v. Middlesex at Lord's, 1889
228	A Mitchell (142) and M Leyland (133) v. Worcestershire at Sheffield, 1933
228	W Barber (141) and M Leyland (114) v. Surrey at The Oval, 1939
228	J V Wilson (132*) and D E V Padgett (115) v. Warwickshire at Birmingham, 1955
226	D E V Padgett (117) and D B Close (198) v. Surrey at The Oval, 1960
224	J V Wilson (110) and D B Close (114) v. Cambridge University at Cambridge, 1955
224	G Boycott (140*) and K Sharp (121) v. Gloucestershire at Cheltenham, 1983
221	A Mitchell (138) and M Leyland (134) v. Nottinghamshire at Bradford, 1933
219	L Hall (116) and W Bates (133) v. Cambridge University at Cambridge, 1884
218	J A Rudolph (127) and A W Gale (121) v. Lancashire at Manchester, 2009
217	A McGrath (144) and J A Rudolph (129) v. Kent at Canterbury, 2008
216	R G Lumb (118) and J H Hampshire (127) v. Surrey at The Oval, 1975
215	A Mitchell (73) and M Leyland (139) v. Surrey at Bradford, 1928
213	E Oldroyd (168) and W Barber (114) v. Glamorgan at Hull, 1929
208	J V Wilson (157*) and E I Lester (112) v. Sussex at Leeds, 1949
206	A McGrath (105) and J A Rudolph (228*) v Durham at Leeds, 2010
205*	E Oldroyd (122*) and M Leyland (100*) v. Hampshire at Harrogate, 1924
205	F S Jackson (124) and D Denton (112) v. Somerset at Taunton, 1897
205	D E V Padgett (83) and D B Close (128) v. Somerset at Bath, 1959
204	M P Vaughan (113) and A McGrath (70) v. Essex at Scarborough, 2001
203	D Denton (132) and J Tunnicliffe (102) v. Warwickshire at Birmingham, 1905
203	A A Metcalfe (216*) and P E Robinson (88) v. Middlesex at Leeds, 1988
201	J Tunnicliffe (101) and T L Taylor (147) v. Surrey at The Oval, 1900
201	H Sutcliffe (87) and W Barber (130) v. Leicestershire at Leicester, 1938
200	M D Moxon (274*) and A P Grayson (100) v. Worcestershire at Worcester, 1994

FOURTH WICKET (Qualification 175 runs)

372	J E Root (213) and J M Bairstow (198) v. Surrey at Leeds, 2016
358	D S Lehmann (339) and M J Lumb (98) v. Durham at Leeds, 2006
330	M J Wood (116) and D R Martyn (238) v. Gloucestershire at Leeds, 2003
312	D Denton (168*) and G H Hirst (146) v. Hampshire at Southampton, 1914
299	P Holmes (277*) and R Kilner (150) v. Northamptonshire at Harrogate, 1921
272	D Byas (138) and A McGrath (137) v. Hampshire at Harrogate, 1996
271	B B Wilson (208) and W Rhodes (113) v. Sussex at Bradford, 1914
269	D J Malan (152) and H C Brook (194) . Kent at Leeds, 2022
259	A Drake (115) and G H Hirst (218) v. Sussex at Hastings, 1911

258   J Tunnicliffe (128) and G H Hirst (152) v. Hampshire at Portsmouth, 1904
258   P E Robinson (147) and D Byas (117) v. Kent at Scarborough, 1989
255   A W Gale (148) and J A Leaning (110) v. Nottinghamshire at Leeds, 2015
254   A W Gale (164) and J M Bairstow (139) v. Worcestershire at Scarborough, 2015
249   W B Stott (143) and G Boycott (145) v. Lancashire at Sheffield, 1963
247*   R G Lumb (165*) and S N Hartley (104*) v. Gloucestershire at Bradford, 1984
247   M Leyland (263) and L Hutton (83) v. Essex at Hull, 1936
238   D S Lehmann (216) and M J Lumb (92) v. Susex at Arundel, 2002
233   D Byas (120) and P E Robinson (189) v. Lancashire at Scarborough, 1991
231   J E Root (236) and J M Bairstow (186) v. Derbyshire at Leeds, 2013
226   W H Wilkinson (89) and G H Hirst (140) v. Northamptonshire at Hull, 1909
225   C H Grimshaw (85) and G H Hirst (169) v. Oxford University at Oxford, 1906
212   B B Wilson (108) and G H Hirst (166*) v. Sussex at Hastings, 1913
212   G Boycott (260*) and J H Hampshire (80) v. Essex at Colchester, 1970
211   J V Wilson (120) and W Watson (108) v. Derbyshire at Harrogate, 1951
210*   A Mitchell (150*) and M Leyland (117*) v. Worcestershire at Worcester, 1933
210   E I. Lester (178) and W Watson (97) v. Nottinghamshire at Nottingham, 1952
207   D Byas (213) and C White (107*) v. Worcestershire at Scarborough, 1995
206   J A Rudolph (121) and A W Gale (150) v. Surrey at The Oval, 2008
205*   G Boycott (151*) and P J Sharpe (79*) v. Leicestershire at Leicester, 1964
205   E Oldroyd (121) and R Kilner (117) v. Worcestershire at Dudley, 1922
205   W Watson (162*) and E I Lester (98) v. Somerset at Leeds, 1953
205   A Lyth (111) and J M Bairstow (246) v. Hampshire at Leeds, 2016
204   A W Gale (148) and G S Ballance (90) v. Surrey at Leeds, 2013
201*   J H Hampshire (105*) and D B Close (101*) v. Surrey at Bradford, 1965
203   P A Jaques (160) and G S Ballance (121*) v. Gloucestershire at Bristol, 2012
201   W H H Sutcliffe (181) and L Hutton (120) v. Kent at Canterbury, 1952
200   J V Wilson (92) and W Watson (122) v. Somerset at Taunton, 1950
198   A A Metcalfe (138) and D Byas (95) v. Warwickshire at Leeds, 1989
198   A W Gale (124) and J M Bairstow (95) v. Durham at Chester-le-Street, 2014
197   N W D Yardley (177) and A Coxon (58) v. Derbyshire at Scarborough, 1947
197   A Lyth (248*) and J M Bairstow (118) v. Leicestershire at Leicester, 2012
196   M D Moxon (130) and D L Bairstow (104) v. Derbyshire at Harrogate, 1987
193   A Drake (85) and G H Hirst (156) v. Lancashire at Manchester, 1911
192   J V Wilson (132) and W Watson (105) v. Essex at Bradford, 1955
191   M Leyland (114) and C Turner (63) v. Essex at Ilford, 1938
190   A W Gale (125) and J A Leaning (76) v. Hampshire at West End, Southampton, 2015
188   H Myers (60) and G H Hirst (158) v. Cambridge University at Cambridge, 1910
188   G S Ballance (159) and J A Leaning (69) v. Kent at Canterbury, 2019
187   E Oldroyd (168) and F E Greenwood (104*) v. Glamorgan at Hull, 1929
187   K Taylor (203*) and W B Stott (57) v. Warwickshire at Birmingham, 1961
186   D S Lehmann (193) and D Byas (100) v. Leicestershire at Leicester, 2001
184   J H Hampshire (96) and R Illingworth (100*) v. Leicestershire at Sheffield, 1968
182*   E I Lester (101*) and W Watson (103*) v. Nottinghamshire at Bradford, 1952
180*   G Boycott (207*) and B Leadbeater (50*) v. Cambridge University
                              at Cambridge, 1976
180   J Tunnicliffe (139*) and G H Hirst (108) v. Surrey at The Oval, 1904
179   J H Hampshire (179) and S N Hartley (63) v. Surrey at Harrogate, 1981
179   M D Moxon (171*) and R J Blakey (71) v. Kent at Leeds, 1993
178   E I Lester (186) and J V Wilson (71) v. Warwickshiire at Scarborough, 1949
177   J D Love (105*) and J H Hampshire (89) v. Lancashire at Manchester, 1980
175   L Hutton (177) and W Barber (84) v. Sussex at Scarborough, 1939
175   A McGrath (188*) and J A Rudolph (82) v. Warwickshire at Birmingham, 2007

FIFTH WICKET (Qualification 150 runs)

340   E Wainwright (228) and G H Hirst (186) v. Surrey at The Oval, 1899
329   F Mitchell (194) and E Wainwright (153) v. Leicestershire at Leicester, 1899
297   A W Gale (272) and G S Ballance (141) v. Nottinghamshire at Scarborough, 2013
276   W Rhodes (104*) and R Kilner (166) v. Northamptonshire at Northampton, 1921

273   L Hutton (270*) and N W D Yardley (136) v. Hampshire at Bournemouth, 1947
245*   H Sutcliffe (107*) and W Barber (128*) v. Northamptonshire at Northampton, 1939
229   D S Lehmann (193) and C White (79) v. Kent at Canterbury, 2006
217   D B Close (140*) and R Illingworth (107) v. Warwickshire at Sheffield, 1962
213   T Kohler-Cadmore (176) and J A Tattersall (135*) v. Leeds/Bradford MCCU
                                              at Weetwood, Leeds, 2019
207   G S Ballance (107) and A U Rashid (180) v. Somerset at Leeds, 2013
200   D J Malan (219) and J A Tattersall (66) v. Derbyshire at Leeds, 2020
198   E Wainwright (145) and R Peel (111) v. Sussex at Bradford, 1896
198   W Barber (168) and K R Davidson (101*) v. MCC at Lord's, 1934
196*   R Kilner (115*) and G H Hirst (82*) v. Gloucestershire at Leeds, 1919
195   M J Lumb (93) and C White (173*) v. Derbyshire at Derby, 2003
194*   Younus Khan (202*) and G L Brophy (100*) v. Hampshire at Southampton, 2007
193   A Mitchell (189) and W Rhodes (88) v. Northamptonshire at Northampton, 1926
193   J D Love (106) and S N Hartley (108) v. Oxford University at Oxford, 1985
192   C W J Athey (114*) and J D Love (123) v. Surrey at The Oval, 1982
191*   L Hutton (271*) and C Turner (81*) v. Derbyshire at Sheffield, 1937
191   M G Bevan (105) and A A Metcalfe (100) v. West Indians at Scarborough, 1995
190*   R J Blakey (204*) and J D Love (79*) v. Gloucestershire at Leeds, 1987
189   J E Root (160) and G S Ballance (87) v. Sussex at Scarborough 2011
188   D E V Padgett (146) and J V Wilson (72) v. Sussex at Middlesbrough, 1960
187   J V Wilson (230) and H Halliday (74) v. Derbyshire at Sheffield, 1952
185   G Boycott (104*) and K Sharp (99) v. Kent at Tunbridge Wells, 1984
182   E Lockwood (208) and E Lumb (40) v. Kent at Gravesend, 1882
182   B B Wilson (109) and W Rhodes (111) v. Sussex at Hove, 1910
182   D B Close (164) and J V Wilson (55) v. Combined Services at Harrogate, 1954
182   A W Gale (126*) and J A Leaning (76) v. Middlesex at Scarborough, 2014
181   A A Metcalfe (149) and J D Love (88) v. Glamorgan at Leeds, 1986
177   Hon F S Jackson (87) and G H Hirst (232*) v. Surrey at The Oval, 1905
176   L Hutton (176*) and A Coxon (72) v. Sussex at Sheffield, 1948
175   A Drake (108) and R Kilner (77) v. Cambridge University at Cambridge, 1913
173   H Sutcliffe (206) and R Kilner (124) v. Warwickshire at Dewsbury, 1925
170   W Rhodes (157) and R Kilner (87) v. Derbyshire at Leeds, 1925
170   J V Wilson (130*) and N W D Yardley (67) v. Lancashire at Manchester, 1954
169   W Watson (147) and A B Sellers (92) v. Worcestershire at Worcester, 1947
168   A T Barber (63) and A Mitchell (122*) v. Worcestershire at Worcester, 1929
167   J M Bairstow (136) and G S Ballance (61) v. Somerset at Taunton 2011
165   E Oldroyd (143) and W Rhodes (110) v. Glamorgan at Leeds, 1922
165   K Sharp (100*) and P Carrick (73) v. Middlesex at Lord's, 1980
164   A A Metcalfe (151) and D L Bairstow (88) v. Northamptonshire at Luton, 1986
159*   J D Love (170*) and D L Bairstow (52*) v. Worcestershire at Worcester, 1979
159   D B Close (128) and R Illingworth (74) v. Lancashire at Sheffield, 1959
159   J H Hampshire (183*) and C Johnson (53) v. Sussex at Hove, 1971
158*   G Boycott (153*) and P E Robinson (74*) v. Derbyshire at Harrogate, 1984
157   T L Taylor (135*) and G H Hirst (72) v. An England XI at Hastings, 1901
157   G H Hirst (142) and F Smith (51) v. Somerset at Bradford, 1903
157   W Barber (87) and N W D Yardley (101) v. Surrey at The Oval, 1937
156   A McGrath (158) and I J Harvey (103) v. Derbyshire at Derby, 2005
155   J M Bairstow (102) and J A Leaning (82) v. Hampshire at Leeds, 2015
153   S N Hartley (87) and M D Moxon (112*) v. Indians at Scarborough, 1986
152   J H Hampshire (83) and S N Hartley (106) v. Nottinghamshire at Nottingham, 1981
151*   G H Hirst (102*) and R Kilner (50*) v. Kent at Bradford, 1913
151   G H Hirst (120) and F Smith (55) v. Kent at Leeds, 1903
151   W Rhodes (57) and R Kilner (90) v. Nottinghamshire at Nottingham, 1925

SIXTH WICKET (Qualification 150 runs)

305   A Lyth (183) and J A Tattersall (180*)v. Surrey at Scarborough, 2022
296   A Lyth (251) and A U Rashid (159*) v. Lancashire at Manchester, 2014
276   M Leyland (191) and E Robinson (124*) v. Glamorgan at Swansea, 1926

252	C White (181) and R J Blakey (109*) v. Lancashire at Leeds, 1996
248	G J Maxwell (140) and A U Rashid (127) v. Durham at Scarborough, 2015
233	M W Booth (210) and G H Hirst (100) v. Worcestershire at Worcester, 1911
229	W Rhodes (267*) and N Kilner (112) v. Leicestershire at Leeds, 1921
225	E Wainwright (91) and Lord Hawke (127) v. Hampshire at Southampton, 1899
217*	H Sutcliffe (200*) and A Wood (123*) v. Worcestershire at Sheffield, 1935
214	W Watson (214*) and N W D Yardley (76) v. Worcestershire at Worcester, 1955
211	D J Malan (87) and H C Brook (123) v. Essex at Chelmsford, 2022
205	G H Hirst (125) and S Haigh (159) v. Nottinghamshire at Sheffield, 1901
200	D Denton (127) and G H Hirst (134) v. Essex at Bradford, 1902
198	M Leyland (247) and W Rhodes (100*) v. Worcestershire at Worcester, 1928
190	W Rhodes (126) and M Leyland (79) v. Middlesex at Bradford, 1923
190	J A Rudolph (122) and A U Rashid (86) v. Surrey at The Oval, 2007
188	W Watson (174) and R Illingworth (53) v. Lancashire at Sheffield, 1955
188	M P Vaughan (161) and R J Blakey (92) v. Essex at Ilford, 1997.
188	G S Ballance (111) and A U Rashid (82) v. Warwickshire at Birmingham 2011
184	R Kilner (104) and M W Booth (79) v. Leicestershire at Leeds, 1913
183	G H Hirst (131) and E Smith (129) v. Hampshire at Bradford, 1899
183	W Watson (139*) and R Illingworth (78) v. Somerset at Harrogate, 1956
178*	D Denton (108*) and G H Hirst (112*) v. Lancashire at Manchester, 1902
178*	N W D Yardley (100*) and R Illingworth (71*) v. Gloucestershire at Bristol, 1955
178	E Robinson (100) and D C F Burton (83) v. Derbyshire at Hull, 1921
178	H Sutcliffe (135) and P A Gibb (157*) v. Nottinghamshire at Sheffield, 1935
175	G M Fellows (88) and R J Blakey (103) v. Warwickshire at Birmingham, 2002
174	D S Lehmann (136) and G M Hamilton (73) v. Kent at Maidstone, 1998
173	T Kohler-Cadmore (81) and A J Hodd (85) v. Somerset at Leeds, 2018
172	A J Dalton (119*) and D L Bairstow (62) v. Worcestershire at Dudley, 1971
170*	A U Rashid 103*) and A J Hodd (68*) v. Somerset at Taunton, 2013
170	A W Gale (101) and T T Bresnan (97) v. Worcestershire at Worcester, 2009
169	W Barber (124) and H Verity (78*) v. Warwickshire at Birmingham, 1933
169	R Illingworth (162) and J Birkenshaw (37) v. Indians at Sheffield, 1959
166	E Wainwright (116) and E Smith (61) v. Kent at Catford, 1900
166	D B Close (161) and F S Trueman (104) v. Northamptonshire at Northampton, 1963
162*	G Boycott (220*) and J G Binks (70*) v. Northamptonshire at Sheffield, 1967
161*	D L Bairstow (100*) and P Carrick (59*) v. Middlesex at Leeds, 1983
159*	D S Lehmann (187*) and R J Blakey (78*) v. Somerset at Bath, 2001
159	J M Bairstow (182) and A McGrath (90) v. Leicestershire at Scarborough, 2012
156	W Rhodes (82*) and E Robinson (94) v. Derbyshire at Chesterfield, 1919
154	C Turner (84) and A Wood (79) v. Glamorgan at Swansea, 1936
153*	J A Rudolph (92*) and A U Rashid (73*) v. Worcestershire at Kidderminster, 2007
153	J A Rudolph (69*) and J M Bairstow (81) v. Warwickshire at Birmingham, 2010
151	D Denton (91) and W Rhodes (76) v. Middlesex at Sheffield, 1904
151	G Boycott (152*) and P Carrick (75) v. Warwickshire at Leeds, 1982
150	G Ulyett (199*) and J M Preston (93) v. Derbyshire at Sheffield, 1887

SEVENTH WICKET (Qualification 125 runs)

366*	J M Bairstow (219*) and T T Bresnan (169*) v. Durham at Chester-le-Street, 2015
254	W Rhodes (135) and D C F Burton (142*) v. Hampshire at Dewsbury, 1919
247	P Holmes (285) and W Rhodes (79) v. Nottinghamshire at Nottingham, 1929
227	J M Bairstow (246) and L E Plunkett (126) v. Hampshire at Leeds, 2016
215	E Robinson (135*) and D C F Burton (110) v. Leicestershire at Leicester, 1921
197	G S Ballance (165*) and T T Bresnan (78) v. Sussex at Hove, 2015
185	E Wainwright (100) and G H Hirst (134) v. Gloucestershire at Bristol, 1897
183	G H Hirst (341) and H Myers (57) v. Leicestershire at Leicester, 1905
183	J A Rudolph (220) and T T Bresnan (101*) v. Warwickshire at Scarborough, 2007
180	C Turner (130) and A Wood (97) v. Somerset at Sheffield, 1936
170	G S Blewett (190) and G M Hamilton (84*) v. Northamptonshire at Scarborough, 1999
168	G L Brophy (99) and A U Rashid (157*) v. Lancashire at Leeds, 2009

CENTURY PARTNERSHIPS *(Continued)*

166 R Peel (55) and I Grimshaw (122*) v. Derbyshire at Holbeck, 1886
162 E Wainwright (109) and S Haigh (73) v. Somerset at Taunton, 1900
162 R J Blakey (90) and R K J Dawson (87) v. Kent at Canterbury, 2002
162 A W Gale (149) and G L Brophy (97) v. Warwickshire at Scarborough, 2006
161 R G Lumb (118) and C M Old (89) v. Worcestershire at Bradford, 1980
160 J Tunnicliffe (158) and D Hunter (58*) v. Worcestershire at Worcester, 1900
157* F A Lowson (259*) and R Booth (53*) v. Worcestershire at Worcester, 1953
157 K S Wiiliamson (189) and T T Bresnan (61) v. Sussex at Scarborough, 2014
155 D Byas (122*) and P Carrick (61) v. Leicestershire at Leicester.1991.
154* G H Hirst (76*) and J T Newstead (100*) v. Nottinghamshire at Nottingham, 1908
148 J Rowbotham (113) and J Thewlis (50) v. Surrey at The Oval, 1873
147 E Wainwright (78) and G Ulyett (73) v. Somerset at Taunton, 1893
147 M P Vaughan (153) and R J Harden (64) v. Kent at Scarborough, 1999
143 C White (135*) and A K D Gray (60) v. Durham at Chester-le-Street, 2003
141 G H Hirst (108*) and S Haigh (48) v. Worcestershire at Worcester, 1905
141 J H Hampshire (149*) and J G Binks (72) v. MCC at Scarborough, 1965
140 E Wainwright (117) and S Haigh (54) v. CI Thornton's XI at Scarborough, 1900
140 D Byas (67) and P J Hartley (75) v. Derbyshire at Chesterfield, 1990
138 D Denton (78) and G H Hirst (103*) v. Sussex at Leeds, 1905
136 GH Hirst (93) and S Haigh (138) v. Warwickshire at Birmingham, 1904
136 E Robinson (77*) and A Wood (65) v. Glamorgan at Scarborough, 1931
133* W Rhodes (267*) and M Leyland (52*) v. Leicestershire at Leeds, 1921
133* E I Lester (86*) and A B Sellers (73*) v. Northamptonshire at Northampton, 1948
133 D Byas (100) and P W Jarvis (80) v. Northamptonshire at Scarborough, 1992
132 W Rhodes (196) and S Haigh (59*) v. Worcestershire at Worcester, 1904
132 A J Hodd (96*) and Azeem Rafiq (74) v. Nottinghamshire at Scarborough, 2016
131* D L Bairstow (79*) and A Sidebottom (52*) v. Oxford University at Oxford, 1981
130 P J Sharpe (64) and J V Wilson (134) v. Warwickshire at Birmingham, 1962
128 W Barber (66) and T F Smailes (86) v. Cambridge University at Cambridge, 1938
128 D B Close (88*) and A Coxon (59) v. Essex at Leeds, 1949
126 E Wainwright (171) and R Peel (46) v. Middlesex at Lord's, 1897
126 W Rhodes (91) and G G Macaulay (63) v. Hampshire at Hull, 1925
126 J C Balderstone (58) and J G Binks (95) v. Middlesex at Lord's, 1964
126 J M Bairstow (70) and A U Rashid (59) v. Kent at Canterbury, 2010
125 A B Sellers (109) and T F Smailes (65) v. Kent at Bradford, 1937

EIGHTH WICKET (Qualification 125 runs)

292 R Peel (210*) and Lord Hawke (166) v. Warwickshire at Birmingham, 1896
238 I J Harvey (209*) and T T Bresnan (74) v. Somerset at Leeds, 2005
192* W Rhodes (108*) and G G Macaulay (101*) v. Essex at Harrogate, 1922
192 A U Rashid (117*) and A Shahzad (78) v. Hampshire at Basingstoke, 2009
180 W Barber (191) and T F Smailcs (89) v. Sussex at Leeds, 1935
167 J A Leaning (118) and J A Brooks (109*) v. Lancashire at Manchester, 2017
165 S Haigh (62) and Lord Hawke (126) v. Surrey at The Oval, 1902
163 G G Macaulay (67) and A Waddington (114) v. Worcestershire at Leeds, 1927
159 E Smith (95) and W Rhodes (105) v. MCC at Scarborough, 1901
157 A Shahzad (88) and D J Wainwright (85*) v. Sussex at Hove, 2009
156 G S Ballance (112) and R J Sidebottom (40) v. Leeds/Bradford MCCU at Leeds, 2013
152 W Rhodes (98) and J W Rothery (70) v. Hampshire at Portsmouth, 1904
151 W Rhodes (201) and Lord Hawke (51) v. Somerset at Taunton, 1905
151 R J Blakey (80*) and P J Hartley (89) v. Sussex at Eastbourne, 1996
149 G L Brophy (177*) and R J Sidebottom (61) v. Worcestershire at Worcester 2011
147 J P G Chadwick (59) and F S Trueman (101) v. Middlesex at Scarborough, 1965
146 S Haigh (159) and Lord Hawke (89) v. Nottinghamshire at Sheffield, 1901
144 G L Brophy (85) and D J Wainwright (102*) v. Warwickshire at Scarborough, 2009
138 E Wainwright (100) and Lord Hawke (81) v. Kent at Tonbridge, 1899
137 E Wainwright (171) and Lord Hawke (75) v. Middlesex at Lord's, 1897
135 P W Jarvis (55) and P J Hartley (69) v. Nottinghamshire at Scarborough, 1992
133 R Illingworth (61) and F S Trueman (74) v. Leicestershire at Leicester, 1955

297

132   G H Hirst (103) and E Smith (59) v. Middlesex at Sheffield, 1904
132   W Watson (119) and J H Wardle (65) v. Leicestershire at Leicester, 1949
131   P E Robinson (85) and P Carrick (64) v. Surrey at Harrogate, 1990
130   E Smith (98) and Lord Hawke (54) v. Lancashire at Leeds, 1904

128   H Verity (96*) and T F Smailes (77) v. Indians at Bradford, 1936
128   D L Bairstow (145) and G B Stevenson (11) v. Middlesex at Scarborough, 1980
127   E Robinson (70*) and A Wood (62) v. Middlesex at Leeds, 1928
126   R Peel (74) and E Peate (61) v. Gloucestershire at Bradford, 1883
126   M W Booth (56) and E R Wilson (104*) v. Essex at Bradford, 1913
126   J D Middlebrook (84) and C E W Silverwood (70) v. Essex at Chelmsford, 2001
126   M J Lumb (115*) and D Gough (72) v. Hampshire at Southampton, 2003
125   M L Revis (106) and J A Thompson (64) v. Derbyshire at Scarborough 2023

NINTH WICKET (Qualification 100 runs)

246   T T Bresnan (116) and J N Gillespie (123*) v. Surrey at The Oval, 2007
192   G H Hirst (130*) and S Haigh (85) v. Surrey at Bradford, 1898
179   R A Hutton (189) and G A Cope (30*) v. Pakistanis at Bradford, 1971
176*   R Moorhouse (59*) and G H Hirst (115*) v. Gloucestershire at Bristol, 1894
173   S Haigh (85) and W Rhodes (92*) v. Sussex at Hove, 1902
171   G S Ballance (194) and J A Brooks (82) v. Worcestershire at Worcester, 2018
167   H Verity (89) and T F Smailes (80) v. Somerset at Bath, 1936
162   W Rhodes (94*) and S Haigh (84) v. Lancashire at Manchester, 1904
161   E Smith (116*) and W Rhodes (79) v. Sussex at Sheffield, 1900
154   R M Pyrah (117) and R J Sidebottom (52) v.Lancashire at Leeds 2011
151   J M Bairstow (205) and R J Sidebottom (45*) v. Nottinghamshire at Nottingham 2011
150   Azeem Rafiq (100) and M J Hoggard (56*) v. Worcestershire at Worcester, 2009
149*   R J Blakey (63*) and A K D Gray (74*) v. Leicestershire at Scarborough, 2002
149   G H Hirst (232*) and D Hunter (40) v. Surrey at The Oval, 1905
146   G H Hirst (214) and W Rhodes (53) v. Worcestershire at Worcester, 1901
144   T T Bresnan (91) and J N Gillespie (44) v. Hampshire at Leeds, 2006
140   A U Rashid (111) and D J Wainwright (104) v. Sussex at Hove, 2008
136   R Peel (210*) and G H Hirst (85) v. Warwickshire at Birmingham, 1896
125*   L Hutton (269*) and A Coxon (65*) v. Northamptonshire at Wellingborough, 1949
124   P J Hartley (87*) and P W Jarvis (47) v. Essex at Chelmsford, 1986
120   G H Hirst (138) and W Rhodes (38) v. Nottinghamshire at Nottingham, 1899
119   A B Sellers (80*) and E P Robinson (66) v. Warwickshire at Birmingham, 1938
118   S Haigh (96) and W Rhodes (44) v. Somerset at Leeds, 1901
118   J E Root (99) and SA Patterson (47*) v. Glamorgan at Cardiff 2021
114   E Oldroyd (194) and A Dolphin (47) v. Worcestershire at Worcester, 1923
114   N Kilner (102*) and G G Macaulay (60) v. Gloucestershire at Bristol, 1923
113   G G Macaulay (125*) and A Waddington (44) v. Nottinghamshire at Nottingham, 1921
113   A Wood (69) and H.Verity (45*) v. MCC at Lord's, 1938
112   G H Hirst (78) and Lord Hawke (61*) v. Essex at Leyton, 1907
109   Lees Whitehead (60) and W Rhodes (81*) v. Sussex at Harrogate, 1899
108   A McGrath (133*) and C E W Silverwood (80) v. Durham at Chester-le-Street, 2005
106   L E Plunkett (86) and S A Patterson (43) v. Warwickshire at Leeds, 2014
105   J V Wilson (134) and A G Nicholson (20*) v. Nottinghamshire at Leeds, 1962
105   C M Old (100*) and H P Cooper (30) v. Lancashire at Manchester, 1978
105   C White (74*) and J D Batty (50) v. Gloucestershire at Sheffield, 1993
104   L Hall (129*) and R Moorhouse (86) v. Gloucestershire at Clifton, 1888
100   G Pollitt (51) and Lees Whitehead (54) v. Hampshire at Bradford, 1899

TENTH WICKET (Qualification 100 runs)

149   G Boycott (79) and G B Stevenson (115*) v. Warwickshire at Birmingham, 1982
148   Lord Hawke (107*) and D Hunter (47) v. Kent at Sheffield, 1898
144   A Sidebottom (124) and A L Robinson (30*) v. Glamorgan at Cardiff, 1977
121   J T Brown (141) and D Hunter (25*) v. Liverpool & District at Liverpool, 1894
118   Lord Hawke (110*) and D Hunter (41) v. Kent at Leeds, 1896
113   P J Hartley (88*) and R D Stemp (22) v. Middlesex at Lord's, 1996

110 C E W. Silverwood (45*) and R D Stemp (65) v. Durham at Chester-le-Street, 1996
109 A Shahzad (70) and R J Sidebottom (28*) v. Worcestershire at Scarborough, 2011
108 Lord Hawke (79) and Lees Whitehead (45*) v. Lancashire at Manchester, 1903
108 G Boycott (129) and M K Bore (37*) v. Nottinghamshire at Bradford, 1973
106 A B Sellers (79) and D V Brennan (30) v. Worcestershire at Worcester, 1948
103 A Dolphin (62*) and E Smith (49) v. Essex at Leyton, 1919
102 D Denton (77*) and D Hunter (45) v. Cambridge University at Cambridge, 1895

Naively planned and gruelling tour

Cricket Tours: The Historic First MCC tour of India and Ceylon 1926/27   **Jeremy Lonsdale**

This is the latest in this author's series of historical books, including many on Yorkshire cricket. This one, however, is the story of a fascinating and political subcontinental tour led by Arthur Gilligan, which yielded an unbeaten run of 34 matches. It was described as a "naively planned and gruelling" trip.

This book, published by the Association of Cricket Statisticians and Historians, has a retail price of £16. It is no longer available via the ACS website, though is directly from the author. Contact

jeremy.lonsdale@btinternet.com

Further titles with Yorkshire interest include — **Yorkshire Grit: The Life of Ray Illingworth** by Mark Peel and **Bazball: The Inside Story of a Test Cricket Revolution** by Lawrence Booth and Nick Hoult.

Graham Hardcastle

FIFTEEN WICKETS OR MORE IN A MATCH

A complete list of 12, 13 and 14 wickets in a match up to and including 2007 is to be found in the 2008 edition

W E BOWES (1)

16 for 35 (8 for 18 and 8 for 17) v. Northamptonshire at Kettering, 1935

A DRAKE (1)

15 for 51 (5 for 16 and 10 for 35) v. Somerset at Weston-super-Mare, 1914

T EMMETT (1)

16 for 38 (7 for 15 and 9 for 23) v. Cambridgeshire at Hunslet, 1869

G H HIRST (1)

15 for 63 (8 for 25 and 7 for 38) v. Leicestershire at Hull, 1907

R ILLINGWORTH (1)

15 for 123 (8 for 70 and 7 for 53) v. Glamorgan at Swansea, 1960

R PEEL (1)

15 for 50 (9 for 22 and 6 for 28) v. Somerset at Leeds, 1895

W RHODES (1)

15 for 56 (9 for 28 and 6 for 28) v. Essex at Leyton, 1899

H VERITY (4)

17 for 91 (8 for 47 and 9 for 44) v. Essex at Leyton, 1933
15 for 129 (8 for 56 and 7 for 73) v. Oxford University at Oxford, 1936
15 for 38 (6 for 26 and 9 for 12) v. Kent at Sheffield, 1936
15 for 100 (6 for 52 and 9 for 48) v. Essex at Westcliffe-on-Sea, 1936

J H WARDLE (1)

16 for 112 (9 for 48 and 7 for 64) v. Sussex at Hull, 1954

TEN WICKETS IN A MATCH
(including best analysis)

61	W Rhodes	15 for	56	v Essex	at Leyton	1899
48	H Verity	17 for	91	v Essex	at Leyton	1933
40	G H Hirst	15 for	63	v Leicestershire	at Hull	1907
31	G G Macaulay	14 for	92	v Gloucestershire	at Bristol	1926
28	S Haigh	14 for	43	v Hampshire	at Southampton	1898
27	R Peel	14 for	33	v Nottinghamshire	at Sheffield	1888
25	W E Bowes	16 for	35	v Northamptonshire	at Kettering	1935
25	J H Wardle	16 for	112	v Sussex	at Hull	1954
22	E Peate	14 for	77	v Surrey	at Huddersfield	1881
20	F S Trueman	14 for	123	v Surrey	at The Oval	1960
19	T Emmett	16 for	38	v Cambridgeshire	at Hunslet	1869
17	R Appleyard	12 for	43	v Essex	at Bradford	1951
15	E Wainwright	14 for	77	v Essex	at Bradford	1896
11	R Illingworth	15 for	123	v Glamorgan	at Swansea	1960
10	A Waddington	13 for	48	v Northamptonshire	at Northampton	1920
9	M W Booth	14 for	160	v Essex	at Leyton	1914
9	R Kilner	12 for	55	v Sussex	at Hove	1924
8	W Bates	11 for	47	v Nottinghamshire	at Nottingham	1881
8	G Freeman	13 for	60	v Surrey	at Sheffield	1869
7	E P Robinson	13 for	115	v Lancashire	at Leeds	1939
7	D Wilson	13 for	52	v Warwickshire	at Middlesbrough	1967
6	G A Cope	12 for	116	v Glamorgan	at Cardiff (Sophia Gardens)	1968
6	A Hill	12 for	59	v Surrey	at The Oval	1871

TEN WICKETS IN A MATCH (Including best analysis) *(Continued)*

6 T F Smailes	14 for 58	v Derbyshire	at Sheffield	1939
5 P Carrick	12 for 89	v Derbyshire	at Sheffield (Abbeydale Pk)	1983
5 J M Preston	13 for 63	v MCC	at Scarborough	1888
5 E Robinson	12 for 95	v Northamptonshire	at Huddersfield	1927
4 J T Newstead	11 for 72	v Worcestershire	at Bradford	1907
3 T W Foster	11 for 93	v Liverpool & District	at Liverpool	1894
3 G P Harrison	11 for 76	v Kent	at Dewsbury	1883
3 F S Jackson	12 for 80	v Hampshire	at Southampton	1897
3 P W Jarvis	11 for 92	v Middlesex	at Lord's	1986
3 S P Kirby	13 for 154	v Somerset	at Taunton	2003
3 A G Nicholson	12 for 73	v Glamorgan	at Leeds	1964
3 R K Platt	10 for 87	v Surrey	at The Oval	1959
3 A Sidebottom	11 for 64	v Kent	at Sheffield (Abbeydale Pk)	1980
3 R J Sidebottom	11 for 43	v Kent	at Leeds	2000
3 G Ulyett	12 for 102	v Lancashire	at Huddersfield	1889
2 T Armitage	13 for 46	v Surrey	at Sheffield	1876
2 R Aspinall	14 for 65	v Northamptonshire	at Northampton	1947
2 J T Brown (Darfield)	12 for 109	v Gloucestershire	at Huddersfield	1899
2 R O Clayton	12 for 104	v Lancashire	at Manchester	1877
2 D B Close	11 for 116	v Kent	at Gillingham	1965
2 B O Coad	10 for 102	v. Warwickshire	at Birmingham	2017
2 M J Cowan	12 for 87	v Warwickshire	at Birmingham	1960
2 A Coxon	10 for 57	v Derbyshire	at Chesterfield	1949
2 D Gough	10 for 80	v Lancashire	at Leeds	1995
2 G M Hamilton	11 for 72	v Surrey	at Leeds	1998
2 P J Hartley	11 for 68	v Derbyshire	at Chesterfield	1995
2 R A Hutton	11 for 62	v Lancashire	at Manchester	1971
2 E Leadbeater	11 for 162	v Nottinghamshire	at Nottingham	1950
2 K A Maharaj	10 for 127	v. Somerset	at Leeds	2019
2 M A Robinson	12 for 124	v Northamptonshire	at Harrogate	1993
2 M Ryan	10 for 77	v Leicestershire	at Bradford	1962
2 E Smith (Morley)	10 for 97	v MCC	at Scarborough	1893
2 G B Stevenson	11 for 74	v Nottinghamshire	at Nottingham	1980
2 S Wade	11 for 56	v Gloucestershire	at Cheltenham	1886
2 E R Wilson	11 for 109	v Sussex	at Hove	1921
1 A B Bainbridge	12 for 111	v Essex	at Harrogate	1961
1 J Birkenshaw	11 for 134	v Middlesex	at Leeds	1960
1 A Booth	10 for 91	v Indians	at Bradford	1946
1 H P Cooper	11 for 96	v Northamptonshire	at Northampton	1976
1 A Drake	15 for 51	v Somerset	at Weston-Super-Mare	1914
1 L Greenwood	11 for 71	v Surrey	at The Oval	1867
1 P M Hutchison	11 for 102	v Pakistan 'A'	at Leeds	1997
1 L Hutton	10 for 101	v Leicestershire	at Leicester (Aylestone Rd)	1937
1 R Iddison	10 for 68	v Surrey	at Sheffield	1864
1 M Leyland	10 for 94	v Leicestershire	at Leicester (Aylestone Rd)	1933
1 J D Middlebrook	10 for 170	v Hampshire	at Southampton	2000
1 F W Milligan	12 for 110	v Sussex	at Sheffield	1897
1 H Myers	12 for 192	v Gloucestershire	at Dewsbury	1904
1 C M Old	11 for 46	v Gloucestershire	at Middlesbrough	1969
1 D Pickles	12 for 133	v Somerset	at Taunton	1957
1 A U Rashid	11 for 114	v Worcestershire	at Worcester	2011
1 W Ringrose	11 for 135	v Australians	at Bradford	1905
1 C E W Silverwood	12 for 148	v Kent	at Leeds	1997
1 W Slinn	12 for 53	v Nottinghamshire	at Nottingham	1864
1 J Waring	10 for 63	v Lancashire	at Leeds	1966
1 F Wilkinson	10 for 129	v Hampshire	at Bournemouth	1938
1 A C Williams	10 for 66	v Hampshire	at Dewsbury	1919

TEN WICKETS IN AN INNINGS

<table>
<tr><td>Bowler</td><td></td><td></td><td align="right">Year</td></tr>
<tr><td>A Drake</td><td>10 for 35</td><td>v. Somerset at Weston-super-Mare</td><td>1914</td></tr>
<tr><td>H Verity</td><td>10 for 36</td><td>v. Warwickshire at Leeds</td><td>1931</td></tr>
<tr><td>*H Verity</td><td>10 for 10</td><td>v. Nottinghamshire at Leeds</td><td>1932</td></tr>
<tr><td>T F Smailes</td><td>10 for 47</td><td>v. Derbyshire at Sheffield</td><td>1939</td></tr>
</table>

*Includes the hat trick.

EIGHT WICKETS OR MORE IN AN INNINGS

(Ten wickets in an innings also listed above)

A complete list of seven wickets in an innings up to and including 2007 is to be found in the 2008 edition

R APPLEYARD (1)

8 for 76 v. MCC at Scarborough, 1951

R ASPINALL (1)

8 for 42 v. Northamptonshire at Northampton, 1947

W BATES (2)

8 for 45 v. Lancashire at Huddersfield, 1878
8 for 21 v. Surrey at The Oval, 1879

M W BOOTH (4)

8 for 52 v. Leicestershire at Sheffield, 1912
8 for 47 v. Middlesex at Leeds, 1912
8 for 86 v. Middlesex at Sheffield, 1913
8 for 64 v. Essex at Leyton, 1914

W E BOWES (9)

8 for 77 v. Leicestershire at Dewsbury, 1929
8 for 69 v. Middlesex at Bradford, 1930
9 for 121 v. Essex at Scarborough, 1932
8 for 62 v. Sussex at Hove, 1932
8 for 69 v. Gloucestershire at Gloucester, 1933
8 for 40 v.Worcestershire at Sheffield, 1935
8 for 18 v. Northamptonshire at Kettering, 1935
8 for 17 v. Northamptonshire at Kettering, 1935
8 for 56 v. Leicestershire at Scarborough, 1936

J T BROWN (Darfield) (1)

8 for 40 v. Gloucestershire at Huddersfield, 1899

P CARRICK (2)

8 for 33 v. Cambridge University at Cambridge, 1973
8 for 72 v. Derbyshire at Scarborough, 1975

R O CLAYTON (1)

8 for 66 v. Lancashire at Manchester, 1877

D B CLOSE (2)

8 for 41 v. Kent at Leeds, 1959
8 for 43 v. Essex at Leeds, 1960

H P COOPER (1)

8 for 62 v. Glamorgan at Cardiff, 1975

EIGHT WICKETS OR MORE IN AN INNINGS *(Continued)*

G A COPE (1)

8 for 73 v. Gloucestershire at Bristol, 1975

M J COWAN (1)

9 for 43 v. Warwickshire at Birmingham, 1960

A COXON (1)

8 for 31 v. Worcestershire at Leeds, 1946

A DRAKE (2)

8 for 59 v. Gloucestershire at Sheffield, 1913
10 for 35 v. Somerset at Weston-super-Mare, 1914

T EMMETT (8)

9 for 34 v. Nottinghamshire at Dewsbury, 1868
9 for 23 v. Cambridgeshire at Hunslet, 1869
8 for 31 v. Nottinghamshire at Sheffield, 1871
8 for 46 v. Gloucestershire at Clifton, 1877
8 for 16 v. MCC at Scarborough, 1877
8 for 22 v. Surrey at The Oval, 1881
8 for 52 v. MCC at Scarborough, 1882
8 for 32 v. Sussex at Huddersfield, 1884

S D FLETCHER (1)

8 for 58 v. Essex at Sheffield, 1988

T W FOSTER (1)

9 for 59 v. MCC at Lord's, 1894

G FREEMAN (2)

8 for 11 v. Lancashire at Holbeck, 1868
8 for 29 v. Surrey at Sheffield, 1869

L GREENWOOD (1)

8 for 35 v. Cambridgeshire at Dewsbury, 1867

S HAIGH (5)

8 for 78 v. Australians at Bradford, 1896
8 for 35 v. Hampshire at Harrogate, 1896
8 for 21 v. Hampshire at Southampton, 1898
8 for 33 v. Warwickshire at Scarborough, 1899
9 for 25 v. Gloucestershire at Leeds, 1912

P J HARTLEY (2)

8 for 111 v. Sussex at Hove, 1992
9 for 41 v. Derbyshire at Chesterfield, 1995

G H HIRST (8)

8 for 59 v. Warwickshire at Birmingham, 1896
8 for 48 v. Australians at Bradford, 1899
8 for 25 v. Leicestershire at Hull, 1907
9 for 45 v. Middlesex at Sheffield, 1907
9 for 23 v. Lancashire at Leeds, 1910
8 for 80 v. Somerset at Sheffield, 1910
9 for 41 v. Worcestershire at Worcester, 1911
9 for 69 v. MCC at Lord's, 1912

EIGHT WICKETS OR MORE IN AN INNINGS *(Continued)*

R ILLINGWORTH (5)

8 for 69 v. Surrey at The Oval, 1954
9 for 42 v. Worcestershire at Worcester, 1957
8 for 70 v. Glamorgan at Swansea, 1960
8 for 50 v. Lancashire at Manchester, 1961
8 for 20 v. Worcestershire at Leeds, 1965

R KILNER (2)

8 for 26 v. Glamorgan at Cardiff, 1923
8 for 40 v. Middlesex at Bradford, 1926

S P KIRBY (1)

8 for 80 v. Somerset at Taunton, 2003

E LEADBEATER (1)

8 for 83 v. Worcestershire at Worcester, 1950

M LEYLAND (1)

8 for 63 v. Hampshire at Huddersfield, 1938

G G MACAULAY (3)

8 for 43 v. Gloucestershire at Bristol, 1926
8 for 37 v. Derbyshire at Hull, 1927
8 for 21 v. Indians at Harrogate, 1932

H MYERS (1)

8 for 81 v. Gloucestershire at Dewsbury, 1904

A G NICHOLSON (2)

9 for 62 v. Sussex at Eastbourne, 1967
8 for 22 v. Kent at Canterbury, 1968

E PEATE (6)

8 for 24 v. Lancashire at Manchester, 1880
8 for 30 v. Surrey at Huddersfield, 1881
8 for 69 v. Sussex at Hove, 1881
8 for 32 v. Middlesex at Sheffield, 1882
8 for 5 v. Surrey at Holbeck, 1883
8 for 63 v. Kent at Gravesend, 1884

R PEEL (6)

8 for 12 v. Nottinghamshire at Sheffield, 1888
8 for 60 v. Surrey at Sheffield, 1890
8 for 54 v. Cambridge University at Cambridge, 1893
9 for 22 v. Somerset at Leeds, 1895
8 for 27 v. South of England XI at Scarborough, 1896
8 for 53 v. Kent at Halifax, 1897

J M PRESTON (2)

8 for 27 v. Sussex at Hove, 1888
9 for 28 v. MCC at Scarborough, 1888

EIGHT WICKETS OR MORE IN AN INNINGS *(Continued)*

W RHODES (18)

9 for 28 v. Essex at Leyton, 1899
8 for 38 v. Nottinghamshire at Nottingham, 1899
8 for 68 v. Cambridge University at Cambridge, 1900
8 for 43 v. Lancashire at Bradford, 1900
8 for 23 v. Hampshire at Hull, 1900
8 for 72 v. Gloucestershire at Bradford, 1900
8 for 28 v. Essex at Harrogate, 1900
8 for 53 v. Middlesex at Lord's, 1901
8 for 55 v. Kent at Canterbury, 1901
8 for 26 v. Kent at Catford, 1902
8 for 87 v. Worcestershire at Worcester, 1903
8 for 61 v. Lancashire at Bradford, 1903
8 for 90 v. Warwickshire at Birmingham, 1905
8 for 92 v. Northamptonshire at Northampton, 1911
8 for 44 v. Warwickshire at Bradford, 1919
8 for 39 v. Sussex at Leeds, 1920
8 for 48 v. Somerset at Huddersfield, 1926
9 for 39 v. Essex at Leyton, 1929

W RINGROSE (1)

9 for 76 v. Australians at Bradford, 1905

E ROBINSON (3)

9 for 36 v. Lancashire at Bradford, 1920
8 for 32 v. Northamptonshire at Huddersfield, 1927
8 for 13 v. Cambridge University at Cambridge, 1928

E P ROBINSON (2)

8 for 35 v. Lancashire at Leeds, 1939
8 for 76 v. Surrey at The Oval, 1946

M A ROBINSON (1)

9 for 37 v. Northamptonshire at Harrogate, 1993

A SIDEBOTTOM (1)

8 for 72 v. Leicestershire at Middlesbrough, 1986

T F SMAILES (2)

8 for 68 v. Glamorgan at Hull, 1938
10 for 47 v. Derbyshire at Sheffield, 1939

G B STEVENSON (2)

8 for 65 v. Lancashire at Leeds, 1978
8 for 57 v. Northamptonshire at Leeds, 1980

F S TRUEMAN (8)

8 for 70 v. Minor Counties at Lord's, 1949
8 for 68 v. Nottinghamshire at Sheffield, 1951
8 for 53 v. Nottinghamshire at Nottingham, 1951
8 for 28 v. Kent at Dover, 1954
8 for 84 v. Nottinghamshire at Worksop, 1962
8 for 45 v. Gloucestershire at Bradford, 1963
8 for 36 v. Sussex at Hove, 1965
8 for 37 v. Essex at Bradford, 1966

EIGHT WICKETS OR MORE IN AN INNINGS *(Continued)*

H VERITY (20)

9 for 60 v. Glamorgan at Swansea, 1930
10 for 36 v. Warwickshire at Leeds, 1931
8 for 33 v. Glamorgan at Swansea, 1931
8 for 107 v. Lancashire at Bradford, 1932
8 for 39 v. Northamptonshire at Northampton, 1932
10 for 10 v. Nottinghamshire at Leeds, 1932
8 for 47 v. Essex at Leyton, 1933
9 for 44 v. Essex at Leyton, 1933
9 for 59 v. Kent at Dover, 1933
8 for 28 v. Leicestershire at Leeds, 1935
8 for 56 v. Oxford University at Oxford, 1936
8 for 40 v. Worcestershire at Stourbridge, 1936
9 for 12 v. Kent at Sheffield, 1936
9 for 48 v. Essex at Westcliff-on-Sea, 1936
8 for 42 v. Nottinghamshire at Bradford, 1936
9 for 43 v. Warwickshire at Leeds, 1937
8 for 80 v. Sussex at Eastbourne, 1937
8 for 43 v. Middlesex at The Oval, 1937
9 for 62 v. MCC at Lord's, 1939
8 for 38 v. Leicestershire at Hull, 1939

A WADDINGTON (3)

8 for 34 v. Northamptonshire at Leeds, 1922
8 for 39 v. Kent at Leeds, 1922
8 for 35 v. Hampshire at Bradford, 1922

E WAINWRIGHT (3)

8 for 49 v. Middlesex at Sheffield, 1891
9 for 66 v. Middlesex at Sheffield, 1894
8 for 34 v. Essex at Bradford, 1896

J H WARDLE (4)

8 for 87 v. Derbyshire at Chesterfield, 1948
8 for 26 v. Middlesex at Lord's, 1950
9 for 48 v. Sussex at Hull, 1954
9 for 25 v. Lancashire at Manchester, 1954

C WHITE (1)

8 for 55 v. Gloucestershire at Gloucester, 1998

A C WILLIAMS (1)

9 for 29 v. Hampshire at Dewsbury, 1919

R WOOD (1)

8 for 45 v. Scotland at Glasgow, 1952

SIX WICKETS IN AN INNINGS AT LESS THAN FOUR RUNS EACH

A complete list of 5 wickets at less than 4 runs each up to and including 2007 is to be found in the 2008 edition

R APPLEYARD (2)

6 for 17 v. Essex at Bradford, 1951
6 for 12 v. Hampshire at Bournemouth, 1954

T ARMITAGE (1)

6 for 20 v. Surrey at Sheffield, 1876

R ASPINALL (1)

6 for 23 v. Northamptonshire at Northampton, 1947

W BATES (5)

6 for 11 v. Middlesex at Huddersfield, 1879
6 for 22 v. Kent at Bradford, 1881
6 for 17 v. Nottinghamshire at Nottingham, 1881
6 for 12 v. Kent at Sheffield, 1882
6 for 19 v. Lancashire at Dewsbury, 1886

A BOOTH (1)

6 for 21 v. Warwickshire at Birmingham, 1946

W E BOWES (4)

6 for 17 v. Middlesex at Lord's, 1934
6 for 16 v. Lancashire at Bradford, 1935
6 for 20 v. Gloucestershire at Sheffield, 1936
6 for 23 v. Warwickshire at Birmingham, 1947

J T BROWN (Darfield) (1)

6 for 19 v. Worcestershire at Worcester, 1899

R.O CLAYTON (1)

6 for 20 v. Nottinghamshire at Sheffield, 1876

A COXON (1)

6 for 17 v. Surrey at Sheffield, 1948

T EMMETT (6)

6 for 7 v. Surrey at Sheffield, 1867
6 for 13 v. Lancashire at Holbeck, 1868
6 for 21 v. Middlesex at Scarborough, 1874
6 for 12 v. Derbyshire at Sheffield, 1878
6 for 19 v. Derbyshire at Bradford, 1881
6 for 22 v. Australians at Bradford, 1882

H FISHER (1)

6 for 11 v. Leicestershire at Bradford, 1932

S HAIGH (10)

6 for 18 v. Derbyshire at Bradford, 1897
6 for 22 v. Hampshire at Southampton, 1898
6 for 21 v. Surrey at The Oval, 1900
6 for 23 v. Cambridge University at Cambridge, 1902
6 for 19 v. Somerset at Sheffield, 1902
6 for 22 v. Cambridge University at Sheffield, 1903
6 for 21 v. Hampshire at Leeds, 1904
6 for 21 v. Nottinghamshire at Sheffield, 1905
6 for 13 v. Surrey at Leeds, 1908
6 for 14 v. Australians at Bradford, 1912

A HILL (2)

6 for 9 v. United South of England XI at Bradford, 1874
6 for 18 v. MCC at Lord's, 1881

G H HIRST (7)

6 for 23 v. MCC at Lord's, 1893
6 for 20 v. Lancashire at Bradford, 1906
6 for 12 v. Northamptonshire at Northampton, 1908
6 for 7 v. Northamptonshire at Northampton, 1908
6 for 23 v. Surrey at Leeds, 1908
6 for 23 v. Lancashire at Manchester, 1909
6 for 20 v. Surrey at Sheffield, 1909

R ILLINGWORTH (2)

6 for 15 v. Scotland at Hull, 1956
6 for 13 v. Leicestershire at Leicester, 1963

F S JACKSON (1)

6 for 19 v. Hampshire at Southampton, 1897

R KILNER (5)

6 for 22 v. Essex at Harrogate, 1922
6 for 13 v. Hampshire at Bournemouth, 1922
6 for 14 v. Middlesex at Bradford, 1923
6 for 22 v. Surrey at Sheffield, 1923
6 for 15 v. Hampshire at Portsmouth, 1924

G G MACAULAY (10)

6 for 10 v. Warwickshire at Birmingham, 1921
6 for 3 v. Derbyshire at Hull, 1921
6 for 8 v. Northamptonshire at Northampton, 1922
6 for 12 v. Glamorgan at Cardiff, 1922
6 for 18 v. Northamptonshire at Bradford, 1923
6 for 19 v. Northamptonshire at Northampton, 1925
6 for 22 v. Leicestershire at Leeds, 1926
6 for 11 v. Leicestershire at Hull, 1930
6 for 22 v. Leicestershire at Bradford, 1933
6 for 22 v. Middlesex at Leeds, 1934

SIX WICKETS IN AN INNINGS AT LESS THAN FOUR RUNS EACH *(Continued)*

E PEATE (5)

6 for 14 v. Middlesex at Huddersfield, 1879
6 for 12 v. Derbyshire at Derby, 1882
6 for 13 v. Gloucestershire at Moreton-in-Marsh, 1884
6 for 16 v. Sussex at Huddersfield, 1886
6 for 16 v. Cambridge University at Sheffield, 1886

R PEEL (4)

6 for 21 v. Nottinghamshire at Sheffield, 1888
6 for 19 v. Australians at Huddersfield, 1888
6 for 22 v. Gloucestershire at Bristol, 1891
6 for 19 v. Leicestershire at Scarborough, 1896

A C RHODES (1)

6 for 19 v. Cambridge University at Cambridge, 1932

W RHODES (12)

6 for 21 v. Somerset at Bath, 1898
6 for 16 v. Gloucestershire at Bristol, 1899
6 for 4 v. Nottinghamshire at Nottingham, 1901
6 for 15 v. MCC at Lord's, 1902
6 for 16 v. Cambridge University at Cambridge, 1905
6 for 9 v. Essex at Huddersfield, 1905
6 for 22 v. Derbyshire at Glossop, 1907
6 for 17 v. Leicestershire at Leicester, 1908
6 for 13 v. Sussex at Hove, 1922
6 for 23 v. Nottinghamshire at Leeds, 1923
6 for 22 v. Cambridge University at Cambridge, 1924
6 for 20 v. Gloucestershire at Dewsbury, 1927

W RINGROSE (1)

6 for 20 v. Leicestershire at Dewsbury, 1903

R J SIDEBOTTOM (1)

6 for 16 v. Kent at Leeds, 2000

W SLINN (1)

6 for 19 v. Nottinghamshire at Nottingham, 1864

G B STEVENSON(1)

6 for 14 v. Warwickshire at Sheffield, 1979

F S TRUEMAN (4)

6 for 23 v. Oxford University at Oxford, 1955
6 for 23 v. Oxford University at Oxford, 1958
6 for 18 v. Warwickshire at Birmingham, 1963
6 for 20 v. Leicestershire at Sheffield, 1968

H VERITY (5)

6 for 11 v. Surrey at Bradford, 1931
6 for 21 v. Glamorgan at Swansea, 1931
6 for 12 v. Derbyshire at Hull, 1933
6 for 10 v. Essex at Ilford, 1937
6 for 22 v. Hampshire at Bournemouth, 1939

SIX WICKETS IN AN INNINGS AT LESS THAN FOUR RUNS EACH *(Continued)*

A WADDINGTON (2)

6 for 21 v. Northamptonshire at Harrogate, 1921
6 for 21 v. Northamptonshire at Northampton, 1923

S WADE (1)

6 for 18 v. Gloucestershire at Dewsbury, 1887

E WAINWRIGHT (4)

6 for 16 v. Sussex at Leeds, 1893
6 for 23 v. Sussex at Hove, 1893
6 for 18 v. Sussex at Dewsbury, 1894
6 for 22 v. MCC at Scarborough, 1894

J H WARDLE (8)

6 for 17 v. Sussex at Sheffield, 1948
6 for 10 v. Scotland at Edinburgh, 1950
6 for 12 v. Gloucestershire at Hull, 1950
6 for 20 v. Kent at Scarborough, 1950
6 for 23 v. Somerset at Sheffield, 1951
6 for 21 v. Glamorgan at Leeds, 1951
6 for 18 v. Gloucestershire at Bristol, 1951
6 for 6 v. Gloucestershire at Bristol, 1955

D WILSON (3)

6 for 22 v. Sussex at Bradford, 1963
6 for 15 v. Gloucestershire at Middlesbrough, 1966
6 for 22 v. Middlesex at Sheffield, 1966

FOUR WICKETS IN FOUR BALLS

A Drake v. Derbyshire at Chesterfield, 1914

FOUR WICKETS IN FIVE BALLS

F S Jackson v. Australians at Leeds, 1902
A Waddington v. Northamptonshire at Northampton, 1920
G G Macaulay v. Lancashire at Manchester, 1933
P J Hartley v. Derbyshire at Chesterfield, 1995
D Gough v. Kent at Leeds, 1995
J D Middlebrook v. Hampshire at Southampton, 2000

BEST BOWLING ANALYSES IN A MATCH
FOR AND AGAINST YORKSHIRE

Best For Yorkshire:
17 for 91 (8 for 47 and 9 for 44) H Verity v Essex at Leyton, 1933

Against Yorkshire:
17 for 91 (9 for 62 and 8 for 29) H Dean for Lancashire at Liverpool, 1913
(non-championship)

County Championship
16 for 114 (8 for 48 and 8 for 66) G Burton for Middlesex at Sheffield, 1888

Yorkshire versus:

Derbyshire	*For Yorkshire:*	14 for 58 (4 for 11 and 10 for 47) T F Smailes at Sheffield, 1939
	Against:	13 for 65 (7 for 33 and 6 for 32) W Mycroft at Sheffield, 1879
Most 10 wickets in a match	*For Yorkshire:* *Against:*	P Carrick and E Peate 4 each W Mycroft 3
Durham	*For Yorkshire:*	10 for 101 (6 for 57 and 4 for 44) M A Robinson at Durham, 1992
	Against:	10 for 144 (7 for 81 and 3 for 63) O D Gibson at Chester-le-Street, 2007
Most 10 wickets in a match	*For Yorkshire:* *Against:*	M A Robinson 1 G R Breese and O D Gibson 1 each
Essex	*For Yorkshire:*	17 for 91 (8 for 47 and 9 for 44) H Verity at Leyton, 1933
	Against:	14 for 127 (7 for 37 and 7 for 90) W Mead at Leyton, 1899
Most 10 wickets in a match	*For Yorkshire:* *Against:*	W Rhodes 7 J K Lever, W Mead 2 each
Glamorgan	*For Yorkshire:*	15 for 123 (8 for 70 and 7 for 53) R Illingworth at Swansea. 1960
	Against:	12 for 76 (7 for 30 and 5 for 46) D J Shepherd at Cardiff, 1957
Most 10 wickets in a match	*For Yorkshire:* *Against:*	H Verity 5 D J Shepherd, J S Pressdee 1 each
Gloucestershire	*For Yorkshire:*	14 for 64 (7 for 58 and 7 for 6) R Illingworth at Harrogate, 1967
	Against:	15 for 79 (8 for 33 and 7 for 46) W G Grace at Sheffield, 1872
Most 10 wickets in a match	*For Yorkshire:* *Against:*	W Rhodes 8 E G Dennett 5
Hampshire	*For Yorkshire:*	14 for 43 (8 for 21 and 6 for 22) S Haigh at Southampton, 1898
	Against:	12 for 145 (7 for 78 and 5 for 67) D Shackleton at Bradford, 1962
Most 10 wickets in a match	*For Yorkshire:* *Against:*	W Rhodes, E Robinson, H Verity 3 each A S Kennedy 3

Yorkshire versus

Kent — *For Yorkshire:* 15 for 38 (6 for 26 and 9 for 12)
H Verity at Sheffield, 1936

Against: 13 for 48 (5 for 13 and 8 for 35)
A Hearne at Sheffield, 1885

Most 10 wickets in a match — *For Yorkshire:* E Peate and J H Wardle 4 each
Against: C Blythe 6

Lancashire — *For Yorkshire:* 14 for 80 (6 for 56 and 8 for 24)
E Peate at Manchester, 1880

Against: 17 for 91 (9 for 62 and 8 for 29)
H Dean at Liverpool, 1913 (non-championship)
14 for 90 (6 for 47 and 8 for 43)
R Tattersall at Leeds, 1956 (championship)

Most 10 wickets in a match — *For Yorkshire:* T Emmett 5
Against: J Briggs 8

Leicestershire — *For Yorkshire:* 15 for 63 (8 for 25 and 7 for 38)
G H Hirst at Hull, 1907

Against: 12 for 139 (8 for 85 and 4 for 54)
A D Pougher at Leicester, 1895

Most 10 wickets in a match — *For Yorkshire:* G H Hirst 5
Against: A D Pougher 2

Middlesex — *For Yorkshire:* 13 for 94 (6 for 61 and 7 for 33)
S Haigh at Leeds, 1900

Against: 16 for 114 (8 for 48 and 8 for 66)
G Burton at Sheffield, 1888

Most 10 wickets in a match — *For Yorkshire:* W Rhodes 5
Against: J T Hearne 7

Northamptonshire — *For Yorkshire:* 16 for 35 (8 for 18 and 8 for 17)
W E Bowes at Kettering, 1935

Against: 15 for 31 (7 for 22 and 8 for 9)
G E Tribe at Northampton, 1958

Most 10 wickets in a match — *For Yorkshire:* W E Bowes, G G Macaulay, H Verity, A Waddington 3 each
Against: G E Tribe 3

Nottinghamshire — *For Yorkshire:* 14 for 33 (8 for 12 and 6 for 21)
R Peel at Sheffield, 1888

Against: 14 for 94 (8 for 38 and 6 for 56)
F Morley at Nottingham, 1878

Most 10 wickets in a match — *For Yorkshire:* G H Hirst 5
Against: F Morley, J C Shaw 4 each

Somerset — *For Yorkshire:* 15 for 50 (9 for 22 and 6 for 28)
R Peel at Leeds, 1895

Against: 15 for 71 (6 for 30 and 9 for 41)
L C Braund at Sheffield, 1902

Most 10 wickets in a match — *For Yorkshire:* G H Hirst 7
Against: L C Braund 3

BEST BOWLING ANALYSES IN A MATCH
FOR AND AGAINST YORKSHIRE *(continued)*

Yorkshire versus

Surrey	*For Yorkshire:*	14 for 77 (6 for 47 and 8 for 30) E Peate at Huddersfield, 1881
	Against:	15 for 154 (7 for 55 and 8 for 99) T Richardson at Leeds, 1897
Most 10 wickets in a match	*For Yorkshire:* *Against:*	W Rhodes 7 G A Lohmann, T Richardson 6 each
Sussex	*For Yorkshire:*	16 for 112 (9 for 48 and 7 for 64) J H Wardle at Hull, 1954
	Against:	12 for 110 (6 for 71 and 6 for 39) G R Cox at Sheffield, 1907
Most 10 wickets in a match	*For Yorkshire:* *Against:*	R Peel, E Wainwright 3 each Twelve players 1 each
Warwickshire	*For Yorkshire:*	14 for 92 (9 for 43 and 5 for 49) H Verity at Leeds, 1937
	Against:	12 for 55 (5 for 21 and 7 for 34) T W Cartwright at Bradford, 1969
Most 10 wickets in a match	*For Yorkshire:* *Against:*	S Haigh 4 E F Field 4
Worcestershire	*For Yorkshire:*	14 for 211 (8 for 87 and 6 for 124) W Rhodes at Worcester, 1903
	Against:	13 for 76 (4 for 38 and 9 for 38) J A Cuffe at Bradford, 1907
Most 10 wickets in a match	*For Yorkshire:* *Against:*	S Haigh, G G Macaulay 4 each N Gifford 2
Australians	*For Yorkshire:*	13 for 149 (8 for 48 and 5 for 101) G H Hirst at Bradford, 1899
	Against:	13 for 170 (6 for 91 and 7 for 79) J M Gregory at Sheffield, 1919
Most 10 wickets in a match	*For Yorkshire:* *Against:*	S Haigh 2 C V Grimmett, F R Spofforth, C T B Turner, H Trumble 2 each

BEST BOWLING ANALYSES IN AN INNINGS
FOR AND AGAINST YORKSHIRE

Best For Yorkshire:

10 for 10 H Verity v Nottinghamshire at Leeds, 1932

Against Yorkshire:

10 for 37 C V Grimmett for Australians at Sheffield, 1930
(non-championship)

County Championship
10 for 51 H Howell for Warwickshire at Birmingham, 1923

Yorkshire versus:

Derbyshire	*For Yorkshire:*	10 for 47	T F Smailes at Sheffield, 1939
	Against:	9 for 27	J J Hulme at Sheffield, 1894
Most 5 wickets in an innings	*For Yorkshire:*	S Haigh, E Peat, W Rhodes 11 each	
	Against:	W Mycroft 10	

BEST BOWLING ANALYSES IN AN INNINGS
FOR AND AGAINST YORKSHIRE *(continued)*

Yorkshire versus

Durham — *For Yorkshire:* 6 for 37 — R D Stemp at Durham, 1994
6 for 37 — J N Gillespie at Chester-le-Street, 2006
Against: 7 for 58 — J Wood at Leeds, 1999
Most 5 wickets in an innings — *For Yorkshire:* D Gough and M J Hoggard 2 each
Against: G R Breese, S J E Brown, S J Harmison and G Onions 2 each

Essex — *For Yorkshire:* 9 for 28 — W Rhodes at Leyton, 1899
Against: 8 for 44 — F G Bull at Bradford, 1896
Most 5 wickets in an innings — *For Yorkshire:* W Rhodes 18
Against: W Mead 14

Glamorgan — *For Yorkshire:* 9 for 60 — H Verity at Swansea, 1930
Against: 9 for 43 — J S Pressdee at Swansea, 1965
Most 5 wickets in an innings — *For Yorkshire:* H Verity 12
Against: D J Shepherd 6

Gloucestershire — *For Yorkshire:* 9 for 25 — S Haigh at Leeds, 1912
Against: 9 for 36 — C W L Parker at Bristol, 1922
Most 5 wickets in an innings — *For Yorkshire:* W Rhodes 22
Against: T W J Goddard 17

Hampshire — *For Yorkshire:* 9 for 29 — A C Williams at Dewsbury, 1919
Against: 8 for 49 — O W Herman at Bournemouth, 1930
Most 5 wickets in an innings — *For Yorkshire:* G H Hirst 10
Against: A S Kennedy 10

Kent — *For Yorkshire:* 9 for 12 — H Verity at Sheffield, 1936
Against: 8 for 35 — A Hearne at Sheffield, 1885
Most 5 wickets in an innings — *For Yorkshire:* W Rhodes 12
Against: A P Freeman 14

Lancashire — *For Yorkshire:* 9 for 23 — G H Hirst at Leeds, 1910
Against: 9 for 41 — A Mold at Huddersfield, 1890
Most 5 wickets in an innings — *For Yorkshire:* T Emmett 16
Against: J Briggs 19

Leicestershire — *For Yorkshire:* 8 for 25 — G H Hirst at Hull, 1907
Against: 9 for 63 — C T Spencer at Huddersfield, 1954
Most 5 wickets in an innings — *For Yorkshire:* G H Hirst 15
Against: H A Smith 7

Middlesex — *For Yorkshire:* 9 for 45 — G H Hirst at Sheffield 1907
Against: 9 for 57 — F A Tarrant at Leeds, 1906
Most 5 wickets in an innings — *For Yorkshire:* W Rhodes 18
Against: J T Hearne 21

Northamptonshire — *For Yorkshire:* 9 for 37 — M A Robinson at Harrogate, 1993
Against: 9 for 30 — A E Thomas at Bradford, 1920
Most 5 wickets in an innings — *For Yorkshire:* G G Macaulay 14
Against: G E Tribe, W Wells 7 each

Nottinghamshire — *For Yorkshire:* 10 for 10 — H Verity at Leeds, 1932
Against: 8 for 32 — J C Shaw at Nottingham, 1865
Most 5 wickets in an innings — *For Yorkshire:* W Rhodes 17
Against: F Morley 17

BEST BOWLING ANALYSES IN AN INNINGS FOR AND AGAINST YORKSHIRE *(continued)*

Yorkshire versus

Somerset   *For Yorkshire:* 10 for 35   A Drake at Weston-super-Mare, 1914

   Against: 9 for 41   L C Braund at Sheffield, 1902

Most 5 wickets   *For Yorkshire:* G H Hirst 16

in an innings   *Against:* E J Tyler 8

Surrey   *For Yorkshire:* 8 for 5   E Peate at Holbeck, 1883

   Against: 9 for 47   T Richardson at Sheffield, 1893

Most 5 wickets   *For Yorkshire:* W Rhodes 17

in an innings   *Against:* W Southerton 19

Sussex   *For Yorkshire:* 9 for 48   J H Wardle at Hull, 1954

   Against: 9 for 34   James Langridge at Sheffield, 1934

Most 5 wickets   *For Yorkshire:* W Rhodes 14

in an innings   *Against:* G R Cox, J A Snow 6 each

Warwickshire   *For Yorkshire:* 10 for 36   H Verity at Leeds, 1930

   Against: 10 for 51   H Howell at Birmingham, 1923

Most 5 wickets   *For Yorkshire:* W Rhodes 18

in an innings   *Against:* E F Field, W E Hollies 7 each

Worcestershire   *For Yorkshire:* 9 for 41   G H Hirst at Worcester, 1911

   Against: 9 for 38   J A Cuffe at Bradford, 1907

Most 5 wickets   *For Yorkshire:* S Haigh, W Rhodes 11 each

in an innings   *Against:* R T D Perks 7

Australians   *For Yorkshire:* 9 for 76   W Ringrose at Bradford, 1905

   Against: 10 for 37   C V Grimmett at Sheffield, 1930

Most 5 wickets   *For Yorkshire:* R Peel 7

in an innings   *Against:* F R Spofforth 7

HAT-TRICKS

G Freeman v. Lancashire at Holbeck, 1868

G Freeman v. Middlesex at Sheffield, 1868

A Hill v. United South of England XI at Bradford, 1874

A Hill v. Surrey at The Oval, 1880

E Peate v. Kent at Sheffield, 1882

G Ulyett v. Lancashire at Sheffield, 1883

E Peate v. Gloucestershire at Moreton-in-Marsh, 1884

W Fletcher v. MCC at Lord's, 1892

E Wainwright v. Sussex at Dewsbury, 1894

G H Hirst v. Leicestershire at Leicester, 1895

J T Brown v. Derbyshire at Derby, 1896

R Peel v. Kent at Halifax, 1897

S Haigh v. Derbyshire at Bradford, 1897

W Rhodes v. Kent at Canterbury, 1901

S Haigh v. Somerset at Sheffield, 1902

H A Sedgwick v. Worcestershire at Hull, 1906

G Deyes v. Gentlemen of Ireland at Bray, 1907

G H Hirst v. Leicestershire at Hull, 1907

J T Newstead v. Worcestershire at Bradford, 1907

S Haigh v. Lancashire at Manchester, 1909

M W Booth v. Worcestershire at Bradford, 1911

A Drake v. Essex at Huddersfield, 1912

M W Booth v. Essex at Leyton, 1912
A Drake v. Derbyshire at Chesterfield, 1914 (4 in 4)
W Rhodes v. Derbyshire at Derby, 1920
A Waddington v. Northamptonshire at Northampton, 1920 (4 in 5)
G G Macaulay v. Warwickshire at Birmingham, 1923
E Robinson v. Sussex at Hull, 1928
G G Macaulay v. Leicestershire at Hull, 1930
E Robinson v. Kent at Gravesend, 1930
H Verity v. Nottinghamshire at Leeds, 1932
H Fisher v. Somerset at Sheffield, 1932 (all lbw)
G G Macaulay v. Glamorgan at Cardiff, 1933
G G Macaulay v. Lancashire at Manchester, 1933 (4 in 5)
M.Leyland v. Surrey at Sheffield, 1935
E Robinson v. Kent at Leeds, 1939
A Coxon v. Worcestershire at Leeds, 1946
F S Trueman v. Nottinghamshire at Nottingham, 1951
F S Trueman v. Nottinghamshire at Scarborough, 1955
R Appleyard v. Gloucestershire at Sheffield, 1956
F S.Trueman v. MCC at Lord's, 1958
D Wilson v. Nottinghamshire at Middlesbrough, 1959
F S Trueman v. Nottinghamshire at Bradford, 1963
D Wilson v. Nottinghamshire at Worksop, 1966
D Wilson v. Kent at Harrogate, 1966
G A Cope v. Essex at Colchester, 1970
A L Robinson v. Nottinghamshire at Worksop, 1974
P W Jarvis v. Derbyshire at Chesterfield, 1985
P J Hartley v. Derbyshire at Chesterfield, 1995 (4 in 5)
D Gough v. Kent at Leeds, 1995 (4 in 5)
C White v. Gloucestershire at Gloucester, 1998
M J Hoggard v. Sussex at Hove, 2009

52 Hat-Tricks: G G Macaulay and F S Trueman took four each, S Haigh and D Wilson three each. There have been seven hat-tricks versus Kent and Nottinghamshire, and six versus Derbyshire.

200 WICKETS IN A SEASON

Bowler	Season	Overs	Maidens	Runs	Wickets	Average
W Rhodes	1900	1366.4	411	3054	240	12.72
W Rhodes	1901	1455.3	474	3497	233	15.00
G H Hirst	1906	1111.1	262	3089	201	15.36
G G Macaulay	1925	1241.2	291	2986	200	14.93
R Appleyard†	1951	1323.2	394	2829	200	14.14

† First full season in First-Class cricket.

100 WICKETS IN A SEASON

Bowler		*Wickets taken*	*Wickets taken*	*Wickets taken*
R Appleyard	(3)	200 in 1951	141 in 1954	110 in 1956
A Booth	(1)	111 in 1946	—	—
M W Booth	(3)	104 in 1912	167 in 1913	155 in 1914
W E Bowes	(8)	117 in 1931	168 in 1932	130 in 1933
		109 in 1934	154 in 1935	113 in 1936
		106 in 1938	107 in 1939	—

100 WICKETS IN A SEASON *(Continued)*

Bowler		Wickets taken	Wickets taken	Wickets taken
D B Close	(2)	105 in 1949	114 in 1952	—
A Coxon	(2)	101 in 1949	129 in 1950	—
A Drake	(2)	115 in 1913	158 in 1914	—
T Emmett	(1)	112 in 1886	—	—
S Haigh	(10)	100 in 1898	160 in 1900	154 in 1902
		102 in 1903	118 in 1904	118 in 1905
		161 in 1906	120 in 1909	100 in 1911
		125 in 1912	—	—
G H Hirst	(12)	150 in 1895	171 in 1901	121 in 1903
		114 in 1904	100 in 1905	201 in 1906
		169 in 1907	164 in 1908	138 in 1910
		130 in 1911	113 in 1912	100 in 1913
R Illingworth	(5)	103 in 1956	120 in 1961	116 in 1962
		122 in 1964	105 in 1968	—
R Kilner	(4)	107 in 1922	143 in 1923	134 in 1924
		123 in 1925	—	—
G G Macaulay	(10)	101 in 1921	130 in 1922	163 in 1923
		184 in 1924	200 in 1925	133 in 1926
		130 in 1927	117 in 1928	102 in 1929
		141 in 1933	—	—
J T Newstead	(1)	131 in 1908	—	—
A G Nicholson	(2)	113 in 1966	101 in 1967	—
E Peate	(3)	131 in 1880	133 in 1881	165 in 1882
R Peel	(6)	118 in 1888	132 in 1890	106 in 1892
		134 in 1894	155 in 1895	108 in 1896
W Rhodes	(22)	141 in 1898	153 in 1899	240 in 1900
		233 in 1901	174 in 1902	169 in 1903
		118 in 1904	158 in 1905	113 in 1906
		164 in 1907	100 in 1908	115 in 1909
		105 in 1911	117 in 1914	155 in 1919
		156 in 1920	128 in 1921	100 in 1922
		127 in 1923	102 in 1926	111 in 1928
		100 in 1929	—	—
E Robinson	(1)	111 in 1928	—	—
E P Robinson	(4)	104 in 1938	120 in 1939	149 in 1946
		108 in 1947	—	—
T F Smailes	(4)	105 in 1934	125 in 1936	120 in 1937
		104 in 1938	—	—
F S Trueman	(8)	129 in 1954	140 in 1955	104 in 1959
		150 in 1960	124 in 1961	122 in 1962
		121 in 1965	107 in 1966	—
H Verity	(9)	169 in 1931	146 in 1932	168 in 1933
		100 in 1934	199 in 1935	185 in 1936
		185 in 1937	137 in 1938	189 in 1939
A Waddington	(5)	100 in 1919	140 in 1920	105 in 1921
		132 in 1922	105 in 1925	—
E Wainwright	(3)	114 in 1893	157 in 1894	102 in 1896
J H Wardle	(10)	148 in 1948	100 in 1949	172 in 1950
		122 in 1951	169 in 1952	126 in 1953
		122 in 1954	159 in 1955	146 in 1956
		106 in 1957	—	—
D Wilson	(3)	100 in 1966	107 in 1968	101 in 1969

BOWLERS WHO HAVE TAKEN OVER 500 WICKETS

Player	M	Runs	Wkts	Av'ge	Best
W Rhodes	883	57634	3598	16.01	9 for 28
G H Hirst	717	44716	2481	18.02	9 for 23
S Haigh	513	29289	1876	15.61	9 for 25
G G Macaulay	445	30554	1774	17.22	8 for 21
F S Trueman	459	29890	1745	17.12	8 for 28
H Verity	278	21353	1558	13.70	10 for 10
J H Wardle	330	27917	1539	18.13	9 for 25
R Illingworth	496	26806	1431	18.73	9 for 42
W E Bowes	301	21227	1351	15.71	9 for 121
R Peel	318	20638	1311	15.74	9 for 22
T Emmett	299	15465	1216	12.71	9 for 23
D Wilson	392	22626	1104	20.49	7 for 19
P Carrick	425	30530	1018	29.99	8 for 33
E Wainwright	352	17744	998	17.77	9 for 66
D B Close	536	23489	967	24.29	8 for 41
Emmott Robinson	413	19645	893	21.99	9 for 36
A G Nicholson	282	17296	876	19.74	9 for 62
R Kilner	365	14855	857	17.33	8 for 26
A Waddington	255	16203	835	19.40	8 for 34
T F Smailes	262	16593	802	20.68	10 for 47
E Peate	154	9986	794	12.57	8 for 5
Ellis P Robinson	208	15141	735	20.60	8 for 35
C M Old	222	13409	647	20.72	7 for 20
R Appleyard	133	9903	642	15.42	8 for 76
W Bates	202	10692	637	16.78	8 for 21
G A Cope	230	15627	630	24.80	8 for 73
P J Hartley	195	17438	579	30.11	9 for 41
A Sidebottom	216	13852	558	24.82	8 for 72
M W Booth	144	11017	557	19.17	8 for 47
A Hill	140	7002	542	12.91	7 for 14
Hon F S Jackson	207	9690	506	19.15	7 for 42

BOWLERS UNCHANGED IN A MATCH
(IN WHICH THE OPPONENTS WERE DISMISSED TWICE)

**There have been 31 instances. The first and most recent are listed below.
A complete list is to be found in the 2008 edition.**

First: L Greenwood (11 for 71) and G Freeman (8 for 73) v. Surrey
at The Oval, 1867
Yorkshire won by an innings and 111 runs

Most Recent: E Robinson (8 for 65) and G G Macaulay (12 for 50) v. Worcestershire
at Leeds, 1927
Yorkshire won by an innings and 106 runs

FIELDERS (IN MATCHES FOR YORKSHIRE)

MOST CATCHES IN AN INNINGS

6	E P Robinson	v. Leicestershire	at Bradford, 1938
6	T Kohler- Cadmore		
		v. Kent	at Canterbury, 2019
5	J Tunnicliffe	v. Leicestershire	at Leeds, 1897
5	J Tunnicliffe	v. Leicestershire	at Leicester, 1900
5	J Tunnicliffe	v. Leicestershire	at Scarborough, 1901
5	A B Sellers	v. Essex	at Leyton, 1933
5	D Wilson	v. Surrey	at The Oval, 1969
5	R G Lumb	v. Gloucestershire	at Middlesbrough, 1972

MOST CATCHES IN A MATCH

7	J Tunnicliffe	v. Leicestershire	at Leeds, 1897
7	J Tunnicliffe	v. Leicestershire	at Leicester, 1900
7	A B Sellers	v Essex	at Leyton, 1933
7	E P Robinson	v. Leicestershire	at Bradford, 1938
7	A Lyth	v. Middlesex	at Scarborough, 2014
7	T Kohler-Cadmore		
		v. Hampshire	at West End, Southampton, 2019

MOST CATCHES IN A SEASON

70	J Tunnicliffe	in 1901
70	P J Sharpe	in 1962
61	J Tunnicliffe	in 1895
60	J Tunnicliffe	in 1904
59	J Tunnicliffe	in 1896
57	J V Wilson	in 1955
54	J V Wilson	in 1961
53	J V Wilson	in 1957
51	J V Wilson	in 1951

MOST CATCHES IN A CAREER

665	J Tunnicliffe	(1.40 per match)
586	W Rhodes	(0.66 per match)
564	D B Close	(1.05 per match)
525	P J Sharpe	(1.27 per match)
520	J V Wilson	(1.09 per match)
518	G H Hirst	(0.72 per match)

WICKET-KEEPERS IN MATCHES FOR YORKSHIRE

MOST DISMISSALS IN AN INNINGS

7	(7ct)	D L Bairstow	v. Derbyshire	at Scarborough	1982
6	(6ct)	J Hunter	v. Gloucestershire	at Gloucester	1887
6	(5ct,1st)	D Hunter	v. Surrey	at Sheffield	1891
6	(6ct)	D Hunter	v. Middlesex	at Leeds	1909
6	(2ct,4st)	W R Allen	v. Sussex	at Hove	1921
6	(5ct,1st)	J G Binks	v. Lancashire	at Leeds	1962
6	(6ct)	D L Bairstow	v. Lancashire	at Manchester	1971
6	(6ct)	D L Bairstow	v. Warwickshire	at Bradford	1978
6	(5ct,1st)	D L Bairstow	v. Lancashire	at Leeds	1980
6	(6ct)	D L Bairstow	v. Derbyshire	at Chesterfield	1984
6	(6ct)	R J Blakey	v. Sussex	at Eastbourne	1990
6	(5ct,1st)	R J Blakey	v. Gloucestershire	at Cheltenham	1992
6	(5ct,1st)	R J Blakey	v. Glamorgan	at Cardiff	1994
6	(6ct)	R J Blakey	v. Glamorgan	at Leeds	2003
6	(6ct)	G L Brophy	v. Durham	at Chester-le-Street	2009
6	(6ct)	J M Bairstow	v. Middlesex	at Leeds	2013
6	(6ct)	J M Bairstow	v. Sussex	at Arundel	2014
6	(6ct)	H G Duke	v. Nottinghamshire	at Nottingham	2021

MOST DISMISSALS IN A MATCH

11	(11ct)	D L Bairstow	v. Derbyshire	at Scarborough	1982
		(Equalled World Record)			
9	(9ct)	J.Hunter	v. Gloucestershire	at Gloucester	1887
9	(8ct,1st)	A Dolphin	v. Derbyshire	at Bradford	1919
9	(9ct)	D L Bairstow	v. Lancashire	at Manchester	1971
9	(9ct)	R J Blakey	v. Sussex	at Eastbourne	1990
8	(2ct,6st)	G Pinder	v. Lancashire	at Sheffield	1872
8	(2ct,6st)	D Hunter	v. Surrey	at Bradford	1898
8	(7ct,1st)	A Bairstow	v. Cambridge University	at Cambridge	1899
8	(8ct)	A Wood	v. Northamptonshire	at Huddersfield	1932
8	(8ct)	D L Bairstow	v. Lancashire	at Leeds	1978
8	(7ct,1st)	D L Bairstow	v. Derbyshire	at Chesterfield	1984
8	(6ct,2st)	D L Bairstow	v. Derbyshire	at Chesterfield	1985
8	(8ct)	R J Blakey	v. Hampshire	at Southampton	1989
8	(8ct)	R J Blakey	v. Northamptonshire	at Harrogate	1993
8	(8ct)	A J Hodd	v. Glamorgan	at Leeds	2012
8	(8ct)	J M Bairstow	v. Middlesex	at Leeds	2013

MOST DISMISSALS IN A SEASON

107	(96ct,11st)	J G Binks, 1960
94	(81ct,13st)	JG Binks, 1961
89	(75ct,14st)	A Wood, 1934
88	(80ct,8st)	J G Binks, 1963
86	(70ct,16st)	J G Binks, 1962
82	(52ct,30st)	A Dolphin, 1919
80	(57ct,23st)	A. Wood, 1935

MOST DISMISSALS IN A CAREER

1186	(863ct,323st)	D Hunter (2.29 per match)
1044	(872ct,172st)	J G Binks (2.12 per match)
1038	(907ct,131st)	D L Bairstow (2.41 per match)
855	(612ct,243st)	A Wood (2.09 per match)
829	(569ct,260st)	A Dolphin (1.94 per match)
824	(768ct, 56st)	R J Blakey (2.43 per match)

YORKSHIRE PLAYERS WHO HAVE COMPLETED THE "DOUBLE"

(all First-Class matches)

Player	Year	Runs	Average	Wickets	Average
M W Booth (1)	1913	1,228	27.28	181	18.46
D B Close (2)	†1949	1,098	27.45	113	27.87
	1952	1,192	33.11	114	24.08
A Drake (1)	1913	1,056	23.46	116	16.93
S Haigh (1)	1904	1,055	26.37	121	19.85
G H Hirst (14)	1896	1,122	28.20	104	21.64
	1897	1,535	35.69	101	23.22
	1901	1,950	42.39	183	16.38
	1903	1,844	47.28	128	14.94
	1904	2,501	54.36	132	21.09
	1905	2,266	53.95	110	19.94
	††1906	2,385	45.86	208	16.50
	1907	1,344	28.38	188	15.20
	1908	1,598	38.97	114	14.05
	1909	1,256	27.30	115	20.05
	1910	1,840	32.85	164	14.79
	1911	1,789	33.12	137	20.40
	1912	1,133	25.75	118	17.37
	1913	1,540	35.81	101	20.13
R Illingworth (6)	1957	1,213	28.20	106	18.40
	1959	1,726	46.64	110	21.46
	1960	1,006	25.79	109	17.55
	1961	1,153	24.53	128	17.90
	1962	1,612	34.29	117	19.45
	1964	1,301	37.17	122	17.45
F S Jackson (1)	1898	1,566	41.21	104	15.67
R Kilner (4)	1922	1,198	27.22	122	14.73
	1923	1,404	32.24	158	12.91
	1925	1,068	30.51	131	17.92
	1926	1,187	37.09	107	22.52
R Peel (1)	1896	1,206	30.15	128	17.50
W Rhodes (16)	1903	1,137	27.07	193	14.57
	1904	1,537	35.74	131	21.59
	1905	1,581	35.93	182	16.95
	1906	1,721	29.16	128	23.57
	1907	1,055	22.93	177	15.57
	1908	1,673	31.56	115	16.13
	1909	2,094	40.26	141	15.89
	1911	2,261	38.32	117	24.07
	1914	1,377	29.29	118	18.27
	1919	1,237	34.36	164	14.42
	1920	1,123	28.07	161	13.18
	1921	1,474	39.83	141	13.27
	1922	1,511	39.76	119	12.19
	1923	1.321	33.02	134	11.54
	1924	1,126	26.18	109	14.46
	1926	1,132	34.30	115	14.86
T F Smailes (1)	1938	1,002	25.05	113	20.84
E Wainwright (1)	1897	1,612	35.82	101	23.06

† First season in First-Class cricket.
†† The only instance in First-Class cricket of 2,000 runs and 200 wickets in a season.

H Sutcliffe (194) and M Leyland (45) hit 102 off six consecutive overs for Yorkshire v. Essex at Scarborough in 1932.

From 1898 to 1930 inclusive, Wilfred Rhodes took no less than 4,187 wickets, and scored 39,969 runs in First-Class cricket at home and abroad, a remarkable record. He also took 100 wickets and scored 1,000 in a season 16 times, and G H Hirst 14 times.

Of players with a qualification of not less than 50 wickets, Wilfred Rhodes was first in bowling in First-Class cricket in 1900, 1901, 1919, 1920, 1922, 1923 and 1926; Schofield Haigh in 1902, 1905, 1908 and 1909; Mr E R Wilson in 1921; G G Macaulay in 1924; H Verity in 1930, 1933, 1935, 1937 and 1939; W E Bowes in 1938; A Booth in 1946; R Appleyard in 1951 and 1955, and F S Trueman in 1952 and 1963.

The highest aggregate of runs made in one season in First-Class cricket by a Yorkshire player is 3,429 by L Hutton in 1949. This total has been exceeded three times, viz: D C S Compton 3,816 and W J Edrich 3,539 in 1947, and 3,518 by T Hayward in 1906. H Sutcliffe scored 3,336 in 1932.

Three players have taken all 10 Yorkshire wickets in an innings. G Wootton, playing for All England XI at Sheffield in 1865, took all 10 wickets for 54 runs. H Howell performed the feat for Warwickshire at Edgbaston in 1923 at a cost of 51 runs; and C V Grimmett, Australia, took all 10 wickets for 37 runs at Sheffield in 1930.

The match against Sussex at Dewsbury on June 7th and 8th, 1894, was brought to a summary conclusion by a remarkable bowling performance on the part of Edward Wainwright. In the second innings of Sussex, he took the last five wickets in seven balls, including the "hat trick". In the whole match he obtained 13 wickets for only 38 runs.

M D Moxon has the unique distinction of scoring a century in each of his first two First-Class matches in Yorkshire — 116 (2nd inns.) v. Essex at Leeds and 111 (1st inns.) v. Derbyshire at Sheffield, June 1981).

In the Yorkshire v. Norfolk match — played on the Hyde Park Ground, Sheffield, on July 14th to 18th, 1834 — 851 runs were scored in the four innings, of which no fewer than 128 were extras: 75 byes and 53 wides. At that time wides were not run out, so that every wide included in the above total represents a wide actually bowled. This particular achievement has never been surpassed in the annals of county cricket.

L Hutton reached his 1,000 runs in First-Class cricket in 1949 as early as June 9th.

W Barber reached his 1,000 runs in 1934 on June 13th. P Holmes reached his 1,000 in 1925 on June 16th, as also did H Sutcliffe in 1932. J T Brown reached his 1,000 in 1899 on June 22nd. In 1905, D Denton reached his 1,000 runs on June 26th; and in 1906 G H Hirst gained the same total on June 27th.

In 1912, D Denton scored over 1,000 runs during July, while M Leyland and H Sutcliffe both scored over 1,000 runs in August 1932.

L Hutton scored over 1,000 in June and over 1,000 runs in August in 1949.

H Verity took his 100th wicket in First-Class cricket as early as June 19th in 1936 and on June 27th in 1935. In 1900, W Rhodes obtained his 100th wicket on June 21st, and again on the same date in 1901, while G H Hirst obtained his 100th wicket on June 28th, 1906.

In 1930, Yorkshiremen (H Sutcliffe and H Verity) occupied the first places by English players in the batting and the bowling averages of First-Class cricket, which is a record without precedent. H Sutcliffe was also first in the batting averages in 1931 and 1932.

G Boycott was the first player to have achieved an average of over 100 in each of two English seasons. In 1971, he scored 2,503 runs for an average of 100.12, and in 1979 he scored 1,538 runs for an average of 102.53.

FIRST-CLASS MATCHES BEGUN AND FINISHED IN ONE DAY

Yorkshire v. Somerset, at Huddersfield, July 9th, 1894.

Yorkshire v. Hampshire, at Southampton, May 27th, 1898

Yorkshire v. Worcestershire, at Bradford, May 7th, 1900

For England

YORKSHIRE TEST CRICKETERS 1877-2024 (Correct to February 5, 2024)

Player	M.	I	NO	Runs	HS.	Av'ge.	100s	50s	Balls	R	W	Av'ge	Best	5wI	10wM	c/st
APPLEYARD, R ...1954-56	9	9	6	51	19*	17.00	0	0	1,596	554	31	17.87	5-51	1	0	4
ARMITAGE, T 1877	2	3	0	33	21	11.00	0	0	12	15	0	—	—	0	0	0
ATHEY, C W .J 1980-88	23	41	1	919	123	22.97	1	4	0	0	0	—	—	0	0	13
BAIRSTOW, D L ...1979-81	4	7	1	125	59	20.83	0	1	0	0	0	—	—	0	0	12/1
BAIRSTOW, J M ...2012-24	97	172	12	5,902	167*	36.88	12	26	0	0	0	—	—	0	0	241/14
BALLANCE, G S 2013/14-17	23	42	2	1,498	156	37.45	4	7	12	5	0	—	—	0	0	22
BARBER, W 1935	2	4	0	83	44	20.75	0	0	2	0	1	0.00	1- 0	0	0	1
BATES, W 1881-87	15	26	2	656	64	27.33	0	5	2,364	821	50	16.42	7-28	4	1	9
BESS D M 2018-20/21	14	19	5	319	57	22.78	0	1	2,502	1,223	36	33.97	5-30	2	0	3
BINKS, J G.........1964	2	4	0	91	55	22.75	0	1	0	0	0	—	—	0	0	8/0
BLAKEY, R J 1993	2	4	0	7	6	1.75	0	0	0	0	0	—	—	0	0	2/0
BOOTH, M W 1913-14	2	2	0	46	32	23.00	0	0	312	130	7	18.57	4-49	0	0	0
BOWES, W E 1932-46	15	11	5	28	10*	4.66	0	0	3,655	1,519	68	22.33	6-33	6	0	2
†BOYCOTT, G 1964-82	108	193	23	8,114	246*	47.72	22	42	944	382	7	54.57	3-47	0	0	33
BRENNAN, D V 1951	2	2	0	16	16	8.00	0	0	0	0	0	—	—	0	0	0/1
BRESNAN, T T ..2009-13/14	23	26	4	575	91	26.13	0	3	4,674	2,357	72	32.73	5-48	1	0	8
BROOK, H C 2022-23	12	20	1	1,181	186	62.15	4	7	84	37	1	37.00	1-25	0	0	9
BROWN, J T 1894-99	8	16	3	470	140	36.15	1	1	35	22	0	—	—	0	0	7
†CLOSE, D B 1949-76	22	37	2	887	70	25.34	0	4	1,212	532	18	29.55	4-35	0	0	24
COPE, G A 1977-78	3	3	0	40	22	13.33	0	0	864	277	8	34.62	3-102	0	0	1
COXON, A 1948	1	2	0	19	19	9.50	0	0	378	172	3	57.33	2-90	0	0	0
DAWSON, R K J ...2002-03	7	13	3	114	19*	11.40	0	0	1,116	677	11	61.54	4-134	0	0	3
DENTON, D 1905-10	11	22	1	424	104	20.19	1	1	0	0	0	—	—	0	0	8
DOLPHIN, A.........1921	1	2	0	1	1	0.50	0	0	0	0	0	—	—	0	0	1/0
EMMETT, T 1877-82	7	13	1	160	48	13.33	0	0	728	284	9	31.55	7-68	1	0	9
FISHER, M D 2021/22	1	1	1	0	0*	—	0	0	162	71	1	71.00	1-67	0	0	1

YORKSHIRE TEST CRICKETERS 1877-2023 *(Continued)*

Player	M.	I	NO	Runs	HS.	Av'ge.	100s	50s	Balls	R	W	Av'ge	Best	5wI	10wM	c/st
GIBB, PA 1938-46	8	13	0	581	120	44.69	2	3	0	0	0	—	—	0	0	3/1
GOUGH, D 1994-2003	58	86	18	855	65	12.57	0	2	11,821	6,503	229	28.39	6-42	9	0	13
GREENWOOD, A 1877	2	4	0	77	49	19.25	0	0	0	0	0	—	—	0	0	2
HAIGH, S 1899-1912	11	18	3	113	25	7.53	0	0	1,294	622	24	25.91	6-11	1	0	8
HAMILTON, G.M. 1999	1	2	0	0	0	0.00	0	0	90	63	0	—	—	0	0	0
HAMPSHIRE, J H . . .1969-75	8	16	1	403	107	26.86	1	2	0	0	0	—	—	0	0	9
†HAWKE, LORD . . .1896-99	5	8	1	55	30	7.85	0	0	0	0	0	—	—	0	0	3
HILL, A 1877	2	4	2	101	49	50.50	0	0	340	130	7	18.57	4-27	0	0	1
HIRST, G H 1897-1909	24	38	3	790	85	22.57	0	5	3,967	1,770	59	30.00	5-48	3	0	18
HOGGARD, M J . .2000-2008	67	92	27	473	38	7.27	0	0	13,909	7,564	248	30.50	7-61	7	1	24
HOLMES, P 1921-32	7	14	1	357	88	27.46	0	4	0	0	0	—	—	0	0	3
HUNTER, J 1884-85	5	7	2	93	39*	18.60	0	0	0	0	0	—	—	0	0	8/3
†HUTTON, L 1937-55	79	138	15	6,971	364	56.67	19	33	260	232	3	77.33	1-2	0	0	57
HUTTON, R A 1971	5	8	2	219	81	36.50	0	2	738	257	9	28.55	3-72	0	0	9
†ILLINGWORTH, R .1958-73	61	90	11	1,836	113	23.24	2	5	11,934	3,807	122	31.20	6-29	3	0	45
†JACKSON, Hon F S1893-1905	20	33	4	1,415	144*	48.79	5	6	1,587	799	24	33.29	5-52	1	0	10
JARVIS, P W 1988-93	9	15	2	132	29*	10.15	0	0	1,912	965	21	45.95	4-107	0	0	2
KILNER, R 1924-26	9	8	1	233	74	33.28	0	2	2,368	734	24	30.58	4-51	0	0	6
LEADBEATER, E . . .1951-52	2	2	0	40	38	20.00	0	0	289	218	2	109.00	1-38	0	0	3
LEYLAND, M 1928-38	41	65	5	2,764	187	46.06	9	10	1,103	585	6	97.50	3-91	0	0	13
LOWSON, F A 1951-55	7	13	0	245	68	18.84	0	2	0	0	0	—	—	0	0	5
LYTH A 2015	7	13	0	265	107	20.38	1	0	6	0	0	—	—	0	0	8
McGRATH, A 2003	4	5	0	201	81	40.20	0	2	102	56	4	14.00	3-16	0	0	3
MACAULAY, G G . .1923-33	8	10	4	112	76	18.66	0	1	1,701	662	24	27.58	5-64	1	0	5
MALAN, D J 2017-21/22	22	39	0	1,074	140	27.53	1	9	222	131	2	65.50	2-33	0	0	13
MILLIGAN, F W 1899	2	4	0	58	38	14.50	0	0	45	29	0	—	—	0	0	1

YORKSHIRE TEST CRICKETERS 1877-2023 *(Continued)*

Player	M.	I	NO	Runs	HS.	Av'ge.	100s	50s	Balls	R	W	Av'ge	Best	5wI	10wM	c/st
MITCHELL, A 1933-36	6	10	0	298	72	29.80	0	2	6	4	0	—	—	0	0	9
* MITCHELL, F 1899	2	4	0	88	41	22.00	0	0	0	0	0	—	—	0	0	2
MOXON, M D 1986-89	10	17	1	455	99	28.43	0	3	48	30	0	—	—	0	0	10
OLD, CM 1972-81	46	66	9	845	65	14.82	0	2	8,858	4,020	143	28.11	7-50	4	0	22
PADGETT, D E V 1960	2	4	0	51	31	12.75	0	0	12	8	0	—	—	0	0	0
PEATE, E 1881-86	9	14	8	70	13	11.66	0	0	2,096	682	31	22.00	6-85	2	0	2
PEEL, R 1884-96	20	33	4	427	83	14.72	0	3	5,216	1,715	101	16.98	7-31	5	1	17
PLUNKETT, L E 2005/6-2014	13	20	5	238	55*	15.86	0	1	2,659	1,536	41	37.46	5-64	1	0	3
RASHID, A U 2015/16-19	19	33	5	540	61	19.28	0	2	3,816	2,390	60	39.83	5-49	2	0	4
RHODES, W 1899-1930	58	98	21	2,325	179	30.19	2	11	8,231	3,425	127	26.96	8-68	6	1	60
† ROOT, J E 2012-24	137	251	20	11,468	254	49.64	30	60	5,283	2,852	65	43.87	5- 8	1	0	188
SHARPE, P J 1963-69	12	21	4	786	111	46.23	1	4	0	0	0	—	—	0	0	17
SHAHZAD, A 2010	1	1	0	5	5	5.00	0	0	102	63	4	15.75	3-45	0	0	2
SIDEBOTTOM, A 1985	1	1	0	2	2	2.00	0	0	112	65	1	65.00	1-65	0	0	0
SIDEBOTTOM, R J .2001-10	22	31	11	313	31	15.65	0	0	4,812	2,231	79	28.24	7-47	5	1	5
SILVERWOOD, CEW1997-2003	6	7	3	29	10	7.25	0	0	828	444	11	40.36	5-91	1	0	2
SMAILES, T F 1946	1	1	0	25	25	25.00	0	0	120	62	3	20.66	3-44	0	0	0
SMITHSON, G A 1948	2	3	0	70	35	23.33	0	0	0	0	0	—	—	0	0	0
†STANYFORTH, R T 1927-28	4	6	1	13	6*	2.60	0	0	0	0	0	—	—	0	0	7/2
STEVENSON, G B ..1980-81	2	2	1	28	27*	28.00	0	0	312	183	5	36.60	3-111	0	0	0
SUTCLIFFE, H 1924-35	54	84	9	4,555	194	60.73	16	23	0	0	0	—	—	0	0	23
TAYLOR, K 1959-64	3	5	0	57	24	11.40	0	0	12	6	0	—	—	0	0	1
TRUEMAN, F S 1952-65	67	85	14	981	39*	13.81	0	0	15,178	6,625	307	21.57	8-31	17	3	64
ULYETT, G 1877-90	25	39	0	949	149	24.33	1	7	2,627	1,020	50	20.40	7-36	1	0	19
†VAUGHAN M P .1999-2008	82	147	9	5,719	197	41.44	18	18	978	561	6	93.50	2-71	0	0	44
VERITY, H 1931-39	40	44	12	669	66*	20.90	0	3	11,173	3,510	144	24.37	8-43	5	2	30
WADDINGTON, A ..1920-21	2	4	0	16	7	4.00	0	0	276	119	1	119.00	1-35	0	0	1

Player	M.	I	NO	Runs	HS.	Av'ge.	100s	50s	Balls	R	W	Av'ge	Best	5wI	10wM	c/st
WAINWRIGHT, E 1893-98	5	9	0	132	49	14.66	0	0	127	73	0	—	—	0	0	2
WARDLE, J H 1948-57	28	41	8	653	66	19.78	0	2	6,597	2,080	102	20.39	7-36	5	1	12
WATSON, W 1951-59	23	37	3	879	116	25.85	2	3	0	0	0	—	—	0	0	8
WHITE, C 1994-2002	30	50	7	1,052	121	24.46	1	5	3,959	2,220	59	37.62	5-32	3	0	14
WILSON, C E M 1899	2	4	1	42	18	14.00	0	0	0	0	0	—	—	0	0	0
WILSON, D 1964-71	6	7	1	75	42	12.50	0	0	1,472	466	11	42.36	2-17	0	0	1
WILSON, E R 1921	1	2	0	10	5	5.00	0	0	123	36	3	12.00	2-28	0	0	0
WOOD, A 1938-39	4	5	1	80	53	20.00	0	1	0	0	0	—	—	0	0	10/1
†YARDLEY, N W D ..1938-50	20	34	2	812	99	25.37	0	4	1,662	707	21	33.66	3-67	0	0	14

†Captained England

*Also represented and captained South Africa

For South Africa

Player	M.	I	NO	Runs	HS.	Av'ge.	100s	50s	Balls	R	W	Av'ge	Best	5wI	10wM	c/st
†MITCHELL, F 1912	3	6	0	28	12	4.66	0	0	0	0	0	—	—	0	0	0

†Captained South Africa

Overseas Players

(Qualification: 20 first-class matches for Yorkshire)

For Australia

Player	M.	I	NO	Runs	HS.	Av'ge.	100s	50s	Balls	R	W	Av'ge	Best	5wI	10wM	c/st
BEVAN, M G 1994-98	18	30	3	785	91	29.07	0	6	1,285	703	29	24.24	6-82	1	1	8
GILLESPIE, J N 1996-2006	71	93	28	1,218	201*	18.73	1	2	14,234	6,770	259	26.13	7-37	8	0	27
JAQUES, P A 2005-2008	11	19	0	902	150	47.47	3	6	0	0	0	—	—	0	0	7
LEHMANN, D S 1999-2004	27	42	2	1,798	177	44.95	5	10	974	412	15	27.46	3-42	0	0	11

For South Africa

Player	M.	I	NO	Runs	HS.	Av'ge.	100s	50s	Balls	R	W	Av'ge	Best	5wI	10wM	c/st
OLIVIER, D 2016/17-2024	16	21	10	66	15*	6.00	0	0	1,192	1,432	59	24.27	6-37	3	1	3
RUDOLPH, J A 2003-12/13	48	83	9	2,622	222*	35.43	6	11	664	432	4	108.00	1- 1	0	0	29

YORKSHIRE TEST CRICKETERS 1877-2023 *(Continued)*

Player	M.	I	NO	Runs	HS.	Av'ge.	100s	50s	Balls	R	W	Av'ge	Best	5wI	10wM	c/st
Overseas Players (Continued)																
For West Indies																
RICHARDSON, R B 1983-84/95	86	146	12	5,949	194	44.39	16	27	66	18	0	—	—	0	0	90
For Zimbabwe																
BALLANCE, G S 2022/23	1	2	1	155	137*	155.00	1	0	0	0	0	—	—	0	0	0

G S Ballance is only the second player to score a Test century for two different countries — the other being K C Wessels for Australia and South Africa

CENTURIES FOR ENGLAND

C W J ATHEY (1)

123 v Pakistan at Lord's, 1987

J M BAIRSTOW (12)

150* v. South Africa at Cape Town, 2016

167* v. Sri Lanka at Lord's, 2016

101 v. New Zealand at Christchurch, 2018

113 v. Australia at Sydney, 2022

136 v. New Zealand at Nottingham, 2022

106 v. India at Birmingham, 2022, 1st innings

140 v. Sri Lanka at Leeds, 2016

119 v. Australia at Perth, 2017

110 v. Sri Lanka at Colombo (SSC), 2018

140 v. West Indies at North Soun, Antigua, 2022

162 v. New Zealand at Leeds, 2022

114* v. India at Birmingham, 2022, 2nd innings

G S BALLANCE (4)

104* v. Sri Lanka at Lord's, 2014

256 v. India at Southampton, 2014

110 v. India at Lord's, 2014

122 v. West Indies at North Sound, 2015

G BOYCOTT (22)

113 v. Australia at The Oval, 1964

117 v. South Africa at Port Elizabeth, 1965

246* v. India at Leeds, 1967

116 v. West Indies at Georgetown, 1968

128 v. West Indies at Manchester, 1969

106 v. West Indies at Lord's, 1969

142* v. Australia at Sydney, 1971

119* v. Australia at Adelaide, 1971

121* v. Pakistan at Lord's, 1971

112 v. Pakistan at Leeds, 1971

115 v. New Zealand at Leeds, 1973

112 v West Indies at Port-of-Spain, 1974

107 v. Australia at Nottingham, 1977

191 v. Australia at Leeds, 1977

100* v. Pakistan at Hyderabad, 1978

131 v. New Zealand at Nottingham, 1978

155 v. India at Birmingham, 1979

125 v. India at The Oval, 1979

128* v. Australia at Lord's, 1980

104* v. West Indies at St John's, 1981

137 v. Australia at The Oval, 1981

105 v. India at Delhi, 1981

H C BROOK (4)

153 v. Pakistan at Rawalpindi, 2022

108 v. Pakistan at Multan, 2022

111 v. Pakistan at Karachi, 2022

186 v. New Zealand at Wellington, 2023

J T BROWN (1)

140 v. Australia at Melbourne, 1895

D DENTON (1)

104 v. South Africa at Old Wanderers, Johannesburg, 1910

P A GIBB (2)

106 v. South Africa at Old Wanderers, Johannesburg, 1938

120 v. South Africa at Kingsmead, Durban, 1939

J H HAMPSHIRE (1)

107 v. West Indies at Lord's, 1969

L HUTTON (19)

100 v. New Zealand at Manchester, 1937

100 v. Australia at Nottingham, 1938

364 v. Australia at The Oval, 1938

196 v. West Indies at Lord's, 1939

165* v. West Indies at The Oval, 1939

122* v. Australia at Sydney, 1947

100 v. South Africa at Leeds, 1947

158 v. South Africa at Ellis Park, J'b'rg, 1948

123 v. South Africa at Ellis Park, J'b'rg, 1949

101 v. New Zealand at Leeds, 1949

206 v. New Zealand at The Oval, 1949

202* v. West Indies at The Oval, 1950

156* v. Australia at Adeladide, 1951

100 v. South Africa at Leeds, 1951

150 v. India at Lord's, 1952

104 v. India at Manchester, 1952

145 v. Australia at Lord's, 1953

169 v. West Indies at Georgetown, 1954

205 v. West Indies at Kingston, 1954

CENTURIES FOR ENGLAND *(Continued)*

R ILLINGWORTH (2)

113 v. West Indies at Lord's, 1969

107 v. India at Manchester, 1971

Hon. F S JACKSON (5)

103 v. Australia at The Oval, 1893

118 v. Australia at The Oval, 1899

128 v. Australia at Manchester, 1902

144* v. Australia at Leeds, 1905

113   v. Australia at Manchester, 1905

M LEYLAND (9)

137 v. Australia at Melbourne, 1929

102 v. South Africa at Lord's, 1929

109 v. Australia at Lord's, 1934

153 v. Australia at Manchester, 1934

110 v. Australia at The Oval, 1934

161   v. South Africa at The Oval, 1935

126   v. Australia at Woolloongabba, Brisbane, 1936

111* v. Australia at Melbourne, 1937

187   v. Australia at The Oval, 1938

A LYTH (1)

107 v. New Zealand at Leeds 2015

W RHODES (2)

179 v. Australia at Melbourne, 1912

152 v. South Africa at Old Wanderers, Johannesburg, 1913

J E ROOT (30)

104 v. New Zealand at Leeds, 2013

200* v. Sri Lanka at Lord's, 2014

149* v. India at The Oval, 2014

134 v. Australia at Cardiff 2015

110 v. South Africa at Johannesburg, 2016

124 v. India at Rajkot, 2016

136 v. West Indies at Birmingham, 2017

124 v. Sri Lanka at Pallekele, 2018

226 v, New Zealand at Hamilton, 2019

186 v. Sri Lanka at Galle, 2021

109 v. India at Nottingham, 2021

121 v. India at Leeds, 2021

180   v. Australia at Lord's, 2013

154* v, India at Nottingham, 2014

182* v. West Indies at St George's, 2015

130   v. Australia at Nottingham, 2015

254   v. Pakistan at Manchester, 2016

190   v. South Africa at Lord's, 2017

125   v. India at The Oval, 2018

122   v. West Indies at Gros Islet, 2019

228   v. Sri Lanka at Galle, 2021

218   v. India at Chennai, 2021

180* v. India at Lord's, 2021

109   v. West Indies at North Sound, Antigua, 2022

153 v. West Indies at Bridgetown, 2022

176 v. New Zealand at Nottingham, 2022

153* v. New Zealand at Wellington, 2023

115* v. New Zealand at Lord's, 2022

142* v, India at Birmingham, 2022

118* v. Australia at Birmingham, 2023

P J SHARPE (1)

111 v. New Zealand at Nottingham, 1969

H SUTCLIFFE (16)

122 v. South Africa at Lord's, 1924

115 v. Australia at Sydney, 1924

176 v. Australia at Melbourne, 1925 (1st Inns)

127 v. Australia at Melbourne, 1925 (2nd Inns)

143 v. Australia at Melbourne, 1925

161 v. Australia at The Oval, 1926

102 v. South Africa at Old Wanderers, Jbg.1927

135 v. Australia at Melbourne, 1929

114 v. South Africa at Birmingham, 1929

100 v. South Africa at Lord's, 1929

104 v. South Africa at The Oval, 1929 (1st inns)

109* v. South Africa at The Oval, 1929 (2nd inns)

161 v. Australia at The Oval, 1930

117 v. New Zealand at The Oval, 1931

109* v. New Zealand at Manchester, 1931

194 v. Australia at Sydney, 1932

CENTURIES FOR ENGLAND *(Continued)*

G ULYETT (1)

149 v. Australia at Melbourne, 1882

M P VAUGHAN (18)

120 v. Pakistan at Manchester, 2001
115 v. Sri Lanka at Lord's, 2002
100 v. India at Lord's, 2002
197 v. India at Nottingham, 2002
195 v. India at The Oval, 2002
177 v. Australia at Adelaide, 2002
145 v. Australia at Melbourne, 2002
183 v. Australia at Sydney, 2003
156 v. South Africa at Birmingham, 2003
105 v. Sri Lanka at Kandy, 2003
140 v. West Indies at Antigua, 2004
103 v. West Indies at Lord's (1st inns) 2004
101* v. West Indies at Lord's (2nd inns) 2004
120 v. Bangladesh at Lord's, 2005
166 v. Australia at Manchester, 2005
103 v. West Indies at Leeds, 2007
124 v. India at Nottingham, 2007
106 v. New Zealand at Lord's, 2008

W WATSON (2)

109 v. Australia at Lord's, 1953
116 v. West Indies at Kingston, 1954

C WHITE (1)

121 v. India at Ahmedabad, 2001

Summary of the Centuries

versus	Total	In England	Away
Australia	45	24	21
Bangladesh	1	1	0
India	25	21	4
New Zealand	19	15	4
Pakistan	6	5	1
Pakistan	9	5	4
South Africa	21	11	10
Sri Lanka	10	5	5
West Indies	24	11	13
Totals	154	93	61

For Australia

J N GILLESPIE (1)

201* v. Bangladesh at Chittagong, 2006

P A JAQUES (3)

100 v. Sri Lanka at Brisbane, 2007
150 v. Sri Lanka at Hobart, 2007
108 v. West Indies at Bridgetown, 2008

D S LEHMANN (5)

160 v. West Indies at Port of Spain, 2003
110 v. Bangladesh at Darwin, 2003
177 v. Bangladesh at Cairns, 2003
129 v. Sri Lanka at Galle, 2004
153 v. Sri Lanka at Columbo, 2004

For South Africa

J A RUDOLPH (6)

222* v. Bangladesh at Chittagong, 2003
101 v West Indies at Cape Town, 2004
154* v. New Zealand at Auckland, 2004
102 v. Sri Lanka at Galle, 2004
102* v Australia at Perth, 2005
105* v. New Zealand at Dunedin, 2012

10 WICKETS IN A MATCH FOR ENGLAND

W BATES (1)
14 for 102 (7 for 28 and 7 for 74) v. Australia at Melbourne, 1882

M J HOGGARD (1)
12 for 205 (5 for 144 and 7 for 61) v. South Africa at Johannesburg, 2005

R PEEL (1)
11 for 68 (7 for 31 and 4 for 37) v. Australia at Mancester, 1888

Note: The scorebook for the Australia v. England Test match at Sydney in February 1888
shows that the final wicket to fall was taken by W Attewell, and not by Peel
Peel therefore took 9, and not 10 wickets, in the match
His career totals have been amended to take account of this alteration

W RHODES (1)
15 for 124 (7 for 56 and 8 for 68) v. Australia at Melbourne, 1904

R J SIDEBOTTOM (1)
10 for 139 (4 for 90 and 6 for 49) v. New Zealand at Hamilton, 2008

F S TRUEMAN (3)
11 for 88 (5 for 58 and 6 for 30) v. Australia at Leeds, 1961
11 for 152 (6 for 100 and 5 for 52) v. West Indies at Lord's, 1963*
12 for 119 (5 for 75 and 7 for 44) v. West Indies at Birmingham, 1963*
consecutive Tests

H VERITY (2)
11 for 153 (7 for 49 and 4 for 104) v. India at Chepauk, Madras, 1934
15 for 104 (7 for 61 and 8 for 43) v. Australia at Lord's, 1934

J H WARDLE (1)
12 for 89 (5 for 53 and 7 for 36) v. South Africa at Cape Town, 1957

Summary of Ten Wickets in a Match

versus	Total	In England	Away
Australia	5	3	2
India	1	—	1
New Zealand	1	—	1
Pakistan	—	—	—
South Africa	2	—	2
Sri Lanka	—	—	—
West Indies	2	2	—
Totals	11	5	6

For Australia

M G BEVAN (1)
10 for 113 (4 for 31and 6 for 82) v. West Indies at Adelaide, 1997

5 WICKETS IN AN INNINGS FOR ENGLAND

R APPLEYARD (1)
5 for 51 v. Pakistan at Nottingham, 1954

W BATES (4)
7 for 28 v. Australia at Melbourne, 1882   5 for 31 v. Australia at Adelaide, 1884
7 for 74 v. Australia at Melbourne, 1882   5 for 24 v. Australia at Sydney, 1885

D M BESS (2)
5 for 51 v. South Africa at Port Elizabeth, 2020   5 for 30 v. Sri Lanka at Galle 2021

5 WICKETS IN AN INNINGS FOR ENGLAND *(Continued)*

W E BOWES (6)

6-34	v. New Zealand	at Auckland	1933	5-100	v. South Africa	at Manchester 1935
6-142	v. Australia	at Leeds	1934*	5-49	v. Australia	at The Oval 1938
5-55	v. Australia	at The Oval	1934*	6-33	v. West Indies	at Manchester 1939

consecutive Test matches

T T BRESNAN (1)

5-48   v. India   at Nottingham   2011

T EMMETT (1)

7-68   v. Australia   at Melbourne   1879

D GOUGH (9)

6-49	v. Australia	at Sydney	1995	5-70	v. South Africa	at Johannesburg 1999
5-40	v. New Zealand	at Wellington	1997	5-109	v. West Indies	at Birmingham 2000
5-149	v. Australia	at Leeds	1997	5-61	v. Pakistan	at Lord's 2001
6-42	v. South Africa	at Leeds	1998	5-103	v. Australia	at Leeds 2001
5-96	v. Australia	at Melbourne	1998			

S HAIGH (1)

6-11   v. South Africa   at Cape Town   1909

G H HIRST (3)

5-77	v. Australia	at The Oval 1902	5-58	v. Australia	at Birmingham 1909
5-48	v. Australia	at Melbourne 1904			

M J HOGGARD (7)

7-63	v. New Zealand	at Christchurch 2002	5-73	v. Bangladesh	at Chester-le-Street	2005
5-92	v. Sri Lanka	at Birmingham 2002				
5-144	v. South Africa	at Johannesburg 2005*	6-57	v. India	at Nagpur	2006
7-61	v. South Africa	at Johannesburg 2005*	7-109	v. Australia	at Adelaide	2006

Consecutive Test innings

R ILLINGWORTH (3)

6-29	v. India	at Lord's	1967	5-70	v. India	at The Oval 1971
6-87	v. Australia	at Leeds	1968			

Hon F S JACKSON (1)

5-52   v. Australia   at Nottingham   1905

G G MACAULAY (1)

5-64   v. South Africa   at Cape Town   1923

C M OLD (4)

5-113	v. New Zealand	at Lord's	1973	6-54	v. New Zealand	at Wellington 1978
5-21	v. India	at Lord's	1974	7-50	v. Pakistan	at Birmingham 1978

E PEATE (2)

5-43	v. Australia	at Sydney 1882	6-85	v. Australia	at Lord's 1884

R PEEL (5)

5-51	v. Australia	at Adelaide	1884	6-67	v. Australia	at Sydney 1894
5-18	v. Australia	at Sydney	1888	6-23	v. Australia	at The Oval 1896
7-31	v. Australia	at Manchester	1888			

L E PLUNKETT (1)

5-64   v. Sri Lanka   at Leeds   2014

A U RASHID (2)

5-64 v. Pakistan   at Abu Dhabi   2015   5-49   v. Sri Lanka   at Colombo (SSC)   2018

5 WICKETS IN AN INNINGS FOR ENGLAND *(Continued)*

W RHODES (6)

7-17	v. Australia	at Birmingham	1902	7-56	v. Australia	at Melbourne	1904*
5-63	v. Australia	at Sheffield	1902	8-68	v. Australia	at Melbourne	1904*
5-94	v. Australia	at Sydney	1903*	5-83	v. Australia	at Manchester	1909

**consecutive Test innings*

J E ROOT (1)

5- 8   v. India   at Ahmedabad   2021

C E W SILVERWOOD (1)

5-91   v. South Africa   at Cape Town   2000

R J SIDEBOTTOM (5)

5-88	v. West Indies	at Chester-le-Street		5-105	v. New Zealand	at Wellington	2008
			2007	7-47	v. New Zealand	at Napier	2008
6-49	v. New Zealand	at Hamilton	2008	6-47	v. New Zealand	at Nottingham	2008

F S TRUEMAN (17)

8-31	v. India	at Manchester	1952	6-31	v. Pakistan	at Lord's	1962
5-48	v. India	at The Oval	1952	5-62	v. Australia	at Melbourne	1963
5-90	v. Australia	at Lord's	1956	7-75	v. New Zealand	at Christchurch	1963
5-63	v. West Indies	at Nottingham	1957	6-100	v. West Indies	at Lord's	1963*
5-31	v. New Zealand	at Birmingham	1958	5-52	v. West Indies	at Lord's	1963*
5-35	v. West Indies	at Port-of-Spain	1960	5-75	v. West Indies	at Birmingham	1963*
5-27	v. South Africa	at Nottingham	1960	7-44	v. West Indies	at Birmingham	1963*
5-58	v. Australia	at Leeds	1961*	5-48	v. Australia	at Lord's	1964
6-30	v. Australia	at Leeds	1961*				

G ULYETT (1)

7-36   v. Australia   at Lord's   1884

H VERITY (5)

5-33	v. Australia	at Sydney	1933	8-43	v. Australia	at Lord's	1934*
7-49	v. India	at Chepauk, Madras	1934	5-70	v. South Africa	at Cape Town	1939
7-61	v. Australia	at Lord's	1934*				

J H WARDLE (5)

7-56	v. Pakistan	at The Oval	1954	7-36	v. South Africa	at Cape Town	1957*
5-79	v. Australia	at Sydney	1955	5-61	v. South Africa	at Kingsmead Durban	1957*
5-53	v. South Africa	at Cape Town	1957*				

C WHITE (3)

5-57	v. West Indies	at Leeds	2000	5-32	v. West Indies	at The Oval	2000
		5-127	v. Australia	at Perth	2002		

**consecutive Test innings*

5 WICKETS IN AN INNINGS *(Continued)*

Summary of Five Wickets in an Innings

versus	Total	In England	Away
Australia	42	22	20
Bangladesh	1	1	0
India	9	6	3
New Zealand	11	3	8
Pakistan	6	5	1
South Africa	14	3	11
Sri Lanka	4	2	2
West Indies	11	10	1
Totals	98	52	46

For Australia

M G BEVAN (1)

6-82	v. West Indies	at Adelaide	1997

J N GILLESPIE (8)

5-54	v. South Africa	at Port Elizabeth	1997
7-37	v. England	at Leeds	1997
5-88	v. England	at Perth	1998
5-89	v. West Indies	at Adelaide	2000
6-40	v. West Indies	at Melbourne	2000
5-53	v. England	at Lord's	2001
5-39	v. West Indies	at Georgetown	2003
5-56	v. India	at Nagpur	2004

For South Africa

D OLIVIER (3)

6-37	v. Pakistan (1st innings)	at Centurion	2018
5-59	v. Pakistan (2nd innings)	at Centurion	2018
5-51	v. Pakistan	at Johannesburg	2019

HAT-TRICKS

W Bates	v. Australia	at Melbourne	1882
D Gough	v. Australia	at Sydney	1998
M J Hoggard	v. West Indies	at Bridgetown	2004
R J Sidebottom	v. New Zealand	at Hamilton	2008

FOUR WICKETS IN FIVE BALLS

C M Old	v. Pakistan	at Birmingham	1978

THREE WICKETS IN FOUR BALLS

R Appleyard	v. New Zealand	at Auckland	1955
D Gough	v. Pakistan	at Lord's	2001

YORKSHIRE PLAYERS WHO PLAYED ALL THEIR TEST CRICKET
AFTER LEAVING YORKSHIRE

For England

Player	M.	I	NO	Runs	HS.	Av'ge.	100s	50s	Balls	R	W	Av'ge	Best	5wI	10wM	c/st
BALDERSTONE, J C ...1976	2	4	0	39	35	9.75	—	—	96	80	1	80.00	1:80	—	—	1
BATTY G J 2003/4-16/17	9	12	2	149	38	14.90	—	—	1,714	914	15	60.93	3-55	—	—	3
BIRKENSHAW, J ...1973-74	5	7	0	148	64	21.14	—	1	1,017	469	13	36.07	5:57	1	—	3
BOLUS, J B1963-64 7	12	0	496	88	41.33	—	4	18	16	0	—	—	—	—	—	2
LEES, A Z 2021/22-2022	10	19	0	453	67	23.84	0	2	—	—	—	—	—	—	—	6
†PARKIN, C H 1920-24	10	16	3	160	36	12.30	—	—	2,095	1,128	32	35.25	5:38	2	—	3
RHODES, S J 1994-95	11	17	5	294	65*	24.50	—	1	—	—	—	—	—	—	—	46/3
†SUGG, F H 1888	2	2	0	55	31	27.50	—	—	—	—	—	—	—	—	—	0
WARD, A 1893-95	7	13	0	487	117	37.46	1	3	—	—	—	—	—	—	—	1
WOOD, B 1972-78	12	21	0	454	90	21.61	—	2	98	50	0	—	—	—	—	6

For South Africa

Player	M.	I	NO	Runs	HS.	Av'ge.	100s	50s	Balls	R	W	Av'ge	Best	5wI	10wM	c/st
THORNTON, P G 1902	1	1	1	1	1*	—	—	—	24	20	1	20.00	1:20	—	—	1

†Born outside Yorkshire

CENTURIES
FOR ENGLAND

A WARD (1)
117 v. Australia at Sydney, 1894

5 WICKETS IN AN INNINGS
FOR ENGLAND

J BIRKENSHAW (1)
5 : 57 v. Pakistan at Karachi, 1973

C H PARKIN (2)
5 : 60 v. Australia at Adelaide, 1921
5 : 38 v. Australia at Manchester, 1921

YORKSHIRE'S TEST CRICKET RECORDS

R APPLEYARD

Auckland 1954-55: took 3 wickets in 4 balls as New Zealand were dismissed for the lowest total in Test history (26).

C W J ATHEY

Perth 1986-87: shared an opening stand of 223 with B C Broad – England's highest for any wicket at the WACA Ground.

J M BAIRSTOW

Cape Town, January 2016: scored his maiden Test Century (150*). His sixth- wicket partnership of 399 with B A Stokes (258) was the highest in Test cricket and the highest First Class partnership for any wicket at Newlands. There was only one higher partnership for England. This was 411 by P B H May and M C Cowdrey for the fourth wicket against the West Indies at Birmingham in 1957.

Chittagong, October 2016: scored 52 in the first innings, which passed his 1,000 Test runs in a calendar year. He became only the third Yorkshire player to do this after M P Vaughan with 1,481 in 2002 and J E Root 1,385 in 2015. He was only the second Test wicket-keeper to pass this mark. His first scoring shot in the second inning broke a 16-year record set by Zimbabwe's A Flower (1,045 in 2000) to give him the highest total of runs scored in a calendar year by a Test wicket-keeper. His final tally for 2016 was 1,470.

Mohali, November 2016: his third catch of India's first innings (U T Yadav) was his 68th dismissal of the year to pass the previous best in a calendar year (67) by I A Healy (Australia) in 1991 and M V Boucher (South Africa) in 1998. Bairstow's final tally for the calendar year was 70 (66 caught and 4 stumped).

Trent Bridge, June 2022: When England were set 299 to win in the Second Test against New Zealand, Bairstow went to his hundred off his 77th ball, one ball more than G Jessop in 1902 against Australia. Bairstow's innings ended on 136, coming off 92 balls with 14 fours and seven sixes. In the rescheduled fifth Test against India at Edgbaston Bairstow, with 106 and 114*, saw England win by seven wickets. He added 269* for the fourth wicket with Root (142*) in England's second innings. Bairstow, despite having to miss the last four Tests of the year through injury, ended 2022 with 1,061 runs, the fourth highest of the year.

W BATES

Melbourne 1882-83 (Second Test): achieved the first hat-trick for England when he dismissed P S McDonnell, G Giffen and G J Bonnor in Australia's first innings. Later in the match, he became the first player to score a fifty (55) and take 10 or more wickets (14 for 102) in the same Test.

W E BOWES

Melbourne 1932-33: enjoyed the unique satisfaction of bowling D G Bradman first ball in a Test match (his first ball to him in Test cricket).

G BOYCOTT

Leeds 1967: scored 246 not out off 555 balls in 573 minutes to establish the record England score against India. His first 100 took 341 minutes (316 balls) and he was excluded from the next Test as a disciplinary measure; shared in hundred partnerships for three successive wickets.

Adelaide 1970-71: with J H Edrich, became the third opening pair to share hundred partnerships in both innings of a Test against Australia.

Port-of-Spain 1973-74: first to score 99 and a hundred in the same Test.

Nottingham 1977: with A P E Knott, equalled England v. Australia sixth-wicket partnership record of 215 – the only England v. Australia stand to be equalled or broken since 1938. Batted on each day of the five-day Test (second after M L Jaisimha to achieve this feat).

Leeds 1977: first to score his 100th First Class hundred in a Test; became the fourth England player to be on the field for an entire Test.

Perth: 1978-79: eighth to score 2,000 runs for England against Australia.

Birmingham 1979: emulated K F Barrington by scoring hundreds on each of England's six current home grounds.

Perth: 1979-80: fourth to carry his bat through a completed England innings (third v. Australia) and the first to do so without scoring 100; first to score 99 not out in a Test.

Lord's 1981: 100th Test for England – second after M C Cowdrey (1968).

The Oval, 1981: second after Hon F S Jackson to score five hundreds v. Australia in England.

Gained three Test records from M C Cowdrey: exceeded England aggregate of 7,624 runs in 11 fewer Tests (Manchester 1981); 61st fifty – world record (The Oval 1981); 189th innings – world record (Bangalore 1981-82).

Delhi, 4.23p.m. on 23 December 1981: passed G St.A Sobers's world Test record of 8,032 runs, having played 30 more innings and batted over 451 hours (cf. 15 complete five-day Tests); his 22nd hundred equalled the England record.

H C BROOK

Rawalpindi, Pakistan, December 2022: Having made his Test debut against South Africa at The Oval, Brook scored his maiden Test century in his second Test, the opening Test in Pakistan. His century, coming off 80 balls, left him in third place for the fastest England century. He was England's fourth centurion on the opening day which ended on 506-4. This was the first time 500 had been scored on the opening day of a Test as was the four centuries. Brook was out for 153. He scored 108 in the second Test and 111 in the third.

J T BROWN

Melbourne 1894-95: his 28-minute fifty remains the fastest in Test cricket, and his 95-minute hundred was a record until 1897-98; his third-wicket stand of 210 with A Ward set a Test record for any wicket.

D B CLOSE

Manchester 1949: at 18 years 149 days he became – and remains – the youngest to represent England.

Melbourne 1950-51: became the youngest (19 years 301 days) to represent England against Australia.

YORKSHIRE'S TEST CRICKET RECORDS *(Continued)*

T EMMETT

Melbourne 1878-79: first England bowler to take seven wickets in a Test innings.

P A GIBB

Johannesburg 1938-39: enjoyed a record England debut, scoring 93 and 106 as well as sharing second-wicket stands of 184 and 168 with E Paynter.

Durban 1938-39: shared record England v. South Africa second-wicket stand of 280 with W J Edrich, his 120 in 451 minutes including only two boundaries.

D GOUGH

Sydney 1998-99: achieved the 23rd hat-trick in Test cricket (ninth for England and first for England v. Australia since 1899).

Lord's 2001: took 3 wickets in 4 balls v. Pakistan.

S HAIGH

Cape Town 1898-99: bowled unchanged through the second innings with A E Trott, taking 6 for 11 as South Africa were dismissed for 35 in the space of 114 balls.

J H HAMPSHIRE

Lord's 1969: became the first England player to score 100 at Lord's on his debut in Tests.

A HILL

Melbourne 1876-77: took the first wicket to fall in Test cricket when he bowled N Thompson, and held the first catch when he dismissed T P Horan.

G H HIRST

The Oval: 1902: helped to score the last 15 runs in a match-winning tenth-wicket partnership with W Rhodes.

Birmingham 1909: shared all 20 Australian wickets with fellow left-arm spinner C Blythe (11 for 102).

M J HOGGARD

Bridgetown 2004: became the third Yorkshire player to take a hat-trick in Test cricket (see W Bates and D Gough). It was the 10th hat-trick for England and the third for England versus West Indies.

L HUTTON

Nottingham 1938: scored 100 in his first Test against Australia.

The Oval 1938: his score (364) and batting time (13 hours 17 minutes – the longest innings in English First-Class cricket) remain England records, and were world Test records until 1958. It remains the highest Test score at The Oval. His stand of 382 with M Leyland is the England second-wicket record in all Tests and the highest for any wicket against Australia. He also shared a record England v. Australia sixth-wicket stand of 216 with J Hardstaff Jr. – the first instance of a batsman sharing in two stands of 200 in the same Test innings. 770 runs were scored during his innings (Test record) which was England's 100th century against Australia, and contained 35 fours. England's total of 903 for 7 declared remains the Ashes Test record.

Lord's 1939: added 248 for the fourth wicket with D C S Compton in 140 minutes.

The Oval 1939: shared (then) world-record third-wicket stand of 264 with W R Hammond, which remains the record for England v. West Indies. Hutton's last eight Tests had brought him 1,109 runs.

The Oval 1948: last out in the first innings, he was on the field for all but the final 57 minutes of the match.

Johannesburg 1948-49: shared (then) world-record first-wicket stand of 359 in 310 minutes with C Washbrook on the opening day of Test cricket at Ellis Park; it remains England's highest opening stand in all Tests.

The Oval 1950: scored England's first 200 in a home Test v. West Indies, and remains alone in carrying his bat for England against them; his 202 not out (in 470 minutes) is the highest score by an England batsman achieving this feat.

Adelaide 1950-51: only England batsman to carry his bat throughout a complete Test innings twice, and second after R Abel (1891-92) to do so for any country against Australia.

Manchester 1951: scored 98 not out, just failing to become the first to score his 100th First Class hundred in a Test match.

The Oval 1951: became the only batsman to be out 'obstructing the field' in Test cricket.

1952: first professional to be appointed captain of England in the 20th Century.

The Oval 1953: first captain to win a rubber after losing the toss in all five Tests.

Kingston 1953-54: scored the first 200 by an England captain in a Test overseas.

R ILLINGWORTH

Manchester 1971: shared record England v. India eighth-wicket stand of 168 with P Lever.

Hon. F S JACKSON

The Oval 1893: his 100 took 135 minutes, and was the first in a Test in England to be completed with a hit over the boundary (then worth only four runs).

The Oval 1899: his stand of 185 with T W Hayward was then England's highest for any wicket in England, and the record opening partnership by either side in England v. Australia Tests.

Nottingham 1905: dismissed M A Noble, C Hill and J Darling in one over (W01W0W).

Leeds 1905: batted 268 minutes for 144 not out – the first hundred in a Headingley Test.

Manchester 1905: first to score five Test hundreds in England.

The Oval 1905: first captain to win every toss in a five-match rubber.

YORKSHIRE'S TEST CRICKET RECORDS *(Continued)*

M LEYLAND

Melbourne 1928-29: scored 137 in his first innings against Australia.

1934: first to score three hundreds in a rubber against Australia in England.

Brisbane 1936-37: scored England's only 100 at 'The Gabba' before 1974-75.

The Oval 1938: contributed 187 in 381 minutes to the record Test total of 903 for 7 declared, sharing in England's highest stand against Australia (all wickets) and record second-wicket stand in all Tests: 382 with L Hutton. First to score hundreds in his first and last innings against Australia.

G G MACAULAY

Cape Town 1922-23: fourth bowler (third for England) to take a wicket (G A L Hearne) with his first ball in Test cricket. Made the winning hit in the fourth of only six Tests to be decided by a one-wicket margin.

Leeds 1926: shared a match-saving ninth-wicket stand of 108 with G Geary.

C M OLD

Birmingham 1978: took 4 wickets in 5 balls in his 19th over (0WW no-ball WW1) to emulate the feat of M J C Allom.

R PEEL

Took his 50th wicket in his ninth Test and his 100th in his 20th Test – all against Australia.

W RHODES

Birmingham 1902: his first-innings analysis of 7 for 17 remains the record for all Tests at Edgbaston.

The Oval 1902: helped to score the last 15 runs in a match-winning tenth-wicket partnership with G H Hirst.

Sydney 1903-04: shared record England v. Australia tenth-wicket stand of 130 in 66 minutes with R E Foster.

Melbourne 1903-04: first to take 15 wickets in England v. Australia Tests; his match analysis of 15 for 124 remains the record for all Tests at Melbourne.

Melbourne 1911-12: shared record England v. Australia first-wicket stand of 323 in 268 minutes with J B Hobbs.

Johannesburg 1913-14: took his 100th wicket and completed the first 'double' for England (in 44

Sydney 1920-21: first to score 2,000 runs and take 100 wickets in Test cricket.

Adelaide 1920-21: third bowler to take 100 wickets against Australia.

The Oval 1926: set (then) record of 109 wickets against Australia.

Kingston 1929-30: ended the world's longest Test career (30 years 315 days) as the oldest Test cricketer (52 years 165 days).

J E ROOT

Chittagong, October 2016: with his score (40) in England's first innings he passed 1,000 runs in a calendar year. He also did this in 2015 (1,385) and became the first Yorkshire player to do this twice. His final tally (1,477) in 2016 left him four short of M P Vaughan's total in 2002

Visakhapatnam, November 2016: Played his 50th Test match, which was also his 100th first-class match

Lord's, July 2017 v. West Indies: His first innings (190) was the highest by an England captain in his first innings in this role.

Galle, January 2021 v. Sri Lanka. In the second Test match Root's first-innings score of 186 took him passed G Boycott's England Test runs total of 8,114, and by the end of that match Root's total runs for England stood at 8,249, leaving him in fourth place behind A N Cook (12,472), G A Gooch (8,900) and A J Stewart (8,463).

Chennai, February 2021 First Test Match v. India. Root with scores of 218 and 40 became the first player to score a double-hundred in their 100th Test Match. Eight others including two England players, M C Cowdrey (1968) and A J Stewart (2000) passed the century mark in their 100th Test Match. Root is now England's third all-time run-scorer.

Root scored a total of 1,708 Test runs in the calendar year 2021 to become the highest England player on this list. M P Vaughan with 1,481 runs in 2002 was the previous best. Only two other players have scored more runs in a calendar year, Mohammad Yousuf (Pakistan) with 1,788 runs and I V A Richards (West Indies) with 1,710.

The Ashes Test Match at Sydney in January 2022 saw Root become the player to captain England most times (60) passing A N Cook (59).

At the end of the fifth Ashes Test at Hobart he had scored 5,006 runs as captain, the first England captain to do this.

2022: After the three-Test series in West Indies Root relinquished the England captaincy. He had captained England 64 times, winning 27 matches and loosing 26. A N Cook, with 24 wins and 22 losses from 59 Tests, was the previous highest. In his first time back in the ranks Root took England to victory in the opening Test against New Zealand at Lord's with his first century in the fourth innings of a Test. He passed 10,000 Test runs in that match, ending the calendar year on 10,629 Test runs, having added 1,098 in that year to finishing second to Babar Azam, who scored 1,184 runs.

H SUTCLIFFE

Birmingham 1924: shared the first of 15 three-figure partnerships with J B Hobbs at the first attempt.

Lord's 1924: shared stand of 268 with J B Hobbs, which remains the first-wicket record for all Lord's Tests, and was then the England v. South Africa record.

Sydney 1924-25: his first opening stands against Australia with J B Hobbs realised 157 and 110.

Melbourne 1924-25 (Second Test): with J B Hobbs achieved the first instance of a batting partnership enduring throughout a full day's Test match play; they remain the only England pair to achieve this feat, and their stand of 283 in 289 minutes remains the longest for the first wicket in this series. Became the first to score 100 in each innings of a Test against Australia, and the first Englishman to score three successive hundreds in Test cricket.

Melbourne 1924-25 (Fourth Test): first to score four hundreds in one rubber of Test matches; it was his third 100 in successive Test innings at Melbourne. Completed 1,000 runs in fewest Test innings (12) – since equalled.

Sydney 1924-25: his aggregate of 734 was the record for any rubber until 1928-29.

YORKSHIRE'S TEST CRICKET RECORDS *(Continued)*

H SUTCLIFFE *(Continued)*

The Oval 1926: shared first-wicket stand of 172 with J B Hobbs on a rain-affected pitch.

The Oval 1929: first to score hundreds in each innings of a Test twice; only England batsman to score four hundreds in a rubber twice.

Sydney 1932-33: his highest England innings of 194 overtook J B Hobbs's world record of 15 Test hundreds.

F S TRUEMAN

Leeds 1952: reduced India to 0 for 4 in their second innings by taking 3 wickets in 8 balls on his debut.

Manchester 1952: achieved record England v. India innings analysis of 8 for 31.

The Oval 1952: set England v. India series record with 29 wickets.

Leeds 1961: took 5 for 0 with 24 off-cutters at a reduced pace v. Australia.

Lord's 1962: shared record England v. Pakistan ninth-wicket stand of 76 with T W Graveney.

Christchurch 1962-63: passed J B Statham's world Test record of 242 wickets; his analysis of 7-75 remains the record for Lancaster Park Tests and for England in New Zealand.

Birmingham 1963: returned record match analysis (12-119) against West Indies in England and for any Birmingham Test, ending with a 6-4 spell from 24 balls.

The Oval 1963: set England v. West Indies series record with 34 wickets.

The Oval 1964: first to take 300 wickets in Tests.

G ULYETT

Sydney 1881-82: with R G Barlow shared the first century opening partnership in Test cricket (122).

Melbourne 1881-82: his 149 was the first Test hundred for England in Australia, and the highest score for England on the first day of a Test in Australia until 1965-66.

M P VAUGHAN

Scored 1481 runs in 2002 – more than any other England player in a calendar year, surpassing the 1379 scored by D L Amiss in 1979. It was the fourth highest in a calendar year.

Scored 633 runs in the 2002-3 series versus Australia – surpassed for England in a five Test series versus Australia only by W R Hammond, who scored 905 runs in 1928-29, H Sutcliffe (734 in 1924-25), J B Hobbs (662 in 1911-12) and G Boycott (657 in 1970-71), when he played in five of the six Tests.

Scored six Test Match centuries in 2002 to equal the record set for England by D C S Compton in 1947.

Lord's 2004: scored a century in each innings (103 and 101*) versus West Indies and so became the third player (after G A Headley and G A Gooch) to score a century in each innings of a Test match at Lord's.

Lord's 2005: only the second player (J B Hobbs is the other) to have scored centuries in three consecutive Test match innings at Lord's. Scored the 100th century for England by a Yorkshire player.

H VERITY

Lord's 1934: took 14 for 80 on the third day (six of them in the final hour) to secure England's first win against Australia at Lord's since 1896. It remains the most wickets to fall to one bowler in a day of Test cricket in England. His match analysis of 15 for 104 was then the England v. Australia record, and has been surpassed only by J C Laker.

W WATSON

Lord's 1953: scored 109 in 346 minutes in his first Test against Australia.

N W D YARDLEY

Melbourne 1946-47: dismissed D G Bradman for the third consecutive innings without assistance from the field. Became the first to score a fifty in each innings for England and take five wickets in the same match.

Nottingham 1947: shared record England v. South Africa fifth-wicket stand of 237 with D C S Compton.

* * *

Facts adapted by Bill Frindall from his *England Test Cricketers – The Complete Record from 1877* (Collins Willow, 1989). With later additions.

Best schools for cricket

Eight Yorkshire schools have been recognised among the best for cricket in *The Cricketer* Magazine's Schools Guide for 2024: Aysgarth School; Huddersfield New College; Queen Ethelburga's Collegiate; Scarborough College; St Peter's School, York, 8-13; St Peter's School, York; Woodhouse Grove School and Yorkshire Cricket College.

TEST MATCHES AT HEADINGLEY, LEEDS 1899-2023

1899 **Australia 172** (J Worrall 76) and **224** (H Trumble 56, J T Hearne hat-trick). **England 220** (A F A Lilley 55, H Trumble 5 for 60) and **19 for 0 wkt.**
Match drawn   Toss: Australia

1905 **England 301** (Hon F S Jackson 144*) and **295 for 5 wkts dec** (J T Tyldesley 100, T W Hayward 60, W W. Armstrong 5 for 122). **Australia 195** (W W Armstrong 66, A R Warren 5 for 57) and **224 for 7 wkts** (M A Noble 62).
Match drawn   Toss: England

1907 **England 76** (G A Faulkner 6 for 17) and **162** (C B Fry 54). **South Africa 110** (C Blythe 8 for 59) and **75** (C Blythe 7 for 40).
England won by 53 runs   Toss: England

1909 **Australia 188** and **207** (S F Barnes 6 for 63). **England 182** (J Sharp 61, J T Tyldesley 55, C G Macartney 7 for 58) and **87** (A Cotter 5 for 38).
Australia won by 126 runs   Toss: Australia

1912 **England 242** (F E Woolley 57) and **238** (R H Spooner 82, J B Hobbs 55). **South Africa 147** (S F Barnes 6 for 52) and **159.**
England won by 174 runs   Toss: England

1921 **Australia 407** (C G Macartney 115, W W Armstrong 77, C E Pellew 52, J M Taylor 50) and **273 for 7 wkts dec** (T J E Andrew 92). **England 259** (J W H T Douglas 75, Hon L H Tennyson 63, G Brown 57) and **202.**
Australia won by 219 runs   Toss: Australia

1924 **England 396** (E H Hendren 132, H Sutcliffe 83) and **60 for 1 wkt. South Africa 132** (H W Taylor 59*, M W Tate 6 for 42) and **323** (H W Taylor 56, R H Catterall 56).
England won by 9 wickets   Toss: England

1926 **Australia 494** (C G Macartney 151, W M Woodfull 141, A J Richardson 100). **England 294** (G G Macaulay 76, C V Grimmett 5 for 88) and **254 for 3 wkts** (H Sutcliffe 94, J B Hobbs 88).
Match drawn   Toss: England

1929 **South Africa 236** (R H Catterall 74, C L Vincent 60, A P Freeman 7 for 115) and **275** (H G Owen-Smith 129). **England 328** (F E Woolley 83, W R Hammond 65, N A Quinn 6 for 92) and **186 for 5 wkts** (F E Woolley 95*).
England won by 5 wickets   Toss: South Africa

1930 **Australia 566** (D G Bradman 334, A F Kippax 77, W M Woodfull 50, M W Tate 5 for 124). **England 391** (W R Hammond 113, C V Grimmett 5 for 135) and **95 for 3 wkts.**
Match drawn   Toss: Australia

1934 **England 200** and **229 for 6 wkts. Australia 584** (D G Bradman 304, W H Ponsford 181, W E Bowes 6 for 142).
Match drawn   Toss: England

1935 **England 216** (W R Hammond 63, A Mitchell 58) and **294 for 7 wkts dec** (W R Hammond 87*, A Mitchell 72, D Smith 57). **South Africa 171** (E A B Rowan 62) and **194 for 5 wkts** (B Mitchell 58).
Match drawn   Toss: England

1938 **England 223** (W R Hammond 76, W J O'Reilly 5 for 66) and **123** (W J O'Reilly 5 for 56). **Australia 242** (D G Bradman 103, B A Barnett 57) and **107 for 5 wkts.**
Australia won by 5 wickets   Toss: England

1947 **South Africa 175** (B Mitchell 53, A Nourse 51) and **184** (A D Nourse 57). **England 317 for 7 wkts dec** (L Hutton 100, C Washbrook 75) and **47 for 0 wkt.**
England won by 10 wickets   Toss: South Africa

1948 **England 496** (C Washbrook 143, W .J Edrich 111, L Hutton 81, A V Bedser 79) and **365 for 8 wkts dec** (D C S. Compton 66, C Washbrook 65, L Hutton 57, W J Edrich 54). **Australia 458** (R N Harvey 112, S J E Loxton 93, R R Lindwall 77, K R Miller 58) and **404 for 3 wkts** (A R Morris 182, D G Bradman 173*).
Australia won by 7 wickets   Toss: England

1949 **England 372** (D C S Compton 114, L Hutton 101, T B Burtt 5 for 97, J Cowie 5 for 127) and **267 for 4 wkts dec** (C Washbrook 103*, W J Edrich 70). **New Zealand 341** (F B Smith 96, M P Donnelly 64, T E Bailey 6 for 118) and **195 for 2 wkts** (B Sutcliffe 82, F Smith 54*).
Match drawn   Toss: England

1951 **South Africa 538** (E A B Rowan 236, P N F Mansell 90, C B. van Ryneveld 83, R A McLean 67) and **87 for 0 wkt** (E A B Rowan 60*). **England 505** (P B H May 138, L Hutton 100, T E Bailey 95, F A Lowson 58, A M B Rowan 5 for 174).
Match drawn   Toss: South Africa

1952 **India 293** (V L Manjrekar 133, V S Hazare 89) and 165 (D G Phadkar 64, V S Hazare 56). **England 334** (T W Graveney 71, T G Evans 66, Ghulam Ahmed 5 for 100) and **128 for 3 wkts** (R T Simpson 51).
England won by 7 wickets   Toss: India

1953 **England 167** (T W Graveney 55, R R Lindwall 5 for 54) and **275** (W J Edrich 64, D C S Compton 61). **Australia 266** (R N Harvey 71, G B Hole 53, A V Bedser 6 for 95) and **147 for 4 wkts.**
Match drawn   Toss: Australia

1955 **South Africa 171** and **500** (D J McGlew 133, W R Endean 116*, T L Goddard 74, H J Keith 73). **England 191** (D C S Compton 61) and **256** (P B H May 97, T L Goddard 5 for 69, H J Tayfield 5 for 94).
South Africa won by 224 runs   Toss: South Africa

1956 **England 325** (P B H May 101, C Washbrook 98). **Australia 143** (J C Laker 5 for 58) and **140** (R N Harvey 69, J C Laker 6 for 55).
England won by an innings and 42 runs   Toss: England

1957 **West Indies 142** (P J Loader 6 for 36, including hat-trick) and **132. England 279** (P B H May 69, M C Cowdrey 68, Rev D S Sheppard 68, F M M Worrell 7 for 70).
England won by an innings and 5 runs   Toss: West Indies

1958 **New Zealand 67** (J C Laker 5 for 17) and **129** (G A R Lock 7 for 51). **England 267 for 2 wkts dec** (P B H May 113*, C A Milton 104*).
England won by an innings and 71 runs   Toss: New Zealand

1959 **India 161** and **149. England 483 for 8 wkts dec** (M C Cowdrey 160, K F Barrington 80, W G A Parkhouse 78, G Pullar 75).
England won by an innings and 173 runs   Toss: India

1961 **Australia 237** (R N Harvey 73, C C McDonald 54, F S Trueman 5 for 58) and **120** (R N Harvey 53, F S Trueman 6 for 30); **England 299** (M C Cowdrey 93, G Pullar 53, A K Davidson 5 for 63) and **62 for 2 wkts.**
England won by 8 wickets   Toss: Australia

1962 **England 428** (P H Parfitt 119, M J Stewart 86, D A Allen 62, Munir Malik 5 for 128). **Pakistan 131** (Alimuddin 50) and **180** (Alimuddin 60, Saeed Ahmed 54).
England won by an innings and 117 runs   Toss: Pakistan

1963 **West Indies 397** (G St A Sobers 102, R B Kanhai 92, J S Solomon 62) and **229** (B F Butcher 78, G St.A Sobers 52). **England 174** (G A R Lock 53, C C Griffith 6 for 36) and **231** (J M Parks 57, D B Close 56).
West Indies won by 221 runs   Toss: West Indies

1964 **England 268** (J M Parks 68, E R Dexter 66, N J N Hawke 5 for 75) and 229 (K F Barrington 85). **Australia 389** (P J P Burge 160, W M Lawry 78) and **111 for 3 wkts** (I R Redpath 58*).
Australia won by 7 wickets   Toss: England

1965 **England 546 for 4 wkts dec** (J H Edrich 310*, K F Barrington 163). **New Zealand 193** (J R Reid 54) and **166** (V Pollard 53, F J Titmus 5 for 19).
England won by an innings and 187 runs   Toss: England

1966 **West Indies 500 for 9 wkts dec** (G St A Sobers 174, S M Nurse 137). **England 240** (B L D'Oliveira 88, G St A Sobers 5 for 41) and **205** (R W Barber 55, L R Gibbs 6 for 39).
West Indies won by an innings and 55 runs   Toss: West Indies

1967 **England 550 for 4 wkts dec** (G Boycott 246*, B L D'Oliveira 109, K F Barrington 93, T W Graveney 59) and **126 for 4 wkts.** **India 164** (Nawab of Pataudi jnr 64) and **510** (Nawab of Pataudi jnr 148, A L Wadekar 91, F M Engineer 87, Hanumant Singh 73). **England won by 6 wickets** Toss: England

1968 **Australia 315** (I R Redpath 92, I M Chappell 65) and **312** (I M Chappell 81, K D Walters 56, R Illingworth 6 for 87). **England 302** (R M Prideaux 64, J H Edrich 62, A N Connolly 5 for 72) and **230 for 4 wkts** (J H Edrich 65). **Match drawn** Toss: Australia

1969 **England 223** (J H Edrich 79) and **240** (G.St A Sobers 5 for 42). **West Indies 161** and **272** (B F Butcher 91, G S Camacho 71). **England won by 30 runs** Toss: England

1971 **England 316** (G Boycott 112, B L D'Oliveira 74) and **264** (B L D'Oliveira 72, D L Amiss 56) **Pakistan 350** (Zaheer Abbas 72, Wasim Bari 63, Mushtaq Mohammad 57) and **205** (Sadiq Mohammad 91). **England won by 25 runs** Toss: England

1972 **Australia 146** (K R Stackpole 52) and **136** (D L Underwood 6 for 45). **England 263** (R Illingworth 57, A A Mallett 5 for 114) and **21 for 1 wkt.** **England won by 9 wickets** Toss: Australia

1973 **New Zealand 276** (M G Burgess 87, V Pollard 62) and **142** (G M Turner 81, G G Arnold 5 for 27). **England 419** (G Boycott 115, K W R Fletcher 81, R Illingworth 65, RO Collinge 5 for 74). **England won by an innings and 1 run** Toss: New Zealand

1974 **Pakistan 285** (Majid Khan 75, Safraz Nawaz 53) and **179.** **England 183** and **238 for 6 wkts** (J H Edrich 70, K W R Fletcher 67*). **Match drawn** Toss: Pakistan

1975 **England 288** (D S Steele 73, J H Edrich 62, A W Greig 51, G J Gilmour 6 for 85) and **291** (D S Steele 92). **Australia 135** (P H Edmonds 5 for 28) and **220 for 3 wkts** (R B McCosker 95*, I M Chappell 62). **Match drawn** Toss: England

1976 **West Indies 450** (C G Greenidge 115, R C Fredericks 109, I V A Richards 66, L G Rowe 50) and **196** (C L King 58, R G D Willis 5 for 42). **England 387** (A W Greig 116, A P E Knott 116) and **204** (A W Greig 76*). **West Indies won by 55 runs** Toss: West Indies

1977 **England 436** (G Boycott 191, A P E Knott 57). **Australia 103** (I T Botham 5 for 21) and **248** (R W Marsh 63). **England won by an innings and 85 runs** Toss: England

1978 **Pakistan 201** (Sadiq Mohammad 97). **England 119 for 7 wkts** (Safraz Nawaz 5 for 39). **Match drawn** Toss: Pakistan

1979 **England 270** (I T Botham 137). **India 223 for 6 wkts** (S M Gavaskar 78, D B Vengsarkar 65*). **Match drawn** Toss: England

1980 **England 143 and 227 for 6 wkts dec** (G A Gooch 55). **West Indies 245.** **Match drawn** Toss: West Indies

1981 **Australia 401 for 9 wkts dec** (J Dyson 102, K J Hughes 89, G N Yallop 58, I T Botham 6 for 95) and **111** (R G D Willis 8 for 43). **England 174** (I T Botham 50) and **356** (I T Botham 149*, G R Dilley 56, T M Alderman 6 for 135). **England won by 18 runs** Toss: Australia

1982 **Pakistan 275** (Imran Khan 67*, Mudassar Nazar 65, Javed Miandad 54) and **199** (Javed Miandad 52, I T Botham 5 for 74). **England 256** (D I Gower 74, I T Botham 57, Imran Khan 5 for 49) and **219 for 7 wkts** (G Fowler 86). **England won by 3 wickets** Toss: Pakistan

1983 **England 225** (C J Tavaré 69, A J Lamb 58, B L Cairns 7 for 74) and **252** (D I Gower 112*, E J Chatfield 5 for 95). **New Zealand 377** (J G Wright 93, B A Edgar 84, R J Hadlee 75) and **103 for 5 wkts** (R G D Willis 5 for 35). **New Zealand won by 5 wickets** Toss: New Zealand

1984 **England 270** (A J Lamb 100) and **159** (G Fowler 50, M D Marshall 7 for 53). **West Indies 302** (H A Gomes 104*, M A Holding 59, P J W Allott 6 for 61) and **131 for 2 wkts.**
West Indies won by 8 wickets   Toss: England

1985 **Australia 331** (A M J Hilditch 119) and **324** (W B Phillips 91, A M J Hilditch 80, K C Wessels 64, J E Emburey 5 for 82). **England 533** (R T Robinson 175, I T Botham 60, P R Downton 54, M W Gatting 53) and **123 for 5 wkts.**
England won by 5 wickets   Toss: Australia

1986 **India 272** (D B Vengsarkar 61) and **237** (D B Vengsarkar 102*). **England 102 (**R M H Binny 5 for 40) and **128.**
India won by 279 runs   Toss: India

1987 **England 136** (D J Capel 53) and **199** (D I Gower 55, Imran Khan 7 for 40). **Pakistan 353** (Salim Malik 99, Ijaz Ahmed 50, N A Foster 8 for 107).
Pakistan won by an innings and 18 runs   Toss: England

1988 **England 201** (A J Lamb 64*) and **138** (G A Gooch 50). **West Indies 275** (R A Harper 56, D L Haynes 54, D R Pringle 5 for 95) and **67 for 0 wkt.**
West Indies won by 10 wickets   Toss: West Indies

1989 **Australia 601 for 7 wkts dec** (S R Waugh 177*, M A Taylor 136, D M Jones 79, M G Hughes 71, A R Border 66) and **230 for 3 wkts dec** (M A Taylor 60, A R Border 60*). **England 430** (A J Lamb 125, K J Barnett 80, R A Smith 66, T M Alderman 5 for 107) and **191.** (G A Gooch 68, T M Alderman 5 for 44).
Australia won by 210 runs   Toss: England

1991 **England 198** (R A Smith 54) and **252** (G A Gooch 154*, C E L Ambrose 6 for 52). **West Indies 173** (I V A Richards 73) and **162** (R B Richardson 68).
England won by 115 runs   Toss: West Indies

1992 **Pakistan 197** (Salim Malik 82*) and **221** (Salim Malik 84*, Ramiz Raja 63, N A Mallinder 5 for 50). **England 320** (G A Gooch 135, M A Atherton 76, Waqar Younis 5 for 117) and **99 for 4 wkts.**
England won by 6 wickets   Toss: Pakistan

1993 **Australia 653 for 4 wkts dec** (A R Border 200*, S R Waugh 157*, D C Boon 107, M J Slater 67, M E Waugh 52). **England 200** (G A Gooch 59, M A Atherton 55, P R Reiffel 5 for 65) and **305** (A J Stewart 78, M A Atherton 63).
Australia won by an innings and 148 runs   Toss: Australia

1994 **England 477 for 9 wkts dec** (M A Atherton 99, A J Stewart 89, G P Thorpe 72, S J Rhodes 65*) and **267 for 5 wkts dec** (G A Hick 110, G P Thorpe 73). **South Africa 447** (P N Kirsten 104, B M McMillan 78, C R Matthews 62*) and **116 for 3 wkts** (G Kirsten 65).
Match drawn   Toss: England

1995 **England 199** (M A Atherton 81, I R Bishop 5 for 32) and **208** (G P Thorpe 61). **West Indies 282** (S L Campbell 69, J C Adams 58, B C Lara 53) and **129 for 1 wkt** (C L Hooper 73*).
West Indies won by 9 wickets   Toss: West Indies

1996 **Pakistan 448** (Ijaz Ahmed 141, Mohin Khan 105, Salim Malik 55, Asif Mujtaba 51, D G Cork 5 for 113) and **242 for 7 wkts dec** (Inzamam-ul-Haq 65, Ijaz Ahmed sen 52) **England 501** (A J Stewart 170, N V Knight 113, J P Crawley 53).
Match drawn   Toss: England

1997 **England 172** (J N. Gillespie 7 for 37) and **268** (N Hussain 105, J P Crawley 72, P R Reiffel 5 for 49). **Australia 501 for 9 wkts dec** (M T G Elliott 199, R T Ponting 127, P R Reiffel 54*, D Gough 5 for 149).
Australia won by an innings and 61 runs   Toss: Australia

1998 **England 230** (M A Butcher 116) and **240** (N Hussain 94, S M Pollock 5 for 53, A A Donald 5 for 71). **South Africa 252** (W J. Cronje 57, A R C Fraser 5 for 42) and **195** (J N Rhodes 85, B M McMillan 54, D Gough 6 for 42).
England won by 23 runs   Toss: England

2000 **West Indies 172** (R R Sarwan 59*, C White 5 for 57) and **61** (A R Caddick 5 for 14). **England 272** (M P Vaughan 76, G A Hick 59).
England won by an innings and 39 runs   Toss: West Indies

2001 **Australia 447** (R T Ponting 144, D R Martyn 118, M E Waugh 72, D Gough 5 for 103) and **176 for 4 wkts dec** (R T Ponting 72). **England 309** (A J Stewart 76*, G D McGrath 7 for 76) and **315 for 4 wkts** (M A Butcher 173*, N Hussain 55).
England won by 6 wickets   Toss: Australia

2002 **India 628 for 8 wkts dec** (S R Tendulkar 193, R S Dravid 148, S C Ganguly 128, S B Bangar 68). **England 273** (A J Stewart 78*, M P Vaughan 61) and **309** (N Hussain 110.)
India won by an innings and 46 runs   Toss: India

2003 **South Africa 342** (G Kirsten 130, M Zondeki 59, J A Rudolph 55) and **365** (A J Hall 99*, G Kirsten 60). **England 307** (M A Butcher 77, M E Trescothick 59, A Flintoff 55) and **209** (M A Butcher 61, A Flintoff 50, J H Kallis 6 for 54.)
South Africa won by 191 runs   Toss: South Africa

2004 **New Zealand 409** (S P Fleming 97, M H W Papps 86, B B McCullum 54) and **161. England 526** (M E Trescothick 132, G O Jones 100, A Flintoff 94, A J Strauss 62) and **45 for 1 wkt**
England won by 9 wickets   Toss: England

2006 **England 515** (K P Pietersen 135, I R Bell 119, Umar Gul 5 for 123) and **345** (A J Strauss 116, M E Trescothick 58, C M W Reid 55). **Pakistan 538** (Mohammad Yousuf 192, Younis Khan 173) and **155**.
England won by 167 runs   Toss: England

2007 **England 570 for 7 wkts dec** (K P Pietersen 226, M P Vaughan 103, M J Prior 75). **West Indies 146** and **141** (D J Bravo 52).
England won by an innings and 283 runs   Toss: England

2008 **England 203** and **327** (S C J Broad 67*, A N Cook 60). **South Africa 522** (A B de Villiers 174, A G Prince 149) and **9 for 0 wkt**.
South Africa won by 10 wickets   Toss: South Africa

2009 **England 102** (P M Siddle 5 for 21) and **263** (G P Swann 62, S C J Broad 61, M G Johnson 5 for 69). **Australia 445** (M J North 110, M J Clarke 93, R T Ponting 78, S R Watson 51, S C J Broad 6 for 91).
Australia won by an innings and 80 runs   Toss: England

2010 **Australia 88** and **349** (R T Ponting 66, M J Clarke 77, S P D Smith 77). **Pakistan 258** (S R Watson 6-33) and **180-7** (Imran Farhat 67, Azhar Ali 51).
Pakistan won by 3 wickets   Toss: Australia
                      (This was a Home Test Match for Pakistan)

2012 **South Africa 419** (A N Petersen 182, G C Smith 52) and **258-9 dec** (J A Rudolph 69, GC Smith 52, S C J Broad 5-69). **England 425** (K P Pietersen 149, M J Prior 68) and **130-4**.
Match drawn   Toss: England

2013 **England 354** (J E Root 104, J M Bairstow 64, T A Boult 5-57) and **287-5 dec** (A N Cook 130, I J L Trott 76). **New Zealand 174** and **220** (L R P L Taylor 70, G P Swann 6-90)
England won by 247 runs   Toss: England

2014 **Sri Lanka 257** (K C Sangakkara 79, L E Plunkett 5-64) and **457** (K C Sangakkara 55, DPMD Jayawardene 79, A D Mathews 160). **England 365** (S D Robson 127, G S Ballance 74, I R Bell 64) and **249** (M M Ali 108*, K T G D Prasad 5-50)
Sri Lanka won by 100 runs   Toss: England

2015 **New Zealand 350** (T W M Latham 84, L Ronchi 88, S C J Broad 5-109) and **454-8 dec** (M J Guptill 70, B B McCullum 55, B J Watling 120, M D Craig 58*). **England 350** (A Lyth 107, A N Cook 75) and **255** (A N Cook 56, J C Buttler 73)
New Zealand won by 199 runs   Toss: England

2016 **England 298** (A D Hales 86, J M Bairstow 140). **Sri Lanka 91** (J M Anderson 5-16) **and 119** (B K G Mendis 53, J N Anderson 5-29)
England won by an innings and 88 runs   Toss: Sri Lanka

2017 **England 258** (J E Root 58, B A Stokes100) and **490-8 dec** (M D Stoneman 52, J E Root 72, D J Malan 61, B A Stokes 58, M M Ali 84, C R Woakes 61*). **West Indies 427** (K C Brathwaite 134, S D Hope 147, J M Anderson 5-76) and **322-5** (K C Brathwaite 95, S D Hope 118*).
West Indies won by 5 wickets   Toss: England

348

2018 **Pakistan 174** (Shadab Khan 56) and **134**. **England 363** (J C Buttler 80*)
England won by an innings and 55 runs Toss: Pakistan

2019 **Australia 179** (M Labuschagne 74, J C Archer 6-45) and **246** (M Labuschagne 80).
England 67 (J R Hazlewood 5-65) and **362-9** (J E Root 77, J L Denly 50,
B A Stokes 135*)
England won by 1 wicket Toss: England

2021 **India 78** and **278** (R G Sharma 59, C A Pujara 91, V Kohli 55, O E Robinson 5-65).
England 432 (R J Burns 61, H Hameed 68, D J Malan 70, J E Root 121)
England won by an innings and 76 runs Toss: India

2022 **New Zealand 329** (D J Mitchell 109, T A Blundell 55, M J Leach 5-100) and **326**
(T W M Latham 76, D J Mitchell 56, T A Blundell 88*, M J Leach 5-66)
England 360 (J M Bairstow 162, J Overton 97) and **296-3** (O J D Pope 82, J E Root 86*
J M Bairstow 71*)
England won by 7 wickets Toss: New Zealand

2023 **Australia 263** (M R Marsh 118, M A Wood 5-34) and **224** (T M Head 77). **England
237** (B A Stokes 80, P J Cummins 6-91) and **254-7** (H C Brook 75, M A Starc 5-78)
England won by 3 wickets Toss: England

SUMMARY OF RESULTS

ENGLAND	First played	Last played	Played	Won	Lost	Drawn
v. Australia	1899	2023	26	9	9	8
v. India	1952	2021	7	4	2	1
v. New Zealand	1949	2022	9	6	2	1
v. Pakistan	1962	2018	10	6	1	3
v. South Africa	1907	2012	13	6	3	4
v. Sri Lanka	2014	2016	2	1	1	0
v. West Indies	1957	2017	13	5	7	1
Totals	1899	2023	80	37	25	18

SIX HIGHEST AGGREGATES

Runs	*Wkts*	
1723	31	in 1948 (England 496 and 365 for 8 wkts dec; Australia 458 and 404 for 3 wkts)
1553	40	in 2006 (England 515 and 345; Pakistan 538 and 155)
1497	33	in 2017 (England 258 and 490-8 dec; West Indies 427 and 322-5)
1452	30	in 1989 (Australia 601 for 7 wkts dec and 230 for 3 wkts dec; England 430 and 191)
1409	40	in 2015 (New Zealand 350 and 454 for 8 wkts dec; England 350 and 255)
1350	28	in 1967 (England 550 for 4 wkts dec and 126 for 4 wkts; India 164 and 510)

Note: The highest aggregate prior to the Second World War

| 1141 | 37 | in 1921 (Australia 407 and 272 for 7 wkts dec; England 259 and 202) |

SIX LOWEST AGGREGATES

Runs	*Wkts*	
423	40	in 1907 (England 76 and 162; South Africa 110 and 75)
463	22	in 1958 (New Zealand 67 and 129; England 267 for 2 wkts)
505	30	in 2000 (West Indies 172 and 61; England 272)
508	30	in 2016 (England 298; Sri Lanka 91 and 119)
553	30	in 1957 (West Indies 142 and 132; England 279)
566	31	in 1972 (Australia 146 and 136; England 263 and 21 for 1 wkt)

SIX HIGHEST TOTALS

653 for 4 wkts dec	Australia	v. England, 1993
608 for 8 wkts dec	India	v. England, 2002
601 for 7 wkts dec	Australia	v. England, 1989
584	Australia	v. England, 1934
570 for 7 wkts dec	England	v. West Indies, 2007
566	Australia	v. England, 1930

SIX LOWEST TOTALS

61	West Indies	v. England, 2000
67	New Zealand	v. England, 1958
67	England	v. Australia, 2019
75	South Africa	v. England, 1907
76	England	v. South Africa, 1907
78	India	v. England, 2021

SIX HIGHEST INDIVIDUAL SCORES

For England

310*	J H Edrich versus New Zealand, 1965
246*	G Boycott versus India, 1967
226	K P Pietersen versusWest Indies, 2007
191	G Boycott versus Australia, 1977
175	R T Robinson versus Australia, 1985
173*	M A Butcher versus Australia, 2001

For Australia

334	D G Bradman, 1930
304	D G Bradman, 1934
200*	A R Border, 1993
199	M T G Elliott, 1997
182	A R Morris, 1948
181	W H Ponsford, 1934

For Pakistan

192	Mohammad Yousuf, 2006
173	Younis Khan, 2006
141	Ijaz Ahmed, 1996
105	Moin Khan, 1996
99	Salim Malik, 1987
97	Sadiq Mohammad, 1978

For India

193	S R Tendulkar, 2002
148	Nawab of Pataudi jnr, 1967
148	R S Dravid, 2002
133	V L Manjrekar, 1952
128	S C Gangulay, 2002
102*	D B Vengsarkar, 1986

For South Africa

236	E A B Rowan, 1951
182	A N Petersen, 2012
174	A B de Villiers, 2008
149	A G Prince, 2008
133	D J McGlew, 1955
130	G Kirsten, 2003

For New Zealand

120	B J Watling, 2015
109	D J Mitchell, 2022
97	S P Fleming, 2004
96	F B Smith, 1949
93	J G Wright, 1983
88*	T A Blundell, 2022
88	L Ronchi, 2015

For Sri Lanka

160*	A D Mathews, 2014
79	K C Sangakkara, 2014
55	K C Sangakkara, 2014
53*	B K G Mendis, 2016
48	H M R K B Herath, 2014
45	L D Chandimal, 2014
45	F D M Karunaratne, 2014

For West Indies

174	G St.A Sobers, 1966
147	S D Hope, 2017 (1st innings)
137	S M Nurse, 1966
134	K C Brathwaite, 2017
118*	S D Hope, 2017 (2nd innings)
115	C G Greenidge, 1976

S D Hope was the first player to score centuries in both innings of a First Class match at Headingley

HUNDRED BEFORE LUNCH

First day

112*	C G Macartney for Australia, 1926
105*	D G Bradman for Australia, 1930

Third day

102	(from 27* to 129) H G Owen-Smith for South Africa, 1929

CARRYING BAT THROUGH A COMPLETED INNINGS

154* out of 252 G A Gooch, England v. West Indies, 1991

MOST CENTURIES IN AN INNINGS

3	1926	C G Macartney (151), W M Woodfull (141) and A J Richardson for Australia
3	1993	A R Border (200*), S R Waugh (157*) and D C Boon (107) for Australia
3	2002	S R Tendulkar (193), R S Dravid (148) and S C Gangulay (128) for India

MOST CENTURIES IN A MATCH

5	1948	C Washbrook (143) and W J Edrich (111) for England; R N Harvey (112), A R Morris (182) and D G Bradman (173*) for Australia
5	2006	K P Pietersen (135), I R Bell (119) and A J Strauss (116) for England: Younis Khan (173) and Mohammad Yousuf (192) for Pakistan
4	1976	C G Greenidge (115) and R C Fredericks (109) for West Indies; A W Greig (116) and A P E Knott (116) for England
4	1996	Ijaz Ahmed (141) and Moin Khan (105) for Pakistan; A J Stewart (170) and N V Knight (113) for England
4	2002	S R Tendulkar (193), R S Dravid (148) and S C Gangulay (128) for India; N Hussain (110) for England
4	2017	B A Stokes (100) for England; K C Brathwaite (134), S D Hope (147 and 118*) for West Indies

CENTURY PARTNERSHIPS

For England
(six highest)
For the 1st wicket

177	A Lyth (107) and A N Cook (75) v. New Zealand, 2015
168	L Hutton (81) and C Washbrook (143) v. Australia, 1948 (1st inns)
168	G A Gooch (135) and M A Atherton (76) v. Pakistan, 1992
158	M E Trescothick (58) and A J Strauss (116) v. Pakistan, 2006
156	J B Hobbs (88) and H Sutcliffe (94) v. Australia, 1926
153	M E Trescothick (132) and A J Strauss (62) v. New Zealand, 2004

For all other wickets

369	(2nd wkt) J H Edrich (310*) and K F Barrington (163) v. New Zealand, 1965
252	(4th wkt) G Boycott (246*) and B L D'Oliveira (109) v. India, 1967
241	(7th wkt) J M Bairstow (162) and J Overton (97) v. New Zealand, 2022
194*	(3rd wkt) C A Milton (104*) and P B H May (113*) v. New Zealand, 1958
193	(4th wkt) M C Cowdrey (160) and K F Barrington (80) v. India, 1959
187	(4th wkt) P B H May (101) and C Washbrook (98) v. Australia, 1956

For Australia
(six highest)
For the 1st wkt – none

For all other wickets

388	(4th wkt) W H Ponsford (181) and D G Bradman (304), 1934
332*	(5th wkt) A R Border (200*) and S R Waugh (157*), 1993
301	(2nd wkt) A R Morris (182) and D G Bradman (173*), 1948
268	(5th wkt) M T G Elliott (199) and R T Ponting (127), 1997
235	(2nd wkt) W M Woodfull (141) and C G Macartney (151), 1926
229	(3rd wkt) D G Bradman (334) and A F Kippax (77), 1930

CENTURY PARTNERSHIPS *(Continued)*

For other countries in total

India

249	(4th wkt)	S R Tendulkar (193)	and S C Gangulay (128)	2002
222	(4th wkt)	V S Hazare (89)	and V L Manjrekar (133)	1952
170	(2nd wkt)	S B Bangar (68)	and R S Dravid (148)	2002
168	(2nd wkt)	F M Engineer (87)	and A L Wadekar (91)	1967
150	(3rd wkt)	R S Dravid (148)	and S R Tendulkar (193)	2002
134	(5th wkt)	Hanumant Singh (73)	and Nawab of Pataudi jnr (148)	1967
105	(6th wkt)	V S Hazare (56)	and D G Phadkar (64)	1952

New Zealand

169	(2nd wkt)	M H W Papps (86)	and S P Fleming (97)	2004
121	(5th wkt)	B B McCullum (55)	and B J Watling (120)	2015
120	(5th wkt)	M P Donnelly (64)	and F B Smith (96)	1949
120	(6th wkt)	T W M Latham (84)	and L Ronchi (88)	2015
120	(6th wkt) 1st innings	D J Mitchell (109)	and T A Blundell (55)	2022
116	(2nd wkt)	J G Wright (93)	and M D Crowe (37)	1983
113	(6th wkt) 2nd innings	D J Mitchel (56)	and T A Blundell (88*),	2022

Pakistan

363	(3rd wkt)	Younis Khan (173)	and Mohammad Yousuf (192)	2006
130	(4th wkt)	Ijaz Ahmed (141)	and Salim Malik (55)	1996
129	(3rd wkt)	aheer Abbas (72)	and Mushtaq Mohammed (57)	1971
112	(7th wkt)	Asif Mujtaba (51)	and Moin Khan (105)	1996
110	(2nd wkt)	Imran Farhat (67)	and Azhar Ali (51)	2010
				v. Australia
100	(3rd wkt)	Mudassar Nazar (65)	and Javed Miandad (54)	1982
100	(4th wkt)	Majid Khan (75)	and Zaheer Abbas (48)	1974

South Africa

212	(5th wkt)	A G Prince (149)	and A B de Villiers (174)	2008
198	(2nd wkt)	E A B Rowan (236)	and C B van Ryneveld (83)	1951
176	(1st wkt)	D J McGlew (133)	and T L Goddard (74)	1955
150	(8th wkt)	G Kirsten (130)	and M Zondeki (59)	2003
120	(1st wkt)	A N Petersen (182)	and G C Smith (52)	2012
120	(1st wkt)	J A Rudolph (69)	and G C Smith (52)	2012
117	(6th wkt)	J N Rhodes (85)	and B M McMillan (54)	1998
115	(7th wkt)	P N Kirsten (104)	and B M McMillan (78)	1994
108	(5th wkt)	E A B Rowan (236)	and R A McLean (67)	1951
103	(10th wkt)	H G Owen-Smith (129)	and A J Bell (26*)	1929

Sri Lanka

| 149 | (8th wkt) | A D Mathews (160) | and H M R K B Herath (48) | 2014 |

West Indies

265	(5th wkt)	S M Nurse (137)	and G St A Sobers (174)	1966
246	(4th wkt)	K C Brathwaite (134)	and S D Hope (147)	2017
192	(1st wkt)	R C Fredericks (109)	and C G Greenidge (115)	1976
144	(3rd wkt)	K C Brathwaite (95)	and S D Hope (118*)	2017
143	(4th wkt)	R B Kanhai (92)	and G St A Sobers (102)	1963
118*	(2nd wkt)	C L Hooper (73*)	and B C Lara (48*)	1995
108	(3rd wkt)	G S Camacho (71)	and B F Butcher (91)	1969
106	(1st wkt)	C G Greenidge (49)	and D L Haynes (43)	1984

6 BEST INNINGS ANALYSES

For England

8-43	R G D Willis	v. Australia	1981
8-59	C Blythe	v. South Africa	1907 (1st inns)
8-107	N A Foster	v. Pakistan	1987
7-40	C Blythe	v. South Africa,	1907 (2nd inns)
7-51	G A R Lock	v. New Zealand	1958
7-115	A P Freeman	v. South Africa	1929

For Australia

7-37	J N Gilliespie	1997	
7-58	C G Macartney	1909	
7-76	G D McGrath	2001	
6-33	S R Watson	2010	v. Pakistan
6-85	G J Gilmour	1975	
6-91	M A Starc	2023	

5 WICKETS IN AN INNINGS

For India (2)

5-40	R M H Binny	1986
5-100	Ghulam Ahmed	1952

For New Zealand (6)

7-74	B L Cairns	1983
5-57	T A Boult	2013
5-74	R O Collinge	1973
5-95	E J Chatfield	1983
5-97	T B Burtt	1949
5-127	J Cowie	1949

For Pakistan (6)

7-40	Imran Khan	1987
5-39	Sarfraz Nawaz	1978
5-49	Imran Khan	1982
5-117	Waqar Younis	1992
5-123	Umar Gul	2006
5 128	Munir Malik	1962

For South Africa (8)

6-17	G A Faulkner	1907
6-92	N A Quinn	1929
6-54	J H Kallis	2003
5-53	S M Pollock	1998
5-69	T L Goddard	1955
5-71	A A Donald	1998
5-94	H J Tayfield	1955
5-174	A M B Rowan	1951

For Sri Lanka

5-50	K T G D Prasad	2014

For West Indies (8)

7-53	M D Marshall	1984
7-70	F M Worrell	1957
6-36	C C Griffith	1963
6-39	L R Gibbs	1996
6-52	C E L Ambrose	1991
5-32	I R Bishop	1995
5-41	G.St.A Sobers	1966
5-42	G.St A Sobers	1969

10 WICKETS IN A MATCH

For England (9)

15-99	(8-59 and 7-40)	C Blythe	v. South Africa	1907
11-65	(4-14 and 7-51)	G A R Lock	v. New Zeland	1958
11-88	(5-58 and 6-30)	F S Trueman	v. Australia	1961
11-113	(5-58 and 6-55)	J C Laker	v. Australia	1956
10-45	(5-16 and 5-29)	J M Anderson	v. Sri Lanka	2016
10-82	(4-37 and 6-45)	D L Underwood	v. Australia	1972
10-115	(6-52 and 4-63)	S F Barnes	v. South Africa	1912
10-132	(4-42 and 6-90)	G P Swann	v. New Zealand	2013
10-166	(5-100 and 5-66)	M J Leach	v. New Zealand	2022
10-207	(7-115 and 3-92)	A P Freeman	v. South Africa	1929

For Australia (3)

11-85	(7-58 and 4-27)	C G Macartney	1909
10-122	(5-66 and 5-56)	W J O'Reilly	1938
10-151	(5-107 and 5-44)	T M Alderman	1989

For New Zealand (1)

10-144	(7-74 and 3-70)	B L Cairns	1983

10 WICKETS IN A MATCH *(Continued)*

For Pakistan (1)

10-77   (3-37 and 7-40)   Imran Khan   1987

Note: Best bowling in a match for:

India	7-58	(5-40 and 2-18)	R M H Binney	1986
Sri Lanka	6-125	(1-75 and 5-50)	K T G D Prasad	2014
South Africa	9-75	(6-17 and 3-58)	G A Faulkner	1907
West Indies	9-81	(6 -36 and 3-45)	C C Griffith	1963

HAT-TRICKS

J T Hearne	v. Australia	1899
P J Loader	v. West Indies	1957
S C J Broad	v. Sri Lanka	2014

TEST MATCH AT BRAMALL LANE, SHEFFIELD 1902

1902 **Australia 194** (S F Barnes 6 for 49) and **289** (C Hill 119, V T Trumper 62, W Rhodes 5 for 63) **England 145** (J V Saunders 5 for 50, M A Noble 5 for 51) and **195** (A C MacLaren 63, G L Jessop 55, M A Noble 6 for 52).

Australia won by 143 runs   Toss: Australia

When everything stops for tea...

Dales, Bails and Cricket Club Tales   John Fuller

The editor of *CricketYorkshire.com* and the author of *Last of the Summer Wickets* is back with another alternative look at club cricket in the Broad Acres. This is a travel-writing style collection of articles from Fuller's website, be it the weird or the wonderful, picturesque grounds and teas to die for.

"I particularly like smaller, rural grounds such as Upper Wharfedale in the Yorkshire Dales village of Grassington, which is the inspiration for the cover," Fuller says. "Two examples of teas that spring to mind are Ripon Cricket Club, who did a joint of gammon, countless home-baked cakes, sausage rolls, salads and quiches. It was an incredible effort.

"Collingham and Linton was mighty impressive. I sat with my wife and hoovered a chilli and rice, then a gooey brownie, while a pair of badminton players sweated and duelled below us in the indoor court."

This self-published book is available via Amazon at £7.99 paperback or £4.99 Kindle.

Graham Hardcastle

LIST OF PLAYERS AND CAREER AVERAGES IN ALL FIRST-CLASS MATCHES FOR YORKSHIRE 1863-2023

Based on research by John T Potter, Paul E Dyson, Mick Pope and the late Roy D Wilkinson and Anthony Woodhouse

Career records date from the foundation of Yorkshire County Cricket Club in 1863. The Club welcome any help in keeping this list up to date. The compilers do not believe that we should alter the status of matches from that determined when they were played. These averages include the match versus Gentlemen of Scotland in 1878, and exclude those versus Liverpool and District in 1889, 1891, 1892 and 1893 in line with what appear to have been the decisions of the Club.

* Played as an amateur   © Awarded County Cap   § Born outside Yorkshire

Player	Date of Birth	Date of Death (if known)	First Played	Last Played	M	Inns	NO	Runs	HS	Av'ge	100s	Runs	Wkts	Av'ge	Ct/St
Ackroyd, A *	Aug. 29, 1858	Oct. 3, 1927	1879	1879	1	1	1	2	2*	—	0	7	0	—	0
Allen, S *	Dec 20, 1893	Oct 9, 1978	1924	1924	1	2	0	8	6	4.00	0	116	2	58.00	0
Allen, W R	Apr14, 1893	Oct 14, 1950	1921	1925	30	32	10	475	95*	21.59	—	—	—	—	45/21
Ambler, J	Feb 12, 1860	Feb 10 1899	1886	1886	4	7	0	68	25	9.71	—	22	0	—	2
Anderson, G	Jan 20, 1826	Nov 27, 1902	1863	1869	19	31	6	520	99*	20.80	0	—	—	—	19
Anderson, P N	Apr. 28, 1966		1988	1988	1	1	0	0	0	0.00	—	47	1	47.00	1
Anson, C E *	Oct 14, 1889	Mar 26, 1969	1924	1924	1	2	0	27	14	13.50	0	—	—	—	1
Appleton, C *	May15, 1844	Feb 26, 1925	1865	1865	3	6	1	56	18	11.20	0	—	—	—	0
Appleyard, R ©	June 27, 1924	Mar 17, 2015	1950	1958	133	122	43	679	63	8.59	0	9,903	642	15.42	70
Armitage, C I *	Apr 28, 1849	Apr 24, 1917	1873	1878	3	5	0	26	12	5.20	0	29	0	—	0
Armitage, T	Apr 25, 1848	Sept 21, 1922	1872	1878	52	85	8	1,053	95	13.67	0	1,614	107	15.08	20
Ash, D L	Feb 18, 1944		1965	1965	3	3	0	22	12	7.33	0	22	0	—	0
Ashman, J R	May 20, 1926	Mar 4, 2019	1951	1951	1	1	1	0	0*	—	0	116	4	29.00	0
Ashraf, Moin A	Jan 5, 1992		2010	2013	21	19	5	56	10	4.00	0	1,268	43	29.48	2
Aspinall, R ©	Oct 26, 1918	Aug 16, 1999	1946	1950	36	48	8	763	75*	19.07	0	2,670	131	20.38	18
Aspinall, W	Mar 24, 1858	Jan 27, 1910	1880	1880	2	3	0	16	14	5.33	0	—	—	—	1
Asquith, F T	Feb 5, 1870	Jan 11, 1916	1903	1903	1	1	0	0	0	0.00	0	—	—	—	2
Athey, C W J ©	Sept 27, 1957		1976	1983	151	246	21	6,320	134	28.08	10	1,003	21	47.76	144/2
Atkinson, G R	Sept 21, 1830	May 3, 1906	1863	1870	27	38	8	399	44	13.30	0	1,146	54	21.22	14
Atkinson, H T	Feb 1, 1881	Dec 23, 1959	1907	1907	1	2	0	0	0	0.00	0	17	0	—	0
§ Azeem Rafiq ©	Feb 27, 1991		2009	2017	35	41	4	814	100	22.00	1	2,511	63	39.85	14
Backhouse, E N	May 13, 1901	Nov 1, 1936	1931	1931	1	1	0	2	2	2.00	0	4	0	—	0
Badger, H D *	Mar 7, 1900	Aug 10, 1975	1921	1922	2	4	2	6	6*	3.00	0	145	6	24.16	1
Bainbridge, A B	Oct 15, 1932		1961	1963	5	10	0	93	24	9.30	0	358	20	17.90	3

LIST OF PLAYERS AND CAREER AVERAGES IN ALL FIRST-CLASS MATCHES FOR YORKSHIRE *(Continued)*

Player	Date of Birth	Date of Death (if known)	First Played	Last Played	M	Inns	NO	Runs	HS	Av'ge	100s	Runs	Wkts	Av'ge	Ct/St
Baines, F E *	June 18, 1864	Nov 17, 1948	1888	1888	1	1	0	0	0	0.00	0	—	—	—	0
Bairstow, A ©	Aug 14, 1868	Dec 7, 1945	1896	1900	24	24	10	69	12	4.92	0	—	—	—	41/18
Bairstow, D L ©	Sept 1, 1951	Jan 5, 1998	1970	1990	429	601	113	12,985	145	26.60	9	192	6	32.00	907/131
Bairstow, J M ©	**Sept 26, 1989**		**2009**	**2023**	**96**	**153**	**23**	**6,528**	**246**	**50.21**	**15**	**1**	**0**	**—**	**247/10**
Baker, G R	Apr 18, 1862	Feb 6, 1938	1884	1884	7	11	1	42	13	4.20	0	—	—	—	5
Baker, R *	July 3, 1849	June 21, 1896	1874	1875	3	5	1	45	22	11.25	0	43	0	—	3
Balderstone, J C	Nov 16, 1940	Mar 6, 2000	1961	1969	68	81	6	1,332	82	17.76	0	790	37	21.35	24
§ Ballance, G S ©	Nov 22, 1989		2008	2021	127	202	21	8,507	203*	47.00	27	143	0	—	70
Barber, A T * ©	June 17, 1905	Mar 10, 1985	1929	1930	42	54	3	1,050	100	20.58	1	0	0	—	40
Barber, W ©	Apr 18, 1901	Sept 10, 1968	1926	1947	354	495	48	15,315	255	34.26	27	404	14	28.85	169
Barraclough, E S	Mar 30, 1923	May 21, 1999	1949	1950	2	4	2	43	24*	21.50	0	136	4	34.00	0
Bates, W	Nov 19, 1855	Jan 8, 1900	1877	1887	202	331	12	6,499	136	20.37	8	10,692	637	16.78	163
Bates, W E ©	Mar 5, 1884	Jan 17, 1957	1907	1913	113	167	15	2,634	81	17.32	0	57	2	28.50	64
Batty G J	Oct 13, 1977		1997	1997	1	2	0	18	18	9.00	0	70	2	35.00	0
Batty, J D	May 15, 1971		1989	1994	64	67	20	703	51	14.95	0	5,286	140	37.75	25
Bayes, G W	Feb 27, 1884	Dec 6, 1960	1910	1921	18	24	11	165	36	12.69	0	1,534	48	31.95	7
Bean, F J	**Apr 16, 2002**		**2022**	**2023**	**16**	**27**	**0**	**1,121**	**135**	**41.51**	**3**	**105**	**0**	**—**	**15**
Beaumont, H	Oct 14, 1916	Nov. 15, 2003	1946	1947	28	46	6	716	60	17.90	0	236	9	26.22	11
Beaumont, J	Sept 16, 1854	May 1, 1920	1877	1878	5	9	3	60	24	10.00	0	50	2	25.00	0
Bedford, H	July 17, 1907	July 5, 1968	1928	1928	5	5	1	57	24	14.25	0	179	8	22.37	0
Bedford, W	Feb 24, 1879	July, 28 1939	1903	1903	2	2	1	38	30*	38.00	0	117	2	58.50	1
Bell, J T	June 16, 1895	Aug 8, 1974	1921	1923	7	8	1	125	54	17.85	0	—	—	—	0
Berry, John	Jan 10, 1823	Feb 26, 1895	1864	1867	18	32	2	492	78	16.40	0	149	8	18.62	12
Berry, Joseph	Nov 29, 1829	Apr 20, 1894	1863	1874	3	4	0	68	30	17.00	0	—	—	—	1
Berry, P J	Dec 28, 1966		1986	1990	7	7	6	76	31*	76.00	0	401	7	57.28	6
§ Bess, D M	**July 22, 1997**		**2019**	**2023**	**39**	**57**	**7**	**1,270**	**91***	**25.40**	**0**	**3,625**	**93**	**38.97**	**16**
§ Best T L	Aug 26, 1981		2010	2010	9	9	0	86	40	9.55	0	793	18	44.05	4
Betts, G	Sept 19, 1841	Sept 26, 1902	1873	1874	2	4	1	56	44*	18.66	0	—	—	—	0
§ Bevan, M G ©	May 8, 1970		1995	1996	32	56	8	2,823	160*	58.81	9	720	10	72.00	24
Binks, J G ©	Oct 5, 1935		1955	1969	491	587	128	6,745	95	14.69	0	66	0	—	872/172

356

LIST OF PLAYERS AND CAREER AVERAGES IN ALL FIRST-CLASS MATCHES FOR YORKSHIRE *(Continued)*

Player	Date of Birth	Date of Death (if known)	First Played	Last Played	M	Inns	NO	Runs	HS	Av'ge	100s	Runs	Wkts	Av'ge	Ct/St
Binns, J	Mar 31, 1870	Dec 8, 1934	1898	1898	1	1	0	4	4	4.00	0	—	—	—	0/3
Bird, H D	Apr 19, 1933		1956	1959	14	25	2	613	181*	26.65	1	—	—	—	3
Birkenshaw, J	Nov 13, 1940		1958	1960	30	42	7	588	42	16.80	0	1,819	69	26.36	21
Birtles, T J D	Oct 26, 1886	Jan 13, 1971	1913	1924	37	57	11	876	104	19.04	1	20	0	—	19
Blackburn, J D H *	Oct 27, 1924	Feb 19, 1987	1956	1956	1	2	0	18	15	9.00	0	—	—	—	0
Blackburn, J S	Sept 24, 1852	July 8, 1922	1876	1877	6	11	1	102	28	10.20	0	173	7	24.71	4
§ Blackburn, W E *	Nov 24, 1888	June 3, 1941	1919	1920	10	13	6	26	6*	3.71	0	1,113	45	24.73	9
§ Blain J A R	Jan 4, 1979		2004	2010	15	17	7	137	28*	13.70	0	1,312	38	34.52	4
Blake, W	Nov 29, 1854	Nov 28, 1931	1880	1880	2	3	0	44	21	14.66	0	17	1	17.00	0
Blakey, R J ....©	Jan 15, 1967		1985	2003	339	541	84	14,150	223*	30.96	12	68	1	68.00	768/56
Blamires, E	July 31, 1850	Mar 22, 1886	1877	1877	1	2	0	23	17	11.50	0	82	5	16.40	0
§ Blewett, G S ....©	Oct 28, 1971		1999	1999	12	23	2	655	190	31.19	1	212	5	42.40	5
Bloom, G R	Sept 13, 1941		1964	1964	1	1	0	2	2	2.00	0	—	—	—	2
Bocking, H	Dec 10, 1835	Feb 22, 1907	1865	1865	2	2	0	14	11	7.00	0	—	—	—	0
Boden, J G *	Dec 27, 1848	Jan 3, 1928	1878	1878	1	1	0	6	6	6.00	0	—	—	—	1
Bolton, B C *	Sept 23, 1861	Nov 18, 1910	1890	1891	4	6	0	25	11	4.16	0	252	13	19.38	2
Bolus, J B ....©	Jan 31, 1934	May 6, 2020	1956	1962	107	179	18	4,712	146*	29.26	7	407	13	31.30	45
Booth, A ....©	Nov 3, 1902	Aug 17, 1974	1931	1947	36	36	16	114	29	5.70	0	1,684	122	13.80	10
Booth, M W ....©	Dec 10, 1886	July 1, 1916	1908	1914	144	218	31	4,244	210	22.69	2	11,017	557	19.77	114
Booth, P A	Sept 5, 1965		1982	1989	23	29	9	193	33*	9.65	0	1,517	35	43.34	7
Booth, R	Oct 1, 1926	Sept 24, 2018	1951	1955	65	76	28	730	53*	15.20	0	—	—	—	79/29
Bore, M K	June 2, 1947	May 2, 2017	1969	1977	74	78	21	481	37*	8.43	0	4,866	162	30.03	27
Borrill, P D	July 4, 1951		1971	1971	2	—	—	—	—	—	—	61	5	12.20	0
Bosomworth W E	Mar 8, 1847	June 7, 1891	1872	1880	4	7	1	20	7	3.33	0	140	9	15.55	2
Bottomley, I H *	Apr 9, 1855	Apr 23, 1922	1878	1880	9	12	0	166	32	13.83	0	75	1	75.00	1
Bottomley, T	Dec 26, 1910	Feb 19, 1977	1934	1935	6	7	0	142	51	20.28	0	188	1	188.00	5
Bower, W H	Oct 17, 1857	Jan 31, 1943	1883	1883	1	2	0	10	5	5.00	0	—	—	—	0
Bowes, W E ....©	July 25, 1908	Sept 4, 1987	1929	1947	301	257	117	1,251	43*	8.93	0	21,227	1,351	15.71	118
Boycott, G ....©	Oct 21, 1940		1962	1986	414	674	111	32,570	260*	57.85	103	665	28	23.75	200
Brackin, T	Jan 5, 1859	Oct 7, 1924	1882	1882	3	6	0	12	9	2.00	0	—	—	—	0

LIST OF PLAYERS AND CAREER AVERAGES IN ALL FIRST-CLASS MATCHES FOR YORKSHIRE *(Continued)*

Player	Date of Birth	Date of Death (if known)	First Played	Last Played	M	Inns	NO	Runs	HS	Av'ge	100s	Runs	Wkts	Av'ge	Ct/St
§ Brathwaite, K C	Dec 1, 1992		2017	2017	2	4	0	40	18	10.00	0	—	—	—	1
Brayshay, P B *	Oct 14, 1916	July 6, 2004	1952	1952	2	3	0	20	13	6.66	0	104	3	34.66	0
Brearley, H *	June 26, 1913	Aug 14, 2007	1937	1937	1	2	0	17	9	8.50	0	—	—	—	0
Brennan, D V * ....©	Feb 10, 1920	Jan 9, 1985	1947	1953	204	221	66	1,653	47	10.66	0	—	—	—	280/100
Bresnan, T T ......©	Feb 28, 1985		2003	2019	163	232	35	5,594	169*	28.39	5	13,663	445	30.70	89
Britton, G ..	Feb 7, 1843	Jan 3, 1910	1867	1867	1	2	0	3	3	1.50	0	—	—	—	0
Broadbent, A	June 7, 1879	July 19, 1958	1909	1910	3	5	0	66	29	13.20	0	252	5	50.40	1
Broadhead, W B	May 31, 1903	Apr 2, 1986	1929	1929	1	2	0	5	3	2.50	0	—	—	—	1
Broadhurst, M	June 20, 1974		1991	1994	5	3	0	7	6	2.33	0	231	7	33.00	0
Brook, H C ......©	**Feb 22, 1999**		**2016**	**2022**	**55**	**88**	**5**	**3,049**	**194**	**36.73**	**7**	**438**	**8**	**54.75**	**44**
Brook, J W	Feb 1, 1897	Mar.3 1989	1923	1923	1	1	0	0	0	0.00	0	—	—	—	0
Brooke, B	Mar 3, 1930	Apr 19, 2021	1950	1950	2	4	0	16	14	4.00	0	191	2	95.50	0
§ Brooks, J A ......©	June 4, 1984		2013	2018	81	102	34	1,229	109*	18.07	1	8,341	316	26.39	21
§ Brophy, G L ....©	Nov 26, 1975		2006	2012	73	112	12	3,012	177*	30.12	3	6	0	—	176/15
Broughton, P N	Oct 22, 1935		1956	1956	6	5	2	19	12	6.33	0	365	16	22.81	1
Brown, A	June 10, 1854	Nov 2, 1900	1872	1872	2	3	0	9	5	3.00	0	47	3	15.66	4
Brown, J T (Driffield) ©	Aug 20, 1869	Nov 4, 1904	1889	1904	345	567	41	15,694	311	29.83	23	5,183	177	29.28	188
Brown, J T (Darfield) ©	Nov 24, 1874	Apr 12, 1950	1897	1903	30	32	3	333	37*	11.48	0	2,071	97	21.35	18
Brown, W	Nov 19, 1876	July 27, 1945	1902	1908	2	2	1	2	2	2.00	0	84	4	21.00	0
Brownhill, T	Oct 10, 1838	Jan 6, 1915	1863	1871	14	20	3	185	25	10.88	0	—	—	—	7
Brumfitt, J *	Feb. 18, 1917	Mar 16, 1987	1938	1938	1	1	0	9	9	9.00	0	—	—	—	0
Buller, J S	Aug 23, 1909	Aug 7, 1970	1930	1930	1	2	0	5	3	2.50	0	—	—	—	2
Bulmer, J R L	Dec 28, 1867	Jan 20, 1917	1891	1891	1	2	0	0	0	0.00	0	79	1	79.00	0
Burgess, T	Oct 1, 1859	Feb 15, 1922	1895	1895	1	2	1	0	0*	0.00	0	—	—	—	2
Burgin, E	Jan 4, 1924	Nov 16, 2012	1952	1953	12	10	3	92	32	13.14	0	795	31	25.64	0
Burman, J	Oct 5, 1838	May 14, 1900	1867	1867	1	2	1	1	1*	1.00	0	—	—	—	0
Burnet, J R * ......©	Oct 11, 1918	Mar 6, 1999	1958	1959	54	75	6	889	54	12.88	0	26	1	26.00	7
§ Burrows, M	Aug 18, 1855	May 29, 1893	1880	1880	6	10	0	82	23	8.20	0	—	—	—	2
Burton, D C F * .....©	Sept 13, 1887	Sept 24, 1971	1907	1921	104	130	15	2,273	142*	19.76	2	—	—	—	44
Burton, R C *	Apr 11, 1891	Apr 30, 1971	1914	1914	2	2	0	47	47	23.50	0	73	6	12.16	2

LIST OF PLAYERS AND CAREER AVERAGES IN ALL FIRST-CLASS MATCHES FOR YORKSHIRE *(Continued)*

Player	Date of Birth	Date of Death (if known)	First Played	Last Played	M	Inns	NO	Runs	HS	Av'ge	100s	Runs	Wkts	Av'ge	Ct/St
Butterfield, E B *	Oct 22, 1848	May 6, 1899	1870	1870	1	2	0	18	10	9.00	0	—	—	—	0
Byas, D ©	Aug 26, 1963		1986	2001	268	449	42	14,398	213	35.37	28	727	12	60.58	351
Byrom, J L *	July 20, 1851	Aug 24, 1931	1874	1874	2	4	0	19	11	4.75	0	—	—	—	1
Callis, E	Nov 8, 1994		2016	2017	2	3	1	131	84	65.50	0	—	—	—	1
Cammish, J W	May 21, 1921	July 16, 1974	1954	1954	2	1	0	0	0	0.00	0	155	3	51.66	0
Carrick, P ©	July, 16 1952	Jan 11, 2000	1970	1993	425	543	102	9,994	131*	22.66	3	30,530	1,018	29.99	183
Carter, Rev E S *	Feb 3, 1845	May 23, 1923	1876	1881	14	21	2	210	39*	11.05	0	104	8	13.00	4
Cartman, W H	June 20, 1861	Jan 16, 1935	1891	1891	3	6	0	57	49	9.50	0	—	—	—	0
Carver, K	Mar 26, 1996		2014	2018	8	13	6	108	20	15.42	0	543	18	30.16	4
Cawthray, G	Sept 28, 1913	Jan 5, 2001	1939	1952	4	6	0	114	30	19.00	0	304	4	76.00	1
Chadwick, J P G	Nov 8, 1934		1960	1965	6	9	3	106	59	17.66	0	67	2	33.50	7
Champion, A	Dec 27, 1851	June 26, 1909	1876	1879	14	23	4	148	29	7.78	0	17	1	17.00	7
Chapman, C A	June 8, 1971		1990	1998	8	13	2	238	80	21.63	0	—	—	—	13/3
Charlesworth, A P	Feb 19, 1865	May 11, 1926	1894	1895	7	12	1	241	63	21.90	0	—	—	—	2
§ Chichester-Constable, R C J *	Dec 21, 1890	May 26, 1963	1919	1919	1	1	0	0	0	0.00	0	6	0	—	0
Clarkson, A	Sept 5, 1939		1963	1963	6	8	1	80	30	11.42	0	92	5	18.40	5
Claughton, H M	Dec 24, 1891	Oct 17, 1980	1914	1919	4	6	0	39	15	6.50	0	176	3	58.66	1
§ Claydon, M E	Nov 25, 1982		2005	2006	3	2	0	38	38	19.00	0	263	3	87.66	0
§ Clayton, R O	Jan 1, 1844	Nov 26, 1901	1870	1879	70	115	23	992	62	10.78	0	2,478	153	16.19	26
§ Cleary, M F	July 19, 1980		2005	2005	2	2	0	23	12	11.50	0	250	8	31.25	0
Clegg, H	Dec 8, 1850	Dec 30, 1920	1881	1881	6	8	1	63	25*	9.00	0	—	—	—	2
Cliff, B M	**Oct 23, 2002**		**2023**	**2023**	**2**	**2**	**1**	**1**	**1**	**1.00**	**0**	**116**	**3**	**38.66**	**0**
Clifford, C C	July, 5, 1942		1972	1972	11	12	4	39	12*	4.87	0	666	26	25.61	5
Close, D B ©	Feb 24, 1931	Sept 14, 2015	1949	1970	536	811	102	22,650	198	31.94	33	23,489	967	24.29	564
Clough, G D	May 23, 1978		1998	1998	1	2	0	34	33	17.00	0	11	0	—	1
Coad, B O ©	**Jan 10, 1994**		**2016**	**2023**	**64**	**84**	**27**	**868**	**69**	**15.22**	**0**	**4,983**	**246**	**20.25**	**4**
Collinson, R W *	Nov 6, 1875	Dec 26, 1963	1897	1897	2	3	0	58	34	19.33	0	—	—	—	0
Cooper, H P	Apr 17, 1949		1971	1980	98	107	29	1,159	56	14.85	0	6,327	227	27.87	60

LIST OF PLAYERS AND CAREER AVERAGES IN ALL FIRST-CLASS MATCHES FOR YORKSHIRE *(Continued)*

Player	Date of Birth	Date of Death (if known)	First Played	Last Played	M	Inns	NO	Runs	HS	Av'ge	100s	Runs	Wkts	Av'ge	Ct/St
Cooper, P E *	Feb 19, 1885	May 21, 1950	1910	1910	1	2	0	0	0	0.00	0	—	—	—	0
Cope, G A ©	Feb 23, 1947		1966	1980	230	249	89	2,241	78	14.00	0	15,627	630	24.80	64
Corbett, A M	Nov 25, 1855	Oct 7, 1934	1881	1881	1	2	0	0	0	0.00	0	—	—	—	1
Coverdale, S P	Nov 20, 1954		1973	1980	6	4	0	31	18	7.75	0	—	—	—	11/4
Coverdale, W *	July 8, 1862	Sept 23, 1934	1888	1888	2	2	0	2	1	1.00	0	—	—	—	2
Cowan, M J ©	June 10, 1933	July 11, 2022	1953	1962	91	84	48	170	19*	4.72	0	6,388	266	24.01	37
Cownley, J M	Feb 24, 1929	Nov 7, 1998	1952	1952	2	2	1	19	19	19.00	0	119	1	119.00	0
Coxon, A ©	Jan 18, 1916	Jan 22, 2006	1945	1950	142	182	33	2,747	83	18.43	0	9,528	464	20.53	124
Craven, V J	July 31, 1980		2000	2004	33	55	6	1,206	81*	24.61	0	584	15	38.93	18
Crawford, G H	Dec 15, 1890	June 28, 1975	1914	1926	9	8	0	46	21	5.75	0	541	21	25.76	3
Crawford, M G *	July 30, 1920	Dec 2, 2012	1951	1951	1	2	0	22	13	11.00	0	—	—	—	1
Creighton, E	July 9, 1859	Feb 17, 1931	1888	1888	4	8	2	33	10	5.50	0	181	10	18.10	0
Crick, H	Jan 29, 1910	Feb 10, 1960	1937	1947	8	10	0	88	20	8.80	0	—	—	—	18/4
Crookes, R	Oct 9, 1846	Feb 15, 1897	1879	1879	1	2	1	2	2*	2.00	0	14	0	—	0
Crossland, S M	Aug 16, 1851	April 11, 1906	1883	1886	4	6	2	32	20	8.00	0	—	—	—	3/5
Crowther, A	Aug 1, 1878	June 4, 1946	1905	1905	1	2	0	0	0	0.00	0	—	—	—	1
Cuttell, W	Jan 28, 1835	June 10, 1896	1863	1871	15	27	6	271	56	12.90	0	596	36	16.55	4
Dalton, A J	Mar 14, 1947		1969	1972	21	31	2	710	128	24.48	3	—	—	—	6
§ Darnton, T	Feb 12, 1836	Oct 18, 1874	1864	1868	13	22	1	314	81*	14.95	0	349	12	29.08	3
Davidson, K R ©	Dec 24, 1905	Dec 25, 1954	1933	1935	30	46	5	1,331	128	32.46	2	—	—	—	18
Dawes, J	Feb 14, 1836	Not known	1865	1865	5	9	2	93	28*	13.28	0	196	5	39.20	3
Dawood, I	July 23, 1976		2004	2005	20	31	7	636	75	26.50	0	—	—	—	46/3
Dawson, E	May 1, 1835	Dec 1, 1888	1863	1874	16	25	1	224	20	9.33	0	—	—	—	5
Dawson, R K J ©	Aug 4, 1980		2001	2006	72	106	9	2,179	87	22.46	0	6,444	157	41.04	39
Dawson, W A *	Dec 3, 1850	Mar 6, 1916	1870	1870	1	2	0	0	0	0.00	0	—	—	—	1
Day, A G *	Sept 20, 1865	Oct 16, 1908	1885	1888	6	10	0	78	25	7.80	0	—	—	—	3
Dennis, F ©	June 11, 1907	Nov 21, 2000	1928	1933	89	100	28	1,332	67	18.50	0	4,517	156	28.95	58
Dennis, S J ©	Oct 18, 1960		1980	1988	67	62	24	338	53*	8.89	0	5,548	173	32.06	19
Denton, D ©	July 4, 1874	Feb 16, 1950	1894	1920	676	1,058	61	33,282	221	33.38	61	957	34	28.14	360/1

Player	Date of Birth	Date of Death (if known)	First Played	Last Played	M	Inns	NO	Runs	HS	Av'ge	100s	Runs	Wkts	Av'ge	Ct/St
Denton, J	Feb 3, 1865	July 19, 1946	1887	1888	15	24	1	222	59	9.65	0	—	—	—	6
Dewse, H	Feb 23, 1836	July 8, 1910	1873	1873	1	2	0	14	12	7.00	0	15	0	—	1
Deyes, G	Feb 11, 1878	Jan 11, 1963	1905	1907	17	24	4	44	12	2.20	0	944	41	23.02	6
Dick, R D *	Apr 16, 1889	Dec 14, 1983	1911	1911	1	1	0	2	2	2.00	0	37	2	18.50	1
Dobson, A	Feb 22, 1854	Sept 17, 1932	1879	1879	2	3	0	1	1	0.33	0	—	—	—	1
Doidge, M J	July 2, 1970		1990	1990	1	—	—	—	—	—	—	106	0	—	0
Dolphin, A ©	Dec 24, 1885	Oct 23, 1942	1905	1927	427	446	157	3,325	66	11.50	0	28	1	28.00	569/260
Douglas, J S	Apr 4, 1903	Dec 27, 1971	1925	1934	23	26	8	125	19	6.94	0	1,310	49	26.73	14
Drake, A ©	Apr 16, 1884	Feb 14, 1919	1909	1914	156	244	24	4,789	147*	21.76	3	8,623	479	18.00	93
Drake, J	Sept 1, 1893	May 22, 1967	1923	1924	3	4	1	21	10	7.00	0	117	1	117.00	2
§ Drakes, D C	June 2, 1998		2022	2022	1	2	0	27	21	13.50	0	86	2	43.00	0
Driver, J	May 16, 1861	Dec 10, 1946	1889	1889	2	4	1	24	8	8.00	0	—	—	—	2
Dury, T S *	June 12, 1854	Mar 20, 1932	1878	1881	13	24	1	329	46	14.30	0	21	0	—	3
Duke, H G	**Sept 6, 2001**		**2021**	**2022**	**17**	**25**	**2**	**436**	**54**	**18.95**	**0**	**1**	**0**	—	**50/1**
Dyson, W L	Dec 11, 1857	May 1, 1936	1887	1887	2	4	0	8	6	2.00	0	—	—	—	2
Earnshaw, W	Sept 20, 1867	Nov 24, 1941	1893	1896	6	7	3	44	23	11.00	0	—	—	—	6/2
Eastwood, D	Mar 30, 1848	May 17, 1903	1870	1877	29	51	2	591	68	12.06	0	349	11	31.72	16
Eckersley, R	Sept 4, 1925	May 30, 2009	1945	1945	1	1	1	9	9*	—	0	62	0	—	0
§ Edwards, M W	**Dec 23, 1994**		**2023**	**2023**	**3**	**5**	**1**	**52**	**19***	**13.00**	**0**	**254**	**5**	**50.80**	**0**
Elam, F W *	Sept 13, 1871	Mar 19, 1943	1900	1902	2	3	1	48	28	24.00	0	—	—	—	0
§ Elliott, M T G	Sept 28, 1971		2002	2002	5	10	1	487	127	54.11	1	77	1	77.00	7
Ellis, J E	Nov 10, 1864	Dec 1, 1927	1888	1892	11	15	6	14	4*	1.55	0	—	—	—	11/10
Ellis, S *	Nov 23, 1851	Oct 28, 1930	1880	1880	2	3	0	12	9	4.00	0	—	—	—	2
Elms, J E	Dec 24, 1874	Nov 1, 1951	1905	1905	1	2	0	20	20	10.00	0	28	1	28.00	1
Elstub, C J	Feb 3, 1981		2000	2002	6	7	6	28	18*	28.00	0	356	9	39.55	2
Emmett, T ©	Sept 3, 1841	June 29, 1904	1866	1888	299	484	65	6,315	104	15.07	1	15,465	1,216	12.71	179
Farrar, A	Apr 29, 1883	Dec 25, 1954	1906	1906	1	1	0	2	2	2.00	0	—	—	—	1
Fearnley, M C	Aug 21, 1936	July 7, 1979	1962	1964	3	4	2	19	11*	9.50	0	133	6	22.16	0
Featherby, W D	Aug 18, 1888	Nov 20, 1958	1920	1920	2	—	—	—	—	—	—	12	0	—	0

LIST OF PLAYERS AND CAREER AVERAGES IN ALL FIRST-CLASS MATCHES FOR YORKSHIRE *(Continued)*

Player	Date of Birth	Date of Death (if known)	First Played	Last Played	M	Inns	NO	Runs	HS	Av'ge	100s	Runs	Wkts	Av'ge	Ct/St
Fellows, G M	July 30, 1978		1998	2003	46	71	6	1,526	109	23.47	1	1,202	32	37.56	23
Fiddling, K	Oct 13, 1917	June 19, 1992	1938	1946	18	24	6	182	25	10.11	0	—	—	—	24/13
§ Finch, A J ©	Nov 17, 1986		2014	2015	8	10	1	415	110	46.11	1	40	1	40.00	11
Firth, A *	Sept 3, 1847	Jan 16, 1927	1869	1869	1	1	0	4	4	4.00	0	—	—	—	0
Firth, Rev E B *	Apr 11, 1863	July 25, 1905	1894	1894	1	1	0	1	1	1.00	0	—	—	—	0
§ Firth, E L *	Mar 7, 1886	Jan 8, 1949	1912	1912	2	4	0	43	37	10.75	0	—	—	—	1
Firth, J	June 26, 1917	Sept 6, 1981	1949	1950	8	8	5	134	67*	44.66	0	—	—	—	14/2
Fisher, H ©	Aug 3, 1903	Apr 16, 1974	1928	1936	52	58	14	681	76*	15.47	0	2,621	93	28.18	22
Fisher, I D	Mar 31, 1976		1996	2001	24	32	9	545	68*	23.69	0	1,382	43	32.13	1
Fisher, M D ©	**Nov 9, 1997**		**2015**	**2023**	**29**	**41**	**12**	**462**	**47***	**15.93**	**0**	**2,495**	**95**	**26.26**	**9**
Flaxington, S	Oct 14, 1860	Mar 10, 1895	1882	1882	4	8	0	121	57	15.12	0	—	—	—	1
§ Fleming, S P	Apr 1, 1973		2003	2003	7	14	2	469	98	39.08	0	—	—	—	13
Fletcher, S D ©	June 8, 1964		1983	1991	107	91	31	414	28*	6.90	0	7,966	234	34.04	25
Fletcher, W	Feb 16, 1866	June 1, 1935	1892	1892	5	8	1	80	31*	11.42	0	157	7	22.42	4
Foord, C W	June 11, 1924	July 8, 2015	1947	1953	51	34	16	114	35	6.33	0	3,412	126	27.07	19
Foster, E	Nov 23, 1873	April 16, 1956	1901	1901	1	1	0	2	2	2.00	0	27	0	—	0
Foster, M J	Sept 17, 1972		1993	1994	5	7	1	165	63*	27.50	0	150	6	25.00	6
§ Foster, T W *	Nov 12, 1871	Jan 31, 1947	1894	1895	14	20	5	138	25*	9.20	0	952	58	16.41	6
Fraine, W A R	June 13, 1996		2019	2022	21	38	2	663	106	18.41	1	—	—	—	17
Frank, J *	Dec 27, 1857	Oct 22, 1940	1881	1881	1	2	0	10	7	5.00	0	17	1	17.00	3
Frank, R W * ©	May 29, 1864	Sept 9, 1950	1889	1903	18	28	4	298	58	12.41	0	9	0	—	8
Freeman, G	July 27, 1843	Nov 18, 1895	1865	1880	32	54	2	752	53	14.46	0	2,079	209	9.94	16
§ Gabriel, S T	Apr 28, 1988		2022	2022	2	3	0	7	5	2.33	0	222	5	44.40	1
Gale, A W ©	Nov 28, 1983		2004	2016	149	235	17	7,726	272	35.44	19	238	1	238.00	46
Geldart, C J	Dec 17, 1991		2010	2011	2	2	0	51	34	25.50	0	—	—	—	1
Gibb, P A * ©	July 11, 1913	Dec 7, 1977	1935	1946	36	54	7	1,545	157*	32.87	2	82	3	27.33	25/8
Gibson, B P **	Mar 31, 1996		2011	2011	1	1	1	1	1*	—	0	—	—	—	6/0
Gibson, R	Jan 22, 1996		2016	2016	1	1	0	0	0	0.00	0	42	1	42.00	0

** At 15 years and 27 days on April 27, 2011, First Day of Yorkshire's match v. Durham MCCU, he became the youngest ever English First Class cricketer.

LIST OF PLAYERS AND CAREER AVERAGES IN ALL FIRST-CLASS MATCHES FOR YORKSHIRE *(Continued)*

Player	Date of Birth	Date of Death (if known)	First Played	Last Played	M	Inns	NO	Runs	HS	Av'ge	100s	Runs	Wkts	Av'ge	Ct/St
§ Gifkins, C J *	Feb 19, 1856	Jan 31, 1897	1880	1880	2	3	0	30	23	10.00	0	—	—	—	1
Gilbert, C R	Apr 16, 1984		2007	2007	1	1	0	64	64	64.00	0	11	0	—	1
Gill, F	Sept 3, 1883	Nov 1, 1917	1906	1906	2	4	0	18	11	4.50	0	—	—	—	0
§ Gillespie, J N	©April 19, 1975		2006	2007	26	34	11	640	123*	27.82	1	2,013	59	34.11	4
Gillhouley, K	Aug 8, 1934		1961	1961	24	31	7	323	56*	13.45	0	1,702	77	22.10	16
Gough, D	© Sept 18, 1970		1989	2008	146	188	29	2,922	121	18.37	1	12,487	453	27.56	30
Goulder, A	Aug 16, 1907	June 11, 1986	1929	1929	2	1	0	3	3	3.00	0	90	3	30.00	0
§ Gray, A K D	May 19, 1974		2001	2004	18	26	3	649	104	28.21	1	1,357	30	45.23	16
Grayson, A P	Mar 31, 1971		1990	1995	52	80	10	1,958	100	27.97	1	846	13	65.07	36
Greenwood, A	Aug 20, 1847	Feb 12, 1889	1869	1880	95	166	12	2,762	91	17.93	0	9	0	—	33
Greenwood, F E *	© Sept 28, 1905	July 30, 1963	1929	1932	57	66	8	1,558	104*	26.86	1	36	2	18.00	37
Greenwood, L	July 13, 1834	Nov 1, 1909	1864	1874	50	84	12	885	83	12.29	0	1,615	85	19.00	24
Grimshaw, C H	May 12, 1880	Sept 25, 1947	1904	1908	54	75	7	1,219	85	17.92	0	221	7	31.57	42
Grimshaw, I	May 4, 1857	Jan 18, 1911	1880	1887	125	194	14	3,354	129*	18.63	4	—	—	—	76/3
Guy S M	Nov 17, 1978		2000	2011	37	52	6	742	52*	16.13	0	8	0	—	98/12
Haggas, S	Apr 18, 1856	Mar 14, 1926	1878	1882	31	47	3	478	43	10.86	0	—	—	—	10
Haigh S	© Mar 19, 1871	Feb 27, 1921	1895	1913	513	687	110	10,993	159	19.05	4	29,289	1,876	15.61	276
Hall, B	Sept 16, 1929	Feb 27, 1989	1952	1952	1	2	0	14	10	7.00	0	55	1	55.00	1
Hall, C H	Apr 5, 1906	Dec 11, 1976	1928	1934	23	22	9	67	15*	5.15	0	1,226	45	27.24	11
§ Hall, J	Nov 11, 1815	Apr 17, 1888	1863	1863	1	2	0	4	3	2.00	0	—	—	—	2
Hall, L	© Nov 1, 1852	Nov 19, 1915	1873	1894	275	477	58	9,757	160	23.28	9	781	15	52.06	173
Halliday, H	© Feb 9, 1920	Aug 27, 1967	1938	1953	182	279	18	8,361	144	32.03	12	3,119	101	30.88	140
Halliley, C	Dec 5, 1852	Mar 23, 1929	1872	1872	3	5	0	27	17	5.40	0	—	—	—	2
Hamer, A	Dec 8, 1916	Nov 3, 1993	1938	1938	2	2	0	3	3	1.50	0	64	1	64.00	2
§ Hamilton, G M	© Sept 16, 1974		1994	2003	73	108	18	2,228	125	24.75	1	5,479	222	24.68	25
Hampshire, A W	Oct 18, 1950		1975	1975	1	2	0	18	17	9.00	0	—	—	—	1
Hampshire, J	Oct 5, 1913	May 23, 1997	1937	1937	3	2	0	5	5	2.50	0	109	5	21.80	1
Hampshire, J H	© Feb 10, 1941	March 1, 2017	1961	1981	456	724	89	21,979	183*	34.61	34	1,108	24	46.16	367
§ Handscomb, P S P	Apr 26, 1991		2017	2017	9	14	1	441	101*	33.92	1	—	—	—	7

LIST OF PLAYERS AND CAREER AVERAGES IN ALL FIRST-CLASS MATCHES FOR YORKSHIRE *(Continued)*

Player	Date of Birth	Date of Death (if known)	First Played	Last Played	M	Inns	NO	Runs	HS	Av'ge	100s	Runs	Wkts	Av'ge	Ct/St
Hannon-Dalby, O J	Jun 20, 1989		2008	2012	24	25	10	45	11*	3.00	0	1,938	43	45.06	2
§ Harbord, W E *	Dec 15, 1908	July 28, 1992	1929	1935	16	21	1	411	109	20.55	1	—	—	—	7
§ Harden, R J	Aug 16, 1965		1999	2000	12	22	3	439	69	23.10	0	—	—	—	2
Hardisty, C H ©	Dec 10, 1885	Mar 2, 1968	1906	1909	38	55	5	991	84	19.82	0	—	—	—	18
Hargreaves, H S	Mar 22, 1912	Sept 29, 1990	1934	1938	18	20	6	51	9	3.64	0	1,145	55	20.81	3
§ Haris Rauf	Nov 7, 1993		2022	4	4	1	15	6	5.00	0	473	15	31.53		2
§ Harmison, S J	Oct 23, 1978		2012	2012	3	3	0	25	23	8.33	0	195	8	24.37	1
Harris, W	Nov 21, 1861	May 23, 1923	1884	1887	4	8	2	45	25	7.50	0	18	0	—	1
Harrison, G P ©	Feb 11, 1862	Sept 14, 1940	1883	1892	59	87	26	407	28	6.67	0	3,276	226	14.49	36
Harrison, H	Jan 26, 1885	Feb 11, 1962	1907	1907	2	1	1	4	4*	—	0	39	2	19.50	1
Harrison, W H	May 27, 1863	July 15, 1939	1888	1888	3	6	1	12	7	2.40	0	—	—	—	0
Hart, H W *	Sept 21, 1859	Nov 2, 1895	1888	1888	1	2	0	6	6	3.00	0	32	2	16.00	0
Hart, P R	Jan 12, 1947		1981	1981	3	5	0	23	11	4.60	0	140	2	70.00	1
Hartington, H E	Sept 18, 1881	Feb 16, 1950	1910	1911	10	10	4	51	16	8.50	0	764	23	33.21	2
Hartley, P J ©	Apr 18, 1960		1985	1997	195	237	51	3,844	127*	20.66	2	17,438	579	30.11	60
Hartley, S N ©	Mar 18, 1956		1978	1988	133	199	27	4,193	114	24.37	4	2,052	42	48.85	47
§ Harvey, I J	Apr 10, 1972		2004	2005	20	31	2	1,045	209*	36.03	2	1,218	37	32.91	12
Hatton, A G	Mar 25, 1937	Nov 1, 2022	1960	1961	3	1	1	4	4*	—	0	202	6	33.66	1
§ Hawke, Lord * ©	Aug 16, 1860	Oct 10, 1938	1881	1911	510	739	91	13,133	166	20.26	10	16	0	—	159
Hayley, H	Feb 22, 1860	June 3, 1922	1884	1898	7	12	1	122	24	11.09	0	48	0	—	3
Haywood, W J	Feb 25, 1841	Jan 7, 1912	1878	1878	1	2	0	7	7	3.50	0	14	1	14.00	0
§ Head, T M	Dec 29, 1993		2016	2016	1	2	0	56	54	28.00	0	16	0	—	0
Hicks, J	Dec 10, 1850	June 10, 1912	1872	1876	15	25	3	313	66	14.22	0	17	0	—	12
Higgins, J	Mar 13, 1877	July 19, 1954	1901	1905	9	14	5	93	28*	10.33	0	—	—	—	10/3
Hill, A	Nov 15, 1843	Aug 28, 1910	1871	1882	140	223	25	1,705	49	8.61	0	7,002	542	12.91	91
Hill, G C H	**Jan 24, 2001**		**2020**	**2023**	**36**	**58**	**4**	**1,719**	**151***	**31.83**	**3**	**1,285**	**47**	**27.34**	**18**
Hill, H *	Nov 29, 1858	Aug 14, 1935	1888	1891	14	27	2	337	34	13.48	0	—	—	—	10
Hill, L G *	Nov 2, 1860	Aug 27, 1940	1882	1882	1	2	0	13	8	6.50	0	—	—	—	1
Hirst, E T *	May 6, 1857	Oct 26, 1914	1877	1888	21	33	2	328	87*	10.58	0	—	—	—	7
Hirst, E W *	Feb 27, 1855	Oct 24, 1933	1881	1881	2	3	0	33	28	11.00	0	3	0	—	0

LIST OF PLAYERS AND CAREER AVERAGES IN ALL FIRST-CLASS MATCHES FOR YORKSHIRE *(Continued)*

Player	Date of Birth	Date of Death (if known)	First Played	Last Played	M	Inns	NO	Runs	HS	Av'ge	100s	Runs	Wkts	Av'ge	Ct/St
Hirst, G H ....©	Sept 7, 1871	May 10, 1954	1891	1921*	717	1,050	128	32,024	341	34.73	56	44,716	2,481	18.02	518
Hirst, T H	May 21, 1865	Apr 3, 1927	1899	1899	1	1	1	5	5*	—	0	27	0	—	0
§ Hodd, A J ....©	Jan 12, 1984		2012	2018	57	79	10	1,803	96*	26.13	0	14	0	—	165/11
Hodgson, D M	Feb 26, 1990		2014	2015	2	3	0	72	35	24.00	0	—	—	—	2
Hodgson, G	July 24, 1938		1964	1964	1	1	0	4	4	4.00	0	—	—	—	0/2
Hodgson, I	Nov 15, 1828	Nov 24, 1867	1863	1866	21	35	14	164	21*	7.80	0	1,537	88	17.46	11
Hodgson, L J	Jun 29, 1986		2009	2010	3	3	0	99	34	33.00	0	158	2	79.00	1
Hodgson, P	Sept 21, 1935	Mar 30, 2015	1954	1956	13	6	2	33	8*	8.25	0	648	22	29.45	6
Hoggard, M J ......©	Dec 31, 1976		1996	2009	102	120	34	956	89*	11.11	0	8,956	331	27.05	23
Holdsworth, W E N ...	Sept 17, 1928	July 31, 2016	1952	1953	27	26	12	111	22*	7.92	0	1,598	53	30.15	7
Holgate, G	June 23, 1839	July 11, 1895	1865	1867	12	19	0	174	38	9.15	0	—	—	—	17/1
Holmes, P ....©	Nov 25, 1886	Sept 3, 1971	1913	1933	485	699	74	26,220	315*	41.95	60	124	1	124.00	319
§ Hope, S D	Nov 10, 1993		2023	2023	2	4	1	187	83	62.33	0	—	—	—	6/1
Horner, N F	May 10, 1926	Dec 24, 2003	1950	1950	2	4	0	114	43	28.50	0	—	—	—	2
Houseman I J	Oct 12, 1969		1989	1991	5	2	1	18	18	18.00	0	311	3	103.66	0
Hoyle, T H	Mar 19, 1884	June 2, 1953	1919	1919	1	2	0	7	7	3.50	0	—	—	—	0/1
Hudson, B	June 29, 1851	Nov 11, 1901	1880	1880	3	4	0	13	5	3.25	0	—	—	—	2
Hunter, D ....©	Feb 23, 1860	Jan 11, 1927	1888	1909	517	681	323	4,177	58*	11.66	0	43	0	—	863/323
Hunter, J	Aug 3, 1855	Jan 4, 1891	1878	1888	143	213	61	1,183	60*	7.78	0	—	—	—	207/102
Hutchison, P M .....©	June 9, 1977		1996	2001	39	39	23	187	30	11.68	0	3,244	143	22.68	8
Hutton, L ....©	June 23, 1916	Sept, 6, 1990	1934	1955	341	527	62	24,807	280*	53.34	85	4,221	154	27.40	278
Hutton, R A ....©	Sept 6, 1942		1962	1974	208	292	45	4,986	189	20.18	4	10,254	468	21.91	160
Iddison, R	Sept 15, 1834	Mar 19, 1890	1863	1876	72	108	15	1,916	112	20.60	1	1,540	102	15.09	70
Illingworth, R ......©	June 8, 1932	Dec 25, 2021	1951	1983	496	668	131	14,986	162	27.90	14	26,806	1,431	18.73	285
§ Imran Tahir	Mar 27, 1979		2007	2007	1	2	0	5	5	2.50	0	141	0	—	0
Ingham, P G	Sept 28, 1956		1979	1981	8	14	0	290	64	20.71	0	—	—	—	0
Inglis, J W	Oct 19, 1979		2000	2000	1	2	0	4	2	2.00	0	—	—	—	0
§ Inzamam-ul-Haq	Mar 3, 1970		2007	2007	3	4	0	89	51	22.25	0	—	—	—	5
Jackson, Hon F S * ..©	Nov 21, 1870	Mar 9, 1947	1890	1907	207	328	22	10,371	160	33.89	21	9,690	506	19.15	129

LIST OF PLAYERS AND CAREER AVERAGES IN ALL FIRST-CLASS MATCHES FOR YORKSHIRE (Continued)

Player	Date of Birth	Date of Death (if known)	First Played	Last Played	M	Inns	NO	Runs	HS	Av'ge	100s	Runs	Wkts	Av'ge	Ct/St
Jackson, S R *	July 15, 1859	July 19, 1941	1891	1891	1	2	0	9	9	4.50	0	—	—	—	0
Jacques, T A *	Feb 19, 1905	Feb 23, 1995	1927	1936	28	20	7	162	35*	12.46	0	1,786	57	31.33	12
Jakeman, F	Jan 10, 1921	May 17, 1986	1946	1947	10	16	2	262	51	18.71	0	—	—	—	3
James, B	Apr 23, 1934	May 26, 1999	1954	1954	4	5	3	22	11*	11.00	0	228	8	28.50	0
§ Jaques, P A ©	May 3, 1979		2004	2013	53	82	3	4,039	243	51.12	11	112	1	112.00	46
Jarvis, P W ©	June 29, 1965		1981	1993	138	160	46	1,898	80	16.64	0	11,990	449	26.70	36
Johnson, C	Sept 5, 1947		1969	1979	100	152	14	2,960	107	21.44	2	265	4	66.25	50
Johnson, J	May 16, 1916	Jan 16, 2011	1936	1939	3	3	2	5	4*	5.00	0	27	5	5.40	1
Johnson, M	Apr 23, 1958		1981	1981	4	4	2	2	2	1.00	0	301	7	43.00	1
Joy, J	Dec 29, 1825	Sept 27, 1889	1863	1867	3	5	0	107	74	21.40	0	5	0	—	3
Judson, A	July 10, 1885	Apr 8, 1975	1920	1920	1	—	—	—	—	—	—	5	0	—	0
§ Karunaratne, F D M	Apr 28, 1988		2022	2022	3	4	0	89	36	22.25	0	—	—	—	1
§ Katich, S M	Aug 21, 1975		2002	2002	1	2	0	37	21	18.50	0	25	0	—	1
Kaye, Harold S *	May 9, 1882	Nov 6, 1953	1907	1908	18	25	1	243	37	10.12	0	—	—	—	9
Kaye, Haven	June 11, 1846	Jan 24, 1892	1872	1873	8	14	0	117	33	8.35	0	—	—	—	3
Keedy, G	Nov 27, 1974		1994	1994	1	1	0	1	1	1.00	0	—	—	—	0
§ Keighley, W G * ©	Jan 10, 1925	June 14, 2005	1947	1951	35	51	5	1,227	110	26.67	1	18	0	—	12
Kellett, S A ©	Oct 16, 1967		1989	1995	86	147	10	4,204	125*	30.68	2	7	0	—	74
Kennie, G	May 17, 1904	Apr 11, 1994	1927	1927	1	2	0	6	6	3.00	0	—	—	—	1
Kettleborough, R A	Mar 15, 1973		1994	1997	13	19	2	446	108	26.23	1	153	3	51.00	9
Kilburn, S	Oct 16, 1868	Sept 25, 1940	1896	1896	1	1	0	8	8	8.00	0	—	—	—	0
Kilner, N	July 21, 1895	Apr 28, 1979	1919	1923	69	73	7	1,253	112	18.98	2	—	—	—	34
Kilner, R ©	Oct 17, 1890	Apr 5, 1928	1911	1927	365	478	46	13,018	206*	30.13	15	14,855	857	17.33	231
King, A M	Oct 8, 1932		1955	1955	1	1	0	12	12	12.00	0	—	—	—	0
Kippax, P J	Oct 15, 1940	Jan 17, 2017	1961	1962	4	7	2	37	9	7.40	0	279	8	34.87	0
§ Kirby, S P ©	Oct 4, 1977		2001	2004	47	61	14	342	57	7.27	0	5,143	182	28.25	11
§ Kohler-Cadmore, T ©	Apr 19, 1994		2017	2022	46	77	5	2,395	176	33.26	6	—	—	—	79/1
§ Kruis, G J ©	May 9, 1974		2005	2009	54	64	31	617	50*	18.69	0	5,431	154	35.26	11
§ Lambert, G A	Jan 4, 1980		2000	2000	2	3	2	6	3*	6.00	0	133	4	33.25	1

LIST OF PLAYERS AND CAREER AVERAGES IN ALL FIRST-CLASS MATCHES FOR YORKSHIRE *(Continued)*

Player	Date of Birth	Date of Death (if known)	First Played	Last Played	M	Inns	NO	Runs	HS	Av'ge	100s	Runs	Wkts	Av'ge	Ct/St
Lancaster, W W	Feb 4, 1873	Dec 30, 1938	1895	1895	7	10	0	163	51	16.30	0	29	0	—	1
§ Landon, C W *	May 30, 1850	Mar 5, 1903	1878	1882	9	13	0	51	18	3.92	0	74	0	—	7
§ Law, W *	Apr 9, 1851	Dec 20, 1892	1871	1873	4	7	0	51	22	7.28	0	—	—	—	3
Lawson, M A K	Oct 24, 1985		2004	2007	15	21	5	197	44	12.31	0	1,699	42	40.45	7
Leadbeater, B ©	Aug 14, 1943		1966	1979	144	236	27	5,247	140*	25.10	1	5	1	5.00	80
Leadbeater, E	Aug 15, 1927	Apr 17, 2011	1949	1956	81	94	29	898	91	13.81	0	5,657	201	28.14	49
Leadbeater, H *	Dec 31, 1863	Oct 9, 1928	1884	1890	6	10	2	141	65	17.62	0	11	0	—	4
§ Leaning, J A ©	Oct 18, 1993		2013	2019	68	108	11	2,955	123	30.46	4	455	8	56.87	52
Leatham, G A B *	Apr 30, 1851	June 19, 1932	1874	1886	12	18	5	61	14	4.69	0	—	—	—	21/7
Leather, R S *	Aug 17, 1880	Jan 3, 1913	1906	1906	1	2	0	19	14	9.50	0	—	—	—	0
Lee, C	Mar 17, 1924	Sept 4, 1999	1952	1952	2	4	0	98	74	24.50	0	—	—	—	1
Lee, F ©	Nov 18, 1856	Sept 13, 1896	1882	1890	105	182	10	3,622	165	21.05	3	—	—	—	53/1
Lee, G H	Aug 24, 1854	Oct 4, 1919	1879	1879	1	2	0	13	9	6.50	0	—	—	—	0
Lee, Herbert	July 2, 1856	Feb 4, 1908	1885	1885	5	6	0	20	12	3.33	0	—	—	—	2
Lee, J E *	Mar 23, 1838	Apr 2, 1880	1867	1867	2	3	0	9	6	3.00	0	—	—	—	0
Lee, J E	Dec 23, 1988		2006	2009	2	3	1	24	21*	12.00	0	149	2	74.50	1
Leech, D J	**Jan 10, 2001**		**2020**	**2023**	**4**	**3**	**1**	**33**	**32**	**16.50**	**0**	**291**	**7**	**41.57**	**1**
Lees, A Z ©	Apr 14, 1993		2010	2018	82	140	11	4,528	275*	35.10	11	77	2	38.50	56
Legard, A D *	June 19, 1878	Aug 15, 1939	1910	1910	4	5	0	50	15	10.00	0	26	0	—	1
§ Lehmann, D S ©	Feb 5, 1970		1997	2006	88	137	8	8,871	339	68.76	26	1,952	61	32.00	35
§ Lehmann, J S	Jul 8, 1992		2016	2016	5	8	1	384	116	54.85	1	—	—	—	2
Lester, E I ©	Feb 18, 1923	Mar 23, 2015	1945	1956	228	339	27	10,616	186	34.02	24	160	3	53.33	106
Leyland, M ©	July 20, 1900	Jan 1, 1967	1920	1946	548	720	82	26,180	263	41.03	62	11,079	409	27.08	204
Lilley, A E	Apr 17, 1992		2011	2011	1	1	0	0	0	0.00	0	34	0	—	0
Linaker, L	Apr 8, 1885	Nov 17, 1961	1909	1909	1	2	0	0	0	0.00	0	28	1	28.00	0
Lister, B	Dec 9, 1850	Dec 3, 1919	1874	1878	7	11	1	36	10	3.60	0	—	—	—	2
Lister, J *	May 14, 1930	Jan 28, 1991	1954	1954	2	4	0	35	16	8.75	0	—	—	—	2
§ Lister-Kaye, K A *	Mar 27, 1892	Feb 28, 1955	1928	1928	2	2	1	13	7*	13.00	0	64	1	64.00	2
Lockwood, E	Apr 4, 1845	Dec 19, 1921	1868	1884	214	364	29	7,789	208	23.25	6	2,265	141	16.06	164/2
Lockwood, H	Oct 20, 1855	Feb 18, 1930	1877	1882	16	27	2	408	90	16.32	0	37	0	—	8

LIST OF PLAYERS AND CAREER AVERAGES IN ALL FIRST-CLASS MATCHES FOR YORKSHIRE *(Continued)*

Player	Date of Birth	Date of Death (if known)	First Played	Last Played	M	Inns	NO	Runs	HS	Av'ge	100s	Runs	Wkts	Av'ge	Ct/St
Lodge, J T	Apr 16, 1921	July 9, 2002	1948	1948	2	3	0	48	30	16.00	0	17	0	—	0
Logan, J E G	Oct 12, 1997		2018	2019	2	3	1	33	20*	16.50	0	85	4	21.25	1
Loten, T W	Jan 8, 1999		2019	2022	7	9	0	137	58	15.22	0	152	4	38.00	2
Love, J D ©	Apr 22, 1955		1975	1989	247	388	58	10,263	170*	31.10	13	835	12	69.58	123
Lowe, G E	Jan 12, 1877	Aug 15, 1932	1902	1902	1	1	1	5	5*	—	0	—	—	—	1
Lowe J R	Oct 19,1991		2010	2010	1	1	0	5	5	5.00	0	—	—	—	0
Lowson, F A ©	July 1, 1925	Sept 8, 1984	1949	1958	252	404	31	13,897	259*	37.25	30	15	0	—	180
§ Lucas, D S	Aug 19, 1978		2005	2005	1	—	—	—	—	—	—	84	8	10.50	0
Lumb, E * ©	Sept 12, 1852	Apr 5, 1891	1872	1886	14	23	4	311	70*	16.36	0	—	—	—	5
§ Lumb, M J ©	Feb 12, 1980		2000	2006	78	135	12	4,194	144	34.09	8	199	5	39.80	43
Lumb, R G ©	Feb 27, 1950		1970	1984	239	395	30	11,525	165*	31.57	22	5	0	—	129
Lupton, A W * ©	Feb 23, 1879	Apr 14, 1944	1908	1927	104	79	15	668	43*	10.43	0	88	0	—	25
Luxton, W A	**May 6, 2003**		**2022**	**2022**	**1**	**2**	**0**	**45**	**31**	**22.50**	**0**	—	—	—	**0**
Lynas, G G	Sept 7, 1832	Dec 8, 1896	1867	1867	2	3	1	4	4*	2.00	0	—	—	—	2
Lyth, A ©	**Sept 25, 1987**		**2007**	**2023**	**207**	**347**	**17**	**12,894**	**251**	**39.07**	**31**	**1,798**	**37**	**48.59**	**284**
Macaulay, G G ©	Dec 7, 1897	Dec 13, 1940	1920	1935	445	430	112	5,717	125*	17.97	3	30,554	1,774	17.22	361
McGrath, A ©	Oct 6, 1975		1995	2012	242	405	29	14,091	211	37.47	34	4,652	128	36.34	168
McHugh, F P	Nov 15, 1925	Feb 21, 2018	1949	1949	3	1	0	0	0	0.00	0	147	4	36.75	1
§ Maharaj, K A	Feb 7, 1990		2019	2019	5	9	0	239	85	26.55	0	719	38	18.92	1
§ Malan, D J ©	**Sept 3,1987**		**2020**	**2023**	**17**	**29**	**0**	**1,622**	**219**	**55.93**	**5**	**64**	**2**	**32.00**	**5**
§ Marsh, S E	Jul 9, 1983		2017	2017	2	3	1	225	125*	112.50	1	—	—	—	1
Marshall, A	July 10, 1849	Aug 3, 1891	1874	1874	1	2	0	2	2	1.00	0	11	0	—	0
§ Martyn, D R	Oct 21, 1971		2003	2003	2	3	1	342	238	171.00	1	—	—	—	2
Mason, A	May 2, 1921	Mar 22, 2006	1947	1950	18	19	3	105	22	6.56	0	1,473	51	28.88	6
Maude, E *	Dec 31, 1839	July 2, 1876	1866	1866	2	2	0	17	16	8.50	0	—	—	—	0
§ Maxwell, G J	Oct 14, 1988		2015	2015	4	7	1	244	140	40.66	1	144	4	36.00	3
Metcalfe, A A ©	Dec 25, 1963		1983	1995	184	317	19	10,465	216*	35.11	25	344	3	114.66	72
Micklethwait, W H *	Dec 13, 1885	Oct 7, 1947	1911	1911	1	1	0	44	44	44.00	0	—	—	—	0
Middlebrook, J D	May 13, 1977		1998	2015	29	38	3	534	84	15.25	0	1,899	66	28.77	1

LIST OF PLAYERS AND CAREER AVERAGES IN ALL FIRST-CLASS MATCHES FOR YORKSHIRE *(Continued)*

Player	Date of Birth	Date of Death (if known)	First Played	Last Played	M	Inns	NO	Runs	HS	Av'ge	100s	Runs	Wkts	Av'ge	Ct/St
Middlebrook, W	May 23, 1858	Apr 26, 1919	1888	1889	17	27	7	88	19*	4.40	0	895	50	17.90	17
Midgley, C A *	Nov 13, 1877	June 24, 1942	1906	1906	4	6	2	115	59*	28.75	0	149	8	18.62	3
§ Mike, B W M	Aug 24, 1998		2022	2023	2	3	0	47	25	15.66	0	91	1	91.00	1
Milburn, S M	Sept 29, 1972		1992	1995	6	8	2	22	7	3.66	0	431	14	30.78	0
§ Milligan, F W * ...©	Mar 19, 1870	Mar 31, 1900	1894	1898	81	113	10	1,879	74	18.24	0	2,736	112	24.42	40
§ Milnes, M E	July 29, 1994		2023	2023	2	2	1	90	75	90.00	0	224	7	32.00	1
Mitchell, A ©	Sept 13, 1902	Dec 25, 1976	1922	1945	401	550	69	18,189	189	37.81	39	291	5	58.20	406
Mitchell, F * ©	Aug 13, 1872	Oct 11, 1935	1894	1904	83	125	5	4,104	194	34.20	10	16	1	16.00	52
Monks, G D	Sept 3, 1929	Jan 3, 2011	1952	1952	1	1	0	3	3	3.00	0	—	—	—	1
Moorhouse, R ©	Sept 7, 1866	Jan 7, 1921	1888	1899	206	315	45	5,217	113	19.32	3	1,232	43	28.65	92
§ Moriarty, D T	Dec 2, 1999		2023	2023	4	3	3	7	4*	—	0	245	7	35.00	1
§ Morkel, M	Oct 6, 1984		2008	2008	1	2	0	8	8	4.00	0	33	1	33.00	0
Morris, A C	Oct 4, 1976		1995	1997	16	23	2	362	60	17.23	0	508	9	56.44	12
Mosley, H	Mar 8, 1850	Nov 29, 1933	1881	1881	2	4	0	1	1	0.25	0	34	3	11.33	1
Motley, A *	Feb 5, 1858	Sept 28, 1897	1879	1879	2	2	1	10	8*	10.00	0	135	7	19.28	1
Mounsey, J T ....©	Aug 30, 1871	Apr 6, 1949	1891	1897	92	145	21	1,939	64	15.63	0	444	10	44.40	45
Moxon, M D ©	May 4, 1960		1981	1997	277	476	42	18,973	274*	43.71	41	1,213	22	55.13	190
Myers, H ©	Jan 2, 1875	June 12, 1944	1901	1910	201	289	46	4,450	91	18.31	0	7,095	282	25.15	106
Myers, M	Apr 12, 1847	Dec 8, 1919	1876	1878	22	40	4	537	49	14.91	0	20	0	—	11
§ Naved-ul-Hasan, Rana	Feb 28, 1978		2008	2009	11	16	3	207	32	15.92	0	1,018	26	39.15	3
Naylor, J E	Dec 11, 1930	June 27, 1996	1953	1953	1	—	—	—	—	—	—	88	0	—	1
Newstead, J T ....©	Sept 8, 1877	Mar 25, 1952	1903	1913	96	128	17	1,791	100*	16.13	1	5,555	297	18.70	75
Nicholson, A G ...©	June 25, 1938	Nov 3, 1985	1962	1975	282	267	125	1,667	50	11.73	0	17,296	876	19.74	85
Nicholson, N G	Oct 17, 1963		1988	1989	5	8	3	134	56*	26.80	0	25	0	—	5
§ Northeast, S A	Oct 16, 1989		2021	2021	2	2	0	4	3	2.00	0	0	0	—	2
Oates, William	Jan 1, 1852	Dec 9, 1940	1874	1875	7	13	7	34	14*	5.66	0	—	—	—	5/1
Oates, W F	June 11, 1929	May 15, 2001	1956	1956	3	3	0	20	9	6.66	0	—	—	—	0
Old, C M ©	Dec 22, 1948		1966	1982	222	262	56	4,785	116	23.22	5	13,409	647	20.72	131
Oldham, S	July 26, 1948		1974	1985	59	39	18	212	50	10.09	0	3,849	130	29.60	18

LIST OF PLAYERS AND CAREER AVERAGES IN ALL FIRST-CLASS MATCHES FOR YORKSHIRE *(Continued)*

Player	Date of Birth	Date of Death (if known)	First Played	Last Played	M	Inns	NO	Runs	HS	Av'ge	100s	Runs	Wkts	Av'ge	Ct/St
Oldroyd, E ....©	Oct 1, 1888	Dec 27, 1964	1910	1931	383	509	58	15,891	194	35.23	37	1,658	42	39.47	203
§ Olivier, D ......©	May 9, 1992		2019	2021	25	32	17	224	24	14.93	0	2,432	75	32.42	7
Oyston, C	May 12, 1869	July 15, 1942	1900	1909	15	21	8	96	22	7.38	0	872	31	28.12	3
Padgett, D E V .....©	July 20, 1934	Jan 20, 2024	1951	1971	487	774	63	20,306	161*	28.55	29	208	6	34.66	250
Padgett, G H	Oct 9, 1931		1952	1952	6	7	4	56	32*	18.66	0	336	4	84.00	5
Padgett, J	Nov 21, 1860	Aug 2, 1943	1882	1889	6	9	0	92	22	10.22	0	—	—	—	2
Parker, B	June 23, 1970		1992	1998	44	71	10	1,839	138*	30.14	2	3	0	—	19
§ Parkin, C H	Feb 18, 1886	June 15, 1943	1906	1906	1	1	0	0	0	0.00	0	25	2	12.50	0
Parratt, J	Mar 24, 1859	May 6, 1905	1888	1890	2	2	0	11	11	5.50	0	75	1	75.00	4
§ Parton, J W	Jan 31, 1863	Jan. 30, 1906	1889	1889	1	2	0	16	14	8.00	0	4	1	4.00	0
§ Patel, A Y ......©	Oct 21, 1988		2019	2019	2	2	1	20	20	20.00	0	231	2	115.50	0
Patterson, S A .....©	Oct 3, 1983		2005	2022	185	226	48	2,699	63*	15.16	0	13,486	489	27.57	37
Pearson, H E	Aug 7, 1851	July 8, 1903	1878	1880	4	7	5	31	10*	15.50	0	90	5	18.00	1
Pearson, J H	May 14, 1915	May 13, 2007	1934	1936	3	3	0	54	44	18.00	0	—	—	—	0
Peate, E ......©	Mar 2, 1855	Mar 11, 1900	1879	1887	154	226	61	1,793	95	10.86	0	9,986	794	12.57	97
Peel, R ......©	Feb 12, 1857	Aug 12, 1941	1882	1897	318	510	42	9,322	210*	19.91	6	20,638	1,311	15.74	141
Penny, J H	Sept 29, 1856	July 29, 1902	1891	1891	1	1	1	8	8*	—	0	31	2	15.50	1
Pickles, C S	Jan 30, 1966		1985	1992	58	76	21	1,336	66	24.29	0	3,638	83	43.83	24
Pickles D	Nov 16, 1935	June 22, 2020	1957	1960	41	40	20	74	12	3.70	0	2,062	96	21.47	10
§ Pillans, M W	Jul 4, 1991		2018	2019	2	2	0	11	8	5.50	0	189	2	94.50	0
Pinder, G	July 15, 1841	Jan 15, 1903	1867	1880	125	199	44	1,639	57	10.57	0	325	19	17.10	145/102
Platt, R K ......©	Dec 26, 1932		1955	1963	96	103	47	405	57*	7.23	0	6,389	282	22.65	35
Plunkett, L E .....©	Apr 6, 1985		2013	2017	36	51	7	1,241	126	28.20	1	2,925	98	29.84	20
Pollard, D	Aug 7, 1835	Mar 26, 1909	1865	1865	1	2	0	3	3	1.50	0	19	0	—	0
Pollitt, G	June 3, 1874	May 19, 1942	1899	1899	1	1	0	51	51	51.00	0	—	—	—	1
§ Poysden, J E	Aug 8, 1991		2018	2018	3	5	2	25	20*	8.33	0	259	7	37.00	0
Prest, C H *	Dec 9, 1841	Mar 4, 1875	1864	1864	2	4	0	57	31	14.25	0	—	—	—	3
Preston, J M ......©	Aug 23, 1864	Nov 26, 1890	1885	1889	79	134	11	1,935	93	15.73	0	3,232	178	18.15	36
Pride, T	July 23, 1864	Feb 16, 1919	1887	1887	1	1	0	1	1	1.00	0	—	—	—	4/3

LIST OF PLAYERS AND CAREER AVERAGES IN ALL FIRST-CLASS MATCHES FOR YORKSHIRE *(Continued)*

Player	Date of Birth	Date of Death (if known)	First Played	Last Played	M	Inns	NO	Runs	HS	Av'ge	100s	Runs	Wkts	Av'ge	Ct/St
Priestley, I M	Sept 25, 1967		1989	1989	2	4	2	25	23	12.50	0	119	4	29.75	1
Pullan, P	Mar 29, 1857	Mar 3, 1901	1884	1884	1	1	0	14	14	14.00	0	5	0	—	1
§ Pujara, C A ©	Jan 25, 1988		2015	2018	10	18	1	436	133*	25.64	1	5	0	—	6
Pyrah, R M ©	Nov 1, 1982		2004	2015	51	61	8	1,621	134*	30.58	3	2527	55	45.94	22
§ Radcliffe, E J R H *©	Jan 27, 1884	Nov 23, 1969	1909	1911	64	89	13	826	54	10.86	0	134	2	67.00	21
Ramage, A	Nov 29, 1957		1979	1983	23	22	9	219	52	16.84	0	1,649	44	37.47	1
Ramsden, G	Mar 2, 1983		2000	2000	1	1	1	0	0*	—	0	68	1	68.00	0
Randhawa, G S	Jan 25, 1992		2011	2011	1	1	0	5	5	5.00	0	62	2	31.00	0
Raper, J R S *	Aug 9, 1909	Mar 9, 1997	1936	1947	3	4	0	24	15	6.00	0	—	—	—	0
Rashid, A U ©	**Feb 17, 1988**		**2006**	**2017**	**140**	**196**	**33**	**5,620**	**180**	**34.47**	**10**	**14,136**	**420**	**33.65**	**70**
§ Raval, J A ©	May 22, 1988		2018	2018	4	7	0	84	21	12.00	0	—	—	—	3
Rawlin, E R	Oct 4, 1897	Jan 11, 1943	1927	1936	8	10	1	72	35	8.00	0	498	21	23.71	2
Rawlin, J T	Nov 10, 1856	Jan 19, 1924	1880	1885	27	36	2	274	31	8.05	0	258	11	23.45	13
Rawlinson, E B	Apr 10, 1837	Feb 17, 1892	1867	1875	37	68	5	991	55	15.73	0	62	5	12.40	16
Read, J	Feb 2, 1998		2016	2016	1	1	0	14	14	14.00	0	—	—	—	4
Redfearn, J	May 13, 1862	Jan 14, 1931	1890	1890	1	1	0	5	5	5.00	0	—	—	—	0
Render, G W A	Jan 5, 1887	Sept 17, 1922	1919	1919	1	1	0	5	5	5.00	0	—	—	—	0
Revis, M L	**Nov 15, 2001**		**2019**	**2023**	**20**	**30**	**7**	**797**	**106**	**34.65**	**2**	**1,207**	**30**	**40.23**	**13**
Rhodes, A C ©	Oct 14, 1906	May 21, 1957	1932	1934	61	70	19	917	64*	17.98	0	3,026	107	28.28	45
§ Rhodes, H E *	Jan 11, 1852	Sept 10, 1889	1878	1883	10	16	1	269	64	17.93	0	—	—	—	1
Rhodes, S J	June 17, 1964		1981	1984	3	2	1	41	35	41.00	0	—	—	—	3
Rhodes, Wilfred ©	Oct 29, 1877	July 8, 1973	1898	1930	883	1,195	162	31,075	267*	30.08	46	57,634	3,598	16.01	586
Rhodes, William	Mar 4, 1883	Aug 5, 1941	1911	1911	1	1	1	1	1*	—	0	40	0	—	0
§ Rhodes, W M H	Mar 2, 1995		2015	2016	15	25	2	689	95	29.95	0	551	16	34.43	8
Richardson, J A *	Aug 4, 1908	Apr 2, 1985	1936	1947	7	12	2	308	61	30.80	0	90	2	45.00	3
§ Richardson, R B ©	Jan 12, 1962		1993	1994	23	39	1	1,310	112	34.47	1	23	1	23.00	18
§ Richardson, S A	Sept 5, 1977		2000	2003	13	23	2	377	69	17.95	0	—	—	—	11
§ Rickelton, R D	July 11, 1996		2023	2023	3	3	0	65	46	21.66	0	—	—	—	2
Riley, H	Aug 17, 1875	Nov 6, 1922	1895	1900	4	5	1	36	25*	9.00	0	54	1	54.00	1

LIST OF PLAYERS AND CAREER AVERAGES IN ALL FIRST-CLASS MATCHES FOR YORKSHIRE *(Continued)*

Player	Date of Birth	Date of Death (if known)	First Played	Last Played	M	Inns	NO	Runs	HS	Av'ge	100s	Runs	Wkts	Av'ge	Ct/St
Riley, M *	Apr 5, 1851	June 1, 1899	1878	1882	17	28	1	361	92	13.37	0	10	0	—	3
Ringrose, W ©	Sept 2, 1871	Sept 14, 1943	1901	1906	57	66	9	353	23	6.19	0	3,224	155	20.80	25
Robinson, A L ©	Aug 17, 1946	Feb 11, 2024	1971	1977	84	69	31	365	30*	9.60	0	4,927	196	25.13	48
Robinson, B L H	May 12, 1858	Dec 14, 1909	1879	1879	1	2	0	5	4	2.50	0	20	1	20.00	0
Robinson, Edward *	Dec 27, 1862	Sept 3, 1942	1887	1887	1	2	1	23	23*	23.00	0	—	—	—	0
Robinson, Emmott ©	Nov 16, 1883	Nov 17, 1969	1919	1931	413	455	77	9,651	135*	25.53	7	19,645	893	21.99	318
Robinson, E P ©	Aug 10, 1911	Nov 10, 1998	1934	1949	208	253	46	2,596	75*	12.54	0	15,141	735	20.60	189
Robinson, M A ©	Nov 23, 1966		1991	1995	90	93	36	240	23	4.21	0	6,866	218	31.49	17
Robinson, P E ©	Aug 3, 1963		1984	1991	132	217	31	6,668	189	35.84	7	238	1	238.00	96
Robinson, W	Nov 29, 1851	Aug 14, 1919	1876	1877	7	14	1	151	68	11.61	0	—	—	—	3
Roebuck C G	Aug 14, 1991		2010	2010	1	1	0	23	23	23.00	0	—	—	—	0
Root, J E ©	**Dec 30, 1990**		**2010**	**2022**	**55**	**90**	**9**	**3,644**	**236**	**44.98**	**9**	**958**	**18**	**53.22**	**34**
Roper, E *	Apr 8, 1851	Apr 27, 1921	1878	1880	5	7	1	85	68	14.16	0	—	—	—	2
Rothery, J W ©	Sept 5, 1876	June 2, 1919	1903	1910	150	236	18	4,614	161	21.16	3	44	2	22.00	45
Rowbotham, J	July 8, 1831	Dec 22, 1899	1863	1876	94	162	9	2,624	113	17.15	3	37	3	12.33	52
§ Rudolph J A ©	May 4, 1981		2007	2011	68	112	8	5,429	228*	52.20	18	311	1	311.00	79
Rudston, H	Nov 22, 1878	Apr 14, 1962	1902	1907	21	30	0	609	164	20.30	1	—	—	—	3
Ryan, M ©	June 23, 1933	Nov 16, 2015	1954	1965	150	149	58	682	26*	7.49	0	9,466	413	22.92	59
Ryder, L	Aug 28, 1900	Jan 24, 1955	1924	1924	2	2	1	1	1	1.00	0	151	4	37.75	2
Sanderson B W	Jan 3, 1989		2008	2010	3	2	1	6	6	6.00	0	190	6	31.66	0
§ Saud Shakeel	Sep 5. 1995		2023	2023	3	5	0	71	35	14.20	0	23	0	—	1
Savile, G *	Apr 26, 1847	Sept 4, 1904	1867	1874	5	7	0	140	65	20.00	0	—	—	—	2
Sayers, J J ©	Nov 5, 1983		2004	2013	97	161	13	4,855	187	32.80	9	166	6	27.66	60
§ Shan Masood	**Oct 14, 1989**		**2023**	**2023**	**7**	**13**	**1**	**720**	**192**	**60.00**	**2**	—	—	—	**2**
Schofield, C J	Mar 21, 1976		1996	1996	1	1	0	25	25	25.00	0	—	—	—	0
Schofield, D	Oct 9, 1947		1970	1974	3	4	4	13	6*	—	0	112	5	22.40	0
Scott, E	July 6, 1834	Dec 3, 1898	1864	1864	1	1	0	8	8	8.00	0	27	2	13.50	1
Sedgwick, H A	Apr 8, 1883	Dec 28, 1957	1906	1906	3	5	2	53	34	17.66	0	327	16	20.43	2
Sellers, Arthur * ©	May 31, 1870	Sept 25, 1941	1890	1899	49	88	1	1,643	105	18.88	2	84	2	42.00	40

LIST OF PLAYERS AND CAREER AVERAGES IN ALL FIRST-CLASS MATCHES FOR YORKSHIRE *(Continued)*

Player	Date of Birth	Date of Death (if known)	First Played	Last Played	M	Inns	NO	Runs	HS	Av'ge	100s	Runs	Wkts	Av'ge	Ct/St
Sellers, A B * ....©	Mar 5, 1907	Feb 20, 1981	1932	1948	334	437	51	8,949	204	23.18	4	653	8	81.62	264
Shackleton, W A	Mar 9, 1908	Nov 16, 1971	1928	1934	5	6	0	49	25	8.16	0	130	6	21.66	3
Shahzad, Ajmal .....©	July 27, 1985		2006	2012	45	58	14	1,145	88	26.02	0	4,196	125	33.56	5
§ Shan Masood	Oct 14, 1989		2023		7	13	1	720	192	60.00	2	0	0	—	2
Sharp, K ....©	Apr. 6, 1959		1976	1990	195	320	35	8,426	181	29.56	11	836	12	69.66	95
§ Sharpe, C M *	Sept 6, 1851	June 25, 1935	1875	1875	1	1	0	15	15	15.00	0	17	0	—	0
Sharpe, P J ....©	Dec 27, 1936	May 19, 2014	1958	1974	411	666	71	17,685	203*	29.72	23	140	2	70.00	526
Shaw C	Feb 17, 1964		1984	1988	61	58	27	340	31	10.96	0	4,101	123	33.34	9
Shaw, James	Mar 12, 1865	Jan 22, 1921	1896	1897	3	3	0	8	7	2.66	0	181	7	25.85	2
Shaw, Joshua	Jan 3, 1996		2016	2019	8	11	2	144	42	16.00	0	617	12	51.41	1
Sheepshanks, E R * ...	Mar 22, 1910	Dec 31, 1937	1929	1929	1	1	0	26	26	26.00	0	—	—	—	0
Shepherd, D A *	Mar 10, 1916	May 29, 1998	1938	1938	1	1	0	0	0	0.00	0	—	—	—	0
Shotton, W	Dec 1, 1840	May 26, 1909	1865	1874	2	4	0	13	7	3.25	0	—	—	—	0
Shutt, J W	June 24, 1997		2020	2022	5	7	5	12	7*	6.00	0	200	5	40.00	3
Sidebottom, A .....©	Apr 1, 1954		1973	1991	216	249	50	4,243	124	22.33	1	13,852	558	24.82	60
Sidebottom, R J .....©	Jan 15, 1978		1997	2017	137	172	55	1,674	61	14.30	0	10,128	450	22.50	37
Sidgwick, R *	Aug 7, 1851	Oct 23, 1933	1882	1882	9	13	0	64	17	4.92	0	—	—	—	7
Silverwood, C E W ..©	Mar 5, 1975		1993	2005	131	179	33	2,369	80	16.22	0	11,413	427	27.62	30
Silvester, S	Mar 12, 1951		1976	1977	6	7	4	30	14	10.00	0	313	12	26.08	2
Simpson, E T B *	Mar 5, 1867	Mar 20, 1944	1889	1889	1	2	0	1	1	0.50	0	—	—	—	0
§ Sims, Rev H M *	Mar 15, 1853	Oct 5, 1885	1875	1877	5	10	1	109	35*	12.11	0	—	—	—	2
Slinn, W	Dec 13, 1826	June 17, 1888	1863	1864	9	14	3	22	11	2.00	0	742	48	15.45	5
Smailes, T F ....©	Mar 27, 1910	Dec 1, 1970	1932	1948	262	339	42	5,686	117	19.14	3	16,593	802	20.68	153
Smales, K	Sept 15, 1927	Mar 10, 2015	1948	1950	13	19	3	165	45	10.31	0	766	22	34.81	4
Smith, A F	Mar 7, 1847	Jan 6, 1915	1868	1874	28	49	4	692	89	15.37	0	—	—	—	11
Smith, E (Morley) .* ©	Oct 19, 1869	April 9, 1945	1888	1907	154	234	18	4,453	129	20.61	2	6,278	248	25.31	112
Smith, E (Barnsley) ...	July 11, 1888	Jan 2, 1972	1914	1926	16	21	5	169	49	10.56	0	1,090	46	23.69	5
Smith, Fred (Yeadcn) ..	Dec 18, 1879	Oct 20, 1905	1903	1903	13	19	1	292	55	16.22	0	—	—	—	3
Smith, Fred (Idle)	Dec 26, 1885	Not known	1911	1911	1	1	0	11	11	11.00	0	45	2	22.50	0
Smith, G	Jan 19, 1875	Jan 16, 1929	1901	1906	2	1	0	7	7	7.00	0	62	0	—	3
Smith, J	Mar 23, 1833	Feb 12, 1909	1865	1865	2	3	0	28	16	9.33	0	72	6	12.00	3

LIST OF PLAYERS AND CAREER AVERAGES IN ALL FIRST-CLASS MATCHES FOR YORKSHIRE *(Continued)*

Player	Date of Birth	Date of Death (if known)	First Played	Last Played	M	Inns	NO	Runs	HS	Av'ge	100s	Runs	Wkts	Av'ge	Ct/St
Smith, N	Apr 1, 1949	Mar 4, 2003	1970	1971	8	11	5	82	20	13.66	0	—	—	—	14/3
Smith, R	Apr 6, 1944		1969	1970	5	8	3	99	37*	19.80	0	—	—	—	0
Smith, Walter	Aug 19, 1845	June 2, 1926	1874	1874	5	9	0	152	59	16.88	0	—	—	—	3
§ Smith, William	Nov 1, 1839	Apr 19, 1897	1865	1874	11	19	3	260	90	16.25	0	—	—	—	8
Smithson, G A ©️	Nov 1, 1926	Sept 6, 1970	1946	1950	39	60	5	1,449	169	26.34	2	84	1	84.00	21
Smurthwaite, J	Oct 17, 1916	Oct 20, 1989	1938	1939	7	9	5	29	20*	7.25	0	237	12	19.75	4
Sowden, A	Dec 1, 1853	July 5, 1921	1878	1887	8	11	0	137	37	12.45	0	22	0	—	1
Squire, D	Dec 31, 1864	Apr 28, 1922	1893	1893	1	2	0	0	0	0.00	0	25	0	—	0
Squires, P J	Aug 4, 1951		1972	1976	49	84	8	1,271	70	16.72	0	32	0	—	14
Stanley, H C *	Feb 16, 1888	May 18, 1934	1911	1913	8	13	0	155	42	11.92	0	—	—	—	6
§ Stanyforth, R T *	May 30, 1892	Feb 20, 1964	1928	1928	3	3	0	26	10	8.66	0	—	—	—	2
§ Starc, M A	Jan 30, 1990		2012	2012	2	1	1	28	28*	—	0	153	7	21.85	0
Stead, B	June 21, 1939	Apr 15, 1980	1959	1959	2	3	0	8	8	2.66	0	115	7	16.42	0
§ Steketee, M T	Jan 1, 1994		2023	2023	4	3	0	31	26	10.33	0	272	6	45.33	0
§ Stemp, R D ©️	Dec 11, 1967		1993	1998	104	135	36	1,267	65	12.79	0	8,557	241	35.50	49
Stephenson, E	June 5, 1832	July 5, 1898	1863	1873	36	61	5	803	67	14.33	0	—	—	—	30/27
Stephenson, J S *	Nov 10, 1903	Oct 7, 1975	1923	1926	16	19	2	182	60	10.70	0	65	0	—	6
Stevenson, G B ©️	Dec 16, 1955	Jan 21, 2014	1973	1986	177	217	32	3,856	115*	20.84	2	13,254	464	28.56	73
Stott, W B ©️	July 18, 1934		1952	1963	187	309	19	9,168	186	31.61	17	112	7	16.00	91
Stringer, P M	Feb 23, 1943		1967	1969	19	17	8	101	15*	11.22	0	696	32	21.75	7
Stuchbury, S	June 22, 1954		1978	1981	3	3	2	7	4*	7.00	0	236	8	29.50	0
§ Sugg, F H	Jan 11, 1862	May 29, 1933	1883	1883	8	12	4	80	13*	10.00	0	—	—	—	4/1
§ Sugg, W	May 21, 1860	May 21, 1933	1881	1881	1	1	0	9	9	9.00	0	—	—	—	0
Sullivan, J H B *	Sept 21, 1890	Feb 8, 1932	1912	1912	1	2	0	41	26	20.50	0	43	0	—	0
Sutcliffe, H ©️	Nov 24, 1894	Jan 22, 1978	1919	1945	602	864	96	38,558	313	50.20	112	381	8	47.62	402
Sutcliffe, W H H * ©️	Oct 10, 1926	Sept 16, 1998	1948	1957	177	273	34	6,247	181	26.13	6	152	6	25.33	80
Swallow, I G	Dec 18, 1962		1983	1989	61	82	18	1,296	114	20.25	1	3,270	64	51.09	28
§ Swanepoel, P J	Mar 30, 1977		2003	2003	2	3	0	20	17	6.66	0	129	3	43.00	1
§ Tait, T	Oct 7, 1872	Sept 6, 1954	1898	1899	2	3	1	7	3	3.50	0	—	—	—	1

Player	Date of Birth	Date of Death (if known)	First Played	Last Played	M	Inns	NO	Runs	HS	Av'ge	100s	Runs	Wkts	Av'ge	Ct/St
Tasker, J * ....©	Feb 4, 1887	Aug 24, 1975	1912	1913	31	43	4	586	67	15.02	0	—	—	—	14
Tattersall, G *	Apr 21, 1882	June 29, 1972	1905	1905	1	2	0	26	26	13.00	0	—	—	—	0
**Tattersall, J A ......©	Dec 15, 1994**		**2018**	**2023**	**48**	**74**	**8**	**2,192**	**180***	**33.21**	**2**	**66**	**2**	**33.00**	**118/10**
Taylor, C R	Feb 21, 1981		2001	2008	16	27	3	416	52*	17.33	0	—	—	—	8
Taylor, H	Dec 18, 1900	Oct 28, 1988	1924	1925	9	13	0	153	36	11.76	0	—	—	—	1
Taylor, H S	Dec 11, 1856	Nov 16, 1896	1879	1879	3	5	0	36	22	7.20	0	—	—	—	0
Taylor, J	Apr 2, 1850	May 27, 1924	1880	1881	9	13	1	107	44	8.91	0	—	—	—	4
Taylor, K ......©	Aug 21, 1935		1953	1968	303	505	35	12,864	203*	27.37	16	3,680	129	28.52	146
Taylor, N S	June 2, 1963		1982	1983	8	6	1	10	4	2.00	0	720	22	32.72	2
Taylor, T L * ......©	May 25, 1878	Mar. 16, 1960	1899	1906	82	122	10	3,933	156	35.11	8	—	—	—	47/2
§ Tendulkar, S R ....©	Apr 24, 1973		1992	1992	16	25	2	1,070	100	46.52	1	195	4	48.75	10
Thewlis, H	Aug 31, 1865	Nov 30, 1920	1888	1888	2	4	1	4	2*	1.33	0	—	—	—	2
Thewlis, John Sen. ...	Mar 11, 1828	Dec 29, 1899	1863	1875	44	80	3	1,280	108	16.62	1	—	—	—	21/1
Thewlis, John Jun. ...	Sept 21, 1850	Aug 9, 1901	1879	1879	3	4	0	21	10	5.25	0	—	—	—	0
**Thompson, J A ......©	Oct 9, 1996**		**2019**	**2023**	**45**	**64**	**5**	**1,257**	**98**	**21.30**	**0**	**3,677**	**138**	**26.64**	**12**
Thornicroft, N D	Jan 23, 1985		2002	2007	7	10	4	50	30	8.33	0	545	16	34.06	2
Thornton, A	July 20, 1854	Apr 18, 1915	1881	1881	3	4	0	21	7	5.25	0	—	—	—	2
Thornton, G *	Dec 24, 1867	Jan 31, 1939	1891	1891	3	4	0	21	16	5.25	0	74	2	37.00	0
Thorpe, G	Feb 20, 1834	Mar 2, 1899	1864	1864	1	2	1	14	9*	14.00	0	—	—	—	2
Threapleton, J W	July 20, 1857	July 30, 1918	1881	1881	1	1	1	8	8*	—	0	—	—	—	2/1
Tinsley, H J	Feb 20, 1865	Dec 10, 1938	1890	1891	9	13	0	56	15	4.30	0	57	4	14.25	1
Townsley, R A J	June 24, 1952		1974	1975	2	4	0	22	12	5.50	0	0	0	—	1
Towse, A D	Apr 22, 1968		1988	1988	1	1	0	1	1	1.00	0	50	3	16.66	1
Trueman, F S ......©	Feb 6, 1931	July 1, 2006	1949	1968	459	533	81	6,852	104	15.15	2	29,890	1,745	17.12	325
Tunnicliffe, J ......©	Aug 26, 1866	July 11, 1948	1891	1907	472	768	57	19,435	243	27.33	22	388	7	55.42	665
Turner, A	Sept 2, 1885	Aug 29, 1951	1910	1911	9	16	1	163	37	10.86	0	—	—	—	7
Turner, B	July 25, 1938	Dec 27, 2015	1960	1961	2	4	2	7	3*	3.50	0	47	4	11.75	2
Turner, C ......©	Jan 11, 1902	Nov 19, 1968	1925	1946	200	266	32	6,132	130	26.20	2	5,320	173	30.75	181
Turner, F I	Sept 3, 1894	Oct 18, 1954	1924	1924	5	7	0	33	12	4.71	0	—	—	—	2

Player	Date of Birth	Date of Death (if known)	First Played	Last Played	M	Inns	NO	Runs	HS	Av'ge	100s	Runs	Wkts	Av'ge	Ct/St
Tyson, C T	Jan 24, 1889	Apr 3, 1940	1921	1921	3	5	2	232	100*	77.33	1	—	—	—	1
Ullathorne, C E	Apr 11, 1845	May 2, 1904	1868	1875	27	46	8	283	28	7.44	0	—	—	—	19
Ulyett, G ....©	Oct 21, 1851	June 18, 1898	1873	1893	355	618	31	14,157	199*	24.11	15	8,181	457	17.90	235
§ Usher, J	Feb 26, 1859	Aug 9, 1905	1888	1888	1	2	0	7	5	3.50	0	31	2	15.50	1
van Geloven, J	Jan 4, 1934	Aug 21, 2003	1955	1955	3	2	1	17	16	17.00	0	224	6	37.33	2
§ Vaughan, M P .....©	Oct 29, 1974		1993	2009	151	267	14	9,160	183	36.20	20	4,268	92	46.39	55
§ Verelst, H W *	July 2, 1846	Apr 5, 1918	1868	1869	3	4	1	66	33*	22.00	0	—	—	—	1
Verity, H ....©	May 18, 1905	July 31, 1943	1930	1939	278	294	77	3,898	101	17.96	1	21,353	1,558	13.70	191
Waddington, A ......©	Feb 4, 1893	Oct 28, 1959	1919	1927	255	250	65	2,396	114	12.95	1	16,203	835	19.40	222
Wade, S ....©	Feb 8, 1858	Nov 5, 1931	1886	1890	65	11	20	1,438	74*	15.80	0	2,498	133	18.78	31
Wainwright D J .....©	Mar 21, 1985		2004	2011	29	36	11	914	104*	36.56	2	2,480	69	35.94	6
Wainwright, E ......©	Apr 8, 1865	Oct 28, 1919	1888	1902	352	545	30	11,092	228	21.53	18	17,744	998	17.77	327
Wainwright, W	Jan 21, 1882	Dec 31, 1961	1903	1905	24	36	3	648	62	19.63	0	582	19	30.63	21
Waite, M J	Dec 24, 1995		2017	2022	13	19	2	358	59	21.05	0	893	27	33.07	2
Wake, W R *	May 21, 1852	Mar 14, 1896	1881	1881	3	3	0	13	11	4.33	0	—	—	—	2
Walker, A *	June 22, 1844	May 26, 1927	1863	1870	9	16	1	138	26	9.20	0	74	1	74.00	3
Walker, C	June 27, 1919	Dec 3, 1992	1947	1948	5	9	2	268	91	38.28	0	71	2	35.50	1
Walker, T	Apr 3, 1854	Aug 28, 1925	1879	1880	14	22	2	179	30	8.95	0	7	0	—	3
Waller, G	Dec 3, 1864	Dec 11, 1937	1893	1894	3	4	0	17	13	4.25	0	70	4	17.50	1
Wallgate, L *	Nov 12, 1849	May 9, 1887	1875	1878	3	3	0	9	6	3.00	0	17	1	17.00	3
Ward, A	Nov 21, 1865	Jan 6, 1939	1886	1886	4	7	1	41	22	6.83	0	1	0	—	1
Ward, F	Aug 31, 1881	Feb 28, 1948	1903	1903	1	1	0	0	0	0.00	0	16	0	—	0
Ward, H P *	Jan 20, 1899	Dec 16, 1946	1920	1920	1	1	1	10	10*	—	0	—	—	—	1
Wardall, T A ....©	Apr 19, 1862	Dec 20, 1932	1884	1894	43	73	2	1,003	106	14.12	2	489	23	21.26	25
Wardlaw, I	Jun 29, 1985		2011	2012	4	3	2	31	17*	31.00	0	368	4	92.00	2
Wardle, J H ....©	Jan 8, 1923	July 23, 1985	1946	1958	330	418	57	5,765	79	15.96	0	27,917	1,539	18.13	210
Waring, J S	Oct 1, 1942	Oct 1, 2023	1963	1966	28	27	15	137	26	11.41	0	1,122	53	21.16	17
Waring, S ....*	Nov 4, 1838	Apr 17, 1919	1870	1870	1	1	0	9	9	9.00	0	—	—	—	0

LIST OF PLAYERS AND CAREER AVERAGES IN ALL FIRST-CLASS MATCHES FOR YORKSHIRE *(Continued)*

Player	Date of Birth	Date of Death (if known)	First Played	Last Played	M	Inns	NO	Runs	HS	Av'ge	100s	Runs	Wkts	Av'ge	Ct/St
Warner, J D	Nov 14, 1996		2020	2020	1	1	0	4	4	4.00	0	23	1	23.00	0
Washington, W A I ..©	Dec 11, 1879	Oct 20, 1927	1900	1902	44	62	6	1,290	100*	23.03	1	—	—	—	18
Watson, H	Sept 26, 1880	Nov 24, 1951	1908	1914	29	35	11	141	41	5.87	0	—	—	—	46/10
Watson, W ©	Mar 7, 1920	Apr 24, 2004	1939	1957	283	430	65	13,953	214*	38.22	26	75	0	—	170
Waud, B W *	June 4, 1837	May 31, 1889	1863	1864	6	10	1	165	42	18.33	0	—	—	—	2
Webster, C	June 9, 1838	Jan 6, 1881	1868	1868	3	5	1	30	10	7.50	0	—	—	—	1
Webster, H H	May 8, 1844	Mar 5, 1915	1868	1868	2	3	0	10	10	3.33	0	—	—	—	0
§ Weekes, L C	July 19, 1971		1994	2000	2	2	0	20	10	10.00	0	191	10	19.10	1
West, J	Oct 16, 1844	Jan 27, 1890	1868	1876	38	64	13	461	41	9.03	0	853	53	16.09	14
Wharf, A G	June 4, 1975		1994	1997	7	9	1	186	62	23.25	0	454	11	41.27	2
Wharton, J H	**Feb 1, 2001**		**2022**	**2023**	**9**	**16**	**1**	**394**	**89**	**26.26**	**0**	**114**	**1**	**114.00**	**4**
Whatmough, F J	Dec 4, 1856	June 3, 1904	1878	1882	7	11	1	51	20	5.10	0	111	5	22.20	4
Wheater, C H *	Mar 4, 1860	May 11, 1885	1880	1880	2	4	1	45	27	15.00	0	—	—	—	3
White, Sir A W * ©	Oct 14, 1877	Dec 16, 1945	1908	1920	97	128	28	1,457	55	14.57	0	7	0	—	50
White, C ©	Dec 16, 1969		1990	2007	221	350	45	10,376	186	34.01	19	7,649	276	27.71	140
Whitehead, J P	Sept 3, 1925	Aug 15, 2000	1946	1951	37	38	17	387	58*	18.42	0	2,610	96	27.47	11
Whitehead, Lees ©	Mar 14, 1864	Nov 22, 1913	1889	1904	119	172	38	2,073	67*	15.47	0	2,408	99	24.32	68
Whitehead, Luther	June 25, 1869	Jan 17, 1931	1893	1893	2	4	0	21	13	5.25	0	—	—	—	0
Whiteley, J P	Feb 28, 1955		1978	1982	45	38	17	231	20	11.00	0	2,410	70	34.42	21
Whiting, C P	Apr 18, 1888	Jan 14, 1959	1914	1920	6	10	2	92	26	11.50	0	416	15	27.73	2
Whitwell, J F *	Feb 22, 1869	Nov 6, 1932	1890	1890	1	2	0	8	4	4.00	0	11	1	11.00	0
§ Whitwell, W F *	Dec 12, 1867	Apr 12, 1942	1890	1890	10	14	2	67	26	5.58	0	518	25	20.72	2
Widdup, S	Nov 10, 1977		2000	2001	11	18	1	245	44	14.41	0	22	1	22.00	5
Wigley, D H	Oct 26, 1981		2002	2002	1	2	1	19	15	19.00	0	116	1	116.00	0
§ Wilkinson, A J A *	May 28, 1835	Dec 11, 1905	1865	1868	5	6	0	129	53	21.50	0	57	0	—	1
Wilkinson, F	May 23, 1914	Mar 26, 1984	1937	1939	14	14	1	73	18*	5.61	0	590	26	22.69	12
Wilkinson, H * ©	Dec 11, 1877	Apr 15, 1967	1903	1905	48	75	3	1,382	113	19.19	1	121	3	40.33	19
Wilkinson, R	Nov 11, 1977		1998	1998	1	1	0	9	9	9.00	0	35	1	35.00	0
Wilkinson, W H ©	Mar 12, 1881	June 4, 1961	1903	1910	126	192	14	3,812	103	21.41	1	971	31	31.32	93
§ Willey, D J ©	Feb 28, 1990		2016	2021	19	26	6	463	46	23.15	0	1,494	50	29.88	4

LIST OF PLAYERS AND CAREER AVERAGES IN ALL FIRST-CLASS MATCHES FOR YORKSHIRE (Continued)

Player	Date of Birth	Date of Death (if known)	First Played	Last Played	M	Inns	NO	Runs	HS	Av'ge	100s	Runs	Wkts	Av'ge	Ct/St
Williams, A C	Mar 1, 1887	June 1, 1966	1911	1919	12	14	10	95	48*	23.75	0	678	30	22.60	6
§ Williamson. K S ...©	Aug 8, 1990		2013	2018	19	32	3	1,292	189	44.55	1	475	11	43.18	20
Wilson, B B ....©	Dec 11, 1879	Sept 14, 1957	1906	1914	185	308	12	8,053	208	27.50	15	278	2	139.00	53
Wilson, C E M * ....©	May 15, 1875	Feb 8, 1944	1896	1899	9	13	3	256	91*	25.60	0	257	12	21.41	3
Wilson, D ....©	Aug 7, 1937	July 21, 2012	1957	1974	392	502	85	5,788	83	13.88	0	22,626	1,104	20.49	235
Wilson, E R * ......©	Mar 25, 1879	July 21, 1957	1899	1923	66	72	18	902	104*	16.70	1	3,106	197	15.76	30
Wilson, Geoffrey * ..©	Aug 21, 1895	Nov 29, 1960	1919	1924	92	94	14	983	70	12.28	0	11	0	—	33
Wilson, G A *	Feb 2, 1916	Sept 24, 2002	1936	1939	15	25	5	352	55*	17.60	0	138	1	138.00	7
Wilson, John *	June 30, 1857	Nov 11, 1931	1887	1888	4	5	1	17	13*	4.25	0	165	12	13.75	3
Wilson, J P *	Apr 3, 1889	Oct 3, 1959	1911	1912	9	14	1	81	36	6.23	0	24	1	24.00	2
Wilson, J V ....©	Jan 17, 1921	June 5, 2008	1946	1962	477	724	75	20,548	230	31.66	29	313	3	104.33	520
Wood, A ....©	Aug 25, 1898	Apr 1, 1973	1927	1946	408	481	80	8,579	123*	21.39	1	33	1	33.00	612/243
Wood, B	Dec 26, 1942		1964	1964	5	7	2	63	35	12.60	0	—	—	—	4
Wood, C H	July 23, 1934	June 28, 2006	1959	1959	4	4	1	22	10	7.33	0	319	11	29.00	1
Wood, G W	Nov 18, 1862	Dec 4, 1948	1895	1895	2	2	0	2	2	1.00	0	—	—	—	0/1
Wood, H *	Mar 22, 1855	July 31, 1941	1879	1880	10	16	1	156	36	10.40	0	212	10	21.20	8
Wood, J H *			1881	1881	2	1	0	14	14	14.00	0	—	—	—	0
Wood, M J ....©	Apr 6, 1977		1997	2007	128	222	20	6,742	207	33.37	16	27	2	13.50	113
Wood, R	June 3, 1929	May 22, 1990	1952	1956	22	18	4	60	17	4.28	0	1,346	51	26.39	5
Woodford, J D	Sept 9, 1943		1968	1972	38	61	2	1,204	101	20.40	1	185	4	46.25	12
Woodhead, F E *	May 29, 1868	Aug 25, 1943	1893	1894	4	8	0	57	18	7.12	0	—	—	—	3
Woodhouse, W H *	Apr 16, 1856	Mar 4, 1938	1884	1885	9	13	0	218	63	16.76	0	—	—	—	6
Wormald, A	May 10, 1855	Feb 6, 1940	1885	1891	7	11	3	161	80	20.12	0	—	—	—	10/2
Worsley, W A * .....©	Apr 5, 1890	Dec 4, 1973	1928	1929	60	50	4	722	60	15.69	0	—	—	—	32
Wrathmell, L F	Jan 22, 1855	Sept 16, 1928	1886	1886	1	2	0	18	17	9.00	0	—	—	—	0
Wright, R	July 19, 1852	Jan 2, 1891	1877	1877	2	4	1	28	22	9.33	0	—	—	—	0
Wright, T J *	Mar 5, 1900	Nov 7, 1962	1919	1919	1	1	0	12	12	12.00	0	—	—	—	0
Yardley, N W D * ...©	Mar 19, 1915	Oct 3, 1989	1936	1955	302	420	56	11,632	183*	31.95	17	5,818	195	29.83	220
Yeadon, J	Dec 10, 1861	May 30, 1914	1888	1888	3	6	2	41	22	10.25	0	—	—	—	5/3

LIST OF PLAYERS AND CAREER AVERAGES IN ALL FIRST-CLASS MATCHES FOR YORKSHIRE *(Continued)*

Player	Date of Birth	Late of Death (if known)	First Played	Last Played	M	Inns	NO	Runs	HS	Av'ge	100s	Runs	Wkts	Av'ge	Ct/St
§ Younus Khan .....©	Nov 29, 1977		2007	2007	13	19	2	824	217*	48.47	3	342	8	42.75	11
§ Yuvraj Singh	Dec 12, 1981		2003	2003	7	12	2	145	56	14.50	0	130	3	43.33	12

In the career averages it should be noted that the bowling analysis for the second Cambridgeshire innings at Ashton-under-Lyne in 1865 has not been found. G R Atkinson took 3 wickets, W Cuttell 2, G Freeman 4 and R Iddison 1.The respective bowling averages have been calculated excluding these wickets.

MOST FIRST-CLASS APPEARANCES FOR YORKSHIRE

Matches	Player	Matches	Player
883	W Rhodes (1898-1930)	477	J V Wilson (1946-1962)
717	G H Hirst (1891-1929)	472	J Tunnicliffe (1891-1907)
676	D Denton (1894-1920)	459	F S Trueman (1949-1968)
602	H Sutcliffe (1919-1945)	456	J H Hampshire (1961-1981)
548	M Leyland (1920-1947)	445	G G Macaulay (1920-1935)
536	D B Close (1949-1970)	429	D L Bairstow (1970-1990)
517	D Hunter (1888-1909)	427	A Dolphin (1905-1927)
513	S Haigh (1895-1913)	425	P Carrick (1970-1993)
510	Lord Hawke (1881-1911)	414	G Boycott (1962-1986)
496	R Illingworth (1951-1983)	413	E. Robinson (1919-1931)
491	† J G Binks (1955-1969)	411	P J Sharpe (1958-1974)
487	D E V Padgett (1951-1971)	408	A Wood (1927-1946)
485	P Holmes (1913-1933)	401	A Mitchell (1922-1945)

† Kept wicket in 412 consecutive Championship matches 1955-1969

MOST TOTAL APPEARANCES FOR YORKSHIRE
(First-Class, Domestic List A and t20)

Matches	Player	Matches	Player
883	W Rhodes (1898-1930)	513	S Haigh (1895-1913)
832	D L Bairstow (1970-1990)	510	Lord Hawke (1881-1911)
729	P Carrick (1970-1993)	502	P J Sharpe (1958-1974)
719	R J Blakey (1985-2004)	485	P Holmes (1913-1933)
717	G H Hirst (1891-1929)	477	J V Wilson (1946-1962)
690	J H Hampshire (1961-1981)	472	J Tunnicliffe (1891-1907)
678	G Boycott (1962-1986)	470	F S Trueman (1949-1968)
676	D Denton (1894-1920)	467	J D Love (1975-1989)
602	H Sutcliffe (1919-1945)	453	D Wilson (1957-1974)
583	A McGrath (1995-2012)	452	A Sidebottom (1973-1991)
581	D Byas (1986-2001)	445	G G Macaulay(1920-1935)
568	D B Close (1949-1970)	443	C M Old (1966-1982)
548	M Leyland (1920-1947)	427	A Dolphin (1905-1927)
546	C White (1990-2007)	414	P J Hartley (1985-1997)
544	D E V Padgett (1951-1971)	413	E Robinson (1919-1931)
537	R Illingworth (1951-1983)	408	A Wood (1927-1946)
521	J G Binks (1955-1969)	402	A G Nicholson (1962-1975)
517	D Hunter (1888-1909)	401	A Mitchell (1922-1945)
514	M D Moxon (1980-1997)		

Yorkshire County Cricket Club thanks Statistician JOHN T. POTTER, who in 2014 revamped and streamlined Yorkshire's One-Day Records Section. John's symbols in the pages that follow are:

$ = Sunday and National Leagues, Pro 40, Clydesdale Bank 40 and Yorkshire Bank 40

= Benson & Hedges Cup

+ = Gillette Cup, NatWest Trophy, Cheltenham & Gloucester Trophy, Friends Provident Trophy and Royal London Cup

Yorkshire played no List A matches in 2020 because of the Covid-19 pandemic

WINNERS OF THE GILLETTE CUP, NATWEST TROPHY, CHELTENHAM & GLOUCESTER TROPHY FRIENDS PROVIDENT TROPHY AND ROYAL LONDON ONE-DAY CUP

Yorkshire's Position

GILLETTE CUP

1963	Sussex	Quarter-Final
1964	Sussex	Round 2
1965	**Yorkshire**	**Winner**
1966	Warwickshire	Round 2
1967	Kent	Quarter-Final
1968	Warwickshire	Round 2
1969	**Yorkshire**	**Winner**
1970	Lancashire	Round 1
1971	Lancashire	Round 2
1972	Lancashire	Round 1
1973	Gloucestershire	Round 1
1974	Kent	Quarter-Final
1975	Lancashire	Round 2
1976	Northamptonshire	Round 1
1977	Middlesex	Round 2
1978	Sussex	Quarter-Final
1979	Somerset	Quarter-Final
1980	Middlesex	Semi-Final

NATWEST TROPHY

1981	Derbyshire	Round 1
1982	Surrey	Semi-Final
1983	Somerset	Round 2
1984	Middlesex	Round 1
1985	Essex	Round 2
1986	Sussex	Quarter-Final
1987	Nottinghamshire	Quarter-Final
1988	Middlesex	Round 2
1989	Warwickshire	Round 2
1990	Lancashire	Quarter-Final
1991	Hampshire	Round 1
1992	Northamptonshire	Round 2
1993	Warwickshire	Quarter-Final

Yorkshire's Position

1994	Worcestershire	Round 2
1995	Warwickshire	Semi-Final
1996	Lancashire	Semi-Final
1997	Essex	Quarter-Final
1998	Lancashire	Round 2
1999	Gloucestershire	Semi-Final
2000	Gloucestershire	Round 4

CHELTENHAM & GLOUCESTER TROPHY

2001	Somerset	Quarter-Final
2002	**Yorkshire**	**Winner**
2003	Gloucestershire	Round 4
2004	Gloucestershire	Semi-Final
2005	Hampshire	Semi-Final
2006	Sussex	North 7 (10)

FRIENDS PROVIDENT TROPHY

2007	Durham	North 5 (10)
2008	Essex	Semi-Final
2009	Hampshire	Group C 3 (5)

ROYAL LONDON ONE-DAY CUP

2014	Durham	Quarter-Final
2015	Gloucestershire	Semi-Final
2016	Warwickshire	Semi-Final
2017	Nottinghamshire	Quarter-Final
2018	Hampshire	Semi-Final
2019	Somerset	North 6 (9)
2020	*Not played: COVID-19 restrictions*	
2021	Glamorgan	Quarter-Final
2022	Kent	Group B 5 (9)

METRO BANK ONE-DAY CUP

2023	Leicestershire	Group A 6 (9)

WINNERS OF THE NATIONAL AND SUNDAY LEAGUES, PRO 40, CLYDESDALE BANK 40 AND YORKSHIRE BANK 40 1969-2014

		Yorkshire's Position			*Yorkshire's Position*
SUNDAY LEAGUE			1993	Glamorgan	9th
1969	Lancashire	8th	1994	Warwickshire	5th
1970	Lancashire	14th	1995	Kent	12th
1971	Worcestershire	15th	1996	Surrey	3rd
1972	Kent	4th	1997	Warwickshire	10th
1973	Kent	2nd	1998	Lancashire	9th
1974	Leicestershire	=6th	**NATIONAL LEAGUE**		
1975	Hampshire	=5th	1999	Lancashire	5th Div 1
1976	Kent	15th	2000	Gloucestershire	2nd Div 1
1977	Leicestershire	=13th	2001	Kent	6th Div 1
1978	Hampshire	7th	2002	Glamorgan	4th Div 1
1979	Somerset	=4th	2003	Surrey	8th Div 1
1980	Warwickshire	=14th	2004	Glamorgan	4th Div 2
1981	Essex	=7th	2005	Essex	8th Div 2
1982	Sussex	16th	2006	Essex	9th Div 2
1983	**Yorkshire**	**1st**	2007	Worcestershire	6th Div 2
1984	Essex	=14th	2008	Sussex	2nd Div 2
1985	Essex	6th	2009	Sussex	7th Div 1
1986	Hampshire	8th	**CLYDESDALE BANK 40**		
1987	Worcestershire	=13th	2010	Warwickshire	Group B 1 (7) (Semi-Final)
1988	Worcestershire	8th			
1989	Lancashire	11th	2011	Surrey	Group A 6 (7)
1990	Derbyshire	6th	2012	Hampshire	Group C 5 (7)
1991	Nottinghamshire	7th	2013	Nottinghamshire	Group C 6 (7)
1992	Middlesex	15th			

BENSON & HEDGES WINNERS 1972-2002

		Yorkshire's Position			*Yorkshire's Position*
1972	Leicestershire	Final	1988	Hampshire	Group B 4 (5)
1973	Kent	Group N 3 (5)	1989	Nottinghamshire	Group C 3 (5)
1974	Surrey	Quarter-Final	1990	Lancashire	Group C 3 (5)
1975	Leicestershire	Quarter-Final	1991	Worcestershire	Semi-Final
1976	Kent	Group D 3 (5)	1992	Hampshire	Group C 5 (5)
1977	Gloucestershire	Group D 3 (5)	1993	Derbyshire	Round One
1978	Kent	Group D 4 (5)	1994	Warwickshire	Round One
1979	Essex	Semi-Final	1995	Lancashire	Quarter-Final
1980	Northamptonshire	Group B 4 (5)	1996	Lancashire	Semi-Final
1981	Somerset	Quarter-Final	1997	Surrey	Quarter-Final
1982	Somerset	Group A 5 (5)	1998	Essex	Semi-Final
1983	Middlesex	Group B 5 (5)	1999	Gloucestershire	Final
1984	Lancashire	Semi-Final	2000	Gloucestershire	Quarter-Final
1985	Leicestershire	Group B 3 (5)	2001	Surrey	Semi-Final
1986	Middlesex	Group B 3 (5)	2002	Warwickshire	Quarter-Final
1987	**Yorkshire**	**Winner**			

SEASON-BY-SEASON RECORD OF ALL LIST A MATCHES PLAYED BY YORKSHIRE 1963-2023

Season	Played	Won	Lost	Tie	N R	Abd	Season	Played	Won	Lost	Tie	N R	Abd
1963	2	1	1	0	0	0	1995	27	15	11	0	1	1
1964	1	0	1	0	0	0	1996	27	18	9	0	0	0
1965	4	4	0	0	0	1	1997	25	14	10	1	0	1
1966	1	0	1	0	0	0	1998	25	14	10	0	1	0
1967	2	1	1	0	0	0	1999	23	13	10	0	0	0
1968	1	0	1	0	0	0	2000	24	13	10	0	1	0
1969	19	12	7	0	0	2	2001	26	13	13	0	0	0
1970	17	5	10	0	2	0	2002	27	16	11	0	0	1
1971	15	5	10	0	0	2	2003	18	6	12	0	0	0
1972	25	15	8	0	2	1	2004	23	13	8	0	2	0
1973	21	14	7	0	0	0	2005	22	8	14	0	0	0
1974	22	12	9	0	1	1	2006	15	4	10	0	1	2
1975	22	12	10	0	0	0	2007	17	8	7	0	2	1
1976	22	9	13	0	0	0	2008	18	10	4	1	3	0
1977	19	5	10	0	4	2	2009	16	6	9	0	1	0
1978	22	10	11	0	1	2	2010	13	10	3	0	0	0
1979	21	12	6	0	3	3	2011	12	5	7	0	0	0
1980	23	9	14	0	0	0	2012	11	4	7	0	0	1
1981	19	9	8	0	2	3	2013	13	4	9	0	0	0
1982	23	7	14	1	1	1	2014	10	6	4	0	0	0
1983	19	11	7	0	1	3	2015	10	5	3	0	2	0
1984	23	10	13	0	0	0	2016	10	5	4	0	1	0
1985	19	9	9	0	1	3	2017	10	6	3	0	1	0
1986	22	11	9	1	1	1	2018	9	6	3	0	0	1
1987	24	14	9	0	1	2	2019	8	2	3	2	0	0
1988	21	9	9	0	3	1	2020	No matched played due to Covid-19					
1989	23	10	13	0	0	0	2021	9	4	3	0	2	0
1990	22	13	9	0	0	1	2022	8	4	4	0	0	0
1991	24	13	10	0	1	0	2023	6	2	4	0	0	2
1992	21	8	13	0	0	2							
1993	21	10	10	0	1	0	1021	505	466	6	44	42	
1994	19	11	8	0	0	1							

Abandoned matches are not included in the list of matches played.

ABANDONED LIST A MATCHES (42)

1965	v. South Africa at Bradford		v. Warwickshire at Birmingham $
1969 (2)	v. Warwickshire at Harrogate $		v. Lancashire at Leeds $
	v. Lancashire at Manchester $	1986	v. Kent at Canterbury $
1971 (2)	v. Gloucestershire at Sheffield $	1987 (2)	v. Sussex at Hull $
	v. Somerset at Weston-Super-Mare $		v. Hampshire at Leeds $
1972	v. Sussex at Leeds $	1988	v. Northamptonshire at Northampton $
1974	v. Warwickshire at Leeds $		
1977 (2)	v. Warwickshire at Birmingham $	1990	v. Glamorgan at Newport $
	v. Surrey at Leeds $	1992 (2)	v. Sussex at Hove $
1978 (2)	v. Essex at Bradford $		v. Durham at Darlington $
	v. Gloucestershire at Hull $	1994	v. Essex at Leeds $
1979 (3)	v. Leicestershire at Middlesbrough $	1995	v. Derbyshire at Chesterfield #
	v. Kent at Huddersfield $	1997	v. Sussex at Scarborough $
	v. Worcestershire at Worcester $	2002	v. Nottinghamshire at Nottingham $
1981 (3)	v. Warwickshire at Birmingham $	2006 (2)	v. Nottinghamshire at Leeds +
	v. Lancashire at Leeds #		v. Derbyshire at Derby $
	v. Sussex at Hove $	2007	v. Warwickshire at Birmingham +
1982	v. Glamorgan at Bradford $	2012	v. Northamptonshire at Leeds $
1983 (3)	v. Derbyshire at Chesterfield #	2018	v. Nottinghamshire at Leeds +
	v. Surrey at Leeds $	2023 (2)	v. Lancashire at Scarborough +
	v. Essex at Chelmsford $		v. Nottinghamshire at Nottingham +
1985 (3)	v. Derbyshire at Scarborough $		

ANALYSIS OF LIST A RESULTS V. ALL TEAMS 1963-2023
DOMESTIC MATCHES

Opponents	Played	HOME				AWAY				
		Won	Lost	Tied	N. R	Won	Lost	Tied	N. R	Abd
Derbyshire	67	20	9	1	1	22	9	1	4	4
Durham	31	10	5	0	1	7	7	0	1	1
Essex	50	12	12	0	0	12	14	0	0	3
Glamorgan	41	9	8	0	0	11	13	0	0	2
Gloucestershire	55	12	12	0	2	8	19	0	2	2
Hampshire	47	11	11	0	1	9	15	0	0	1
Kent	57	13	12	0	1	10	21	0	0	2
Lancashire	65	10	18	0	2	15	18	0	2	4
Leicestershire	70	20	16	0	0	14	17	1	2	1
Middlesex	49	14	4	0	3	9	17	0	2	0
Northamptonshire	62	19	11	0	4	20	7	0	1	2
Nottinghamshire	61	19	8	1	3	10	17	0	3	4
Somerset	55	13	14	0	1	11	16	0	0	1
Surrey	58	13	16	0	0	11	18	0	0	2
Sussex	46	11	11	0	1	11	12	0	0	5
Warwickshire	64	12	18	1	2	13	17	1	0	6
Worcestershire	66	14	20	0	2	17	13	0	0	1
Bedfordshire	1	0	0	0	0	1	0	0	0	0
Berkshire	2	0	0	0	0	2	0	0	0	0
Cambridgeshire	3	2	0	0	0	1	0	0	0	0
Cheshire	1	0	0	0	0	1	0	0	0	0
Combined Universities	3	0	2	0	0	1	0	0	0	0
Devon	4	0	0	0	0	4	0	0	0	0
Dorset	1	0	0	0	0	1	0	0	0	0
Durham (M C)	3	1	1	0	0	1	0	0	0	0
Herefordshire	1	0	0	0	0	1	0	0	0	0
Ireland	4	3	0	0	0	1	0	0	0	0
Minor Counties	11	6	0	0	0	5	0	0	0	0
Netherlands	4	1	1	0	0	1	1	0	0	0
Norfolk	2	1	0	0	0	1	0	0	0	0
Northumberland	1	1	0	0	0	0	0	0	0	0
Scotland	16	8	0	0	0	8	0	0	0	0
Shropshire	2	0	0	0	0	1	1	0	0	0
Unicorns	4	2	0	0	0	2	0	0	0	0
Wiltshire	1	0	0	0	0	1	0	0	0	0
Yorkshire Cricket Board	1	0	0	0	0	1	0	0	0	0
Total	**1009**	**257**	**209**	**3**	**24**	**244**	**252**	**3**	**17**	**41**

OTHER MATCHES

Opponents	Played	Won	Lost	Tied	N. R	Won	Lost	Tied	N. R	Abd
Australia	3	0	1	0	2	0	0	0	0	0
Bangladesh A	1	1	0	0	0	0	0	0	0	0
South Africa	0	0	0	0	0	0	0	0	0	1
South Africa A	1	0	0	0	1	0	0	0	0	0
Sri Lanka A	3	0	3	0	0	0	0	0	0	0
West Indies	1	1	0	0	0	0	0	0	0	0
West Indies A	1	0	1	0	0	0	0	0	0	0
Young Australia	1	1	0	0	0	0	0	0	9	0
Zimbabwe	1	1	0	0	0	0	0	0	0	0
Total	**12**	**4**	**5**	**0**	**3**	**0**	**0**	**0**	**0**	**1**
Grand Total	**1021**	**261**	**214**	**3**	**27**	**244**	**252**	**3**	**17**	**42**

Abandoned matches are not included in the list of matches played.

LIST A HIGHEST AND LOWEST SCORES BY AND AGAINST YORKSHIRE
PLUS INDIVIDUAL BEST BATTING AND BOWLING

The lowest score is the lowest all-out total or the lowest score at completion of the allotted overs, 10-over matches not included

Yorkshire versus:

Derbyshire

		By Yorkshire			Against Yorkshire		
Highest Score:	In Yorkshire	349:7		at Leeds 2017 +	334:8		at Leeds 2017 +
	Away	288:6		at Derby 2002 #	268:8		at Chesterfield 2010 $
Lowest Score:	In Yorkshire	117		at Huddersfield 1978 $	87		at Scarborough 1973 $
	Away	132		at Chesterfield 1986 $	109		at Chesterfield 2022 +
Best Batting:	In Yorkshire	140	P S P Handscomb	at Leeds 2017 +	112	W L Madsen	at Leeds 2017 +
	Away	115*	M J Wood	at Derby 2002 #	109*	C J Adams	at Derby 1997 $
Best Bowling:	In Yorkshire	6-32	S A Patterson	at Leeds 2010 $	4-20	F E Rumsey	at Bradford 1973 #
	Away	5-35	C W J Athey	at Chesterfield 1981 $	5-24	C J Tunnicliffe	at Derby 1981 #

Durham

		By Yorkshire			Against Yorkshire		
Highest Score:	In Yorkshire	339:4		at Leeds 2017 +	335:5		at Leeds 2017 +
	Away	328:4		at Chester-le-Street 2018 +	281:7		at Chester-le-Street 2016 +
Lowest Score:	In Yorkshire	133		at Leeds 1995 $	121		at Scarborough 1997 $
	Away	122		at Chester-le-Street 2007 $	136		at Chester-le-Street 1996 $
Best Batting:	In Yorkshire	174	J M Bairstow	at Leeds 2017 +	114	W Larkins	at Leeds 1993 $
	Away	164	T Kohler-Cadmore	at Chester-le-Street 2018 +	124*	J P Maher	at Chester-le-Street 2006 +
Best Bowling	In Yorkshire	4-18	C White	at Scarborough 1997 $	4-20	S J E Brown	at Leeds 1995 $
	Away	4-26	C E W Silverwood	at Chester-le-Street 1996 $	4-31	P D Collingwood	at Chester-le-Street 2000 #

Essex

		By Yorkshire			Against Yorkshire		
Highest Score:	In Yorkshire	290:6		at Scarborough 2014 +	291:5		at Scarborough 2014 +
	Away	307:3		at Chelmsford 1995 +	317:7		at Chelmsford 2021 +
Lowest Score:	In Yorkshire	54		at Leeds 2003 $	108		at Leeds 1996 $
	Away	119:8		at Colchester 1987 $	123		at Colchester 1974 $
Best Batting:	In Yorkshire	111*	J A Leaning	at Scarborough 2014 +	119*	R N ten Doeschate	at Scarborough 2014 +
	Away	125*	A W Gale	at Chelmsford 2010 $	136*	N Hussain	at Chelmsford 2002 #
Best Bowling:	In Yorkshire	4-20	G B Stevenson	at Barnsley 1977 #	6-18	R E East	at Hull 1969 $
	Away	5-37	D M Bess	at Chelmsford 2023 +	5-20	R E East	at Colchester 1979 $

LIST A HIGHEST AND LOWEST SCORES BY AND AGAINST YORKSHIRE
PLUS INDIVIDUAL BEST BATTING AND BOWLING *(Continued)*

Yorkshire versus:

Glamorgan

		By Yorkshire			Against Yorkshire		
Highest Score:	In Yorkshire	253:4		at Leeds 1991 $	216:6		at Leeds 2013 $
	Away	257		at Colwyn Bay 2013 $	285:7		at Colwyn Bay 2013 $
		257:9		at Cardiff 2022 +			
Lowest Score:	In Yorkshire	139		at Hull 1981 $	83		at Leeds 1987 +
	Away	93-8		at Swansea 1985 $	90		at Neath 1969 $
Best Batting:	In Yorkshire	96	A A Metcalfe	at Leeds 1991 $	97*	G P Ellis	at Leeds 1976 $
	Away	141*	M D Moxon	at Cardiff 1991 #	127	A R Butcher	at Cardiff 1991 #
Best Bowling:	In Yorkshire	5-22	P Carrick	at Leeds 1991 $	5-26	D S Harrison	at Leeds 2002 $
	Away	6-40	R J Sidebottom	at Cardiff 1998 $	5-16	G C Holmes	at Swansea 1985 $

Gloucestershire

		By Yorkshire			Against Yorkshire		
Highest Score:	In Yorkshire	263:9		at Leeds 2015 +	269		at Leeds 2009 +
	Away	262:7		at Bristol 1996 $	294:6		at Cheltenham 2010 $
Lowest Score:	In Yorkshire	115		at Leeds 1973 $	91		at Scarborough 2001 $
	Away	133		at Cheltenham 1999 $	90		at Tewkesbury 1972 $
Best Batting:	In Yorkshire	118	J A Rudolph	at Leeds 2009 +	146*	S Young	at Leeds 1997 $
	Away	100*	J D Love	at Gloucester in 1985 $	143*	C M Spearman	at Bristol 2004 $
		100*	R J Blakey	at Cheltenham 1990 $			
Best Bowling:	In Yorkshire	5-42	N D Thornicroft	at Leeds 2003 $	5-33	M C J Ball	at Leeds 2003 $
	Away	4-25	R D Stemp	at Bristol 1996 $	5-42	M C J Ball	at Cheltenham 1999 $

Hampshire

		By Yorkshire			Against Yorkshire		
Highest Score:	In Yorkshire	259:4		at Middlesbrough 1985 $	313:9		at Scarborough 2022 +
	Away	264:2		at Southampton 1995 $	348:9		at West End, Southampton, 2018 +
Lowest Score:	In Yorkshire	74:9		at Hull 1970 $	50		at Leeds 1991 #
	Away	118		at Southampton 1990 +	133		at Bournemouth 1976 $
Best Batting:	In Yorkshire	104*	D Byas	at Leeds 1999 #	155*	B A Richards	at Hull 1970 $
	Away	97*	M G Bevan	at Southampton 1995 $	171	J M Vince	at West End, Southampton, 2018 +
Best Bowling:	In Yorkshire	5-16	G M Hamilton	at Leeds 1998 $	5-33	A J Murtagh	at Huddersfield 1977 $
	Away	5-33	A U Rashid	at Southampton 2014 +	5-31	D W White	at Southampton 1969 $

LIST A HIGHEST AND LOWEST SCORES BY AND AGAINST YORKSHIRE
PLUS INDIVIDUAL BEST BATTING AND BOWLING *(Continued)*

Yorkshire versus:

Kent

		By Yorkshire			Against Yorkshire		
Highest Score:	In Yorkshire	299:3		at Leeds 2002 $	282:9		at Scarborough 2023 +
	Away	282:6		at Canterbury 2022 +	297:7		at Canterbury 2022 +
Lowest Score:	In Yorkshire	75		at Leeds 1995 $	133		at Leeds 1974 $
					133		at Leeds 1979 #
	Away	114		at Canterbury 1978 #	105		at Canterbury 1969 $
Best Batting:	In Yorkshire	130*	R J Blakey	at Scarborough 1991 $	136	J D M Evison	at Scarborough 2023 +
	Away	102	A McGrath	at Canterbury 2001 $	118*	C J Tavare	at Canterbury 1981 +
Best Bowling:	In Yorkshire	4-15	A G Nicholson	at Leeds 1974 $	6-32	M T Coles	at Leeds 2012 $
	Away	6-18	D Wilson	at Canterbury 1969 $	5-25	B D Julien	at Canterbury 1971 +

Lancashire

		By Yorkshire			Against Yorkshire		
Highest Score:	In Yorkshire	310		at Leeds 2019 +	311:6		at Leeds 2019 +
	Away	379:7		at Manchester 2018 +	363		at Manchester 2018 +
Lowest Score:	In Yorkshire	81		at Leeds 1998 $	68		at Leeds 2000 $
		81		at Leeds 2002 #			
	Away	125		at Manchester 1973 #	84		at Manchester 2016 +
Best Batting:	In Yorkshire	111*	D Byas	at Leeds 1996 $	102*	N J Speak	at Leeds 1992 $
	Away	144	A Lyth	at Manchester 2018 +	141*	B J Hodge	at Manchester 2007 +
Best Bowling:	In Yorkshire	5-25	C White	at Leeds 2000 #	6-25	G Chapple	at Leeds 1998 $
	Away	4-18	G S Blewett	at Manchester 1999 +	5-49	M Watkinson	at Manchester 1991 #

Leicestershire

		By Yorkshire			Against Yorkshire		
Highest Score:	In Yorkshire	379:7		at Leeds 2019 +	302:7		at Leeds 2008 $
	Away	376:3		at Leicester 2016 +	327:7		at Leicester 2021 +
Lowest Score:	In Yorkshire	93		at Leeds 1998 $	141		at Hull 1975 $
	Away	89:9		at Leicester 1989 $	53		at Leicester 2000 $
Best Batting:	In Yorkshire	156	G S Ballance	at Leeds 2019 +	108	N E Briers	at Bradford 1984 $
	Away	176	T M Head	at Leicester 2016 +	127	M S Harris	at Leicester 2021 +
Best Bowling:	In Yorkshire	5-29	M W Pillans	at Leeds 2019 +	5-24	C W Henderson	at Leeds 2004 $
	Away	5-16	S Stuchbury	at Leicester 1982 $	4-25	J Ormond	at Leicester 2001 #

LIST A HIGHEST AND LOWEST SCORES BY AND AGAINST YORKSHIRE PLUS INDIVIDUAL BEST BATTING AND BOWLING *(Continued)*

Yorkshire versus:

Middlesex

		By Yorkshire			Against Yorkshire		
Highest Score:	In Yorkshire	271:7		at Scarborough 1990 $	245:8		at Scarborough 2010 $
	Away	275:4		at Lord's 2011 $	273:6		at Southgate 2004 $
Lowest Score:	In Yorkshire	148		at Leeds 1974 $	23		at Leeds 1974 $
	Away	90		at Lord's 1964 +	107		at Lord's 1979 #
Best Batting:	In Yorkshire	124*	J A Rudolph	at Scarborough 2010 $	104	P N Weekes	at Leeds 1996 +
	Away	116	A A Metcalfe	at Lord's 1991	125*	O A Shah	at Southgate 2004 $
Best Bowling:	In Yorkshire	4-6	R Illingworth	at Hull 1983 $	4-24	N G Cowans	at Leeds 1986 +
	Away	4-28	H P Cooper	at Lord's 1979 #	5-44	T M Lamb	at Lord's 1975 #

Northamptonshire

		By Yorkshire			Against Yorkshire		
Highest Score:	In Yorkshire	353:5		at York 2022 +	320		at York 2022 +
	Away	341:3		at Northampton 2006 +	351		at Northampton 2019 +
Lowest Score:	In Yorkshire	129		at Leeds 2000 $	127		at Huddersfield 1974 $
	Away	112		at Northampton 1975 $	109		at Northampton 2000 $
Best Batting:	In Yorkshire	143	W A R Fraine	at York 2022 +	132	U Afzaal	at Leeds 2007 +
	Away	152*	G S Ballance	at Northampton in 2017 +	161	D J G Sales	at Northampton 2006 +
Best Bowling:	In Yorkshire	5-38	C M Old	at Sheffield 1972 $	5-16	B S Crump	at Bradford 1969 $
	Away	5-29	P W Jarvis	at Northampton 1992 $	5-15	Sarfraz Nawaz	at Northampton 1975 $

Nottinghamshire

		By Yorkshire			Against Yorkshire		
Highest Score:	In Yorkshire	352:6		at Scarborough 2001 $	251:5		at Scarborough 1996 $
					251:9		at Scarborough 2016 +
	Away	280:4		at Nottingham 2007 +	291:6		at Nottingham 2004 $
Lowest Score:	In Yorkshire	120:9		at Scarborough 1998 +	66		at Bradford 1969 $
	Away	147		at Nottingham 1975 $	134:8		at Nottingham 1973 $
Best Batting:	In Yorkshire	191	D S Lehmann	at Scarborough 2001 $	101	M J Harris	at Hull 1973 #
	Away	103	R B Richardson	at Nottingham 1993 $	123	D W Randall	at Nottingham 1987 $
Best Bowling:	In Yorkshire	5-17	A G Nicholson	at Hull 1972 $	5-41	C L Cairns	at Scarborough 1996 $
	Away	4-12	C M Old	at Nottingham 1977 $	5-30	F D Stephenson	at Nottingham 1991 #

LIST A HIGHEST AND LOWEST SCORES BY AND AGAINST YORKSHIRE PLUS INDIVIDUAL BEST BATTING AND BOWLING *(Continued)*

Yorkshire versus:

Somerset

		By Yorkshire			Against Yorkshire		
Highest Score:	In Yorkshire	283:9		at Scarborough 2002 $	338;5		at Leeds 2013 $
	Away	343:9		at Taunton 2005 $	345:4		at Taunton 2005 $
Lowest Score:	In Yorkshire	110		at Scarborough 1977 $	103		at Sheffield 1972 $
	Away	120		at Taunton 1992 #	63		at Taunton 1965 +
Best Batting:	In Yorkshire	127	J A Rudolph	at Scarborough 2007 $	113	R T Ponting	at Scarborough 2004 $
	Away	148	A McGrath	at Taunton 2006 $	140*	P D Trego	at Taunton 2013 $
Best Bowling:	In Yorkshire	6-36	A G Nicholson	at Sheffield 1972 $	4-10	I T Botham	at Scarborough 1979 $
	Away	6-15	F S Trueman	at Taunton 1965 +	5-27	J Garner	at Bath 1985 $

Surrey

		By Yorkshire			Against Yorkshire		
Highest Score:	In Yorkshire	289:9		at Leeds 2017 +	375:4		at Scarborough 1994 $
	Away	334:5		at The Oval 2005 $	329:8		at The Oval 2009 +
Lowest Score:	In Yorkshire	76		at Harrogate 1970 +	90		at Leeds 1996 $
	Away	128:8		at The Oval 1971 $	134		at The Oval 1969 +
Best Batting:	In Yorkshire	118*	J D Love	at Leeds 1987 $	136	M A Lynch	at Bradford 1985 $
	Away	146	G Boycott	at Lord's 1965 +	177	S A Newman	at The Oval 2009 +
Best Bowling:	In Yorkshire	5-25	D Gough	at Leeds 1998 $	7-33	R D Jackman	at Harrogate 1970 +
	Away	5-29	R Illingworth	at Lord's 1965 +	5-22	R D Jackman	at The Oval 1978 $

Sussex

		By Yorkshire			Against Yorkshire		
Highest Score:	In Yorkshire	302:4		at Scarborough 2011 $	267		at Scarborough 2011 $
	Away	270		at Hove 1963 +	292		at Hove 1963 +
Lowest Score:	In Yorkshire	89:7		at Huddersfield 1969 $	85		at Bradford 1972 #
	Away	89		at Hove 1998 $	108		at Hove 1971 $
Best Batting:	In Yorkshire	132*	J A Rudolph	at Scarborough 2011 $	129	A W Greig	at Scarborough 1976 $
	Away	111*	J H Hampshire	at Hastings 1973 $	103	L J Wright	at Hove 2012 $
Best Bowling:	In Yorkshire	5-34	G M Hamilton	at Scarborough 2000 $	4-15	Imran Khan	at Sheffield 1985 $
	Away	5-13	D Gough	at Hove 1994 $	4-10	M H Yardy	at Hove 2011 $

LIST A HIGHEST AND LOWEST SCORES BY AND AGAINST YORKSHIRE
PLUS INDIVIDUAL BEST BATTING AND BOWLING *(Continued)*

Yorkshire versus:

Warwickshire

		By Yorkshire			Against Yorkshire		
Highest Score:	In Yorkshire	320:7		at York 2021 +	283:6		at Leeds 2016 +
	Away	281:8		at Birmingham 2017 +	309-3		at Birmingham 2005 $
Lowest Score:	In Yorkshire	158		at Scarborough 2012 $	59		at Leeds 2001 $
	Away	56		at Birmingham 1995 $	158:9		at Birmingham 2003 $
Best Batting:	In Yorkshire	139*	S P Fleming	at Leeds 2003 $	118	I J L Trott	at Leeds 2016 +
	Away	100*	J H Hampshire	at Birmingham 1975 $	137	I R Bell	at Birmingham 2005 $
Best Bowling:	In Yorkshire	5-31	M D Moxon	at Leeds 1991 #	4-16	N M Carter	at Scarborough 2012 $
	Away	4-27	H P Cooper	at Birmingham 1973 $	7-32	R G D Willis	at Birmingham 1981 #

Worcestershire

		By Yorkshire			Against Yorkshire		
Highest Score:	In Yorkshire	346:9		at Leeds 2018 +	350:6		at Leeds 2018 +
	Away	346:6		at Worcester 2015 +	342		at Worcester 2017 +
Lowest Score:	In Yorkshire	88		at Leeds 1995 #	86		at Leeds 1969 $
	Away	90		at Worcester 1987 $	122		at Worcester 1975 $
Best Batting:	In Yorkshire	130	G C H Hill	at Scarborough 2022 +	113*	G A Hick	at Scarborough 1995 $
		101	C A Pujara	at Leeds 2018 +	115	Younis Ahmed	at Worcester 1980 #
	Away	142	G Boycott	at Worcester 1980 #			
Best Bowling:	In Yorkshire	7-15	R A Hutton	at Leeds 1969 $	5-36	Kabir Ali	at Leeds 2002 $
	Away	6-14	H P Cooper	at Worcester 1976 $	5-25	W D Parnell	at Worcester 2019 +

Bedfordshire +

		By Yorkshire			Against Yorkshire		
Highest Score:	Away	212:6		at Luton 2001	211:9		at Luton 2001
Best Batting:	Away	88	D S Lehmann	at Luton 2001	34	O J Clayton	at Luton 2001
Best Bowling:	Away	4-39	R J Sidebottom	at Luton 2001	4-54	S R Rashid	at Luton 2001

Berkshire +

		By Yorkshire			Against Yorkshire		
Highest Score:	Away	131:3		at Reading 1983	128:9		at Reading 1983
Lowest Score:	Away				105		at Finchampstead 1988
Best Batting:	Away	74*	A A Metcalfe	at Finchampstead 1988	29	G R J Roope	at Reading 1983
Best Bowling:	Away	5-27	G B Stevenson	at Reading 1983	1-15	M Lickley	at Reading 1983

LIST A HIGHEST AND LOWEST SCORES BY AND AGAINST YORKSHIRE
PLUS INDIVIDUAL BEST BATTING AND BOWLING *(Continued)*

Yorkshire versus:

Cambridgeshire +

		By Yorkshire			Against Yorkshire		
Highest Score:	In Yorkshire	177:1		at Leeds 1986	176: 8		at Leeds 1986
	Away	299:5		at March 2003	214:8		at March 2003
Lowest Score:	In Yorkshire				176: 8		at Leeds 1986
	Away	299:5		at March 2003	214:8		at March 2003
Best Batting:	In Yorkshire	75	M D Moxon	at Leeds 1986	85	J D R Benson	at Leeds 1986
	Away	118*	M J Wood	at March 2003	53	N T Gadsby	at March 2003
Best Bowling:	In Yorkshire	3-11	A G Nicholson	at Castleford 1967	2-8	D H Fairey	at Castleford 1967
	Away	3-37	A K D Gray	at March 2003	3-53	Ajaz Akhtar	at March 2003

Cheshire +

		By Yorkshire			Against Yorkshire		
Highest Score:	Away	160:0		at Oxton 1985	159:7		at Oxton 1985
Best Batting:	Away	82*	M D Moxon	at Oxton 1985	46	K Teasdale	at Oxton 1985
Best Bowling:	Away	2-17	G B Stevenson	at Oxton 1985			

Combined Universities #

		By Yorkshire			Against Yorkshire		
Highest Score:	In Yorkshire	197:8		at Leeds 1990	200:8		at Leeds 1990
	Away	151:1		at Oxford 1980	150:7		at Oxford 1980
Lowest Score:	In Yorkshire	197:8		at Leeds 1990	200:8		at Leeds 1990
	Away	151:1		at Oxford 1980	150:7		at Oxford 1980
Best Batting:	In Yorkshire				63	S P James	at Leeds 1990
	Away	74*	C W J Athey	at Oxford 1980	63	J O D Orders	at Oxford 1980
Best Bowling:	In Yorkshire	3-34	P J Hartley	at Leeds 1990	3-44	M E W Brooker	at Barnsley 1976
	Away	2-43	H P Cooper	at Oxford 1980	1-16	C J Ross	at Oxford 1980

Devon +

		By Yorkshire			Against Yorkshire		
Highest Score:	Away	411:6		at Exmouth 2004	279-8		at Exmouth 2004
Lowest Score:	Away	259:5		at Exmouth 2002	80		at Exmouth 1998
Best Batting:	Away	160	M J Wood	at Exmouth 2004	83	P M Roebuck	at Exmouth 1994
Best Bowling:	Away	4-26	D S Lehmann	at Exmouth 2002	2-42	A O F Le Fleming	at Exmouth 1994

LIST A HIGHEST AND LOWEST SCORES BY AND AGAINST YORKSHIRE
PLUS INDIVIDUAL BEST BATTING AND BOWLING *(Continued)*

Yorkshire versus:

Dorset +

		By Yorkshire			Against Yorkshire		
Highest Score:	Away	101:2		at Bournemouth 2004	97		at Bournemouth 2004
Best Batting:	Away	71*	M J Wood	at Bournemouth 2004	23	C L Park	at Bournemouth 2004
Best Bowling:	Away	4-18	C E W Silverwood	at Bournemouth 2004	2-31	D J Worrad	at Bournemouth 2004

Durham M C +

		By Yorkshire			Against Yorkshire		
Highest Score:	In Yorkshire	249:6		at Middlesbrough 1978	138:5		at Harrogate 1973
	Away	214:6		at Chester-le-Street 1979	213:9		at Chester-le-Street 1979
Lowest Score:	In Yorkshire	135		at Harrogate 1973	136:7		at Middlesbrough 1978
	Away				213:9		at Chester-le-Street 1979
Best Batting:	In Yorkshire	110	J H Hampshire	at Middlesbrough 1978	52	N A Riddell	at Middlesbrough 1978
	Away	92	G Boycott	at Chester-le-Street 1979	52	Wasim Raja	at Chester-le-Street 1979
Best Bowling:	In Yorkshire	4-9	C M Old	at Middlesbrough 1978	5-15	B R Lander	at Harrogate 1973
	Away	3-39	H P Cooper	at Chester-le-Street 1979	2-35	B L Cairns	at Chester-le-Street 1979

Herefordshire +

		By Yorkshire			Against Yorkshire		
Highest Score:	Away	275:8		at Kington 1999	124:5		at Kington 1999
Best Batting:	Away	77	G S Blewett	at Kington 1999	39	R D Hughes	at Kington 1999
Best Bowling:	Away	2-22	G M Hamilton	at Kington 1999	2-41	C W Boroughs	at Kington 1999

Ireland +

		By Yorkshire			Against Yorkshire		
Highest Score:	In Yorkshire	299:6		at Leeds 1995	228:7		at Leeds 1995
	Away	202:4		at Belfast 2005	201:7		at Belfast 2005
Lowest Score:	In Yorkshire	249		at Leeds 1997	53		at Leeds 1997
	Away				201:7		at Belfast 2005
Best Batting:	In Yorkshire	113	C White	at Leeds 1995	82	S J S Warke	at Leeds 1995
	Away	58	M P Vaughan	at Belfast 2005	59	E J G Morgan	at Belfast 2005
Best Bowling:	In Yorkshire	7-27 D Gough		at Leeds 1997	3-26	P McCrum	at Leeds 1997
	Away	4-43	C White	at Belfast 2005	1-29	W K McCallan	at Belfast 2005

LIST A HIGHEST AND LOWEST SCORES BY AND AGAINST YORKSHIRE PLUS INDIVIDUAL BEST BATTING AND BOWLING *(Continued)*

Yorkshire versus:

Minor Counties #

		By Yorkshire		Against Yorkshire		
Highest Score:	In Yorkshire	309:5		at Leeds 1997	206:6		at Leeds 1988
	Away	218:3		at Scunthorpe 1975	182		at Scunthorpe 1975
		218:9		at Jesmond 1979			
Lowest Score:	In Yorkshire	309:5		at Leeds 1997	109		at Leeds 1974
	Away	218:3		at Scunthorpe 1975	85		at Jesmond 1979
		218:9		at Jesmond 1979			
Best Batting:	In Yorkshire	109*	A McGrath	at Leeds 1997	80*	J D Love	at Leeds 1991
	Away	83*	G Boycott	at Chester-le-Street 1973	61	N A Folland	at Jesmond 1989
Best Bowling:	In Yorkshire	6-27	A G Nicholson	at Middlesbrough 1972	3-37	S Oakes	at Leeds 1997
	Away	5-32	S Oldham	at Scunthorpe 1975	3-27	I E Conn	at Jesmond 1989

Netherlands $

		By Yorkshire		Against Yorkshire		
Highest Score:	In Yorkshire	204:6		at Leeds 2010	200:8		at Leeds 2010
	Away	158:5		at Rotterdam 2010	154:9		at Rotterdam 2010
Lowest Score:	In Yorkshire	188:9		at Leeds 2011	190:8		at Leeds 2011
	Away	123		at Amsterdam 2011	154:9		at Rotterdam 2010
Best Batting:	In Yorkshire	83*	J A Rudolph	at Leeds 2010	62	M G Dighton	at Leeds 2010
	Away	46*	J M Bairstow	at Rotterdam 2010	34	P W Borren	at Amsterdam 2011
Best Bowling:	In Yorkshire	3-34	S A Patterson	at Leeds 2010	3-26	Mudassar Bukhari	at Leeds 2011
	Away	4-24	R M Pyrah	at Rotterdam 2010	3-28	Mudassar Bukhari	at Amsterdam 2011

Norfolk +

		By Yorkshire		Against Yorkshire		
Highest Score:	In Yorkshire	106:0		at Leeds 1990	104		at Leeds 1990
	Away	167		at Lakenham 1969	78		at Lakenham 1969
Lowest Score:	In Yorkshire				104		at Leeds 1990
	Away	167		at Lakenham 1969	78		at Lakenham 1969
Best Batting:	In Yorkshire	56*	M D Moxon	at Leeds 1990	25	R J Finney	at Leeds 1990
	Away	55	J H Hampshire	at Lakenham 1969	21	G J Donaldson	at Lakenham 1969
Best Bowling:	In Yorkshire	3-8	P Carrick	at Leeds 1990			
	Away	3-14	C M Old	at Lakenham 1969	6-48	T I Moore	at Lakenham 1969

LIST A HIGHEST AND LOWEST SCORES BY AND AGAINST YORKSHIRE
PLUS INDIVIDUAL BEST BATTING AND BOWLING *(Continued)*

Yorkshire versus:

Northumberland +

		By Yorkshire			Against Yorkshire		
Highest Score:	In Yorkshire	138: 2		at Leeds 1992	137		at Leeds 1992
Best Batting:	In Yorkshire	38	S A Kellett	at Leeds 1992	47	G R Morris	at Leeds 1992
Best Bowling:	In Yorkshire	3-18	M A Robinson	at Leeds 1992	2-22	S Greensword	at Leeds 1992

Scotland

		By Yorkshire			Against Yorkshire		
Highest Score:	In Yorkshire	317:5		at Leeds 1986 #	244		at Leeds 2008 +
	Away	259:8		at Edinburgh 2007 +	217		at Edinburgh 2007 +
Lowest Score:	In Yorkshire	228:6		at Bradford 1981 #	142		at Leeds 1996 #
	Away	199:8		at Edinburgh 2004 $	129		at Glasgow 1995 #
Best Batting:	In Yorkshire	118*	J D Love	at Bradford 1981 #	73	I L Philip	at Leeds 1989 +
	Away	91	A A Metcalfe	at Glasgow 1987 #	78	J A Beukes	at Edinburgh 2005 $
Best Bowling:	In Yorkshire	5-28	C E W Silverwood	at Leeds 1996 #	2-22	P J C Hoffman	at Leeds 2006 +
	Away	4-20	R K J Dawson	at Edinburgh 2004 $	3-42	Asim Butt	at Linlithgow 1998 #

Shropshire +

		By Yorkshire			Against Yorkshire		
Highest Score:	Away	192		at Telford 1984	229:5		at Telford 1984
Lowest Score:	Away	192		at Telford 1984	185		at Wellington 1976
Best Batting:	Away	59	J H Hampshire	at Wellington 1976	80	Mushtaq Mohammad	at Telford 1984
Best Bowling:	Away	3-17	A L Robinson	at Wellington 1976	3-26	Mushtaq Mohammad	at Telford 1984

Unicorns $

		By Yorkshire			Against Yorkshire		
Highest Score:	In Yorkshire	266:6		at Leeds 2013	234		at Leeds 2013
	Away	191:5		at Chesterfield 2013	189:9		at Chesterfield 2013
Lowest Score:	In Yorkshire				150:6		at Leeds 2012
	Away				184		at Scarborough 2012
Best Batting:	In Yorkshire	139	G S Ballance	at Leeds 2013	107	M S Lineker	at Leeds 2013
	Away	103*	G S Ballance	at Scarborough 2012	83*	T J New	at Scarborough 2012
	In Yorkshire	5-22	J A Leaning	at Leeds 2013	2-25	R J Woolley	at Leeds 2012
Best Bowling:	Away	3-34	R M Pyrah	at Chesterfield 2013	2-31	W W Lee	at Chesterfield 2013

LIST A HIGHEST AND LOWEST SCORES BY AND AGAINST YORKSHIRE
PLUS INDIVIDUAL BEST BATTING AND BOWLING *(Continued)*

Yorkshire versus:

Wiltshire +

		By Yorkshire			Against Yorkshire		
Highest Score:	Away	304:7		at Trowbridge 1987	175		at Trowbridge 1987
Best Batting:	Away	85	A A Metcalfe	at Trowbridge 1987	62	J J Newman	at Trowbridge 1987
Best Bowling:	Away	4-40	K Sharp	at Trowbridge 1987	2-38	R C Cooper	at Trowbridge 1987

Yorkshire Cricket Board +

Highest Score:	Away	240:5		at Harrogate 2000	110		at Harrogate 2000
Best Batting:	Away	70	M P Vaughan	at Harrogate 2000	31	R A Kettleborough	at Harrogate 2000
Best Bowling:	Away	5-30	D Gough	at Harrogate 2000	1-25	A E McKenna	at Harrogate 2000

Australians

Highest Score:	In Yorkshire	188		at Leeds 1989	297:3		at Leeds 1989
Lowest Score:	In Yorkshire	140		at Bradford 1972	297:3		at Leeds 1989
Best Batting:	In Yorkshire	105	G Boycott	at Bradford 1972	172	D C Boon	at Leeds 1989
Best Bowling:	In Yorkshire	2-23	D Wilson	at Bradford 1972	3-30	D J Colley	at Bradford 1972

Bangladesh A

Highest Score:	In Yorkshire	198		at Leeds 2013	191		at Leeds 2013
Best Batting:	In Yorkshire	47*	L E Plunkett	at Leeds 2013	69	Anamul Haque	at Leeds 2013
Best Bowling:	In Yorkshire	5-30	Azeem Rafiq	at Leeds 2013	3-25	Elias Sunny	at Leeds 2013

South Africa A

Highest Score:	In Yorkshire				129:4		at Leeds 2017
Best Batting:	In Yorkshire				56*	K Zonda	at Leeds 2017
Best Bowling:	In Yorkshire	2-16	S A Patterson	at Leeds 2017			

Sri Lanka A

Highest Score:	In Yorkshire	249		at Leeds 2014	275:9		at Leeds 2014
Lowest Score:	In Yorkshire	179:7		at Leeds 2004			
Best Batting:	In Yorkshire	81	A W Gale	at Leeds 2007	100	L D Chandimal	at Leeds 2014
Best Bowling:	In Yorkshire	5-51	A Shahzad	at Leeds 2007	4-42	S Prasanna	at Leeds 2014

LIST A HIGHEST AND LOWEST SCORES BY AND AGAINST YORKSHIRE PLUS INDIVIDUAL BEST BATTING AND BOWLING *(Continued)*

Yorkshire versus:

West Indians — **By Yorkshire** / **Against Yorkshire**

		By Yorkshire				Against Yorkshire		
Highest Score:	In Yorkshire	253:4		at Scarborough 1995	242		at Scarborough 1995
Best Batting:	In Yorkshire	106	A McGrath	at Scarborough 1995	54	R B Richardson	at Scarborough 1995
Best Bowling:	In Yorkshire	3-42	G M Hamilton	at Scarborough 1995	3-48	R Dhanraj	at Scarborough 1995

West Indians A

		By Yorkshire				Against Yorkshire		
Highest Score:	In Yorkshire	139		at Leeds 2002	140:2		at Leeds 2002
Best Batting:	In Yorkshire	48	M J Wood	at Leeds 2002	57	D Ganga	at Leeds 2002
Best Bowling:	In Yorkshire	1-31	C J Elstub	at Leeds 2002	4-24	J J C Lawson	at Leeds 2002

Young Australians

		By Yorkshire				Against Yorkshire		
Highest Score:	In Yorkshire	224:6		at Leeds 1995	156		at Leeds 1995
Best Batting:	In Yorkshire	76	M P Vaughan	at Leeds 1995	51	A C Gilchrist	at Leeds 1995
Best Bowling:	In Yorkshire	5-32	A C Morris	at Leeds 1995	2-21	S Young	at Leeds 1995

Zimbabwe

		By Yorkshire				Against Yorkshire		
Highest Score:	In Yorkshire	203:7		at Sheffield 1982	202		at Sheffield 1982
Best Batting:	In Yorkshire	98*	G Boycott	at Sheffield 1982	53	D A G Fletcher	at Sheffield 1982
Best Bowling:	In Yorkshire	3-47	P W Jarvis	at Sheffield 1982	3-30	D A G Fletcher	at Sheffield 1982

LIST A HIGHEST TEAM TOTALS

BY YORKSHIRE

411:6	v.	Devon at Exmouth	2004 +
379:7	v.	Lancashire at Manchester	2018 +
379:7	v.	Leicestershire at Leeds	2019 +
376:3	v.	Leicestershire at Leicester	2016 +
353:5	v.	Northamptonshire at York	2022 +
352:6	v.	Nottinghamshire at Scarborough	2001 $
349:7	v.	Derbyshire at Leeds	2017 +
346:9	v.	Worcestershire at Leeds	2018 +
345:5	v.	Nottinghamshire at Leeds	1996 +
345:6	v.	Worcestershire at Worcester	2015 +
343:9	v.	Somerset at Taunton	2005 $
341:3	v.	Northamptonshire at Northampton	2006 +
339:4	v.	Durham at Leeds	2017 +
334:5	v.	Surrey at The Oval	2005 $
330:6	v	Surrey at The Oval	2009 +
329:3	v.	Leicestershire at Leicester	2021 +
328:4	v.	Durham at Chester-le-Street	2018 +
325:7	v.	Lancashire at Manchester	2016 +
324:7	v.	Lancashire at Manchester	2014 +
320:7	v.	Warwickshire at York	2021 +
318:7	v.	Leicestershire at Leicester	1993 $
317:4	v.	Surrey at Lord's	1965 +
317:5	v.	Scotland at Leeds	1986 #
314:8	v.	Northamptonshire at Scarboough	2016 +
310:5	v.	Leicestershire at Leicester	1997 +
310	v.	Lancashire at Leeds	2019 +
309:5	v.	Minor Counties at Leeds	1997 #
307:3	v.	Essex at Chelmsford	1995 +
307:4	v.	Somerset at Taunton	2002 $
304:7	v.	Wiltshire at Trowbridge	1986 +

LIST A HIGHEST TEAM TOTALS

AGAINST YORKSHIRE

375:4	for Surrey at Scarborough	1994 $
363	for Lancashire at Manchester	2018 +
351	for Northamptonshire at Northampton	2019 +
350:6	for Worcestershire at Leeds	2018 +
348:9	for Hampshire at West End	2018 +
345:4	for Somerset at Taunton	2005 $
342	for Worcestershire at Worcester	2017 +
339:7	for Northamptonshire at Northampton	2006 +
338:5	for Somerset at Leeds	2013 $
335:5	for Durham at Leeds	2017 +
334:8	for Derbyshire at Leeds	2017 +
329:8	for Surrey at The Oval	2009 +
327:7	for Leicestershire at Leicester	2021 +
325:7	for Northamptonshire at Northampton	1992 $
320	for Northamptonshire at York	2022 +
317:7	for Essex at Chelmsford	2021 +
314:4	for Northamptonshire at Leeds	2007 +
313:7	for Surrey at Leeds	2017 +
313:9	for Hampshire at Scarborough	2022 +
311:6	for Lancashire at Leeds	2019 +
311:6	for Hampshire at York	2023 +
310:7	for Northamptonshire at Scarborough	2016 +
309:3	for Warwickshire at Birmingham	2005 $
308:6	for Surrey at The Oval	1995 $
306:8	for Somerset at Taunton	2002 $
302:7	for Leicestershire at Leeds	2008 $
298:9	for Leicestershire at Leicester	1997 $
297:3	for Australians at Leeds	1989
297:7	for Kent at Canterbury	2022 +
294:6	for Gloucestershire at Cheltenham	2010 $

LIST A HIGHEST INDIVIDUAL SCORES

BY YORKSHIRE

191	D S Lehmann	v.	Nottinghamshire at Scarborough	2001 $
175	T M Head	v.	Leicestershire at Leicester	2016 +
174	J M Bairstow	v.	Durham at Leeds	2017 +
164	T Kohler-Cadmore	v.	Durham at Chester-le-Street	2018 +
160	M J Wood	v.	Devon at Exmouth	2004 +
156	G S Ballance	v.	Leicestershire at Leeds	2019 +
152 *	G S Ballance	v.	Northamptonshire at Northampton	2017 +
148	C White	v.	Leicestershire at Leicester	1997 $
148	A McGrath	v.	Somerset at Taunton	2006 $
146	G Boycott	v.	Surrey at Lord's	1965 +
144	A Lyth	v.	Lancashire at Manchester	2018 +
143	W A R Fraine	v.	Northamptonshire at York	2022 +
142	G Boycott	v.	Worcestershire at Worcester	1980 #
141*	M D Moxon	v	Glamorgan at Cardiff	1991 #
140	P S P Handscomb	v.	Derbyshire at Leeds	2017 +
139*	S P Fleming	v.	Warwickshire at Leeds	2003 $
139	G S Ballance	v.	Unicorns at Leeds	2013 $

AGAINST YORKSHIRE

177	S A Newman	for	Surrey at The Oval	2009 +
172	D C Boon	for	Australia at Leeds	1989
171	J M Vince	for	Hampshire at West End	2018 +
161	D J G Sales	for	Northamptonshire at Northampton	2006 +
155*	B A Richards	for	Hampshire at Hull	1970 $
146*	S Young	for	Gloucestershire at Leeds	1997 $
143*	C M Spearman	for	Gloucestershire at Bristol	2004 $
141*	B J Hodge	for	Lancashire at Manchester	2007 +
140*	P D Trego	for	Somerset at Taunton	2013 $
137*	M Klinger	for	Gloucestershire at Leeds	2015 +
137	I R Bell	for	Warwickshire at Birmingham	2005 $
136*	N Hussain	for	Essex at Chelmsford	2002 #
136	M A Lynch	for	Surrey at Bradford	1985 $
136	J D M Evison	for	Kent at Scarborough	2023 +
135*	D J Bicknell	for	Surrey at The Oval	1989 +
133	A D Brown	for	Surrey at Scarborough	1994 $

MOST RUNS IN LIST A MATCHES

742	v.	Lancashire at Manchester	2018 +	Y 379:7	L 363
696	v.	Worcestershire at Leeds	2018 +	W 350:6	Y 346:9
690	v.	Devon at Exmouth	2004 +	Y 411:6	D 279:8
688	v.	Somerset at Taunton	2005 $	S 345:4	Y 343:9
683	v.	Derbyshire at Leeds	2017 +	Y 349:7	D 334:8
680	v.	Northamptonshire at Northampton	2006 +	Y 342:3	N 339:7
674	v.	Durham at Leeds	2017 +	D 335:5	Y: 339-4
673	v.	Northamptonshire at York	2022 +	Y 353:5	N 320
659	v.	Surrey at The Oval	2009 +	S 329:8	Y 330:6
656	v.	Leicestershire at Leicester	2021 +	L 327:7	Y 329:3
633	v.	Worcestershire at Worcester	2017 +	W 342	Y 291
625	v.	Surrey at The Oval	2005 $	Y 334:5	S 291
624	v.	Northamptonshire at Scarborough	2016 +	N 310:7	Y 314·8
621	v.	Lancashire at Leeds	2019 +	L 311:6	Y 310
613	v.	Somerset at Taunton	2002 $	Y 307:4	S 306:8
605	v.	Leicestershire at Leeds	2008 $	Y 303:4	L 302:7
604	v.	Surrey at The Oval	1995 $	S 308:6	Y 296:6
602	v.	Surrey at Leeds	2017 +	S 313:7	Y 289:9
601	v.	Lancashire at Manchester	2014 +	Y 324:7	L 277
601	v.	Warwickshire at York	2021+	Y 320:7	W 281

LIST A BEST BOWLING

BY YORKSHIRE

7-15	R A Hutton	v.	Worcestershire at Leeds	1969 $
7-27	D Gough	v.	Ireland at Leeds	1997 +
6-14	H P Cooper	v.	Worcestershire at Worcester	1975 $
6-15	F S Trueman	v.	Somerset at Taunton	1965 +
6-18	D Wilson	v.	Kent at Canterbury	1969 $
6-27	A G Nicholson	v.	Minor Counties at Middlesbrough	1972 #
6-27	P W Jarvis	v.	Somerset at Taunton	1989 $
6-32	S A Patterson	v.	Derbyshire at Leeds	2010 $
6-36	A G Nicholson	v	Somerset At Sheffield	1972 $
6-40	R J Sidebottom	v.	Glamorgan at Cardiff	1998 $
5-13	D Gough	v.	Sussex at Hove	1994 $
5-16	S Stuchbury	v.	Leicestershire at Leicester	1982 $
5-16	G M Hamilton	v.	Hampshire at Leeds	1998 $
5-17	A G Nicholson	v.	Nottinghamshire at Hull	1972 $
5-18	P W Jarvis	v.	Derbyshire at Leeds	1990 $

AGAINST YORKSHIRE

7-32	R G D Willis	for	Warwickshire at Birmingham	1981 #
7-33	R D Jackman	for	Surrey at Harrogate	1970 +
6-15	A A Donald	for	Warwickshire at Birmingham	1995 $
6-18	R E East	for	Essex at Hull	1969 $
6-25	G Chapple	for	Lancashire at Leeds	1998 $
6-32	M T Coles	for	Kent at Leeds	2012 $
6-48	T I Moore	for	Norfolk at Lakenham	1969 +
5-15	B R Lander	for	Durham M C at Harrogate	1973 +
5-15	Sarfraz Nawaz	for	Northamptonshire at Northampton	1975 $
5-16	B S Crump	for	Northamptonshire at Bradford	1969 $
5-16	G C Holmes	for	Glamorgan at Swansea	1985 $
5-20	R E East	for	Essex at Colchester	1979 $
5-22	R D Jackman	for	Surrey at The Oval	1978 $
5-24	C J Tunnicliffe	for	Derbyshire at Derby	1981 #
5-24	C W Henderson	for	Leicestershire at Leeds	2004 $

LIST A ECONOMICAL BOWLING

BY YORKSHIRE

11-9-3-1	C M Old	v.	Middlesex at Lord's	1979 #
8-5-3-3	A L Robinson	v.	Derbyshire at Scarborough	1973 $

AGAINST YORKSHIRE

8-4-6-2	P J Sainsbury	for	Hampshire at Hull	1970 $
8-5-6-3	M J Procter	for	Gloucestershire at Cheltenham	1979 $

LIST A MOST EXPENSIVE BOWLING

BY YORKSHIRE

9-0-87-1	T T Bresnan	v.	Somerset at Taunton	2005 $

AGAINST YORKSHIRE

12-1-96-0	M E Waugh	for	Essex at Chelmsford	1995 +

LIST A HAT-TRICKS FOR YORKSHIRE (4)

P W Jarvis v. Derbyshire at Derby 1982 $ D Gough v. Ireland at Leeds 1997 +
D Gough v. Lancashire at Leeds 1998 $ C White v. Kent at Leeds 2000 $

LIST A MAN-OF-THE-MATCH AWARDS (137)

M D Moxon	12	M P Vaughan	5	M J Wood	3
G Boycott	11	A Sidebottom	4	R J Blakey	2
D L Bairstow	8	C E W Silverwood	4	G L Brophy	2
C White	8	D Byas	3	P Carrick	2
A A Metcalfe	7	D Gough	3	R A Hutton	2
J H Hampshire	6	P J Hartley	3	L E Plunkett	2
D S Lehmann	6	J D Love	3	P J Sharpe	2
C W J Athey	5	A McGrath	3	G B Stevenson	2
M G Bevan	5	C M Old	3		

One each: T T Bresnan, D B Close, M T G Elliott, G M Fellows, S D Fletcher, G M Hamilton, S N Hartley, P M Hutchinson, R Illingworth, C Johnson, S A Kellett, B Leadbeater, M J Lumb, A G Nicholson, S Oldham, S A Patterson, R M Pyrah, P E Robinson, R D Stemp, F S Trueman and D Wilson.

ALL LIST A CENTURIES 1963-2023 (121)

C W J ATHEY (2)

118	v. Leicestershire	at Leicester	1978 $
115	v. Kent	at Leeds	1980 +

D L BAIRSTOW (1)

103 *	v. Derbyshire	at Derby	1981 #

J M BAIRSTOW (2)

114	v. Middlesex	at Lord's	2011 $
174	v. Durham	at Leeds	2017 +

G S BALLANCE (4)

139	v. Unicorns	at Leeds	2013 $
103 *	v. Unicorns	at Scarborough	2012 $
152 *	v. Northamptonshire	at Northampton	2017 +
156	v Leicestershire	at Leeds	2019 +

M G BEVAN (2)

103 *	v Gloucestershire	at Middlesbrough	1995 $
101	v Worcestershire	at Scarborough	1995 $

G BOYCOTT (7)

146	v Surrey	at Lord's	1965 +
142	v Worcestershire	at Worcester	1980 #
108 *	v Northamptonshire	at Huddersfield	1974 $
106	v Northamptonshire	at Bradford	1984 #
105	v Australians	at Bradford	1972
104 *	v Glamorgan	at Colwyn Bay	1973 $
102	v Northamptonshire	at Middlesbrough	1977 #

R J BLAKEY (3)

130	v Kent	at Scarborough	1991 $
105 *	v Warwickshire	at Scarborough	1992 $
100 *	v Gloucestershire	at Cheltenham	1990 $

H C BROOK (1)

103	v Leicestershire	at Leeds	2019 +

D BYAS (5)

116 *	v.	Surrey	at The Oval	1996 #
111 *	v.	Lancashire	at Leeds	1996 $
106 *	v.	Derbyshire	at Chesterfield	1993 $
104 *	v.	Hampshire	at Leeds	1999 #
101 *	v.	Nottinghamshire	at Leeds	1994 $

H G DUKE (2)

125	v. Leicestershire	at Leicester	2021 +
111	v. Northamptonshire	York	2022 +

M T G ELLIOTT (3)

128 *	v.	Somerset	at Lord's	2002 +
115 *	v.	Kent	at Leeds	2002 $
109	v.	Leicestershire	at Leicester	2002 $

S P FLEMING (1)

139 *	v.	Warwickshire	at Leeds	2003 $

M J FOSTER (1)

118	v. Leicestershire	at Leicester	1993 $

W A R FRAINE (1)

143	v. Northamptonshire	at York	2022 +

A W GALE (2)

125 *	v.	Essex	at Chelmsford	2010 $
112	v.	Kent	at Canterbury	2011 $

J H HAMPSHIRE (7)

119	v.	Leicestershire	at Hull	1971 $
114 *	v.	Northamptonshire	at Scarborough	1978 $
111 *	v.	Sussex	at Hastings	1973 $
110	v.	Durham M C	at Middlesbrough	1978 +
108	v.	Nottinghamshire	at Sheffield	1970 $
106 *	v.	Lancashire	at Manchester	1972 $
100 *	v.	Warwickshire	at Birmingham	1975 $

P S P HANDSCOMB (1)

140	v. Derbyshire	at Leeds	2017 +

T M HEAD (1))

175	v. Leicestershire	at Leicester	2016 +

G C H HILL (1)

130	v. Worcestershire	at Scarborough	2022 +

P A JAQUES (1)

105	v. Sussex	at Leeds	2004 $

S A KELLETT (2)

118 *	v.	Derbyshire	at Leeds	1992 $
107	v.	Ireland	at Leeds	1995 +

T KOHLER-CADMORE (1)

164	v. Durham	at Chester-le-Street	2018 +

J A LEANING (2)

131 *	v.	Leicestershire	at Leicester	2016 +
111 *	v.	Essex	at Scarborough	2014 +

ALL LIST A CENTURIES 1963-2022 *(Continued)*

A Z LEES (1)

102	v.	Northamptonshire	at Northampton	2014 +

D S LEHMANN (8)

191	v.	Nottinghamshire	at Scarborough	2001 $
119	v.	Durham	at Leeds	1998 #
118 *	v.	Northamptonshire	at Northampton	2006 +
105	v.	Glamorgan	at Cardiff	1995 +
104	v.	Somerset	at Taunton	2002 $
103	v.	Derbyshire	at Leeds	2001 #
103	v.	Leicestershire	at Scarborough	2001 $
102 *	v.	Derbyshire	ar Derby	1998 #

J D LOVE (4)

118 *	v.	Scotland	at Bradford	1981 #
118 *	v.	Surrey	at Leeds	1987 $
104 *	v.	Nottinghamshire	at Hull	1986 $
100 *	v.	Gloucestershire	at Gloucester	1985 $

R G LUMB (1)

101	v.	Nottinghamshire	at Scarborough	1976 $

A LYTH (5)

144	v.	Lancashire	at Manchester	2018 +
136 §	v.	Lancashire	at Manchester	2016 +
132*	v.	Leicestershire	at Leicester	2018 +
125 §	v.	Northamptonshire	at Scarborough	2016 +
109 *	v.	Sussex	at Scarborough	2009 $

(§ consecutive days)

A McGRATH (7)

148	v.	Somerset	at Taunton	2006 $
135 *	v.	Lancashire	at Manchester	2007 +
109 *	v.	Minor Counties	at Leeds	1997 #
106	v.	West Indies	at Scarborough	1995
105 *	v.	Scotland	at Leeds	2008 +
102	v.	Kent	at Canterbury	2001 $
100	v.	Durham	at Leeds	2007 +

G J MAXWELL (1)

111	v.	Worcestershire	at Worcester	2015 +

A A METCALFE (4)

127 *	v.	Warwickshire	at Leeds	1990 +
116	v.	Middlesex	at Lord's	1991 $
115 *	v.	Gloucestershire	at Scarborough	1984 $
114	v.	Lancashire	at Manchester	1991 #

M D MOXON (7)

141 *	v.	Glamorgan	at Cardiff	1991 #
137	v.	Nottinghamshire	at Leeds	1996+
129 *	v.	Surrey	at The Oval	1991 $
112	v.	Sussex	at Middlesbrough	1991 $
107 *	v.	Warwickshire	at Leeds	1990 +
106 *	v.	Lancashire	at Manchester	1986 #
105	v.	Somerset	at Scarborough	1990 $

C A PUJARA (1)

| 101 | v. | Worcestershire | at Leeds | 2018 + |

R B RICHARDSON (1)

| 103 | v. | Nottinghamshire | at Nottingham | 1993 $ |

J A RUDOLPH (9)

132 *	v.	Sussex	at Scarborough	2011 $
127	v.	Somerset	at Scarborough	2007 $
124 *	v.	Middlesex	at Scarborough	2010 $
120	v.	Leicestershire	at Leeds	2008 $
118	v.	Gloucestershire	at Leeds	2009 +
106	v.	Warwickshire	at Scarborough	2010 $
105	v.	Derbyshire	at Chesterfield	2010 $
101 *	v.	Essex	at Chelmsford	2010 $
100	v.	Leicestershire	at Leeds	2007 +

K SHARP (3)

114	v.	Essex	at Chelmsford	1985 $
112 *	v.	Worcestershire	at Worcester	1985 $
105 *	v.	Scotland	at Leeds	1984 #

S R TENDULKAR (1)

| 107 | v. | Lancashire | at Leeds | 1992 $ |

M P VAUGHAN (3)

125 *	v.	Somerset	at Taunton	2001 #
116 *	v.	Lancashire	at Manchester	2004 +
116 *	v.	Kent	at Leeds	2005 $

C WHITE (5)

148	v.	Leicestershire	at Leicester	1997 $
113	v.	Ireland	at Leeds	1995 +
112	v.	Northamptonshire	at Northampton	2006 +
101 *	v.	Durham	at Chester-le-Street	2006 +
100 *	v.	Surrey	at Leeds	2002 +

D J WILLEY (1)

| 131 | v. | Lancashire | at Manchester | 2018 + |

M J WOOD (5)

160	v.	Devon	at Exmouth	2004 +
118 *	v.	Cambridgeshire	at March	2003 +
115 *	v.	Derbyshire	at Derby	2002 #
111	v.	Surrey	at The Oval	2005 $
105 *	v.	Somerset	at Taunton	2002$

YOUNUS KHAN (1)

| 100 | v. | Nottinghamshire | at Nottingham | 2007 + |

LIST A PARTNERSHIPS OF 150 AND OVER 1963-2023 (53)

274 3rd wkt T M Head (175)   and J A Leaning (131*)   v. Leicestershire at Leicester
                                                                                          2016+
242* 1st wkt M D Moxon (107*) and A A Metcalfe (127*) v. Warwickshire at Leeds   1990 +
235 2nd wkt A Lyth (144)   and D J Willey (131)   v. Lancashire at Manchester
                                                                                          2018 +
233* 1st wkt A W Gale (125*)   and J A Rudolph (101*) v. Essex at Chelmsford   2010 $
213 1st wkt M D Moxon (141*) and A A Metcalfe (84)   v. Glamorgan at Cardiff   1991 #
211* 1st wkt M D Moxon (93*)   and A A Metcalfe (94*) v. Warwickshire at Birmingham
                                                                                          1987 #
211 4th wkt H C Brook (103)   and G S Ballance (156) v. Leicestershire at Leeds   2019 +
209 1st wkt W A R Fraine (143) and H G Duke (111)   v.   Northamptonshire at York
                                                                                          2022 +
207 4th wkt S A Kellett (107)   and C White (113)   v. Ireland at Leeds   1995 +
202 2nd wkt G Boycott (87)   and C W J Athey (115) v. Kent at Leeds   1980 +
201 1st wkt J H Hampshire (86) and C W J Athey (118) v. Leicestershire at Leicester
                                                                                          1978 $
198* 4th wkt M T G Elliott (115*) and A McGrath (85*)   v. Kent at Leeds   2002 $
195 1st wkt A Lyth (84)   and A Z Lees (102)   v. Northamptonshire
                                                                    at Northampton 2014 +
192 2nd wkt G Boycott (146)   and D B Close (79)   v. Surrey at Lord's   1965 +
190 1st wkt G Boycott (89*)   and R G Lumb (101)   v. Nottinghamshire
                                                                    at Scarborough 1976 $
190 5th wkt R J Blakey (96)   and M J Foster (118)   v. Leicestershire at Leicester
                                                                                          1993 $
189 2nd wkt J M Bairstow (174) and J E Root (55)   v. Durham at Leeds   2017 +
186 1st wkt G Boycott (99)   and J H Hampshire (92*) v. Gloucestershire
                                                                    at Scarborough 1975 $
186 1st wkt G S Blewett (71)   and D Byas (104*)   v. Hampshire at Leeds   1999 #
184 3rd wkt M P Vaughan (70)   and D S Lehmann (119) v. Durham at Leeds   1998 #
181 5th wkt M T G Elliott (109) and A McGrath (78)   v. Leicestershire at Leicester
                                                                                          2002 $
176 3rd wkt R J Blakey (86)   and S R Tendulkar (107) v. Lancashire at Leeds   1992 $
176 2nd wkt T Kohler-Cadmore (164)
                                     and C A Pujara (82)   v. Durham at Chester-le-Street
                                                                                          2018 +
172 2nd wkt D Byas (86)   and D S Lehmann (99)   v. Kent at Maidstone   1998 $
172 3rd wkt A McGrath (38)   and D S Lehmann (191) v. Nottinghamshire
                                                                    at Scarborough 2001 $
172 3rd wkt H G Duke (125)   and G C H Hill (90*)   v.   Leicestershire at Leicester
                                                                                          2021 +
171 1st wkt M D Moxon (112)   and A A Metcalfe (68) v. Sussex at Middlesbrough 1991 $
170 4th wkt M J Wood (105*)   and D S Lehmann (104) v. Somerset at Taunton   2002 $
170 1st wkt A W Gale (89)   and J A Rudolph (120) v. Leicestershire at Leeds   2008 $
167* 6th wkt M G Bevan (95*)   and R J Blakey ((80*) v. Lancashire at Manchester
                                                                                          1996 #
167* 1st wkt C White (100*)   and M J Wood (57*)   v. Surrey at Leeds   2002 +
167 1st wkt M D Moxon(64)   and A A Metcalfe (116) v. Middlesex at Lord's   1991 $
167 1st wkt M J Wood (65)   and S P Fleming (139*) v. Warwickshire at Leeds   2003 $
166 1st wkt M D Moxon (82*)   and A A Metcalfe (70) v. Northamptonshire at Leeds
                                                                                          1988 #
165 1st wkt M D Moxon (80)   and D Byas (106*)   v. Derbyshire at Chesterfield
                                                                                          1993 $

LIST A PARTNERSHIPS OF 150 AND OVER *(Continued)*

165 1st wkt M D Moxon (70)   and D Byas (88*)   v. Northamptonshire at Leeds
                                                                                 1993 $

164* 2nd wkt G Boycott (91*)   and C W J Athey (79*)   v. Worcestershire at Worcester
                                                                                 1981 $

164 3rd wkt A McGrath (105*)   and J A Rudolph (82)   v. Scotland at Leeds   2008 +
164 3rd wkt J A Rudolph (84)   and A McGrath (73)   v. Glamorgan at Scarborough
                                                                                 2008 $

161 1st wkt M D Moxon (74)   and A A Metcalfe (85)   v. Wiltshire at Trowbridge 1987 +

160* 1st wkt G Boycott (70*)   and M D Moxon (82*)   v. Cheshire at Oxton   1985 +
160* 5th wkt G M Fellows (80*)   and C White (73*)   v. Surrey at Leeds   2001 +
160* 3rd wkt A Lyth (60*)   and G S Ballance (103*) v. Unicorns at Scarborough
                                                                                 2012 $

160 1st wkt G Boycott (67)   and J H Hampshire (84) v. Warwickshire at Birmingham
                                                                                 1973 $

159 2nd wkt G Boycott (92)   and D B Close (96)   v. Surrey at The Oval   1969 +
157 2nd wkt K Sharp (71)   and R J Blakey (79)   v. Worcestershire at Worcester
                                                                                 1990 $

157 1st wkt T Kohler-Cadmore (79)
                                  and A Lyth (78)   v. Derbyshire at Leeds   2019 +
156 4th wkt P S P Handscomb (140)
                                  and G S Ballance (63)   v. Derbyshire at Leeds   2017 +
155* 1st wkt A Lyth (67*)   and A Z Lees (69*)   v. Derbyshire at Scarborough
                                                                                 2014 +

154* 2nd wkt J H Hampshire (111*)
                                  and B Leadbeater (57*) v. Sussex at Hove   1973 $
153 4th wkt Younus Khan (100)   and A W Gale ((69*)   v. Nottinghamshire
                                                                      at Nottingham 2007 +

153 1st wkt A Lyth (132*)   and T Kohler-Cadmore (74)
                                                          v. Leicestershire at Leicester
                                                                                 2018 +

150* 5th wkt S N Hartley (67*)   and J D Love (82*)   v. Hampshire at Middlesbrough
                                                                                 1983 $

LIST A HIGHEST PARTNERSHIPS FOR EACH WICKET

1st wkt   242* M D Moxon (107*) and A A Metcalfe (127*) v Warwickshire at Leeds 1990 +
2nd wkt   235   A Lyth (144)   and D J Willey (131)   v. Lancashire at Manchester
                                                                                 2018 +

3rd wkt   274   T M Head (175)   and J A Leaning (131*) v.Leicestershire at Leicester
                                                                                 2016+

4th wkt   211   H C Brook (103)   and G S Ballance (156) v.Leicestershire at Leeds 2019 +
5th wkt   190   R J Blakey (96)   and M J Foster (118)   v. Leicestershire at Leicester
                                                                                 1993 $

6th wkt   167* M G Bevan (95*)   and R J Blakey ((80*)   v. Lancashire at Manchester
                                                                                 1996 #

7th wkt   149* J D Love (118*)   and C M Old (78*)   v. Scotland at Bradford   1981 #
8th wkt   89   R J Blakey (60)   and R K J Dawson (41)   v. Leicestershire at Scarborough
                                                                                 2002 $

9th wkt   88   S N Hartley (67) and A Ramage (32*)   v. Middlesex at Lord's   1982 $
10th wkt 80*   D L Bairstow (103*)
                                  and M Johnson (4*)   v. Derbyshire at Derby   1981 #

ALL LIST A 5 WICKETS IN AN INNINGS 1963-2023 (59)

C W J ATHEY (1)

| 5-35 | v | Derbyshire | at Chesterfield | 1981 $ |

AZEEM RAFIQ (1)

| 5-30 | v | Bangladesh A | at Leeds | 2013 |

D M BESS (1)

| 5-37 | v | Essex | Chelmsford | 2023 + |

M G BEVAN (1)

| 5-29 | v | Sussex | at Eastbourne | 1996 $ |

P CARRICK (2)

| 5-22 | v | Glamorgan | at Leeds | 1991 $ |
| 5-40 | v | Sussex | at Middlesbrough | 1991 $ |

H P COOPER (2)

| 6-14 | v | Worcestershire | at Worcester | 1975 $ |
| 5-30 | v | Worcestershire | at Middlesbrough | 1978 $ |

D GOUGH (4)

5-13	v	Sussex	at Hove	1994 $
7-27	v	Ireland	at Leeds	1997 +
5-25	v	Surrey	at Leeds	1998 $
5-30	v	Yorkshire C B	at Harrogate	2000 +

G M HAMILTON (2)

| 5-16 | v | Hampshire | at Leeds | 1998 $ |
| 5-34 | v | Sussex | at Scarborough | 2000 $ |

P J HARTLEY (4)

5-36	v	Sussex	at Scarborough	1993 $
5-38	v	Worcestershire	at Worcester	1990 $
5-43	v	Scotland	at Leeds	1986 #
5-46	v	Hampshire	at Southampton	1990 +

M J HOGGARD (3)

5-28	v	Leicestershire	at Leicester	2000 $
5-30	v	Northamptonshire	at Northampton	2000 $
5-65	v	Somerset	at Lord's	2002 +

R A HUTTON (1)

| 7-15 | v | Worcestershire | at Leeds | 1969 $ |

R ILLINGWORTH (1)

| 5-29 | v | Surrey | at Lord's | 1965 + |

P W JARVIS (3)

6-27	v	Somerset	at Taunton	1989 $
5-18	v	Derbyshire	at Leeds	1990 $
5-29	v	Northamptonshire	at Northampton	1992 $

J A LEANING (1)

| 5-22 | v | Unicorns | at Leeds | 2013 $ |

A C MORRIS (1)

| 5-32 | v | Young Australia | at Leeds | 1995 |

M D MOXON (1)

| 5-31 | v | Warwickshire | at Leeds | 1991 # |

ALL LIST A 5 WICKETS IN AN INNINGS *(Continued)*

A G NICHOLSON (4)

6-27	v	Minor Counties	at Middlesbrough	1972 #
6-36	v	Somerset	at Sheffield	1972 $
5-17	v	Nottinghamshire	at Hull	1972 $
5-24	v	Derbyshire	at Bradford	1975 #

C M OLD (2)

| 5-33 | v | Sussex | at Hove | 1971 $ |
| 5-38 | v | Northamptonshire | at Sheffield | 1972 $ |

S OLDHAM (1)

| 5-32 | v | Minor Counties | at Scunthorpe | 1975 # |

S A PATTERSON (2)

| 6-32 | v | Derbyshire | at Leeds | 2010 $ |
| 5-24 | v | Worcestershire | at Worcester | 2015 + |

M W PILLANS (1)

| 5-29 | v | Leicestershire | Leeds | 2019 + |

A U RASHID (1)

| 5-33 | v | Hampshire | at Southampton | 2014 + |

A SHAHZAD (1)

| 5-51 | v | Sri Lanka A | at Leeds | 2007 |

C SHAW (1)

| 5-41 | v | Hampshire | at Bournemouth | 1984 $ |

A SIDEBOTTOM (2)

| 5-27 | v | Worcestershire | at Bradford | 1985 # |
| 5-27 | v | Glamorgan | at Leeds | 1987 + |

R J SIDEBOTTOM (2)

| 6-40 | v | Glamorgan | at Cardiff | 2003 $ |
| 5-42 | v | Leicestershire | at Leicester | 2003 $ |

C E W SILVERWOOD (1)

| 5-28 | v | Scotland | at Leeds | 1996 # |

G B STEVENSON (4)

5-27	v	Berkshire	at Reading	1983 +
5-28	v	Kent	at Canterbury	1978 #
5-41	v	Leicestershire	at Leicester	1976 $
5-50	v	Worcestershire	at Leeds	1982 #

S STUCHBURY (1)

| 5-16 | v | Leicestershire | at Leicester | 1982 $ |

N D THORNICROFT (1)

| 5-42 | v | Gloucestershire | at Leeds | 2003 $ |

F S TRUEMAN (1)

| 6-15 | v | Somerset | at Taunton | 1965 + |

M J WAITE (1)

| 5-50 | v. | Leicestershire | at Leicester | 2021 + |

ALL LIST A 5 WICKETS IN AN INNINGS *(Continued)*

C WHITE (2)

5-19	v	Somerset	at Scarborough	2002 $
5-25	v	Lancashire	at Leeds	2000 #

D WILSON (2)

6-18	v	Kent	at Canterbury	1969 $
5-25	v	Lancashire	at Bradford	1972 #

ALL LIST A PLAYERS WHO HAVE TAKEN 4 WICKETS IN AN INNINGS 1963-2023 (175) AND BEST FIGURES

11	C M Old	4-9	v	Durham M C	at Middlesbrough	1978 +
10	C White	4-14	v	Lancashire	at Leeds	2000 $
		4-14	v	Surrey	at The Oval	2005 $
9	A Sidebottom	4-15	v	Worcestershire	at Leeds	1987 #
8	P W Jarvis	4-13	v	Worcestershire	at Leeds	1986 $
8	D Gough	4-17	v	Nottinghamshire	at Nottingham	2000 #
8	G B Stevenson	4-20	v	Essex	at Barnsley	1977 #
7	S D Fletcher	4-11	v	Kent	at Canterbury	1988 $
6	C E W Silverwood	4-11	v	Leicestershire	at Leicester	2000 $
6	H P Cooper	4-18	v	Leicestershire	at Leeds	1975 +
5	S Oldham	4-13	v	Nottinghamshire	at Nottingham	1989 #
5	R M Pyrah	4-24	v	Netherlands	at Rotterdam	2010 $
4	P Carrick	4-13	v	Derbyshire	at Bradford	1983 $
4	R K J Dawson	4-13	v	Derbyshire	at Derby	2002 #
4	T T Bresnan	4-25	v	Somerset	at Leeds	2005 $
4	G M Hamilton	4-27	v	Warwickshire	at Birmingham	1995 $
3	R A Hutton	4-18	v	Surrey	at The Oval	1972 $
3	A G Nicholson	4-15	v	Kent	at Leeds	1974 $
3	P J Hartley	4-21	v	Scotland	at Glasgow	1995 #
3	A L Robinson	4-25	v	Surrey	at The Oval	1974 $
3	R D Stemp	4-25	v	Gloucestershire	at Bristol	1996 $
3	M P Vaughan	4-27	v	Gloucestershire	at Bristol	2000 $
3	S A Patterson	4-28	v	Worcestershire	at Worcester	2011 $
3	A U Rashid	4-38	v	Northamptonshire	at Northampton	2012 $
2	M K Bore	4-21	v	Sussex	at Middlesbrough	1970 $
		4-21	v	Worcestershire	at Worcester	1970 $
2	J D Woodford	4-23	v	Northamptonshire	at Northampton	1970 $
		4-23	v	Warwickshire	at Middlesbrough	1971 $
2	G J Kruis	4-17	v	Derbyshire	at Leeds	2007 $
2	D Wilson	4-22	v	Nottinghamshire	at Bradford	1969 $
2	V J Craven	4-22	v	Kent	at Scarborough	2003 $
2	M A Robinson	4-23	v	Northamptonshire	at Leeds	1993 $
2	M W Pillans	4-26	v.	Nottinghamshire	at York	2021 +
2	S N Hartley	4-32	v	Derbyshire	at Leeds	1989 #
2	A U Rashid	4-38	v	Northamptonshire	at Northampton	2012 $
2	A McGrath	4-41	v	Surrey	at Leeds	2003 $
2	J W Shutt	4-46	v	Glamorgan	at Cardiff	2022 +
2	D J Willey	4-47	v	Derbyshire	at Derby	2018 +
2	M L Revis	4-54	v	Essex	at Chelmsford	2023 +
1	R Illingworth	4-6	v	Middlesex	at Hull	1983 $
1	J R Sullivan	4-11	v	Derbyshire	at Chesterfield	2021 +
1	M Johnson	4-18	v	Scotland	at Bradford	1981 #
1	G S Blewett	4-18	v	Lancashire	at Manchester	1999 +

1	M Johnson	4-18	v	Scotland	at Bradford	1981	#
1	G S Blewett	4-18	v	Lancashire	at Manchester	1999	+
1	G M Fellows	4-19	v	Durham	at Leeds	2002	$
1	A P Grayson	4-25	v	Glamorgan	at Cardiff	1994	$
1	C J Elstub	4-25	v	Surrey	at Leeds	2001	$
1	D S Lehmann	4-26	v	Devon	at Exmouth	2002	+
1	C Shaw	4-29	v	Middlesex	at Leeds	1988	+
1	A G Wharf	4-29	v	Nottinghamshire	at Leeds	1996	#
1	F S Trueman	4-30	v	Nottinghamshire	at Middlesbrough	1963	+
1	J D Batty	4-33	v	Kent	at Scarborough	1991	$
1	P M Hutchinson	4-34	v	Gloucestershire	at Gloucester	1998	$
1	A K D Gray	4-34	v	Kent	at Leeds	2002	$
1	A Shahzad	4-34	v	Middlesex	at Lord's	2010	$
1	P M Stringer	4-35	v	Derbyshire	at Sheffield	1969	$
1	C S Pickles	4-36	v	Somerset	at Scarborough	1990	$
1	M J Hoggard	4-39	v	Surrey	at Leeds	2000	#
1	R J Sidebottom	4-39	v	Bedfordshire	at Luton	2001	+
1	K Sharp	4-40	v	Wiltshire	at Trowbridge	1987	+
1	B W M Mike	4-40	v	Surrey	at York	2023	+
1	T L Best	4-46	v	Essex	at Chelmsford	2010	$
1	Azeem Rafiq	4-47	v.	Lancashire	at Leeds	2017	+
1	A C Morris	4-49	v	Leicestershire	at Leicester	1997	$
1	L E Plunkett	4-52	v	Kent	Canterbury	2016	+
1	D B Close	4-60	v	Sussex	at Hove	1963	+
1	B O Coad	4-63	v.	Derbyshire	at Leeds	2017	+
1	M J Waite	4-65	v.	Worcestershire	at Worcester	2017	+
1	M L Revis	4-77	v.	Hampshire	at Scarborough	2022	+

LARGEST MARGINS OF VICTORY IN LIST A CRICKET

By 242 runs	v. Lancashire	at Old Trafford	June 15, 2016
By 10 wickets (13 occasions):			
First	v. Middlesex	at Lord's	July 27, 1975
Latest	v. Derbyshire	at Scarborough	August 12, 2014

LARGEST MARGINS OF DEFEAT IN LIST A CRICKET

By 205 runs	v. Surrey	at Scarborough	September 11, 1994
By 10 wickets (3 occasions):			
First	v. Sussex	at Bradford	August 13, 1978
Latest	v Kent	at Canterbury	May 26, 1996

ALL LIST A MATCHES OF 40 TO 65 OVERS 1963-2023

Player	M	Inns	NO	Runs	HS	Av'ge	100s	50s	Runs	Wkts	Av'ge	Ct/St
Ashraf, M A ...	22	6	4	3	3*	1.50	0	0	895	23	38.91	4
Athey, C W J ...	140	129	14	3,662	118	31.84	2	25	431	19	22.68	46
Azeem Rafiq ...	30	21	8	222	52*	17.07	0	1	1,160	41	28.29	12
Bairstow, D L ..	403	317	71	5,180	103*	21.05	1	19	17	0	—	390/31
Bairstow, J M .	**43**	**39**	**4**	**1,051**	**174**	**30.02**	**2**	**3**	**0**	**0**	**—**	**33/3**
Baker, T M	4	1	0	3	3	3.00	0	0	89	4	22.25	3
Balderstone, J C	13	11	2	173	46	19.22	0	0	38	2	19.00	3
Ballance, G S ..	76	70	10	3,033	156	50.55	4	19	0	0	—	32
Batty, J D	38	16	7	50	13*	5.55	0	0	1,297	42	30.88	18
Bean, F J	**9**	**9**	**0**	**164**	**61**	**18.22**	**0**	**1**	**0**	**0**	**—**	**4**
Berry, P J	1	0	0	0	—	—	0	0	28	0	—	0
Bess, D M	**17**	**14**	**4**	**217**	**51**	**21.70**	**0**	**1**	**799**	**16**	**49.93**	**11**
Best, T L	5	1	1	8	8*	—	0	0	166	10	16.60	1
Bevan, M G	48	45	12	2,110	103*	63.93	2	19	540	28	19.28	11
Binks, J G	30	21	3	247	34	13.72	0	0	0	0	—	26/8
Birkhead, B D ..	1	0	0	0	—	—	0	0	0	0	—	1
Blain, J A R	15	8	3	34	11*	6.80	0	0	462	14	33.00	3
Blakey, R J	373	319	84	7,361	130*	31.32	3	35	0	0	—	369/59
Blewett, G S ...	17	17	0	345	77	20.29	0	2	196	11	17.81	7
Booth, P A	5	2	1	7	6*	7.00	0	0	147	3	49.00	1
Bore, M K	55	24	10	90	15	6.42	0	0	1,600	50	32.00	15
Boycott, G	264	255	38	8,699	146	40.08	7	63	1,095	25	43.80	92
Bresnan, T T ...	181	130	31	2,124	95*	21.45	0	8	6,536	196	33.34	52
Broadhurst, M ..	1	0	0	0	—	—	0	0	27	0	—	0
Brook, H C	**15**	**12**	**1**	**343**	**103**	**31.18**	**1**	**1**	**19**	**0**	**—**	**4**
Brooks, J A	12	4	1	7	6	2.33	0	0	461	15	30.73	3
Brophy, G L ...	68	57	12	1,240	93*	27.55	0	9	0	0	—	67/14
Byas, D	313	301	35	7,782	116*	29.25	5	44	659	25	26.36	128
Callis, E	1	1	0	0	0	0.00	0	0	0	0	—	0
Carrick, P	304	206	53	2,159	54	14.11	0	2	7,408	236	31.38	70
Carver, K	15	4	4	52	35*	—	0	0	440	14	31.42	2
Chapman, C A ..	10	7	4	94	36*	31.33	0	0	0	0	—	7
Claydon, M E ..	7	2	0	15	9	7.50	0	0	293	8	36.62	0
Cleary, M F	4	3	1	50	23*	25.00	0	0	159	2	79.50	0
Cliff, B M	**2**	**1**	**0**	**0**	**0**	**0.00**	**0**	**0**	**84**	**1**	**84.00**	**0**
Close, D B	32	31	2	631	96	21.75	0	3	475	23	20.65	14
Coad, B O	**38**	**17**	**9**	**142**	**45**	**17.75**	**0**	**0**	**1,472**	**41**	**35.90**	**9**
Cooper, H P ...	142	74	34	483	29*	12.07	0	0	4,184	177	23.63	26
Cope, G A	37	20	13	96	18*	13.71	0	0	1,020	24	42.50	9
Coverdale, S P .	3	3	2	18	17*	18.00	0	0	0	0	—	3
Craven, V J	42	39	5	580	59	17.05	0	2	353	21	16.80	14
Dalton, A J	17	16	1	280	55	18.66	0	1	0	0	—	7
Dawood, I	25	20	4	260	57	16.25	0	1	0	0	—	18/8
Dawson, R K J .	92	58	12	431	41	9.36	0	0	2,784	91	30.59	31
Dennis, S J	56	24	11	114	16*	8.76	0	0	1,736	42	41.33	7
Duke, H G	**23**	**21**	**1**	**737**	**125**	**36.85**	**2**	**3**	**0**	**0**	**—**	**20/3**
Elliott, M T G ..	6	6	3	394	128*	131.33	3	0	0	0	—	0
Elstub, C J	10	4	4	6	4*	—	0	0	290	12	24.16	0
Fellows, G M ..	95	79	15	1,342	80*	20.96	0	6	836	22	38.00	27
Fisher, I D	28	12	3	68	20	7.55	0	0	708	29	24.41	6
Fisher, M D ...	**27**	**14**	**9**	**201**	**36***	**40.20**	**0**	**0**	**1,039**	**27**	**38.48**	**7**
Fleming, S P ...	7	7	1	285	139*	47.50	1	1	0	0	—	3

Player	M	Inns	NO	Runs	HS	Av'ge	100s	50s	Runs	Wkts	Av'ge	Ct/St
Fletcher, S D . . .	129	32	18	109	16*	7.78	0	0	4,686	164	28.57	34
Foster, M J	20	14	1	199	118	15.30	1	0	370	6	61.66	6
Fraine, W A R . .	22	20	2	613	143	34.05	1	2	0	0	—	11
Gale, A W	125	116	11	3,256	125*	31.00	2	17	0	0	—	24
Gibson, R	6	4	1	19	9	6.33	0	0	158	5	31.60	1
Gilbert, C R	5	4	0	55	37	13.75	0	0	199	8	24.87	2
Gillespie, J N . .	18	4	1	29	15*	9.66	0	0	601	18	33.38	6
Gough, D	214	120	33	1,280	72*	14.71	0	1	6,798	291	23.36	43
Gray, A K D . . .	31	19	7	130	30*	10.83	0	0	843	25	33.72	8
Grayson, A P . . .	66	49	8	587	55	14.31	0	1	1,441	39	36.94	19
Guy, S M	32	23	4	282	40	14.84	0	0	0	0	—	35/11
Hamilton, G M .	101	70	18	1,059	57*	20.36	0	2	2,803	121	23.16	15
Hampshire, A W	4	3	0	3	3	1.00	0	0	0	0	—	1
Hampshire, J H .	234	223	24	6,296	119	31.63	7	36	26	1	26.00	69
Hannon-Dalby, O J	5	1	1	21	21*	—	0	0	202	5	40.40	3
Handscomb, P S P	9	9	1	504	140	63.00	1	3	0	0	—	5
Harden, R J	19	16	2	230	42	16.42	0	0	0	0	—	1
Hartley, P J	219	145	49	1,609	83	16.76	0	4	7,476	283	26.41	40
Hartley, S N . . .	171	154	31	2,815	83*	22.88	0	13	2,153	67	32.13	52
Harvey, I J	28	27	2	637	74	25.48	0	3	950	30	31.66	8
Head, T M	4	4	0	277	175	69.25	1	1	0	0	—	1
Hill, G C H	**22**	**20**	**3**	**473**	**130**	**27.82**	**1**	**2**	**391**	**15**	**26.06**	**3**
Hodd, A J	32	23	5	368	69*	20.44	0	1	0	0	—	39/8
Hodgson, D M .	12	10	1	272	90	30.22	0	3	0	0	—	10/2
Hodgson, L J . . .	6	2	0	9	9	4.50	0	0	161	4	40.25	1
Hoggard, M J . .	83	28	19	41	7*	4.55	0	0	2,682	118	22.72	7
Hutchison, P M .	32	11	8	18	4*	6.00	0	0	844	43	19.62	3
Hutton, R A	107	80	25	1,075	65	19.54	0	4	3,000	128	23.43	27
Illingworth, R . .	41	15	11	171	45	42.75	0	0	793	40	19.82	14
Ingham, P G . . .	12	10	4	312	87*	52.00	0	2	0	0	—	2
Inzamam ul Haq	3	3	0	69	53	23.00	0	1	0	0	—	0
Jaques, P A	43	42	2	1,588	105	39.70	1	13	0	0	—	16
Jarvis, P W	144	74	28	529	42	11.50	0	0	4,684	213	21.99	33
Johnson, C	129	102	22	1,615	73*	20.18	0	4	28	2	14.00	33
Johnson, M	14	6	3	34	15*	11.33	0	0	455	12	37.91	2
Katich, S M	3	3	2	79	40*	79.00	0	0	0	0	—	2
Kellett, S A	56	51	3	1,207	118*	25.14	2	4	16	0	—	13
Kettleborough, R A	10	6	3	71	28	23.66	0	0	72	3	24.00	4
Kirby, S P	29	12	3	38	15	4.22	0	0	1,061	24	44.20	6
Kohler -Cadmore, T . . .	17	16	0	762	164	47.62	1	6	0	0	—	16
Kruis, G J	55	22	11	138	31*	12.54	0	0	1,793	62	28.91	9
Lawson, M A K .	4	4	0	30	20	7.50	0	0	141	3	47.00	1
Leadbeater, B . .	105	100	19	2,245	90	27.71	0	11	95	5	19.00	26
Leaning, J A . . .	47	40	7	1,024	131*	31.03	2	5	204	7	29.14	24
Lee, J E	4	0	0	0	0	—	0	0	116	7	16.57	0
Leech, D J	**5**	**3**	**2**	**42**	**23**	**42.00**	**0**	**0**	**224**	**5**	**44.80**	**1**
Lees, A Z	42	39	2	1,109	102	29.97	1	8	0	0	—	15
Lehmann, D S . .	130	126	20	5,229	191	49.33	8	38	1,990	79	25.18	41
Lester, E I	1	1	0	0	0	0.00	0	0	0	0	—	0
Loten, T W	8	4	2	85	43*	42.50	0	0	240	6	40.00	1
Love , J D	220	203	33	4,298	118*	25.28	4	18	129	5	25.80	44
Lucas, D S	5	2	0	40	32	20.00	0	0	187	3	62.33	1
Lumb, M J	104	98	8	2,606	92	28.95	0	18	28	0	—	31

Player	M	Inns	NO	Runs	HS	Av'ge	100s	50s	Runs	Wkts	Av'ge	Ct/St
Lumb, R G	137	123	13	2,784	101	25.30	1	16	0	0	—	21
Luxton, W	**14**	**13**	**1**	**300**	**84**	**25.00**	**0**	**2**	**0**	**0**	**—**	**4**
Lyth, A	**121**	**114**	**8**	**3,754**	**144**	**35.41**	**5**	**18**	**373**	**6**	**62.16**	**53**
McGrath, A	275	253	39	7,220	148	33.73	7	44	2,514	79	31.82	91
Maxwell, G J ...	8	7	1	312	111	52.00	1	2	144	3	48.00	4
Metcalfe, A A ..	194	189	15	5,584	127*	32.09	4	36	44	2	22.00	44
Middlebrook, J D	18	11	3	61	15*	7.62	0	0	530	13	40.76	5
Mike, B W M ..	**5**	**4**	**0**	**12**	**7**	**3.00**	**0**	**0**	**237**	**7**	**33.85**	**0**
Milburn, S M ..	4	2	1	14	13*	14.00	0	0	118	2	59.00	1
Miller, D A	3	3	0	45	44	15.00	0	0	0	0	—	3
Morris, A C	27	17	5	212	48*	17.66	0	0	464	21	22.09	5
Moxon, M D ...	237	229	21	7,380	141*	35.48	7	49	1,202	34	35.35	77
Nicholson, A G .	120	46	22	155	15*	6.45	0	0	2,951	173	17.05	16
Nicholson, N G .	2	2	1	1	1*	1.00	0	0	0	0	—	2
Old, C M	221	169	38	2,572	82*	19.63	0	10	5,841	308	18.96	56
Oldham, S	106	40	21	192	38*	10.10	0	0	3,136	142	22.08	17
Olivier, D	6	3	3	17	8*	—	0	0	322	3	107.33	2
Padgett, D E V .	57	54	3	1,069	68	20.96	0	2	25	1	25.00	13
Parker, B	73	61	8	965	69	18.20	0	1	18	0	—	12
Patterson, S A ..	95	40	20	249	25*	12.45	0-	0-	3,436	118	29.11	17
Pickles, C S	71	48	20	375	37*	13.39	0	0	2,403	63	38.14	23
Pillans, M W ...	14	8	2	115	40	19.16	0	0	595	24	24.79	3
Plunkett, L E ...	28	21	10	327	53	29.72	0	1	1,060	33	32.12	17
Poysden, J E ...	8	4	1	2	1	0.66	0	0	303	6	50.50	0
Pyrah, R M	114	75	20	978	69	17.78	0	2	3,572	133	26.85	35
Pujara, C A	8	8	1	370	101	52.85	1	3	0	0	—	4
Ramage, A	34	17	8	134	32*	14.88	0	0	1,178	30	39.26	3
Ramsden, G	1	0	0	0	—	—	0	0	26	2	13.00	0
Rana Naved -ul-Hasan	17	16	1	375	74	25.00	0	3	681	26	26.19	5
Rashid, A U ...	**107**	**75**	**22**	**1,063**	**71**	**20.05**	**0**	**1**	**3,986**	**137**	**29.09**	**34**
Read, J	1	0	0	0	—	—	0	0	0	0	—	1
Revis, M L	**23**	**20**	**3**	**393**	**58***	**23.11**	**0**	**2**	**858**	**27**	**31.77**	**11**
Rhodes, S J	2	1	0	6	6	6.00	0	0	0	0	—	3
Rhodes, W M H	21	17	2	252	46	16.80	0	0	364	11	33.09	8
Richardson. R B	28	28	6	993	103	45.13	1	8	0	0	—	5
Richardson, S A	1	1	0	7	7	7.00	0	0	0	0	—	0
Robinson, A L ..	92	36	19	127	18*	7.47	0	0	2,588	105	24.64	14
Robinson, M A .	89	30	16	41	7	2.92	0	0	2,795	91	30.71	7
Robinson, O E ..	3	2	2	16	12*	—	0	0	66	0	—	4
Robinson, P E ..	135	123	15	2,738	78*	25.35	0	14	0	0	—	47
Root, J E	**23**	**22**	**3**	**747**	**83**	**39.31**	**0**	**5**	**280**	**7**	**40.00**	**10**
Rudolph, J A ...	65	62	10	3,090	132*	59.42	9	19	37	0	—	32
Ryan, M	3	2	1	7	6*	7.00	0	0	149	5	29.80	3
Sadler, J L	1	1	0	19	19	19.00	0	0	0	0	—	0
Sanderson, B W	10	2	1	14	12*	14.00	0	0	247	8	30.87	5
Sayers, J J	31	30	2	594	62	21.21	0	5	79	1	79.00	2
Scofield, D	3	1	0	0	0	0.00	0	0	111	2	55.50	1
Shahzad. A	30	22	7	243	59*	16.20	0	1	1,182	34	34.76	7
Shan Masood ..	**6**	**6**	**0**	**217**	**96**	**36.16**	**0**	**2**	**0**	**0**	**—**	**0**
Sharp, K	206	191	18	4,776	114	27.60	3	28	48	4	12.00	68
Sharpe, P J	91	86	4	1,515	89*	18.47	0	8	11	0	—	53
Shaw, C	48	20	10	127	26	12.70	0	0	1,396	58	24.06	8
Shutt, J W	14	6	4	9	6*	4.50	0	0	437	15	29.13	7

ALL LIST A MATCHES OF 40 TO 65 OVERS 1963-2023 *(Continued)*

Player	M	Inns	NO	Runs	HS	Av'ge	100s	50s	Runs	Wkts	Av'ge	Ct/St
Sidebottom, A . .	236	131	47	1,279	52*	15.22	0	1	6,918	260	26.60	51
Sidebottom, R J .	113	51	22	303	30*	10.44	0	0	3,631	124	29.28	24
Silverwood, C E W												
	166	94	33	892	61	14.62	0	4	5,212	224	23.26	25
Smith, N	7	2	1	5	5	5.00	0	0	0	0	—	2
Smith, R	3	2	0	17	17	8.50	0	0	0	0	—	1
Squires, P J	56	48	5	708	79*	16.46	0	3	4	0	—	10
Starc, M A	4	2	2	5	4*	—	0	0	181	8	22.62	1
Stemp, R D	88	28	10	118	23*	6.55	0	0	2,996	100	29.96	14
Stevenson, G B .	217	158	23	1,710	81*	12.66	0	2	6,820	290	23.51	38
Stott, W B	2	2	0	30	30	15.00	0	0	0	0	—	0
Stringer, P M . . .	11	8	6	29	13*	14.50	0	0	256	15	17.06	0
Stuchbury, S . . .	22	8	4	21	9*	5.25	0	0	677	29	23.34	2
Sullivan, H A . .	5	3	1	21	12	10.50	0	0	193	6	32.16	3
Sullivan, J R . . .	3	1	0	6	6	6.00	0	0	79	5	15.80	0
Swallow, I G . . .	8	5	3	37	17*	18.50	0	0	198	2	99.00	5
Swanepoel, P J .	3	2	2	9	8*	—	0	0	100	3	33.33	0
Tattersall, J A .	**32**	**25**	**3**	**697**	**89**	**31.68**	**0**	**7**	**0**	**0**	**—**	**27/3**
Taylor, C R	6	5	0	102	28	20.40	0	0	0	0	—	0
Taylor, K	10	10	0	135	30	13.50	0	0	168	11	15.27	3
Taylor, N S	1	0	0	0	0	—	0	0	45	1	45.00	1
Tendulkar, S R .	17	17	2	540	107	36.00	1	1	167	6	27.83	3
Thompson, J A	**1**	**0**	**0**	**0**	**—**	**—**	**0**	**0**	**43**	**0**	**—**	**0**
Thornicroft, N D	14	7	4	52	20	17.33	0	0	591	17	34.76	3
Townsley, R A J	5	4	1	81	34	27.00	0	0	62	0	—	1
Trueman, F S . .	11	9	1	127	28	15.87	0	0	348	21	16.57	5
Vaughan, M P . .	183	178	13	4,966	125*	30.09	3	29	1,860	60	31.00	56
Wainman, J C . .	4	3	1	51	33	25.50	0	0	201	5	40.20	1
Wainwright, D J	48	21	13	150	26	18.75	0	0	1,427	38	37.55	16
Waite, M J	29	23	5	606	71	33.66	0	1	1,102	42	26.23	1
Wardlaw, I	17	10	4	56	18	9.33	0	0	686	24	28.58	3
Waring, J	1	1	1	1	1*	—	0	0	11	0	—	0
Warner, J D	1	0	0	0	—	—	0	0	32	0	—	0
Warren, A C . . .	1	1	0	3	3	3.00	0	0	35	1	35.00	0
Wharf, A G	6	1	1	2	2*	—	0	0	176	8	22.00	1
Wharton, J H . .	**6**	**6**	**2**	**89**	**54***	**22.25**	**0**	**1**	**0**	**0**	**—**	**5**
White, C	292	266	39	6,384	148	28.12	5	28	6,120	248	24.67	84
Whiteley, J P . . .	6	4	0	19	14	4.75	0	0	195	2	97.50	1
Widdup, S	4	4	0	49	38	12.25	0	0	0	0	—	2
Wigley, D H . . .	1	1	0	0	0	0.00	0	0	38	0	—	0
Willey, D J	20	16	2	448	131	32.00	1	2	808	33	24.48	5
Williamson, K A	13	11	0	279	70	25.36	0	1	42	1	42.00	6
Wilson, D	61	47	8	430	46	11.02	0	0	1,527	76	20.09	22
Wood, G L	1	1	0	26	26	26.00	0	0	0	0	—	0
Wood, M J	145	134	14	3,270	160	27.25	5	14	76	3	25.33	57
Woodford, J D . .	72	57	14	890	69*	20.69	0	2	1,627	77	21.12	25
Younus Khan . . .	11	8	0	248	100	31.00	1	0	144	2	72.00	5
Yuvraj Singh . . .	9	9	0	196	50	21.77	0	1	197	3	65.66	1

Player	M	I	NO	Runs	HS	Av'ge	100s	50s	Balls	Runs	W	Av'ge	Best	4wI	Ct/St
ATHEY, C W J 1980-88	31	30	3	848	142*	31.40	2	4	—	—	—	—	—	0	16
BAIRSTOW, D L 1979-84	21	20	6	206	23*	14.71	0	0	—	—	—	—	—	0	17/4
BAIRSTOW, J M 2011-23	107	98	8	3,868	141*	42.97	11	17	—	—	—	—	—	0	55/3
BALLANCE, G S .2013-14/15	16	15	1	297	79	21.21	0	2	—	—	—	—	—	0	8
BLAKEY, R J 1992-93	3	2	0	25	25	12.50	0	0	—	—	—	—	—	0	2/1
BOYCOTT, G 1971-81	36	34	4	1,082	105	36.06	1	9	168	105	5	21.00	2-14	0	5
BRESNAN, T T 2006-15	85	64	20	871	80	19.79	0	1	4,221	3,813	109	34.98	5-48	4	20
BROOK, H C 2022/23-23	15	15	1	407	80	29.07	0	3	—	—	—	—	—	0	2
COPE, G A 1977-78	2	1	1	1	1*	—	0	0	112	35	2	17.50	1-16	0	0
GOUGH, D 1994-2006	158	87	38	609	46*	12.42	0	0	8,422	6,154	234	26.29	5-44	10	24
HAMPSHIRE, J H ...1971-72	3	3	1	48	25*	24.00	0	0	—	—	—	—	—	0	0
HOGGARD, M J 2001-06	26	6	2	17	7	4.25	0	0	1,306	1,152	32	36.00	5-49	1	5
JARVIS, P W 1988-93	16	8	2	31	16*	5.16	0	0	879	672	24	28.00	5-35	2	1
LOVE, J D 1981	3	3	0	61	43	20.33	0	0	—	—	—	—	—	0	1
MALAN, D J 2019-23	30	30	4	1,450	140	55.76	6	7	15	17	1	17.00	1- 5	0	11
McGRATH, A 2003-04	14	12	2	166	52	16.60	0	1	228	175	4	43.75	1-13	0	4
MOXON, M D 1985-88	8	8	0	174	70	21.75	0	1	—	—	—	—	—	0	5
OLD, C M 1973-81	32	25	7	338	51*	18.77	0	1	1,755	999	45	22.20	4-8	2	8
PLUNKETT, L E 2005/6-2019	89	50	19	646	56	20.83	0	1	4,137	4,010	135	29.70	5-52	7	24
RASHID, A U 2009-23	135	68	23	826	69	18.35	0	1	6,789	6,377	199	32.04	5-27	10	43
ROOT, J E 2012/13-23	171	160	23	6,522	133*	47.60	16	39	1,638	1587	27	58.77	3-52	0	85
SHAHZAD, A 2010-11	11	8	2	39	9	6.50	0	0	588	490	17	28.82	3-41	0	4
SIDEBOTTOM, P J .2001-10	25	18	8	133	24	13.30	0	0	1,277	1,039	29	35.82	3-19	0	6
SILVERWOOD, C E W 1996-2001	7	4	0	17	12	4.25	0	0	306	244	6	40.66	3-43	0	0
STEVENSON, G B ..1980-81	4	4	3	43	28*	43.00	0	0	192	125	7	17.85	4-33	1	2
VAUGHAN, M P 2001-07	86	83	10	1,982	90*	27.15	0	16	796	649	16	40.56	4-22	1	25
WHITE, C 1994-2003	51	41	5	568	57*	15.77	0	1	2,364	1,726	65	26.55	5-21	2	12
WILLEY, D J 2015-2023	73	46	19	663	51	24.55	0	2	3,230	2,975	100	29.75	5-30	5	27

YORKSHIRE ONE-DAY INTERNATIONAL CRICKETERS 1971-2022 (Correct to February 23, 2023)

For Scotland

Player	M	I	NO	Runs	HS	Av'ge	100s	50s	Balls	Runs	W	Av'ge	Best	4wI	Ct/St
BLAIN, J A R 1999-2009	33	25	6	284	41	14.94	0	0	1,329	1,173	41	28.60	5-22	4	8
HAMILTON, G M .1999-2010	38	38	3	1,231	119	35.17	2	7	220	160	3	53.33	2-36	0	6/1
WARDLAW, I 2012/14/15	22	14	8	21	7*	3.50	0	0	1,108	1,036	36	28.77	4-22	2	1

YORKSHIRE PLAYERS WHO PLAYED ALL THEIR ONE-DAY INTERNATIONAL CRICKET AFTER LEAVING YORKSHIRE

For England

Player	M	I	NO	Runs	HS	Av'ge	100s	50s	Balls	Runs	W	Av'ge	Best	4wI	Ct/St
BATTY, G J 2002-09	10	8	2	30	17	5.00	0	0	440	366	5	73.20	2-40	—	4
CLOSE, D B 1972	3	3	0	49	43	16.33	0	0	18	21	0	—	—	—	1
GRAYSON, A P 2000-01	2	2	0	6	6	3.00	0	0	90	60	3	20.00	3-40	—	1
ILLINGWORTH, R ..1971-72	3	2	0	5	4	2.50	0	0	130	84	4	21.00	3-50	—	1
LUMB, M J 2013/14	3	3	0	165	106	55.00	1	0	—	—	—	—	—	—	1
RHODES, S J 1989-95	9	8	2	107	56	17.83	0	1	—	—	—	—	—	—	9/2
WHARF, A G 2004-05	13	5	3	19	9	9.50	0	0	584	428	18	23.77	4-24	1	1
WOOD, B 1972-82	13	12	2	314	78*	31.40	0	2	420	224	9	24.88	2-14	—	6

Overseas Players

(Qualification: 20 List A matches for Yorkshire)

For Australia

Player	M	I	NO	Runs	HS	Av'ge	100s	50s	Balls	Runs	W	Av'ge	Best	4wI	Ct/St
BEVAN, M G 1994-2004	232	196	67	6,912	108*	53.58	6	46	1,966	1,655	36	45.97	3-36	—	128
HARVEY, I J ...1997/98-2004	73	51	11	715	48*	17.87	0	0	3,279	2,577	85	30.31	4-16	4	17
JAQUES, P A 2006-2007	6	6	0	125	94	20.83	0	1	—	—	—	—	—	—	3
LEHMANN, D S . 1996-2005	117	101	22	3,078	119	38.96	4	17	1,793	1,445	52	27.78	4-7	1	26

For South Africa

Player	M	I	NO	Runs	HS	Av'ge	100s	50s	Balls	Runs	W	Av'ge	Best	4wI	Ct/St
RUDOLPH, J A 2003-06	43	37	6	1,157	81	37.32	0	7	24	26	0	—	—	—	11

YORKSHIRE PLAYERS WHO PLAYED ALL THEIR ONE-DAY INTERNATIONAL CRICKET AFTER LEAVING YORKSHIRE *(Continued)*

Player	M	I	NO	Runs	HS	Av'ge	100s	50s	Balls	Runs	W	Av'ge	Best	4wI	Ct/St
For West Indies															
RICHARDSON, R B .1983-96	224	217	30	6,248	122	33.41	5	44	58	46	1	46.00	1-4	0	75
For Zimbabwe															
BALLANCE, G S ...2022/23	2	2	0	75	52	37.50	0	1	0	0	0	—	—	0	4

LIMITED-OVERS INTERNATIONAL MATCHES AT NORTH MARINE ROAD, SCARBOROUGH 1976-1978

1976 England 202 for 8 wkts (55 overs) (G D Barlow 80*, A M E Roberts 4 for 32). West Indies 207 for 4 wkts (41 overs) (I V A Richards 119*)
West Indies won by 6 wickets
Award: I V A Richards

1978 England 206 for 8 wkts (55 overs) (G A Gooch 94, B L Cairns 5 for 28). New Zealand 187 for 8 wkts (55 overs) (B E Congdon 52*).
England won by 19 runs
Award: G A Gooch

LIMITED-OVERS INTERNATIONAL MATCHES
AT HEADINGLEY, LEEDS 1973-2023

1973 **West Indies 181** (54 overs) (R B Kanhai 55). **England 182 for 9 wkts** (54.3 overs) (M H Denness 66).
England won by 1 wicket   **Award: M H Denness**

1974 **India 265** (53.5 overs) (B P Patel 82, A L Wadekar 67). **England 266 for 6 wkts** (51.1 overs) (J H Edrich 90).
England won by 4 wickets   **Award: J H Edrich**

1975 **Australia 278 for 7 wkts** (60 overs) (R Edwards 80*). **Pakistan 205** (53 overs) (Majid Khan 65, Asif Iqbal 53, D K Lillee 5 for 34).
Australia won by 73 runs   **Award: D K Lillee**

1975 **East Africa 120** (55.3 overs). **India 123 for 0 wkt** (29.5 overs) (S M Gavaskar 65* F M Engineer 54*).
India won by 10 wickets   **Award: F M Engineer**

1975 **England 93** (36.2 overs) (G J Gilmour 6 for 14). **Australia 94 for 6 wkts** (28.4 overs).
Australia won by 4 wickets   **Award: G J Gilmour**

1979 **Canada 139 for 9 wkts** (60 overs). **Pakistan 140 for 2 wkts** (40.1 overs) (Sadiq Mohammed 57*).
Pakistan won by 8 wickets   **Award: Sadiq Mohammed**

1979 **India 182 (55.5 overs)** (S M Gavaskar 55). **New Zealand 183 for 2 wkts** (57 overs) (B A Edgar 84*).
New Zealand won by 8 wickets   **Award: B A Edgar**

1979 **England 165 for 9 wkts** (60 overs). **Pakistan 151** (56 overs) (Asif Iqbal 51, M Hendrick 4 for 15)
England won by 14 runs   **Award: M Hendrick**

1980 **West Indies 198** (55 overs) (C G Greenidge 78). **England 174** (51.2 overs) (C J Tavaré 82*).
West Indies won by 24 runs   **Award: C J Tavaré**

1981 **Australia 236 for 8 wkts** (55 overs) (G M Wood 108). **England 165** (46.5 overs) (R M Hogg 4 for 29).
Australia won by 71 runs   **Award: G M Wood**

1982 **India 193** (55 overs) (Kapil Dev 60, I T Botham 4 for 56). **England 194 for 1 wkt** (50.1 overs) (B Wood 78*, C J Tavaré 66).
England won by 9 wickets   **Award: B Wood**

1983 **West Indies 252 for 9 wkts** (60 overs) (H A Gomes 78). **Australia 151** (30.3 overs) (W W Davis 7 for 51).
West Indies won by 101 runs   **Award: W W Davis**

1983 **Pakistan 235 for 7 wkts** (60 overs) (Imran Khan 102*, Shahid Mahboob 77, A L F de Mel 5 for 39). **Sri Lanka 224** (58.3 overs) (S Wettimuny 50, Abdul Qadir 5 for 44).
Pakistan won by 11 runs   **Award: Abdul Qadir**

1983 **Sri Lanka 136** (50.4 overs). **England 137 for 1 wkt** (24.1 overs) (G Fowler 81*).
England won by 9 wickets   **Award: R G D Willis**

1986 **New Zealand 217 for 8 wkts** (55 overs) (J J Crowe 66). **England 170** (48.2 overs).
New Zealand won by 47 runs   **Award: J J Crowe**

1988 **England 186 for 8 wkts** (55 overs). **West Indies 139** (46.3 overs).
England won by 47 runs   **Award: D R Pringle**

1990 **England 295 for 6 wkts** (55 overs) (R A Smith 128, G A Gooch 55). **New Zealand 298 for 6 wkts** (54.5 overs) (M J Greatbatch 102*, J G Wright 52, A H Jones 51).
New Zealand won by 4 wickets   **Award: M J Greatbatch**

1990 **England 229** (54.3 overs) (A J Lamb 56, D I Gower 50). **India 233 for 4 wkts** (53 overs) (S V Manjrekar 82, M Azharuddin 55*)
India won by 6 wickets   **Award: A Kumble**

1996 **India 158** (40.2 overs). **England 162 for 4 wkts** (39.3 overs) (G P Thorpe 79*).
England won by 6 wickets   **Award: G P Thorpe**

1997 **Australia 170 for 8 wkts** (50 overs).**England 175 for 4 wkts** (40.1 overs) (G P
Thorpe 75*, A J Hollioake 66*).
England won by 6 wickets   **Award: G P Thorpe**

1998 **South Africa 205 for 8 wkts** (50 overs) (S M Pollock 56). **England 206 for 3 wkts**
(35 overs) (A D Brown 59, N V Knight 51).
England won by 7 wickets   **Award: A D Brown**

1999 **Pakistan 275 for 8 wkts** (50 overs) (Inzamam-ul-Haq 81, Abdur Razzaq 60). **Australia
265** (49.5 overs) (M G Bevan 61, Wasim Akram 4-40).
Pakistan won by 10 runs   **Award: Inazmam-ul-Haq**

1999 **Zimbabwe 175** (49.3 overs) (M A Goodwin 57). **New Zealand 70 for 3 wkts** (15
overs).
No result   **No Award**

1999 **South Africa 271 for 7 wkts** (50 overs) (H H Gibbs 101, D J Cullinan 50). **Australia
275 for 5 wkts** (49.4 overs) (S R. Waugh 120*, R T Ponting 69).
Australia won by 5 wickets   **Award: S R Waugh**

2001 **England 156 (45.2 overs)** (B C Hollioake 53, Waqar Younis 7 for 36). **Pakistan 153
for 4 wkts** (39.5 overs) (Abdur Razzaq 75).
Pakistan won — England conceding the match following a pitch invasion.
                    Award: Waqar Younis

2002 **Sri Lanka 240 for 7 wkts** (32 overs) (S T Jayasuriya 112). **England 241 for 7 wkts**
(31.2 overs) (M E Trescothick 82).
England won by 3 wkts   **Award: S T Jayasuriya**

2003 **England 81 for 4 wkts. Zimbabwe** did not bat.
No result   **No Award**

2004 **West Indies 159** (40.1 overs). **England 160 for 3 wkts** (22 overs) (M E Trescothick 55).
England won by 7 wickets   **Award: S J Harmison**

2005 **Bangladesh 208 for 7 wkts** (50 overs) (Belim 81, A Flintoff 4-29). **England 209
for 5 wkts** (38.5 overs) (A J Strauss 98)
England won by 5 wickets   **Award: A J Strauss**

Australia 219 for 7 wkts (50 overs) (P D Collingwood 4-34). **England 221 for 1 wkt**
(46 overs) (M E Trescothick 104*, M P Vaughan 59*).
England won by 9 wickets   **Award: M E Trescothick**

2006 **England 321 for 7 wkts** (50 overs) (M E Trescothick 121, S L Malinga 4-44).
Sri Lanka 324 for 2 wkts (37.3 overs) (S T Jayasuriya 152, W U Tharanga 109).
Sri Lanka won by 8 wickets   **Award: S T Jayasuriya**

2007 **India 324 for 6 wkts** (50 overs) (Yuvraj Singh 72, S R Tendulkar 71, S C Ganguly
59, G Gambhir 51). **England 242 for 8 wkts** (39 overs) (P D Collingwood 91*)
India won by 38 runs *(D/L Method)*   **Award: S C Ganguly**

2008 **England 275 for 4 wkts** (50 overs) (K P Pietersen 90*, A Flintoff 78). **South Africa 255**
(J H Kallis 52).
England won by 20 runs   **Award: K P Pietersen**

2009 **England v. West Indies**   **Match abandoned without a ball bowled**

2010 **Pakistan 294 for 8 wkts** (50 overs) (Kamran Akmal 74, Asad Shafiq 50, S C J Broad
4-81). **England 295 for 6 wkts** (A J Strauss 126, I J L Trott 53)
England won by 4 wickets   **Award: A J Strauss**

2011 **Sri Lanka 309 for 5 wkts** (50 overs) (D P M D Jayawardene 144, K C Sangakkara 69)
England 240 all out (E J G Morgan 52)
Sri Lanka won by 69 runs   **Award: D P M D Jayawardene**

2012 **England v. West Indies**   **Match abandoned without a ball bowled**

2013 **England v. Australia**   **Match abandoned without a ball bowled**

2014 **England 294 for 7 wkts** (50 overs) (J E Root 113). **India** 253 all out (48.4 overs) (R A Jadeja 87)
England won by 41 runs   Award: **J E Root**

2015 **Australia 299 for 7 wkts** (50 overs) (G J Bailey 75, G J Maxwell 85, M S Wade 50*). **England 304 for 7 wkts** (48.2 overs) (E J G Morgan 92, P J Cummins 4-49)
England won by 7 wickets   Award: **E J G Morgan**

2016 **Pakistan 247 for 8 wkts** (50 overs) (Azhar Ali 80, Imad Wasim 57*); **England 252 for 6 wkts** (48 overs) (B A Stokes 69, J M Bairstow 61)
England won by 6 wickets   Award: **J M Bairstow**

2017 **England 339 for 6 wkts** (50 overs) (A D Hales 61, E J G Morgan 107, M M Ali 77*) **South Africa 267** (45 overs) (H M Amla 72, F du Plessis 67, C R Woakes 4-38)
England won by 72 runs   Award **M M Ali**

2018 **India 256 for 8 wkts** (50 overs) (V Kohli 71). **England 260 for 2 wkts** (44.3 overs) (J E Root 100*, E J G Morgan 88*)
England won by 8 wickets   Award: **A U Rashid**

2019 **England 351 for 9 wkts** (50 overs) (J E Root 84, E J G Morgan 76, Shaheen Afridi 4-82). **Pakistan 297** (46.5 overs) (Babar Azam 80, Sarfaraz Ahmed 97, C R Woakes 5-54)
England won by 54 runs   Award: **C R Woakes**

2019 **Sri Lanka 232 for 9 wkts** (50 overs) (A D Mathews 85*). **England 212 (47 overs)** (B A Stokes 82*, S L Malinga 4-43)
Sri Lanka won by 20 runs   Award: **S L Malinga**

2019 **Afghanistan 227 for 9 wkts** (50 overs) (Shaheen Afridi 4-47). **Pakistan 230 for 7 wkts** (49.4 overs)
Pakistan won by 3 wickets   Award: **Imad Wasim**

2019 **West Indies 311 for 6 wkts** (50 overs) (E Lewis 58, S D Hope 77). **Afghanistan 288** (50 overs) (Rahmat Shah 62, Ikram Ali Khil 86, C R Brathwaite 4-63)
West Indies won by 23 runs   Award: **S D Hope**

2019 **Sri Lanka 264 for 7 wkts** (50 overs) (A D Mathews 113). **India 265 for 3 wkts** (43.3 overs) (K L Rahul 111, R G Sharma 103)
India won by 7 wickets   Award: **R G Sharma**

2022 **South Africa 159 for 2 wkts** (27.4 overs) (Q de Kock 92*)   **England did not bat**
No result

2023 **England v. Ireland**   **Match abandoned without a ball bowled**

SUMMARY OF RESULTS

ENGLAND	Played	Won	Lost	No Result
v. Australia	5	3	2	0
v. Bangladesh	1	1	0	0
v. India	7	5	2	0
v. New Zealand	2	0	2	0
v. Pakistan	5	4	1	0
v. South Africa	4	3	0	1
v. Sri Lanka	5	2	3	0
v. West Indies	4	3	1	0
v. Zimbabwe	1	0	0	1
Totals	34	21	11	2

In addition to two matches v. West Indies, one v. Australia and one v. Ireland abandoned

AFGHANISTAN	Played	Won	Lost	No Result
v. Pakistan	1	0	1	0
v. West Indies	1	0	1	0
Totals	2	0	2	0

SUMMARY OF RESULTS *(Continued)*

AUSTRALIA	Played	Won	Lost	No Result
v. England	5	2	3	0
v. Pakistan	2	1	1	0
v. South Africa	1	1	0	0
v. West Indies	1	0	1	0
Totals	9	4	5	0

In addition to one match abandoned

BANGLADESH	Played	Won	Lost	No Result
v. England	1	0	1	0

INDIA	Played	Won	Lost	NoResult
v. England	7	2	5	0
v. East Africa	1	1	0	0
v. New Zealand	1	0	1	0
v. Sri Lanka	1	1	0	0
Totals	10	4	6	0

NEW ZEALAND	Played	Won	Lost	No Result
v. England	2	2	0	0
v. India	1	1	0	0
v. Zimbabwe	1	0	0	1
Totals	4	3	0	0

PAKISTAN	Played	Won	Lost	No Result
v. Afghanistan	1	1	0	0
v. Australia	2	1	1	0
v. Canada	1	1	0	0
v. England	5	1	4	0
v. Sri Lanka	1	1	0	0
Totals	10	5	5	0

SOUTH AFRICA	Played	Won	Lost	No Result
v. Australia	1	0	1	0
v. England	3	0	2	1
Totals	4	0	3	1

SRI LANKA	Played	Won	Lost	No Result
v. England	5	3	2	0
v. India	1	0	1	0
v. Pakistan	1	0	1	0
Totals	7	3	4	0

WEST INDIES	Played	Won	Lost	No Result
v. Afghanistan	1	1	0	0
v. Australia	1	1	0	0
v. England	4	1	3	0
Totals	6	3	3	0

In addition to two matches abandoned

SUMMARY OF RESULTS *(Continued)*

ZIMBABWE	Played	Won	Lost	No Result
v. England	1	0	0	1
v. New Zealand	1	0	0	1
Totals	2	0	0	2

CANADA	Played	Won	Lost	No Result
v. Pakistan	1	0	1	0
EAST AFRICA	Played	Won	Lost	No Result
v. India	1	0	1	0

CENTURIES

152	S J Jayasuriya	for Sri Lanka	v. England	2006
144	D P M D Jayawardene	for Sri Lanka	v. England	2011
128	R A Smith	for England	v. New Zealand	1990
126	A J Strauss	for England	v. Pakistan	2010
121	M E Trescothick	for England	v. Sri Lanka	2006
120*	S R Waugh	for Australia	v. South Africa	1999
113	J E Root	for England	v. India	2014
113	A D Mathews	Sri Lanka	v. India	2019
112	S J Jayasuriya	for Sri Lanka	v. England	2002
111	K L Rahul	for India	v. Sri Lanka	2019
109	W U Tharanga	for Sri Lanka	v. England	2006
108	G M Wood	for Australia	v. England	1981
104*	M E Trescothick	for England	v. Australia	2005
103	R G Sharma	for India	v. Sri Lanka	2019
102*	Imran Khan	for Pakistan	v. Sri Lanka	1983
102*	M J Greatbatch	for New Zealand	v. England	1990
101	H H Gibbs	for South Africa	v. Australia	1999
100*	J E Root	for England	v. India	2018

4 WICKETS IN AN INNINGS

7-36	Waqar Younis	for Pakistan	v. England	2001
7-51	W W Davis	for West Indies	v. Australia	1983
6-14	G J Gilmour	for Australia	v. England	1975
5-34	D K Lillee	for Australia	v. Pakistan	1975
5-39	A L F de Mel	for Sri Lanka	v. Pakistan	1983
5-44	Abdul Qadir	for Pakistan	v. Sri Lanka	1983
5-54	C R Woakes	for England	v. Pakistan	2019
4-15	M Hendrick	for England	v. Pakistan	1979
4-29	R M Hogg	for Australia	v England	1981
4-29	A Flintoff	for England	v. Bangladesh	2005
4-34	P D Collingwood	for England	v. Australia	2005
4-38	C R Woakes	for England	v. South Africa	2017
4-40	Wasim Akram	for Pakistan	v. Australia	1999
4-43	S L Malinga	for Sri Lanka	v. England	2019
4-44	S L Malinga	for Sri Lanka	v. England	2006
4-47	Shaheen Afridi	for Pakistan	v. Afghanistan	2019
4-49	P J Cummins	Australia	v. England	2015
4-56	I T Botham	for England	v. India	1982
4-81	S J C Broad	for England	v. Pakistan	2010

Player	M	I	NO	Runs	HS	Av'ge	100s	50s	Balls	Runs	W	Av'ge	Best	4wI	Ct/St
BAIRSTOW, J M 2011-23	70	64	13	1,512	90	29.64	0	10	0	0	0	—	—	0	45/1
BRESNAN, T T ..2006-13/14	34	22	9	216	47*	16.61	0	0	663	887	24	36.95	3-10	0	10
BROOK, H C 2021/22-23	29	26	6	544	81*	27.20	0	2	0	0	0	—	—	0	18
MALAN, D J 2017-23	62	60	8	1,892	103*	36.38	1	16	12	27	1	27.00	1-27	0	22
PLUNKETT, L E 2006-19	22	11	4	42	18	6.00	0	0	476	627	25	25.08	3-21	0	7
RASHID, A U 2009-23	104	33	16	101	22	5.94	0	0	2,192	2,698	107	25.21	4- 2	2	29
ROOT, J E 2012-19	32	30	5	893	90*	35.72	0	5	84	139	6	23.16	2- 9	0	18
SHAHZAD, A 2010-11	3	1	1	0	0*	—	0	0	66	97	3	32.33	2-38	0	1
VAUGHAN, M P 2005-7	2	2	0	27	27	13.50	0	0	0	0	0	—	—	0	0
WILLEY, D J 2015-22/23	43	26	11	226	33*	15.06	0	0	865	1,180	51	23.13	4- 7	1	17

For Scotland

Player	M	I	NO	Runs	HS	Av'ge	100s	50s	Balls	Runs	W	Av'ge	Best	4wI	Ct/St
BLAIN, J A R 2007-8	6	3	1	4	3*	2.00	0	0	120	108	6	18.00	2-23	0	1
HAMILTON, G M ...2007-10	12	8	0	90	32	11.25	0	0	0	0	0	—	—	0	3
WARDLAW, I .2012/13-13/14	4	1	0	1	1	1.00	0	0	96	145	9	16.11	4-40	0	0

YORKSHIRE PLAYERS WHO PLAYED ALL THEIR T20i CRICKET AFTER LEAVING YORKSHIRE

For England

Player	M	I	NO	Runs	HS	Av'ge	100s	50s	Balls	Runs	W	Av'ge	Best	4wI	Ct/St
BATTY, G J 2009	1	1	0	4	4	4.00	0	0	18	17	0	—	—	0	0
GOUGH, D 2005-06	2	0	0	0	—	—	—	—	41	49	3	16.33	3-16	0	0
LUMB, M J 2010-13/14	27	27	1	552	63	21.23	0	3	0	0	0	—	—	0	8
SIDEBOTTOM, R J .2007-10	18	1	1	5	5*	—	0	0	367	437	23	19.00	3-16	0	5

Overseas Players
(Qualification: 20 t20 matches for Yorkshire)

For South Africa

Player	M	I	NO	Runs	HS	Av'ge	100s	50s	Balls	Runs	W	Av'ge	Best	4wI	Ct/St
RUDOLPH, J A 2006	1	1	1	6	6*	—	0	0	—	—	—	—	—	0	0

For Zimbabwe

Player	M	I	NO	Runs	HS	Av'ge	100s	50s	Balls	Runs	W	Av'ge	Best	4wI	Ct/St
BALLANCE, G S ...2022/23	1	1	0	30	30	30.00	0	0	—	—	—	—	—	0	0

T20 RECORDS SECTION
TROPHY WINNERS 2003-2023

		Yorkshire's Position			*Yorkshire's Position*
2003	Surrey	Group N 2 (6)	2014	Warwickshire	Group N 5 (9)
2004	Leicestershire	Group N 5 (6)	2015	Lancashire	Group N 8 (9)
2005	Somerset	Group N 4 (6)	2016	Northamptonshire	Semi-Final
2006	Leicestershire	Quarter-Final	2017	Nottinghamshire	Group N 5 (9)
2007	Kent	Quarter-Final	2018	Worcestershire	Group N 5 (9)
2008	Middlesex	Group N 3 (6)	2019	Essex	Group N 5 (9)
2009	Sussex	Group N 5 (6)	2020	Nottinghamshire	Group N 5 (6)
2010	Hampshire	Group N 6 (9)	2021	Kent	Quarter-Final
2011	Leicestershire	Group N 6 (9)	2022	Hampshire	Semi-Final
2012	Hampshire	Final	2023	Somerset	Group N 8 (9)
2013	Northamptonshire	Group N 6 (6)			

SEASON-BY-SEASON RECORD OF ALL T20 MATCHES PLAYED BY YORKSHIRE 2003-2023

Season	Played	Won	Lost	Tie	N R	Abd	Season	Played	Won	Lost	Tie	N R	Abd
2003	5	3	2	0	0	0	2014	11	6	5	0	0	3
2004	5	2	3	0	0	0	2015	14	5	8	1	0	0
2005	8	3	5	0	0	0	2016	15	8	6	0	1	1
2006	9	4	4	0	1	0	2017	12	6	5	1	0	2
2007	8	4	4	0	0	1	2018	16	8	8	0	0	0
2008	9	5	3	1	0	1	2019	10	4	5	1	0	4
2009	10	4	6	0	0	0	2020	8	3	5	0	0	2
2010	16	6	9	1	0	0	2021	13	7	6	0	0	1
2011	15	6	7	0	2	1	2022	16	8	7	1	0	0
2012	12	9	2	0	1	1	2023	13	6	6	0	1	1
2012/13	6	2	3	0	1	0		241	111	116	7	7	18
2013	10	2	7	1	0	0							

ANALYSIS OF T20 RESULTS V. ALL TEAMS 2003-2023
DOMESTIC MATCHES

Opponents	Played	HOME Won	HOME Lost	HOME Tied	HOME N. R	AWAY Won	AWAY Lost	AWAY Tied	AWAY N. R	Abd
Derbyshire	36	11	9	0	0	9	6	0	1	0
Durham	39	11	6	1	0	9	10	0	2	2
Essex	1	0	0	0	0	0	1	0	0	0
Glamorgan	1	0	0	0	0	1	0	0	0	0
Hampshire	1	0	0	0	0	0	1	0	0	0
Lancashire	36	10	7	1	0	4	12	2	0	5
Leicestershire	29	7	6	0	0	5	10	1	0	2
Northamptonshire	16	5	4	0	0	5	1	1	0	3
Nottinghamshire	34	7	7	0	1	5	14	0	0	3
Surrey	1	0	0	0	0	1	0	0	0	0
Sussex	3	0	1	0	0	1	1	0	0	0
Warwickshire	20	5	5	1	0	2	5	0	2	2
Worcestershire	16	7	2	0	0	3	4	0	0	1
Total	**233**	**63**	**47**	**3**	**1**	**45**	**65**	**4**	**5**	**18**

Abandoned matches are not included in the list of matches played.

ANALYSIS OF T20 RESULTS V. ALL TEAMS 2003-2023 *(Cont)*
OTHER MATCHES

Opponents	Played	HOME				AWAY				Abd
		Won	Lost	Tied	N. R	Won	Lost	Tied	N. R	
Uva	1	0	0	0	0	1	0	0	0	0
Trinidad and Tobago	1	0	0	0	0	1	0	0	0	0
Sydney Sixers	1	0	0	0	0	0	1	0	0	0
Mumbai	1	0	0	0	0	0	0	0	1	0
Highveld	1	0	0	0	0	0	1	0	0	0
Chennai	1	0	0	0	0	0	1	0	0	0
Lahore Qalandars	1	0	0	0	0	0	1	0	0	0
Hobart Hurricanes	1	0	0	0	1	0	0	0	0	0
Total	**8**	**0**	**0**	**0**	**0**	**3**	**4**	**0**	**1**	**0**
Grand Total	**241**	**63**	**47**	**3**	**1**	**48**	**69**	**4**	**6**	**18**

Abandoned matches are not included in matches played

ABANDONED T20 MATCHES (18)

2007	v. Lancashire at Leeds		v. Warwickshire at Birmingham
2008	v. Leicestershire at Leeds	2019	v. Nottinghamshire at Leeds
2011	v. Northamptonshire at Leeds		v. Northamptonshire at Northampton
2012	v. Lancashire at Manchester		v. Lancashire at Manchester
2014	v. Warwickshire at Birmingham		v. Durham at Leeds
	v. Lancashire at Leeds	2020	v. Nottinghamshire at Leeds
	v. Worcestershire at Worcester		v. Leicestershire at Leeds
2016	v. Nottinghamshire at Leeds	2021	v. Durham at Leeds
2017	v. Northamptonshire at Northampton	2023	v. Lancashire at Manchester

T20 HIGHEST TEAM TOTALS

BY YORKSHIRE

260-4	v.	Northamptonshire at Leeds	2017
255:2	v.	Leicestershire at Leicester	2019
240:4	v.	Leicestershire at Leeds	2021
233-6	v.	Worcestershire at Leeds	2017
227-5	v.	Nottinghamshire at Leeds	2017
226:8	v.	Birmingham Bears at Leeds	2018
224:3	v.	Northamptonshire at Leeds	2021
224:4	v.	Worcestershire at Leeds	2023
223-5	v.	Nottinghamshire at Nottingham	2017
223:6	v.	Durham at Leeds	2016
220:5	v.	Derbyshire at Leeds	2020
216:6	v.	Worcestershire at Worcester	2021
215:6	v.	Northamptonshire at Leeds	2016
213:7	v.	Worcestershire at Leeds	2010
212:5	v.	Worcestershire at Leeds	2012
211:6	v.	Leicestershire at Leeds	2004
210:3	v.	Derbyshire at Derby	2006
209:4	v.	Nottinghamshire at Leeds	2015
209:8	v.	Lancashire at Leeds	2022
208:4	v.	Durham at Leeds	2022
207	v.	Birmingham Bears at Leeds	2022
204:7	v.	Lancashire at Birmingham	2022
207:7	v.	Nottinghamshire at Nottingham	2004
202:5	v.	Nottinghamshire at Leeds	2022
202:8	v.	Lancashire at Manchester	2015

T20 HIGHEST TEAM TOTALS

AGAINST YORKSHIRE

238:5	for Birmingham Bears at Leeds	2022
231:6	for Lancashire at Manchester	2015
225:5	for Nottinghamshire at Nottingham	2017
222:6	for Derbyshire at Leeds	2010
222:8	for Leicestershire at Leeds	2021
221:3	for Leicestershire at Leeds	2004
217:3	for Durham at Leeds	2023
215:6	for Nottinghamshire at Nottingham	2011
215:6	for Durham at Chester-le-Street	2013
213:5	for Lancashire at Leeds	2022
212:4	for Derbyshire at Chesterfield	2023
212:5	for Nottinghamshire at Nottingham	2018
211:7	for Leicestershire at Leicester	2022
210:7	for Nottinghamshire at Nottingham	2004
208:4	for Lancashire at Birmingham	2022
208:7	for Worcestershire at Worcester	2010
207:3	for Leicestershire at Leicester	2021
207:5	for Derbyshire at Leeds	2019
207:6	for Lancashire at Manchester	2005
207:8	for Durham at Leeds	2022
201:4	for Leicestershire at Leicester	2019
201:5	for Nottinghamshire at Leeds	2014
204:7	for Lancashire at Manchester	2016
200:6	for Birmingham Bears at Birmingham	2023
198:6	for Worcestershire at Leeds	2023
196:7	for Worcestershire at Leeds	2017

T20 HIGHEST INDIVIDUAL SCORES

BY YORKSHIRE

161	A Lyth	v.	Northamptonshire at Leeds	2017
118	D J Willey	v.	Worcestershire at Leeds	2017
112	J M Bairstow	v.	Worcestershire at Worcester	2021
111*	J H Wharton	v.	Worcestershire at Leeds	2023
109	I J Harvey	v.	Derbyshire at Leeds	2005
108*	I J Harvey	v.	Lancashire at Leeds	2004
102*	J M Bairstow	v	Durham at Chester-le-Street	2014
101*	H H Gibbs	v.	Northamptonshire at Northampton	2010
96*	M J Wood	v.	Nottinghamshire at Nottingham	2004
96*	T Kohler-Cadmore	v.	Leicestershire at Leicester	2019
95*	D J Malan	v,	Nottinghamshire at Nottingham	2023
94*	T Kohler-Cadmore	v.	Birmingham Bears at Birmingham	2019
92*	G J Maxwell	v.	Nottinghamshire at Leeds	2015
92*	J E Root	v.	Lancashire at Manchester	2016
92*	A Lyth	v.	Durham at Leeds	2018
92	P A Jaques	v.	Leicestershire at Leeds	2004
92	J M Bairstow	v.	Durham at Leeds	2015
91*	H C Brook	v.	Lancashire at Leeds	2021
91	A W Gale	v.	Nottinghamshire at Leeds	2009
90*	A Lyth	v.	Leicestershire at Leeds	2023
89	A J Finch	v.	Nottinghamshire at Leeds	2014
88	A J Finch	v.	Lancashire at Manchester	2014
87	A Lyth	v.	Durham at Leeds	2017

T20 HIGHEST INDIVIDUAL SCORES

AGAINST YORKSHIRE

111	D L Maddy	for	Leicestershire at Leeds	2004
101	S G Law	for	Lancashire at Manchester	2005
101	A D Hales	for	Nottinghamshire at Nottingham	2017
100*	G M Smith	for	Derbyshire at Leeds	2008
100	Sohail Akhtar	for	Lahore Qalandars at Abu Dhabi	2018
99*	A M Lilley	for	Leicestershire at Leicester	2021
97	B J Hodge	for	Leicestershire at Leicester	2003
96*	A B McDonald	for	Leicestershire at Leeds	2011
94	L E Bosman	for	Derbyshire at Leeds	2010
91*	G Clark	for	Durham at Leeds	2015
91*	R A Whiteley	for	Worcestershire at Leeds	2015
91	M A Ealham	for	Nottinghamshire at Nottingham	2004
91	P Mustard	for	Durham at Chester-le-Street	2013
91	M H Wessels	for	Worcestershire at Leeds	2019
90*	S R Patel	for	Nottinghamshire at Leeds	2015
90*	B A Stokes	for	Durham at Leeds	2018
90	A Z Lees	for	Durham at Leeds	2023
88*	P D Collingwood	for	Durham at Chester-le-Street	2017
85*	B M Duckett	for	Nottinghamshire at Nottingham	2020
85	A Flintoff	for	Lancashire at Leeds	2004

T20 BEST BOWLING

BY YORKSHIRE

6-19	T T Bresnan	v.	Lancashire at Leeds	2017
5-11	J W Shutt	v.	Durham at Chester-le-Street	2019
5-16	R M Pyrah	v.	Durham at Scarborough	2011
5-19	Azeem Rafiq	v.	Northamptonshire at Leeds	2017
5-21	J A Brooks	v.	Leicestershire at Leeds	2013
5-21	J A Thompson	v.	Leicestershire at Leicester	2023
5-22	M D Fisher	v.	Derbyshire at Leeds	2015
5-31	A Lyth	v.	Nottinghamshire at Nottingham	2019
4-18	M A Ashraf	v.	Derbyshire at Derby	2012
4-18	D J Willey	v.	Northamptonshire at Leeds	2019
4-19	A U Rashid	v.	Durham at Leeds	2017
4-20	R M Pyrah	v.	Durham at Leeds	2008
4-20	A U Rashid	v.	Leicestershire at Leeds	2010
4-21	R M Pyrah	v.	Worcestershire at Leeds	2011
4-21	B W Sanderson	v.	Derbyshire at Derby	2011
4-21	J A Brooks	v.	Derbyshire at Leeds	2013
4-23	Rana Naved	v.	Nottinghamshire at Leeds	2009
4-24	A U Rashid	v.	Nottinghamshire at Nottingham	2008
4-24	L H Ferguson	v.	Lancashire at Leeds	2021
4-25	R J Sidebottom	v.	Durham at Chester-le-Street	2012

T20 BEST BOWLING

AGAINST YORKSHIRE

5-28	T A I Taylor	for	Northamptonshire at Leeds	2023
5-43	L J Fletcher	for	Nottinghamshire at Nottingham	2020
4- 9	C K Langeveldt	for	Derbyshire at Leeds	2008
4-17	L V van Beek	for	Derbyshire at Leeds	2019
4-19	K H D Barker	for	Warwickshire at Birmingham	2010
4-19	J S Patel	for	Warwickshire at Leeds	2014
4-19	R Rampaul	for	Derbyshire at Chesterfield	2018
4-19	M R J Watt	for	Derbyshire at Chesterfield	2019
4-20	L Wood	for	Lancashire at Manchester	2021
4-28	D R Mousley	for	Birmingham Bears at Leeds	2023
4-21	J Needham	for	Derbyshire at Leeds	2009
4-23	A J Hall	for	Northamptonshire at Northampton	2011
4-23	M W Parkinson	for	Lancashire at Leeds	2017
4-24	D Y Pennington	for	Worcestershire at Leeds	2021
4-25	J A Morkel	for	Derbyshire at Chesterfield	2013
4-25	I G Butler	for	Northamptonshire at Leeds	2014
4-25	M A Wood	for	Durham at Birmingham	2016
4-28	D R Mousley	for	Birmingham Bears at Leeds	2023
4-31	Shakib al Hasan	for	Worcestershire at Worcester	2011
4-31	B J Dwarshuis	for	Worcestershire at Worcester	2021
4-32	C A Ingram	for	Glamorgan at Cardiff	2016
4-32	H J H Brookes	for	Birmingham Bears at Birmingham	2023

T20 ECONOMICAL BOWLING

BY YORKSHIRE

4-0-11-5	J W Shutt	v. Durham at Chester-le-Street	2019

AGAINST YORKSHIRE

4-0-9-4	C K Langeveldt for Derbyshire at Leeds	2008

T20 MOST EXPENSIVE BOWLING

BY YORKSHIRE

4-0-65-2	M J Hoggard	v. Lancashire at Leeds	2005

AGAINST YORKSHIRE

4-0-77-0	B W Sanderson for Northamptonshire at Leeds	2017

T20 MAN OF THE MATCH AWARDS (109)

A Lyth	10	R M Pyrah	5	A J Finch	2
A W Gale	8	Azeem Rafiq	4	H H Gibbs	2
T Kohler-Cadmore	7	I J Harvey	3	P A Jaques	2
D J Willey	7	J A Leaning	3	A Z Lees	2
A McGrath	6	D A Miller	3	M J Lumb	2
J M Bairstow	5	A U Rashid	3	J E Root	2
H C Brook	5	J A Thompson	3		
T T Bresnan	5	K S Williamson	3		

One each: G S Ballance, J A Brooks, M E Claydon, D C Drakes, M D Fisher, S P Fleming, D S Lehmann, D J Malan, G J Maxwell, J A Rudolph, B W Sanderson, J J Sayers, A Shahzad, J W Shutt, D J Wainwright, C White and D Wiese (1 each)..

T20 HIGHEST AND LOWEST SCORES BY AND AGAINST YORKSHIRE PLUS INDIVIDUAL BEST BATTING AND BOWLING 2003-2023

The lowest score is the lowest all-out score or the lowest score at completion of the allotted overs, five-over matches not included.

Yorkshire versus:

Derbyshire

		By Yorkshire			Against Yorkshire		
Highest Score:	In Yorkshire	220:5	at Leeds 2020		222:5	at Leeds 2010	
	Away	210:3	at Derby 2006		212:4	at Chesterfield 2023	
Lowest Score:	In Yorkshire	102	at Leeds 2018		124	at Chesterfield 2014	
	Away	68	at Chesterfield 2023		119:7	at Leeds 2007	
Best Batting:	In Yorkshire	109	I J Harvey	at Leeds 2005	100*	G M Smith	at Leeds 2008
	Away	79*	A W Gale	at Chesterfield 2009	71*	B A Godleman	at Chesterfield 2018
Best Bowling:	In Yorkshire	5-22	M D Fisher	at Leeds 2015	4-9	C K Langeveldt	at Leeds 2008
	Away	4-18	M A Ashraf	at Derby 2012	4-19	R Rampaul	at Chesterfield 2018
					4-19	M R J Watt	at Chesterfield 2019

Durham

		By Yorkshire			Against Yorkshire		
Highest Score:	In Yorkshire	223:6	at Leeds 2016		217:8	at Leeds 2023	
	Away	201:5	at Chester-le-Street 2022		215:6	at Chester-le-Street 2013	
Lowest Score:	In Yorkshire	95	at Leeds 2014		116:8	at Leeds 2009	
	Away	90:9	at Chester-le-Street 2009		98	at Chester-le-Street 2006	
Best Batting:	In Yorkshire	92	J M Bairstow	at Leeds 2015	91*	G Clark	at Leeds 2015
	Away	102*	J M Bairstow	at Chester-le-Street 2014	91	P Mustard	at Chester-le-Street 2013
Best Bowling:	In Yorkshire	5-16	R M Pyrah	at Scarborough 2011	4-38	S J Harmison	at Leeds 2008
	Away	5-11	J W Shutt	at Chester-le-Street 2019	4-25	M A Wood	at Birmingham 2016

Essex

		By Yorkshire			Against Yorkshire		
Highest Score:	Away	143:7	at Chelmsford 2006		149:5	at Chelmsford 2006	
Best Batting:	Away	43	G L Brophy	at Chelmsford 2006	48*	J S Foster	at Chelmsford 2006
Best Bowling:	Away	2-22	A Shahzad at Chelmsford 2006		2-11	T J Phillips	at Chelmsford 2006

Glamorgan

		By Yorkshire			Against Yorkshire		
Highest Score:	Away	180:8	at Cardiff 2016		90	at Cardiff 2016	
Best Batting:	Away	79	D J Willey	at Cardiff 2016	26	J A Rudolph	at Cardiff 2016
Best Bowling:	Away	4-26	A U Rashid	at Cardiff 2016	4-32	C A Ingram	at Cardiff 2016

T20 HIGHEST AND LOWEST SCORES BY AND AGAINST YORKSHIRE
PLUS INDIVIDUAL BEST BATTING AND BOWLING 2003-2023 *(Continued)*

The lowest score is the lowest all-out score or the lowest score at completion of the allotted overs, five-over matches not included.

Yorkshire versus:

	Hampshire	**By Yorkshire**			**Against Yorkshire**		
Highest Score:	Away	140:6	at Cardiff 2012		150:6	at Cardiff 2012	
Best Batting:	Away	72*	D A Miller at Cardiff 2012		43	J H K Adams	at Cardiff 2012
Best Bowling:	Away	2-20	R J Sidebottom at Cardiff 2012		3-26	C P Wood	at Cardiff 2012

	Lancashire	**Against Yorkshire**					
Highest Score:	In Yorkshire	209:9	at Leeds 2022		213:5	at Leeds 2022	
	Away	204:7	at Birmingham 2022		231:4	at Manchester 2015	
Lowest Score:	In Yorkshire	111:8	at Leeds 2009		131:9	at Leeds 2004	
	Away	97	at Manchester 2005		104:3	at Manchester 2003	
Best Batting:	In Yorkshire	108*	I J Harvey	at Leeds 2004	85	A Flintoff	at Leeds 2004
	Away	92*	J E Root	at Manchester 2016	101	S G Law	at Manchester 2005
Best Bowling	In Yorkshire	6-19	T T Bresnan	at Leeds 2017	4-23	M W Parkinson	at Leeds 2017
	Away	3-15	Azeem Rafiq	at Manchester 2011	4-20	L Wood	at Manchester 2021

	Leicestershire						
Highest Score:	In Yorkshire	240:4	at Leeds 2021		221:3	at Leeds 2004	
	Away	255:2	at Leicester 2019		211:7	at Leicester 2022	
Lowest Score:	In Yorkshire	134	at Leeds 2006		113:9	at Leeds 2013	
	Away	105	at Leicester 2013		126	at Leicester 2023	
Best Batting:	In Yorkshire	92	P A Jaques	at Leeds 2004	111	D L Maddy	at Leeds 2004
	Away	96 *	T Kohler-Cadmore	at Leicester 2019	99*	A M Lilley	at Leicester 2021
Best Bowling:	In Yorkshire	5-21	J A Brooks	at Leeds 2013	4-34	Naveen ul Haq	at Leeds 2022
	Away	5-21	J A Thompson	at Leicester 2023	4-35	C F Parkinson	at Leicester 2021

T20 HIGHEST AND LOWEST SCORES BY AND AGAINST YORKSHIRE
PLUS INDIVIDUAL BEST BATTING AND BOWLING 2003-2023 *(Continued)*

The lowest score is the lowest all-out score or the lowest score at completion of the allotted overs, five-over matches not included.

Yorkshire versus:

Northamptonshire — By Yorkshire / Against Yorkshire

		By Yorkshire			Against Yorkshire		
Highest Score:	In Yorkshire	260:4	at Leeds 2017		180:6	at Leeds 2023	
	Away	190:7	at Northampton 2022		180:5	at Northampton 2010	
Lowest Score:	In Yorkshire	102	at Leeds 2023		107	at Leeds 2019	
	Away	144	at Northampton 2011		128	at Northampton 2022	
Best Batting:	In Yorkshire	161	A Lyth	at Leeds 2017	65	R E Levi	at Leeds 2017
	Away	101*	H H Gibbs	at Northampton 2010	76	R E Levi	at Northampton 2014
	In Yorkshire	5-19	Azeem Rafiq	at Leeds 2017	5-28	T A I Taylor	at Leeds 2023
	Away	3-15	T T Bresnan	at Northampton 2016	4-23	A J Hall	at Northampton 2011

Nottinghamshire

		By Yorkshire			Against Yorkshire		
Highest Score:	In Yorkshire	227:5	at Leeds 2017		201:4	at Leeds 2014	
	Away	223:5	at Nottingham 2017		225:5	at Nottingham 2017	
Lowest Score:	In Yorkshire	141:8	at Leeds 2008		155:6	at Leeds 2009	
	Away	112:7	at Nottingham 2010		136:6	at Nottingham 2008	
Best Batting:	In Yorkshire	92*	G J Maxwell	at Leeds 2015	90*	S R Patel	at Leeds 2015
	Away	96*	M J Wood	at Nottingham 2004	101	A D Hales	at Nottingham 2017
Best Bowling:	In Yorkshire	4-23	Rana Naved-ul-Hasan	at Leeds 2009	3-29	J T Ball	at Leeds 2022
	Away	5-31	A Lyth	at Nottingham 2019	5-43	L J Fletcher	at Nottingham 2020

Surrey

		By Yorkshire			Against Yorkshire		
Highest Score:	Away	160:5	at The Oval 2022		159:7	at The Oval 2022	
Best Batting:	Away	62	T Kohler-Cadmore	at The Oval 2022	40	J Overton	at The Oval 2022
Best Bowling:	Away	2-26	D J Willey	at The Oval 2022	2-28	A A P Atkinso	at The Oval 2022

T20 HIGHEST AND LOWEST SCORES BY AND AGAINST YORKSHIRE
PLUS INDIVIDUAL BEST BATTING AND BOWLING 2003-2023 *(Continued)*

The lowest score is the lowest all-out score or the lowest score at completion of the allotted overs, five-over matches not included.

Yorkshire versus:

Sussex

		By Yorkshire			Against Yorkshire		
Highest Score:	Home	177:7	at Chester-l -Street 2021		178:5	at Chester-le-Street 2021	
	Away	172:6	at Cardiff 2012		193:5	at Hove 2007	
Lowest Score:	Away	155	at Hove 2007		136:8	at Cardiff 2012	
Best Batting:	Home	55	T Kohler-Cadmore and G S Ballance at Chester-le-Street 2021		54	L J Wright	at Chester-le-Street 2021
	Away	68*	J M Bairstow	at Cardiff 2012	80*	C D Nash	at Cardiff 2012
Best Bowling:	Home	3-28	J A Thompson	at Chester-le-Street 2021	3-39	T S Mills	at Chester-le-Street 2021
	Away	2-22	T T Bresnan	at Cardiff 2012	3-22	S B Styris	at Cardiff 2012

Warwickshire

		By Yorkshire			Against Yorkshire		
Highest Score:	In Yorkshire	226:8	at Leeds 2018		238:5	at Leeds 2022	
	Away	200:3	at Birmingham 2019		158:2	at Birmingham 2018	
Lowest Score:	In Yorkshire	121:9	at Leeds 2010		145	at Leeds 2015	
	Away	81	at Birmingham 2021		101	at Birmingham 2022	
Best Batting:	In Yorkshire	76*	T Kohler-Cadmore	at Leeds 2019	83*	S R Hain	at Leeds 2023
	Away	94*	T Kohler-Cadmore	at Birmingham 2019	64*	S R Hain	at Birmingham 2019
	In Yorkshire	3-21	T T Bresnan	at Leeds 2017	4-19	J S Patel	at Leeds 2014
	Away	3-17	D J Willey	at Birmingham 2022	4-19	K H D Barker	at Birmingham 2010

Worcestershire

		By Yorkshire			Against Yorkshire		
Highest Score:	In Yorkshire	233:6	at Leeds 2017		198:6	at Leeds 2023	
	Away	216:6	at Worcester 2021		208:7	at Worcester 2010	
Lowest Score:	In Yorkshire	117	at Leeds 2015		109	at Leeds 2010	
	Away	142	at Worcester 2011		120	at Worcester 2021	
Best Batting:	In Yorkshire	118	D J Willey	at Leeds 2017	91*	R A Whiteley	at Leeds 2015
					91	M H Wessels	at Leeds 2019
	Away	112	J M Bairstow	at Worcester 2021	56	A N Kervezee	at Worcester 2011
Best Bowling:	In Yorkshire	4-21	R M Pyrah	at Leeds 2011	4-24	D Y Pennington	at Leeds 2021
	Away	3-18	D Wiese	at Worcester 2023	4-31	Shakib al Hasan	at Worcester 2011
					4-31	B J Dwarshuis	at Worcester 2021

T20 HIGHEST AND LOWEST SCORES BY AND AGAINST YORKSHIRE
PLUS INDIVIDUAL BEST BATTING AND BOWLING 2003-2023 *(Continued)*

The lowest score is the lowest all-out score or the lowest score at completion of the allotted overs, five-over matches not included.

Yorkshire versus:

Chennai

		By Yorkshire			Against Yorkshire		
Highest Score:	Away	140:6	at Durban 2012		141:6	at Durban 2012	
Best Batting:	Away	58	G S Ballance	at Durban 2012	47	S Badrinath	at Durban 2012
Best Bowling:	Away	3-23	I Wardlaw	at Durban 2012	2-12	J A Morkel	at Durban 2012

Highveld

Highest Score:	Away	131:7	at Johannesburg 2012		134:5	at Johannesburg	
Best Batting:	Away	31	P A Jaques	at Johannesburg 2012	32	Q de Kock	at Johannesburg 2012
Best Bowling:	Away	2-21	S A Patterson	at Johannesburg 2012	2-23	A M Phangiso	at Johannesburg

Hobart Hurricanes   By Yorkshire · Against Yorkshire

Highest Score:	Away	144:1	at Abu Dhabi 2018		140:7	at Abu Dhabi 2018	
Best Batting:	Away	72*	T Kohler-Cadmore	at Abu Dhabi 2018	38	C P Jewell	at Abu Dhabi 2018
Best Bowling:	Away	2-29	K Carver	at Abu Dhabi 2018	1-24	J Clark	at Abu Dhabi 2018

Lahore Qalandars

Highest Score:	Away	184:5	at Abu Dhabi 2018		189:4	at Abu Dhabi 2018	
Best Batting:	Away	37	H C Brook	at Abu Dhabi 2018	100	Sohail Akhtar	at Abu Dhabi 2018
Best Bowling:	Away	2-26	J E Poysden	at Abu Dhabi 2018	2-36	Shaheen Shah Afridi	at Abu Dhabi 2018

Mumbai

Highest Score:	Away				156: 6	at Cape Town 2012	
Best Batting:	Away				37	D R Smith	at Cape Town
Best Bowling:	Away	2-36	Azeem Rafiq	at Cape Town 2012			

Sydney Sixers

Highest Score:	Away	96:9	at Cape Town 2012		98:2	at Cape Town 2012	
Best Batting:	Away	25	J E Root	at Cape Town 2012	43*	M J Lumb	at Cape Town 2012
Best Bowling:	Away	1-21	Azeem Rafiq	at Cape Town 2012	3-22	M A Starc	at Cape Town 2012

T20 HIGHEST AND LOWEST SCORES BY AND AGAINST YORKSHIRE
PLUS INDIVIDUAL BEST BATTING AND BOWLING 2003-2023 *(Continued)*

The lowest score is the lowest all-out score or the lowest score at completion of the allotted overs, five-over matches not included.

Yorkshire versus:

Trinidad and Tobago

Highest Score:	Away	154:4	at Centurion 2012	148:9	at Centurion 2012	
Best Batting:	Away	64*	G S Ballance	at Centurion 2012	59	D Ramdin	at Centurion 2012
Best Bowling:	Away	3-13	R J Sidebottom	at Centurion 2012	1-16	K Y G Ottley	at Centurion 2012

Uva

Highest Score:	Away	151:5	at Johannesburg 2012	150:7	at Johannesburg 2012	
Best Batting:	Away	39*	D A Miller	at Johannesburg 2012	29	S H T Kandamby	at Johannesburg 2012
Best Bowling:	Away	2-29	M A Ashraf	at Johannesburg 2012	3-32	E M D Y Munaweera	at Johannesburg 2012

CAREER AVERAGES FOR YORKSHIRE

ALL T20 MATCHES 2003-2023

Player	M	Inns	NO	Runs	HS	Av'ge	100s	50s	Runs	Wkts	Av'ge	Ct/St
Allen, F H	9	9	0	190	48	21.11	0	0	0	0	—	4
Ashraf, M A ...	17	1	0	4	4	4.00	0	0	462	17	27.17	1
Azeem Rafiq ...	95	37	24	153	21*	11.76	0	0	2,489	102	24.40	36
Bairstow, J M .	**68**	**63**	**11**	**1,533**	**112**	**29.48**	**2**	**6**	**0**	**0**	**—**	**29/8**
Ballance, G S ..	88	76	9	1,549	79	23.11	0	5	0	0	—	43
Bess, D M	**43**	**18**	**10**	**118**	**42***	**14.75**	**0**	**0**	**909**	**30**	**30.30**	**8**
Best, T L	8	3	2	10	10*	10.00	0	0	243	7	34.71	4
Birkhead, B D ..	1	0	0	0	—	—	0	0	0	0	—	1
Blakey, R J	7	5	1	119	32	29.75	0	0	0	0	—	5/1
Bresnan, T T ...	118	91	35	1,208	51	21.57	0	1	2,918	118	24.72	41
Brook, H C	**51**	**50**	**12**	**1,478**	**91***	**38.89**	**0**	**7**	**26**	**1**	**26.00**	**32**
Brooks, J A	23	0	0	0	—	—	0	0	582	22	26.45	11
Brophy, G L ...	54	46	9	717	57*	19.37	0	2	0	0	—	25/7
Carver, K	10	2	1	2	2	2.00	0	0	208	8	26.00	5
Chohan, J A ...	**13**	**5**	**2**	**55**	**37**	**18.33**	**0**	**0**	**246**	**5**	**49.20**	**3**
Claydon, M E ..	7	2	2	14	12*	—	0	0	188	5	37.60	2
Coad, B O	**12**	**4**	**1**	**14**	**7**	**4.66**	**0**	**0**	**323**	**13**	**24.84**	**6**
Craven, V J	6	6	4	76	44*	38.00	0	0	67	0	—	3
Dawood, I	11	8	3	44	15	8.80	0	0	0	0	—	5/2
Dawson, R K J .	22	8	3	71	22	14.20	0	0	558	24	23.25	7
Drakes, D C ...	5	1	0	4	4	4.00	0	0	168	10	16.80	3
Duke, H G	**4**	**0**	**0**	**0**	**—**	**—**	**0**	**0**	**0**	**0**	**—**	**3**
Ferguson, L H ..	10	2	1	2	2	2.00	0	0	269	14	19.21	1
Finch, A J	16	16	0	332	89	20.75	0	2	24	1	24.00	16
Fisher, M D ...	**42**	**11**	**5**	**61**	**19**	**10.16**	**0**	**0**	**1,197**	**45**	**26.60**	**12**
Fleming, S P ...	4	4	0	62	58	15.50	0	1	0	0	—	1
Fraine, W A R ..	29	27	10	362	44*	21.29	0	0	0	0	—	16
Gale, A W	104	97	8	2,260	91	25.39	0	16	0	0	—	30
Gibbs, H H	15	15	3	443	101*	36.91	1	2	0	0	—	8
Gibson, R	3	2	0	32	18	16.00	0	0	30	0	—	1
Gilbert, C R	13	9	2	107	38*	15.28	0	0	0	0	—	7
Gillespie, J N ..	17	4	2	14	8*	7.00	0	0	422	17	24.82	5
Gough, D	17	7	3	42	20*	10.50	0	0	416	16	26.00	2
Gray, A K D ...	8	3	0	17	13	5.66	0	0	211	9	23.44	4
Guy, S M	10	6	1	44	13	8.80	0	0	0	0	—	2
Hamilton, G M .	3	3	1	41	41*	20.50	0	0	0	0	—	1
Handscomb, P S P	7	6	0	97	31	16.16	0	0	0	0	—	3/3
Hannon-Dalby, O J	2	0	0	0	—	—	0	0	58	3	19.33	0
Haris Rauf	4	1	1	5	5*	—	0	0	111	4	27.75	0
Harvey, I J	10	10	1	438	109	48.66	2	2	258	10	25.80	4
Head, T M	4	4	0	113	40	28.25	0	0	4	0	—	0
Hill, G C H	**14**	**8**	**2**	**72**	**19***	**12.00**	**0**	**0**	**85**	**2**	**42.50**	**6**
Hodd, A J	26	17	4	147	70	11.30	0	1	0	0	—	9/6
Hodgson, D M .	16	14	2	213	52*	17.75	0	1	0	0	—	9/1
Hodgson, L J ...	2	1	1	39	39*	—	0	0	59	2	29.50	1
Hoggard, M J ..	15	2	1	19	18	19.00	0	0	472	13	36.30	4
Jaques, P A	34	32	3	907	92	31.27	0	6	15	0	—	5
Kirby, S P	3	0	0	0	—	—	0	0	119	4	29.75	1
Kohler-Cadmore, T												
	59	57	8	1,790	96*	36.53	0-	17	0	0	—	32/1
Kruis, G J	20	5	3	41	22	20.50	0	0	486	19	25.57	6
Lawson, M A K .	2	1	1	4	4*	—	0	0	87	3	29.00	1
Leaning, J A ...	52	45	11	952	64	28.00	0	2	45	1	45.00	25

Player	M	Inns	NO	Runs	HS	Av'ge	100s	50s	Runs	Wkts	Av'ge	Ct/St
Leech, D J	**4**	**2**	**1**	**1**	**1***	**—**	**0**	**0**	**90**	**6**	**15.00**	**0**
Lees, A Z	37	36	2	857	67*	25.20	0	4	0	0	—	12
Lehmann, D S ..	9	9	3	252	48	42.00	0	0	180	8	22.50	4
Lumb, M J	26	26	3	442	84*	19.21	0	4	65	3	21.66	8
Luxton, W A ..	**3**	**3**	**0**	**11**	**7**	**3.66**	**0**	**0**	**0**	**0**	**—**	**3**
Lyth, A	**161**	**152**	**5**	**3,921**	**161**	**26.67**	**1**	**25**	**628**	**22**	**28.54**	**80**
McGrath, A	66	61	12	1,403	73*	28.63	0	8	698	23	30.34	26
McKay, C J	8	6	3	54	21*	18.00	0	0	258	10	25.80	1
Maharaj, K A ..	5	2	2	10	10*	—	0	0	126	2	63.00	2
Malan, D J	**30**	**30**	**4**	**857**	**95***	**32.96**	**0**	**7**	**16**	**0**	**—**	**13**
Marsh, S E	11	11	4	289	60*	41.28	0	2	0	0	—	1
Maxwell, G J ...	12	12	1	229	92*	20.81	0	1	264	12	22.00	6
Middlebrook, J D	4	2	2	33	29*	—	0	0	101	4	25.25	1
Mike, B W M ..	**11**	**9**	**4**	**84**	**30***	**16.80**	**0**	**0**	**359**	**13**	**27.61**	**7**
Miller, D A	14	13	4	457	74*	50.77	0	4	0	0	—	7
Northeast, S A ..	1	1	1	0	0*	—	0	0	0	0	—	0
Olivier, D	8	3	0	10	8	3.33	0	0	264	11	24.00	1
Patterson, S A ..	63	9	4	9	3*	1.80	0	0	1,811	61	29.68	10
Pillans, M W ...	9	3	0	18	8	6.00	0	0	246	5	49.20	2
Plunkett, L E ..	42	31	10	353	36	16.80	0	0	1,146	44	26.04	13
Pooran, N	3	3	0	122	67	40.66	0	1	0	0	—	2
Poysden, J E ...	8	1	1	0	0*	—	0	0	205	8	25.62	2
Pyrah, R M	105	71	21	593	42	11.86	0	0	2,315	108	21.43	40
Rana												
Naved-ul-Hasan	8	8	2	63	20*	10.50	0	0	159	11	14.45	2
Rashid, A U ...	**116**	**64**	**21**	**584**	**36***	**13.58**	**0**	**0**	**3,061**	**122**	**25.09**	**36**
Revis, M L	**31**	**17**	**5**	**205**	**42**	**17.08**	**0**	**0**	**766**	**23**	**33.30**	**8**
Rhodes, W M H	18	16	3	128	45	9.84	0	0	283	13	21.76	2
Robinson, O E..	7	3	0	5	3	1.66	0	0	162	6	27.00	3
Root, J E	**45**	**41**	**9**	**1,063**	**92***	**33.21**	**0**	**8**	**490**	**15**	**32.66**	**16**
Rudolph, J A ...	39	35	5	710	61	23.66	0	3	145	6	24.16	7
Sanderson, B W	4	0	0	0	—	—	0	0	74	6	12.33	0
Sarfraz Ahmed .	5	4	0	53	42	13.25	0	0	0	0	—	3/1
Sayers, J J	17	14	0	253	44	18.07	0	0	0	0	—	5
Shadab Khan ...	12	11	1	134	34	13.40	0	0	376	9	41.77	2
Shahzad, A	22	16	4	129	20	10.75	0	0	576	17	33.88	5
Shan Masood ..	**13**	**11**	**1**	**189**	**35***	**18.90**	**0**	**0**	**0**	**0**	**—**	**7**
Shaw, J	5	2	1	1	1	1.00	0	0	138	2	69.00	1
Shutt, J W	13	4	3	0	0*	0.00	0	0	327	16	20.43	3
Sidebottom, R J .	40	16	10	87	16*	14.50	0	0	1,069	42	25.45	9
Silverwood, C E W	9	5	2	32	13*	10.66	0	0	264	7	37.71	4
Starc, M A	10	2	1	0	0*	0.00	0	0	218	21	10.38	1
Stoneman, M D .	4	4	0	58	50	14.50	0	1	0	0	—	2
Swanepoel, P J .	2	1	1	2	2*	—	0	0	60	3	20.00	1
Tattersall, J A .	**54**	**35**	**10**	**526**	**53***	**21.04**	**0**	**1**	**0**	**0**	**—**	**36/6**
Taylor, C R	2	2	1	10	10*	10.00	0	0	0	0	—	0
Thompson, J A	**66**	**51**	**15**	**702**	**74**	**19.50**	**0**	**4**	**1,866**	**71**	**26.28**	**25**
Vaughan, M P ..	16	16	1	292	41*	19.46	0	0	81	1	81.00	2
Wainman, J C ..	2	1	1	12	12*	—	0	0	49	1	49.00	0
Wainwright, D J	26	9	6	23	6*	7.66	0	0	551	21	26.23	9
Waite, M J	22	13	6	91	35*	13.00	0	0	476	15	31.73	5
Wardlaw, I	10	1	1	1	1*	—	0	0	179	5	35.80	0

ALL T20 MATCHES 2003-2023 *(Continued)*

Player	M	Inns	NO	Runs	HS	Av'ge	100s	50s	Runs	Wkts	Av'ge	Ct/St
Warren, A C ...	2	0	0	0	—	—	0	0	70	4	17.50	0
Wharton, J H ..	**8**	**8**	**1**	**157**	**111***	**22.42**	**1**	**0**	**0**	**0**	**—**	**3**
White, C	33	31	0	570	55	18.38	0	2	132	2	66.00	8
Wiese, D	12	11	3	197	50*	24.62	0	1	359	11	32.63	6
Willey, D J	59	54	5	1,586	118	32.36	1	9	1,585	63	25.15	28
Williamson, K S	12	11	0	302	65	27.45	0	1	37	3	12.33	3
Wisniewski, S A	2	0	0	0	—	—	0	0	32	0	—	0
Wood, M J	15	15	3	328	96*	27.33	0	2	32	2	16.00	11
Younus Khan ...	2	2	0	55	40	27.50	0	0	32	2	16.00	0
Yuvraj Singh ...	5	5	0	154	71	30.80	0	1	51	5	10.20	0

T20 HIGHEST PARTNERSHIPS FOR EACH WICKET

1st wkt 158 A Lyth (90*) and D J Malan (79) v.Leicestershire at Leeds 2023

2nd wkt 159 D J Malan (79) and J H Wharton (111*)
v.Worcestershire at Leeds 2023

2nd wkt 150 A Lyth (66) and D J Willey (79) v.Northamptonshire
at Northampton 2018

3rd wkt 146 J M Bairstow (112) and T Kohler-Cadmore
(53) v.Worcestershire at Worcester 2021

4th wkt 115 T Kohler-Cadmore
(67) and H C Brook (72) v.Lancashire at Manchester 2022

5th wkt 103* G S Ballance (64*) and A U Rashid (33*) v.Trinidad & Tobago
at Centurion 2012/13

6th wkt 141* H C Brook (83*) and J A Thompson (66*) v.Worcestershire at Leeds 2021

7th wkt 68* T T Bresnan (45*) and A U Rashid (29*) v.Warwickshire at Leeds 2014

8th wkt 78* D Wiese (50*) and B W M Mike (30*) v.Leicestershire at Leicester 2023

9th wkt 62 D M Bess (42*) and J A Chohan (37) v.Birmingham Bears
at Birmingham 2023

10th wkt 28* A U Rashid (28*) and G J Kruis (12*) v.Durham at Chester-le-Street
2009

LARGEST MARGINS OF VICTORY IN T20 CRICKET

| By 124 runs | v. Northamptonshire | at Headingley | August 17, 2017 |
| By 10 wickets | v. Birmingham | at Birmingham | June 10, 2022 |

LARGEST MARGINS OF DEFEAT IN T20 CRICKET

By 144 runs v. Derbyshire at Chesterfield June 18, 2023
By 10 wickets (3 occasions):
First v. Leicestershire at Grace Road July 28, 2013
Latest v. Nottinghamshire at Trent Bridge July 9, 2021

T20 PARTNERSHIPS OF 100 AND OVER 2003-2023 (34)

159 2nd wkt D J Malan   (79)   and J H Wharton (111*) v. Worcestershire at Leeds   2023
158 1st wkt A Lyth   (90*) and D J Malan   (79) v. Leicestershire at Leeds   2023
150 2nd wkt A Lyth   (66)   and D J Willey   (79) v. Northamptonshire at
                                                             Northampton 2018

146 3rd wkt J M Bairstow (112)   and T Kohler-Cadmore (53)
                                       v.Worcestershire at Worcester 2021

141* 6th wkt H C Brook   (83*) and J A Thompson (66*)
                                       v. Worcestershire at Leeds   2021

137* 2nd wkt A W Gale   (60*) and H H Gibbs   (76*) v. Durham at Leeds   2010
131 1st wkt A Lyth   (78)   and P A Jaques   (64) v. Derbyshire at Leeds   2012
129 2nd wkt A W Gale   (91)   and M P Vaughan (41*) v. Nottinghamshire at Leeds 2009
129 2nd wkt T Kohler-Cadmore
                      (46)   and D J Willey   (80) v. Lancashire at Leeds   2018
127 1st wkt A Lyth   (161)   and T Kohler-Cadmore
                                 (41) v. Northamptonshire at Leeds 2017

124 2nd wkt I J Harvey   (109) and P A Jaques   (37) v. Derbyshire at Leeds   2005
124 2nd wkt A Lyth   (161)   and D J Willey   (40) v. Northamptonshire at Leeds 2017
121 3rd wkt J A Rudolph   (56)   and A McGrath   (59) v. Leicestershire at Leicester 2008
121 2nd wkt T Kohler-Cadmore
                     (96*) and N Pooran   (67) v. Leicestershire at Leicester 2019
119 2nd wkt A Lyth   (38)   and T Kohler-Cadmore
                               (77) v. Lancashire at Leeds   2022
116 1st wkt A W Gale   (70)   and P A Jaques   (48) v. Leicestershire at Leeds   2012
116 1st wkt A Lyth   (69)   and T Kohler-Cadmore
                            (96*) v. Leicestershire at Leicester 2019

115 4th wkt T Kohler-Cadmore
                     (67)   and H C Brook (72)   v. Lancashire at Manchester 2022
113 1st wkt A Lyth   (51)   and J M Bairstow (82) v. Leicestershire at Leeds   2021
110* 4th wkt A Lyth   (92*) and J A Tattersall (53*) v. Durham at Leeds   2018
108 2nd wkt I J Harvey   (108*) and P A Jaques   (39) v. Lancashire at Leeds   2004
108 2nd wkt A Lyth   (59)   and H H Gibbs   (40) v. Worcestershire at Leeds   2010
106* 1st wkt A Lyth   (58*) and D J Malan   (38*) v. Birmingham Bears
                                         at Birmingham 2022
106 2nd wkt D J Willey   (74)   and A Z Lees   (35) v. Northamptonshire at Leeds 2016
105 1st wkt A Lyth   (81)   and F H Allen   (48) v. Durham at Chester-le-Street
                                                 2022
104 1st wkt A W Gale   (43)   and J A Rudolph (61) v. Leicestershire at Leicester 2009
104 2nd wkt A Z Lees   (63)   and J A Leaning (60*) v. Warwickshire at Leeds   2015
104 1st wkt A Lyth   (68)   and T Kohler-Cadmore
                             (40) v. Worcestershire at Leeds   2019
103* 5th wkt G S Ballance   (64*) and A U Rashid (33*) v. Trinidad & Tobago at Centurion
                                             2012/13
103 1st wkt A W Gale   (65*) and J A Rudolp   (53) v. Leicestershire at Leicester 2010
102 1st wkt T Kohler-Cadmore
                     (94*) and A Lyth   (42) v. Birmingham Bears
                                         at Birmingham 2019
101 2nd wkt M J Wood   (57)   and M J Lumb   (55) v. Nottinghamshire at Leeds 2003
101 3rd wkt A J Hodd   (70)   and G J Maxwell (92*) v. Nottinghamshire at Leeds 2015
100 4th wkt A Z Lees   (59)   and J A Leaning (64) v. Northamptonshire
                                           at Northampton 2016

ALL WHO HAVE TAKEN 4 WICKETS IN AN INNINGS (28)

M A ASHRAF (1)

4-18	v.	Derbyshire	at Derby	2012

AZEEM RAFIQ (1)

5-19	v.	Northamptonshire	at Leeds	2017

T T BRESNAN (1)

6-19	v.	Lancashire	at Leeds	2017

J A BROOKS (2)

5-21	v.	Leicestershire	at Leeds	2013
4-21	v.	Derbyshire	at Leeds	2013

L H FERGUSON (1)

4-24	v.	Lancashire	at Leeds	2021

M D FISHER (1)

5-22	v.	Derbyshire	at Leeds	2015

A LYTH (1)

5-31	v.	Nottinghamshire	at Nottingham	2019

C J MCKAY (1)

4-33	v.	Derbyshire	at Leeds	2010

RANA NAVED-UL-HASAN (1)

4-23	v.	Nottinghamshire	at Leeds	2009

S A PATTERSON (1)

4-30	v.	Lancashire	at Leeds	2010

R M PYRAH (3)

5-16	v.	Durham	at Scarborough	2011
4-20	v.	Durham	at Leeds	2006
4-21	v.	Worcestershire	at Leeds	2011

A U RASHID (5)

4-19	v.	Durham	at Leeds	2017
4-20	v.	Leicestershire	at Leeds	2011
4-24	v.	Nottingham	at Nottingham	2008
4-26	v.	Lancashire	at Leeds	2011
4-26	v.	Glamorgan	at Cardiff	2016

B W SANDERSON (1)

4-21	v.	Derbyshire	at Derby	2011

J W SHUTT (2)

5-11	v.	Durham	at Chester-le-Street	2019
4-35	v.	Durham	at Chester-le-Street	2022

R J SIDEBOTTOM (1)

4-25	v.	Durham	at Chester-le-Street	2012

J A THOMPSON (4)

5-21	v. Leicestershire	at Leicester	2023
4-32	v. Durham	at Leeds	2022
4-34	v. Worcestershire	at Leeds	2023
4-44	v. Durham	at Chester-le-Street	2021

D J WILLEY

4-18	v.	Northamptonshire	at Leeds	2019

SECOND ELEVEN CHAMPIONS

In the seasons in which Yorkshire have competed.

From 2009 the Championship was divided into two groups, each team playing each other once. The two group winners played for the Championship.

For 2021 the Championship reverted to one league of 18 teams, each team playing between seven and 12 games Final positions were decided on average points per game.

Season	Champions	Yorkshire's Position	Season	Champions	Yorkshire's Position
1959	Gloucestershire	7th	2000	Middlesex	5th
1960	Northamptonshire	14th	2001	Hampshire	2nd
1961	Kent	11th	2002	Kent	3rd
1975	Surrey	4th	**2003**	**Yorkshire**	**1st**
1976	Kent	5th	2004	Somerset	8th
1977	**Yorkshire**	**1st**	2005	Kent	10th
1978	Sussex	5th	2006	Kent	3rd
1979	Warwickshire	3rd	2007	Sussex	10th
1980	Glamorgan	5th	2008	Durham	5th
1981	Hampshire	11th	2009	Surrey	A 2nd
1982	Worcestershire	14th	2010	Surrey	A 8th
1983	Leicestershire	2nd	2011	Warwickshire	A 10th
1984	**Yorkshire**	**1st**	2012	Kent	(North) 9th
1985	Nottinghamshire	12th	2013	Lancashire & Middlesex	
1986	Lancashire	5th			(North) 4th
1987	**Yorkshire** and Kent	**1st**	2014	Leicestershire	(North) 4th
1988	Surrey	9th	2015	Nottinghamshire	(North) 7th
1989	Middlesex	9th	2016	Durham	(North) 5th
1990	Sussex	17th	2017	Lancashire	(North) 4th
1991	**Yorkshire**	**1st**	2018	Durham	(North) 5th
1992	Surrey	5th	2019	Leicestershire	(North) 2nd
1993	Middlesex	3rd	2020	*No Second Eleven*	
1994	Somerset	2nd		*Championship fixtures*	
1995	Hampshire	5th		*were played because of*	
1996	Warwickshire	4th		*the Coronovirus outbreak*	
1997	Lancashire	2nd	2021	Hampshire	5th
1998	Northamptonshire	9th	**2022**	**Yorkshire**	**1st**
1999	Middlesex	14th	2023	Leicestershire	3rd

SECOND ELEVEN CHAMPIONSHIP 1959-1961 AND 1975-2023

SUMMARY OF RESULTS BY SEASON

Season	Played	Won	Lost	Drawn	Tied	Abandoned	Position in Championship
1959	10	4	1	5	0	0	7
1960	10	1	3	6	0	0	14
1961	9	2	2	5	0	1	11
1975	14	4	0	10	0	0	4
1976	14	5	5	4	0	0	5
1977	**16**	**9**	**0**	**7**	**0**	**1**	**1**
1978	15	5	2	8	0	1	4
1979	16	5	0	11	0	0	3
1980	14	5	2	7	0	1	5
1981	16	2	3	11	0	0	11
1982	16	2	3	11	0	0	14 =
1983	11	5	1	5	0	3	2
1984	**15**	**9**	**3**	**3**	**0**	**0**	**1**
1985	14	3	3	8	0	1	12
1986	16	5	1	10	0	0	5
1987	**15**	**5**	**2**	**8**	**0**	**1**	**1 =**
1988	16	4	1	11	0	0	9
1989	17	2	3	12	0	0	9 =
1990	16	1	6	9	0	0	17
1991	**16**	**8**	**1**	**7**	**0**	**0**	**1**
1992	17	5	2	10	0	0	5
1993	17	6	1	10	0	0	3
1994	17	6	2	9	0	0	2
1995	17	7	1	9	0	0	5
1996	17	6	3	8	0	0	4
1997	16	8	5	3	0	1	2
1998	15	4	2	9	0	0	9
1999	16	3	8	5	0	1	14
2000	14	5	2	7	0	1	5
2001	12	8	2	2	0	1	2
2002	12	5	1	6	0	0	3
2003	**10**	**7**	**1**	**2**	**0**	**0**	**1**
2004	7	2	0	5	0	1	8
2005	12	2	4	6	0	0	10
2006	14	6	4	4	0	0	3
2007	12	4	5	3	0	0	10
2008	12	4	4	4	0	2	5
2009	9	5	0	4	0	0	(Group A) 2
2010	9	2	4	3	0	0	(Group A) 8
2011	9	0	4	4	1	0	(Group A) 10
2012	7	1	2	4	0	2	(North) 9
2013	9	3	4	2	0	0	(North) 4
2014	9	2	1	6	0	0	(North) 4
2015	9	2	4	3	0	0	(North) 7
2016	9	2	3	4	0	0	(North) 5
2017	8	2	0	6	0	1	(North) 4
2018	9	3	1	5	0	0	(North) 5
2019	8	3	1	4	0	0	(North) 2
2021	10	3	1	6	0	2	5
2022	**9**	**5**	**0**	**4**	**0**	**0**	**1**
2023	11	6	3	2	0	0	3
Totals	648	213	117	317	1	21	

Matches abandoned without a ball bowled are not counted as matches played. The 1976 match between Yorkshire and Northamptonshire at Bradford was cancelled after the fixtures had been published.

ANALYSIS OF RESULTS AGAINST EACH OPPONENT

County	Played	Won	Lost	Drawn	Tied	Abandoned	First Played
Derbyshire	62	16	8	38	0	3	1959
Durham	37	13	7	17	0	3	1992
Essex	15	11	2	2	0	0	1990
Glamorgan	41	11	3	27	0	2	1975
Gloucestershire	12	5	3	4	0	0	1990
Hampshire	12	4	1	7	0	0	1990
Kent	27	5	4	18	0	1	1981
Lancashire	77	16	21	40	0	3	1959
Leicestershire	35	14	9	11	1	2	1975
MCC Young Cricketers	7	4	1	2	0	0	2005
MCC Universities	4	1	1	2	0	0	2011
Middlesex	18	7	2	9	0	0	1977
Northamptonshire	53	17	6	30	0	2	1959
Nottinghamshire	64	18	13	33	0	3	1959
Scotland	2	1	0	1	0	0	2007
Somerset	18	9	3	6	0	0	1988
Surrey	38	10	9	19	0	2	1976
Sussex	16	6	5	5	0	0	1990
Warwickshire	65	24	13	28	0	0	1959
Worcestershire	45	21	6	18	0	0	1961
Totals	648	213	117	317	1	21	

Note: Matches abandoned are not included in the total played.

Largest Victory   An innings and 230 runs v. Glamorgan at Headingley, 1986
Largest Defeat   An innings and 124 runs v. Gloucestershire at Bradford, 1994
Narrowest Victory By 1 run v. Lancashire at Old Trafford, 2003
Narrowest Defeat By 8 runs v. Derbyshire at Harrogate, 1982

Highest Total
By Yorkshire: 814-7 dec v. Nottinghamshire at Notts Sports Ground, 2022)
Against Yorkshire: 567 for 7 wkts dec by Middlesex at RAF Vine Lane, Uxbridge, 2000

Lowest Total
By Yorkshire   66 v. Nottinghamshire at Trent College, 2016
Against Yorkshire: 36 by Lancashire at Elland, 1979

Highest Match Aggregate
1,470 for 39 wkts   v. Gloucestershire at Cheltenham, 2001

Highest Individual Score
For Yorkshire: 441 by F J Bean . Nottinghamshire at Notts Sports Ground, 2022)
Against Yorkshire: 235 by O A Shah for Middlesex at Leeds, 1999

Best Bowling In An Innings
For Yorkshire: 9-27 by G A Cope v. Northamptonshire at Northampton, 1979
Against Yorkshire: 8-15 by I Folley for Lancashire at Heywood, 1983

Best Bowling In A Match
For Yorkshire: 13-92 by M K Bore v. Lancashire at Harrogate, 1976)
Against Yorkshire: 13-100 by N J Perry for Glamorgan at Cardiff, 1978)

Most Career Runs: 7,450 by Bradley Parker in 122 matches, average 40.48

Most Career Wickets: 248 by Paul A Booth in 85 matches, average 29.33

Century in Each Innings

For Yorkshire

C White	209* and 115*	v. Worcestershire at Worcester, 1990

(The only instance of two unbeaten centuries in the same match)

K Sharp	150* and 127	v. Essex at Elland, 1991
A A Metcalfe	109 and 136*	v. Somerset at North Perrott, 1994
R A Kettleborough	123 and 192*	v. Nottinghamshire at Todmorden, 1996
C R Taylor	201* and 129	v. Sussex at Hove, 2005
A W Gale	131 and 123	v. Somerset at Taunton, 2006
J J Sayers	157 and 105	v. Lancashire at Leeds, 2007

Against Yorkshire

N Nannan	100 and 102*	for Nottinghamshire at Harrogate, 1979
G D Lloyd	134 and 103	for Lancashire at Scarborough, 1989
A J Swann	131 and 100	for Northamptonshire at York, 1998
G J Kennis	114 and 114	for Somerset at Taunton, 1999

Totals of 450 and over

By Yorkshire (36)

Score	Versus	Ground	Season
814 for 7 wkts dec	Nottinghamshire	Notts Sports Ground	2022
602 for 8 wkts dec	Gloucestershire	Bristol	2021
585 for 8 wkts dec	Lancashire	Scarborough	2017
538 for 9 wkts dec	Worcestershire	Stamford Bridge	2007
534 for 5 wkts dec	Lancashire	Stamford Bridge	2003
530 for 8 wkts dec	Nottinghamshire	Middlesbrough	2000
526 for 8 wkts dec	MCC Young Cricketers	High Wycombe	2017
526 for 9 wkts dec	Nottinghamshire	Headingley	2023
514 for 3 wkts dec	Somerset	Taunton	1988
509 for 4 wkts dec	Northamptonshire	Northampton	1986
508	Durham	Riverside	2017
505 for 6 wkts dec	Worcestershire	Scarborough	2021
502	Derbyshire	Chesterfield	2003
501 for 5 wkts dec	MCC Young Cricketers	Stamford Bridge	2009
497	Derbyshire	Chesterfield	2005
495 for 5 wkts dec	Somerset	Taunton	2006
488 for 8 wkts dec	Warwickshire	Harrogate	1984
486 for 6 wkts dec	Glamorgan	Leeds	1986
481	Durham	Richmond CC	2022
480	Leicestershire	Market Harborough	2013
477	Surrey	Guildford	2023
476 for 3 wkts dec	Glamorgan	Gorseinon	1984
475 for 9 wkts dec	Nottinghamshire	Nottingham	1995
474 for 3 wkts dec	Glamorgan	Todmorden	2003
474	Durham	Stamford Bridge	2003
470	Lancashire	Leeds	2006
469	Warwickshire	Castleford	1999
462	Scotland	Stamford Bridge	2007
461 for 8 wkts dec	Essex	Stamford Bridge	2006
459 for 3 wkts dec	Leicestershire	Oakham	1997
459 for 6 wkts dec	Glamorgan	Bradford	1992
457 for 9 wkts dec	Kent	Canterbury	1983
456 for 5 wkts dec	Gloucestershire	Todmorden	1990
456 for 6 wkts dec	Nottinghamshire	York	1986
454 for 9 wkts dec	Derbyshire	Chesterfield	1959
452 for 9 wkts dec	Glamorgan	Cardiff	2005

Totals of 450 and over

Against Yorkshire (19)

Score	For	Ground	Season
567 for 7 wkts dec	Middlesex	RAF Vine Lane, Uxbridge	2000
555 for 7 wkts dec	Derbyshire	Stamford Bridge	2002
534	Nottinghamshire	Notts Sports Ground	2022
530 for 9 wkts dec	Leicestershire	Hinckley	2015
525 for 7 wkts dec	Sussex	Hove	2005
518 for 8 wkts dec	Essex	Weetwood	2022
502 for 4 wkts dec	Warwickshire	Edgbaston Community Foundation Sports Ground	2016
497	Leicestershire	Weetwood	2022
493 for 8 wkts dec	Nottinghamshire	Lady Bay, Nottingham	2002
488 for 8 wkts dec	Warwickshire	Castleford	1999
486 for 8 wkts dec	Lancashire	Scarborough	2022
486	Essex	Chelmsford	2000
485	Gloucestershire	North Park, Cheltenham	2001
477	Lancashire	Headingley	2006
471	Warwickshire	Clifton Park, York	2010
458	Lancashire	Bradford	1997
454 for 7 wkts dec	Lancashire	Todmorden	1993
450 for 7 wkts (inns closed)	Derbyshire	Bradford	1980
450 for 7 wkts dec	Derbyshire	Weetwood	2023

Completed Innings under 75

By Yorkshire (6)

Score	Versus	Ground	Season
66	Nottinghamshire	Trent College	2016
67	Worcestershire	Barnt Green (1st inns)	2013
68	Worcestershire	Barnt Green (2nd inns)	2013
69	Lancashire	Heywood	1983
72	Leicestershire	Kibworth	2019
74	Derbyshire	Chesterfield	1960
74	Nottinghamshire	Bradford	1998

Against Yorkshire (11)

Score	By	Ground	Season
36	Lancashire	Elland	1979
49	Leicestershire	Leicester	2008
50	Lancashire	Liverpool	1984
60	Derbyshire	Bradford	1977
60	Surrey	Sunbury-on-Thames	1977
62	MCC YC	High Wycombe	2005
64	Nottinghamshire	Brodsworth	1959
66	Leicestershire	Lutterworth	1977
71	Lancashire	Blackpool	2022
72	Sussex	Horsham	2003
74	Worcestershire	Barnsley	1978

Individual Scores of 150 and over (73)

Score	Player	Versus	Ground	Season
441	FJ Bean	Nottinghamshire	Notts Sports Ground	2022
273*	R J Blakey	Northamptonshire	Northampton	1986
238*	K Sharp	Somerset	Taunton	1988
233	P E Robinson	Kent	Canterbury	1983
230	T Kohler-Cadmore	Derbyshire	York	2017
221*	K Sharp	Gloucestershire	Todmorden	1990
219	G M Hamilton	Derbyshire	Chesterfield	2003
218*	A McGrath	Surrey	Elland	1994
212	G S Ballance	MCC Young Cricketers	Stamford Bridge	2009
209*	C White	Worcestershire	Worcester	1990
207	G C H Hill	Gloucestershire	Bristol	2021
205	C R Taylor	Glamorgan	Todmorden	2003
204	B Parker	Gloucestershire	Bristol	1993
203	A McGrath	Durham	Headingley	2005
202*	J M Bairstow	Leicestershire	Oakham	2009
202	A Z Lees	Durham	Riverside	2017
202	M J Wood	Essex	Stamford Bridge	2006
201*	C R Taylor	Sussex	Hove	2005
200*	D Byas	Worcestershire	Worcester	1992
200*	A McGrath	Northamptonshire	Northampton	2012
192*	R A Kettleborough	Nottinghamshire	Todmorden	1996
191	P E Robinson	Warwickshire	Harrogate	1984
191	M J Wood	Derbyshire	Rotherham	2000
191	M J Lumb	Nottinghamshire	Middlesbrough	2000
189*	C S Pickles	Gloucestershire	Bristol	1991
186 .	A McGrath	MCC Universities	York	2011
186	W A R Fraine	Gloucestershire	Bristol	2021
184	J D Love	Worcestershire	Headingley	1976
183	A W Gale	Durham	Stamford Bridge	2006
174	G L Brophy	Worcestershire	Stamford Bridge	2007
173	S N Hartley	Warwickshire	Edgbaston	1980
173	A A Metcalfe	Glamorgan	Gorseinon	1984
173	B Parker	Sussex	Hove	1996
173	R A Kettleborough	Leicestershire	Oakham School	1997
173	T Kohler-Cadmore	Northamptonshire	Desborough	2018
172	A C Morris	Lancashire	York	1995
170*	R A J Townsley	Glamorgan	Harrogate	1975
170	M J Waite	Essex	Billericay	2021
169	J E Root	Warwickshire	York	2010
168	M J Wood	Leicestershire	Oakham School	1997
166	A A Metcalfe	Lancashire	York	1984
166	C A Chapman	Northamptonshire	York	1998
165*	A Lyth	Durham	Stamford Bridge	2006
165	J J Sayers	Sussex	Hove	2006
164*	A W Gale	Leicestershire	Harrogate	2002
164	J C Balderstone	Nottinghamshire	Harrogate	1960
163*	J E Root	Leicestershire	Oakham	2009
163	A A Metcalfe	Derbyshire	Chesterfield	1992
162*	D Byas	Surrey	Scarborough	1987
162*	R Gibson	Leicestershire	York	2016
161	H C Brook	Lancashire	Scarborough	2017
160	A A Metcalfe	Somerset	Bradford	1993
157*	W A R Fraine	Worcestershire	Kidderminster	2019
157	J J Sayers	Lancashire	Headingley	2007

Score	Player	Versus	Ground	Season
155	S M Guy	Derbyshire	Chesterfield	2005
154*	C R Taylor	Surrey	Whitgift School	2005
153*	A A Metcalfe	Warwickshire	Bingley	1995
153	C White	Worcestershire	Marske-by-the-Sea	1991
153	R A Stead	Surrey	Todmorden	2002
152	A A Metcalfe	Gloucestershire	Bristol	1993
151*	P E Robinson	Nottinghamshire	York	1986
151*	S J Foster	Kent	Elland	1992
151*	J J Sayers	Durham	Stamford Bridge	2004
151	P J Hartley	Somerset	Clevedon	1989
151	A McGrath	Somerset	Elland	1995
151	V J Craven	Glamorgan	Todmorden	2003
150*	K Sharp	Essex	Elland	1991
150*	G M Fellows	Hampshire	Todmorden	1998
150*	S M Guy	Nottinghamshire	Headingley	2005
150*	J A Leaning	Worcestershire	Worcester	2011
150	K Sharp	Glamorgan	Ebbw Vale	1983
150	S N Hartley	Nottinghamshire	Worksop	1988
150	C R Taylor	Derbyshire	Chesterfield	2003

7 Wickets in an Innings (31)

Analysis	Player	Versus	Ground	Season
9 for 27	G A Cope	Northamptonshire	Northampton	1977
9 for 62	M K Bore	Warwicshire	Scarborough	1976
8 for 33	B O Coad	MCC Young Cricketers	York	2018
8 for 53	S J Dennis	Nottinghamshire	Nottingham	1983
8 for 57	M K Bore	Lancashire	Manchester	1977
8 for 79	P J Berry	Derbyshire	Harrogate	1991
7 for 13	P Carrick	Northamptonshire	Marske-by-the-Sea	1977
7 for 21	S Silvester	Surrey	Sunbury-on-Thames	1977
7 for 22	J A R Blain	Surrey	Purley	2004
7 for 32	P W Jarvis	Surrey	The Oval	1984
7 for 34	P Carrick	Glamorgan	Leeds	1986
7 for 37	P M Hutchison	Warwickshire	Coventry	2001
7 for 39	G M Hamilton	Sussex	Leeds	1995
7 for 40	M K Bore	Worcestershire	Old Hill	1976
7 for 44	M K Bore	Lancashire	Harrogate	1976
7 for 44	J P Whiteley	Worcestershire	Leeds	1979
7 for 51	J D Middlebrook	Derbyshire	Rotherham	2000
7 for 53	J P Whiteley	Warwickshire	Birmingham	1980
7 for 55	C White	Leicestershire	Bradford	1990
7 for 58	K Gillhouley	Derbyshire	Chesterfield	1960
7 for 58	P J Hartley	Lancashire	Leeds	1985
7 for 63	M J Hoggard	Worcestershire	Harrogate	1998
7 for 65	M K Bore	Nottinghamshire	Steetley	1976
7 for 70	J D Batty	Leicestershire	Bradford	1992
7 for 71	J D Batty	Hampshire	Harrogate	1994
7 for 81	K Gillhouley	Lancashire	Scarborough	1960
7 for 84	I J Houseman	Kent	Canterbury	1989
7 for 88	I G Swallow	Nottinghamshire	Nottingham	1983
7 for 90	A P Grayson	Kent	Folkestone	1991
7 for 93	D Pickles	Nottinghamshire	Nottingham	1960
7 for 94	K Gillhouley	Northamptonshire	Redcar	1960

12 Wickets in a Match (6)

Analysis		Player	Versus	Ground	Season
13 for 92	(6-48 and 7-44)	M K Bore	Lancashire	Harrogate	1976
13 for 110	(7-70 and 6-40)	J D Batty	Leicestershire	Bradford	1992
13 for 111	(4-49 and 9-62)	M K Bore	Warwickshire	Scarborough	1976
12 for 69	(5-32 and 7-37)	P M Hutchison	Warwickshire	Coventry	2001
12 for 120	(5-39 and 7-81)	K Gillhouley	Lancashire	Scarborough	1960
12 for 162	(5-78 and 7-84)	I J Houseman	Kent	Canterbury	1989

Hat-tricks (4)

Player	Versus	Ground	Season
I G Swallow	Warwickshire	Harrogate	1984
S D Fletcher	Nottinghamshire	Marske-by-the-Sea	1987
I G Swallow	Derbyshire	Chesterfield	1988
M Broadhurst	Essex	Southend-on-Sea	1992

Second Eleven Performance Of The Year Award

The Trophy was instituted in 2013 to reward a Second Eleven performance with either bat or ball that stood out from the ordinary and turned the course of the game.

2013 M D Fisher 6-25 v. Leicestershire (One-Day Trophy)
Grace Road, Leicester
2014 J A Leaning 102 v. Nottinghamshire (T20) Trent College, Nottingham
2015 M J Waite 143 v. Lancashire (Friendly) Scarborough
2016 W M H Rhodes 137
and 114* v Lancashire (Friendly) Liverpool
2017 J W Jack Shutt 4-19 v. Middlesex in the Trophy Final Headingley
and 4-12 v. Derbyshire in the T20 Alvaston and Boulton
to secure two victories.
2018 J H Wharton 162 v. Leiestershire (Friendly) Kibworth CC
in only his second Second Eleven match.
2019 M L Revis 177 v Sussex (Friendly) Hove
2020 No Award The Coronoviris epidemic prevented any Second Eleven
cricket being played in 2020
2021 G C H Hill 207 v. Gloucestershire. His maiden Championship century
2022 F J Bean 441 v. Nottinghamshire.
This is the highest score ever recorded in the Second Eleven Championship.
2023 W A R Fraine 113 not out and 107 not out in consecutive Second XI T20 matches v. Nottinghamshire at Worksop College on the same day. This
was the first time the feat of scoring two centuries on the same day
had been achieves in this competition since it began in 2011.

SECOND ELEVEN TROPHY

WINNERS 1986-2019

1986   **Northamptonshire**, who beat Essex by 14 runs
1987   **Derbyshire**, who beat Hampshire by 7 wickets
1988   **Yorkshire**, who beat Kent by 7 wickets
1989   **Middlesex**, who beat Kent by 6 wickets
1990   **Lancashire**, who beat Somerset by 8 wickets
1991   **Nottinghamshire**, who beat Surrey by 8 wickets
1992   **Surrey**, who beat Northamptonshire by 8 wickets
1993   **Leicestershire**, who beat Sussex by 142 runs
1994   **Yorkshire**, who beat Leicestershire by 6 wickets
1995   **Leicestershire**, who beat Gloucestershire by 3 runs
1996   **Leicestershire**, who beat Durham by 46 runs
1997   **Surrey**, who beat Gloucestershire by 3 wickets
1998   **Northamptonshire**, who beat Derbyshire by 5 wickets
1999   **Kent**, who beat Hampshire by 106 runs.
2000   **Leicestershire,** who beat Hampshire by 25 runs.
2001   **Surrey**, who beat Somerset by 6 wickets
2002   **Kent**, who beat Hampshire by 5 wickets
2003   **Hampshire**, who beat Warwickshire by 8 wickets
2004   **Worcestershire**, who beat Essex by 8 wickets
2005   **Sussex**, who beat Nottinghamshire by 6 wickets
2006   **Warwickshire**, who beat Yorkshire by 93 runs
2007   **Middlesex**, who beat Somerset by 1 run
2008   **Hampshire**, who beat Essex by 7 runs
2009   **Yorkshire,** who beat Lancashire by 2 wickets
2010   **Essex**, who beat Lancashire by 14 runs
2011   **Nottinghamshire**, who beat Lancashire by 4 wickets
2012   **Lancashire**, who beat Durham by 76 runs
2013   **Lancashire**, who beat Nottinghamshire by 76 runs
2014   **Leicestershire**, who beat Lancashire by 168 runs
2015   **Derbyshire**, who beat Durham by 10 runs
2016   **Lancashire,** who beat Somerset by 10 wickets *(DLS)*
2017   **Yorkshire,** who beat Middlesex by 99 runs *(DLS)*
2018   **Middlesex,** who beat Somerset by 1 wicket
2019   **Kent**, who beat Durham by 16 runs

SECOND ELEVEN TWENTY20

WINNERS 2011-2023

2011   **Sussex**, who beat Durham by 24 runs
2012   **England Under-19s**, who beat Sussex by eight wickets
2013   **Surrey**, who beat Middlesex by six runs
2014   **Leicesterhire**, who beat Somerset by 11 runs
2015   **Middlesex**, who beat Kent by four wickets
2016   **Middlesex**, who beat Somerset by two wickets
2017   **Sussex**, who beat Hampshire by 24 runs
2018   **Lancashire**, who beat Essex by 25 runs
2019   **Glamorgan**, who beat Hampshire by 1 run
2021   **Warwickshire,** who beat Sussex by 54 runs
2022   **Glamorgan,** who beat Leicestershire by five wickets *(DLS)*
2023   **Derbyshire,** who beat Glamorgan by 5 runs